Lecture Notes in Computer Science   11486

Commenced Publication in 1973
Founding and Former Series Editors:
Gerhard Goos, Juris Hartmanis, and Jan van Leeuwen

More information about this series at http://www.springer.com/series/7407

José Manuel Ferrández Vicente ·
José Ramón Álvarez-Sánchez ·
Félix de la Paz López ·
Javier Toledo Moreo ·
Hojjat Adeli (Eds.)

Understanding the Brain Function and Emotions

8th International Work-Conference on the Interplay
Between Natural and Artificial Computation, IWINAC 2019
Almería, Spain, June 3–7, 2019
Proceedings, Part I

 Springer

Editors
José Manuel Ferrández Vicente
Universidad Politécnica de Cartagena
Cartagena, Spain

José Ramón Álvarez-Sánchez
Universidad Nacional de Educación
a Distancia
Madrid, Spain

Félix de la Paz López
Universidad Nacional de Educación
a Distancia
Madrid, Madrid, Spain

Javier Toledo Moreo
Universidad Politécnica de Cartagena
Cartagena, Spain

Hojjat Adeli
The Ohio State University
Columbus, OH, USA

ISSN 0302-9743   ISSN 1611-3349   (electronic)
Lecture Notes in Computer Science
ISBN 978-3-030-19590-8   ISBN 978-3-030-19591-5   (eBook)
https://doi.org/10.1007/978-3-030-19591-5

LNCS Sublibrary: SL1 – Theoretical Computer Science and General Issues

This Springer imprint is published by the registered company Springer Nature Switzerland AG
The registered company address is: Gewerbestrasse 11, 6330 Cham, Switzerland

Preface

Bio-inspired computing methods take inspiration from nature to develop optimization and search algorithms or metaheuristics, typically in order to tackle the search for optimal solutions of complex problems in science and engineering, which usually imply a high dimensionality of the search space. The interplay between natural and artificial computation creates new paradigms not only in computer science but also in medicine and biology. The hybridization between social sciences and social behaviors with robotics, between neurobiology and computing, between ethics and neuroprosthetics, between cognitive sciences and neurocomputing, and between neurophysiology and marketing, will give rise to new concepts and tools that can be applied to ICT systems, as well as to natural science fields. Through IWINAC, we provide a forum in which research in different fields can converge to create new computational paradigms that are on the frontier between neural and biomedical sciences and information technologies.

As a multidisciplinary forum, IWINAC is open to any established institutions and research laboratories actively working in the field of natural or neural technologies. But beyond achieving cooperation between different research realms, we wish to actively encourage cooperation with the private sector, particularly SMEs, as a way of bridging the gap between frontier science and societal impact. In this edition, four main themes outline the conference topics: Affective Computing, Machine Learning Applied to NeuroScience, Deep Learning, and Biomedical Applications.

Emotions are essential in human–human communication, cognition, learning and rational decision-making processes. However, human–machine interfaces (HMIs) are still not able to understand human feelings and react accordingly. With the aim of endowing HMIs with the emotional intelligence they lack, affective computing science focuses on the development of artificial intelligence by means of the analysis of affects and emotions, such that systems and devices may be able to recognize, interpret, process and simulate human feelings.

Today, the evaluation of electrophysiological signals plays a key role in the advancement toward that purpose since they are an objective representation of the emotional state of an individual. Hence, the interest in physiological variables like electroencephalogram, electrocardiogram, or electrodermal activity, among many others, has notably grown in the field of affective states detection. Furthermore, emotions have also been widely identified by means of the assessment of speech characteristics and facial gestures of people under different sentimental conditions. It is also worth noting that the development of algorithms for the classification of affective states in social media has experienced a notable boost in the last years. In this sense, language of posts included in social networks, such as Facebook or Twitter, is evaluated with the aim of detecting the sentiments of the users of these media tools. Affective computing and sentiment analysis is intended to be a meeting point for researchers that are interested in any of those areas of expertise related to sentiment analysis and who want to initiate their studies or are currently working on these topics. Hence, manuscripts introducing new proposals based on the analysis of physiological measures, facial recognition, speech recognition, or natural language processing in social media are examples on affective computing and sentiment analysis.

Currently, machine learning holds great promise in the development of new models and theories in the field of neuroscience, in conjunction with classic statistical hypothesis testing. Machine learning algorithms have the potential to reveal interactions, hidden patterns of abnormal activity, brain structure and connectivity, and physiological mechanisms of the brain and behavior. In addition, several approaches for testing the significance of the machine learning outcomes have been successfully proposed to avoid "the dangers of spurious findings or explanations void of mechanism" by means of proper replication, validation, and hypothesis-driven confirmation. Therefore, machine learning can effectively provide relevant information to take great strides toward understanding how the brain works. The main goal of this field is to build a bridge between two scientific communities, the machine learning community, including lead scientists in deep learning and related areas in pattern recognition and artificial intelligence, and the neuroscience community.

Deep learning has represented a breakthrough for the artificial intelligence community. The best performances attained so far in many fields, such as computer vision or natural language processing, have been overtaken by these novel paradigms up to a point that only ten years ago was just science fiction. In addition, this technology has been open sourced by the main AI companies, hence making it quite straightforward to design, train, and integrate deep-learning based systems. Moreover, the amount of data available every day is not only enormous, but growing at an exponential rate. Over the past few years there has been increasing interest in using machine learning methods to analyze and visualize massive data generated from very different sources and with many different features: social networks, surveillance systems, smart cities, medical diagnosis, business, cyberphysical systems or media digital data. This topic is designed to serve researchers and developers to publish original, innovative, and state-of-the art machine learning algorithms and architectures to analyze and visualize large amounts of data.

Finally, biomedical applications are essential in IWINAC meetings. For instance, brain–computer interfaces (BCI) implement a new paradigm in communication networks, namely, brain area networks. In this paradigm, our brain receives input data (external stimuli), performs multiple media-access controls by means of cognitive tasks (selective attention), processes the information (perception), takes a decision (cognition) and, eventually, transmits data back to the source (by means of a BCI), thus closing the communication loop. Image understanding is a research area involving both feature extraction and object identification within images from a scene, and a posterior treatment of this information in order to establish relationships between these objects with a specific goal. In biomedical and industrial scenarios, the main purpose of this discipline is, given a visual problem, to manage all aspects of prior knowledge, from study start-up and initiation through data collection, quality control, expert independent interpretation, to design and development of systems involving image processing capable of tackle with these tasks. These areas are clear examples of innovative applications in biology or medicine.

The wider view of the computational paradigm gives us more elbow room to accommodate the results of the interplay between nature and computation. The IWINAC forum thus becomes a methodological approximation (set of intentions, questions, experiments, models, algorithms, mechanisms, explanation procedures, and engineering and computational methods) to the natural and artificial perspectives of the mind embodiment problem, both in humans and in artifacts. This is the philosophy that continues in IWINAC meetings, the "interplay" movement between the natural and the artificial, facing this same problem every two years. This synergistic approach will permit us not only to build new computational systems based on the natural measurable phenomena, but also to understand many of the observable behaviors inherent to natural systems.

The difficulty of building bridges between natural and artificial computation is one of the main motivations for the organization of IWINAC 2019. The IWINAC 2019 proceedings contain the works selected by the Scientific Committee from nearly 200 submissions, after the refereeing process. The first volume, entitled *Understanding the Brain Function and Emotions*, includes all the contributions mainly related to the new tools for analyzing neural data, or detecting emotional states, or interfacing with physical systems. The second volume, entitled *From Bioinspired Systems and Biomedical Applications to Machine Learning*, contains the papers related to bioinspired programming strategies and all the contributions oriented to the computational solutions to engineering problems in different application domains, as biomedical systems, or big data solutions.

An event of the nature of IWINAC 2019 cannot be organized without the collaboration of a group of institutions and people whom we would like to thank now, starting with Universidad Nacional de Educación a Distancia (UNED) and Universidad Politécnica de Cartagena. The collaboration of the Universidad de Granada and Universidad de Almeria was crucial, as was the efficient work of the local Organizing Committee, chaired by Juan Manuel Gorriz Sáez with the close collaboration of Manuel Cantón Garbín, Manuel Berenguel Soria, Javier Ramírez Pérez de Inestrosa, Andrés Ortiz García, Francisco Jesús Martínez Murcia, Diego Salas González, Ignacio Álvarez Illán, Fermín Segovia Román, and Diego Castillo Barnés. In addition to our universities, we received financial support from the Spanish CYTED, Red Nacional en Computación Natural y Artificial, Programa de Grupos de Excelencia de la Fundación Séneca and Apliquem Microones 21 s.l.

We want to express our gratitude to our invited speakers, Prof. Hojjat Adeli (Ohio State University, USA), Prof. Francisco Herrera (Universidad de Málaga, Spain), Prof. John Suckling (University of Cambridge, UK), and Prof. Hiroaki Wagatsuma (Kyushu Institute of Technology, Japan), for accepting our invitation and for their magnificent plenary talks. We would also like to thank the authors for their interest in our call and the effort in preparing the papers, condition sine qua non for these proceedings. We thank the Scientific and Organizing Committees, in particular the members of these committees who acted as effective and efficient referees and as promoters and managers of preorganized sessions on autonomous and relevant topics under the IWINAC global scope. Our sincere gratitude also goes to Springer and to Alfred Hofmann and his colleagues, Anna Kramer and Elke Werner, for the continuous receptivity, help efforts, and collaboration in all our joint editorial ventures on the interplay between neuroscience and computation. Finally, we want to express our special thanks to Viajes Hispania, our technical secretariat, and to Chari García and Beatriz Baeza, for making this meeting possible, and for arranging all the details that comprise the organization of this kind of event.

Last year, in 2018, was 10 years without Professor Mira, without his close and friendly presence. We want to dedicate these two volumes of the IWINAC proceedings to Professor Mira's memory.

June 2019

José Manuel Ferrández Vicente
José Ramón Álvarez-Sánchez
Félix de la Paz López
Javier Toledo Moreo
Hojjat Adeli

Organization

General Chair

José Manuel Ferrández Vicente, Spain

Organizing Committee

José Ramón Álvarez-Sánchez, Spain
Félix de la Paz López, Spain
Javier Toledo Moreo, Spain

Honorary Chairs

Hojjat Adeli, USA
Zhou Changjiu, Singapore
Rodolfo Llinás, USA

Local Organizing Committee

Ignacio Álvarez Illán, Spain
Manuel Berenguel Soria, Spain
Manuel Cantón Garbín, Spain
Diego Castillo Barnés, Spain
Juan Manuel Górriz Sáez, Spain

Francisco Jesús Martínez Murcia, Spain
Andrés Ortiz García, Spain
Javier Ramírez Pérez de Inestrosa, Spain
Diego Salas González, Spain
Fermín Segovia Román, Spain

Invited Speakers

Hojjat Adeli, USA
Francisco Herrera, Spain

John Suckling, UK
Hiroaki Wagatsuma, Japan

Field Editors

Jose Santos Reyes, Spain
Ramiro Varela Arias, Spain
Arturo Martínez-Rodrigo, Spain
Antonio Fernández-Caballero, Spain
Jose García-Rodríguez, Spain
Enrique Domínguez, Spain
David Tomás, Spain

Jaime Oswaldo Salvador Meneses,
  Ecuador
Zoila Ruiz, Ecuador
Rafael Verdú Monedero, Spain
José Luis Sancho Gómez, Spain
Rafael Martínez Tomás, Spain
Mariano Rincón Zamorano, Spain

Javier de Lope Asiain, Spain
Manuel Graña, Spain
Alfredo Cuesta Infante, Spain
Juan José Pantrigo, Spain

Antonio S. Montemayor, Spain
Juan Manuel Górriz Sáez, Spain
Javier Ramirez Pérez de Inestrosa, Spain

International Scientific Committee

Ajith Abraham, Norway
Michael Affenzeller, Austria
Peter Ahnelt, Austria
Boris Almonacid, Chile
Amparo Alonso Betanzos, Spain
Antonio Anaya, Spain
Davide Anguita, Italy
Manuel Arias Calleja, Spain
Jose Luis Aznarte Mellado, Spain
José M. Azorín, Spain
Jorge Azorin Lopez, Spain
Margarita Bachiller Mayoral, Spain
Antonio Bahamonde, Spain
Emilia I. Barakova, The Netherlands
Alvaro Barreiro, Spain
Senén Barro Ameneiro, Spain
María Consuelo Bastida Jumilla, Spain
Francisco Bellas, Spain
Rafael Berenguer Vidal, Spain
Guido Bologna, Italy
Maria Bonomini, Argentina
Juan Carlos Burguillo Rial, Spain
Enrique J. Carmona Suarez, Spain
Juan Castellanos, Spain
German Castellanos Dominguez,
    Colombia
José Carlos Castillo, Spain
Miguel Cazorla, Spain
Joaquin Cerda Boluda, Spain
Alexander Cerquera, USA
Santi Chillemi, Italy
Carlos Colodro Conde, Spain
Ricardo Contreras, Chile
Carlos Cotta, Spain
José Manuel Cuadra Troncoso, Spain
Adriana Dapena, Spain
Angel P. del Pobil, Spain
Ana E. Delgado García, Spain
Jose Dorronsoro, Spain

Richard Duro, Spain
Patrizia Fattori, Italy
Paulo Félix Lamas, Spain
Eduardo Fernandez, Spain
Manuel Fernández Delgado, Spain
Miguel A. Fernandez Graciani, Spain
Jose Luis Fernández Vindel, Spain
Cipriano Galindo, Spain
Vicente Garceran Hernandez, Spain
Francisco Javier Garrigos Guerrero,
    Spain
Elena Gaudioso, Spain
Pedro Gomez Vilda, Spain
Pascual González, Spain
Francisco Guil Reyes, Spain
Juan Carlos Herrero, Spain
Cesar Hervas Martinez, Spain
Tom Heskes, The Netherlands
Eduardo Iáñez, Spain
Roberto Iglesias, Spain
Fernando Jimenez Barrionuevo, Spain
Jose M. Juarez, Spain
Joost N. Kok, The Netherlands
Elka Korutcheva, Spain
Ryo Kurazume, Japan
Jorge Larrey Ruiz, Spain
Jerome Leboeuf, Mexico
Álvar-Ginés Legaz Aparicio, Spain
Emilio Leton Molina, Spain
Maria Teresa Lopez Bonal, Spain
Mguel Angel Lopez Gordo, Spain
Tino Lourens, The Netherlands
Manuel Luque, Spain
Saturnino Maldonado, Spain
Ángeles Manjarrés, Spain
Dario Maravall, Spain
Jose Javier Martinez Alvarez, Spain
Antonio Martínez Álvarez, Spain
Rosa-María Menchón Lara, Spain

Sergio Miguel Tomé, Spain
Jesus Minguillon, Spain
Victor Mitrana, Spain
Jose Maria Molina Garcia Pardo, Spain
Jose Manuel Molina Lopez, Spain
Juan Morales Sanchez, Spain
Ana Belen Moreno Diaz, Spain
Roberto Moreno Diaz, Spain
Elena Navarro, Spain
Pablo Padilla, Spain
Jose T. Palma Mendez, Spain
Miguel Angel Patricio Guisado, Spain
Francisco Peláez, Brazil
Francisco Pelayo, Spain
Mario J. Perez Jimenez, Spain
Maria Pinninghoff, Chile
Blanca Priego, Spain
Carlos Puntonet, Spain
Alexis Quesada Arencibia, Spain
Andonie Razvan, USA
José C. Riquelme, Spain
Victoria Rodellar, Spain
Miguel Rodriguez Artacho, Spain

Jesus Rodriguez Presedo, Spain
Daniel Ruiz, Spain
Ramon Ruiz Merino, Spain
Jose M Sabater Navarro, Spain
Pedro Salcedo Lagos, Chile
Angel Sanchez, Spain
Eduardo Sánchez Vila, Spain
Olga C. Santos, Spain
Ricardo Sanz, Spain
Antonio Sanz, Spain
Luis Sarro, Spain
Guido Sciavicco, Italy
Amari Shun-ichi, Japan
Juan A. Sigüenza, Spain
Jordi Solé i Casals, Spain
Maria Jesus Taboada, Spain
Antonio J. Tallón Ballesteros, Spain
Rafael Toledo Moreo, Spain
Jan Treur, The Netherlands
Daniel Varela, Spain
Hujun Yin, UK
Juan Zapata, Spain
Changjiu Zhou, Singapore

Contents – Part I

Affective Computing

Contents – Part II

Applications

Bioinspired Systems

Machine Learning for Big Data and Visualization

Biomedical Applications

Deep Learning

Neuroscience Applications

The Effect of tDCS on EEG-Based Functional Connectivity in Gait Motor Imagery

J. A. Gaxiola-Tirado[1](✉) , M. Rodríguez-Ugarte[2], E. Iáñez[2] , M. Ortiz[2] ,
D. Gutiérrez[1] , and J. M. Azorín[2]

[1] CINVESTAV, Monterrey's Unit, Vía del Conocimiento 201,
PIIT, km 9.5 de la autopista nueva al aeropuerto, 66600 Apodaca, NL, Mexico
jgaxiola@cinvestav.mx, dgtz@ieee.org
[2] Brain-Machine Interface Systems Lab, Systems Engineering and Automation
Department at Miguel Hernández University of Elche,
Avda. de la Universidad s/n. Ed. Innova, 03202 Elche (Alicante), Spain
{maria.rodriguezu,eianez,mortiz,jm.azorin}@umh.es
http://www.monterrey.cinvestav.mx/, https://psblab.gutierrezruiz.com/,
http://bmi.umh.es/

Abstract. Transcranial direct current stimulation (tDCS) is a non-invasive technique for brain stimulation capable of modulating brain excitability. Although beneficial effects of tDCS have been shown, the underlying brain mechanisms have not been described. In the present study, we aim to investigate the effects of tDCS on EEG-based functional connectivity, through a partial directed coherence (PDC) analysis, which is a frequency-domain metric that provides information about directionality in the interaction between signals recorded at different channels. The tDCS montage used in our study, was focused on the lower limbs and it was composed of two anodes and one cathode. A single-blind study was carried out, where eight healthy subjects were randomly separated into two groups: sham and active tDCS. Results showed that, for the active tDCS group, the central EEG electrodes Cz, C3 and C4 turned out to be highly connected within alpha and beta frequency bands. On the contrary, the sham group presented a tendency to be more random at its functional connections.

Keywords: PDC · Functional connectivity · Motor imagery · BCI · EEG · Gait · tDCS

1 Introduction

Transcranial direct current stimulation (tDCS) is a non-invasive technique for brain stimulation capable of modulating brain excitability [1]. It delivers low intensity, direct current (transferred between electrodes from anode to cathode) to cortical areas facilitating or inhibiting spontaneous neuronal activity. Specifically, anodal direct current stimulation has been shown to increase cortical

© Springer Nature Switzerland AG 2019
J. M. Ferrández Vicente et al. (Eds.): IWINAC 2019, LNCS 11486, pp. 3–10, 2019.
https://doi.org/10.1007/978-3-030-19591-5_1

excitability, whereas cathodal stimulation decreased it [2,3]. This technique has shown potential to improve motor performance and motor learning [4,5]. Thus, tDCS application is now explored as a promising tool applied in motor neurorehabilitation [6]. However, even though the beneficial effects of tDCS have been shown, its effects on functional connectivity and the underlying brain mechanisms have still not been described.

The majority of the studies have investigated the effects of tDCS as an augmentative technique to improve the performance of upper limbs [7–9]. Up to this date, only relative few studies have investigated how tDCS affects the lower limbs performance [10,11]. Hence, we are interested in to investigate the effects of tDCS in gait motor imagery (IM). From a cognitive perspective, brain activity during gait, involves the supplementary motor area (SMA), the primary motor cortex (M1), the primary somatosensory cortex (S1) and the premotor area (PM) [12]. Moreover, it has been shown that IM relies on neural processes also associated with these areas [13,14].

In the present study, we aim to investigate tDCS effects in functional connectivity, through a partial directed coherence (PDC) analysis, which is a frequency-domain metric that provides information about directionality in the interaction between electroencephalography (EEG) signals recorded at different channels. In this context, in [15] authors examined time and frequency-based measures of EEG-based brain networks, connectivity analysis, and their applications on brain-computer interfaces (BCI). They also reported connections between the sensorimotor cortex and frontal areas during IM. Therefore, with better understanding of the mechanisms and dynamics of brain activity, it may be obtain useful and informative features for BCI applications as well as in motor neurorehabilitation.

2   Materials and Methods

In this section, we present the experimental procedure and the tDCS montage focused on lower limbs. Furthermore, we introduce the PDC, in order to evaluate the effects of tDCS in EEG-based functional connectivity.

2.1   EEG Acquisition

The brain activity was recorded using an EEG array of 30 electrodes (The StarStim R32 system) placed on the scalp according to the extended 10–20 placing system (P7, P4, CZ, PZ, P3, P8, O1, O2, C2, C4, F4, FP2, FZ, C3, F3, FP1, C1, OZ, PO4, FC6, FC2, AF4, CP6, CP2, CP1, CP5, FC1, FC5, AF3, PO3) at a sampling frequency of 500 Hz.

2.2   TDCS Supply

The StarStim R32 system was used to provide tDCS to the subject's brain. The tDCS montage was composed by one anode located over the right cerebrocerebellum (two centimeters right and one centimeter down of the inion), the other one over the motor cortex in Cz on M1, and the cathode over FC2 (using the International 10-10 system). The idea was to excite simultaneously the right cerebrocerebelum and the motor cortex considering that both areas are implicated in IM. The intensity was established to 0.2 mA and 0.3 mA for the cerebrocerebellum and Cz anodes respectively. The cathode current density was of 0.16 $\frac{mA}{cm^2}$. All the electrodes were 1 cm of radius (surface area of π cm^2), 3 mm of thickness and with 4 mm of space for the conductive gel.

2.3 Experimental Procedure

The experiment was based on visual cues in order to detect gait IM. Eight subjects were separated into two groups: *active tDCS* (labeled as S1t, S2t, S3t and S4t) and *sham* (labeled as S5s, S6s, S7s and S8s). After the initial stimulation, subjects stood in front of a screen that provided instructions while their EEG signals were being recorded. Two types of instructions were indicated: Imagine and +. During Imagine periods, they had to imagine a gait movement. Subjects were instructed to avoid blinking, head movements or any other artifact during the Imagine periods, postponing these actions to the + periods. The *sham* group received 15 min of fake stimulation to create a placebo effect, while the *active tDCS* group received 15 min of real stimulation. Participants performed one session each day for five consecutive days.

2.4 Partial Directed Coherence

The partial directed coherence (PDC) is a frequency domain measure of the relationships (information about directionality in the interaction) between pairs of signals in a multivariate data set for application in functional connectivity inference in neuroscience [16]. If one assumes a set $S = \{x_m, 1 \leq m \leq M\}$ of M EEG signals (simultaneously observed time series)

$$\boldsymbol{x}(n) = [x_1(n), x_2(n), \ldots, x_M(n)]^T \tag{1}$$

is adequately represented by a multivariate autoregressive (MVAR) model of order p, or simply MVAR(p):

$$\boldsymbol{x}(n) = \sum_{k=1}^{p} A_p \boldsymbol{x}(n-k) + \boldsymbol{e}(n), \tag{2}$$

where $\boldsymbol{A}_1, \boldsymbol{A}_2, \ldots, \boldsymbol{A}_p$ are the coefficient matrices (dimensions $M \times M$), containing the coefficients $a_{ij}(k)$ which represent the linear interaction effect of $x_j(n-k)$ onto $x_i(n)$ and where

$$\boldsymbol{e}(n) = [e_1(n), e_2(n), \ldots, e_M(n)]^T \tag{3}$$

is the noise vector (uncorrelated error process). A measure of the direct causal relations (directional connectivity) of x_j to x_i is given by the PDC defined by [16]

$$\pi_{i \leftarrow j}(f) = \frac{A_{ij}(f)}{\sqrt{\boldsymbol{a}_j(f)\boldsymbol{a}_j^T(f)}} \tag{4}$$

where $A_{ij}(f)$ and $\boldsymbol{a}_j$ are, respectively, the i, j element and the j-th column of

$$\boldsymbol{A}(f) = \boldsymbol{I} - \sum_{k=1}^{p} A_k e^{-2\pi i f k}. \tag{5}$$

PDC values range between 0 and 1; $\pi_{i \leftarrow j}$ measures the outflow of information from channel x_j to x_i in relation to the total outflow of information from x_j to all of the channels.

2.5   EEG Processing and Analysis of Connectivities

The methods presented in this paper are implemented in the Matlab package ARfit [17]. For the purpose of this paper, we jointly analyze data from five experimental sessions. The first two seconds of each trial were discarded to assure the concentration of the subject in the task and to get rid of the visual cue artifacts on the EEG. A digital band-pass filter between 0.5 and 50 Hz, a notch filter with 50 Hz cut-off frequency and a laplacian filter as in [12], were applied to the data. Signals were processed in 2 s epochs (400 epochs for each subject). Each epoch undergoes independent component analysis (ICA) with EEGLAB toolbox [18] in order to detect visually the presence of blinking artifacts as in [4]. From now on, we will refer to EEG channel as an electrode.

Once preprocessing was performed, we chose to analyze the directed interconnections in a set of $M = 9$ electrodes from the M1, SMA and PM regions: $S = \{$Cz, CP1, CP2, C1, C2, C3, C4, FC1, FC2$\}$. Under these conditions, the computation of the PDC was based on a method similar to the one used in [19], where a significance threshold for testing for nonzero PDC at a given frequency proposed in [20] was assessed.

In our case, in order to compute the PDC, the signals were fitted with a MVAR(9), where the model order was determined by the Akaike Information Criterion [21]. We analyzed the frequency range of 1 to 30 Hz, as they are within the range considered for the sensorimotor rhythm modulation. For the given set of frequencies, the PDC values from electrode j to electrode i ($i = 1, 2, \ldots, 9; j = 1, 2, \ldots, 9$) were obtained for each 2 s epoch (400 epochs for each subject) obtaining 9×9 matrixes. In all cases (epoch, frequency and direction), the threshold for the PDC to be significant was stored with a statistical significance for $\alpha = 0.05$ for all possible directions at a given frequency (for details see [19]). Then, those epochs for which the PDC value was higher than the significance threshold (i.e., the PDC whose confidence was enough to be regarded as indicative of directional connectivity) were retained in our calculations. For every directed interconnection at a given frequency, we found those more likely (in terms of the total number of epochs with significant interconnections) to be present.

3 Results

The preliminary results of the analysis proposed in Sect. 2.5 are shown in Figs. 1a and 1b for the cases of *active tDCS* and *Sham*, respectively. For each subject, we present the mean value of directed interconnections (in terms of the total number of epochs with significant interconnections) at the frequency bands theta (4–7 Hz), alpha (8–12 Hz) and beta (13–30 Hz). The color bar indicates the normalized number of epochs (out of 400) in which the corresponding directed interconnection was significant. Thus, red regions indicate high levels of connectivity (e.g., 1 indicates 100% of significative epochs) among the nine electrodes.

The results showed that brain connectivity of both groups increase mainly at the alpha and beta bands. Regarding the spatial distribution of the directed interconnections revealed by our analysis in these frequency bands, we note that for the *active tDCS* group (Fig. 1a), the central EEG electrodes Cz, C3 and C4 turned out to be highly connected. Specifically, we note the following cases:

- An outflow greater than 90% (Subjects S1t, S2t and S3t) and 75% (Subject S4t) from Cz to all electrodes;
- An outflow greater than 80% (Subjects S2t, S3t and S4t) and 65% (Subject S1t) from C4, mainly in beta band;
- An outflow greater than 60% (Subjects S2t and S4) from C3;
- An outflow greater than 90% (Subject S1t) from C2 and 50% (Subjects S2t and S3t).

On the contrary, the *sham* (Fig. 1b) group presented a tendency to be more random at its functional connections. The characteristic patterns of this group presented relevant differences among subjects in the resulted interconnections. Expressly, the largest percent of outflows was presented in C3/CP2/FC2 (Subject S5s), C4 (Subject S6s), CP1/CP2 (Subject S7s) and C3/C4 (Subject S8s). It is important to note that the outflow number in this group, in the central electrodes Cz, C3 and C4 is always lower than the *active tDCS* group. It is important to note that the outflow number in this group, in the central electrodes Cz, C3 and C4 is always lower than the *active tDCS* group.

So far, based on preliminary findings more directional connectivity existed in the *active tDCS* group in comparison with the *sham* group. These results are in accordance with the tDCS montage used. As we mentioned above, the montage was composed by one anode located over the right cerebrocerebellum (two centimeters right and one centimeter down of the inion). The effects of the stimulation over the cerebellum are still nuclear [22]. However, recent studies have reported that anodal stimulation over the cerebellum, produces cortical excitability changes in a polarity-specific manner [23]. Furthermore, a second anode was placed over Cz on M1 with a slightly higher current, exciting the motor area, which can explain why the central EEG electrodes Cz, C3 and C4 turned out to be highly connected in the *active tDCS* group.

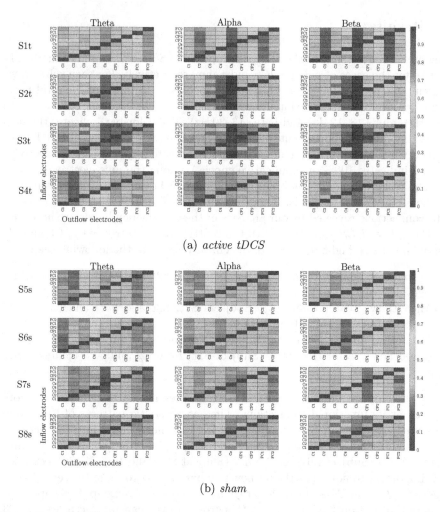

(a) *active tDCS*

(b) *sham*

Fig. 1. Functional brain connectivity during IM for the groups of (a) *active tDCS* and (b) *sham*. For each subject, the mean value of directed interconnections (in terms of the total number of epochs with significant interconnections) at the frequency bands theta (4–7 Hz), alpha (8–12 Hz) and beta (13–30 Hz) is presented. The color bar indicates the normalized number of epochs (out of 400) in which the corresponding directed interconnection was significant. Thus, blue regions indicate low and red regions indicate high levels of connectivity (e.g., 1 indicates 100% of significative epochs) among the 9 electrodes. In all cases the diagonal elements were set to zero. (Color figure online)

4   Conclusions

In conclusion, in this preliminary study we demonstrated that EEG-based PDC analysis is able to detect changes in functional connectivity mediated by the application of transcranial direct current stimulation (one anode located over the right cerebrocerebellum, the other one over the motor cortex in Cz on M1, and the cathode over FC2) in healthy subjects. Our future work will include a more rigorous assessment of our connectivity-based analysis in more complex sensor networks and extending our approach to the study of resting-state brain networks. Furthermore, in the context of BCI applications, we will study the effects of tDCS in the relationship between the brain connectivity (assessed through PDC) and the IM detection accuracy in operating a BCI, in order to development of brain plasticity over the course of training sessions. This information can be useful to help understanding the neuroplastic modifications induced by tDCS, and design therapies to motor neurorehabilitation.

Acknowledgments. This research has been carried out in the framework of the project Associate - Decoding and stimulation of motor and sensory brain activity to support long term potentiation through Hebbian and paired associative stimulation during rehabilitation of gait (DPI2014-58431-C4-2-R), funded by the Spanish Ministry of Economy and Competitiveness and by the European Union through the European Regional Development Fund (ERDF) "A way to build Europe". Also, the Mexican Council of Science and Technology (CONACyT) provided J. A. Gaxiola-Tirado his scholarship, under Grant 220145.

References

1. Gandiga, P.C., Hummel, F.C., Cohen, L.G.: Transcranial DC stimulation (tDCS): a tool for double-blind sham-controlled clinical studies in brain stimulation. Clin. Neurophysiol. **117**(4), 845–850 (2006)
2. Brunoni, A.R., et al.: Clinical research with transcranial direct current stimulation (tDCS): challenges and future directions. Brain Stimul. **5**(3), 175–195 (2012)
3. Nitsche, M.A., Paulus, W.: Excitability changes induced in the human motor cortex by weak transcranial direct current stimulation. J. Physiol. **527**(3), 633–639 (2000)
4. Angulo-Sherman, I.N., Rodríguez-Ugarte, M., Sciacca, N., Iáñez, E., Azorín, J.M.: Effect of tDCS stimulation of motor cortex and cerebellum on EEG classification of motor imagery and sensorimotor band power. J. Neuroeng. Rehabil. **14**(1), 31 (2017)
5. Matsumoto, J., Fujiwara, T., Takahashi, O., Liu, M., Kimura, A., Ushiba, J.: Modulation of mu rhythm desynchronization during motor imagery by transcranial direct current stimulation. J. Neuroeng. Rehabil. **7**(1), 27 (2010)
6. Reis, J., Fritsch, B.: Modulation of motor performance and motor learning by transcranial direct current stimulation. Curr. Opin. Neurol. **24**(6), 590–596 (2011)
7. Lee, S.J., Chun, M.H.: Combination transcranial direct current stimulation and virtual reality therapy for upper extremity training in patients with subacute stroke. Arch. Phys. Med. Rehabil. **95**(3), 431–438 (2014)
8. Butler, A.J., Shuster, M., O'hara, E., Hurley, K., Middlebrooks, D., Guilkey, K.: A meta-analysis of the efficacy of anodal transcranial direct current stimulation for upper limb motor recovery in stroke survivors. JJ. Hand Ther. **26**(2), 162–171 (2013)
9. Kim, D.Y., et al.: Effect of transcranial direct current stimulation on motor recovery in patients with subacute stroke. Am. J. Phys. Med. Rehabil. **89**(11), 879–886 (2010)

10. Foerster, Á., Dutta, A., Kuo, M.F., Paulus, W., Nitsche, M.A.: Effects of anodal transcranial direct current stimulation over lower limb primary motor cortex on motor learning in healthy individuals. Eur. J. Neurosci. **47**(7), 779–789 (2018)
11. Fernandez, L., et al.: Cathodal transcranial direct current stimulation (tDCS) to the right cerebellar hemisphere affects motor adaptation during gait. Cerebellum **16**(1), 168–177 (2017)
12. Rodriguez-Ugarte, M., Iáñez, E., Ortiz-Garcia, M., Azorín, J.M.: Effects of tDCS on real-time BCI detection of pedaling motor imagery. Sensors **18**(4), 1136 (2018)
13. Bakker, M., De Lange, F., Stevens, J., Toni, I., Bloem, B.: Motor imagery of gait: a quantitative approach. Exp. Brain Res. **179**(3), 497–504 (2007)
14. Parsons, L.M., et al.: Use of implicit motor imagery for visual shape discrimination as revealed by PET. Nature **375**(6526), 54 (1995)
15. Hamedi, M., Salleh, S.H., Noor, A.M.: Electroencephalographic motor imagery brain connectivity analysis for BCI: a review. Neural Comput. **28**(6), 999–1041 (2016)
16. Baccalá, L.A., Sameshima, K.: Partial directed coherence: a new concept in neural structure determination. Biol. Cybern. **84**(6), 463–474 (2001)
17. Neumaier, A., Schneider, T.: Estimation of parameters and eigenmodes of multivariate autoregressive models. ACM Trans. Math. Softw. (TOMS) **27**(1), 27–57 (2001)
18. Delorme, A., Makeig, S.: EEGLAB: an open source toolbox for analysis of single-trial EEG dynamics including independent component analysis. J. Neurosci. Methods **134**(1), 9–21 (2004)
19. Gaxiola-Tirado, J.A., Salazar-Varas, R., Gutiérrez, D.: Using the partial directed coherence to assess functional connectivity in electroencephalography data for brain-computer interfaces. IEEE Trans. Cogn. Dev. Syst. **10**(3), 776–783 (2018)
20. Schelter, B., et al.: Testing for directed influences among neural signals using partial directed coherence. J. Neurosci. Methods **152**(1–2), 210–219 (2006)
21. Akaike, H.: A new look at the statistical model identification. IEEE Trans. Autom. Control. **19**(6), 716–723 (1974)
22. van Dun, K., Bodranghien, F.C., Mariën, P., Manto, M.U.: tDCS of the cerebellum: where do we stand in 2016? Technical issues and critical review of the literature. Front. Hum. Neurosci. **10**, 199 (2016)
23. Galea, J.M., Jayaram, G., Ajagbe, L., Celnik, P.: Modulation of cerebellar excitability by polarity-specific noninvasive direct current stimulation. J. Neurosci. **29**(28), 9115–9122 (2009)

Distinguishing Aging Clusters and Mobile Devices by Hand-Wrist Articulation: A Case of Study

Daniel Palacios-Alonso[1,2](✉) , Carlos Lázaro-Carrascosa[1,2] ,
Raquel Mas-García[1] , José Manuel Ferrández Vicente[3] ,
Andrés Gómez-Rodellar[2] , and Pedro Gómez-Vilda[2]

[1] Escuela Técnica Superior de Ingeniería Informática, Universidad Rey Juan Carlos,
Campus de Móstoles, Tulipán, s/n, 28933 Móstoles, Madrid, Spain
daniel.palacios@urjc.es
[2] Neuromorphic Speech Processing Lab, Center for Biomedical Technology,
Universidad Politécnica de Madrid, Campus de Montegancedo,
28223 Pozuelo de Alarcón, Madrid, Spain
[3] Universidad Politécnica de Cartagena,
Campus Universitario Muralla del Mar, Pza. Hospital 1, 30202 Cartagena, Spain

Abstract. Nowadays, video games are not considered only mere hobbies. The use of these tools is increased in last years. On the other hand, gamification and usability techniques have empowered the improvement of communication between player/user and Aided Communication Devices (ACD). New ACDs provide a novel approach to capture biomechanical features or indicators. This work consists of a novel methodology development to capture biomechanical indicators throughout multiplatform video games. The present work has an exploratory nature to measure, hand-wrist articulation features estimated from the smartphone's accelerometer. The intention of the study is to answer some hypothesis for instance, if the device is crucial to evaluate player's movement capabilities or if the age of the person as a key biomarker. Once these indicators have been tested, it will be able to use them in studies of neurodegenerative diseases, where involuntary tremor is one of the most important observable correlates.

Keywords: Hand-wrist articulation · Video games ·
Gamification · Mobile devices · Neurodegenerative diseases

1 Introduction

When speaking about a case of study or proof of concept, one of the aims is to find an objective method which produces always consistent results. However, some well-known scales, such as Hoëhn-Yahr [9] or UPDRS [7], which are used to diagnose the grade or level of symptom severity in Parkinson's Disease (PD) patients do not satisfy this premise because two raters could produce different

© Springer Nature Switzerland AG 2019
J. M. Ferrández Vicente et al. (Eds.): IWINAC 2019, LNCS 11486, pp. 11–21, 2019.
https://doi.org/10.1007/978-3-030-19591-5_2

scores for the same patient using the same rating scale. This methodology is based on the subjective opinion of the clinician. The rater is going to review a list of items where each item has a lower and upper limit. That is where a subjective decision of the professional comes in. This decision could be crucial due to the waiting list in health services. Depending on the speciality and clinical diagnosis, patients must wait between four and eighteen months for their next clinical revision. Furthermore, it must also be remembered that posology and dosing must be subject to frequent revision and updating. For this reason, it is necessary to design and develop a methodology reproducible, simple and ubiquitous to assess the conditions of the patient in any circumstance.

According to the results of Tardon's work [8], the serious video games and gamification are a powerful tool for direct social transformation in several fields: health improvement [4], learning [10], work performance [11], etc. Furthermore, as is well known, the industry of video games has clearly grown fast in last years and the use of video games in biomedical research has been notable [17] but not without critical voices in this approach [2,3]. On the other hand, the use of video consoles such as Wii of Nintendo® in biomedicine is a reality [14]. Moreover, in the rehabilitation area, video games are a novel approach and are used as well [16,18].

The contribution of this work is to propose and assess a methodology to capture and monitor biomechanical features throughout the use of a hand-held video game. The calculated trait and the hand-wrist articulation, were estimated from the smartphone's accelerometer through a video game using a mobile device.

This paper is organized as follows. In Sect. 2, we introduce the proposed methods. The following section, the materials used. Results are shown and discussed in Sect. 4. And finally, conclusions are presented in Sect. 5.

2   Methods

2.1   Objectives

In what follows, the objectives that are to be achieved at the beginning of this work will be presented. To monitor player's activity it is necessary to design and develop two questionnaires. The first one is based on an enrolment form to know the initial conditions of the user, and consists of items such as user code, age, gender, region, country, current diseases, and in its case, prescriptions and dosage in the moment of the enrolment. This form is presented only the first time. The second one is the dialy questionnaire, which must take into account occasional data, as the circumstantial use of a painkiller, antihistaminics, antibiotics, etc., to have into account any possible factors which could alter patient's neuromotor conditions beforehand at each session start. Once the state of the player is assessed, the a priori conditions of the hand-wrist articulation will be monitored using the smart device accelerometer, to be saved in the server database.

2.2   Methodology

The experiment consists of three stages: Home, Game and Scores. During the Game, the player must turn the wrist from the right to left, and vice-versa, as in driving a car in both directions. This movement is similar to turn the steering wheel in a car. In Fig. 1a an example of the game interface is illustrated.

The experiment is based on the development of a first-person racing video game, where the player has to collect the highest number of coins on the road, as it may be seen in Fig. 1b. The number of coins collected is an indication of the ability of the player to stay within the road limits, if this number is below a given value, an alarm will warn the players to improve their performance. Furthermore, the game has some props for a high quality immersive experience, for example, trees, road, grass, and other details. On the other hand, there are distractor objects such as stones and fences. The last ones are obstacles that slow down the race. If the player crashes with these objects, the car stops. However, if the players pulls back the mobile device towards their chest, the car jumps these obstacles and continue the race. In every single moment of the game, the device captures the accelerometer's outcomes. This information is sent via a 4G connection to the database server.

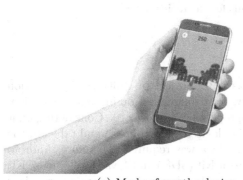

(a) Mode of use the device.

(b) Screenshot of racing game.

Fig. 1. Capture of racing video game.

2.3   Technical Description of Video Game

The game controller is in charge of starting the game, managing the objects and ending the game. This controller generates the roadmap dynamically in real time, using eleven different roads aspects as the ones depicted in Fig. 2a and b, respectively. It was necessary to create checkpoints, which informed the controller when it had to draw the next road. The checkpoints are hidden to players.

Simple and little overloaded interfaces have been contemplated because the target user may not be familiar with video games lore. Big font sizes to facilitate the reading and large buttons were used as well. The naming of the screens and texts were very descriptive.

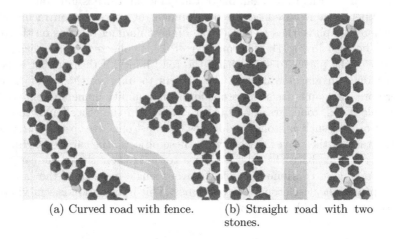

(a) Curved road with fence.

(b) Straight road with two stones.

Fig. 2. Kind of roads for the racing game.

2.4 Framework and Hardware

The application has been developed as a 3D project in Unity [1]. The version used was 5.6.1 because of its stability, fixed bugs, and online documentation. The operative system used in the laptop was Windows 10. Considering that the application was addressed to mobile devices (smartphones and tablets), the use of external libraries of Android and Java was required. Therefore, Android version 24.4.1 of the Software Development Kit (SDK) and Java Development Kit (version 1.8.0) were included. On the other hand, e-mail management required the use of a Dynamic Link Library (DLL) as a project dependency.

Two groups were involved in the proof of concept: end-users and contrast-users. Each group tested the proof in different devices. The first group used a smartphone Huawei P8 Lite with two GB of RAM, sixteen GB of memory, octa-core, a screen of 5.2 in., and Android version 6.0. The contrast group used a tablet Bq Elcano with a GB of RAM, sixteen GB of memory, dual-core, a screen of seven inches, and Android version 4.1.2.

2.5 Statistical Methods

One-Sample Kolmogorov-Smirnov Test is a non-parametric statistical test which is used to assess if a variable follows a given distribution in a population [13]. The null hypothesis for the Kolmogorov-Smirnov test is rejected if its $p-value < 0.05$, this means that the data is normally distributed, otherwise, the distribution is not normally distributed [5]. The K-S test measures the largest distance between the empirical distribution function(EDF) $F_{data}(x)$ and the theoretical function $F_0(x)$ [19]. Let $F_0(x)$ is the cumulative distribution function (cdf) of the hypothesized distribution and $F_{data}(x)$ is the EDF of your observed data. The expression of KS-test:

$$D = sup_x|F_0(x) - F_{data}(x)| \tag{1}$$

Parametric test: t-Student is a statistical test which is used to compare the mean of two groups of samples, assessing if the means of the two sets of data are significantly different from each other [5]. The unpaired two sample T test has been used, used to compare the mean of two independent samples, where its expression is given in Eq. (2) X and Y represent the two groups to compare; m_X and m_Y being the means of groups, respectively. Finally, n_X and n_Y represent the group sizes.

$$T = \frac{m_X - m_Y}{\sqrt{\frac{\sigma^2}{n_X} + \frac{\sigma^2}{n_Y}}} \tag{2}$$

Non-Parametric test: Mann-Whitney U test is the non-parametric alternative to the independent T-test [12]. The test compares two distributions. If these samples are part of the same population, the null hypothesis is not rejected. Otherwise, an alternate null hypothesis is that the two samples belong to the same distribution, that is to say, both samples have the same median. Let X and Y are the distributions, respectively. R is the sum of ranks in the sample, and n is the number of items in the sample.

$$U_1 = R_1 - \frac{n_X(n_X + 1)}{2}; U_2 = R_2 - \frac{n_Y(n_Y + 1)}{2} \tag{3}$$

Cohen's Coefficient or Size effect is determined by calculating the mean difference between two groups M_1 and M_2, respectively, and then dividing the result by the standard deviation of the pooled population [6,15]. This coefficient is used to measure the differences among samples when the T-Student or U-Mann-Whitney tests are used.

$$d = \frac{M_1 - M_2}{\sigma} \tag{4}$$

3   Materials

3.1   Corpora

The corpus consists of two groups, control (nine volunteers) and contrast (four volunteers). The number of participant users was thirteen of different ages and genders and they did not have any neurodegenerative disease at the moment of the experiment. The *Kolmogorov-Smirnov test* was used to assess the distributions and it was concluded that both distributions are normal as their p-values were higher than 0.05 as shown in Fig. 3. In Fig. 4 the boxplots of both datasets are shown.

One-Sample Kolmogorov-Smirnov Test

		AVERAGE
N		13
Normal Parameters(a,b)	Mean	1,80581681
	Std. Deviation	,889302271
Most Extreme Differences	Absolute	,226
	Positive	,226
	Negative	-,196
Kolmogorov-Smirnov Z		,814
Asymp. Sig. (2-tailed)		,521
a Test distribution is Normal.		
b Calculated from data.		

Fig. 3. Summary of one-sample Kolmogorov-Smirnov test with 95% confidence interval.

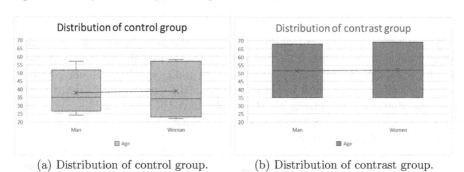

(a) Distribution of control group.   (b) Distribution of contrast group.

Fig. 4. Capture of both datasets.

3.2   Control Group

The control group was composed of the nine volunteers (familiars and friends) with ages between 22 and 58 years old, five of whom were women and four men. The details are shown in Table 1.

3.3   Contrast Group

The contrast group was composed of four volunteers (relatives and friends) with ages between 35 and 69 years old, of whom two were women and two men. The details are shown in Table 2.

Table 1. Corpus of control group.

ID	Age	Gender	Competence in video games
A1	24	Male	High
A2	22	Female	Medium
A3	23	Female	High
B1	34	Female	Medium
B2	36	Male	High
B3	34	Male	High
C1	56	Female	High
C2	57	Male	Medium
C3	58	Female	Low

Table 2. Corpus of contrast group.

ID	Age	Gender	Competence in video games
ContrastB1	35	Male	High
ContrastB2	35	Female	Medium
ContrastC1	68	Male	High
ContrastC2	69	Female	Low

4 Results

The results presented in this paper are extracted from a game session with a duration of 2 min. The volunteers did not know this game in advance. In this way, all participants had the same opportunities and level of knowledge about the test, game, and the scenario at the beginning of test.

As it was explained before, the statistical tests used in the evaluation were T-test, U-test and Cohen's Coefficient. Given the number of samples in both dataset it was necessary to check the values with parametric and non-parametric approaches, because parametric methods assume a statistical distribution in data. However, non-parametric techniques do not require these initial conditions.

The outcomes of the test are depicted in the following pictures Fig. 5a for the control group and Fig. 5b for the contrast group, respectively.

The results are divided into three categories, such as *aging test, smartphone tests, and tablet tests*. Cluster A includes people between 20 and 30 years old. The second cluster (B) includes volunteers between 31 and 50 years old. Finally, the last cluster is composed of players between 51 to 70 years old.

The outcomes are depicted in Table 3 for women and men, regardless of the specific device used. Analyzing the results, it may be noticed that the significant results were obtained in comparing cluster C with A and B, being both tests, parametric and non-parametric, the null hypothesis being rejected with 95% confidence interval. Furthermore, Cohen's coefficient reveals a negative value

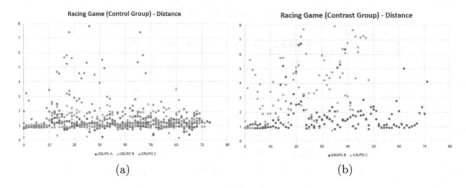

Fig. 5. Results to a session of racing game. Left (a): values of distance respect the middle of road of control group. Cluster A (blue), Cluster B (orange) and Cluster C (grey). Right (b): values of distance respect the middle of road of contrast group. Cluster B (blue) and Cluster C (orange). (Color figure online)

greater than −1.15 (kappa value), in others words, the distributions can be considered different.

Table 3. Summary of results according to the age of volunteers.

Test	T-student	Mann-Whitney test	Cohen coefficient
Cluster A vs B	0.057 (No)	0.101 (No)	
Cluster A vs C	**0.021 (Yes)**	**0.025 (Yes)**	−1.762
Cluster A vs (B U C)	0.101 (No)	0.028 (Yes)	−1.10
Cluster B vs C	**0.042 (Yes)**	**0.016 (Yes)**	−1.515
Cluster B vs (A U C)	0.260 (No)	0.380 (No)	
Cluster C vs (A U B)	0.032 (No)	0.005 (No)	−1.98

Table 4 shows results using only the smartphone. Once again, cluster C seems to be different in both techniques and Cohen's coefficient asserts this condition with respect to cluster A and B even when the third cluster is compared with the union of both.

Table 4. Summary of results from the smartphone.

Test	T-student	Mann-Whitney test	Cohen coefficient
Cluster A vs B	0.215 (No)	0.275 (No)	
Cluster A vs C	**0.015 (Yes)**	**0.05 (Yes)**	−5.06
Cluster A vs (B U C)	0.078 (No)	0.071 (No)	
Cluster B vs C	**0.012 (Yes)**	**0.05 (Yes)**	−2.86
Cluster B vs (A U C)	0.411 (No)	0.606 (No)	
Cluster C vs (A U B)	**0.006 (Yes)**	**0.02 (Yes)**	−4.15

Table 5. Summary of results according to the tablet.

Test	T-student	Mann-Whitney test	Cohen Coefficient
Cluster B vs C	**0.008 (Yes)**	0.121 (No)	**−13.45**

Table 6. Summary of results according to devices and age.

Test	T-student	Mann-Whitney test	Cohen coefficient
Smartphone vs Tablet	0.097(No)	**0.045 (Yes)**	−1.76
Smartphone vs Tablet with Cluster B	**0.033 (Yes)**	0.083 (No)	−2.15
Smartphone vs Tablet with Cluster C	**0.002 (Yes)**	0.083 (No)	−7.61

The test results obtained with the tablet are given in Table 5, where T-Student rejects the initial hypothesis with a rather low value (0.008). However, the U-test does not reject the hypothesis. Nevertheless, Cohen's coefficient returns a high negative value (−13.45), being the lowest value obtained for all tests.

Finally, Table 6 describes the results having into account the devices and the age of players. In this case, T-Student rejects the initial hypothesis in two tests and the U-test only on one occasion. However, both tests have never coincided.

5 Conclusions

The use of video games in biomedical applications is a hot topic. Through the present exploratory study a first approach to this problem under a systematic methodology has been presented. Although limited by the small number of samples included, the most relevant findings derived are the following:

- The third cluster, the elder players, had produced the highest difference respect to the two other groups, that is to say, the young and middle-aged populations. This fact is illustrated when the tests reject the null hypothesis with a p-value less than 0.05 and with a rather high Cohen's coefficient.
- It seems that the devices are a key point in producing this kind of results. The use of a tablet or smartphone produces distinct outcomes. Of course, there are several factors to be taken into account such as weight, performance, and size of devices. It is worth to highlight that the smartphone used is a medium-range device but the tablet is a bottom-range device. Nevertheless, this fact allows a further reflection: it is not necessary to use a top-range device to produce significant results in this type of study.
- Although the outcomes of this research are very promising, a drawback in this exploratory study is the number of samples. For this reason, the continuation of the study foresees two main ideas: Firstly, increasing the number of samples with both devices using another game mode, for example, a third-person mode, where the player can visualize the car instead of being inside the car. Secondly, releasing the video game in Play Store (Android) or App Store (Apple) to recruit more samples.

Acknowledgments. This work is being funded by grants TEC2016 – 77791 – C4 – 4 – R (MINECO, Spain) and CENIE – TECA – PARK_55_02 INTERREG V – A Spain – Portugal (POCTEP).

References

1. Unity Homepage. https://unity3d.com/. Accessed 3 Jan 2019
2. Anderson, C.A.: An update on the effects of playing violent video games. J. Adolesc. **27**(1), 113–122 (2004)
3. Anderson, C.A., Bushman, B.J.: Effects of violent video games on aggressive behavior, aggressive cognition, aggressive affect, physiological arousal, and prosocial behavior: A meta-analytic review of the scientific literature. Psychol. Sci. **12**(5), 353–359 (2001)
4. Anguera, J.A., et al.: Video game training enhances cognitive control in older adults. Nature **501**(7465), 97 (2013)
5. Boslaugh, S.: Statistics in a Nutshell: A Desktop Quick Reference. O'Reilly Media Inc., Sebastopol (2012)
6. Cohen, J.: Statistical Power Analysis for the Behavioural Sciences. Routledge, Abingdon (1988)
7. Goetz, C.G., Tilley, B.C., Shaftman, S.R., Stebbins, G.T., Fahn, S., Martinez-Martin, P., Poewe, W., Sampaio, C., Stern, M.B., Dodel, R., et al.: Movement disorder society-sponsored revision of the unified parkinson's disease rating scale (MDS-UPDRS): scale presentation and clinimetric testing results. Mov. Disord.: Off. J. Mov. Disord. Soc. **23**(15), 2129–2170 (2008)
8. González, C.: Videojuegos para la transformación social. Aportaciones conceptuales y metodológicas. Ph.D. thesis, Tesis para optar a grado de Doctor: Universidad de Deusto. Recuperado el 27 (2014)
9. Hoehn, M.M., Yahr, M.D., et al.: Parkinsonism: onset, progression, and mortality. Neurology **50**(2), 318–318 (1998)
10. Jiménez-Hernández, E.M., Oktaba, H., Piattini, M., Arceo, F.D.B., Revillagigedo-Tulais, A.M., Flores-Zarco, S.V.: Methodology to construct educational video games in software engineering. In: 2016 4th International Conference in Software Engineering Research and Innovation (CONISOFT), pp. 110–114. IEEE (2016)
11. Korn, O.: Industrial playgrounds: how gamification helps to enrich work for elderly or impaired persons in production. In: Proceedings of the 4th ACM SIGCHI Symposium on Engineering Interactive Computing Systems, pp. 313–316. ACM (2012)
12. Mann, H.B., Whitney, D.R.: On a test of whether one of two random variables is stochastically larger than the other. Ann. Math. Stat., 50–60 (1947)
13. Massey Jr., F.J.: The Kolmogorov-Smirnov test for goodness of fit. J. Am. Stat. Assoc. **46**(253), 68–78 (1951)
14. Mhatre, P.V., et al.: Wii fit balance board playing improves balance and gait in Parkinson disease. PM&R **5**(9), 769–777 (2013)
15. Rosnow, R.L., Rosenthal, R.: Effect sizes for experimenting psychologists. Can. J. Exp. Psychol./Rev. Can. Psychol. expérimentale **57**(3), 221 (2003)
16. Silva, K.G., et al.: Effects of virtual rehabilitation versus conventional physical therapy on postural control, gait, and cognition of patients with Parkinsons disease: study protocol for a randomized controlled feasibility trial. Pilot Feasibility Stud. **3**(1), 68 (2017)
17. Staiano, A.E., Flynn, R.: Therapeutic uses of active videogames: a systematic review. Games Health J. **3**(6), 351–365 (2014)

18. Stanmore, E., Stubbs, B., Vancampfort, D., de Bruin, E.D., Firth, J.: The effect of active video games on cognitive functioning in clinical and non-clinical populations: a meta-analysis of randomized controlled trials. Neurosci. Biobehav. Rev. **78**, 34–43 (2017)
19. Stephens, M.: Introduction to kolmogorov (1933) on the empirical determination of a distribution. In: Kotz, S., Johnson, N.L. (eds.) Breakthroughs in Statistics, pp. 93–105. Springer, Heidelberg (1992). https://doi.org/10.1007/978-1-4612-4380-9_9

Hardware and Software for Integrating Brain–Computer Interface with Internet of Things

Francisco Laport$^{(\boxtimes)}$, Francisco J. Vazquez-Araujo , Paula M. Castro ,
and Adriana Dapena

Department of Computer Engineering,
Universidade da Coruña, Campus de Elviña s/n, 15071 A Coruña, Spain
francisco.laport@udc.es
http://www.gtec.udc.es

Abstract. This work shows a system that appropriately integrates a Brain–Computer Interface and an Internet of Things environment based on eye state identification. The Electroencephalography prototype for brain electrical signal acquisition has been designed by the authors. This prototype uses only one electrode and its size is very small, which facilitates its use for all type of applications. We also design a classifier based on the simple calculation of a threshold ratio between alpha and beta rhythm powers. As shown from some experiment results, this threshold-based classifier shows high accuracies for medium response times, and according to that state identification any smart home environment with those response requirements could correctly act, for example ON–OFF switching room lights.

Keywords: Brain–Computer Interface · EEG devices ·
Internet of Things

1 Introduction

A Brain–Computer Interface (BCI) is defined as a hardware and software communication system that records brain electrical activity, commonly obtained by means of Electroencephalography (EEG), and translates it into control commands for external devices [12]. These systems are especially interesting for people with severe motor disabilities since they allow them to interact with their environment without physical activity requirements.

Recent development of low-cost EEG devices together with emerging Internet of Things (IoT) have promoted the creation of new daily-used BCI applications

This work has been funded by the Xunta de Galicia (ED431C 2016-045, ED341D R2016/012), the Agencia Estatal de Investigacin of Spain (TEC2015-69648-REDC, TEC2016-75067-C4-1-R) and ERDF funds of the EU (AEI/FEDER, UE), and the predoctoral grant (ED481A-2018/156).

J. M. Ferrández Vicente et al. (Eds.): IWINAC 2019, LNCS 11486, pp. 22–31, 2019.
https://doi.org/10.1007/978-3-030-19591-5_3

in several domains [11]. As an extension of our proposal presented in [8], we will consider the utilization of BCI to determine the eye state and its integration with IoT.

Eye state identification or the eye-gaze analysis have become emerging topics of study in recent years due to its implication in human machine interfaces [10,14]. In particular, EEG eye state detection has been successfully applied in a wide variety of domains [19], such as infant sleep-waking state classification [6], driving drowsiness detection [20], stress features identification [18] and home automation control [7], among others.

Different approaches have been applied in the literature to classify and distinguish both eye states: closed eyes (cE) and open eyes (oE). Rösler and Suendermann [16] tested 42 different machine learning algorithms to predict the eye state from an EEG dataset of 117 s and 14 channels. The best performance was achieved by the K-star classifier with an error rate of 2.7 %.

Another study of Saghafi et al. based on that dataset employed Multivariate Empirical Mode Decomposition (MEMD) for feature extraction and Logistic Regression (LR), Artificial Neural Networks (NN), and Support Vector Machine (SVM) classifiers for detection of eye state changes [17]. Their proposed algorithm detected the eye state change with an accuracy of 88.2 % in less than 2 s. In this sense, Wang et al. [19] extracted the channel standard deviation and mean as features for an Incremental Attribute Learning (IAL) algorithm and achieved an error rate of 27.45 % from that dataset. In a recent study, Piatek et al. [13] tested 23 machine learning algorithms using four different datasets obtained from a 19-channels EEG device to classify three eye states: cE, oE and blinking. They showed that it is possible to predict eye states using EEG recordings with an accuracy range from about 96 % to 99 % in a real-time scenario.

Although some related work already achieve efficient and accurate detection of eye states, most of them collect brain activity using at least 14 electrodes and big–size EGG devices. Therefore, the main limitation of those devices is the user comfort and their difficulty to be used for long time periods or daily-life activities.

In contrast to these approaches, in this work we develop a BCI software tool integrated in an IoT system for non–critical real situations which only employs a single–channel EEG device to capture user's brain activity. This system monitors alpha (8–3 Hz) and beta (14–19 Hz) rhythms and extracts the mean power ratio between those bands as novel feature to determine user eye states. The extracted knowledge is then communicated to the rest of IoT devices as control commands using Message Queue Telemetry Transport (MQTT) [4].

This paper is organized as follows. Section 2 is devoted to show the system design and its architecture. Section 3 shows the main results achieved with the proposed system and some concluding remarks are made in Sect. 4.

2   System Design and Architecture

For the integration of both BCI application and IoT environment we propose the architecture shown in Fig. 1. The aim of this system is to capture the user's brain activity during its daily-life home activities and detect his/her eye states to control different environment devices. The main details about this architecture are described in this section.

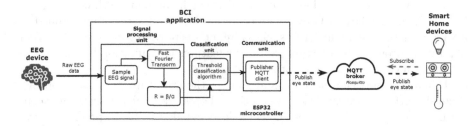

Fig. 1. Proposed system architecture.

2.1 EEG Device

The developed wireless EEG prototype is shown in Fig. 2. It employs three electrodes to capture EEG signals: input, reference and ground electrodes. The prototype uses the AD8221 instrumentation amplifier followed by a 50 Hz notch filter, a second order low pass filter with a cutoff frequency of 29.20 Hz, a second order high pass filter with a cutoff frequency of 4.74 Hz and a final bandpass filter with a frequency range from 4.7 Hz to 22 Hz with adjustable gain. The resulting EEG signal is sampled by the ESP32 microcontroller module [3] at a rate of 128 Hz.

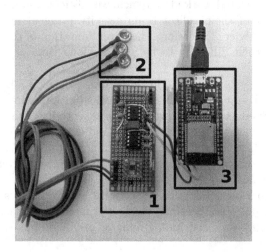

Fig. 2. Proposed EGG device prototype. (1) Amplifier; (2) Electrodes; (3) ESP32 microcontroller.

2.2   Signal Processing and Classification

The ESP32 microcontroller captures the brain signal received from the EEG device and carries out its processing and classification. Due to its dual core nature, complex processing tasks, such as Fast Fourier Transform (FFT), can be performed while the signal is sampled and the extracted knowledge is sent to the IoT environment. For the FFT implementation we will use an Arduino library [1].

The proposed eye state classifier makes use of the mean power value of the alpha (α) and beta (β) brain rhythms. Several studies have proved that the α power increases during closed eyes state while significant reductions are produced when subjects open their eyes. On the other hand, beta power does not show relevant differences between both eye states [5,9].

According to these studies, the proposed classifier obtains both powers considering a fixed time window and their ratio, defined as $R = \beta/\alpha$, is then calculated. This will be the extracted feature to be fed back to the threshold–based system responsible for deciding the user's eyes state. Thus, low ratios are associated to cE state due to the higher alpha, while higher ratios are connected to oE states due to lower alpha powers. Consequently, those ratio values smaller than a predetermined threshold will be classified as closed eyes. By contrast, the values higher than that threshold will represent the open eyes state. The classifier criteria is then defined by the following decision rule,

$$\begin{aligned} \text{cE}, \quad & R \leq T_{\mathbf{h}}, \\ \text{oE}, \quad & R > T_{\mathbf{h}}, \end{aligned} \tag{1}$$

where $T_{\mathbf{h}}$ and R are the threshold and ratio values, respectively.

The threshold value is calibrated from different EEG recordings and eye states. Thus, $T_{\mathbf{h}}$ is defined as follows

$$T_{\mathbf{h}} = \frac{\max(R_{\text{cE}}) + \min(R_{\text{oE}})}{2}, \tag{2}$$

where R_{cE} and R_{oE} respectively represent the ratio value for closed and open eyes.

Once the user's eye state is classified, that state is communicated to the IoT environment using the MQTT protocol.

2.3   IoT Environment

The IoT ecosystem is composed firstly by the EEG device and its BCI application and secondly, by the rest of household devices which consult the received information to determine its behavior.

The communication between different IoT agents is based on the MQTT protocol. It is a publish/subscribe, extremely simple and lightweight messaging protocol, designed for constrained devices and low-bandwidth networks. The publish/subscribe model is built around a central broker and a number of clients connected to the broker. The broker acts like an intermediary agent, responsible for relating that information provided by the publishers with the subscribers clients [15].

These publishers send messages to the broker about an specific topic and the subscribers register their interest in some of them with the broker. The broker acts as a matchmaker, dealing with authentication and controlling who is allowed to publish or subscribe to which topics. These topics can be easily combined and created, so the system could be expanded by the inclusion of new devices or applications into the new topics.

The BCI application, running on the ESP32, is the first publisher client of the IoT ecosystem. It detects the user's eye state and, making use of the Wi-Fi module incorporated in the microcontroller, publishes the extracted information to the broker.

The MQTT broker deals with the messages received from the BCI application and forwards it to interested subscribers. The sent data correspond to 1–byte data, which represents the user's eye state. The broker is deployed in a Raspberry Pi 2 model B and implemented using Eclipse Mosquitto [2], an open source and lightweight MQTT broker.

A wide variety of household devices could be incorporated to the system as subscriber clients (e.g light bulbs, kitchen burners, heating system, and so on). These devices receive information from the broker and react accordingly to it i.e., if the kitchen burner client receives that the user had the eyes closed for a long time, which likely means that he/she has fallen asleep, then the subscriber client should turn off burners in order to avoid risks.

3   Experimental Results

The experiments conducted in this study will aim to prove the accuracy in classification of the proposed system and its possible implementation in a real-life scenario. For this purpose, two different experiments have been developed: firstly, an off-line experiment, which tests classifier performances and secondly, an on-line experiment, which demonstrates the integration of both BCI and IoT environments. The details of these experiments are described in this section.

3.1   Off-line Experiments

The proposed classifier uses 42 EEG recordings captured from four healthy male volunteers, i.e. a total of 168 recordings is considered. Each one is composed by 20 s of each eye state. Therefore, we have 84 of them corresponding to cE and also 84 to oE. The subjects were asked not to move or speak during the experiment. Brain signals were captured at 128 Hz and, according to the 10–20 International System, the input electrode was located at the FP2 position, while reference and ground electrodes were placed in O2 and right mastoid positions, respectively. Figure 3 shows this electrode position (left) and a picture of a subject during the closed eyes recording using the proposed EEG device.

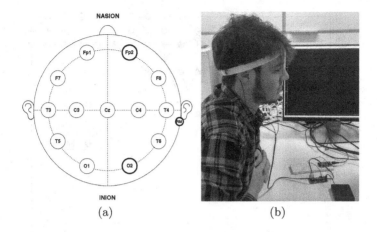

NASION

INION

(a)   (b)

Fig. 3. Electrode position (left) and a subject's photo in a closed eyes task (right).

The classifier is trained by selecting 8 random recordings, 4 for each eye state. Then, considering these training recordings, the threshold value is obtained by applying Eq. (2). According to this threshold value, the test recordings will be classified applying the criterion defined in Eq. (1), i.e. instances with a ratio value smaller than this threshold are classified as closed eyes, while those with higher values are classified as open eyes.

Depending on system applications, T_h and R parameters could be calculated considering different sizes for the time windows. Figure 4 shows the classifier accuracy as a function of time window size. It can be observed that as this size increases, the obtained accuracy improves, and vice versa. Thus, the accuracy is smaller than 70 % for all the subjects with windows of 1 s and greater than 90 % for a size of 13 s. Therefore, there is an important trade-off between system response time and classifier accuracy.

As can be observed from the figure, the proposed algorithm is appropriate for non–critical applications where short response times are not required. Consequently, optimal window sizes will be those with higher classifier accuracy for medium response times. For that reason, the window sizes range from 10 s to 19 s are selected. Figure 5 shows the corresponding threshold values obtained for these window sizes.

On the other hand, it is also important to highlight that those thresholds are highly user-dependent and, as a consequence, the classifier accuracy also depends on the brain characteristics of each subject.

3.2 On-line Experiments

The integration of both BCI and IoT environments will be tested now using a more realistic scenario. For this purpose, the BCI application will perform an on-line detection of user's eye state and according to this information the IoT ecosystem will control different elements of its surroundings.

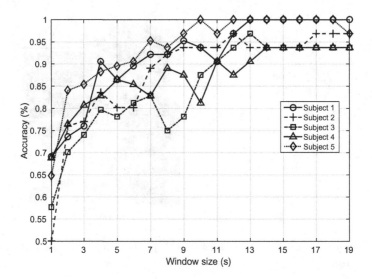

Fig. 4. Accuracy of the proposed classifier for different time window sizes.

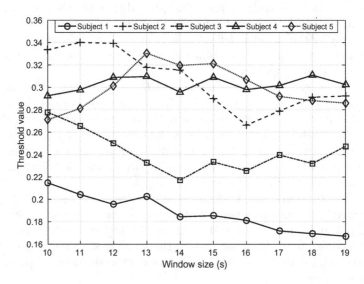

Fig. 5. Threshold values of each subject for different time window sizes.

Figure 6 shows the user's flowchart for a recording starting from an open eyes state. Forty EEG recordings were captured from subject 1 with the electrode position used for the off-line experiment described in the previous subsection. Each recording is composed of 277 s constituted by a short training period, for threshold calibration, and a longer test period, for system performance evaluation. As shown from off-line experiments, the window size should be of 10 s as minimum, and according to that, we choose a size of 13 s. Consequently, the

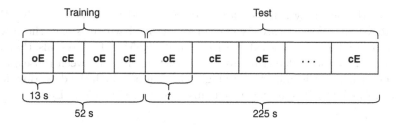

Fig. 6. User's experiment flowchart, with $t \in \{25\,\mathrm{s}, 45\,\mathrm{s}\}$ (cE and oE for closed and open eyes state, respectively).

training period is constituted by four windows of that size, two for cE state and two for oE state. On the other hand, for the test period, EEG recordings were captured using different time intervals, denoted as t, for the eye tasks, specifically 25 s and 45 s, having captured 20 recordings for each time interval. Moreover, in order to avoid any data correlation, half of the test recordings started with the oE task and the other half with cE.

EEG data captured from training period is processed and then used to calculate the threshold value according to Eq. (2). Applying this T_h value and following the criterion defined in Eq. (1), 13 s–windows are classified during the test period. Note that there are three types of windows: oE, cE and overlapped. It is important to say that, since eye state changes occur every 45 or 25 s, some windows could contain information from both eye states. In the transition windows, the window state is considered as that with a greater number of seconds during that time slot. As a consequence, the response time of the detection system will vary according to the window type to be classified i.e.,

- *Non–overlapped windows*, which only contain information related to a single state (cE or oE). In such a case, the response time is equal to the window size i.e., 13 s.
- *Overlapped windows*, which contain information related to both eye states. Since the window state corresponds to the dominant state, two possibilities can be considered. In the first one, *cE state is dominant*, and therefore the response time may be less than the window size. For example, this occurs when a window starts with oE and the state changes only 2 s later. Thus, the window state will be cE, since it contains 2 s for oE against 11 s for cE, and the system detects only 11 s later than the eye state switching. In the second one, *oE state is dominant* and the response time is equal to the window size, although it produces a delay in the following detection. For example, think about a window with 7 s of oE and 6 s of cE. After 13 s the window state is detected and classified as oE, but the following detection of cE will suffer from that delay of 6 s.

According to this criterion, the detection delay of the system will range between 7 s and 19 s. Table 1 shows the accuracy and the mean delay obtained by our classifier considering two time intervals for the eye task duration. It should be noted that the accuracy achieved for non–overlapped windows (i.e. only oE or cE) is above 93 % for all cases, while for overlapped windows (i.e. those with information of both eye states) it drops until 69.55 %. This reveals that our system better performs detecting eye states than changes between those states. On the other hand, it is important to highlight that although the detection delay can vary from 7 s to 19 s, its mean remains close to the window size.

Table 1. Accuracy and mean delay obtained by our classifier considering two time intervals for the eye task duration.

t	oE accuracy	cE accuracy	Overlapped accuracy	Mean delay
25 s	100 %	96.93 %	69.55 %	11.93 s
45 s	93.47 %	94.17 %	87.50 %	13.12 s

Remember that a 13 s–window is processed and on-line classified using the ESP32 microcontroller while the EEG signal is being sampled. Once the eye state has been determined, the system employs the MQTT publisher client to communicate that decision to the IoT ecosystem. The broker receives this information and forwards it to interested subscriber clients. In this experiment, an Arduino UNO connected to a light system has been implemented as a Smart Home (SH) subscriber client. This SH device monitors the user's eye state during long time periods and according to that information that light is regulated. All these MQTT messages were received by the subscriber with a latency lower than 40 ms.

4   Conclusions

In this work we demonstrate the appropriate integration of both Brain–Computer Interface and Internet of Things when Electroencephalography signals are acquired, the accurate identification of closed and open eyes states using a threshold–based classifier and how that extracted information can be correctly transmitted to a simple smart home environment consisting on on–off light switching. The experiments show high classifier accuracies and a correct working of the whole system. Experiment results have shown that classification accuracies, mean delays for detection or system working are sound enough for non-critical and monitoring applications. As future work, we have in mind to incorporate more electrodes to our prototype which will allow us to detect more complex mental states.

References

1. ArduinoFFT library. https://github.com/kosme/arduinoFFT
2. Eclipse Mosquitto. https://mosquitto.org/

3. ESP32 Series. https://www.espressif.com/sites/default/files/documentation/esp32_datasheet_en.pdf/
4. MQTT. http://mqtt.org/
5. Barry, R.J., Clarke, A.R., Johnstone, S.J., Magee, C.A., Rushby, J.A.: EEG differences between eyes-closed and eyes-open resting conditions. Clin. Neurophysiol. **118**(12), 2765–2773 (2007)
6. Estévez, P., et al.: Polysomnographic pattern recognition for automated classification of sleep-waking states in infants. Med. Biol. Eng. Comput. **40**(1), 105–113 (2002)
7. Kirkup, L., Searle, A., Craig, A., McIsaac, P., Moses, P.: EEG-based system for rapid on-off switching without prior learning. Med. Biol. Eng. Comput. **35**(5), 504–509 (1997)
8. Laport, F., Vazquez-Araujo, F.J., Castro, P.M., Dapena, A.: Brain-computer interfaces for Internet of Things. Multi. Digit. Publishing Inst. Proc. **2**(18), 1179 (2018)
9. Li, L., Xiao, L., Chen, L.: Differences of EEG between eyes-open and eyes-closed states based on autoregressive method. J. Electron. Sci. Technol. **7**(2), 175–179 (2009)
10. Ma, J., Zhang, Y., Cichocki, A., Matsuno, F.: A novel EOG/EEG hybrid human-machine interface adopting eye movements and ERPs: application to robot control. IEEE Trans. Biomed. Eng. **62**(3), 876–889 (2015)
11. Narayana, S., Prasad, V., Warmerdam, K.: Mind your thoughts: BCI using single EEG electrode. IET Cyber-Phys. Syst.: Theor. Appl. (2018). https://doi.org/10.1049/iet-cps.2018.5059
12. Nicolas-Alonso, L.F., Gomez-Gil, J.: Brain computer interfaces, a review. Sensors **12**(2), 1211–1279 (2012)
13. Piatek, L., Fiedler, P., Haueisen, J., et al.: Eye state classification from electroencephalography recordings using machine learning algorithms. Digital Med. **4**(2), 84 (2018)
14. Reddy, T.K., Behera, L.: Online eye state recognition from EEG data using deep architectures. In: 2016 IEEE International Conference on Systems, Man, and Cybernetics (SMC), pp. 000712–000717. IEEE (2016)
15. Robinson, J.M., Frey, J.G., Stanford-Clark, A.J., Reynolds, A.D., Bedi, B.V.: Sensor networks and grid middleware for laboratory monitoring. In: 2005 First International Conference on E-Science and Grid Computing, pp. 8-pp. IEEE (2005)
16. Rösler, O., Suendermann, D.: A first step towards eye state prediction using EEG. In: Proceedings of the AIHLS (2013)
17. Saghafi, A., Tsokos, C.P., Goudarzi, M., Farhidzadeh, H.: Random eye state change detection in real-time using EEG signals. Expert Syst. Appl. **72**, 42–48 (2017)
18. Sulaiman, N., Taib, M.N., Lias, S., Murat, Z.H., Aris, S.A., Hamid, N.H.A.: Novel methods for stress features identification using EEG signals. Int. J. Simul.: Syst. Sci. Technol. **12**(1), 27–33 (2011)
19. Wang, T., Guan, S.U., Man, K.L., Ting, T.: Time series classification for EEG eye state identification based on incremental attribute learning. In: 2014 International Symposium on Computer, Consumer and Control (IS3C), pp. 158–161. IEEE (2014)
20. Yeo, M.V., Li, X., Shen, K., Wilder-Smith, E.P.: Can SVM be used for automatic EEG detection of drowsiness during car driving? Saf. Sci. **47**(1), 115–124 (2009)

How to Improve Spatial and Numerical Cognition with a Game-Based and Technology-Enhanced Learning Approach

Michela Ponticorvo[1]([⊠]), Massimiliano Schembri[2], and Orazio Miglino[1]

[1] Department of Humanistic Studies, University of Naples "Federico II", Naples, Italy
michela.ponticorvo@unina.it
[2] Federica Web Learning, Naples, Italy

Abstract. In this paper, the connection between spatial and numerical cognition is highlighted and some applications to improve them are discussed. Indeed, in children, it is possible to promote numerical cognition, which is the base of mathematical cognition and academic achievement in later years, by strengthening their natural endowment to deal both with numerical stimuli and spatial stimuli.

Together with a brief review about spatial and numerical cognition, two tools that are meant to improve them with a Game-based and Technology enhanced approach are reported.

Keywords: Numerical cognition · Spatial cognition ·
Game-based learning · Technology-enhanced learning ·
Cognitive development

1 Introduction

Spatial and numerical cognition represent two of the four core knowledge systems at the foundation of human knowledge [44]. They are strictly connected with many issues that are relevant in different branches of research, including cognitive development.

Studying the development of spatial and numerical skills can be the starting point of relevant applications to educational context for geometry, science [26], mathematics, but also music [25].

The importance of spatial and numerical cognition is evident if we consider the developmental pathways that lead from the basic abilities that can be observed in human beings since the very first moment of their lives to the formal education in school context. Indeed, even if there is a common basis to start from, many different possible outcomes can be observed, including notable differences in math achievement at difference age, between genders [43] and in different cultures [46].

J. M. Ferrández Vicente et al. (Eds.): IWINAC 2019, LNCS 11486, pp. 32–41, 2019.
https://doi.org/10.1007/978-3-030-19591-5_4

These differences cannot be explained by disparity in natural endowment and are therefore likely to depend on other cultural and socio-cognitive factors, for example related to education methodology.

What we propose in this paper is a twofold startegy to improve numerical cognition and, possibly, the later school achievement in math, by addressing directly numerical cognition and by improving numerical skills through spatial cognition. Moreover we propose to adopt an approach relying on Game-based learning and Technology Enhanced learning to improve spatial and numerical cognition in an effective and involving way. In particular we describe two tools that aim at improving numerical and spatial cognition: Velocicards and Flatlandia creatures.

2   Spatial and Numerical Cognition

Human beings, as well as the other species are able to deal with numerical and spatial information without being instructed to do so. This indicates that there are some abilities that are innate and some others that can be acquired by the proper instruction, especially in human beings. This natural predisposition can be the basis of future academic abilities: an intervention on them can affect later achievement in school context.

2.1   Numerical Cognition

Considering numerical cognition, many evidence suggest that human infants possess an intuitive sense of number, the so-called number sense [6]. It is connected with the Approximate Number System (ANS) [14,16]: a cognitive system that supports the estimation of the magnitude of a group with more than four elements without relying on language or symbols, together with the parallel individuation system, or object tracking system for smaller magnitudes. Number sense in infancy predicts math skills in childhood. In the study by Starr and colleagues [45], we find the evidence that the number sense, before language acquisition, "may serve as a developmental building block for the uniquely human capacity for mathematics". These authors show that the performance on numerical preference scores at 6 months of age is correlated with math test scores at 3.5 years of age. This indicates that number sense may facilitate the acquisition of numerical symbols and mathematical abilities.

This evidence supports the theory of innate numerical abilities [3,15], according to which humans have, since the first of life, innate numerical skills to classify small sets of elements (4–5 items), and to distinguish in a rapid and accurate way a small amount of objects and elements, an ability called subitizing [20]. Only later, the culture teaches how to use this mathematical expertise in a more advanced manner. The study by Starr and colleagues goes a step forward, indicating that a stronger number sense predicts later numerical abilities, opening the way to the chance to foresee educational intervention which trains and strengthens the number sense to improve mathematical achievement in later years, as we will see in next section.

2.2 Spatial Cognition

Spatial competence undoubtedly represent a key competence for human adaptation [28]. Indeed spatial knowledge allows to represent elements in the world around and it has a huge adaptive value from every animals who moves in an environment, as they have to organize their action according to their spatial world.

This is true also for artificial agents: simulated or real robots can acquire the competence to act in the environment, only if they possess some kind of representation of the space around them, deriving from their perception [23,24,31]. In analogy with what we have described about numerical cognition, human children have also a predisposition to treat spatial information. For example, Huttenlocher and colleagues [18] show that the basic framework for coding location is present early in life and later development allows to increase this initial ability by organizing a broader range of bounded spaces.

2.3 The Connection Between Spatial and Numerical Cognition

Many studies have underlined the strong connection between spatial and numerical cognition. There is a wide literature on spatial associations during number processing which correlates these two core knowledge. One notable findings is the SNARC effect, spatial numerical association of response codes [9]. This effect consists in the fact that small numbers are reacted to faster with the left hand, large numbers with the right hand and gives a strong witness of this connection [49]. Moreover Fischer and Shaki [13] describe spatial biases found for single digits and pairs of numbers and numbers can be represented by humans on a logarithmic number line [8].

Another interesting effect that connects spatial and numerical cognition is the NIPE effect [30,32,39]. This effect [11], Number Interval Position Effect has been observed in the mental bisection of number intervals both in adults and in children. A systematic error bias in the subjective midpoint of number intervals is found: for intervals of equal size there is a shift of the subjective midpoint towards numbers higher than the true midpoint for intervals at the beginning of decades while for intervals at the end of decades the error bias is directionally reversed towards numbers lower than the true midpoint. This trend of the bisection error is recursively present across consecutive decades.

3 Spatial and Numerical Cognition in Education

Spatial and numerical cognition are not only crucial in adaptation process, but they also are relevant building blocks for human children and adolescents in school context, as hinted at in the introduction.

The pre-requisites on maths are important predictors of school achievement and success. The school readiness is a multidimensional concept that identifies the competences that a child needs before entering school [42]. Crucial indicators are the pre-requisites of learning, knowledge and abilities that develop before acquiring reading, writing and calculation skills and valuable up to preschool years [40]. Literature highlights consistently the importance of pre-requisites of calculation for the success in primary school and beyond [17,21,38].

Pre-requisites and later achievement connection has threats and opportunities. The transition between pre-requisites and advanced math skills can be problematic as it implies a switch from embodied elements to symbolic one. After kindergarten where children use their fingers and physical objects to count, the learning approach strategy soon becomes abstract, mainly relying on working memory [1]. Whereas some children are able to follow this step, some others do not and this can generate difficulties at school. On the opportunity side, if pre-requisites are strengthened also later achievement can be improved, a relevant intervention chance.

Also spatial and numerical cognition connection can be exploited to improve math achievement. Many studies indicate that math and science learning can be improved by spatial thinking [27,41]. Interventions that target spatial abilities can improve math performance and, at an early age, the intervention can have the shape of a game, as we will see in the next section.

4   Game-Based Learning to Improve Spatial and Numerical Cognition

Jirout and Newcombe [19] show that children's play with spatial toys (e.g., puzzles and blocks) correlates with spatial development. These authors underline that spatial skills can be improved, as they are malleable. It is possible to foster spatial skills in children as we teach them, as students' spatial skills are correlated with their success in learning science, both concurrently and predictively. This means that spatial skills can be trained also in early childhood, even before school entrance, also in home context [2]. In this study, the authors underline that, whereas language skills acquisition is supported at home by caregivers, math skills are stimulated in school context only. But, if a little help is given, for example, in the form of a mobile app, math skills improve. This means that together with a theoretical understanding on spatial and numerical cognition, it is relevant to design an educational approach which promotes spatial and numerical skills in the form of games. At the same time of training, these tools can be used for assessing spatial abilities [4,5] or related abilities such as reasoning [12] and soft-skills [22,29] also in children. Existing games that can be used for this goal are cards game and building blocks. Cards games not only implies counting and using symbolic representation of numbers, but also improve memory skills and strategic thinking. Building blocks is a game loved by children that stimulates spatial thinking [47,48].

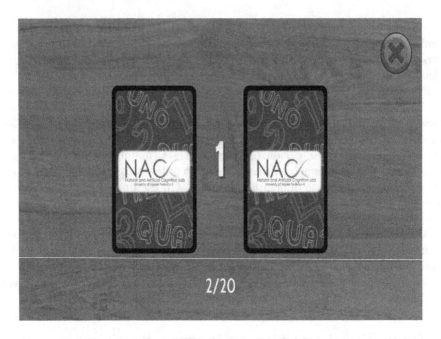

Fig. 1. A screenshot from Velocicards app in Android environment showing the moment before the cards are displayed

5 Examples of Technology Enhanced Version of Cards and Building Blocks

5.1 Velocicards: An Application to Strenghten Numerical Abilities

The first application we would like to introduce is the App Velocicards, an application that can be played on Android devices, shown in Fig. 1.

The games consists in selecting the card with the highest value between 2 cards. It records the speed of the selection on 20 attempts. The cards report the numbers from 0 to 9, represented in different codes, according to triple-code Dehaene model [7].

These codes are analogical (with dots or little characters) and symbolic (verbal and arabic numbers) and are pictured in Figs. 2 and 3.

The application allows to train people, including children, to shift quickly between the different codes, thus favouring the transition between analogic representation, connected with the natural endowment described above and the symbolic one, connected to formal education in maths. These cards represent a Technology-enhanced version of traditional card games where many statistics can be collected and which favours the involvement by children (see [10, 33–37]).

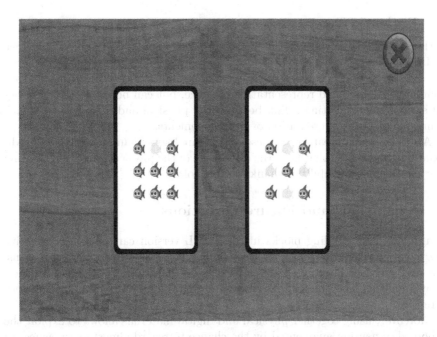

Fig. 2. An example of number analogic representation with little characters. The other one (not shown) is with black dots

Fig. 3. An example of number symbolic representation with arabics. The other one (not shown) is with words

5.2   Flatlandia Creatures

Flatlandia creatures, whose name derives from the book "Flatland: A Romance of Many Dimensions" by Edwin Abbott are building blocks with different shapes and colours to build geometric features. These blocks are physical blocks that stimulate the embodied representation of space, but can be connected to a digital environment, creating a link between the physical and digital world which stimulates mental representation of spatial elements.

Also Flatlandia creatures represent a Technology-enhanced version of traditional building blocks that keep the advantage of the physical game, augmenting their educational possibilities thanks to technology.

6   Conclusions and Future Directions

Using cards and building blocks in their TEL version can be a very effective way to promote spatial and numerical skills. This is true for different reasons. The first one is related with the involvement that these tools have. In fact, today's children have the habit to play with digital materials and find them very attractive.

Moreover, using together physical and digital materials allows to exploit the embodied dimension augmented by the chance to record almost every aspect of children-game interaction. Embodied learning approaches underline that action can support educational objectives and also help the transition between analogic and symbolic dimension which is crucial in math learning. Another important aspect is related to the use of these tools in different context, included non-formal educational contexts such as home. In fact, whereas linguistic abilities are commonly strengthened informally by parents and caregivers, for example reading stories or with the daily linguistic interaction between children and adults, it is not so common that numerical skills are trained this way.

The next step will be to extensively test these tools with a longitudinal and experimental procedure that will follow groups of children at different ages to verify if the use of these tools can improve numerical abilities and later math school achievement, training spatial and numerical predispositions.

References

1. Ashcraft, M.H., Kirk, E.P.: The relationships among working memory, math anxiety, and performance. J. Exp. Psychol.: Gen. **130**(2), 224 (2001)
2. Berkowitz, T., et al.: Math at home adds up to achievement in school. Science **350**(6257), 196–198 (2015)
3. Butterworth, B.: What Counts: How Every Brain is Hardwired for Math (p. pp). The Free Press (1999)
4. Cerrato, A., Ponticorvo, M.: Enhancing neuropsychological testing with gamification and tangible interfaces: the baking tray task. In: Ferrández Vicente, J.M., Álvarez-Sánchez, J.R., de la Paz López, F., Toledo Moreo, J., Adeli, H. (eds.) IWINAC 2017. LNCS, vol. 10338, pp. 147–156. Springer, Cham (2017). https://doi.org/10.1007/978-3-319-59773-7_16

5. Cerrato, A., Ponticorvo, M., Bartolomeo, P., Miglino, O.: Btt-Scan: Uno Strumento Per La Valutazione Della Negligenza Spaziale Unilaterale. SISTEMI INTELLI-GENTI **2019**(1), Il Mulino (2019, in press)
6. Dehaene, S.: The Number Sense: How the Mind Creates Mathematics. OUP USA (2011)
7. Dehaene, S.: Varieties of numerical abilities. Cognition **44**(1–2), 1–42 (1992)
8. Dehaene, S.: The neural basis of the Weber-Fechner law: a logarithmic mental number line. Trends Cogn. Sci. **7**(4), 145–147 (2003)
9. Dehaene, S., Bossini, S., Giraux, P.: The mental representation of parity and number magnitude. J. Exp. Psychol.: Gen. **122**(3), 371 (1993)
10. Di Fuccio, R., Ponticorvo, M., Ferrara, F., Miglino, O.: Digital and multisensory storytelling: narration with smell, taste and touch. In: Verbert, K., Sharples, M., Klobučar, T. (eds.) EC-TEL 2016. LNCS, vol. 9891, pp. 509–512. Springer, Cham (2016). https://doi.org/10.1007/978-3-319-45153-4_51
11. Doricchi, F., et al.: Spatial orienting biases in the decimal numeral system. Curr. Biol. **19**(8), 682–687 (2009)
12. Ferrara, F., Ponticorvo, M., Di Ferdinando, A., Miglino, O.: Tangible interfaces for cognitive assessment and training in children: LogicART. In: Uskov, V.L., Howlett, R.J., Jain, L.C. (eds.) Smart Education and e-Learning 2016. SIST, vol. 59, pp. 329–338. Springer, Cham (2016). https://doi.org/10.1007/978-3-319-39690-3_29
13. Fischer, M.H., Shaki, S.: Spatial associations in numerical cognition-from single digits to arithmetic. Q. J. Exp. Psychol. **67**(8), 1461–1483 (2014)
14. Gilmore, C., Attridge, N., Inglis, M.: Measuring the approximate number system. Q. J. Exp. Psychol. **64**(11), 2099–2109 (2011)
15. Girelli, L., Lucangeli, D., Butterworth, B.: The development of automaticity in accessing number magnitude. J. Exp. Child Psychol. **76**(2), 104–122 (2000)
16. Halberda, J., Feigenson, L.: Developmental change in the acuity of the "number sense": the approximate number system in 3-, 4-, 5-, and 6-year-olds and adults. Dev. Psychol. **44**(5), 1457 (2008)
17. Hindman, A.H., Skibbe, L.E., Miller, A., Zimmerman, M.: Ecological contexts and early learning: contributions of child, family, and classroom factors during Head Start, to literacy and mathematics growth through first grade. Early Child. Res. Q. **25**(2), 235–250 (2010)
18. Huttenlocher, J., Newcombe, N., Sandberg, E.H.: The coding of spatial location in young children. Cogn. Psychol. **27**(2), 115–147 (1994)
19. Jirout, J.J., Newcombe, N.S.: Building blocks for developing spatial skills: evidence from a large, representative US sample. Psychol. Sci. **26**(3), 302–310 (2015)
20. Kaufman, E.L., Lord, M.W., Reese, T.W., Volkmann, J.: The discrimination of visual number. Am. J. Psychol. **62**(4), 498–525 (1949)
21. Lonigan, C.J.: Development, assessment, and promotion of preliteracy skills. Early Educ. Dev. **17**(1), 91–114 (2006)
22. Marocco, D., Pacella, D., Dell'Aquila, E., Di Ferdinando, A.: Grounding serious game design on scientific findings: the case of ENACT on soft skills training and assessment. In: Conole, G., Klobučar, T., Rensing, C., Konert, J., Lavoué, É. (eds.) EC-TEL 2015. LNCS, vol. 9307, pp. 441–446. Springer, Cham (2015). https://doi.org/10.1007/978-3-319-24258-3_37
23. Miglino, O., Ponticorvo, M., Bartolomeo, P.: Place cognition and active perception: a study with evolved robots. Connect. Sci. **21**(1), 3–14 (2009)
24. Miglino, O., Ponticorvo, M.: Place cognition as an example of situated cognition: a study with evolved agents. Cogn. Process. **10**(2), 250–252 (2009)

25. Möhring, W., Ramsook, K.A., Hirsh-Pasek, K., Golinkoff, R.M., Newcombe, N.S.: Where music meets space: children's sensitivity to pitch intervals is related to their mental spatial transformation skills. Cognition **151**, 1–5 (2016)

26. Newcombe, N.S.: Thinking spatially in the science classroom. Curr. Opin. Behav. Sci. **10**, 1–6 (2016)

27. Newcombe, N.S.: Picture this: increasing math and science learning by improving spatial thinking. Am. Educ. **34**(2), 29 (2010)

28. Newcombe, N.S., Huttenlocher, J.: Making Space: The Development of Spatial Representation and Reasoning. MIT Press, Cambridge (2003)

29. Pacella, D., Di Ferdinando, A., Dell Aquila, E., Marocco, D.: Online assessment of negotiation skills through 3D role play simulation (2015)

30. Ponticorvo, M., Rotondaro, F., Doricchi, F., Miglino, O.: A neural model of number interval position effect (NIPE) in children. In: Ferrández Vicente, J.M., Álvarez-Sánchez, J.R., de la Paz López, F., Toledo-Moreo, F.J., Adeli, H. (eds.) IWINAC 2015. LNCS, vol. 9107, pp. 9–18. Springer, Cham (2015). https://doi.org/10.1007/978-3-319-18914-7_2

31. Ponticorvo, M., Miglino, O.: Encoding geometric and non-geometric information: a study with evolved agents. Anim. Cogn. **13**(1), 157 (2010)

32. Ponticorvo, M., Gigliotta, O., Miglino, O.: Simulative models to understand numerical cognition. In: Ferrández Vicente, J.M., Álvarez-Sánchez, J.R., de la Paz López, F., Toledo Moreo, J., Adeli, H. (eds.) IWINAC 2017. LNCS, vol. 10337, pp. 75–84. Springer, Cham (2017). https://doi.org/10.1007/978-3-319-59740-9_8

33. Ponticorvo, M., Di Ferdinando, A., Marocco, D., Miglino, O.: Bio-inspired computational algorithms in educational and serious games: some examples. In: Verbert, K., Sharples, M., Klobučar, T. (eds.) EC-TEL 2016. LNCS, vol. 9891, pp. 636–639. Springer, Cham (2016). https://doi.org/10.1007/978-3-319-45153-4_80

34. Ponticorvo, M., Di Fuccio, R., Ferrara, F., Rega, A., Miglino, O.: Multisensory educational materials: five senses to learn. In: Di Mascio, T., et al. (eds.) MIS4TEL 2018. AISC, vol. 804, pp. 45–52. Springer, Cham (2019). https://doi.org/10.1007/978-3-319-98872-6_6

35. Ponticorvo, M., Rega, A., Miglino, O.: Toward tutoring systems inspired by applied behavioral analysis. In: Nkambou, R., Azevedo, R., Vassileva, J. (eds.) ITS 2018. LNCS, vol. 10858, pp. 160–169. Springer, Cham (2018). https://doi.org/10.1007/978-3-319-91464-0_16

36. Ponticorvo, M., Rega, A., Di Ferdinando, A., Marocco, D., Miglino, O.: Approaches to embed bio-inspired computational algorithms in educational and serious games. In: CEUR Workshop Proceedings (2018)

37. Ponticorvo, M., Di Fuccio, R., Di Ferdinando, A., Miglino, O.: An agent-based modelling approach to build up educational digital games for kindergarten and primary schools. Expert Syst. **34**(4), e12196 (2017)

38. Romano, E., Babchishin, L., Pagani, L.S., Kohen, D.: School readiness and later achievement: replication and extension using a nationwide Canadian survey. Dev. Psychol. **46**(5), 995 (2010)

39. Rotondaro, F., et al.: The Number Interval Position Effect (NIPE) in the mental bisection of numerical intervals might reflect the influence of the decimal-number system on the Gaussian representations of numerosities: a combined developmental and computational-modeling study. Cortex (2018)

40. Shaul, S., Schwartz, M.: The role of the executive functions in school readiness among preschool-age children. Read. Writ. **27**(4), 749–768 (2014)

41. Sorby, S., Casey, B., Veurink, N., Dulaney, A.: The role of spatial training in improving spatial and calculus performance in engineering students. Learn. Individ. Differ. **26**, 20–29 (2013)
42. Snow, K.L.: Measuring school readiness: conceptual and practical considerations. Early Educ. Dev. **17**(1), 7–41 (2006)
43. Spelke, E.S.: Sex differences in intrinsic aptitude for mathematics and science?: A critical review. Am. Psychol. **60**(9), 950 (2005)
44. Spelke, E.S., Kinzler, K.D.: Core knowledge. Dev. Sci. **10**(1), 89–96 (2007)
45. Starr, A., Libertus, M.E., Brannon, E.M.: Number sense in infancy predicts mathematical abilities in childhood. Proc. Natl. Acad. Sci. **110**(45), 18116–18120 (2013)
46. Stevenson, H.W., Chen, C., Lee, S.Y.: Mathematics achievement of Chinese, Japanese, and American children: ten years later. Science, 53–58 (1993)
47. Verdine, B.N., Golinkoff, R.M., Hirsh-Pasek, K., Newcombe, N.S.: I. Spatial skills, their development, and their links to mathematics. Monogr. Soc. Res. Child Dev. **82**(1), 7–30 (2017)
48. Verdine, B.N., Golinkoff, R.M., Hirsh-Pasek, K., Newcombe, N.S., Filipowicz, A.T., Chang, A.: Deconstructing building blocks: preschoolers' spatial assembly performance relates to early mathematical skills. Child Dev. **85**(3), 1062–1076 (2014)
49. Wood, G., Willmes, K., Nuerk, H.-C., Fischer, M.: On the cognitive link between space and number: a meta-analysis of the SNARC effect. Psychol. Sci. Q. **50**(4), 489–525 (2008)

Ontologies for Early Detection
of the Alzheimer Disease and Other
Neurodegenerative Diseases

Alba Gomez-Valadés[(✉)], Rafael Martínez-Tomás,
and Mariano Rincón-Zamorano

Dpto. Inteligencia Artificial,
Universidad Nacional de Educación a Distancia UNED, Madrid, Spain
albagvb@dia.uned.es

Abstract. Nowadays technologies allow an exponential generation of
biomedical data, which must be indexed according to some standard
criteria to be useful to the scientific and medical community, being neurology one of the areas in which the standardization is more necessary.
Ontologies have been highlighted as one of the best options, with their
capability of homogenise information, allowing their integration with
other kind of information, and the inference of new information based on
the data that is stored. We analyse and compare the approaches taken by
different research groups inside the area of the Alzheimer's disease, and
the ontologies they developed with the objective of providing a common
framework to standardize information, data recovery or as a part of an
expert system. However, to make this approach work the ontologies must
be maintained over the time, a critical point which is not been followed
by any of the ontologies reviewed.

1 Introduction

During the last decade has been a revolution in the volume and complexity of
data created in the life sciences, and with them, in the possibility of studying
such data [12] . However, their utility depends fundamentally on the ability to
know how to handle and interpret large heterogeneous datasets [8] scattered
[4] across different databases and under different formats, so the integration
and standardization of the data it's necessary in order to make information
useful [6] while allow the data interoperability, to facilitate the extraction and
retrieval of information [3], with diverse scientific and clinical objectives. Thus,
the generation of adequate infrastructures to allow standardization, exchange
and sharing information have become a key objective for the success of the
current and future research and clinic [4].

In this framework, the development of ontologies has been established as one
of the most adequate solutions to confront these problems, as in the domains
of biomedical research, where specific ontologies have been developed across

© Springer Nature Switzerland AG 2019
J. M. Ferrández Vicente et al. (Eds.): IWINAC 2019, LNCS 11486, pp. 42–50, 2019.
https://doi.org/10.1007/978-3-030-19591-5_5

the different fields [3]. Within biomedicine, neurology is one of the fields where integration is more necessary to make the data useful, since mental processes extend across very heterogeneous levels [11]. Mild cognitive impairment (MCI) has attracted significant attention in neurological research, as it is a transition phase between normal aging and dementia, especially that related to Alzheimer's disease (AD), making MCI one of the main indicators of developed AD, that's why the development of methods that allows their early detection of AD is essential to improve the quality of life of patients [22].

For this purpose, various types of tests have been developed, which evaluate in different ways the state of the patients: biological test (such as the concentration measurement of beta-amyloid); imaging test (as Nuclear Magnetic Resonance or MRI), or neuropsychological tests. The underlying theory of those last tests is that these neurodegenerative diseases cause damage in certain areas of the brain, which affect different mental functions and cognitive processes. In the neuropsychological tests, these dysfunctions created by the MCI are reflected as different types of errors or deficiencies committed at the time of performing of each test. Those tests are the only ones capable of measuring the cognitive abilities in patients, such as short-term memory versus long-term memory, or the executive functioning [11]. In addition, neuropsychological tests have the advantage of being non-invasive, versatile and low cost.

The purpose of this article is to review the different approaches and objectives carried out by different research groups in this area, not only to solve the problems of interoperability and standardization in the AD domain, and other neurodegenerative diseases related to the MCI, but also to allow storage, recovery and making inferences from the information, as well as to help the MCI diagnosis.

2   Ontologies and Neurodegenerative Diseases

An ontology is a formal definition of classes, properties, and relationships between them, which is integrated inside some knowledge area, allowing the homogenization and consensus in the representation and reutilization of a domain [19]. It facilitates the exchange of information in biomedicine [17], the integration and recovery of heterogeneous data from a diverse variety of sources, with the aim to improve the diagnosis or the treatment of the disease. Depending on the approach and the final goal sought during the development of the ontology, it can be distinguished 3 main groups [21]:

- Ontologies for the standardization in the terminology: They seek to allow both the direct reutilization of the terminology by third parties, and the compatibility of the ontology with most of reasoning engines. In design they are characterized by a strong hierarchy of classes and a large amount of different types of metadata for a correct definition of the terms.
- Ontologies for the storage and recovery of the information: They seek to allow the recovery and inference of new knowledge from the stored data, as well as achieve a standardization of the domain. In design, they tend to display less

nesting in the class hierarchy than in the previous case, and the metadata usually are scarce or reduced to the minimum, although their axiomatic tends to be more specific.
- Ontologies as a diagnosis support: they are normally designed from scratch for a practical purpose, to be integrated into a larger system as a module or subsystem, normally working as a knowledge database. They usually are linked to the target application, being difficult their reutilization in other contexts. In design, the class hierarchy usually has only relevant term to the system, few levels of nesting and scarce metadata, although their axiomatic are heavy.

However, there are also some problems associated to the usage of the ontologies. The main and more immediate problem are the low reutilization of the existing terminology, generating redundancy problems and conflict in the term names, unstable references, redundancy in the class hierarchy, and inconsistencies between them [15]. To avoid this situation, a priority during the development of new ontologies must be the reutilization of already existent ontologies as much as possible, only adding new classes and instances when they are not covered by any of the consulted ontologies [10].

In the following sections, the main approaches are presented. They are organized according to the final objective of the ontologies described above.

2.1   Ontologies for the Standardization in the Terminology

The project of Gao et al. [9] of the Semantic Web Application in neuromedicine (SWAN) was one of the first biomedicine ontologies focus in the storage and contextualization of the existent information about the AD. The project was developed as an infrastructure that integrate in an effective way the scientific knowledge of the AD allowing the construction of a semantic web of hypothesis, publications and digital repositories [5]. SWAN was considered as the reference repository about the data regarding to the AD that were available in the web. However, this ontology and the associated application has been discontinued from all the online repositories where it had been stored, being no possible to retrieve it.

On the other hand, Jensen et al. [14] propose Neurological Disease (ND) Ontology, which seeks to provide a framework for the representation the key aspects of neurodegenerative diseases for study and treatment, providing a set of controlled classes connected in a logical way to describe the range of the neurodegenerative diseases, as well as their signs and symptoms, evaluations, diagnosis and interventions that have been found in the course of clinical practice. It can also serve to link and extend other ontologies of the same domain. In the Fig. 1, it can be observed the extension in those domain areas that ND performs to the Basic Formal Ontology (BFO) [1]base ontology.

Later, in the paper published by Cox et al. [7] is described NeuroPsychological Testing Ontology (NPT), which seeks to extend and to complete ND, specifically in the part of the domain relating to the neuropsychological tests. NPT provides a set of classes for the realistic representation and the annotation of a wide variety of neuropsychological tests which evaluate similar or overlapping domains of the cognitive function, such as the MMSE, as well as other associated data, allowing the integration of the results. This provides a realistic and detailed representation of the functioning of the cognitive process and the functions they involve. However, NPT also has the problem of excess of complexity, which make it little manageable due to that. This makes difficult to locate and focus in the relevant classes, since it has classes from very heterogeneous domains that have little to do with the domain in which this ontology is focused.

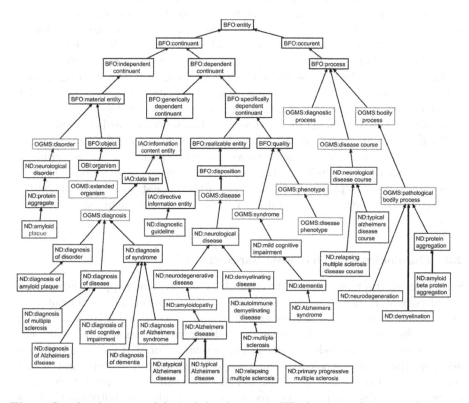

Fig. 1. Graphic depiction of the high-level terms in ND. A subset of classes of ND that shows the is_a relations between BFP [14]

2.2   Ontologies for the Storage and Recovery of the Information

According to the authors of SWAN, this ontology, was designed both as a standardization system and as a storage and information retrieval system [18] stored in the Alzforum digital library, in order to make information inference and generation, among other reasons. The information retrieval would be done through two methods: SWAN Workbench, available only for a reduce group of users, and the SWAN Browser, designed to be used more generally [5].

Malhotra et al. [16] propose Alzheimer Disease Ontology (ADO), following the guide of the BFO. This ontology seeks the widest possible coverage of the different aspects of the AD domain in a structured way, from diagnosis to treatments. Like SWAN, ADO was designed with the idea of allowing retrieval and inference of the information, that will be done through queries about the stored data. However, ADO has the problem of having a low reutilization of already existed ontologies, as well as an obtuse axiomatic of interpreting. For example, the classes generically_dependent_continuant and specifically_dependent_continuant are disjointed classes, but they are also marked as equivalent to dependent_continuant. Since they are subclases of dependent_continuant, this makes those classes both equivalent and disjointed between them. This kind of situations appears more than once across the ontology.

In other hand, the OntoNeuroLOG ontology from Batrancourt et al. [2] is a multilayer ontology of the instruments used to evaluate the brain and cognitive functions. OntoNeuroLOG is a multilayer ontology organized in sub-ontologies or modules located in three different levels of abstraction. It has been built using DOLCE as its main basis, which has been complemented in the different modules with other ontologies. Also, new terms were defined specifically for the ontology when necessary. Although it has the benefit of being one of the most complete ones, it also has the problem of being one of the biggest ontologies, making it impossible to integrate the 3 modules in which it's splitted up as a whole in Protégé.

2.3   Ontologies as a Diagnosis Support

Sanchez et al. [18] propose the MIND ontology as a decision support system that aid physicians in the early diagnosis of AD. This project merges an ontology and a semantic reasoner able to infer logic consequences starting from a series of facts or given axioms to help physicians in the early detection of AD using the multidisciplinary knowledge stored in the ontology. For that case the ontology describes the neuropsychological, neurological, radiological, metabolomical and genetic tests carried out to patients. Despite everything, this ontology does not relate with the different cognitive process, or the mistakes committed in the tests during their performance; instead it employs only in the final score.

The Ontology driven decision support for the diagnosis of MCI was proposed by Zhang et al. [22] as a method of decision support supported by ontologies designed to avoid subjectivity in the diagnosis of MCI through magnetic resonance imaging, for the detection of the cortical cortex thickness, since it is reduced in patients with MCI [20]. However, it has the disadvantage that the C4.5 decision tree used to developed the model is sensitive to the training data, with the consequent problem of overfitting. Also, this ontology is focused only on an imaging approach of MRI, modelling the ontology according to this criterion, and ignoring other systems such as neuropsychological tests.

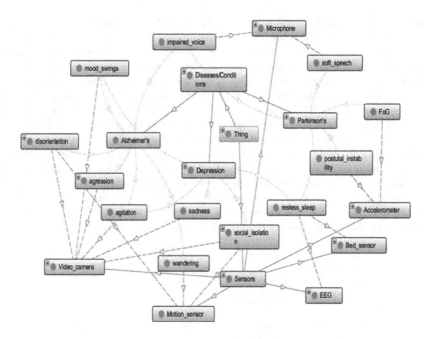

Fig. 2. DSS (Disease-Symptom-Sensor) ontology model [13].

Ivascu et al. [13] propose a multiagent ontology, designed to facilitate remote monitoring of patients who are susceptible to develop cognitive impairment disease. To achieve that goal, this ontology is built using a combination between an ontology developed as a Disease-Symptom-Sensor (DSS) system, which serves as a diagnosis component, which is shown in Fig. 2, and a multiagent system, to which the ontology complements, and which is a group of programs specialized in a task and capable of working together. This way, the system can predict the disease based on the registered symptoms. However, there are still some elements that must be solved before this system can be release, such as data privacy improvements, automated devices/sensors discovery, context sensitive information aggregation and activities correlations for users that match the same profile.

Finally, [21] propose an ontology based in the fuzzy logic, AlzFuzzyOnto, which are developed using MIND as the basis to model an expert system to aid to physicians in the early diagnosis of AD. The motivation is that there is a significant number of terms and concepts that constitute a source of imprecision and uncertainty. To solve this, fuzzy classes were added, and the concepts were connected using a fuzzy relationship of belonging, in which a crisp concept are related to a fuzzy one. Those relations have different weights of degrees of membership with each class with a value in the interval [0, 1], allowing the developed of a fuzzy ontology for the AD. However, the experimentation, validation and instantiation of this ontology has not carried out, but are left as a future work, as well as the construction of a fuzzy inference engine.

Table 1. Summary table of the ontologies. The Reutilization column is according to the paper if the ontology was not found. Axiomatics: High (high number of relationships between low or concrete clases) Medium (relationships between high or more abstract clases, which are inherited by the concrete ones) Low (scarce number of relationships in general). Reutilization: High (they use of different kind of ontologies to model the ontology domain, usually high level) Medium (they reuse no more of 1 or 2 ontologies) Low (they only use the squeme of one ontology for the more upper classes, or no reutilization at all). Hierarchy: High (great depth in nesting, usually a high number of classes -more than 1000-) Medium (presence of more classes in the root, great depth in nesting are more uncommon) Low (the nesting usually no overpass a 5 classes depth, and the number of classes are usually less than 100). Metadata: High (label, description, comments and other metadata tend to appear in most classes), Medium (label and a short description, they can also count with synonyms, comments, etc, rarely surpassing one line), Low (usually just the label; occacionally short descriptions, comments, synonyms, etc, usually of only a few words long)

Name	Publicly available	Last update	Focus	Axiomatics/ relations	Reutilization	Class hierarchy	Metadata
SWAN	No	2009	Terms standardization/Knowledge inference	–	–	–	–
ND	Yes	2012	Terms standardization	Medium	High	High	High
NPT	Yes	2013	Terms standardization	Medium	High	High	High
ADO	Yes	2013	Knowledge inference	Low	Low	Medium	Medium
OntoNeuroLOG	Yes	2013	Knowledge inference	High	High	High	Low
MIND	No	2011 (paper)	Part of an expert system	–	Low	–	–
Ontology Driven Decision	No	2013 (paper)	Part of an expert system	–	No	–	–
Multiagent	No	2015 (paper)	Part of an expert system	High	No	Low	Low
AlzFuzzyOnto	No	2015 (paper)	Part of an expert system	–	Low	–	–

3   Conclusions

The new technologies are allowing an exponential generation of biomedical data, which must be stored and indexed correctly to allow easy access and management, so they can be useful to the scientific and medical community. Inside the area of biomedicine, neurology, and more specifically, MCI related to the early detection of neurodegenerative diseases, has become one of the fields where such integration has become more necessary. Ontologies are a powerful tool in achieving the goal of integration and easy access to the data, since they can provide a standardized vocabulary for the representation, sharing and reuse of the knowledge, as well as storage, retrieval and inference of information. Moreover, they can be integrated into expert systems, working as a knowledge database during the early detection of MCI.

Throughout this article the main ontologies developed in this domain has been shown, either with the shared objective of standardizing and providing a common framework of existing information, data recovery or as a part of an expert system. The summary of the ontologies described is shown in Table 1. But for this to work, ontologies must be maintained, something that are not happening with any of the revised ones. Although this can be understandable in those ontologies designed to work as a part of an expert system to fulfil a specific function, in which case an operative version them would be enough, this situation would apply to standardization-oriented ontologies, though the absence of maintenance is common to all ontologies. Some of them only receive a single update, corresponding to the years of publication of the article. Those that received subsequent updates, they were made in the close years to the first publication, being ND and OntoNeuroLog the ones which received more support during more time, even though both have not received any updates in the recent years. Finally, there are several ontologies described in papers that were not possible to locate in any internet repository. Those are the ones oriented with a more practical goal, with the exception of SWAN, which was deleted from internet for unknown reasons.

Lastly, it has been found that term reuse between different ontologies is, on average, scarce or non-existent, the main exception being the ontologies of ND and the derivative ontology NPT.

Funding. We thanks to the Ministry of Education, Youth and Sports of the Community of Madrid, and the European Social Fund for a contract to A.G.-V. B. (PEJD-2017-PRE/TIC-4406) in the program of Youth Employment and the Youth Employment Initiative (YEI) 2018.

References

1. Arp, R., Smith, B.: Realizable entities in basic formal ontology. In: Proceedings of Bio-Ontologies Workshop, Intelligent Systemas for Molecular Biology (ISMB), p. 10 (2011)
2. Batrancourt, B., Dojat, M., Gibaud, B., Kassel, G.: A multilayer ontology of instruments for neurological behavioral and cognitive assessments. Neuroinformatics **13**(1), 93–110 (2015)
3. Blake, J.A., Bult, C.J.: Beyond the data deluge: data integration and bio-ontologies. J. Biomed. Inf. **39**(3), 314–320 (2006)
4. Burgun, A., Bodenreider, O.: Accessing and integrating data and knowledge for biomedical research. Yearb. Med. Inf. **17**(01), 91–101 (2008)
5. Ciccarese, P., et al.: The SWAN biomedical discourse ontology. J. Biomed. Inf. **41**(5), 739–751 (2008)
6. Costa, F.F.: Big data in biomedicine. Drug Disc. Today **19**(4), 433–440 (2014)
7. Cox, A.P., Jensen, M., Ruttenberg, A., Szigeti, K., Diehl, A.D.: Measuring cognitive functions: hurdles in the development of the neuropsychological testing ontology. In: Proceedings of the 4th International Conference on Biomedical Ontology 2013, Montreal, Canada, p. 6, July 2013

8. Decety, J., Cacioppo, J.: Frontiers in human neuroscience: the golden triangle and beyond. Perspect. Psychol. Sci. **5**(6), 767–771 (2010)
9. Gao, Y., et al.: SWAN: a distributed knowledge infrastructure for Alzheimer disease research. Web Seman.: Sci. Serv. Agents World Wide Web **4**(3), 222–228 (2006)
10. Gomez-Perez, A., Fernandez-Lopez, M., Corcho, O.: Ontological Engineering: with Examples from the Areas of Knowledge Management, E-Commerce and the Semantic Web. Advanced Information and Knowledge Processing. Springer, New York (2004). https://doi.org/10.1007/b97353
11. Hastings, J., et al.: Interdisciplinary perspectives on the development, integration, and application of cognitive ontologies. Front. Neuroinf. **8**, 62 (2014)
12. Hoehndorf, R., Schofield, P.N., Gkoutos, G.V.: The role of ontologies in biological and biomedical research: a functional perspective. Briefings Bioinf. **16**(6), 1069–1080 (2015)
13. Ivascu, T., Manate, B., Negru, V.: A multi-agent architecture for ontology-based diagnosis of mental disorders. In: 2015 17th International Symposium on Symbolic and Numeric Algorithms for Scientific Computing (SYNASC), pp. 423–430. IEEE. September 2015
14. Jensen, M., et al.: The neurological disease ontology. J. Biomed. Semant. **4**(1), 42 (2013)
15. Klein, M.: Combining and Relating Ontologies: an analysis of problems and solutions. In: Ontologies and Information Sharing, vol. 47, May 2001
16. Malhotra, A., Younesi, E., Gndel, M., Mller, B., Heneka, M.T., Hofmann-Apitius, M.: ADO: a disease ontology representing the domain knowledge specific to Alzheimer's disease. Alzheimer's Dement. **10**(2), 238–246 (2014)
17. Mead, C.N.: Data interchange standards in healthcare IT - computable semantic interoperability: now possible but still difficult, do we really need a better mousetrap? J. healthc. Inf. Manage. (JHIM) **20**, 71–78 (2006)
18. Sanchez, E., et al.: A knowledge-based clinical decision support system for the diagnosis of Alzheimer disease. In: 2011 IEEE 13th International Conference on e-Health Networking, Applications and Services, pp. 351–357. IEEE. June 2011
19. Trokanas, N., Cecelja, F.: Ontology evaluation for reuse in the domain of process systems engineering. Comput. Chem. Eng. **85**, 177–187 (2016)
20. Whitwell, J.L., et al.: MRI patterns of atrophy associated with progression to AD in amnestic mild cognitive impairment. Neurology **70**(7), 512–520 (2008)
21. Zekri, F., Bouaziz, R., Turki, E.: A fuzzy-based ontology for Alzheimer's disease decision support. In 2015 IEEE International Conference on Fuzzy Systems (FUZZ-IEEE), pp. 1–6. IEEE. August 2015
22. Zhang, X., Bin, H., Ma, X., Moore, P., Chen, J.: Ontology driven decision support for the diagnosis of mild cognitive impairment. Comput. Methods Programs Biomed. **113**(3), 781–791 (2014)

Gaming the Attention
with a SSVEP-Based
Brain-Computer Interface

M. A. Lopez-Gordo[1]([⊠]), Eduardo Perez[2], and Jesus Minguillon[3]

[1] Department of Signal Theory, Telematics and Communications,
University of Granada, Granada, Spain
malg@ugr.es
[2] Tyndall National Institute, University College Cork,
Wireless Sensors Networks Group, Cork, Ireland
eduardo.perez@tyndall.ie
[3] Department of Information and Communication Technologies,
Pompeu Fabra University, Barcelona, Spain
jesus.minguillon@upf.edu

Abstract. Steady-State Visually Evoked Potentials (SSVEPs) have been widely used in neuroscience for the characterization of dynamic processes from the retina to the visual cortex. In Neuro-engineering, SSVEP-based Brain-computer Interfaces (SSVEP-BCIs) have been used in variety of applications (e. g., communication, entertainment, etc.) for the detection of attention to visual stimuli. In this work, we propose a hands-free videogame in which the player joystick is a SSVEP-BCI. In the videogame, hostile avatars fire weapons against the player who could deflect them if enough attention is exerted. Attention is detected based on the analysis of SSVEP and Alphaband powers. For this purpose, weapons are mobile checkerboards that flicker at a constant frequency. We presented this videogame as a demo in a technologic event for students of engineering who freely tried it. The main findings were: (i) the attention detection algorithm based on SSVEPs is robust enough to be performed in few seconds even with mobile visual stimuli and in a non-isolated room; (ii) the videogame is capable to dose and quantify the amount of cognitive attention that a player exerts on mobile stimuli by controlling their time and position. The results suggest that this videogame could be used as a serious game to play/train the attentional and visual tracking capabilities with direct application in Special Needs Education or in attention disorders.

Keywords: Attention · SSVEP · Gamification · EEG ·
Brain-computer Interface

Supported by the University of Granada.

J. M. Ferrández Vicente et al. (Eds.): IWINAC 2019, LNCS 11486, pp. 51–59, 2019.
https://doi.org/10.1007/978-3-030-19591-5_6

1   Introduction

Visually Evoked Potentials (VEPs) are visually evoked electrophysiological signals generated by the visual cortex. Steady State Visually Evoked Potentials (SSVEPs) consist in periodic VEPs generated in response to a train of periodic stimuli [1,2]. The spectral power of SSVEPs extends over a very narrow band that matches that of the stimulation [3]. Among other uses, SSVEPs are clinically utilized to investigate the visual processing in patients who experience migraine with aura, identify abnormal potentials in children with a history of febrile seizures, assessment of covert attention at work [4–6] and others.

In neuro-engineering, SSVEPs are utilized as indicators of intention or volition in an extended number of Brain-computer Interfaces, namely the SSVEP-BCIs. A BCI is a device that provides the brain with a new, non-muscular communication and control channel [7], thus allowing a subject (e.g. a male) to interact with an external device by means of his neural activity. The two main reasons why SSVEPs are extensively utilized in BCIs are: (i) most part of their spectral energy is concentrated within a narrow band and (ii) this energy can be voluntarily modulated by attention [8,9]. Some examples of health-related SSVEP-BCIs or daily life applications can be reviewed in [10–13]. In the field of videogames, BCIs have been used as an alternative interface. For instance, Mind the sheep, The Mindgame, Brain Driver and Tetris [14–17].

In this work, we propose a hands-free videogame that uses a SSVEP-BCI. This SSVEP-BCI consists of an EEG acquisition system, a computer screen to present the visual stimuli and a server that coordinates the entire system. The game is designed to detect the attention that a player exerts on attacks that hostile avatars fire from the background in a virtual scenario. Attention is detected by measuring changes in the energy of SSVEPs and Alpha band. For this purpose, hostile avatars weapons are texturized as moving checkerboards that reverse their contrast at a constant frequency, thus eliciting SSVEPs [18]. Detection decision is based on a combination of SSVEP amplitude, signal-to-noise-ratio and Alpha band power. As it is indicated in [19], SSVEP power is a valuable biomarker in BCI applications. Moreover, Alpha band power has been proved to be useful for detecting attention since it increases in periods of visual inattention or relaxation [20]. If the detection process assesses that a player is paying enough attention to the attack of an avatar, the attack is immediately deflected, otherwise, the attack will reach the foreground of the virtual scenario and the player will be defeated.

This game was demonstrated in technologic events celebrated at the University of Granada, the UGR LAN Party 2018 (http://ulp.ugr.es/). The game involves the use of gamification principles such as continuous progress feedback, immediate success feedback and autonomy support. Students reported to be an exciting and challenging entertainment that kept their attention focused for periods of time with increasing difficulty. Our proposal arises as an alternative way to train/play with the attention capabilities that could be used as a serious game to play/train the attentional and visual tracking capabilities with direct application in Special Needs Education or in attention disorders.

2   Materials and Methods

2.1   Subjects and Recording

A total of 3 healthy subjects (3 males; age 15–24) tested the game. No cognitive or visual disease was reported that could affect the experience. The game was played in a broad and noisy room filled with people passing by during a technologic event. Therefore, external disturbances were present throughout the experience.

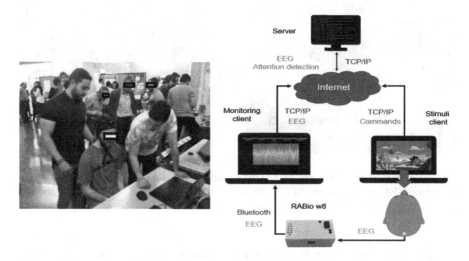

Fig. 1. Left: A student playing the game during a technologic event. Right: Schema of the closed-loop system.

Electroencephalographic activity was acquired using a RABio w8 [21] with a sample rate of 500 Hz. An electrode was placed on the Oz position of the International 10-20 System [22] and a reference electrode was placed on the ear lobe. The RABio w8 transmitted raw EEG to the Monitoring client via Bluetooth (see Fig. 1). The raw EEG was filtered using a 2nd order bandpass Butterworth filter with cutoff frequencies of 0.25 Hz and 40 Hz. The resulting signals were z-scored and averaged. Finally, a Tukey window was applied to them.

2.2   Gameplay

The game advances over a maximum of five stages. In each stage, hostile avatars sequentially appear in random positions in a 3D scenario. The position of the avatar is defined by depth, horizontal vertical components (Z, X and Y coordinates respectively) (see Fig. 2). Once an avatar appears on the screen, it fires an attack consisting in a circular checkerboard with a fixation cross in its center. This mobile stimulus reverses contrasts at a constant frequency of 15 Hz. The checkerboard advances from the position of the avatar to the foreground, thus causing both increasing its size and changing the location. The player goal is to visually track this mobile stimulus by keeping his attention on the fixation cross. If the player exerts enough visual attention, the attack will be deflected and the player will score. Otherwise, the player will be defeated, and the enemy will score.. Immediate feedback is shown on the computer by updating the scoreboard.

Fig. 2. Initial positions of enemies: in this example, the random initial position of the first avatar (left) corresponds to ($z = 10$, $x = 1$, $y = 1$). The random initial position of the second avatar (right) corresponds to ($z = 5$, $x = 3$, $y = 3$).

Each stage ends under two possible conditions: (i) when the running time exceeds a prefixed limit; (ii) when either the player or the avatar scores five times. If the player wins, the game advances to the next stage. Otherwise, the same stage is played again. To achieve a challenging experience consecutive stages have higher and higher difficulty (e.g., by increasing the speed of the checkerboard or closer initial positions of avatars) that require additional attentional effort.

2.3   Application Design

The application proposed in this work consists of four functional modules: a client for presenting the videogame, a RABio w8 for the EEG acquisition, a client for monitoring the bio-signals and a remote server for the coordination of the entire system (see Fig. 1). The stimuli client uses Matlab (Windows 7) to run the game and present the visual stimuli that elicit the SSVEPs. The monitoring client runs a GUI on Matlab to visualize the bio-signals in real time and store them for a future statistical analysis. This client sends online the raw EEG every second to the remote server for the attention detection process by means of a TCP/IP socket. After signal preprocessing, the server executes an attention detection algorithm and makes a decision over the game. The decision is transmitted o the stimuli client to update the game.

2.4 Stimulation

The display was configured with a resolution of 900 × 600 pixels and a screen refresh rate of 60 Hz. A Psych toolbox (Matlab) is utilized to create the stimuli and to control the vertical synchronization (V-sync) of the screen for optimal precision of the stimulus onset. The stimulus consists in a circular checkerboard that reverses its pattern to elicit SSVEPs. The checkerboard is texturized using functions of Psych toolbox. Using these functions, the checkerboard reverses contrast at a rate of 15 Hz, thus evoking a SSVEP of the same frequency. Along with the reversal, the checkerboard changes the position and size, thus creating the effect of a continuous movement (see Fig. 3).

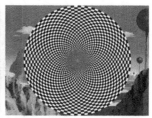

Fig. 3. Trajectory of the mobile visual stimulus. Left: at the beginning, the enemy fires the reversal checkerboard. Center: then, it moves forward. Right: the reversal checkerboard enlarges at the foreground.

2.5 Attention Detection

Two facts are considered during the attention detection algorithm: attentional efforts lead to both enhancing of the amplitude of the SSVEP and suppression of Alpha rhythm [20, 23, 24]. Therefore, two decision parameters for the attention detection process were defined.

Param1: It was defined as the spectral energy of the SSVEP (band 14–16 Hz) compared with that of the background (band 12–13 Hz and 17–18 Hz)

$$Param1 = P_{[14-16]Hz}(dB) - (P_{[12-13]Hz} + P_{[17-18]Hz})(dB) \qquad (1)$$

Param 2: It was defined as the spectral energy of the SSVEP (band 14–16 Hz) compared with that of the Alpha rhythm (band 8–12 Hz)

$$Param2 = P_{[14-16]Hz}(dB) - P_{[8-12]Hz}(dB) \qquad (2)$$

For each parameter we manually defined a threshold for the detection process. The two thresholds were stablished according to the gaming expertise and age of the participants and previous training.

Table 1. Performance of the three players.

Player	Stage	Points won	Points played	Duration
1	1	5	5	41 s
1	2	5	6	53 s
1	3	5	9	68 s
1	4	1	6	44 s
1	4	5	9	59 s
1	5	1	6	41 s
1	5	5	5	29 s
2	1	5	5	51 s
2	2	5	5	44 s
2	3	5	5	41 s
2	4	5	6	40 s
2	5	1	6	57 s
2	5	5	6	40 s
3	1	5	5	38 s
3	2	5	5	37 s
3	3	1	6	60 s
3	3	5	5	29 s
3	4	5	6	40 s
3	5	5	6	41 s

3   Results

Table 1 shows the results of the three players.

Once the scores of the three players were compiled, the ratio of successful detections was 71%. The ratio of successful detection was modelled as a binomial distribution. The 95% confidence interval was calculated as described in [25] and yielded a result of [62–78]%. Figure 4 shows the average time spent on each stage and the ratio of winning stages averaged across the three players.

4   Discussion

In this manuscript we have demonstrated a ludic use of SSVEP as an effective way to train the attention. The global accuracy of the experiment was 71% (CI [0.62, 0.78]), which is far from random choice (50% in binary detection). It evidences that our approach for the detection of attention to mobile visual stimuli based on SSVEP succeeded. Table 1 shows the performance of the three players. It shows that all players were able to defeat the enemies by means of the attention and move on up to the last stage. Only in few cases the enemies

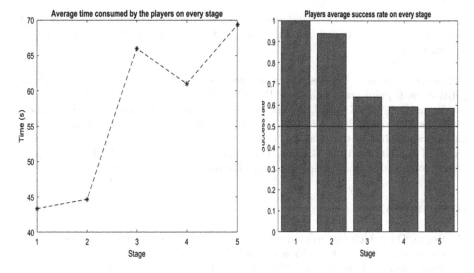

Fig. 4. Left: average time consumed on every stage. Right: average success rate of each stage.

defeated the players. This mainly happened during the second half of the sessions (Player 1: stages 4 and 5; Player 2: stage 5; Player 3: stage 3). It is justified by the increasing level of difficulty that demands to exert more attentional effort in less time. The game has been designed to require players to gradually augment the focus and intensity of their visual attention. The fact that players repeated two times stage 5, one time stage 4 and 3 and cero times stages 2 and 1 evidences it. Figure 4 shows the average time that participants needed to complete each stage. As expected, the time increases with the level of difficulty. Whereas for basic levels (stage 1 and 2) the time needed is approximately the same (43 and 44 s respectively), for the latest stages (stages 4 and 5) the time increases approximately 50% (61 and 69 s respectively). In the same figure, average success rate evidences that our design indeed increased the attentional difficulty stage by stage.

5 Conclusions

In this work, we propose a hands-free videogame in which the players joystick is a SSVEP-BCI tailored to detect user attention. Detection decision is based on a combination of SSVEP and Alpha-band powers. We designed the game with increasing levels of difficulty by means of stages in which the speed and proximity of the enemies increase. It has been evidenced the suitability of our approach to make participants to exert attentional efforts. Our proposal is a simple way to play/train the attention capabilities that could be used as a serious game in education or in mental health. In the future, we plan to include some additional features to increases the potential use of the game. Among others we will add

(i) more than one mobile visual stimulus at a time; (ii) collaborative play with more than one user at a time; (iii) combination of visual and auditory stimulus and distractors.

Acknowledgments. This research was funded by the Ministry of Economy and Competitiveness (Spain) grant number [TIN2015-67020P], the Junta of Andalucia (Spain) grant number [P11-TIC-7983], the Spanish National Youth Guarantee Implementation Plan, the Association Nicolo for the R+D in Neurotechnologies for the disability. The authors would like to thank all the volunteers who participated in the study, participants of the University of Granada Lan Party (ULP) 2018 and the I Workshop of Telecommunication Engineering at the ETSIT of the University of Granada.

References

1. Regan, D.: A high frequency mechanism which underlies visual evoked potentials. Electro-encephalogr. Clin. Neurophysiol. **25**, 231–237 (1968)
2. Minguillon, J., Lopez-Gordo, M.A., Pelayo, F.: Trends in EEG-BCI for daily-life: requirements for artifact removal. Biomed. Sig. Process. Control **31**, 407–418 (2017)
3. Kelly, S.P., Lalor, E.C., Finucane, C., McDarby, G., Reilly, R.B.: Visual spatial atten-tion control in an independent brain-computer interface. IEEE Trans. Biomed. Eng. **52**, 1588–1596 (2005)
4. Shibata, K., Yamane, K., Otuka, K., Iwata, M.: Abnormal visual processing in migraine with aura: a study of steady-state visual evoked potentials. J. Neurol. Sci. **271**, 119–126 (2008)
5. Sheppard, E., et al.: Children with a history of a typical febrile seizures show abnormal steady state visual evoked potential brain responses. Epilepsy Behav. **27**, 90–94 (2013)
6. Grgiĉ, R.G., Calore, E., de'Sperati, C.: Covert enaction at work: recording the continuous movements of visuospatial attention to visible or imagined targets by means of Steady-State Visual Evoked Potentials (SSVEPs). Cortex **74**, 31–52 (2016)
7. Wolpaw, J.R., Birbaumer, N., McFarland, D.J., Pfurtscheller, G., Vaughan, T.M.: Braincomputer interfaces for communication and control. Clin. Neurophysiol. **113**, 767–791 (2002)
8. Russo, F.D., Teder-Sälejärvi, W.A., Hillyard, S.A.: Steady-state VEP and attentional visual processing. In: The Cognitive Electrophysiology of Mind and Brain, pp. 259–274. Elsevier (2003). https://doi.org/10.1016/B978-012775421-5/50013-3
9. Walter, S., Quigley, C., Andersen, S.K., Mueller, M.M.: Effects of overt and covert attention on the steady-state visual evoked potential. Neurosci. Lett. **519**, 37–41 (2012)
10. Yin, E., Zhou, Z., Jiang, J., Yu, Y., Hu, D.: A dynamically optimized SSVEP Brain-Computer Interface (BCI) speller. IEEE Trans. Biomed. Eng. **62**, 1447–1456 (2015)
11. Lim, J.-H., Lee, J.-H., Hwang, H.-J., Kim, D.H., Im, C.-H.: Development of a hybrid mental spelling system combining SSVEP-based braincomputer interface and webcam-based eye tracking. Biomed. Sig. Process. Control **21**, 99–104 (2015)
12. Brennan, C., et al.: Accessing tele-services using a hybrid BCI approach. In: Rojas, I., Joya, G., Catala, A. (eds.) Advances in Computational Intelligence. LNCS, vol. 9094, pp. 110–123. Springer, Cham (2015). https://doi.org/10.1007/978-3-319-19258-1_10

13. Wang, Y.-T., Wang, Y., Jung, T.-P.: A cell-phone-based braincomputer interface for communication in daily life. J. Neural Eng. **8**, 025018 (2011)
14. Gürkök, H., Nijholt, A., Poel, M., Obbink, M.: Evaluating a multiplayer brain-computer interface game: challenge versus co-experience. Entertain. Comput. **4**, 195–203 (2013)
15. Finke, A., Lenhardt, A., Ritter, H.: The MindGame: a P300-based braincomputer interface game. Neural Netw. **22**, 1329–1333 (2009)
16. Krepki, R., Blankertz, B., Curio, G., Müller, K.-R.: The Berlin Brain-Computer Interface (BBCI) towards a new communication channel for online control in gaming applications. Multimed. Tools Appl. **33**, 73–90 (2007)
17. Pires, G., Torres, M., Casaleiro, N., Nunes, U., Castelo-Branco, M.: Playing Tetris with non-invasive BCI, pp. 1–6. IEEE (2011). https://doi.org/10.1109/SeGAH. 2011.6165454
18. Lopez-Gordo, M.A., Prieto, A., Pelayo, F., Morillas, C.: Customized stimulation enhances performance of independent binary SSVEP-BCIs. Clin. Neurophysiol. **122**, 128–133 (2011)
19. Lopez, M.A., Pelayo, F., Madrid, E., Prieto, A.: Statistical characterization of steady-state visual evoked potentials and their use in braincomputer interfaces. Neural Process. Lett. **29**, 179–187 (2009)
20. Klimesch, W.: EEG alpha and theta oscillations reflect cognitive and memory performance: a review and analysis. Brain Res. Rev. **29**, 169–195 (1999)
21. BCI Lab—Universidad de Granada. Available at
22. Klem, G.H., Lüders, H.O., Jasper, H.H., Elger, C.: The ten-twenty electrode system of the International Federation. Electroencephalogr. Clin. Neurophysiol. **52**(Suppl. 3), 3–6 (1999). The International Federation of Clinical Neurophysiology
23. Lopez, M.A., Pomares, H., Damas, M., Prieto, A., de la Plaza Hernandez, E.M.: Use of Kohonen maps as feature selector for selective attention brain-computer interfaces. In: Mira, J., Álvarez, J.R. (eds.) Bio-inspired Modeling of Cognitive Tasks. LNCS, vol. 4527, pp. 407–415. Springer, Heidelberg (2007). https://doi. org/10.1007/978-3-540-73053-8_41
24. Liu, N.-H., Chiang, C.-Y., Chu, H.-C.: Recognizing the degree of human attention Using EEG signals from mobile sensors. Sensors **13**, 10273–10286 (2013)
25. Wilson, E.B.: Probable inference, the law of succession, and statistical inference. J. Am. Stat. Assoc. **22**, 209 (1927)

Analysis of the Consumption of Household Appliances for the Detection of Anomalies in the Behaviour of Older People

Miguel A. Patricio[1]($\boxtimes$) , Daniel González[2], José M. Molina[1] ,
and Antonio Berlanga[1]

[1] Applied Artificial Intelligence Group, Universidad Carlos III de Madrid,
Madrid, Spain
mpatrici@inf.uc3m.es
{molina,aberlang}@ia.uc3m.es
[2] BQ Engineering, Madrid, Spain
daniel.gonzalez@bq.com,
http://www.giaa.inf.uc3m.es,
http://www.bq.com

Abstract. Nowadays, modern societies are facing the important problem of ageing of their population. On many occasions, older people must leave their homes to be cared for by their relatives or to enter specialised centres for the elderly. On the other hand, something similar happens with disabled people who need the support of other people for their daily activity. This phenomenon brings with it important social and economic consequences. In the activities of the daily life of the elderly it is necessary to have the monitoring of different aspects of their physical activity, such as the detection of critical situations (such as falls) or dangerous situations (such as flooding or gas leaks). The aim of this paper is to analyse the consumption of the different household appliances in order to model a normal behaviour within the daily activities of a house. By means of the consumption of the electrical appliances the aim is to detect anomalous behaviours that induce the appearance of possible problems due to the change in the consumption pattern.

Keywords: Anomaly detection · Support for daily activities ·
Elderly · Behaviour analysis

1 Introduction

The world population is ageing rapidly. Projections are that people 60 years old or older will outnumber children by 2030 and adolescents and youth by 2050 [10]. Therefore, concepts such as "independent living", "active ageing", "ageing at home" form the nucleus of proposals for integrated care services for the elderly.

© Springer Nature Switzerland AG 2019
J. M. Ferrández Vicente et al. (Eds.): IWINAC 2019, LNCS 11486, pp. 60–68, 2019.
https://doi.org/10.1007/978-3-030-19591-5_7

In recent years, research is being conducted to monitor the electricity consumption of homes. In this sense, there are works related to non-intrusive appliance load monitoring (NIALM) [2]. NIALM is the process of dis-aggregating a household's total electricity consumption into its contributing appliances.

Neural Networks have been used for the detection of anomalies in Electric Power Systems with auto-associative neural networks [8] or autoencoders [11]. Autoencoders are a kind of neural network that allows to represent a compressed version of the input. The aim of the paper is to analyse the typical or normal behaviour modelling from the consumption of different appliances, so that they can be used in the prediction of anomalous behaviours within the daily activities of the elderly. The best appliance will be evaluated to be used in a detection system of anomalous behaviours within the daily activity of older people.

The paper is organised with a first part where the problem to be solved is presented based on the information of the UK-DALE dataset. Next, we describe the complete process carried out for the modeling of behaviors based on the analysis of the electrical consumption of household appliances. In the last part of the paper, the results obtained and a discussion of the results are described.

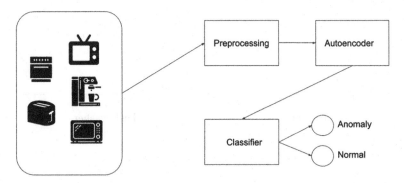

Fig. 1. Phases in the process of detecting anomalous behaviours from the electrical consumption of household appliances.

2 Problem Statement

The problem that arises in this work is divided into different phases (see Fig. 1). Starting from the real electrical consumption of different domestic appliances, a pre-processing of the signals will be carried out. This pre-processing is related to the elimination of outliers (days considered as vacations, for example), as well as the organisation of the information in a set of variables that indicate the summary of the daily behaviour of a house in terms of the electrical consumption of household appliances. The pre-processed signals will be used to model a normal behaviour in the electrical consumption of the different appliances. For each of the appliances, a typical or normal behaviour model will be obtained. In order to validate all the models associated with each appliance, a set of anomalous values will be obtained by shifting the original consumption and varying the amplitude values of the signals in a random way. Each of the models will be evaluated through the use of a classifier. This classifier will be designed using the value of the internal neurons of the autoencoder when at the entrance of the network both typical and abnormal behavioural samples are presented (Fig. 2).

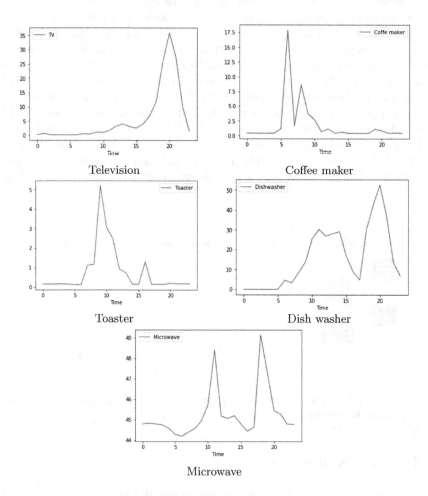

Fig. 2. Histogram of mean power demand on each appliance measure in watts.

2.1 Dataset

The dataset used in this work is the UK-DALE dataset [7], where the power demand of five houses has been collected every 6 s for 4 years. The electrical consumption is measured in watts. Only one house has been considered since the habits of use of each appliance can vary significantly between houses.

The appliance used in this paper are the television, the coffee maker, the toaster, the microwave and the dishwasher since this are the most common appliances in all homes and their consumption habits are relevant for the detection of anomalies.

2.2 Data Preprocessing

This section describes the actions carried out for the preprocessing of each one of the electrical consumption distributions of the different domestic appliances. It has been decided to group the power demand in hours, since the average use of the appliances usually lasts several minutes or even hours. Below it is shown the average electricity demand per hour in the selected home for the five selected appliances. It can be seen that the appliance usage pattern of each appliance varies significantly.

To work effectively with the data, a Data Engineering work has been done. The proposed model has 24 variables, each variable reflects the total watt consumption of the appliance at each hour of a day. The average power consumption at each hour is not used because some relevant information can be lost with this metric. After a work of Data Science, there has been detected some outliers. These outliers are the days in which no use of the appliance has been registered and it might be vacation days or a failure in the sensor or in the appliance, so it has been decided to eliminate this days from the dataset because this entries may affect the performance of the model.

Once the data processing has been done, it is necessary to generate the anomalies. As stated in [5], a nocturnal activity may be associated with Dementia or Alzheimer, so the data has been displaced 8 hours forward. In addition, these values have been multiplied by a random value between $[0.25, 2]$, since a variation in the use of appliance can be associated with anomalous behaviour. The data has been separated by 80% for training and 20% for validation. Below at Fig. 3 it is shown a comparison between the distribution of typical data and anomalies for each appliance.

2.3 Autoencoders for Anomaly Detection

An autoencoder is a neural network where the number of input nodes is equal to the number of output nodes. The autoencoders has an intermediate layer with a lower number of neurons. The autoencoders are part of unsupervised learning, since they do not require labels for their training. This architecture tries to find an arbitrary function $f(W, b)x = x$ that makes the input equal to the output, being W and b the weights and biases of the neural network [1].

The autoencoder of this paper has 24 input nodes as shown in Fig. 4, where each input node is one hour of the day. In the intermediate layer it has two nodes. The popularity of this architecture has increased since at the intermediate layer, the data is represent in a smaller dimension, so the autoencoders are able to simplify the representation of the data and it makes the classification task

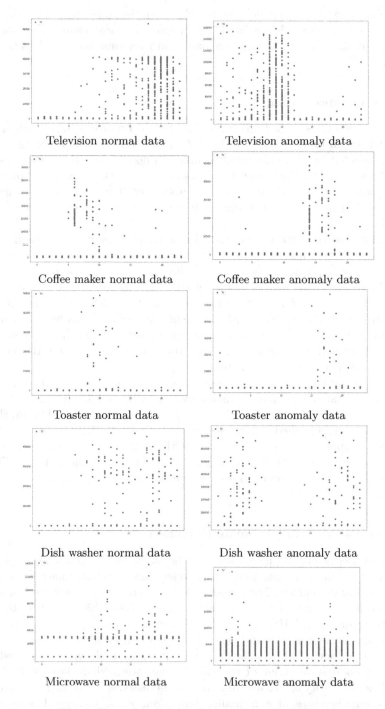

Fig. 3. Normal and anomaly data for each appliance.

easier. At the following figures, it is shown how the autoencoder represent the data of each appliances. As shown in the graphs, the autoencoder represents the data in a simplified way, the classification of said data is now easier (Fig. 5).

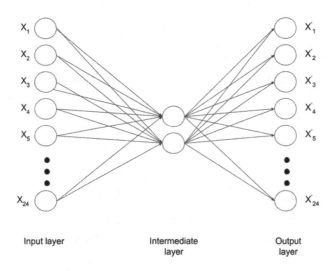

Fig. 4. Architecture of the autoencoder used.

2.4 Anomalies Classification

For the classification task, there has been selected a Random Forest Classifier. The Random Forest is a Bagging method [3], where some Decision Trees are put in parallel. This classifier is part of Ensemble Learning. To find the better parameters for the model, the Grid Search [9] has been used, where the data is split and this framework evaluate the performance of some possible values defined for the parameters. The metrics used for evaluate the performance of the model are:

- AUC (ROC): Measures the capacity of the model to differentiate the classes [4].
- Precision: Success on all the data.
- Recall: True positives on all the positive data.
- F1 Score: Average of the precision and recall [6].

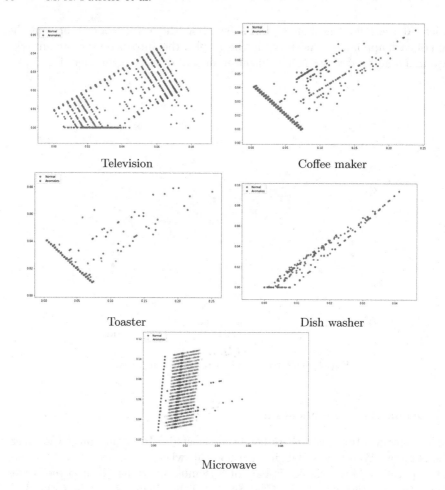

Fig. 5. Representation of the data of each appliance at the intermediate layer.

3 Experimentation

With all the treatment of the dataset and with the autoencoder trained, the results of the described model are shown. In the following table, the results of each appliance with the optimal parameters found with the Grid Search are showed (Table 1).

The appliance that has given better results has been the microwave with an 88% of accuracy, being the one that has obtained the best result in the other metrics too. The confusion matrix this appliance is showed below (Fig. 6).

With the data from the microwave, not only the best precision is achieved, but also the lowest percentage of false negatives is achieved. It is very important that the number of false positives be low since this type of failure occurs when the model is not able to detect an anomaly. The false positives in this model are not so important, since they do not produce dangerous situations for the user.

Table 1. Results of each appliance on autoencoder.

	AUC (ROC)	Precision	Recall	F1 Score
Television	0.73	0.71	0.73	0.72
Coffee maker	0.73	0.73	0.71	0.72
Toaster	0.70	0.72	0.65	0.69
Dish washer	0.62	0.65	0.60	0.63
Microwave	**0.86**	**0.88**	**0.84**	**0.86**

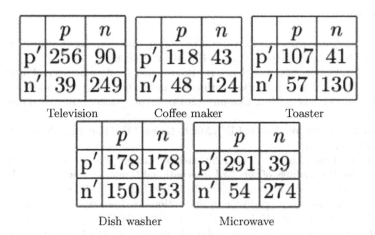

Fig. 6. Confusion matrix of the model with each appliance.

4   Conclusions

The autoencoders are a neural network that simplify the classification work. Finding an autoencoder that suits in a data allows to build a strong classifier that achieves a good performance. The model use combine an Autoencoder to represent the data in a simpler way a Random Forest Classifier, whose parameters has been tuned by Grid Search. The proposed model is capable of detect anomalies in the behaviour of the user with only the power demand of the TV. The model only requires to be trained with previous data of the power demand of this appliance. The appliance that appears to be more relevant in anomalies detection is the toaster and this may be due to the fact that the daily use of the toaster follows a very stable pattern, and the use of other appliances is more random.

This method is a non-intrusive way of caring for people with Dementia or Alzheimer, as it will be able to detect in a precise way situations where the user requires attention and avoid possible dangerous situations derived from these diseases. For the future work, a better performance of the model can be achieved with other anomalies data. It would be interesting to test the model with real anomaly data or use a more precise method to generate anomalies. On the other hand, a combination of some appliances might achieve a better performance and it should be tested.

Acknowledgements. This work was funded by private research project of Company BQ and public research projects of Spanish Ministry of Economy and Competitivity (MINECO), references TEC2017-88048-C2-2-R, RTC-2016-5595-2, RTC-2016-5191-8 and RTC-2016-5059-8.

References

1. Baldi, P.: Autoencoders, unsupervised learning, and deep architectures. J. Mach. Learn. Res. (2012). https://doi.org/10.1561/2200000006
2. Belley, C., Gaboury, S., Bouchard, B., Bouzouane, A.: An efficient and inexpensive method for activity recognition within a smart home based on load signatures of appliances. Pervasive Mob. Comput. (2014). https://doi.org/10.1016/j.pmcj.2013.02.002
3. Breiman, L.: Random forests LEO. Mach. Learn. (2001). https://doi.org/10.1023/A:1010933404324
4. Davis, J., Goadrich, M.: The relationship between Precision-Recall and ROC curves. In: Proceedings of the 23rd International Conference on Machine Learning - ICML 2006 (2006). https://doi.org/10.1145/1143844.1143874
5. Evans, L.K.: Sundown syndrome in institutionalized elderly. J. Am. Geriatr. Soc. (1987). https://doi.org/10.1111/j.1532-5415.1987.tb01337.x
6. Goutte, C., Gaussier, E.: A probabilistic interpretation of precision, recall and F-score, with implication for evaluation. In: Losada, D.E., Fernández-Luna, J.M. (eds.) ECIR 2005. LNCS, vol. 3408, pp. 345–359. Springer, Heidelberg (2005). https://doi.org/10.1007/978-3-540-31865-1_25
7. Kelly, J., Knottenbelt, W.: The UK-DALE dataset, domestic appliance-level electricity demand and whole-house demand from five UK homes. Sci. Data (2015). https://doi.org/10.1038/sdata.2015.7
8. Martinelli, M., Tronci, E., Dipoppa, G., Balducelli, C.: Electric power system anomaly detection using neural networks. In: Negoita, M.G., Howlett, R.J., Jain, L.C. (eds.) KES 2004. LNCS (LNAI), vol. 3213, pp. 1242–1248. Springer, Heidelberg (2004). https://doi.org/10.1007/978-3-540-30132-5_168
9. Pedregosa, F., et al.: Scikitlearn: machine learning in Python. J. Mach. Learn. Res. (2011). https://doi.org/10.1007/s13398-014-0173-7.2
10. United Nations: World Population Ageing 2015. Technical report (2015). ST/ESA/SER.A/390
11. Yuan, Y., Jia, K.: A distributed anomaly detection method of operation energy consumption using smart meter data. In: 2015 International Conference on Intelligent Information Hiding and Multimedia Signal Processing (IIH-MSP), pp. 310–313 (2015)

Autonomic Modulation During a Cognitive Task Using a Wearable Device

Maria Paula Bonomini[1,2], Mikel Val-Calvo[3,5]([✉]), Alejandro Díaz-Morcillo[4],
José Manuel Ferrández Vicente[5], and Eduardo Fernández-Jover[6]

[1] Instituto Argentino de Matemáticas Alberto Calderón,
Saavedra 15, CABA, Argentina
[2] Instituto Tecnológico de Buenos Aires (ITBA),
Av Eduardo Madero 399, CABA, Argentina
[3] Dpto. de Inteligencia Artificial,
Universidad Nacional de Educación a Distancia (UNED),
Juan del Rosal, 16, 28040 Madrid, Spain
mikel1982mail@gmail.com
[4] Dpto. Tecnologías de la Información y las Comunicaciones,
Univ. Politécnica de Cartagena, Cartagena, Spain
[5] Dpto. Electrónica, Tecnología de Computadoras y Proyectos,
Univ. Politécnica de Cartagena, Cartagena, Spain
[6] Instituto de Bioingeniería, Univ. Miguel Hernández, Elche, Spain

Abstract. Heart-brain interaction is by nature bidirectional, and then, it is sensible to expect the heart, via the autonomic nervous system (ANS), to induce changes in the brain. Respiration can originate differentiated ANS states reflected by HRV. In this work, we measured the changes in performance during a cognitive task due to four autonomic states originated by breath control: at normal breathing (NB), fast breathing (FB), slow breathing (SB) and control phases. ANS states were characterized by temporal (SDNN) and spectral (LF and HF power) HRV markers. Cognitive performance was measured by the response time (RT) and the success rate (SR). HRV parameters were acquired with the wristband Empatica E4. Classification was accomplished, firstly, to find the best ANS variables that discriminated the breathing phases (BPH) and secondly, to find whether ANS parameters were associated to changes in RT and SR. In order to compensate for possible bias of the test sets, 1000 classification iterations were run. The ANS parameters that better separated the four BPH were LF and HF power, with changes about 300% from controls and an average classification rate of 59.9%, a 34.9% more than random. LF and HF explained RT separation for every BPH pair, and so was HF for SR separation. The best RT classification was 63.88% at NB vs SB phases, while SR provided a 73.39% at SB vs NB phases. Results suggest that breath control could show a relation with the efficiency of certain cognitive tasks. For this goal the Empatica wristband together with the proposed methodology could help to clarify this hypothesis.

Keywords: ANS · HRV · Response time · Cognition

© Springer Nature Switzerland AG 2019
J. M. Ferrández Vicente et al. (Eds.): IWINAC 2019, LNCS 11486, pp. 69–77, 2019.
https://doi.org/10.1007/978-3-030-19591-5_8

1   Introduction

Brain-heart interactions have been a focus of attention for more than 150 years, with the pioneer work of Claude Bernard, whose suggestions and intuitive framework was strengthened recently, relying on solid physiological backgrounds. Cerebral arousal and autonomic control over the cardiovascular system are bidirectionally linked. Then, modifying one will affect the other, and vice versa. For instance, a growing body of evidence suggests that heart rate variability (HRV) reflects emotion regulation and autonomic responses in the body [11]. Furthermore, there exist a model, the neurovisceral integration model, that use HRV to monitor the activity of a neural network regulating physiological, cognitive, and emotional responses [4,5].

On the other hand, it has also been known that breathing frequency influences amplitude of heart rate variability [2,3], evidencing a maximum heart rate oscillation at a 0.1 Hz (5.5 breaths per minute) respiratory frequency. Indeed, it is in this frequency that heart rate oscillates in phase with respiration, taking place a maximum respiratory sinus arrhythmia (RSA) and the most efficient gas exchange. Practices in slow breathing have shown beneficial effects in many psychological or physiological conditions such as pain and anxiety [6], stress and hypertension [8], coronary artery disease [13] and even in sports [1].

In parallel, wearable devices have widely spread in the last decade and measuring HRV indirectly from photoplethysmography (PPG) has gained increasing attention due to its portability, low cost and flexibility [9]. The pulse rate variability (PRV), however, may lack of accuracy due to measurement errors and/or physiological factors such as transmission of the pulse wave through the tissues or EMG artifacts obscuring the signal. In the recent past, a number of studies have indicated a reasonable agreement between HRV and PRV, encouraging the use of PPG as an indirect measure of HRV [14].

Although great efforts were made on identifying the connections of the neural-autonomic drive of the heart, the system has been extensively studied along one direction; from brain to heart. Moreover, most of the research has focused on emotions, but not on cognitive processes. Thus, experimental paradigms are usually designed to induce emotions and measure their reflex on the HRV. In this work, the feasibility of the Empatica wristband for measuring ANS states has been proved by designing an experiment to investigate to what extent a local cardiovascular autonomic state can afferently change cortical activity. To pursue this, an autonomic procedure was designed based on breath control that directly affects the autonomic drive in the heart. Then, ANS-induced cardiovascular changes were measured to check whether this affected the response times and hit rate in a cognitive task.

2   Materials and Methods

Study Population and Experimental Paradigm. Twenty one young healthy subjects were enrolled aged 34.4 ± 7.2 years old (12 male). From this population, two subjects were discarded due to noisy respiratory phases and two subjects due to invalid recordings in the cognitive task.

Groups were defined according to three respiratory frequencies; normal breathing at about 12 breaths per minute (NB), fast breathing at about 20 breaths per minute (FB) and slow breathing, below 6 breaths per minute (SB). In addition, a control group without breath control was included. During respiratory phases NB, FB and SB, subjects were asked to close their eyes, except for control, where remained with their eyes opened. All experiments were accomplished in the morning, in the same room. Blood volume pulse (BVP) was obtained from photoplethysmography (PPG) using the wearable device E4 Empatica wristband [10].

After the control period and every breathing phase, subjects were asked to complete a cognitive task consisting in the N-Back task with $N = 2$. From these tests, two variables describing performance were recorded, the time to answer, called Response Time (RT) and the hit rate, denominated as Success Rate (SR). The order of the respiratory sessions was randomized to avoid bias due to training.

Autonomic Assessment. Maxima of blood volume pressure waveform were detected, and the n-th pulse-to-pulse interval (PPI) was measured as the temporal distance between the n-th and (n+1)-th blood pulse maxima. From these PPI series, NN series were constructed by concatenating normal PP intervals ignoring the gaps in the time domain, while for frequency-domain analysis, gaps were filled out with artificial PP intervals obtained by linear interpolation. Recordings lasted from one to five minutes, from which sections free of noise and missing beats were cropped and used for analysis. The temporal HRV index chosen was the standard deviation of the NN series (SDNN). Prior to frequency domain analysis, the time series were preprocessed by lowpass filtering at 2 Hz (zero-phase Butterworth filter, order 4th) and subtracting the mean value. Then, resampling at 4 Hz by cubic splines interpolation was accomplished to obtain evenly spaced samples. Afterwards, the periodogram was carried out to estimate the power spectrum of the interpolated NN series. Spectral power of the low frequency band around 0.04–0.15 Hz (LF) and that of the high frequency band around 0.15–0.4 Hz (HF) were computed.

Statistical Analysis and Classification. Kruskal-Wallis ANOVA was used to compare within and between group comparisons, followed by Mann-Whitney post-hoc comparisons. Statistical significance was defined for $p < 0.05$.

A classification step has been performed in order to prove the plausibility of estimating breathing phase (BPH), RT and SR, taking into account the set of measured variables: HR, SDNN, LF and HF. For performance evaluation a test set about (20%) was used and min-max normalization was performed over each variable. As the number of samples is very low, 17 subjects for four experiments make a total of 68 samples, test sets are biased, not being representative of the whole population, therefore, the performance has been evaluated over 1000 classification iterations to evaluate its distribution. For each iteration, the training and test sets have been chosen randomly. A multi-layer perceptron has been used for classification with a L2 regularization term $\alpha = 1e-5$.

The classification process has been split into three stages. First, feature ranking was carried out using recursive feature elimination technique in order to select the best two features for the task of estimating the BPH, resulting in the selection of LF and HF variables. Second, estimation of RT was accomplished by the discretization of the values around the mean, that is, greater values were labeled as 1 and lower ones as 0. With the same feature ranking method, the best two variables have been used for the following classifications: NB versus FB, NB versus SB and FB versus SB. Analogously, estimation of SR implemented SR discretization around its mean and followed the classification processes as for the RT variable.

3   Results

Figure 1 shows a representative example of the heart rate (HR), power spectral density (PSD) and blood volume pressure signal (Bvp) for a subject at Control, NB, FB and SB groups (from top to bottom, respectively). Notice the strong oscillations in the HR and in the Bvp for the slow breathing group, product of the resonance of the respiratory frequency with baroreflex activity.

Figure 2, on the other hand, shows the boxplot distributions expressed as percentages of control values of the low frequency and high frequency energy for the different respiratory groups. Notice that the LF band produced two increases in the order of 300% with respect to control at NB ($p = 2e-4$) and SB ($p = 8e-6$) groups, while in the HF band, only the NB group showed an increased activity in the order of 200% with respect to control ($p = 0.001$) and FB ($p = 0.001$). This evidences a significant increase in autonomic activity from eyes opened to eyes closed, suggesting a modulation of this effect over the remaining respiratory groups. In FB, however, there is a supression of autonomic activity, while a marked increase appears in the SB group at the LF band, reflecting the shift of the respiratory peak, usually centered about 0.25 Hz in the HF band to frequencies below 0.15 Hz, in the LF band. The latter is compatible with cardiac coherence and biofeedback techniques.

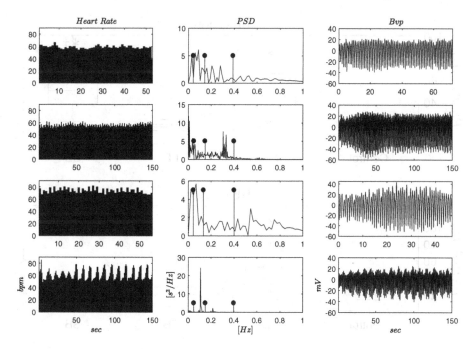

Fig. 1. HRV signals. Tachogram, PSD and Bvp signals for a representative subject at the three breathing phases (NB, FB and SB, from top to bottom) and control. Notice the HR greatest variability evidenced as marked oscillations in the tachogram as well as the Bvp signal at SB and its respective shift in frequency of the breath peak, as observed in the PSD. Stems mark the limits of the LF (0.04–0.15 Hz) and HF (0.15–0.4 Hz) frequency bands.

Analogously, Fig. 3 shows the mean heart rate (HR), SDNN, response time (RT) and success rate (SR) for the different respiratory groups. Even though not significant, RT was uptrended for SB and downtrended for FB, while SDNN produced the highest value at SB. Accordingly, SR showed a trend for the highest CR at SB with the lowest dispersion. HR, on the other hand, was lower than control and FB at NB, although no statistical significance was achieved.

For the classification process, Fig. 4a shows the performance distribution of 1000 classifications for estimating the BPH, where the chance is 25% for the four cases: Control, NB, FB and SB. Results shown that on average the classifiers perform the estimation with a 59.9 ± 12.48% of accuracy. In Fig. 4b three cases are taken into account: NB, FB and SB. For this case, the mean average performance is 83.52% ± 10.23. Therefore, LF and HF are suitable features for the estimation of the BPH. On the other hand, the classification process has been performed for binary cases on both RT and SR features. For a better comparison, mean accuracy performances are shown in Table 1.

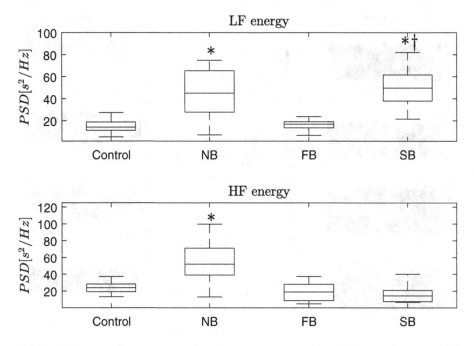

Fig. 2. HRV spectral parameters. Boxplot representations for LF energy (top) and HF energy (bottom) at NB, FB, SB and control for the entire population. Variables were normalized to control values. Notice the remarkable increase of LF at SB, which is not accompanied by a HF increase. $^*p < 0.0005$ vs control, $^\dagger < 0.0005$ vs FB.

Table 1. Obtained estimation performances on RT and CR variables.

Classification	Label	Average accuracy	Selected features
FB vs SB	RT	52.61% ± 15.56	HF, LF
FB vs NB	RT	52.38% ± 16.68	HF, LF
SB vs NB	RT	63.88% ± 17.18	HF, LF
FB vs SB	SR	66.97% ± 15.64	HR, HF
FB vs NB	SR	49.30% ± 16.46	SDNN, HF
SB vs NB	SR	**73.39% ± 14.65**	SDNN, HF

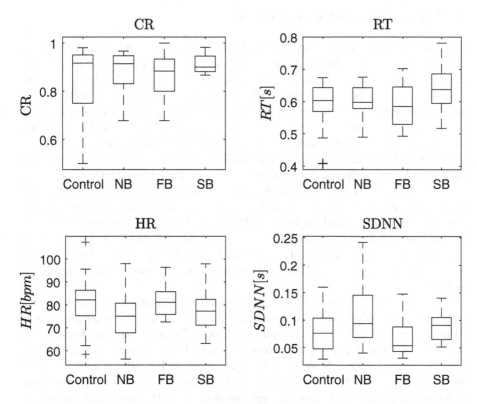

Fig. 3. Trend for cardiovascular and cognitive parameters. Boxplot representation of Heart Rate (HR), SDNN, reaction times (RT) and success rates (SR). Variables were normalized to control values.

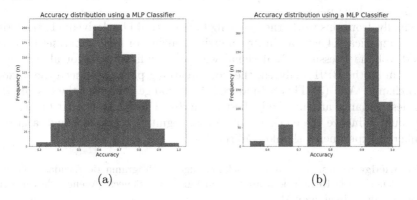

Fig. 4. Accuracy distributions. (a) Classification performance using HF and LF features on the BPH with four experiments: control, NB, FB and SB. (b) Classification performance using HF and LF features on the BPH with three experiments: NB, FB and SB.

4   Discussion and Conclusions

The spectral HRV parameters (LF and HF) significantly changed throughout the breathing phase. Findings related to such parameters are consistent with the literature, particularly for the SB phase, where a state of cardiac coherence was achieved, evidenced by large HR oscillations and maximum HRV power [3]. Accordingly to our results, a higher SDNN, LF power and LF/HF ratio, and no significant differences in HF power was found in [7,15] for all paced breathing sessions as compared to the control condition (spontaneous breathing). Moreover, HRV transitions through respiratory phases were presented, allowing for a complete description between respiratory frequency and ANS system.

Regarding the cognitive parameters, they failed to produce statistical significance although a trend for a higher response time and higher hit rate for the slow breathing phase can be appreciated in Fig. 3. Moreover, the neural networks classification confirmed the trend, with both SR and RT differentiating SB from NB, producing performances of 73.39% and 63.88% respectively. These results suggest a relation between HRV and cognitive parameters at least during SB and NB.

According to RT and SR changes, it could be inferred that SB induces a relaxation state that slows down the reactivity but enhances efficiency. These findings partially agree with Maman et al., who found significant decreases in the response time of basketball players together with significant increases in the shooting performance [12]. A possible explanation of this difference in RT could be attributed to the time elapsed between the breathing session and the task, which is immediate, while due to a long-term effect in the basketball players. It is also worth noting that in order to avoid for training bias, we have changed the order of the breathing phases throughout subjects, so that NB, FB and SB had a roughly balanced amount of sessions in the last trial. Then, the better efficiency in the congruence rate at SB should not be attributed to training but to slow breathing per se.

Finally, from this work, the following findings could be derived: (1) the wristband Empatica E4 was accurate enough to allow for HRV analysis from the Blood Volume Pressure (Bvp) signal without significant loss for about 5 min. (2) From all the BPH analyzed, the slow breathing phase produced the clearest ANS change. And (3) This SB-induced ANS change produced the distribution with less variance around the highest mean SR. This suggests that breath control could influence the efficiency of certain cognitive tasks, although a greater number of experiments should confirm this.

Acknowledgements. We want to acknowledge to Programa de Ayudas a Grupos de Excelencia de la Región de Murcia, from Fundación Séneca, Agencia de Ciencia y Tecnología de la Región de Murcia.

References

1. Increasing performance of professional soccer players and elite track and field athletes with peak performance training and biofeedback: a pilot study
2. Respiratory modulation of muscle sympathetic and vagal cardiac outflow in man. J. Physiol. **365**, 181–89 (1985)
3. Respiratory modulation of human autonomic rhythms. Am. J. Physiol.-Heart Circ. Physiol. **280**(6), H2674–H2688 (2001)
4. Claude Bernard and the heart-brain connection: further elaboration of a model of neurovisceral integration. Neurosci. Biobehav. Rev. **33**(2), 81–88 (2009). The Inevitable Link between Heart and Behavior: New Insights from Biomedical Research and Implications for Clinical Practice
5. Neural correlates of heart rate variability during emotion. NeuroImage. **44**, 213–222 (2009)
6. The effect of mindfulness-based therapy on anxiety and depression: a meta-analytic review. J. Consult. Clin. Psychol. **78**, 169–183 (2010)
7. Breathing at a rate of 5.5 breaths per minute with equal inhalation-to-exhalation ratio increases heart rate variability. Int. J. Psychophysiol. **91**(3), 206–211 (2014)
8. Effects of heart rate variability biofeedback on cardiovascular responses and autonomic sympathovagal modulation following stressor tasks in prehypertensives. J. Hum. Hypertens. **30**, 105–111 (2015)
9. Allen, J.: Photoplethysmography and its application in clinical physiological measurement. Physiol. Meas. **28**(3), R1–R39 (2007)
10. Cogan, D., Birjandtalab, J., Nourani, M., Harvey, J., Nagaraddi, V.: Multi-biosignal analysis for epileptic seizure monitoring. Int. J. Neural Syst. **27**(01), 1650031 (2017)
11. Holzman, J.B., Bridgett, D.J.: Heart rate variability indices as bio-markers of top-down self-regulatory mechanisms: a meta-analytic review. Neurosci. Biobehav. Rev. **74**, 233–255 (2017)
12. Maman, P., Garg, K., Singh Sandhu, J.: Role of biofeedback in optimizingpsychomotor performance in sports. Asian J. Sports Med. **3**, 29 (2012)
13. Pozo, J.M.D., Gevirtz, R.N., Scher, B., Guarneri, E.: Biofeedback treatment increases heart rate variability in patients with known coronary artery disease. Am. Heart J. **147**(3), 545 (2004)
14. Schäfer, A., Vagedes, J.: How accurate is pulse rate variability as an estimate of heart rate variability?: A review on studies comparing photoplethysmographic technology with an electrocardiogram. Int. J. Cardiol. **66**, 15–29 (2013)
15. Van Diest, I., Verstappen, K., Aubert, A., et al.: Inhalation/exhalation ratio modulates the effect of slow breathing on heart rate variability and relaxation. Appl. Psychophysiol. Biofeedback **39**, 171–180 (2014)

The Assessment of Visuospatial Abilities with Tangible Interfaces and Machine Learning

Antonio Cerrato[1(✉)], Michela Ponticorvo[1], Onofrio Gigliotta[1], Paolo Bartolomeo[3], and Orazio Miglino[1,2]

[1] Department of Humanistic Studies,
University of Naples "Federico II", Naples, Italy
`antonio.cerrato@unina.it`
[2] Institute of Cognitive Sciences and Technologies,
National Research Council, Rome, Italy
[3] Inserm U 1127, CNRS UMR 7225, Sorbonne Université,
Institut du Cerveau et de la Moelle épinière, Hôpital de la Pitié-Salpêtriére,
Paris, France

Abstract. Visuospatial abilities are framed in the capacity of perceiving, acting and reasoning in function of spatial coordinates, permitting to identify visual and spatial relationships among objects. They represent the set of skills conferring individuals the ability to interact with the surrounding world. Whenever spatial cognition is impaired it is important to correctly assess visuospatial abilities. Scientific literature, for this purpose, reports many diagnostic tools that have been adopted by clinicians and neuropsychologists.

In this paper we present a prototype that aims to evaluate the visuospatial abilities that are related to how individuals explore their peripersonal space. In particular, the presented tool makes use of tangible interfaces and augmented reality systems.

In the final part of this study we describe the implementation of an ecological test for the assessment of visuospatial abilities through our prototype by highlighting its advantage in terms of data collection and analysis.

Keywords: Visuospatial abilities · Spatial cognition ·
Neuropsychological assessment · Machine learning ·
Unilateral Spatial Neglect

1 Introduction

1.1 The Importance of Visuospatial Abilities

Visuospatial abilities (or spatial abilities) can be defined as the capacity of perceiving, acting and reasoning, as well as operating on mental representations, in function of spatial coordinates. Visuospatial skills permit to identify visual

J. M. Ferrández Vicente et al. (Eds.): IWINAC 2019, LNCS 11486, pp. 78–87, 2019.
https://doi.org/10.1007/978-3-030-19591-5_9

and spatial relationships among objects. In particular, they permit to individuate targets in the surrounding space, visually perceive objects, and understand the multidimensional spatial relationships among objects and our environment. These abilities allow us to safely navigate our environment through the accurate judgment of direction and distance. Moreover, these abilities are evaluated in term of the capacity to locate objects, to make global shapes by individuating small components, or to understand the differences and similarities between objects.

Spatial information related to the internal and external reality of an organism comes from all sensory modalities, but the visual system contributes most to spatial cognition of people. According to Mishkin and Ungerleider [24], the brain has two way to process visual information: one is named ventral pathway, located in the occipito-temporal zone, that is responsible for the object identification and recognition; the other way is named dorsal pathway, located in the occipito-parietal zone, that is involved in object localization. In the last years, the difference between these two systems has been revised, for example Goodale and colleagues [19] sustain that both pathways contribute in the same way in the localization and identification of objects, but, while the ventral pathway elaborates visual information to construct a object-to-object (allocentric) spatial representation, the dorsal pathway process visual information in terms of coordinates to make a self-to-object (egocentric) spatial representation (Fig. 1).

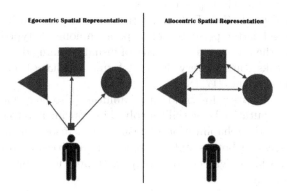

Fig. 1. A model representing egocentric vs allocentric spatial representation

Both pathways consent to act in the external environment and encode information useful to reach and manipulate objects, to recognize familiar places or to get a correct topographical orientation.
Visuospatial abilities are involved in many activities performed in everyday life, so it is important to accurately evaluate and assess them in the context of daily-life routine, in order to identify their impairment that, in certain circumstances, can evolve in a visuospatial disorder.

2 Assessment of Visuospatial Cognition

Visuospatial disorders have been described since the dawn of neuropsychology but they have often received less emphasis than, for example, language disorders. While a language or memory impairment implies an alteration in the behavior immediately evident, spatial impairments assume a brunt only when people undertake their usual activities. In fact, the knowledge of the corporeal and extracorporeal spatial coordinates is the prerequisite of every action: reaching or moving objects, conducting any manual activity, navigating in the streets, driving a car and so on.

The assessment of visuospatial abilities is usually part of the neuropsychologists duties. To evaluate visuospatial impairments it is necessary to consider that a definitive conceptualization of the argument is still missing and that a certain variability persists in identifying which are the basic visuospatial abilities and the appropriate tests to assess them.

A common neuropsychological testing approach is to utilize batteries, consisting in a plethora of tests, to evaluate cognitive functions, including spatial skills. Amongst the many test adopted by clinicians to evaluate visuospatial cognition we can list some of the bestknown:

- *Judgment of Line Orientation* [5], a standardized test of visuospatial skills measuring a person's ability to match the angle and orientation of lines in space. It regards the visuospatial perception.
- *Single Letter Cancellation Test* [12], a task that requires to individuate and delete the target letter presented on a paper among 52 typed letters. It is aimed to asses the presence and severity of visual scanning deficits. Moreover, cancellation tasks come in very different forms and have been administered even to artificial agents [17,18,26].
- *TERADIC* [1], a battery for visuospatial abilities (also known as BVA) developed to analyse putative basic skills involved in drawing and to plan and monitor outcomes after rehabilitation of visuospatial disorders. It encompasses eight tasks assessing both simple "perceptual" abilities, such as line length and line orientation judgments and complex "representational" abilities, such as mental rotation.
- *Behavioral Inattention Test (BIT)* [34], a short screening battery of tests to assess the presence and the extent of spatial exploration impairments on a sample of everyday problems faced by patients with visuo-attentional deficits.
- *ReyOsterrieth complex figure test (ROCF)* [25,30], a neuropsychological test based on the reproduction of a complicated drawing, first by copying it freehand (recognition), and then drawing from memory (recall). Many different cognitive abilities are needed for a correct performance, from visuospatial abilities to attention and planning functions; it allows to highlight even the slightest visual-constructive disorders and to investigate the different copying strategies adopted by people.
- *Visual Object and Space Perception (VOSP) Battery* [21], a battery evaluating spatial and object perception, proceeding from the assumption that these

perceptions are functionally independent. The items require simple responses, and each of them focuses on one component of visual perception, minimizing the effect of other cognitive skills.

Despite the massive adoption and the high reliability of the classical neuropsychological tests, it is possible to notice certain problems such as the long time administration (becoming time-consuming for examiners and participants) or the tiredness generated by it for many participants and patients, who, sometimes, do not complete or incorrectly perform the assessment [2].

To overcome some issues represented by traditional assessment tools, modern and digital technologies have opened new opportunities for neuropsychological testing, allowing new computerized testing tools to be developed and paper-and-pencil testing tools to be translated into new computerized devices. Computerized tests have been used in research since 1970s, and also the American Psychological Association [3] has recognized the importance of computerized psychological testing suggesting how to implement and interpret computerized test results.

In recent times, another choice of assessment is represented by the adoption of digital, augmented and virtual environment to evaluate cognitive and spatial skills, and some successful application are listed by different authors [10,27].

A digitalized evaluation of cognitive functions can present advantages such as a shorter duration (e.g., by reducing downtime in stimuli presentation), great objectivity, precision, and standardization. The computerized assessment can also minimize the so called *floor and ceiling effects*, occurring when differences among participant performance are not fully detected; thus, they can provide more standardized measures of subjects performance, crucial for an accurate and early detection of specific impairments.

It appears clearly that digital assessment will represent an essential part of the clinical setting in the future, specially in screening procedures, providing an automatized score of performances useful for the diagnosis, on condition that these new instruments become supportive for examiners. Given the significance and the increasing use of technology enhanced assessment tools, we proposed a new tool to assess spatial skills and it will be described in the next section.

3   ETAN: The Assessment of Visuospatial Abilities by Means of a Technology Enhanced Platform

In this work we present ETAN, a platform that supports the use of tangible user interfaces ([11,23], physical manipulable object technologically enhanced) to assess and train spatial abilities; the use of *tangibles* in assessment field is not unusual as showed by several research, both for diagnostic and training purposes [14] This prototype is based on a precedent version of a tool designed for the evaluation of visuospatial cognition [6,8].

More specifically, we developed this prototype to investigate visuospatial behaviors of people in their proximal/peripersonal space, that is commonly defined as the space immediately surrounding our bodies [31]. In peripersonal space it is possible to interact immediately and physically with some stimuli present in the external world inasmuch they are inside the limited portion of space around us, reachable by our arms/hands. In this perspective, personal space is what it is covers the entire body surface of a person, peripersonal space refers to the space defining our field of action, and, lastly, the extra-personal space is instead the furthest one and not reachable by the arts (Fig. 2).

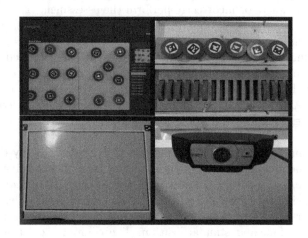

Fig. 2. Materials of the prototype ETAN

The materials of ETAN consist in small disks that are detectable by a camera connected to a PC. It is possible to recreate on the PC the disposition of these objects thanks to a particular kind of tags, popular in augmented reality technology [7] named ArUco Markers [16], that can be traced by a specific software developed with an artificial vision module. Moreover, for each session it is possible to store data about it, both in local that in an online database. The first use of ETAN consisted in the implementation of a well known neuropsychological test: the Baking Tray Task.

3.1   The Baking Tray Task (BTT)

The Baking Tray Task (BTT) represents an ecological test, ideated by Tham e Tegner [32], aimed to assess a specific visuospatial disorder named Unilateral Spatial Neglect (USN), consisting in the inability to analyze and be aware of stimuli and events occurring in half hemispace (usually the left), compromising actions towards that side of the space [33].

During the administration of BTT, subjects are asked to dispose 16 cubes as evenly over a board, *as if they were buns on a baking tray to put in the oven*. The 16 cubes have a dimension of 3.5 cm and they are placed in front of the subject; over the years, the BTT, while maintaining the initial settings and the way of administration, has been re-proposed in different forms, other materials to be disposed (like small disks) and in both digital and virtual environment [9,13,15].

For the administration of BTT there is no time limit and all the cubes have to be disposed. As regards the scoring of the test, the performance is evaluated clinically counting the cubes in each half of the tray, left and right; left - (minus) right differences greater than 2 are a sign of USN.

The baking tray task proved to be a sensitive test, suitable for screening purposes and longitudinal studies, and as opposed to standard USN tests BTT appears to pick up all cases of at least moderately severe neglect, while standard tests missed a few patients [20]. Moreover, BTT seems requiring low-effort attentional resources in contrast to other neglect task like Cancellation Task [29] and it results to be insensitive to practice and set effects.

3.2 Implementing BTT with ETAN

We decided to implement BTT with ETAN for two main reasons: the first is related to the possibility of obtaining a new kind of data, more informative, based on the spatial coordinates (x, y) of the objects arranged on the surface; the second consists in the fact that with our tool it is possible to carry out a massive data collection and store the performances of the subjects both in the local database and the online one. Moreover, with our platform, it is also possible to track the position of every object. The administration of the task strictly followed the directions proposed by Tham e Tegner, and the only differences with the original task refer to the adoption of disks instead of cubes and the use of a board with smaller dimension (adjustments already proposed by other scientists [4,13]). Upon completion of the task, the platform allows to access individuals' performance on the local database. The data can be easily exported in a CSV file for further analyses.

In this manner it is possible to score the performance not only counting how many objects have been placed in each half of the board but, using the X and Y coordinates, it is possible to develop new statistics to make a more informative diagnostic procedure. One example it will be described in the next paragraph.

3.3 A Machine Learning Approach in Analyzing BTT Data

In the Fig. 3, we can see the spatial arrangements of two participants (c and d) at the traditional baking tray task. Although it is not possible to evaluate these patterns as a sign of neglect, surely they show some sort of cognitive impairment. The problem with the scoring of the traditional BTT is that in this specific case, the two arrangements are not diagnosable as a form of disorder inasmuch the difference of the number of cubes between the left and right side of the board is no greater than 2. At first instance, it would help a measure to discriminate normal arrangements (the ones similar the figure a), from abnormal ones (such as the 3 figures) regardless of whether or not they are signs of USN.

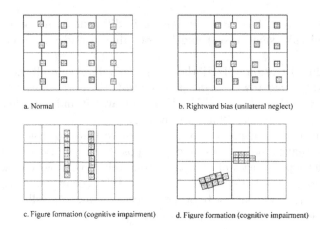

a. Normal   b. Rightward bias (unilateral neglect)

c. Figure formation (cognitive impairment)   d. Figure formation (cognitive impairment)

Fig. 3. Example of BTT dispositions (from Appelros and colleagues [2])

Thanks to the X and Y coordinates collected through our prototype it is possible to differentiate the different patterns by using a machine learning technique based on novelty detection approach [22]. Novelty Detection techniques consist of discriminating instances according to whether or not they belong to a given class. This class can be thought of as a concept to be learned. Usually, concept learning involves learning correct classification of a training set containing both positive and negative instances of a concept, followed by a testing phase in which novel examples are classified. In our case, the concept that represents the class that has to be learned is represented by the correct dispositions at the BTT (like the participants a in the Fig. 3).

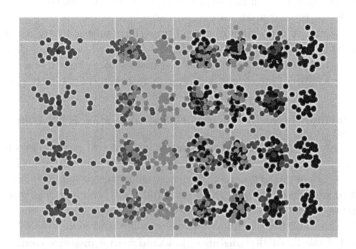

Fig. 4. Simulated BTT dispositions: Normal (medium gray dots), USN (black dots), Other disposition (light gray dots)

In order to test the goodness of the chosen method, we simulated, in terms of X and Y coordinates, three types of dispositions: normal, USN, and dispositions that, while maintaining 8 objects for each side of the board, cannot be assimilated to a proper correct disposition (Fig. 4).

Then, using Sci-kit learn [28], we tested our simulated data with a method from Support vector machines (SVMs) named One-class SVM, that is an unsupervised algorithm that learns a decision function for novelty detection, and is thus able to classify new data as similar or different to a training set. In our case, the application of the ONE-class SVM method proved to be effective in discriminating normal dispositions from the abnormal ones. This means that thanks to our prototype, having more informative data (such as the coordinates) about the BTT, it is also possible to have a more in-depth analysis of the performances, in order to support the diagnostic investigation.

4   Future Directions and Conclusions

The aims of this paper has been to present a new kind of tool designed to assess and evaluate visuospatial abilities. Our prototype ETAN represents an alternative to the traditional tools for assessing peripersonal spatial behaviors, being able to count on the use of tangible interfaces and on the acquisition of previously undetectable data (such as the coordinates of the objects); please notice that BTT is just one possible application of ETAN. The platform, in fact, can be used to implement other forms of visuospatial assessment.

Moreover, ETAN, thanks to its tangible interface, makes the assessment less boring and tiresome for the participants. Additionally, alongside the diagnostic purposes of the use of ETAN, it is also possible to implement a rehabilitative module able to adapt task requests on the users specific requirements, keeping trace of their singular level of abilities; starting from this point, it would be possible integrate a training and rehabilitation program for patients with visuospatial impairments, enriching the potentialities of the assessment tool.

Regarding the technical aspect of the prototype linked to the storage of data, the fact of having available a local and an online database allows us to perform a massive data collection, with which to proceed to an in depth analysis of the data on the spatial skills of the healthy and clinical populations. The adoption of the One-class SVM algorithm described in the previous section represents just one type of possible data analysis to perform; we think that the use of Machine Learning techniques is well suitable for the data that we acquire through our tool, in order to individuate and classify specific alterations of visuospatial abilities.

Once collected data through ETAN, it will be possible develop also a learning analytics module able to track individuals' performances through time and compare them with the rest of the population.

References

1. Angelini, R., Grossi, D.: La terapia razionale dei disturbi costruttivi. TeRaDic (1993)
2. Appelros, P., Karlsson, G., Thorwalls, A., Tham, K., Nydevik, I.: Unilateral neglect: further validation of the baking tray task. J. Rehabil. Med. **36**, 258–261 (2004)
3. American Psychological Association: Committee on professional standards, American psychological Association, Board of Scientific Affairs, and committee on Psychological Tests and Assessment. Guidelines for computer-based tests and interpretations (1986)
4. Bailey, M.J., Riddoch, M.J., Crome, P.: Test-retest stability of three tests for unilateral visual neglect in patients with stroke: Star Cancellation, Line bisection, and the Baking Tray Task. Neuropsychol. Rehabil. **14**, 403–419 (2004)
5. Benton, A.L., Varney, N.R., deS Hamsher, K.: Visuospatial judgment: a clinical test. Arch. Neurol. **35**, 364–367 (1978)
6. Cerrato, A., Ponticorvo, M.: Enhancing neuropsychological testing with gamification and tangible interfaces: the baking tray task. In: Ferrández Vicente, J.M., Álvarez-Sánchez, J.R., de la Paz López, F., Toledo Moreo, J., Adeli, H. (eds.) IWINAC 2017. LNCS, vol. 10338, pp. 147–156. Springer, Cham (2017). https://doi.org/10.1007/978-3-319-59773-7_16
7. Cerrato, A., Siano, G., De Marco, A.: Augmented reality: from education and training applications to assessment procedures. Qwerty-Open Interdisc. J. Technol. Culture Educ. **13**, 11–27 (2018)
8. Cerrato, A., Ponticorvo, M., Bartolomeo, P., Miglino, O.: BTT-scan: An ecological and technology enhanced tool to assess visual neglect. Cogn. Process. **19**, S36–S36 (2018)
9. Chung, S.J., et al.: The computerized table setting test for detecting unilateral neglect. PloS one **11**(1), e0147030 (2016)
10. Colom, R., Contreras, M., Shih, P.C., Santacreu, J., et al.: The assessment of spatial ability with a single computerized test. Eur. J. Psychol. Assess. **19**(2), 92 (2003)
11. Di Fuccio, R., Ponticorvo, M., Ferrara, F., Miglino, O.: Digital and multisensory storytelling: narration with smell, taste and touch. In: Verbert, K., Sharples, M., Klobučar, T. (eds.) EC-TEL 2016. LNCS, vol. 9891, pp. 509–512. Springer, Cham (2016). https://doi.org/10.1007/978-3-319-45153-4_51
12. Diller, L., et al.: Studies in cognition and rehabilitation in hemiplegia (1974)
13. Facchin, A., Beschin, N., Pisano, A., Reverberi, C.: Normative data for distal line bisection and baking tray task. Neurol. Sci. **37**, 1531–1536 (2016)
14. Ferrara, F., Ponticorvo, M., Di Ferdinando, A., Miglino, O.: Tangible interfaces for cognitive assessment and training in children: LogicART. In: Uskov, V.L., Howlett, R.J., Jain, L.C. (eds.) Smart Education and e-Learning 2016. SIST, vol. 59, pp. 329–338. Springer, Cham (2016). https://doi.org/10.1007/978-3-319-39690-3_29
15. Fordell, H., Bodin, K., Bucht, G., Malm, J.: A virtual reality test battery for assessment and screening of spatial neglect. Acta Neurologica Scandinavica **123**, 167–174 (2011)
16. Garrido-Jurado, S., Muñoz-Salinas, R., Madrid-Cuevas, F.J., Marín-Jiménez, M.J.: Automatic generation and detection of highly reliable fiducial markers under occlusion. Pattern Recogn. **47**(6), 2280–2292 (2014)

17. Gigliotta, O., Bartolomeo, P., Miglino, O.: Approaching neuropsychological tasks through adaptive neurorobots. Connect. Sci. **27**, 153–163 (2015)
18. Gigliotta, O., Seidel Malkinson, T., Miglino, O., Bartolomeo, P.: Pseudoneglect in visual search: behavioral evidence and connectional constraints in simulated neural circuitry. eNeuro **4** (2017). https://doi.org/10.1523/ENEURO.0154-17.2017. eprint: http://www.eneuro.org/content/4/6/ENEURO.0154-17
19. Goodale, M.A., Westwood, D.A., Milner, A.D.: Two distinct modes of control for object-directed action. Prog. Brain Res. **144**, 131–144 (2004)
20. Halligan, P.W., Marshall, J.C.: Left visuo-spatial neglect: a meaningless entity? Cortex **28**, 525–535 (1992)
21. James, M., Warrington, E.: Visual object and space perception battery (VOSP) (1991)
22. Japkowicz, N., Myers, C., Gluck, M., et al.: A novelty detection approach to classification. In: IJCAI, vol. 1, pp. 518–523 (1995)
23. Miglino, O., Ponticorvo, M.: Enhancing multi-sensory and handling-based psycho-pedagogical approaches through new technologies (2018)
24. Mishkin, M., Ungerleider, L.G., Macko, K.A.: Object vision and spatial vision: two cortical pathways. Trends Neurosci. **6**, 414–417 (1983)
25. Osterieth, P.A.: Filetest de copie dune figure complex, contribution B letudede la perception et de la m&moire. Archives de Psychologie **30**, 205–353 (1945)
26. Pacella, D., Ponticorvo, M., Gigliotta, O., Miglino, O.: Basic emotions and adaptation. A computational and evolutionary model. PLOS ONE **12**, 1–20 (2017)
27. Parsons, T.D.: Advanced Computational Intelligence Paradigms in Health-Care 6. Virtual Reality in Psychotherapy, Rehabilitation, and Assessment. Studies in Computational Intelligence, vol. 337, pp. 271–289. Springer, Heidelberg (2011). https://doi.org/10.1007/978-3-642-17824-5
28. Pedregosa, F., et al.: Scikit-learn: machine learning in Python. J. Mach. Learn. Res. **12**, 2825–2830 (2011)
29. Rapcsak, S.Z., Verfaellie, M., Fleet, S., Heilman, K.M.: Selective attention in hemispatial neglect. Arch. Neurol. **46**, 178–182 (1989)
30. Rey, A.: L'examen psychologique dans les cas d'encéphalopathie traumatique. (Les problems.). Archives de psychologie (1941)
31. Rizzolatti, G., Fadiga, L., Fogassi, L., Gallese, V.: The space around us. Science **277**, 190–191 (1997)
32. Tham, K.: The baking tray task: a test of spatial neglect. Neuropsychol. Rehabil. **6**, 19–26 (1996)
33. Urbanski, M., et al.: Négligence spatiale unilatérale: une conséquence dramatique mais souvent négligée des lésions de lhémisphère droit. Revue Neurologique **163**, 305–322 (2007)
34. Wilson, B., Cockburn, J., Halligan, P.: Development of a behavioral test of visuospatial neglect. Arch. Phys. Med. Rehabil. **68**, 98–102 (1987)

Midpoint: A Tool to Build Artificial Models of Numerical Cognition

Onofrio Gigliotta[1]([⊠]), Michela Ponticorvo[1], Fabrizio Doricchi[3],
and Orazio Miglino[1,2]

[1] Department of Humanistic Studies, University of Naples "Federico II", Naples, Italy
onofrio.gigliotta@unina.it
[2] Institute of Cognitive Sciences and Technologies, National Research Council,
Rome, Italy
[3] University of Rome "Sapienza", Rome, Italy

Abstract. The present paper describes a tool developed to model and simulate tasks related to numerical cognition, a very important element of both animal and human cognition. In particular, we describe how this software has been used to study a bias that has been consistently observed in humans, both adults and children, about the calculation of the middle point between two numbers and related with the position of numbers in intervals, called NIPE (number interval position effect). Along with the description of the software and the experimental results about the NIPE effect, some results are reported which show the potential of this approach.

Keywords: Simulative models · Numerical cognition · NIPE effect · Developmental studies · Numerical and Spatial cognition

1 Introduction

Numbers are everywhere around us and dealing with them covers an important part of our cognitive activity throughout our life. Number, together with objects, actions, and space represent what has been called the core knowledge [1]. A number of studies have suggested that when left/right response codes must be associated to number magnitudes, healthy participants belonging to western cultures with left-to-right reading habits map numbers upon a mental number line (MNL) with small integers positioned to the left of larger ones. This is reflected in the SNARC effect, (Spatial-Numerical Association of Response Codes) first demonstrated by Dehaene, Bossini, and Giraux [5] who argued that a representation of number magnitude is automatically accessed during parity judgments of Arabic digits.

This representation may be likened to a mental number line, because it bears a natural and seemingly irrepressible correspondence with the left/right coordinates of external space. More recently an inherent spatial and spatial-response-code independent nature of the MNL was suggested by the finding that during the mental

J. M. Ferrández Vicente et al. (Eds.): IWINAC 2019, LNCS 11486, pp. 88–96, 2019.
https://doi.org/10.1007/978-3-030-19591-5_10

bisection of number intervals right brain damaged patients with attentional neglect for the left side of space shift the subjective midpoint of number intervals toward numbers higher than the true midpoint, i.e. supposedly to the right of the true midpoint [2]. However, several ensuing studies have demonstrated that this numerical bias is unrelated to left spatial neglect and that it is rather linked to a deficit in the abstract representation of small numerical magnitudes [7]. This conclusion was suggested by the finding that in right brain damaged patient the pathological bias toward numbers higher than the midpoint in the mental bisection of number interval is correlated to a similar bias in the bisection of time intervals on an imagined clock face where higher number are positioned to the left, rather than to the right, of the mental display. In a quite recent study, Doricchi and colleagues [26] have discovered a new interesting psychophysical property of the number interval bisection task. It was found that in this task, human participants show a systematic error bias which is linked to the position occupied by the number interval in a decade (Number Interval Position Effect, NIPE). The subjective midpoint of number intervals of the same length is placed on numbers higher than the true midpoint the closer the interval is to the beginning of a decade and on numbers lower than the midpoint the closer the interval is to the end of the same decade. For example, in case of 7 units intervals the bias is positive for the intervals at the beginning of the decade (1–7) and negative for the intervals at the end of the decade (3–9). This effect has been observed in healthy adults [7], right brain damaged patients [1, 5] and in pre-school children [22] thus suggesting that it is not related to learning of formal arithmetic and that it could be linked to some fundamental properties of the neural representation of number magnitudes.

The NIPE effect, which has been observed in children and adults consistently, can be explained as a direct effect of numerosity neural coding. Neurophysiological studies have demonstrated a neuronal representations of numerosity in the prefrontal and parietal cortex of rhesus monkeys [17]. In these areas different neuronal populations code for different numerosities. For small numerosities, the neural discharge is narrowly tuned, according to a Gaussian function, to the neuron preferred numerosity so that the discharge is weak for adjacent numerosities. This Gaussian tuning becomes progressively larger, i.e. less selective, for increasing numerosities, so that neurons tuned to larger numerosities show some discharge also for numerosities that are immediately adjacent to the preferred one. The organization of the Gaussian curves linked to the different and progressively increasing numerosities is best described by a nonlinearly logarithmic compressed scaling of numerical information. This result is found in many organisms both with concrete numerosities (such as dots) or Arabic digits, number symbols and suggest that the Fechner law is also valid for numbers [27]. In humans, numerosity coding with neurons tuning has been observed in the intraparietal sulcus, compatible with results on macaque monkeys, thus suggesting a common evolutionary basis for numerical cognition [29].

2   The Number Interval Position Effect in Children and Adults

When healthy adults provide estimates of a number interval midpoint, error biases vary as a function of the interval length and, length being equal, as a function of the position occupied by the interval within tens (i.e. Number Interval Position Effect) [9]. When 7-unit and 5-unit intervals are positioned at the beginning of tens, subjective midpoints are shifted toward values higher than true midpoints. When the same intervals are positioned at the end of tens, subjective midpoints are shifted toward values lower than true midpoints. With 3-unit intervals a progressively increasing negative bias is found the more intervals are placed at the end of tens. This bias has been observed consistently in healthy adults, right-brain damaged patients and children.

To understand the functional origins of this phenomenon an artificial model was conceived.

2.1   The Task

As illustrated in the previous section, one method of study of numerical cognition is to propose simple arithmetic questions to human participants, demanding an immediate response. In this way, participants cannot rely on their formal education and related tips and procedures.

One such task foresees that participants have to identify the natural number that divides equally a numerical series that is delimited by two natural numbers: a bisection task.

For example, if we consider the series of the first natural ten (1–10), the participant can be asked to identify the middle number between 3 (lower bound) and 7 (upper bound) or between 4 (lower bound) and 6 (upper bound) and so on. As the first natural ten includes even and odd numbers, this task takes different forms: the limits may have an even or odd sum. The odd sum permits two solutions.

For example, the middle number between 1 and 8 can be 4 or 5. To reply indicating a natural number, the participant must choose the number that is closer to the lower bound, rounding down, or the upper, rounding up. For this reason, it is preferred to propose the task form with even sum.

This task has been used in neuropsychological literature, applying the traditional bisection task, used for investigating spatial neglect [21] to the study of numerical representation. It has been administered to healthy adults right-brain damaged patients [9] and children [22].

2.2   The Model

The model relies on two well studied neuronal principles:

a. Representations of natural numbers: basic numbers in a certain notation are encoded in an amodal way by distinct neural groups. In other words there is a neural group whose activation is more probable when a specific number is presented regardless of the presentation form.

b. Neural accumulation mechanisms: neural elaboration relies on energy transfer between neural groups and arrives to its conclusion when some neural group accumulates a certain energy level.

In this model we adopt an approach which considers nodes as clusters of neurons; it is a functional representation of brain areas, rather than a single-cell simulation. As hinted above, in order to understand which are the functional bases of the NIPE, a simple model consisting of two modules was developed.

The first module implements the encoding process of natural numbers, it defines how numbers are internally represented. The second one computes the midpoint for each interval. To focus the investigation on number representation, the second module is a perfect calculator whose output correctly bisects the interval received as input.

Number representations have been modeled through networks provided with a probabilistic winner-take-all dynamic. Typically, a probabilistic network is a system of interconnected nodes in which information injected into an input node to nearby connected nodes according to a certain probability. Figure 1 presents a perfect encoding of the number 3, in this case when provided to the input layer, the inner representation will be always correct because the probability that internal node 3 is active when input node 3 is active as well is set to 1. Information is given in input nodes and is transferred, in winner-take-all fashion, to one of inner nodes. This information transfer happens according to a discrete probability density function that, in the network, is translated into the connection weights between nodes.

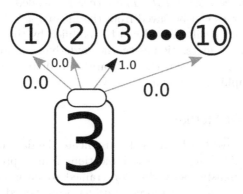

Fig. 1. Perfect representation of number 3. The probability that inner node 3 is active when input node is active as well is set to 1.0.

In case of a perfect representation, as described above, the bisection error would be 0 because the midpoint calculation would be carried out without any error introduced by the encoding process.

In order to model number interval bisection for different limits of intervals, the activation was spread through the dedicated probabilistic network for one step, then active nodes were used to compute the midpoint and the related error.

3   The Simulation Software: Midpoint

Midpoint is a desktop application, developed in C#, implementing the model described in the previous section.

Midpoint can be used to run simulation of numerical bisection task by means of probabilistic networks. Its user-friendly interface allows users to easily run simulation experiments. The interface, reported in Fig. 2 displays every number as a node and it is possible to set the connection weights (expressed as probabilities) to the nearby nodes.

These connection weights in the probabilistic network correspond to the probability that an activation is transmitted from one node to another node. A set of 10 sliders allows users to easily set connections for each node representing numbers from 1 to 10. To each slider, the probability, multiplied by 100, is pictured.

Resulting curves are displayed beneath the sliders panel. Each time a slider is modified, Midpoint runs a new experiment by administering to the probabilistic network model 3-, 5- and 7-unit intervals for 200 times. Collected bisection errors are then displayed through three graphs in the main window of the application.

To run new experiments users have to select the menu *Experiment* where *Run and save* option allows to save the average performance of 200 artificial subjects for each interval described above. Data are saved in a data file that can be easily imported in software for data analyses such as R.

The sliders indicate the probability that the number that is selected with the radio button under *select input number code* is encoded as another number. Every pattern of curves can be saved from the menu *File* in a file .data. Some initial sets are already available and can be modified by the users to easily see how the error changes in relation with the underlying probabilistic network. Every time a slider is modified, the software immediately runs the requested simulations and graphics are updated.

3.1   Materials and Methods

The Midpoint simulator has been used to replicate the data observed in adults and children [9,22,25], confirming the indications from a previous model [18]. Three sets of probabilistic networks, constrained to be unimodal, expressing three different form of number representations, were tested against real data collected on 91 adults by Doricchi and colleagues [26]. The three networks were:

a. Random networks. In which number representations are randomly chosen.
b. Gaussian networks. In which each number is represented by a gaussian probability distribution with $\sigma = .5$.
c. Bio-inspired networks: unimodal and positively skewed gaussian distributions (see [25]).

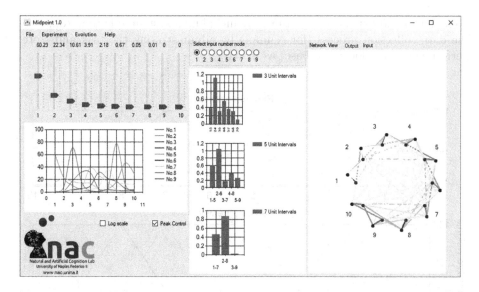

Fig. 2. Midpoint user interface with the slider to modify connection weights and the representation of numbers connection in network form

3.2   Results and Discussion

For each set of number coding networks we simulated 200 performances on the interval bisection task including seven 3-unit intervals, five 5-unit intervals and three 7-unit intervals. Average errors were collected and analyzed against adult individuals' data, by using the statistic software R, for random networks (an unimodal random representation of numerosities), gaussian networks and bio-inspired networks (see Fig. 3).

Among the tested coding models, only the bio-inspired one resulted very close to human subjects' data. Thus the difference between data and model, evaluated by means of the multivariate test on a mean vector (Hotelling's test, [28]), was highly not significant ($p = 0.7408361$). By contrast, differences with the other number representations were highly significative (random networks, $p = 1.777496e{-}100$ and gaussian networks with $\sigma = .5$), $p = 9.33615e{-}28$).

These results indicate that the NIPE effect is likely linked to number representation rather than calculation. In other words, the functional origins of the NIPE effect, investigated in adults and through a biologically plausible computational model of the neural coding of numbers, can be traced back to the logarithmic representation of number magnitudes that has been found in prefrontal and parietal neuronal populations in macaque-monkeys.

Although effective in modeling the representation on numbers, Midpoint in future works should be complemented with an embodied approach able to shed light on the ecological roots behind the formation of a specific representation of numbers. Such kind of work can be carried out by putting together robotics, genetic algorithms and neural networks [10, 30–33]. Finally, another future direction should expand the platform by including a system able to automatize the data collection process (for example by administrating the task and store performances in a local database) as in [34].

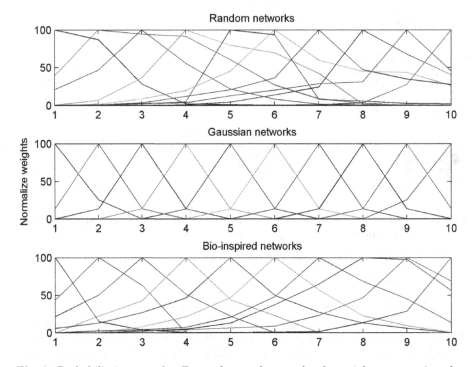

Fig. 3. Probabilistic networks. For each set of networks the weights, expressing the probability of a number to be represented by another, have been normalized in the range [0, 100]

4   Additional Materials

More details about the model and the related code can be provided upon request by emailing Onofrio Gigliotta (onofrio.gigliotta@unina.it).

References

1. Spelke, E.S., Kinzler, K.D.: Core knowledge. Dev. Sci. **10**(1), 89–96 (2007)
2. Zorzi, M., Priftis, K., Umiltà, C.: Neglect disrupts the mental number line. Nature **417**, 138 (2002)
3. Chittka, L., Geiger, K.: Can honey bees count landmarks? Anim. Behav. **49**(1), 159–164 (1995)
4. Dehaene, S.: Varieties of numerical abilities. Cognition **44**(1), 1–42 (1992)

5. Dehaene, S., Bossini, S., Giraux, P.: The mental representation of parity and number magnitude. J. Exp. Psychol.: Gener. **122**(3), 371–396 (1993)
6. Dehaene, S., Molko, N., Cohen, L., Wilson, A.J.: Arithmetic and the brain. Curr. Opin. Neurobiol. **14**(2), 218–224 (2004)
7. Aiello, M., Merola, S., Doricchi, F.: Small numbers in the right brain: evidence from patients without and with spatial neglect. Cortex **49**(1), 348–351 (2013)
8. Di Ferdinando, A., Parisi, D., Bartolomeo, P.: Modeling orienting behavior and its disorders with "ecological" neural networks. J. Cogn. Neurosci. **19**(6), 1033–1049 (2007)
9. Doricchi, F., et al.: Spatial orienting biases in the decimal numeral system. Curr. Biol. **19**(8), 682–687 (2009)
10. Gigliotta, O., Bartolomeo, P., Miglino, O.: Approaching neuropsychological tasks through adaptive neurorobots. Connection Sci. **27**(2), 153–163 (2015)
11. Gilmore, C., Attridge, N., Inglis, M.: Measuring the approximate number system. Q. J. Exp. Psychol. **64**(11), 2099–2109 (2011)
12. Halberda, J., Feigenson, L.: Developmental change in the acuity of the "Number Sense": the approximate number system in 3-, 4-, 5-, and 6-year-olds and adults. Dev. Psychol. **44**(5), 1457 (2008)
13. Matsuzawa, T.: Use of numbers by a chimpanzee. Nature **315**(6014), 57–59 (1985)
14. Miglino, O., Ponticorvo, M.: Place cognition as an example of situated cognition: a study with evolved agents. Cogn. Process. **10**(2), 250–252 (2009)
15. Miglino, O., Ponticorvo, M.: Exploring the roots of (spatial) cognition in artificial and natural organisms. Evol. Robot. Approach Horiz. Evol. Robot. 93–123 (2014)
16. Miglino, O., Ponticorvo, M., Bartolomeo, P.: Place cognition and active perception: a study with evolved robots. Connection Sci. **21**(1), 3–14 (2009)
17. Nieder, A., Miller, E.K.: Coding of cognitive magnitude: compressed scaling of numerical information in the primate prefrontal cortex. Neuron **37**(1), 149–157 (2003)
18. Ponticorvo, M., Rotondaro, F., Doricchi, F., Miglino, O.: A neural model of number interval position effect (NIPE) in children. In: Ferrández Vicente, J.M., Álvarez-Sánchez, J.R., de la Paz López, F., Toledo-Moreo, F.J., Adeli, H. (eds.) IWINAC 2015. LNCS, vol. 9107, pp. 9–18. Springer, Cham (2015). https://doi.org/10.1007/978-3-319-18914-7_2
19. Ponticorvo, M., Miglino, O.: Encoding geometric and non-geometric information: a study with evolved agents. Anim. Cogn. **13**(1), 157 (2010)
20. Ponticorvo, M., Walker, R., Miglino, O.: Evolutionary robotics as a tool to investigate spatial cognition in artificial and natural systems. In: Artificial Cognition Systems, pp. 210–237 (2007)
21. Reuter-Lorenz, P.A., Posner, M.I.: Components of neglect from right-hemisphere damage: an analysis of line bisection. Neuropsychologia **28**(4), 327–333 (1990)
22. Rotondaro, F., Gazzellini, S., Peris, M., Doricchi, F.: The mental number line in children: number interval bisection and number to position performance. Poster presented at the European Workshop Cognitive Neuroscience 2012, Bressanone, Italy (2012)
23. Stoianov, I., Zorzi, M.: Emergence of a 'visual number sense' in hierarchical generative models. Nat. Neurosci. **15**(2), 194–196 (2012)
24. Urbanski, M., et al.: Negligence spatiale unilaterale: une consequence dramatique mais souvent negligee des lesions de l'hemisphere droit. Revue Neurologique **163**(3), 305–322 (2007)

25. Rotondaro, F., et al.: The number interval position effect (NIPE) in the mental bisection of numerical intervals might reflect the influence of the decimal-number system on the Gaussian representations of numerosities: a combined developmental and computational-modeling study. Cortex (2018)
26. Doricchi, F., et al.: Spatial orienting biases in the decimal numeral system. Curr. Biol. **19**(8), 682–7 (2009)
27. Geary, D., Berch, D.B., Mann, K. (eds.): Evolutionary Origins and Early Development of Number Processing. Academic Press, Cambridge (2015)
28. Rencher, A.C.: Methods of Multivariate Analysis. Wiley, Hoboken (2002)
29. Piazza, M., Izard, V., Pinel, P., Bihan, D.L., Dehaene, S.: Tuning curves for approximate numerosity in the human intraparietal sulcus. Neuron **44**(3), 547–555 (2004)
30. Broz, F., et al.: The ITALK project: a developmental robotics approach to the study of individual, social, and linguistic learning. Top. Cogn. Sci. **6**(3), 534–544 (2014)
31. Gigliotta, O., Malkinson, T.S., Miglino, O., Bartolomeo, P.: Pseudoneglect in visual search: behavioral evidence and connectional constraints in simulated neural circuitry. eNeuro **4**(6) (2017)
32. Pacella, D., Ponticorvo, M., Gigliotta, O., Miglino, O.: Basic emotions and adaptation. A computational and evolutionary model. PLOS ONE **12**(11), 1–20 (2017)
33. Pagliuca, P., Milano, N., Nolfi, S.: Maximizing adaptive power in neuroevolution. PLOS ONE **13**(7), e0198788 (2018)
34. Cerrato, A., Ponticorvo, M.: Enhancing neuropsychological testing with gamification and tangible interfaces: the baking tray task. In: Ferrández Vicente, J.M., Álvarez-Sánchez, J.R., de la Paz López, F., Toledo Moreo, J., Adeli, H. (eds.) IWINAC 2017. LNCS, vol. 10338, pp. 147–156. Springer, Cham (2017). https://doi.org/10.1007/978-3-319-59773-7_16

Cognitive AI Systems Contribute to Improving Creativity Modeling and Measuring Tools

Faheem Hassan Zunjani$^{(\boxtimes)}$ ⓘ and Ana-Maria Olteţeanu ⓘ

Freie Universität, Berlin, Germany
{zunjani.faheem,ana-maria.olteteanu}@fu-berlin.de

Abstract. Cognitive science and cognitive psychology have long used creativity tests to measure and investigate the relationships between creativity, creative problem solving and other cognitive abilities. Implementing cognitive systems that can model and/or solve creativity tests can shed light on the cognitive process, and presents the possibility of building much more precise creativity measuring tools. This paper describes four cognitive AI systems related to the Remote Associates Test (RAT) and their contributions to creativity science. comRAT-C is a system that solves the RAT, correlating with human performance. comRAT-G reverse engineers this process to generate RAT queries with a high degree of parameter control. fRAT generates functional RAT queries, resurrecting a theoretical concept proposed by researchers many decades ago. The visual RAT takes advantage of the formal conceptualization necessary for computational implementation, to expand the RAT to the visual domain. All the cognitive systems and generated RAT queries have been successfully validated with human participants and have contributed in improving creativity modeling and measuring tools.

Keywords: Remote Associates Test · Human creativity ·
Visual associates · Computational creativity · Cognitive systems

1 Introduction

Creativity and creative problem solving, though not uniquely human traits, have contributed to technological, scientific and cultural advances that lay at the foundation of human civilization. They are still cognitive tools which make humans adaptable and able to progress in conditions in which not all knowledge or resources are available.

Various streams of research have been connecting creativity research and the computational sciences. One of these is computational creativity - which

Supported by the German Research Foundation (Deutsche Forschungsgemeinschaft) through the Creative Cognitive Systems project OL 518/1-1 (CreaCogs).

© Springer Nature Switzerland AG 2019
J. M. Ferrández Vicente et al. (Eds.): IWINAC 2019, LNCS 11486, pp. 97–107, 2019.
https://doi.org/10.1007/978-3-030-19591-5_11

focuses on the development of computational creativity systems capable of various creativity feats - like poetry and painting [3] and on coming up with ways of evaluating computational creativity systems.

However, this research does not bring us closer to understanding human (cognitive) creativity. Cognitive creativity is generally explored in cognitive science and cognitive psychology. Computational implementations of hypotheses from the cognitive science community are very valuable, because they offer the chance to test cognitive theories via computational systems [7]. Some such systems have been implemented in the literature to study metaphor, insight, object replacement, etc. Furthermore, cognitive AI systems able to perform or model creativity tasks studied in the cognitive science domain may be used to later (i) build cognitive AI systems that act as a more natural interface for humans and (ii) improve creativity in human participants, by intuiting and supporting the weaknesses of their human counterparts.

This paper focuses on describing a research arc consisting of four cognitive AI systems, focused on one initial type of task - creative association. Besides providing a shortened eagle-eye overview of these systems, this paper's goal is to showcase how this type of research on cognitive AI systems contributes towards improving the tools used for modeling and measuring creativity.

The rest of the paper has been organized as follows. The first section describes the Remote Associates Test as a measure for the associativity factor in creativity, and briefly summarizes the principles of the CreaCogs framework. Section 2 describes the initial formalization of the RAT for adaptation to the CreaCogs framework, its implementation as the comRAT-C cognitive system and relation to human performance.

2   The Remote Associates Test and CreaCogs

Building AI systems which solve tasks that have an empirical creativity measure attached has not been explored systematically. With creativity being a multi-faceted cognitive skill, many empirical creativity measures exist.

Among many other tests, one of the most popular and widely used tests to measure creativity in humans is the Remote Associates Test (RAT) proposed by Mednick and Mednick in 1971 [5]. Inspired from Mednick's belief that the creative process has an associative bias [4], the RAT was designed to measure the creativity of a participant based on their ability to draw remote associations. The RAT comprises a number of test queries where each query consists of 3 words and the participant is supposed to answer the word that is connected to all 3 of the query words. For example, for the "SWISS-COTTAGE-CAKE" query the answer would be "CHEESE" as "CHEESE" appears with each of the three query words forming a compound word in the English language.

CreaCogs [8, 17] is a theoretical framework aiming to implement a set of creativity related abilities with a minimal set of processes and the same type of knowledge organization and cognitive architecture. This is in accord with main principles of cognitive architectures [7], in which one architecture should be flexible enough to solve a multiplicity of tasks within a certain domain. CreaCogs proposed processes [8] to solve associativity related tasks (treated here), creative use and inferences related to objects [18], and more complex insight problems using objects from the practical domain [9,16], using a multilayered type of knowledge organization. In the following, we focus on the impact of this knowledge organization on constructing cognitive AI systems related to the associative ability.

3   Computational Solver for the Compound RAT - comRAT-C

A computational solver of the RAT named comRAT-C was proposed [10] to test the CreaCogs abilities related to associative process. For this, the Remote Associates Test was formalized as a succession of queries, in which three words w_a, w_a and w_c are shown to the system, and an answer word is expected.

In order to test its knowledge organization hypothesis, comRAT-C sequentially extracted 2-grams from the Corpus of Contemporary American English (COCA: http://corpus.byu.edu/coca/) and used them to organize its knowledge base (RAT-KB) with three primary atomic structures: EXPRESSION, CONCEPT and LINK. Whenever comRAT-C arrives at a 2-gram EXPRESSION (two words representing two CONCEPTS), it checks for the presence of each of the two CONCEPTS in its existing KB. If both CONCEPTS are present, only a LINK between them is added. The LINK contains a numerical tag of the frequency of the 2-gram in the corpus attached to it, and represents a form of encoding the trace of cognitive association strength. If one or both of the words are unknown, they are added as CONCEPTS and a LINK between them is also added. When the comRAT-C is done constructing its RAT-KB, each CONCEPT then contains LINKS to all other CONCEPTS that it has been in an EXPRESSION with. This is then used to solve the Remote Associates Test.

comRAT-C performs a convergence process based on its associations. This process is meant as a hypothesis for a cognitive process humans may use when solving the task, and uses the strength of associations. It is known for example that some human participants, when given a query, reach the answer by what they perceive as insight: the answer seems to just "pop in" to their mind. The comRAT-C convergence process aims to replicate a form of associative search in the memory, in which the answer is revealed through the strength of the associations.

The probability of reaching an answer is calculated by comRAT-C based on association strength. The probability that w_i' is the answer is:

$$P[w_i'] = 1/3 * P[w_i'|w_a] * P[w_i'|w_b] * P[w_i'|w_c] \tag{1}$$

Figure 1 shows a visualization of the convergence process when comRAT-C searches for solutions to a query in RAT-KB. The words surrounded by green circles represent the query words. The blue ones are the words associated with LINKS to the query words. The yellow ones represent a 2-item convergence and the red one represents a 3-item convergence which is chosen as a plausible solution by comRAT-C.

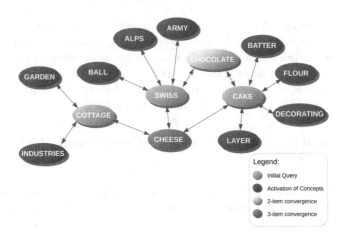

Fig. 1. Visual representation of the comRAT-C activation and convergence. (Color figure online)

The performance of comRAT-C was measured over the Bowden and Jung-Beeman normative dataset [2] of compound RAT queries. Out of 144 queries in the dataset, in 64 of them comRAT-C provided the exact answers to the queries. In more than 20 cases, comRAT-C provided an answer that could be considered as a plausible answer but it was not considered in the Bowden & Jung-Beeman dataset. In 97.92% of the cases in which comRAT-C had all the query words present in its KB, it gave the correct answer. It was interesting to note that in 30.36% of the cases comRAT-C gave the correct answer when it had only 2 query items in its KB demonstrating the robustness of the system.

In terms of its promise as a tool for future modeling, comRAT-C's process probability to solve a RAT query significantly correlated with the Accuracy of human participants, and correlated negatively with their reponse times (the higher the probability, the less time human participants take to solve a query).

4   Computational Generator of Compound RAT Queries - comRAT-G

The RAT was found be the second most used creativity test in a meta analysis study [1]. There are few repositories of normative data for the RAT, like Bowden and Jung-Beeman dataset of 144 RAT queries which was used in the validation of comRAT-C. These repositories still do not provide the ability to vary the query items on the basis of the frequency of occurrence of query words or answer words.

To deal with this bottleneck, after the successful validation of the comRAT-C, it was found that the knowledge organization used by it could not only be used to solve the RAT queries but also to generate them by reversing the convergence process. Hence, comRAT-G was created as a variant of comRAT-C that generates RAT queries using the same knowledge base (KB).

The intuition of the query creation process is the following: each query word in this type of knowledge organization can, in turn, be seen as a potential answer word. For example, in Fig. 1 – SWISS can be seen as an answer word for query ALPS, ARMY, CHOCOLATE.

The comRAT-G first iterated over the KB and provided nouns which were the potential answer words (w_{ans}) along with their linked query words (w_qs). Only the w_{ans}s that had at least three w_qs were selected by comRAT-G. This process yielded around 81500 unique (w_{ans}, w_q) combinations out of 9601 unique w_{ans}s. The probability of w_{ans} as answer for a query word w_q was calculated as:

$$P[w_{ans}|w_q] = \frac{fr(w_q w_{ans})}{\sum_{k=1}^{n}(w_q, w_k)} \tag{2}$$

To make constructing all the combinations computationally feasible, comRAT-G used Alan Tucker's combinatorics formula [20] and capped n at 100. With this, 17 million possible RAT queries were obtained. The probability of answering the generated queries was calculated as the conditional probability of w_{ans} being triggered by each of the query words (w_a, w_b, w_c) was calculated as in comRAT-C.

Table 1 shows a few examples from the generated queries. Frequency and frequency based probability of finding an answer was computed for all the queries.

Table 1. Example queries generated by comRAT-G.

w_a	w_b	w_c	w_{ans}	$P(w_{ans})$
box	panes	shades	window	0.4016
penalty	suit	toll	death	0.5243
paddle	roulette	steering	wheel	0.5582
checking	escrow	deficits	account	0.5626

To validate the generated queries, a study was conducted in which human performance in comRAT-G queries was compared to that in a normative dataset [2]. 113 native English speakers (72 females and 41 males) recruited from the University of Pittsburg and Figure-Eight (F8, https://figure-eight.com) participated in the study. The test consisted of 50 queries randomly selected from the Bowden & Jung-Beeman dataset and 50 queries randomly picked from the queries generated by comRAT-G.

An average significant correlation of $r = 0.54$ ($p < 0.0001$) was observed between the accuracy in comRAT-G queries and Bowden & Jung-Beeman queries. A highly significant large correlation of $r = 0.75$ ($p < 0.0001$) was observed between the response times for the two sets of queries. Cronbach's alpha on accuracy was 0.932 for Bowden & Jung-Beeman queries, 0.851 for comRAT-G queries and 0.936 for both the sets combined. The average and high correlations obtained between the performance of human participants on both the datasets validated the comRAT-G queries. The high Cronbach's alphas show that both the datasets are highly reliable and consistent with each other.

This showed the first implementation in which a cognitive AI system was used for the generation of new queries – displaying applications to improving creativity tests and other psychometric tools related to creativity science. Later on, this system was shown to provide a stronger control over factors and allow new empirical designs [13].

5   Functional RAT and Its Computational Generator - fRAT and comRAT-G_F

Worthen and Clark [21] argued that Mednick's original queries were not uniform, and could be broadly categorized into at least two types: structural and functional. "TOOTH-POTATO-HEART" (answer: "SWEET") is an example of a structural query since "SWEET" occurs together with each of the three query words syntactically in the English language. Whereas, in "DAISY-TULIP-VASE" (answer: "FLOWER"), "FLOWER" shares a language-independent functional relationship with the query words.

As the functional queries examples proposed by Worthen and Clark were lost in transport between two libraries, and this concept was thus never fully explored in the scientific community, [12] set as a goal the resurrection of the concept by computationally constructing a set of functional queries. This set of queries was to then allow comparisons between compound and functional queries for cognitive scientists.

comRAT-G_F [12] is thus a cognitive AI system that aims to computationally generate functional RAT (fRAT) queries. This approach modifies the comRAT-G (Sect. 4) to generate functional queries instead of compound (structural) ones. As Worthen and Clarke considered Palermo-Jenkins word association norms [19] a good source for validating Mednick's initial queries, comRAT-G_F uses a more modern dataset of free association, rhyme and word fragment norms [6] to extract the data for building the knowledge base. This dataset recorded words that were produced by human participants when presented with cue words. For example, when presented with "ABUNDANCE" as a cue word, participants came up with words like "FAMINE", "FOOD", "FULL".

For the creation of functional queries, items were extracted from the dataset and the knowledge base was organized in a structure similar to that of comRAT-G. Words with more than three associates were considered as possible answers and were used as the basis for generating potential functional queries in further stages. The number of subjects producing a target word from the University of South Florida association norms was used as a stand-in for frequency metric. Similarly, the number of participants producing a target word when given a cue over the total participants given that cue was used as a stand-in for probability.

Out of the 13,534,865 fRAT queries generated by comRAT-G_F, Table 2 shows a few examples. To evaluate the created queries, and establish human performance baselines on them, two studies were conducted.

Table 2. Example fRAT queries generated by comRAT-G_F.

w_a	w_b	w_c	w_p	Probability
exhausted	sleepy	weary	tired	0.7202
frame	photo	portrait	picture	0.6897
bassinet	crib	infant	baby	0.6916
daisy	tulip	vase	flower	0.6914
bulb	dark	dim	light	0.5530

In the first study, Figure-Eight users who had previously solved compound queries in a previous study were invited. In the test, 75 fRAT queries with probabilities of obtaining the answer word distributed over the range of 0 to 0.5 were presented to every participant in randomized order. The number of correct answers (accuracy) of every participant was computed and correlated to their performance in the comRAT-G study with compound queries. The accuracy scores on fRAT queries show a large positive significant correlation of $r = 0.55$ ($p < 0.005$) with accuracy on compound queries. For the response times, a medium sized correlation of $r = 0.41$ ($p < 0.05$) was observed.

The second study aimed to further investigate the relationships observed in the first study with a larger sample of 61 participants (44 females and 17 males). Participants were presented with 96 queries consisting of 48 fRAT queries and 48 compound RAT queries (24 comRAT-G queries and 24 Bowden & Jung-Beeman queries) in randomized order. A significant correlation of $r = 0.44$ ($p < 0.001$) was observed between the accuracy in fRAT and compound RAT queries. A highly significant and strong correlation of $r = 0.88$ ($p < 0.001$) was found between the response times for fRAT and compound RAT queries. A measure of reliability, Cronbach's alpha was found to be 0.79 for the accuracy on fRAT queries and 0.87 on compound RAT queries. Cronbach's alpha on response items of the correct answers also showed a high reliability, 0.90 for fRAT queries, compared to 0.96 for compound RAT queries.

The comRAT-G_F cognitive system was thus successful at creating functional queries of high reliability, that correlate in both accuracy and reponse times with compound queries. This offers a new point of measurement and psychometric tool for creativity science.

6   Visual Remote Associates Test - vRAT

The Remote Associates Test is a language based test, and has been widely used in literature to explore linguistic creativity and problem-solving in humans. However, solving complex insight problems may require forms of creativity beyond the linguistic - for example visual and/or spatial creativity. Though empiric evaluation methods for both visual and linguistic creativity exist, these are different: there is no one test through which visual and linguistic performance can be assessed cross-domain.

In order to provide such a tool, a visual adaptation of the RAT was attempted [11]. The formalization of the linguistic RAT supposes that three words are given (w_1, w_2 and w_3), and an answer word (w_{ans}) is to be found. This word is subsequently searched for with the knowledge organization boost from comRAT-C – by using associations, their strength and convergence. In adapting the RAT to the visual domain, the elements of this formalization were considered to more abstractly be sensory elements (e_1, e_2 and e_3), with a related answer element (e_{ans}) to be found.

Specifically for the visual domain, the three elements were considered to be visual elements (e.g. objects), with the answer a visual element as well, For example, such a visual query can be seen in Fig. 2, where visual elements in the three pictures – the chimney, the blacksmith in his workshop and the wood – are meant to elicit a visual association answer (fire).

Fig. 2. An example vRAT query ("chimney-blacksmith-wood"). Answer: "fire".

Two separate studies were conducted to investigate the human response to the created vRAT queries and comparability with linguistic RAT [15].

In Study 1 (n = 38), previous participants to a compound RAT study were presented with 46 vRAT queries in a randomized sequence. Study 2 investigated how people performed when they were administered with vRAT and linguistic RAT one after the other in the same session. Study 2 was administered via two platforms: F8 and Amazon Mechanical Turk (MTurk, http://mturk.com). Participants (n = 170) were presented with 46 vRAT queries (same as Study-1) followed by a set of 24 comRAT-G queries and 24 queries from the Bowden and Jung-Beeman dataset [2].

Table 3 shows the correlations of vRAT scores with linguistic queries from the comRAT-G and Bowden & Jung-Beeman (B-JB) datasets scored for both the studies. In Study-1, a significant correlation of 0.431 was observed between the *vRAT score* and *comRAT-G score*. The significance of this correlation was corroborated by Study-2 where the correlation between *vRAT score* and *comRAT-G score* was significant for each of the platforms independently and both of them combined.

This showed that the initial computational formalization of the RAT for a cognitive AI system can be used to create valid queries in the visual domain, and thus expand the reach of creativity evaluation tools.

Table 3. Correlations between the visual RAT and the linguistic RAT scores

Correlated with *vRAT score*	Study-1	Study-2		
		F8	MTurk	Combined
comRAT-G score	0.431**	0.447*	0.307***	0.331***
B-JB score	0.022	0.395*	0.169*	0.210**
linguistic RAT score	0.202	0.465*	0.266**	0.302***

Correlations significance level indicated as follows: 0.05 - *; 0.01 - **; 0.001 - ***.

7   Discussion and Perspectives

Various cognitive AI systems have been implemented and experimented with – they showed to contribute to improving creativity modeling and measuring tools.

In the creative association domain, comRAT-C was the first system to use the knowledge organization proposed under the CreaCogs framework. comRAT-C was successful in solving the compound RAT queries from the normative Bowden & Jung Beeman dataset and the system's performance significantly correlated with the performance of humans on compound RAT queries. comRAT-G was the first system to computationally generate RAT queries and contributed a large set of generated and validated queries to the existing normative data for RAT. This computational approach to generating new queries has shown to be fruitful by both correlating to human data on a compound normative dataset [14], and also allowing for more refined empirical designs with a better ability to record previously unexplored factors influencing creativity [13].

Before the comRAT-G_F system, functional queries were a theoretical idea [21], the examples of which have been lost to the influence of time and lack of digitalization. No normative data was available for functional RAT queries, thus no researchers could explore this idea further. comRAT-G_F generated a large sized dataset for functional RAT which was successfully evaluated with human participants.

Finally, even formalizing a task in the computational manner required by constructing a subsequent cognitive AI system can have an impact. The visual RAT test is the proof of how this formalization can help grasp a task with more precision, and deploy it in new fields. The visual RAT takes the Remote Associates Test beyond the linguistic domain, creating visual queries which can help gain cross-modal strength when investigating the associative factor in creativity.

In summary, computational cognitive approaches to creativity science can be very fruitful. The formalization and implementation of cognitive AI systems has had and can further have a deep impact on cognitive science tools and models.

As further work on the research arc regarding creativity and association, the authors plan to focus on (i) building a computational solver for the visual RAT, (ii) exploring multiple answer queries in the linguistic RAT, which were suspected to exist but first discovered computationally using comRAT-C and can be addressed in a systemic manner using comRAT-G, and on (iii) taking the RAT to other sensory domains.

References

1. Arden, R., Chavez, R.S., Grazioplene, R., Jung, R.E.: Neuroimaging creativity: a psychometric view. Behav. Brain Res. **214**(2), 143–156 (2010)
2. Bowden, E.M., Jung-Beeman, M.: Normative data for 144 compound remote associate problems. Behav. Res. Methods Instrum. Comput. **35**(4), 634–639 (2003)
3. Colton, S., Wiggins, G.A.: Computational creativity: the final frontier? In: Proceedings of the 20th European Conference on Artificial Intelligence, pp. 21–26. IOS Press (2012)
4. Mednick, S.: The associative basis of the creative process. Psychol. Rev. **69**(3), 220 (1962)
5. Mednick, S.A., Mednick, M.: Remote Associates Test: Examiner's Manual. Houghton Mifflin, Boston (1971)
6. Nelson, D.L., McEvoy, C.L., Schreiber, T.A.: The University of South Florida free association, rhyme, and word fragment norms. Behav. Res. Methods Instrum. Comput. **36**(3), 402–407 (2004)
7. Newell, A.: Unified Theories of Cognition. Harvard University Press, Cambridge (1994)
8. Olteţeanu, A.M.: Two general classes in creative problem-solving? An account based on the cognitive processes involved in the problem structure - representation structure relationship. In: Proceedings of the International Conference on Computational Creativity, January 2014. Institute of Cognitive Science, Osnabrück (2014)
9. Olteţeanu, A.M.: Proceedings of the Workshop on Computational Creativity, Concept Invention, and General Intelligence (C3GI2016), vol. 1767. CEUR-Ws, Osnabrück (2016)
10. Olteţeanu, A.M., Falomir, Z.: comRAT-C - A computational compound remote associates test solver based on language data and its comparison to human performance. Pattern Recogn. Lett. **67**, 81–90 (2015). https://doi.org/10.1016/j.patrec.2015.05.015
11. Olteţeanu, A.M., Gautam, B., Falomir, Z.: Towards a visual remote associates test and its computational solver. In: Proceedings of the Third International Workshop on Artificial Intelligence and Cognition 2015, vol. 1510, pp. 19–28. CEUR-Ws (2015)
12. Olteţeanu, A.M., Schottner, M., Schuberth, S.: Computationally resurrecting the functional remote associates test using cognitive word associates and principles from a computational solver. Knowl. Based Syst. **168**, 1–9 (2019)
13. Olteţeanu, A.M., Schultheis, H.: What determines creative association? Revealing two factors which separately influence the creative process when solving the remote associates test. J. Creat. Behav. (2017). https://doi.org/10.1002/jocb.177
14. Olteţeanu, A.M., Schultheis, H., Dyer, J.B.: Computationally constructing a repository of compound remote associates test items in American English with comRAT-G. Behav. Res. Methods Instrum. Comput. (2017). https://doi.org/10.3758/s13428-017-0965-8
15. Olteţeanu, A.M., Zunjani, F.H.: A visual remote associates test and its validation. Behav. Res. Methods (Submitted)

16. Olteteanu, A.M.: A cognitive systems framework for creative problem solving. Ph.D. thesis, Universität Bremen (2016)

17. Oltețeanu, A.-M.: From simple machines to eureka in four not-so-easy steps: towards creative visuospatial intelligence. In: Müller, V.C. (ed.) Fundamental Issues of Artificial Intelligence. SL, vol. 376, pp. 159–180. Springer, Cham (2016). https://doi.org/10.1007/978-3-319-26485-1_11

18. Oltețeanu, A.M., Falomir, Z.: Object replacement and object composition in a creative cognitive system. Towards a computational solver of the alternative uses test. Cogn. Syst. Res. **39**, 15–32 (2016)

19. Palermo, D.S., Jenkins, J.J.: Word Association Norms: Grade School Through College (1964)

20. Tucker, A.: Applied Combinatorics. Wiley, Hoboken (2006)

21. Worthen, B.R., Clark, P.M.: Toward an improved measure of remote associational ability. J. Educ. Meas. **8**(2), 113–123 (1971)

Neurolight Alpha: Interfacing Computational Neural Models for Stimulus Modulation in Cortical Visual Neuroprostheses

Antonio Lozano[1], Juan Sebastián Suárez[2,3], Cristina Soto-Sánchez[2,3], Javier Garrigós[1]([✉])(iD), Jose-Javier Martínez[1](iD), José Manuel Ferrández Vicente[1], and Eduardo Fernández-Jover[2,3]

[1] Dpto. Electrónica, Tecnología de Computadoras y Proyectos, Universidad Politécnica de Cartagena, Cartagena, Spain
{amlo,javier.garrigos,jjavier.martinez,jm.ferrandez}@upct.es
[2] Instituto de Bioingeniería, Universidad Miguel Hernández, Alicante, Spain
{jsuarez,csoto,e.fernandez}@umh.es
[3] CIBER-BBN, Madrid, Spain
http://gruposinvestigacion.upct.es/grupos_ID/info_grupo.php?id=7,
http://bioingenieria.umh.es/,
https://www.ciber-bbn.es/

Abstract. Visual neuroprostheses that provide electrical stimulation along several sites of the human visual system constitute a potential tool for vision restoring for the blind. In the context of a NIH approved human clinical trials project (CORTIVIS), we now face the challenge of developing not only computationally powerful, but also flexible tools that allow us to generate useful knowledge in an efficient way. In this work, we address the development and implementation of computational models of different types of visual neurons and design a tool -Neurolight alpha- that allows interfacing these models with a visual neural prosthesis in order to create more naturalistic electrical stimulation patterns. We implement the complete pipeline, from obtaining a video stream to developing and deploying predictive models of retinal ganglion cell's encoding of visual inputs into the control of a cortical microstimulation device which will send electrical train pulses through an Utah Array to the neural tissue.

Keywords: Visual neuroprostheses · Neural encoding · Computational models · Artificial vision

1 Introduction

To restore the ability of the human neural system to function properly is one of the main purposes of neural engineering. In the context of this broad and multidisciplinary research field, where disciplines ranging from clinical neurology

© Springer Nature Switzerland AG 2019
J. M. Ferrández Vicente et al. (Eds.): IWINAC 2019, LNCS 11486, pp. 108–119, 2019.
https://doi.org/10.1007/978-3-030-19591-5_12

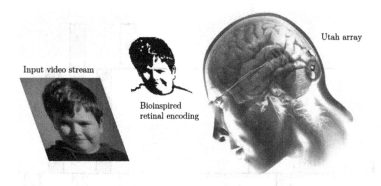

Fig. 1. A general idea of a cortical visual neuroprosthesis is composed of a camera obtaining a video stream, a encoding module and a stimulator which sends electrical pulses throughout an intracortical microelectrode interface.

to computational neuroscience, scientific advancement and engineering development has taken us until today's achievements: EEG-Based BCI [1], motor control BCIs with UTAH arrays [2,3], cochlear implants [5], retinal prosthesis [6], and Deep Brain Stimulation systems [7]. Regarding visual function recovering, several approaches are being extensively explored, such as optogenetics [8], biocompatible material design for neural interfaces [4] and neuromorphic computing for neuroprosthesis [9]. Specifically, several advances have been done in retinal prostheses, where several devices have been already clinically tested or are currently in use [10,11]. These devices are limited to a very specific causes of blindness, where the optic nerve function is intact. Cortical prosthesis appears as a potential solution to those blindness conditions for people with a functional visual cortex, regardless of their retinal or optic nerve condition.Several research groups around the globe are pursuing this goal [13–16,18]. In this context, the main goal of this work is to create and integrate the actual knowledge on neural function, psychophysics, signal processing and neural encoding modeling, and build a working pipeline which leads us towards further experiments and techniques that advance in the development of cortical visual prostheses. A general idea of the complete pipeline of a functional cortical prosthesis is composed of a video camera which receives the visual information, sends its to a signal processing device which sends orders to the neurostimulator that sends electrical pulse trains to the neural tissue accordingly to that commands (see Fig. 1) [13,14]. In the scenario of a NIH approved human clinical trials project named Development of a Cortical Visual Neuroprosthesis for the Blind [17], we now face the challenge of creating not only powerful but also flexible tools that overcome the limitations and needs of the current neurostimulation systems, allowing for new experimental trials.

Inspired by the success of cochlear implants, who greatly benefited from the developing and tuning of signal processing models according to psychophysics [19], we designed an end-to-end image processing and stimulation control

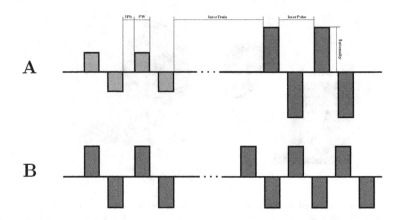

Fig. 2. Two main train modulation strategies are contemplated: Intensity modulation (A) and Frequency modulation (B).

workflow aimed to constitute a useful tool for neuroprosthesis research. In order to allow the designed system to incorporate bioinspired control capabilities of the electrical stimulation parameters (Amplitude of the phases, Pulse Width, Pulse Frequency, Inter Pulse, Inter Phase, Inter-Train, see Fig. 2), we created a neural encoding module which makes use of Deep Learning libraries Keras and Tensorflow [32,33], allowing us to create and make use of custom-defined or data-driven models of neural encoding of light patterns, simulating this way a retina-like visual processing, which output will be used for the stimulation control.

The possibility of reproducing neuronal activity present on the retina during natural vision has been studied with regards of electrical stimulation in epiretinal prosthesis [21], with promising results. In addition, techniques for computing population coding distances on retina have been proposed [22], along with visual perception simulation frameworks [20,23]. These results are encouraging, and the new methodologies could apply and be tested on the visual cortex.

In addition, diverse models of animal and human neural visual encoding systems of different nature have been created until today, targeting different processing stages, some of them focusing on the retina [24–27], which is the primary stage of visual processing.

2   System Overview

In this work, an end-to-end stimulation pipeline has been designed, integrating both hardware and software components into a flexible tool for visual neuroprosthesis research. This system, schematized in Fig. 3, is composed of several stages. First, a commercial USB camera device mounted on a pair of glasses captures the video signal that is received by a computer with a Linux operating system. We implemented the system with both a custom local computer and a Raspberry Pi model 3B+. The input images are then processed and sent to a model's

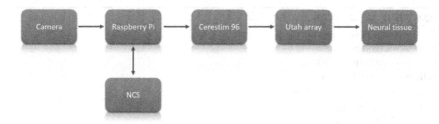

Fig. 3. Illustration of the main system's pipeline.

prediction module, an artificial retina, in our case. Finally, the model's output is interpreted as the main command for the neural stimulation (Cerestim96, Blackrock Microsystems, Inc., Salt Lake City, UT), which provides customized electrical pulse trains to the visual cortex through intracortical microelectrodes such as the Utah Electrode Array [31].

In order to handle the video stream, open source python libraries for scientific computing have been used: openCV scipy, numpy [28–30], along with state-of-the-art deep learning libraries: Tensorflow and Keras [32,33] as the tools to implement the neural coding previous to the stimulation control signals. In addition, we explored the possibility of deploying the visual coding models into a specialized deep learning acceleration hardware device [34], which relies on a Vision Processing Unit (VPU).

In the next section, we detail the function and features of the main blocks of the proposed system.

3 Software Interface Design

3.1 Modules Organization

In order to provide a modular, easy to use and extendable software corpus, we organized our python library, named Neurolight alpha, in the following structure:

Main_experiment. Contains the main thread on which the needed submodules are imported and the camera and stimulation devices configurations are set, before launching the "experiment" code.

Experiments. Each experiment is defined as a sequence of common steps: retrieving a new frame from the camera, preprocessing the incoming image (image normalization and resizing), optionally updating the video buffer (in case of a spatial-only retina model), performing the model's firing rate predictions, adapting the prediction to create stimulation commands, and sending those commands to the stimulator. The main workflow in the experiment module is detailed in Algorithm 1 (an example of an experimental workflow is described in Sect. 3.3).

Algorithm 1. Experiments module

Create train configurations
Select electrodes to use
Create encoding model
while processFlag **do**
  Obtain and process frame
  Update video buffer
  Model processing
  Stimulation command
  if *exitCondition* $==$ *True* **then**
    processFlag $\leftarrow$ *True*
  end if
end while

VisionModels. This module allows to define Keras (TensorFlow) retinal processing models. It also contains model's prediction normalization functions, which are necessary to interface the neurostimulator correctly. In addition, it wraps the Neural Compute Stick API functions necessary to compile the designed Tensorflow models in order to deploy them into the Vision Processing Unit.

StimAPI. This module incorporates the main functions which builds the necessary messages that allows us to interact with the neurostimulator. Those are the basic commands blocks which are used by "StimControl".

StimControl. A higher level API that performs the communication operations needed to control the stimulator. Each StimControl function calls StimAPI one or more times in order to create and send functional commands.

NCSControl. This module can be used to accelerate the model's predictions upon the videostream on the Intel's Neural Compute Stick device. Contains functions for communication with the NCS device, loading models and performing inference over the input.

Utils. Contains various helper functions, as generating custom image filters(for example, Gaussian filters), or mapping the desired electrodes to the actual stimulator output channels.

3.2 Computational Neural Models and Image Preprocessing

The VisionModels module allows to define simple and complex, retina-like visual preprocessing models, which are defined as Keras Sequential models or Tensorflow Graphs. This models can be deployed using a CPU, GPU or specialized architectures, such as FPGAs. In this first design version, we prepared two modalities: spatial processing models and spatiotemporal processing models, where the defined filters are 2D and 3D, respectively.

Custom Linear-Nonlinear 2D/3D filter can be custom-defined or created using data-driven, machine learning techniques, as Linear-Nonlinear models or Convolutional Neural Networks (see Fig. 4).

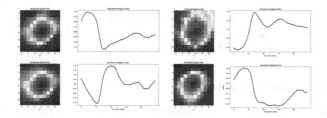

Fig. 4. Spatiotemporal filters can be defined and used as part of the pipeline. In the image, a selection of four of the linear part of the Linear-Nonlinear models after a rank-one decomposition performed with pyret [43]. The ganglion cell's retinal recordings were performed as mentioned in [24].

In order demonstrate the naturalistic stimulation control capability of our system, we fitted ganglion cell's firing responses to light patterns of different nature: full-field light flashes, checkerboard patterns, moving bars and natural scenes, following procedures similar of what is described in [24]. The natural scenes images were obtained from [35], and the rest of the stimuli was created by code scripts.

The ganglion cell's firing rates were fitted by means of a two-stage iterative process, in which each single neuron is modeled by means of a L2 regularized spatiotemporal Linear-Nonlinear process [36] (LN), which parameters are obtained with the Adam optimizer [37], which is a variant of the Gradient Descent optimization. The loss function utilized was a weighted sum of the mean squared error and the cross entropy between the biological retina's responses and the model's output.

In the first modeling stage, the input of the model consists on the flattened spatiotemporal visual stimulus that was projected into the retina during each time bin, and the output is the smoothed firing rate of the neuron as a response to the input [24]. The discrete time binning was 10 ms.

Due to the high dimensionality of the input (50 pixels × 50 pixels × 30 frames), the LN models created struggle to converge and are usually suboptimal. In order to tackle this, in the first stage we used a high regularization factor. This will promote that the model's parameters tends to zero in the spatial pixels which are out of the ganglion cell's receptive field, which is convenient in order to figure out which parts of the image are being encoded by the neuron. For the second modeling stage, we centered the model's target around the most relevant 15 × 15 pixels for each neuron, decreasing this way the number of parameters from 75000 to 6750, this is, 11x less parameters, leading the model to a more robust and faster convergence.

Once the Linear-Nonlinear models of the neurons are created, they can be loaded as the weights of a 1-layer Convolutional Neural Network either into a Keras sequential model (for quick deployment into the working pipeline) or TensorFlow graph, which will allow to compile it into a specific graph format to be used by a Neural Compute Stick (see Sect. 3.4).

Both the Keras and Tensorflow libraries allow for application-specific customization, by selecting the convolution stride or making spatial or spatiotemporal predictions over batches of images.

3.3 Neurostimulator Control and Stimulation Strategy

We developed and implemented a python version of the Blackrock Microsystems' API for the control of the CereStim96 neurostimulation device (briefly described in Sect. 3.1). This device allows for 16 simultaneous active channels, and 15 different pulse train configurations, that can be dynamically created (by overriding previous configurations on demand). After checking the correct operation of the device's current modules, a base pulse train configuration is defined. Then, modified versions of the base pulse trains are created, with different pulse intensity/frequency/pulse width values. This configurations, which shapes the pulse trains that will be delivered through the corresponding channels, are defined by the following parameters: Amplitude1, Amplitude2, PulseWidth1, PulseWidth2, InterPhase, InterPulse (see Fig. 2). Another key parameter to take in consideration its the InterTrain, this is, time between train pulses.

In this experiment, we select a list of electrodes which will be activated and map them into the actual channels which the device connects to.

After this, the camera configuration parameters are set, taking into consideration the dimensions of the input image, and the number of frames to buffer for the spatiotempoal processing. The retina model is defined by loading, reshaping and normalizing the ganglion cell's Linear-Nonlinear -or any other customized filter-based- model's weights into a Keras or Tensorflow model which will handle the convolution operations and strides. In the case of using a hardware acceleration device like the NCS for offloading the model's computations, we compile the desired model and load it into the device.

Once the main configurations are set, the main thread starts. Each input frame from the camera device is handled by openCV, resized and normalized, and stored into a buffer variable of the desired length. This buffer will be processed by the retina model, either in the main computer of in the acceleration device. The model's predictions are then normalized between 0 and 1 and matched to the closest of the 15 configurations selected for each electrode, which vary either in the intensity of frequency, depending on the desired train modulation strategy. Then, a single group stimulation sequence is generated for the corresponding electrodes and configurations and the command is sent to the stimulation device. If desired, a prompt windows will be updated, showing the camera input and stimulation information. After checking that the stimulation operation was properly performed, the next frame is obtained from the camera, and the whole process is repeated.

The stimulation strategies must be shaped by decisions of diverse nature: the actual knowledge of the psychophysics, computational modeling needs, software design decisions, hardware features and limitations. Two main strategies are contemplated currently: Amplitude Modulation and Frequency modulation (see Fig. 2), where the model's predictions for each electrode are mapped to the closest matching configurations, which are previously set and loaded into the stimulator device.Clinical studies will reveal the most optimal way of operating. [12,38–41].

3.4 Hardware Implementation

In order to explore the possibilities that dedicated hardware acceleration offers, we deployed the vision models into a Intel's Neural Compute Stick [34], a low-power consuming, edge-computing device designed to deploy Deep Learning models for inference, which incorporates an Intel® Movidius™ Vision Processing Unit (VPU). This device is connected to the main computer, and the preprocessed image/video data its passed to it through an USB port, returning the model's predictions after the processing.

After creating single Linear-Nonlinear ganglion cell's models, they were loaded into a Tensorflow graph. The Linear-Nonlinear models, as described in Sect. 3.2 consists of a spatial or spatiotemporal filter with a nonlinear activation function which is convoluted through the image/video input, returning the predicted ganglion cell's firing rates, predictions which can be used for the stimulator control after proper normalization and configuration-matching (see Fig. 5). The created graph its prepared for inference-only mode and compiled into a compatible format to be used into the device.

4   Discussion and Future Work

Since many questions regarding the psychophysics of the phosphene generation are either still unanswered or in need of a more extensive exploration, cortical neurostimulators control tools must be smooth and easy to use and at the same time they have to permit to be adapted to the ongoing experimental findings as the theoretical and experimental hyopothesis are confirmed or discarded in the clinical research.

In this work, a cortical prosthesis control framework prototype is developed, having at its core the design principles of robustness and flexibility, allowing custom adaptation to the needs of clinical research. This functional working pipeline allows to incorporate both simple and complex computational neural encoding models of visual inputs (such as data-driven or custom linear-nonlinear models of retinal ganglion cells) for prosthesis control and to define different stimulation strategies, such as amplitude and frequency modulation, based on the implemented models. This framework has been designed and implemented into an experimental setup with a commercial neurostimulator that can be used on both animal an human research. The core pipeline modules, as the image capturing and preprocessing, the neural encoding module and the stimulator control API are based on open-source python libraries commonly used by the scientific community, which we believe is a fundamental feature for scientific tools and knowledge sharing.

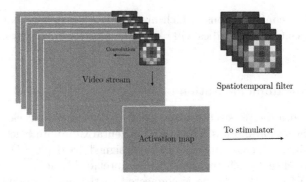

Fig. 5. Illustration of a spatiotemporal filter being applied to a video stream. The output of the model is an array of activation values that can be mapped to the stimulator's electrodes, after a proper normalization and matching with the pre-configured stimulus configuration values.

Among the weaknesses of the current system its the fact that its pipeline is sequential: every new image has to be processed before sending the image/video data for the model to return its output. After that, the stimulator has to finish its function before a new image its fetched. With this operation mode, the system is able to change the running stimulation parameters at 14 FPS. This bottleneck can be avoided by using threading, and its one of the main improvements to be made in future works. As a future planned improvement, Neurolight will allow to parallelize the image/video inputs pre-processing with the model encoding modules and the stimulation control, obtaining this way a better maximum system's performance in terms of FPS and more diverse possibilities for stimulation strategies development.

The fact that the electrical pulse trains are sent after the image processing-model prediction stage leads to a blinking stimulation strategy: train pulses are interleaved with an inter-train resting period. This way of stimulation on the visual cortex has been tested previously [39], and prevents the neural tissue to be permanently under the influence of external electrical fields, although the implications of this stimulation strategy has yet to be elucidated. In this matter, the inter-train interval necessary to generate a separated or continuous phosphene will be one of the main features of study in the clinical phases, along with the effects of temporal summation, and phosphene size and brightness.

Among the main challenges that a visual prosthesis designer faces is how to convey the most useful information trough the prosthesis. One of the most promising alternative pre-processing strategies is semantic segmentation [42] - which can already be implemented into our working pipeline by compiling a U-NET-like semantic segmentation CNN. The main idea of this approach is to simplify the transmitted visual information in a meaningful way, such that the complexity of the environment is diminished without disregarding the important information necessary for scene understanding and navigation.

In future works, we expect to implement several psychophysics modules which complement the tool and allow for a better fine-tuning of the whole system. Regarding the visual encoding models, it is hypothesized that retina-like image preprocessing could be beneficial for visual prosthesis [13], by performing a bioinspired feature extraction of visual information, although this remains unanswered. Along with the technical achievements made, new experiments need to be designed accordingly to provide answers. In this way, more complex, CNN-RNN based retina models which are proven to mimic the retinal encoding will be compiled and tested, and a tradeof between model's complexity and overall system's performance in terms of computing speed will be extensively studied.

We hope that the present work constitutes a step forward towards integrating knowledge from many scientific and engineering fields into a useful clinical research tool, and it is designed under the aim that neural engineers dream of: to help people achieving a level of neural function recovery sufficient to improve their life's quality.

Acknowledgments. This work is supported by the Programa de Ayudas a Grupos de Excelencia de la Región de Murcia, Fundación Séneca, Agencia de Ciencia y Tecnología de la Región de Murcia.

References

1. Wolpaw, J.R., et al.: Brain-computer interface technology: a review of the first international meeting (2000)
2. Davis, T.S., et al.: Restoring motor control and sensory feedback in people with upper extremity amputations using arrays of 96 microelectrodes implanted in the median and ulnar nerves. J. Neural Eng. **13**(3), 36001 (2016)
3. Nuyujukian, P., et al.: Cortical control of a tablet computer by people with paralysis. PLoS ONE **13**(11), e0204566 (2018)
4. Fattahi, P., Yang, G., Kim, G., Abidian, M.R.: A review of organic and inorganic biomaterials for neural interfaces. Adv. Mater. **26**(12), 1846–85 (2014)
5. House, W.F.: Cochlear implants. Ann. Otol. Rhinol. Laryngol. **85**(Suppl. 3), 3 (1976)
6. Weiland, J.D., Liu, W., Humayun, M.S.: Retinal prosthesis. Annu. Rev. Biomed. Eng. **7**(1), 361–401 (2005)
7. Mayberg, H.S., et al.: Deep brain stimulation for treatment-resistant depression. Neuron **45**(5), 651–660 (2005)
8. Sengupta, A., et al.: Red-shifted channelrhodopsin stimulation restores light responses in blind mice, macaque retina, and human retina. EMBO Mol. Med. **8**(11), 1248–1264 (2016)
9. Vassanelli, S., Mahmud, M.: Trends and challenges in neuroengineering: toward intelligent neuroprostheses through brain inspired systems; communication. Front. Neurosci. **10**, 438 (2016)
10. da Cruz, L., et al.: Five-year safety and performance results from the argus II retinal prosthesis system clinical trial. Ophthalmology **123**(10), 2248–2254 (2016)
11. Hornig, R., et al.: Pixium vision: first clinical results and innovative developments. In: Gabel, V. (ed.) Artificial Vision, pp. 99–113. Springer, Cham (2017). https://doi.org/10.1007/978-3-319-41876-6_8

12. Fernandez, E.: Development of visual neuroprostheses: trends and challenges. Bioelectron. Med. **4**(1), 12 (2018)
13. Normann, R.A., Greger, B.A., House, P., Romero, S.F., Pelayo, F., Fernandez, E.: Toward the development of a cortically based visual neuroprosthesis. J. Neural Eng. **6**(3), 35001 (2009)
14. Dobelle, W.H.: Artificial vision for the blind by connecting a television camera to the visual cortex. ASAIO J. **46**(1), 3–9 (2000)
15. Troyk, P., et al.: A model for intracortical visual prosthesis research. Artif. Organs **27**(11), 1005–1015 (2003)
16. Lowery, A.J.: Introducing the Monash vision group's cortical prosthesis. In: IEEE International Conference on Image Processing 2013, pp. 1536–1539 (2013)
17. Development of a Cortical Visual Neuroprosthesis for the Blind (CORTIVIS). ClinicalTrials.gov. Identifier: NCT02983370
18. Early Feasibility Study of the Orion Visual Cortical Prosthesis System. ClinicalTrials.gov. Identifier: NCT03344848
19. Shannon, R.V.: A model of threshold for pulsatile electrical stimulation of cochlear implants. Hear. Res. **40**(3), 197–204 (1989). https://doi.org/10.1016/0378-5955(89)90160-3
20. Golden, J.R., et al.: Simulation of visual perception and learning with a retinal prosthesis. J. Neural Eng. **16**, 025003 (2019)
21. Jepson, L.H., Hottowy, P., Weiner, G.A., Dabrowski, W., Litke, A.M., Chichilnisky, E.J.: High-fidelity reproduction of spatiotemporal visual signals for retinal prosthesis. Neuron **83**(1), 87–92 (2014)
22. Shah, N.P., Madugula, S., Chichilnisky, E.J., Shlens, J., Singer, Y.: Learning a neural response metric for retinal prosthesis (2018)
23. Beyeler, M., Boynton, G., Fine, I., Rokem, A.: pulse2percept: A Python-based simulation framework for bionic vision. In: Proceedings of the 16th Python in Science Conference, pp. 81–88 (2017)
24. Lozano, A., Soto-Sánchez, C., Garrigós, J., Martínez, J.J., Ferrández, J.M., Fernández, E.: A 3D convolutional neural network to model retinal ganglion cell's responses to light patterns in mice. Int. J. Neural Syst. **28**(10), 1850043 (2018)
25. Crespo-Cano, R., Martínez-Álvarez, A., Díaz-Tahoces, A., Cuenca-Asensi, S., Ferrández, J.M., Fernández, E.: On the automatic tuning of a retina model by using a multi-objective optimization. In: Artificial Computation in Biology and Medicine, Elche, Spain, pp. 108–118 (2015)
26. Mcintosh, L., Maheswaranathan, N., Nayebi, A., Ganguli, S., Baccus, S.: Deep learning models of the retinal response to natural scenes. In: Advances in Neural Information Processing Systems, Barcelona, Spain, vol. 29, pp. 1369–1377 (2016)
27. Yan, Q., et al.: Revealing fine structures of the retinal receptive field by deep learning networks (2018). (Lateral geniculate nucleus, V1, V4...). In our work, we focus on the first stage of visual processing: the retina
28. Bradski, G.: The openCV library. Dr. Dobb's J. Softw. Tools **25**, 120–125 (2000)
29. Jones, E., Oliphant, T.E., Peterson, P., et al.: SciPy: open source scientific tools for Python (2001)
30. Travis E, Oliphant. A Guide to NumPy. Trelgol Publishing, USA (2006)
31. Maynard, E.M., Nordhausen, C.T., Normann, R.A.: The utah intracortical electrode array: a recording structure for potential brain-computer interfaces. Electroencephalogr. Clin. Neurophysiol. **102**(3), 228–239 (1997). https://doi.org/10.1016/s0013-4694(96)95176-0

32. Abadi, M., et al.: TensorFlow: large-scale machine learning on heterogeneous distributed systems. In: Computer Science - Distributed, Parallel, and Cluster Computing, Computer Science - Learning (2016)
33. Chollet, F.: Keras (2015). https://github.com/fchollet/keras
34. Intel's Neural Compute Stick. https://movidius.github.io/ncsdk/ncs.html
35. Deng, J., et al.: ImageNet: a large-scale hierarchical image database. In: CVPR (2009)
36. Baccus, S.A., Meister, M.: Fast and slow contrast adaptation in retinal circuitry. Neuron **36**(5), 909–919 (2002)
37. Kingma, D.P., Ba, J.L.: ADAM: a method for stochastic optimization
38. Dobelle, W.H., Mladejovsky, M.G.: Phosphenes produced by electrical stimulation of human occipital cortex, and their application to the development of a prosthesis for the blind. J. Physiol. **243**(2), 553–576 (1974)
39. Schmidt, E.M., Bak, M.J., Hambrecht, F.T., Kufta, C.V., O'Rourke, D.K., Vallabhanath, P.: Feasibility of a visual prosthesis for the blind based on intracortical micro stimulation of the visual cortex. Brain **119**(2), 507–522 (1996)
40. Davis, T.S., et al.: Spatial and temporal characteristics of V1 microstimulation during chronic implantation of a microelectrode array in a behaving macaque. J. Neural Eng. **9**(6), 65003 (2012)
41. Foroushani, A.N., Pack, C.C., Sawan, M.: Cortical visual prostheses: from microstimulation to functional percept. J. Neural Eng. **15**(2), 21005 (2018)
42. Long, J., Shelhamer, E., Darrell, T.: Fully convolutional networks for semantic segmentation (2015)
43. Benjamin Naecker, N.M.: pyret: retinal data analysis in Python - pyret 0.6.0 documentation

Bootstrapping Autonomous Skill Learning in the MDB Cognitive Architecture

Alejandro Romero, Francisco Bellas, Jose A. Becerra, and Richard J. Duro$^{(\boxtimes)}$

Integrated Group for Engineering Research, Universidade da Coruña,
A Coruña, Spain
{alejandro.romero.montero,francisco.bellas,
jose.antonio.becerra.permuy,richard}@udc.es

Abstract. This paper is concerned with motivation in autonomous robots. In particular we focus on the basic structure that is necessary for bootstrapping the initial stages of multiple skill learning within the motivational engine of the MDB cognitive architecture. To this end, taking inspiration from a series of computational models of the use of motivations in infants, we propose an approach that leverages two types of cognitive motivations: exploratory and proficiency based. The latter modulated by the concept of interestingness. We postulate that these make up the minimum set of motivational components required to initiate the unrewarded learning of a skill toolbox that may later be used in order to achieve operational goals. The approach is illustrated through an experiment with a real robot that is learning skills in a real environment.

Keywords: Cognitive Developmental Robotics ·
Motivational system · Skill learning · Open-ended learning

1 Introduction

Making robots able to learn in open-ended manner throughout their lives implies that the robot is expected to learn an unbounded sequence of a priori unknown tasks in unknown domains [6]. At design time, the designer does not know what competences or knowledge the robot will need to achieve its objectives. Consequently, the problem is not that of providing a robot with competences to perform particular tasks in known environments, but to provide the robot with mechanisms that allow it to figure out what tasks to carry out, and how, to achieve its objectives in the situations faces. This is, obviously, a much more difficult problem.

In order to try to find ways to solve it, many authors have drawn inspiration from natural systems. This has been the focus of Cognitive Developmental Robotics (CDR) [1], which addresses the design of robotic systems based on insights from the onto-genetic development of cognition, mostly in children. It deals with the progressive acquisition of competences which are later used as scaffolding to acquire new, more complex, competences.

© Springer Nature Switzerland AG 2019
J. M. Ferrández Vicente et al. (Eds.): IWINAC 2019, LNCS 11486, pp. 120–129, 2019.
https://doi.org/10.1007/978-3-030-19591-5_13

However, a CDR approach implies establishing a series of innate competences that allow for autonomous learning and adaptation. Taking inspiration from the way infants autonomously learn, it is easy to see that they have a tendency to explore their environment and to address and learn from new problems they select by themselves without any explicit external reward. In other words, the individual is the one that defines what to do and what, when, and how learning will take place as a function of its internal state and the needs that emerge from its interaction with the different environments it may face.

Obviously, from a roboticist point of view, the purpose of the robot cannot be defined in terms of what it must do but rather in terms of what it must achieve with respect to its internal state and needs. One way to do this is for the designer to establish an internal state space, which is usually called the motivational space [5], given by a set of domain independent variables that reflect the robot needs in terms of meeting some criteria. Any deviation from these criteria implies a need the robot must fulfill and the amount of deviation the intensity of the need or the drive.

Now the problem becomes how can the robot figure out what tasks to carry out when confronted with an unknown domain as a in order to fulfill its needs. In other words, it needs to self-discover and self-select goals, defined as desired end-states in the domain [14], end-states that will lead to an increase in the fulfillment of its needs. It is important to emphasize here that a goal determines a task the robot must carry out (to reach the goal) and, consequently, a skill it must learn in order to be able to achieve it.

On the other hand, the robot also needs to determine how valuable any goal is (what is its utility) and, by extension, what may the expected utility of any point in state space be with regards to that goal (defining expected utility as the probability of reaching a goal from that point multiplied by the utility of the goal). The mechanisms in charge of this are generally called motivational mechanisms or value systems and, as stated by Begum et al. "The success of designing truly developmental robot depends largely on the design of a value system" [2].

In the classical psychological and educational literature on motivation [5], most authors distinguish two classes of motivations from an external observer's point of view. On the one hand, when the agent is perceived as trying "to obtain some separable outcome" [15], it is said to be extrinsically motivated [12]. The observer sees the agent seeking goal states where some observable explicit utility can be obtained. On the other hand, animals and humans spend time and effort carrying out behaviors that produce no observable explicit utility. This has been explained away as driven by intrinsic motivations [15] arising from within the individual because the behavior is naturally satisfying.

This work is framed within the problem of creating adequate motivational systems for autonomous robots, in particular, within the MDB cognitive architecture [3,7], to be able to efficiently learn and purposefully behave in open-ended settings. For this purpose, the aforementioned traditional classification of motivations is not satisfying. In fact, from an engineering point of view, intrinsic motivations only differ from extrinsic ones in the fact that their drives are usually related to cognitive aspects of the operation of the system. However, no matter what type of drive it is, it is always fulfilled by acquiring utility, whether in terms of a cognitive aspect (e.g. found something new) or an operational one (e.g. increased my energy level). For this reason, we believe a classification of drives into cognitive drives and operational drives is much more useful for engineering purposes and this is the classification we will use in the rest of the paper.

In this paper we describe the motivational engine that has been designed for the MDB cognitive architecture focusing on the initial stages of skill learning. That is, taking inspiration from a series of computational models of the use of cognitive motivations in infants to explore and learn that have been proposed in the last decade [8,13], we will address the problem of how to bootstrap the system to opportunistically start learning skills in domains where multiple skills can be learned at the same time.

2   MDB Motivational Engine

As we have previously indicated in the introduction, motivation should be the driver that makes a cognitive robot perform some action [10] directing its activities. It does this, by providing an evaluation of states determining how good they are for the robot survival or design objectives in the form of an utility value that reflects how much the satisfaction of a drive or drives has improved when the state was reached. This evaluation can be carried out over the real current state of the robot or over prospective states in order to decide on which future state would be the best choice for the robot.

When prospectively evaluating states, a utility value needs to be estimated by a utility model U^k, which is associated to goal k. Goals are points or areas in state space that, when reached, increase the satisfaction of one or more drives of the robot (produce utility). Given the set of goals the system has at any moment in time, the motivational engine must provide their corresponding activation levels depending on the needs it wants to fulfill. This way, states can be evaluated depending on the drives related to those goals. To be able to achieve this, the motivational engine must perform three main processes: select the goal activation for the current context, discover new goals, and learn the utility functions that allow it to evaluate the states depending on the goals.

Figure 1 displays a schematic representation of the Motivational Engine, called MotivEn, that was designed for the MDB architecture. The black boxes delimit the main components of the system: *Goal Manager*, *State Evaluator* and *Utility Modeler*. The red blocks are output elements that are transferred to the rest of the cognitive architecture: the *goal activation vector* and the *discovered goals*, provided by the Goal Manager, the *utility models* provided by the Utility Modeler, and the *evaluation* of the perceptual states, provided by the State Evaluator.

As a general overview of the operation of the motivational engine, we can start from the left block, the *Trace Buffer (TB)*. The episodes in the *TB* are traces, that is, a limited number of consecutive states that lead to a goal, as in classical reinforcement learning. These traces are used by the Goal Manager to define the new goal states, and by the Utility Modeler to carry out Utility Model learning processes. The top part of the *TB* contains a sub-block called Current State, which represents the last perceptual state, required to define the goal activation vector. This definition is performed by the Goal Manager component, taking into account the set of innate drives of the robot. This Goal Activation Vector is used by the State Evaluator to provide the evaluation of the Candidate State when necessary (green block in Fig. 1).

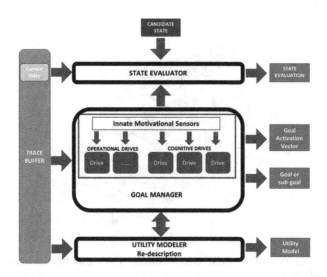

Fig. 1. Motivational engine diagram. (Color figure online)

The utility modeler component is in charge of obtaining models of the utility function associated to each goal. The utility model provides an internally useful representation of expected utility for any point in state-space with regards to a particular goal aimed at establishing clues on how to reach goals. Utility can be modeled in different ways and in this paper we will make use of Value Functions (VFs) in the form of ANNs as utility models in the examples we will present in the experimental section.

The Goal Manager component is tasked with creating and maintaining a goal graph (Fig. 2) that represents the relationships among goals. The goal graph is rooted in the innate motivational vector (top vector of Fig. 2), that is, the vector of drives of the system. This vector provides an indication of the needs of the robot each moment in time as a function of the values of the innate motivational sensors that were established at design time and that constitute the motivational state space. Goals are areas of the operational state space of the system (which has to do with the external sensorial apparatus of the robot and the domain it is immersed in) and they are related to the drives by the fact that achieving a particular goal produces an increase in the satisfaction of the associated drives (utility). As the robot discovers goals in the different environments it finds itself in, the Goal Manager links these goals through a weighed connection to the particular drive they satisfy. Some of the goals may not directly satisfy an innate drive, but may be stepping stones towards another goal, that is, they may be sub-goals. Operationally, given a set of values for the drives, these are propagated along the goal graph to determine the activation level of each goal. This way, the motivational engine uses its experience in the form of stored goals to try to determine goal paths to satisfy the active drives that instant of time in that particular domain.

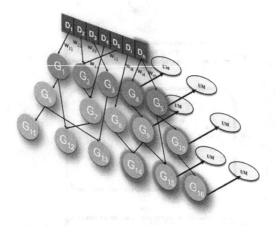

Fig. 2. A representation of the drive-goal hierarchy. Each goal has, at least, one utility model associated to it.

3   Unrewarded Skill Acquisition and Interestingness

This paper deals with the problem of bootstrapping the operation of a developmental cognitive robot in its initial stages of autonomous interaction with an unknown world or a series of worlds. At this stage the robot can only rely on what it has been innately endowed with by the designer and it must use it to progressively acquire new skills that will allow it to become more proficient. Consequently, designing an appropriate set of innate drives is key to the adequate performance of the robot.

As indicated before, operational drives, which are the ones most authors assimilate to classical extrinsic goals, or what the Reinforcement Learning literature calls external rewards, and that reflect the main objectives of the robot, are relatively straightforward to design. However, for practical reasons, the utility (rewards) they provide in state space is usually very sparse, slowing down learning and forcing the robots to perform many "useless" or non-informative interactions with the environment before finding goals and starting to learn skills to achieve them.

This problem was initially addressed, for instance in the field of Reinforcement Learning, through hand designing "well-shaped" reward functions [11]. But this has proven to be a very difficult endeavor in all but the simplest problems [4], especially when considering real life robotic environments. Consequently, inspired by the observations of child cognitive development, a different approach based on supplementing the sparse operational rewards using cognitive (or intrinsic) drives to generate dense utility landscapes was proposed in the last few years [13].

This is the approach chosen within the motivational engine of the MDB. Thus, in order to initially bootstrap the operation of the system, even before any operational goals have been found, we postulate that the designer must define a set of cognitive drives that allow for an efficient exploration of the state-space of the robot and that lead to the concentration of sampling and learning effort where it is more productive. This permits learning skills to be stored in the Long Term Memory so that they can later be used to simplify the process of finding and achieving operational utility, which is the main driver of any robot.

Here we postulate that two types of drives constitute the minimum set of cognitive drives required for this process. On the one hand, the robot needs to explore its state space in order to find utility. This exploration must be efficient and, consequently, some type of cognitive drive related to exploration must be included. In particular, in the experiments we present in the next section, we have made use of a drive related to novelty [9]. However, to learn a skill, it is also necessary to train and become proficient at it. That is, the robot needs to be motivated to concentrate its interaction with the environment on cases that can lead to learning the skill. That is, to establish a virtual goal in that point and learn its utility model. We will call this a Proficiency based type of motivation. In particular, as skills are usually learned in order to be able produce some effect on the environment, we will make use of an effectance based motivation in the experiments and associate it to sensors that determine when unpredicted change has occurred.

To induce training, we incorporate the concept of interestingness within the related proficiency based motivation as a virtual utility value that can change in time as the robot becomes more proficient at achieving the corresponding goal. Thus, when an effect is produced by chance for the first time, the point in state space where that occurred becomes interesting (its interestingness level increases). This is reflected within the motivational engine as a virtual utility value when the goal is achieved and within the attention mechanism of the robot by increasing the saliency of the state-space point in the process of choosing where to go next. However, interestingness is also modulated by the proficiency in achieving the goal: the more proficient the robot becomes, the less interesting the virtual goal becomes. Once the robot is very proficient, the skill for achieving the goal will have been acquired and it can be sent to Long Term Memory for storage and future recall.

Summarizing, to be able to explore and learn skills that may later be useful to achieve operational goals before any operational goal has been found, we postulate that the designer of the robot cognitive architecture and motivational system needs to provide, at least, two types of innate basic motivations: Exploratory motivations and a Proficiency based motivations. The former allow for efficient exploration of state-space (some type of babbling). The latter allow for temporally focusing efforts to learning skills through virtual goals even though no real operational utility is achieved.

4   Experiment with Real Robot

To test how interestingness coupled with a proficiency based motivation allows the motivational engine to autonomously learn new skills while interacting with its environment, a simple but very illustrative real robot setup has been defined. The experiment is carried out using the Baxter robot, which is placed in front of a white table with three different objects it can detect: a brown box, a red ball and a small plastic jar which lights up when it is grabbed. The robot can detect the distance to the objects by using their color and shape. Regarding its actuation, it is equipped with two 7 DOF arms with gripper effectors. The grippers automatically grab an object when it is detected between the gripper plates.

Fig. 3. The left image corresponds to the pushing skill, while the right image corresponds to the grasping skill.

Thus, in this particular experiment, we, as designers, have endowed MotivEn with one exploratory (novelty based) motivation that makes the Baxter right arm move around the table in a sort of babbling pattern seeking states that it has not experienced before. Obviously, for novelty, the objects are more attractive than an empty table and we have included a basic attention mechanism for which, other aspects being equal, the closest one is the most attractive. In addition, we have provided a proficiency based motivation in the form of an effectance drive. That is, a drive towards causing changes in the environment. In this case, the changes it detects have to do with changes in the positions of objects or changes in color. In particular, in this experiment, the jar lights up when it is grabbed and all of the objects can be pushed around.

The execution of the experiment, illustrated in the images of Fig. 3, can be described as follows: the robot started its operation without any explicit goal nor skill apart from the two innate motivations mentioned above. Consequently, it started moving its right arm guided by the novelty motivation. Eventually, this novelty seeking motivation leads it to hitting and pushing a an object, in this case the ball (see left image in Fig. 3), thus generating a change in the perceptions of the robot that it will interpret as an effect of its actions on the environment (it has caused effectance). This increases the interestingness value of the point in state space where the change occurred (defined by the color of the object, a distance of zero between the gripper and the object and a speed of the arm that is different from zero) and establishes it as a virtual goal to be achieved.

The interestingness value triggers the effectance drive through an increase of the drive value. This drive is only satisfied when the robot is able to consistently achieve the virtual goal, which is when interestingness drops to zero. Consequently, the robot concentrates on finding ways to reach the goal point in state space from any initial point it is in. In other words, if the object is the red ball, as in the left of Fig. 3, it explores how to make the ball move and progressively creates a utility model that allows it to consistently make the ball move (push the ball) by selecting actions that follow its positive gradient. In the case of this experiment, the utility models took the form of a value function that was encoded as an ANN that was progressively trained using the ADAM algorithm on the samples the robot produced.

As the robot becomes more proficient, that is, as the utility model improves, the level of interestingness in moving the ball decreases, thus reducing the effectance drive. Depending on the level of its other drives, this may imply a change of activity on the part of the robot. In this particular example, the only other drive is the novelty drive and it does not become dominant until the effectance drive is very low. Once this happens, the robot looses interest in moving the ball and goes back to seeking novelty. At this point the value function obtained for the push-ball skill, shown in Fig. 4(b), is stored in the Long Term Memory (LTM) of the MDB for future use.

As the robot continues to explore, some object may end up between its gripper pads triggering the close gripper reflex action. This action really does not cause any effect in any of the objects except for the jar. Thus, when the object is not the jar, the robot continues with its novelty seeking behavior. When it is the jar the one the gripper closes on, it lights up. This obviously is an effect and, as in the previous case, an interestingness value is assigned (see right image of Fig. 3). Again, the proficiency based motivation starts guiding the robot response and a second value function learning process is launched. As the grasping skill associated to this VF improves the interestingness value decreases until the corresponding value function (displayed in Fig. 4(a)) has been correctly learnt and is stored in the LTM.

The process continues with a new exploratory stage and, if pertinent, new activations of the effectance drive that will allow learning new skills. What is important here is that in this experiment MotivEn was able to learn two primitive skills (grabbing and pushing) in a very efficient manner while it was autonomously interacting with the world, without any extrinsic reward.

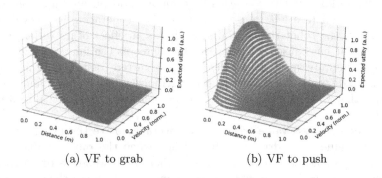

(a) VF to grab   (b) VF to push

Fig. 4. 3D representation of the primitive skills learned.

To illustrate the response of the learned skills, Fig. 4 shows a 3D representation of the value functions in terms of distance and speed of the gripper that were learnt. The VF associated with the grabbing skill (Fig. 4(a)) shows how the expected utility is higher the closer the robot is to the object and the lower the speed of the gripper. Something logical, since the robot will need to be close to the object and stopped to grab it. On the other hand, in the VF associated to the push-object skill (Fig. 4(b)) the expected utility is maximum when the distance to the object is zero and the gripper speed is greater than a threshold so that it can push it.

5   Conclusions

In this paper we have addressed the problem of bootstrapping autonomous robotic learning when operational reward is sparse in terms of the basic drives that should be present within the motivational engine of the MDB cognitive architecture in order to make this bootstrapping possible and efficient. Thus, we have established that a minimum of two types of cognitive drives need to be put in by the designer: Exploratory drives and Proficiency based drives. Exploratory drives are quite common in the motivation literature and provide a way for the system to efficiently explore its state space. Proficiency based drives are the ones that allow the system to concentrate on promising points in state space and learn possible skills in order to consistently reach them. In our case, this focusing is achieved through the use of the concept of interestingness in order to provide temporal virtual reward and saliency, thus allowing the system to learn multiple skills in an environment. This approach was successfully tested in a real robot operating in a real, albeit simple, environment.

Acknowledgments. This work has been funded by the EU's H2020 research programme (grant No 640891 DREAM), MINECO/FEDER (grant TIN2015-63646-C5-1-R), Xunta de Galicia/FEDER (grant ED431C 2017/12), and Spanish Ministry of Education, Culture and Sports for the FPU grant of A. Romero.

References

1. Asada, M., et al.: Cognitive developmental robotics: a survey. IEEE Trans. Auton. Ment. Dev. **1**(1), 12–34 (2009)
2. Begum, M., Karray, F.: Computational intelligence techniques in bio-inspired robotics. In: Liu, D., Wang, L., Tan, K.C. (eds.) Design and Control of Intelligent Robotic Systems. SCI, vol. 177, pp. 1–28. Springer, Heidelberg (2009). https://doi.org/10.1007/978-3-540-89933-4_1
3. Bellas, F., Duro, R.J., Faina, A., Souto, D.: Multilevel darwinist brain (MDB): artificial evolution in a cognitive architecture for real robots. IEEE Trans. Auton. Ment. Dev. **2**(4), 340–354 (2010)
4. Burda, Y., Edwards, H., Pathak, D., Storkey, A., Darrel, T., Efros, A.: Large-scale study of curiosity-driven learning. arXiv preprint arXiv:1808.04355 (2018)
5. Deci, E.L., Ryan, R.M.: Cognitive evaluation theory. In: Deci, E.L., Ryan, R.M. (eds.) Intrinsic Motivation and Self-Determination in Human Behavior. PSPS, pp. 43–85. Springer, Boston (1985). https://doi.org/10.1007/978-1-4899-2271-7_3
6. Doncieux, S., et al.: Open-ended learning: a conceptual framework based on representational redescription. Front. Neurorob. **12**, 59 (2018)
7. Duro, R.J., Becerra, J., Monroy, J., Bellas, F.: Perceptual generalization and context in a network memory inspired long term memory for artificial cognition. Int. J. Neural Syst. (2019, accepted for publication)
8. Forestier, S., Mollard, Y., Oudeyer, P.Y.: Intrinsically motivated goal exploration processes with automatic curriculum learning. arXiv:1708.02190 (2017)
9. Huang, X., Weng, J.: Novelty and reinforcement learning in the value system of developmental robots. In: Proceedings of the Second International Workshop on Epigenetic Robotics, pp. 47–55 (2002)
10. Maslow, A.H.: A theory of human motivation. Psychol. Rev. **50**(13), 370–396 (1943)
11. Mnih, V., et al.: Human-level control through deep reinforcement learning. Nature **518**, 529–533 (2015)
12. Di Nocera, D., Finzi, A., Rossi, S., Staffa, M.: The role of intrinsic motivations in attention allocation and shifting. Front. Psychol. **5**, 273 (2014)
13. Oudeyer, P.Y., Kaplan, F.: What is intrinsic motivation? A typology of computational approaches. Front. Neurorob. **1**, 6 (2009)
14. Rolf, M., Asada, M.: What are goals ? And if so, how many ? In: Proceedings of Joint IEEE International Conference on Development and Learning and Epigenetic Robotics (ICDL-EpiRob), pp. 332–339 (2015)
15. Ryan, R., Deci, E.: Intrinsic and extrinsic motivations: classic definitions and new directions. Contemp. Educ. Psychol. **25**(1), 54–67 (2000)

HAPAN: Support Tool for Practicing Regional Anesthesia in Peripheral Nerves

J. A. Hernández-Muriel$^{(\boxtimes)}$, J. C. Mejía-Hernández, J. D. Echeverry-Correa,
A. A. Orozco, and D. Cárdenas-Peña

Automatic Research Group, Faculty of Engineerings,
Universidad Tecnológica de Pereira, Pereira, Colombia
j.hernandez12@utp.edu.co

Abstract. Ultrasound (US) medical imaging rises as a technique used to visualize nerve structures, among other applications. It has been used, typically, as a tool for assisting in the practice of peripheral nerve anesthesia. Due to its non-invasive nature, US may reduce the risk of injury to medical patients during surgical procedures. Despite its usefulness, it is challenging for anesthesiologists to perform the anesthesia process, mainly due to the presence of speckle and acoustic multiplicative noise, significantly degrading the image quality. Besides, the lack of homogeneity in the imaged structures disorients the anesthesiologist in the effective localization of the nerve structure. In this paper, we present the design and implementation of the software toolkit HAPAN (HAPAN is a Spanish acronym for *Herramienta de Asistencia para la Práctica de Anestesia en Nervios periféricos*-Assistance tool for the anesthesia of peripheral nerves.), developed in MATLAB, for the segmentation of different peripheral nerves in ultrasound images. HAPAN includes algorithms for automatic nerve segmentation based on appearance shape models, and image resolution enhancement.

Keywords: Peripheral nerves · Regional anesthesia · Support tool

1 Introduction

Medical ultrasound (US) imaging stands as a technology widely used by anesthesiologists for the localization of nerves structures [14]. Despite being the standard tool for peripheral nerve blocking, the US strongly suffers from multiplicative acoustic noise and lack of structure homogeneity [16]. To deal with above issues, researches focus on the automatic segmentation of US including fetal catches [1,8], blood vessels [10,15], and pathological tissue [11,19]. In general, the approaches of US segmentation are grouped into statistical approaches [9,13], superpixel or patch-based approaches [2,18], and texture and classification approaches [7,12].

Nonetheless, there are few relevant approaches for peripheral nerve segmentation that provide on-line assistance to the anesthesiologists. Some of them

© Springer Nature Switzerland AG 2019
J. M. Ferrández Vicente et al. (Eds.): IWINAC 2019, LNCS 11486, pp. 130–137, 2019.
https://doi.org/10.1007/978-3-030-19591-5_14

include are clustering algorithms [4], Bayesian shape models [3]; and Gaussian processes [5,6]. Despite reporting promising results, most of the works only test small US collections. Therefore, there is a need for tools allowing anesthesiologist visualization, validation, and analysis of automatic US processing.

This paper presents the design and development of software for the automatic segmentation of ultrasound images, termed HAPAN. HAPAN includes conventional segmentation and appearance and shape models as user alternatives. Besides, HAPAN as a support software deploys complementary tools ranging from digital filters to image resolution enhancement algorithms, developed to facilitate the visualization and localization of the nerve in ultrasound images.

The rest of the article is organized as follows. Section 2 provides a detailed analysis of materials and methods. Section 3 discusses the experimental results. Section 4 presents the concluding remarks and future research directions.

2   Materials and Methods

2.1   Database

The database used for building the HAPAN Software contains a collection of approximately 200 ultrasound images. Two peripheral nerves from 6 different patients were captured. Ultrasonic images were obtained by an acquisition system consisting of the combination of a portable NanoMaxx SONOSITE ultrasound system with a video converter (EASYCAP). The ultrasound system is used to acquire the image of the nerve to study by means of an ultrasonic transducer, and the EASYCAP system allows the scanner to communicate directly with the computer in which the processing will be performed. Any scanner that has similar characteristics to the one used in HAPAN could be compatible with the software. Acquired images go through a pre-processing stage which performs a series of adjustments in order to enhance the quality of the image.

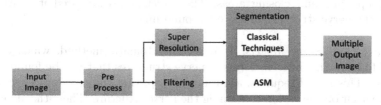

Fig. 1. HAPAN software structure.

2.2   Software Development

HAPAN's interface is comprised of two processing methods and two processing tools, which can be used at any time. The software structure can be seen in Fig. 1. Hapan allows many actions, Zoom In, Zoom Out, Open Images or Projects, Save Images or Projects, Helps and Captures Images directly from the scanner. Figure 2 shows the application interface in which the user can appreciate the different images generated by the software.

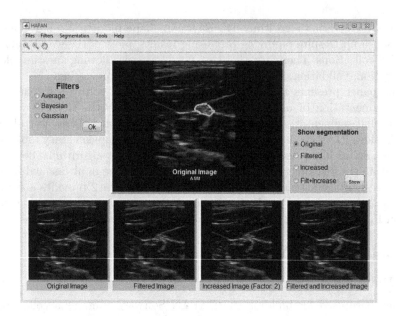

Fig. 2. Software interface for processing ultrasonic images.

2.3   Methodologies

Two different methodologies were used in the segmentation of the peripheral nerve: Classical Techniques and Appearance and Shape Models.

Classical Techniques. This methodology is based on the classical techniques of digital image processing, such as identifying edges, thresholding, dilation, erosion, opening, and closing areas. These techniques are used iteratively to identify the nerve structure in the ultrasound image.

Appearance and Shape Models. It is a semiautomatic method, which can be trained to learn the different forms of nerve structures that can be found in the database. This model requires, as an initial step, that the user locates an ellipsoidal contour on the region containing the nerve structure. Then, the algorithm adjust the contour to the nerve structure in the image. One of the drawbacks of this method is that it requires that the initial region (the ellipsoidal contour placed by the user) contains the nerve structure. If this constraint is not fulfilled, the algorithm would perform the segmentation to a different region of the image.

2.4   Tools

The HAPAN's tools are used to improve the quality of the image and therefore to obtain a more accurate segmentation of the nerve structure. The user is allowed to change the parameters of these tools.

Image Filtering. When an echography is acquired by the scanner, the image is commonly corrupted either by Speckle noise, random variations in intensity, poor contrast or illumination variations as a result of changes in gain or depth of the scanner. The segmentation algorithms used in HAPAN were designed to tackle these effects to some extent. In some cases, these algorithms do not accomplish this goal; however, in those cases an improved segmentation is possible by using image filtering techniques. HAPAN includes the following filters:

- Average filter: This is a two dimensional digital filter which averages the neighborhood of pixels. The default size for this filter is 3×3 pixels.
- Gaussian: A Gaussian low pass digital filter with a symmetric rotation, with standard deviation sigma. The default size of this filter is 3×3 pixels and the default sigma's value is 0,5.
- Bayesian: A Bayesian framework is used to adapt the Non Local (NL) means filter for removing speckle noise in ultrasound images. This algorithm introduces the Pearson distance as a relevant measure for region comparison [20].

Super-Resolution. This tool allows to create a new image, based on the original, performing an increase of the resolution by an user-adjustable factor (2, 3, 4, and so on). The objective is to generate a high-resolution image from a single low-resolution image without any external training set. It uses a framework for both magnification and de-blurring using only the original low-resolution image and its blurred version. In this method, each pixel is predicted by its neighbors through a Gaussian process regression [17].

3   Experimental Results and Discussion

3.1   System Efficiency

The leftmost columns in Table 1 shows the results of the performance of the methodologies implemented in HAPAN in terms of computational consumption (CC) for each of the techniques used during the segmentation process. The test was performed on a Intel Core i3 with 4 GB RAM. The nomenclature used in Table 1 is **CT:** Classical Techniques, **ASM:** Appearance and Shape Models, **AF:** Average Filter, **BF:** Bayesian Filter, **GF:** Gaussian Filter, **IR:** Increased Resolution.

The results show that the computational consumption is considerably low when the user do not use any of the additional tools provided by the software. The results also show that the most efficient methodology (in terms of CC) are the classical techniques. This efficiency is due basically to the fact that its processes and algorithms have a low computational cost. The tools with the lowest cost (in terms of time) are IR[1] and BF.

---

[1] The average execution time of the algorithm with a $\times 2$ factor is about one hour.

3.2   Validation

This software has been tested using a database composed of ultrasound images. These images have been manually labeled by an anesthesiologist. The performance of the system was evaluated using two parameters: dice similarity coefficient and F1 score. These metrics have been computed for measuring the efficiency of both segmentation methods and the additional software tools.

Dice Similarity Coefficient (DSC). DSC is a commonly used metric for evaluating the accuracy of automated or semi-automated segmentation methods. In this work, DSC has been used as a statistical validation metric to evaluate the similarity between two samples (the labels created by the anesthesiologist and the labels provided by HAPAN).

F1 Score. F1 score is a measure of a test's accuracy. It considers both the precision (the number of true positive results divided by the number of all positive results) and the recall (the number of true positive results divided by the number of true positive plus false negative results) of the test. The F1 score can be interpreted as a weighted average of the precision and recall, where an F1 score reaches its best value at 1 and worst at 0.

3.3   Practical Results and Discussion

This section presents the results obtained by HAPAN in the segmentation of the ultrasound images of the database. Figure 3 shows an example of an ASM segmentation process by using an image of a Median nerve. Figure 3(a) shows the original image without segmentation. Figure 3(b) presents the original image after the segmentation process. Figure 3(c) shows the image after both filtering and segmentation processes. Figure 3(d) illustrates the segmented image by taking as input an increased resolution version of the original image. Figure 3(e) shows the image obtained by increasing the resolution, filtering and applying the segmentation process on the original image.

The rightmost columns in Table 1 show the global performance results of the HAPAN software. These results were obtained by processing all the ultrasound images of the database. Both methodologies and all the additional tools were evaluated. Remind that the database was previously described in Sect. 2.1.

Results in Table 1 show that the best segmentation performance, using DSC, can be obtained in the Cubital nerve $(0{,}672 \pm 0{,}04)$. This result is achieved using a Bayesian filter in the preprocessing stage and the ASM methodology for the segmentation process. However, it must be noticed that this performance is not statistically significant when compared to the same procedure in the Median nerve $(0{,}604 \pm 0{,}047)$.

When using the F1 score for comparing the effectiveness of the methodologies, results show that the best performance is achieved in the Median nerve $(0{,}573 \pm 0{,}042)$ by means of an Average filter and Classical techniques. This result improves significantly the performance obtained in the Cubital nerve by the same techniques.

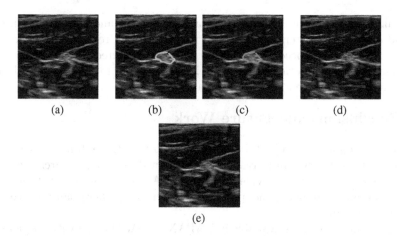

(a)   (b)   (c)   (d)

(e)

Fig. 3. Example of a practical result obtained with HAPAN. (a) Original image. (b) Original image segmented using ASM. (c) Filtered image and segmented using ASM. (d) Increased resolution (×2 factor) and segmented image using ASM. (e) Increased resolution (×2 factor), filtered and segmented image using ASM.

Table 1. Global performance results of the HAPAN software

Process	Median nerve Time (s)	Cubital nerve Time (s)	Median nerve Dice	F1 score	Cubital nerve Dice	F1 score
CT	$0,330 \pm 0,003$	$0,328 \pm 0,007$	$0,647 \pm 0,041$	$0,567 \pm 0,041$	$0,519 \pm 0,063$	$0,437 \pm 0,065$
CT+AF	$0,336 \pm 0,003$	$0,380 \pm 0,019$	$\mathbf{0,663 \pm 0,041}$	$\mathbf{0,573 \pm 0,042}$	$0,532 \pm 0,062$	$0,452 \pm 0,064$
CT+BF	$14,88 \pm 0,234$	$15,36 \pm 0,521$	$0,653 \pm 0,041$	$0,571 \pm 0,041$	$0,565 \pm 0,053$	$0,487 \pm 0,060$
CT+GF	$0,364 \pm 0,009$	$0,368 \pm 0,015$	$0,653 \pm 0,041$	$0,570 \pm 0,041$	$0,539 \pm 0,059$	$0,455 \pm 0,062$
CT+IR	$0,521 \pm 0,022$	$0,973 \pm 0,035$	$0,577 \pm 0,030$	$0,447 \pm 0,034$	$0,479 \pm 0,073$	$0,425 \pm 0,055$
CT+AF+IR	$0,514 \pm 0,021$	$0,945 \pm 0,032$	$0,581 \pm 0,031$	$0,450 \pm 0,035$	$0,491 \pm 0,070$	$0,439 \pm 0,052$
CT+BF+IR	$26,51 \pm 1,131$	$44,69 \pm 1,934$	$0,579 \pm 0,030$	$0,447 \pm 0,034$	$0,493 \pm 0,071$	$0,426 \pm 0,055$
CT+GF+IR	$0,640 \pm 0,038$	$0,895 \pm 0,026$	$0,578 \pm 0,031$	$0,447 \pm 0,034$	$0,478 \pm 0,073$	$0,426 \pm 0,055$
ASM	$3,174 \pm 0,035$	$4,355 \pm 0,182$	$0,628 \pm 0,045$	$0,496 \pm 0,046$	$0,661 \pm 0,042$	$0,542 \pm 0,042$
ASM+AF	$3,345 \pm 0,047$	$4,277 \pm 0,120$	$0,628 \pm 0,045$	$0,520 \pm 0,043$	$0,646 \pm 0,037$	$\mathbf{0,555 \pm 0,044}$
ASM+BF	$3,530 \pm 0,057$	$4,265 \pm 0,053$	$0,604 \pm 0,047$	$0,509 \pm 0,044$	$\mathbf{0,672 \pm 0,040}$	$0,548 \pm 0,041$
ASM+GF	$3,631 \pm 0,067$	$4,289 \pm 0,031$	$0,619 \pm 0,044$	$0,502 \pm 0,043$	$0,668 \pm 0,040$	$0,554 \pm 0,043$
ASM+IR	$4,608 \pm 0,121$	$5,533 \pm 0,126$	$0,649 \pm 0,031$	$0,536 \pm 0,040$	$0,604 \pm 0,022$	$0,521 \pm 0,025$
ASM+AF+IR	$4,838 \pm 0,137$	$5,813 \pm 0,057$	$0,662 \pm 0,025$	$0,561 \pm 0,038$	$0,597 \pm 0,023$	$0,524 \pm 0,032$
ASM+BF+IR	$30,904 \pm 1,20$	$43,640 \pm 1,370$	$0,630 \pm 0,041$	$0,565 \pm 0,040$	$0,585 \pm 0,027$	$0,505 \pm 0,025$
ASM+GF+IR	$5,415 \pm 0,187$	$5,070 \pm 0,070$	$0,636 \pm 0,027$	$0,561 \pm 0,038$	$0,603 \pm 0,023$	$0,521 \pm 0,028$

Overall results show higher rates for the Median nerve. This may be a consequence of a more uniform anatomic structure of the Median nerve along the arm. Also, between the Cubital nerve and skin exist different anatomical structures that may degenerate the image capture.

Better results can be obtained with the combination of IR images and ASM rather than IR combined with Classical techniques. In contrast to ASM, CT is not fully compatible with IR. Take into account that IR tool increases image resolution and therefore changes its parameters. This may be a drawback since

CT makes use of morphological operations with masks and cuts, which in turn depend on the parameters of the image (i.e. depth and resolution). Thereby, a manual readjustment becomes necessary in order to correct this problem. Nevertheless, it must be noticed that ASM is a supervised method while CT does not require user intervention, it is fully automatic.

4   Conclusions and Future Work

This work presents the HAPAN software supporting the automatic segmentation of peripheral nerves in ultrasound images for developing research, and clinical procedures. The results evidence that HAPAN as an interactive tool allows medical specialists to save time, providing a safer and higher quality process for patient healthcare.

Among the algorithms available in HAPAN, the ASM along with IR yield the best segmentation results thanks to including both supervised and unsupervised information. Particularly, ASM drastically reduces the search area of the nerve structure, thus avoiding undesired structures to appear in the ultrasound image.

As a future work, we plan to develop GPU algorithms to achieve real-time processing. Besides, we will extend the coverage of the database by including additional nerve structures.

Acknowledgments. This work was developed for the research project 111074455958 funded by Colciencias. The authors also acknowledge the electrical engineering master program of Universidad Tecnologica de Pereira for supporting the research project development.

References

1. Chen, S.A., Ong, C.S., Hibino, N., Baschat, A.A., Garcia, J.R., Miller, J.L.: 3D printing of fetal heart using 3D ultrasound imaging data. Ultrasound Obstet. Gynecol. **52**(6), 808–809 (2018)
2. Daoud, M.I., Atallah, A.A., Awwad, F., Al-Najjar, M., Alazrai, R.: Automatic superpixel-based segmentation method for breast ultrasound images. Expert Syst. Appl. **121**, 78–96 (2019)
3. García, H.F., Giraldo, J.J., Álvarez, M.A., Orozco, Á.A., Salazar, D.: Peripheral nerve segmentation using speckle removal and bayesian shape models. In: Paredes, R., Cardoso, J.S., Pardo, X.M. (eds.) IbPRIA 2015. LNCS, vol. 9117, pp. 387–394. Springer, Cham (2015). https://doi.org/10.1007/978-3-319-19390-8_44
4. Giraldo, J.J., Álvarez, M.A., Orozco, Á.A.: Peripheral nerve segmentation using nonparametric Bayesian hierarchical clustering. In: 2015 37th Annual International Conference of the IEEE Engineering in Medicine and Biology Society (EMBC), pp. 3101–3104. IEEE (2015)
5. González, J.G., Álvarez, M.A., Orozco, Á.A.: Automatic segmentation of nerve structures in ultrasound images using graph cuts and Gaussian processes. In: 2015 37th Annual International Conference of the IEEE Engineering in Medicine and Biology Society (EMBC), pp. 3089–3092. IEEE (2015)
6. González, J.G., Álvarez, M.A., Orozco, Á.A.: Peripheral nerves segmentation in ultrasound images using non-linear wavelets and Gaussian processes. In: Paredes, R., Cardoso, J.S., Pardo, X.M. (eds.) IbPRIA 2015. LNCS, vol. 9117, pp. 603–611. Springer, Cham (2015). https://doi.org/10.1007/978-3-319-19390-8_68

7. Illanes, A., Esmaeili, N., Poudel, P., Balakrishnan, S., Friebe, M.: Parametrical modelling for texture characterizationa novel approach applied to ultrasound thyroid segmentation. PloS One **14**(1), e0211215 (2019)
8. Kim, B., Kim, K.C., Park, Y., Kwon, J.Y., Jang, J., Seo, J.K.: Machine-learning-based automatic identification of fetal abdominal circumference from ultrasound images. Physiol. Meas. **39**(10), 105007 (2018)
9. Liu, C., Liu, W., Xing, W.: A weighted edge-based level set method based on multi-local statistical information for noisy image segmentation. J. Vis. Commun. Image Represent. **59**, 89–107 (2019)
10. Ma, L., Kiyomatsu, H., Nakagawa, K., Wang, J., Kobayashi, E., Sakuma, I.: Accurate vessel segmentation in ultrasound images using a local-phase-based snake. Biomed. Sig. Process. Control **43**, 236–243 (2018)
11. Meiburger, K.M., Acharya, U.R., Molinari, F.: Automated localization and segmentation techniques for B-mode ultrasound images: a review. Comput. Biol. Med. **92**, 210–235 (2018)
12. Molinari, F., Caresio, C., Acharya, U.R., Mookiah, M.R.K., Minetto, M.A.: Advances in quantitative muscle ultrasonography using texture analysis of ultrasound images. Ultrasound Med. Biol. **41**(9), 2520–2532 (2015)
13. Moradi, M., Mahdavi, S.S., Guerrero, J., Rohling, R., Salcudean, S.E.: Ultrasound segmentation based on statistical unit-root test of B-scan radial intensity profiles. In: CMBES Proceedings, vol. 33, no. 1 (2018)
14. Nieuwveld, D., Mojica, V., Herrera, A., Pomés, J., Prats, A., Sala-Blanch, X.: Medial approach of ultrasound-guided costoclavicular plexus block and its effects on regional perfussion. Rev. Española de Anestesiología y Reanimación (Engl. Ed.) **64**(4), 198–205 (2017)
15. Smistad, E., Løvstakken, L.: Vessel detection in ultrasound images using deep convolutional neural networks. In: Carneiro, G., et al. (eds.) LABELS/DLMIA -2016. LNCS, vol. 10008, pp. 30–38. Springer, Cham (2016). https://doi.org/10.1007/978-3-319-46976-8_4
16. Srivastava, A., Bhateja, V., Gupta, A., Gupta, A.: Non-local mean filter for suppression of speckle noise in ultrasound images. In: Satapathy, S.C., Bhateja, V., Das, S. (eds.) Smart Intelligent Computing and Applications. SIST, vol. 105, pp. 225–232. Springer, Singapore (2019). https://doi.org/10.1007/978-981-13-1927-3_23
17. Wang, H., Gao, X., Zhang, K., Li, J.: Single-image super-resolution using active-sampling Gaussian process regression. IEEE Trans. Image Process. **25**(2), 935–948 (2016)
18. Wang, W., Li, J., Jiang, Y., Xing, Y., Xu, X.: An automatic energy-based region growing method for ultrasound image segmentation. In: 2015 IEEE International Conference on Image Processing (ICIP), pp. 1553–1557. IEEE (2015)
19. Wieclawek, W., Rudzki, M., Wijata, A., Galinska, M.: Preliminary development of an automatic breast tumour segmentation algorithm from ultrasound volumetric images. In: Pietka, E., Badura, P., Kawa, J., Wieclawek, W. (eds.) ITIB 2018. AISC, vol. 762, pp. 77–88. Springer, Cham (2019). https://doi.org/10.1007/978-3-319-91211-0_7
20. Zhou, Y., Zang, H., Xu, S., He, H., Lu, J., Fang, H.: An iterative speckle filtering algorithm for ultrasound images based on Bayesian nonlocal means filter model. Biomed. Sig. Process. Control **48**, 104–117 (2019)

Group Differences in Time-Frequency Relevant Patterns for User-Independent BCI Applications

L. F. Velasquez-Martinez[1]([✉]), F. Y. Zapata-Castaño[1], J. I. Padilla-Buritica[1,2],
José Manuel Ferrández Vicente[2], and G. Castellanos-Dominguez[1]

[1] Signal Processing and Recognition Group,
Universidad Nacional de Colombia, Manizales, Colombia
lfvelasquezm@unal.edu.co
[2] Universidad Politécnica de Cartagena, Cartagena, Spain

Abstract. We present a comparison of two known methodologies for group analysis in EEG signals, which are the analysis by Group ICA on synchronization and desynchronization ERS/ERD, and brain connectivity analysis by measuring wPLI, both analyzes based on the brain synchronization information. For comparison, we have taken into account different frequency bands related to sensorimotor stimuli and time segmentation in order to overcome the nonstationary of the EEG signal. In addition, we have used a threshold algorithm to reduce the dimension of the connectivity matrix, conserving the connections that are most important for both methodologies. The results obtained from the BCI competition IV-2a database show that the variable can be measured between two different measurement spaces, using the Euclidean distance, conserving spatial zones with more meaningful physiological interpretation.

Keywords: Event-related Synchronization/Desynchronization ·
Functional connectivity · Group analysis · wPLI

1 Introduction

The brain is a vastly complex network of interconnected elements, having different brain regions interacting in the resting state as well as in response to a given stimulus or task by synchronization of oscillatory activities. In this regard, brain response could be useful in the development of Media and Information literacy applications. Functional connectivity is defined as the temporal correlation of neural activity between brain regions, measured by functional MRI, magneto or electroencephalography (MEG/EEG) signals that are very convenient because of their low cost and high temporal resolution.

Among the widely used applications, computer-based technologies are employed to communicate the brain with external devices. In particular, Motor Imagery (MI) is a mental process by which an individual rehearses or simulates

J. M. Ferrández Vicente et al. (Eds.): IWINAC 2019, LNCS 11486, pp. 138–145, 2019.
https://doi.org/10.1007/978-3-030-19591-5_15

some actions without involving muscle activities [2]. This cognitive neuroscience paradigm operates the signals measured from the sensorimotor cortex regions, which are the most directly linked to the motor output pathway in the brain, assuming that the imagination of movement execution attenuates the brain sensorimotor rhythms (SMRs).

Here, with the aim of enhancing the interpretation of MI tasks, we develop a group-level comparison between two different methods to analyze the synchronization, ss a result, the use of thresholding allows performing a reduced set of relevant brain connections, but with enough confidence to construct a meaningful explanation in time and frequency of the brain activity [3, 4].

Although further adaptations are to be performed to optimally address the sources of inter-subject and inter-trial variance commonly found in EEG recordings, the presented group-level approach can be considered valid and promising to infer the latent structure of multi-subject datasets [5].

2   Materials

2.1   EEG Database and Preprocessing

We carry out experimental validation using the Dataset 2a from the BCI Competition IV, publicly available at[1], holding EEG signals recorded from nine subjects and measured with a 22-channels montage. All signals are sampled at $F_s = 250$ Hz and bandpass-filtered between 0.5 and 100 Hz. The dataset holds a trial set of four MI tasks, i.e., left hand, right hand, both feet, and tongue. The recordings were carried out in six runs separated by short breaks. Each run contained $N = 48$ trials lasting of 7 s and distributed. A short beep indicated the trial beginning followed by a fixation cross that appeared on the black screen within the first 2 s. Further, as the cue, an arrow (pointing to the left, right, up or down) appeared during 1.25 s, indicating the each MI task to imagine: left hand, right hand, both feet or tongue movement, respectively. In the following time interval, ranging from 3.25 to 6 s, each subject performed the demanded MI task while the cross re-appeared. In our analysis, a bi-class task (left and right hand) set is used, from which artifacts had been removed previously.

As a result, we have a set of N raw EEG data trials $\mathcal{X} = \{X_n : r = 1, \ldots, N \in \mathbb{N}\}$ together with the respective class label set $\mathcal{L} = \{l_n\}$, with $l_r \in \{l, l'\}$, where $X_n \in \mathbb{R}^{C \times T}$ is n-th EEG trial, with $C \in \mathbb{N}$ channels and $T \in \mathbb{N}$ time samples. Over this raw data set, each raw EEG channel is band-pass filtered using 17 five-order overlapped bandpass Butterworth filters within the range 4 Hz to 40 Hz. Each filter bandwidth is adjusted to 4 Hz with overlapping rate at 2 Hz as suggested in [6].

2.2   Subject-Level Feature Extraction

At this stage, we compare the following two feature extraction methods:

---

[1] www.bbci.de/competition/iv/.

Event-Related Desynchronization/Synchronization. This change of the ongoing EEG is a somatotopical organized control mechanism that can be generated intentionally by mental imagery and is frequency band specific. Using each band-pass filtered event-related trial $\boldsymbol{X}_r^c$, the ERD/S estimation is performed by squaring of samples and averaging over EEG trials, computing the variational percentage (decrease or increase) in EEG signal power regarding a reference period, at specific frequency band f and sample t [7]:

$$\zeta_{ft} = (\xi_{ft} - \bar{\xi}_f)/\bar{\xi}_{f\,[\%]}, \quad t \in T \tag{1}$$

where $\xi_{ft} = \mathbb{E}\left\{|x_t^2|_{rf} \in \boldsymbol{x}_{rf} : \forall r\right\}$ is the power scatter averaged across the trial set and $\bar{\xi}_f = \mathbb{E}\left\{\xi_{ft} : \forall t \in \tau_R\right\}$ is the trial power scatter averaged on the reference interval τ_R.

Functional Connectivity Estimation. Weighted Phase Locking Index (wPLI) is commonly used for estimation of functional connectivity between two EEG channels, due to its nonparametric nature and easy implementation [1]. wPLI quantifies the asymmetry of phase difference distribution between two specific channels c, c' (with $\forall c, c' \in C, c \neq c'$), being defined within the recording time span $T \in \mathbb{R}^+$. Initially, the instantaneous phase difference $\Delta\Phi_{ft}(; c, c') \in \mathbb{R}[0, \pi]$ is the angle computed through the continuous wavelet transform coefficients $W_{ft}(;) \in \mathbb{R}^+$,

$$\Delta\Phi_{ft}(n; c, c') = \frac{W_{ft}(n; c)W_{ft}(n; c')}{|W_{ft}(n; c)||W_{ft}(n; c')|}, \, t \in T, \tag{2}$$

Thus, the pair-wise connectivity estimation $y_{ft}^s(c, c')$ for subject is computed as,

$$y_{f,\tau}^s(c, c'), = \frac{\left|\mathbb{E}\left\{|(\Delta\Phi_{f\tau}(n; c, c'))|\,\mathrm{sgn}\left(\Delta\Phi_{f\tau}(n; c, c')\right) : \forall n\right\}\right|}{\mathbb{E}\left\{|(\Delta\Phi_{f\tau}(n; c, c'))| : \forall n\right\}} \tag{3}$$

where notations sgn and $\mathbb{E}\left\{\cdot : \forall n\right\}$ stand for *sign* function and averaging operator over n, respectively. The metric is normalized to highlight the connectivity patterns generated by each induced stimulus, being each $y_{f\tau}^s(c, c')$ mean-value averaged over the trial set $\{n \in N\}$ and on a given baseline interval [8]. Accordingly, $\hat{y}_{f\tau}(c, c') = \mathbb{E}_s\left\{y_{f\tau}^s(c, c')\right\}$ contains the pair-wise connectivity measures of each subject group.

2.3   Group Independent Components Analysis

With the aim of inferring about the source configuration at the group-level, all components constantly expressed across subjects can be estimated using a single ICA decomposition, which is performed on aggregate data sets built from EEG recordings of multiple subjects. Specifically, provided the computed ERD/S of the k-th subject $\boldsymbol{Z}^k \in \mathbb{R}^{c \times T}$, the aggregate data set $\boldsymbol{Y} \in \mathbb{R}^{c \times (T * N_s)}$ is given by the temporal concatenation $\boldsymbol{Y} = [\boldsymbol{y}_1, ..., \boldsymbol{y}_k, ..., \boldsymbol{y}_{N_s}]$, with $k \in N_s$, being N_s the total number of subjects included in the analysis. Furthermore, we apply centering and whitening via principal component analysis (PCA) to $\boldsymbol{Y}$, yielding the principal components $\boldsymbol{R}^\top \boldsymbol{Y}$, where $\boldsymbol{R}$ is the orthonormal transformation matrix obtained from PCA. Applying the basic ICA model to the preprocessed data leads to $\boldsymbol{R}^\top \boldsymbol{Y} = \boldsymbol{A}\boldsymbol{S}$ where $\boldsymbol{S} = [\boldsymbol{s}_1, \ldots, \boldsymbol{s}_k, \ldots, \boldsymbol{s}_{N_s}]$ is the matrix holding the temporally concatenated component time-courses of N_s subjects [3].

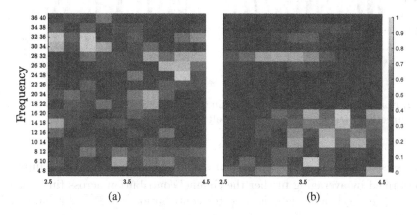

Fig. 1. Differences between classes from the estimated group patterns based on both methods Group-ICA (a) and connectivity (b).

3   Experimental Set-Up and Results

To measure the group differences in time-frequency relevant pattern, we perform a piecewise time segmentation. In each case of contrasting feature extraction, EEG and ERS/D, we split the whole time recording span (ranging from 2.5–4.5 s) into 10 segments, each one lasting 0.2 s. The segment length is adjusted, considering that a short segment leads to bias and variance at estimation level, while a long segment imposes a high computational load and restrain implementation on real-time system operation [9]. The subject analysis is carried out in the supervised mode, extracting separately the feature set for each class.

In the case of ERD/S, to estimate the variational percentage (decrease or increase) in EEG signal power regarding a reference period T_R, we fix $T_R = [0.5 - 1.5]$ s as in [10]. Accordingly, we build a matrix by class for each frequency band and time segment $\hat{\boldsymbol{Z}}_{f\tau} \in \mathbb{R}^{22 \times 450}$ that holds the concatenated ERD/S response for all subjects. Afterward, ICA is applied by mean of the fastICA algorithm using a nonlinear tangent hyperbolic function to obtain $\hat{\boldsymbol{Y}}_{f\tau}^{g-ica} \in \mathbb{R}^{22 \times 22}$ with columns holding the channel weights of the assessed independent components by class. In the case of functional connectivity extraction, we obtain a matrix $\hat{\boldsymbol{Y}}_{f,\tau}^{wpli} \in \mathbb{R}^{22 \times 22}$ by mean of wPLI measure to encode the estimated pairwise changes in phase synchronization of the subject group.

As a result, the feature extraction stage provides a total of 170 matrices $\hat{\boldsymbol{Y}}_{f,\tau}$ by each class and estimated for all frequencies and time partitions. For the purpose of comparison, the contribution of across the channel set, at values τ and

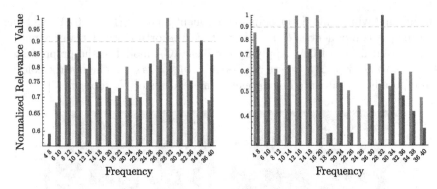

Fig. 2. Normalized frequency relevance value obtained based on both Group-ICA (left) and connectivity (right). – right class, – left class.

f, is assessed by $\boldsymbol{\rho}_{f,\tau} = \mathbb{E}_c\left\{\hat{\boldsymbol{Y}}_{f,\tau}\right\}$, being $\boldsymbol{\rho}_{f,\tau} \in \mathbb{R}^{22}$. However, the comparison is performed by averaging further the channel contribution across time, that is, $\eta_f = \mathbb{E}_\tau\left\{\|\boldsymbol{\rho}_{f,\tau}\|_2\right\}$, and yielding a vector contribution $\boldsymbol{\eta} \in \mathbb{R}^{17}$. $\|\cdot\|_2$ stands for ℓ_2−norm.

Further, using the conventional Euclidean distance, we assess the difference of contribution vectors between classes as seen in Fig. 1 that shows the normalized distances values. Besides, the marginal estimates of contribution by frequency are presented in Fig. 2, i.e., the normalized relevance values in terms of the frequencies that show more differences between time by class.

In this work, we consider as a relevant frequency the value overcoming 0.9. Accordingly, Figs. 3 and 4 exhibits the normalized time-frequency relevance values obtained for all channels by class for the selected relevant frequencies. Bright color designates high relevance values.

4   Discussion and Concluding Remarks

The estimation of cerebral synchronization and desynchronization allows highlighting the information contained in the domains of time and frequency. According to Fig. 1(a), we observe spurious differences for all segments and frequency bands with values lower than 0.7. However, the frequency bands from [24–28] Hz to [32–36] Hz shows high differences values in different time segments. Some lower differences are shown for the frequency bands [6–10] Hz and [14–18] Hz at different time segments. In the case of Fig. 1(b), we see a marked difference in the frequency [28–32] Hz the beginning of MI interval. However, we observe spurious differences for the end of MI period at frequencies belonging to μ band. However, we observe spurious differences for the end of MI period at frequencies belonging to μ band.

The contributions by frequency in Sect. 3, Group-ICA presents as the higher frequencies contributions in μ and β bands being the highest contributor the frequency band [8–12] Hz and [28–32] Hz, frequencies that are normally related

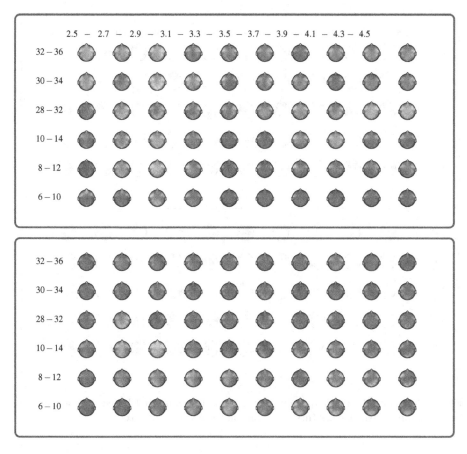

Fig. 3. Normalized time-frequency relevance values obtained by channel. Right class (first box) and left class (second box).

to MI tasks [10,11]. On the other hand, Sect. 3 shows the highest frequencies contributors in [16–20] Hz and [28–32] Hz bands.

Figures 3 and 4 show the change of channels contribution through the segment windows. For both classes, in Fig. 3 the highest channel contributions are at the MI period beginning. Nevertheless, the analysis finds highest channel contribution values in [24–36] Hz frequency band at the end of the trial. Regarding to Fig. 4, the highest contribution values appears at the frequency band [28–32] Hz.

In order to guarantee the interpretability in imagery motor tasks, the group analysis was carried out on brain synchronization information. Due to each subject has its own brain dynamics is necessary to include a group model that allows estimating similar patterns for all subjects. In this work, we used Group ICA and a connectivity analysis to perform this task. Group ICA is widely known and used to analyze tasks of multiple subjects through EEG. For both methods differents partens were found in the bands which are part of the rhythms μ and

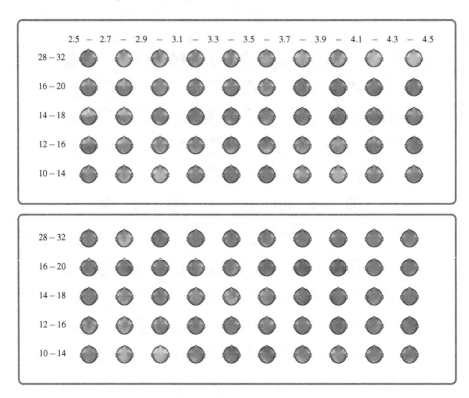

Fig. 4. Normalized time-frequency relevance values computed based on connectivity for all channels. Right class (first box) and left class (second box).

β frequencies which are known as sensorimotor rhythms. The obtained results on a concrete attention task show that the developed relevant connectivity analysis on group-level synchronization, improve the interpretation, although the proposed comparison for connectivity analysis depends on the time interval. As future work, we intend to validate EEG data with more complicated dynamics. To overcome more effectively nonstationarities of neural responses and structural homogeneity of latent processes across the sample, we plan to introduce an elaborate group-level strategy, including more complex approaches for graph analysis as well as enhanced relevance metrics.

Acknowledgements. This work is supported by the project Programa de reconstrucción del tejido social en zonas de pos-conflicto en Colombia del proyecto Fortalecimiento docente desde la alfabetización mediática Informacional y la CTel, como estrategia didáctico-pedagógica y soporte para la recuperación de la confianza del tejido social afectado por el conflicto. Código SIGP 58950 Financiado por Fondo Nacional de Financiamiento para la Ciencia, la Tecnología y la Innovación, Fondo Francisco José de Caldas con contrato No 213-2018 con Código 58960.

References

1. Hardmeier, M., Hatz, F., Bousleiman, H., Schindler, C., Stam, C.J., Fuhr, P.: Reproducibility of functional connectivity and graph measures based on the phase lag index (PLI) and weighted phase lag index (wPLI) derived from high resolution EEG. PloS One **9**(10), e108648 (2014)
2. Allison, B.Z., Wolpaw, E.W., Wolpaw, J.R.: Brain-computer interface systems: progress and prospects. Expert Rev. Med. Dev. **4**(4), 463–474 (2007)
3. Huster, R., Plis, S.M., Calhoun, V.D.: Group-level component analyses of EEG: validation and evaluation. Front. Neurosci. **9**, 254 (2015)
4. Allen, E., Damaraju, E., Eichele, T., Wu, L., Calhoun, V.D.: EEG signatures of dynamic functional network connectivity states. Brain Topogr. **31**(1), 101–116 (2018)
5. Labounek, R., et al.: Stable scalp EEG spatiospectral patterns across paradigms estimated by group ICA. Brain Topogr. **31**(1), 76–89 (2018)
6. Zhang, Y., Zhou, G., Jin, J., Wang, X., Cichocki, A.: Optimizing spatial patterns with sparse filter bands for motor-imagery based brain-computer interface. J. Neurosci. Methods **255**, 85–91 (2015)
7. Dai, S., Wei, Q.: Electrode channel selection based on backtracking search optimization in motor imagery brain-computer interfaces. J. Integr. Neurosci. **16**(3), 241–254 (2017)
8. Aviyente, S., Tootell, A., Bernat, E.M.: Time-frequency phase-synchrony approaches with ERPs. Int. J. Psychophysiol. **111**, 88–97 (2017)
9. Terrien, J., Germain, G., Marque, C., Karlsson, B.: Bivariate piecewise stationary segmentation; improved pre-treatment for synchronization measures used on non-stationary biological signals. Med. Eng. Phys. **35**(8), 1188–1196 (2013)
10. Reinhold Scherer, C.V.: Motor imagery based brain-computer interfaces, chap. 8, pp. 171 – 195 (2018)
11. Wolpaw, J.R., Birbaumer, N., McFarland, D.J., Pfurtscheller, G., Vaughan, T.M.: Brain-computer interfaces for communication and control. Clin. Neurophysiol. **113**(6), 767–791 (2002)

Affective Computing

Assessing an Application of Spontaneous Stressed Speech - Emotions Portal

Daniel Palacios-Alonso[1,2(✉)] ⓘ, Carlos Lázaro-Carrascosa[1,2] ⓘ,
Agustín López-Arribas[1] ⓘ, Guillermo Meléndez-Morales[1] ⓘ,
Andrés Gómez-Rodellar[2] ⓘ, Andrés Loro-Álavez[4] ⓘ, Victor Nieto-Lluis[2] ⓘ,
Victoria Rodellar-Biarge[2] ⓘ, Athanasios Tsanas[3] ⓘ, and Pedro Gómez-Vilda[2] ⓘ

[1] Escuela Técnica Superior de Ingeniería Informática - Universidad Rey Juan Carlos,
Campus de Móstoles, Tulipán, s/n, 28933 Móstoles, Madrid, Spain
daniel.palacios@urjc.es
[2] Neuromorphic Speech Processing Lab, Center for Biomedical Technology,
Universidad Politécnica de Madrid, Campus de Montegancedo,
28223 Pozuelo de Alarcón, Madrid, Spain
[3] Usher Institute of Population Health Sciences and Informatics,
University of Edinburgh, Edinburgh, UK
[4] Hermosilla 60 Legal Counselors, Hermosilla 60, 28001 Madrid, Spain

Abstract. Detecting and identifying emotions expressed in speech signals is a very complex task that generally requires processing a large sample size to extract intricate details and match the diversity of human expression in speech. There is not an emotional dataset commonly accepted as a standard test bench to evaluate the performance of the supervised machine learning algorithms when presented with extracted speech characteristics. This work proposes a generic platform to capture and validate emotional speech. The aim of the platform is collaborative-crowdsourcing and it can be used for any language (currently, it is available in four languages such as Spanish, English, German and French). As an example, a module for elicitation of stress in speech through a set of online interviews and other module for labeling recorded speech have been developed. This study is envisaged as the beginning of an effort to establish a large, cost-free standard speech corpus to assess emotions across multiple languages.

Keywords: Characterizing stress · Data acquisition ·
Stress behavior in human-computer interaction ·
Cooperative framework · Emotional stress

1 Introduction

Nowadays, multimedia show machines, robots and other interactive agents endowed with an unusual intelligence. An example of that is the film, "Her" [7], where the main character falls in love with a new generation of a talking operative system, which is designed to act, feel and evolve as a human being. Another

© Springer Nature Switzerland AG 2019
J. M. Ferrández Vicente et al. (Eds.): IWINAC 2019, LNCS 11486, pp. 149–160, 2019.
https://doi.org/10.1007/978-3-030-19591-5_16

example is "Robot and Frank" [12]. Frank is an old man with a serious mental deterioration and the robot is looking after him. The robot is programmed to provide Frank therapeutic care, it fixes his daily routine and helps him to do cognitive enhancing activities. The examples mentioned above are not far from being real nowadays, but a large body of research is being done in order to provide the machines cognitive capabilities and emotional abilities similar to those of humans beings.

This study has two main aims: determining a robust feature set extracted from voice signals to characterize an emotion and identify emotions using classification algorithms [14]. Speech emotion characterization is an arduous task that starts with an enormous work of data acquisition.

Emotion identification is a very complex task because is dependent on culture, language, gender and age of the subject, among other factors. The available literature mentions a few databases and data collections of emotional speech in different languages but in many cases this information is not open to the community and not available for research. There is not an emotional voice data set recognized for the research community as a basic test bench, which impedes progress in this exciting and challenging research field, due to the difficulty in evaluating the quality of new proposals in features for characterization and in the classification algorithms obtained using the same input data.

On the other hand, it should be noted that this type of work is linked to the new regulation of Personal Data Protection Act. These regulations set the general principles according to which biometric data is considered amongst the "special categories of personal data", categories that are consequently protected by a more restrictive set of rules than common data, based on the thought that an adequate processing of this type of data depends on the result of a very severe risk analysis [1]. Therefore, researchers need to take into account and work in full alignment with these new regulations towards making data accessible.

The contribution of this work is to promote the idea of establishing a community to collaborate in collecting and analyzing emotional speech data and define a standard corpus in different languages. In this sense, this paper is a first step to propose the design and development of an online collaborative research community for multilingual data acquisition of emotional speech. This paper is organized as follows. In Sect. 2 preliminary research is reviewed. In Sect. 3 Materials and Methods are described. In Sect. 4 results are presented and discussed. Conclusions are drafted in Sect. 5.

2 Previous Works

The study of emotions is a multidisciplinary field that involves neurological, physiological, psychological, sociological and cultural aspects.

Regarding speech, most databases have been recorded by actors simulating emotional discourses and there are very few studies of spontaneous speech [11,15]. The emotions are rated and labeled by a panel of experts or by a voting system. Most of the databases include few speakers and sometimes they are heavily skewed in terms of gender bias [10, 13], whereas in many cases, age is not recorded to be taken into account. It can be noticed that in several publications the data are produced just for a specific study, and not made available to the community. Some databases related to our research work are briefly mentioned next.

Two of the well-known emotional databases for speech are the Danish Emotional Speech Database (DES) [5] in Danish and the Berlin Emotional Speech Database (BES) [4] in German. Regarding stress in speech, the SUSAS database in English (Speech Under Simulated and Actual Stress) is publically accessible and is widely used [6]. It contains a set of 35 aircraft communication words, which are spoken spontaneously by aircraft pilots during a flight, and also contains other samples of non-spontaneous speech. Another stress database is ATCOSIM - Air Traffic Control Simulation Speech. It consists of ten hours of speech data, which were recorded during ATC real-time simulations. The utterances are in English and pronounced by ten non-native speakers. The data are not categorized into emotional states and is freely available. Besides, it includes orthographic transcriptions and additional information on speakers and recording sessions. The corpus is provided by Graz University of Technology (TUG) and Eurocontrol Experimental Centre (EEC) [8].

3 Methods and Materials

3.1 The Framework

The aim of this work is the elaboration of a multilingual cooperative database. The idea is that the database collects stressed voice in different languages, with different accents and origins. These stressed speeches are labeled in a subjective way using a first-past-the-post system. These utterances will be labeled and classified with the state that seems to express (stressed and non-stressed). This framework can be defined as **collaborative, modular** and **unbiased**.

According to Fig. 1, the provided framework is divided into three main stages: *User identification, Voice donation and Speech validation* (it has been highlighted with three distinct colors). At the top of the sketch, an individual using devices with internet connection, is interacting with the framework. The user identification step starts once the user is connected to the framework. It consists of a sign-up process through a web form through which, users provide personal data, as a nickname, native language, country, gender, age and email. This last requirement, email address, is convenient in order to keep contact with users and to give them information about the progress of the project. Once logged in the platform, the user can choose either to donate voice or validate speech. The actions to follow the options mentioned before are explained next.

3.2 Voice Donation

First of all, the platform checks if the current user has donated speech samples before. If the answer is affirmative, the application informs the user that the process cannot be repeated again. However, the user can contribute validating other samples from other users.

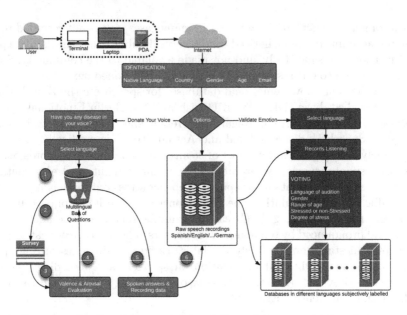

Fig. 1. Overview of online framework for multilingual data acquisition of stress speech (Color figure online)

The method used to elicit stress is based on Arciuli's work [3]. The main idea of this method consists of asking a controversial question about one trending topic. The user is compelled to defend their opinion and the opposite, as well. It is important to highlight that users are differently stressed when producing a statement in agreement with their ideas than when producing a statement contrary to them. This stress is manifested in phonation [9].

The method works as follows: the first survey is composed of ten questions which have been extracted of a multilingual bag of questions, depicted as a bucket in Fig. 1. Next, the survey assesses the arousal and valence about personal opinions as illustrated in Fig. 2(a). Some questions could be "Is the globalization a big problem for society?", "Is the public health system self-sufficient?", "Is it fair that student grant funding has been reduced, whereas football players do not pay taxes?", and other related statements. Afterwards, users have to give their opinion about each topic grading it from 1 to 7 (strongly disagree = 1, strongly agree = 7) and they have also to grade their feelings or confidence about each topic using the same scale (indifference = 1, very strong feelings = 7). These steps are shown from 2 to 4 in Fig. 1.

Once the survey has been answered (see Fig. 2a), the application selects any topic, where the user expressed a strong opinion or valence (agreement or disagreement) and strong feelings or confidence in the arousal. After that, users are asked to defend their self-consistent opinion about one of the topics and to sustain a self-contradictory opinion. Each answer is recorded during 40 s (see Fig. 2b). The complication of this kind of exercise is based on artificial discourse.

The mind must build an intelligible speech intended to convince a fictitious inter-locutor as the time allowed is too short. Moreover, the time is brief to construct a good discourse. In this period of time, a number of stops, long vowels, fillers, and delays are produced.

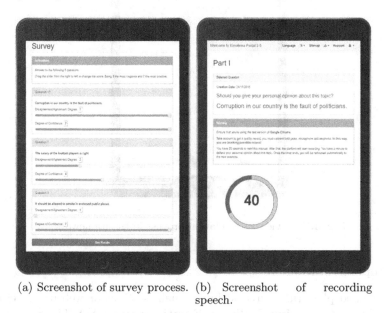

(a) Screenshot of survey process. (b) Screenshot of recording speech.

Fig. 2. Test answer and speech recording interfaces.

3.3   Stress Validation

This procedure is seeking to improve the biased labeling of the raw speech record-ings which are given in step 6 of the previous procedure. The process is divided in two parts. The first one consists of answering six questions on the web form such as language, gender, age range, type of response (agreement, disagreement or politically correct), and whether the person is under stress or not (see Fig. 3). The option politically correct is used to express a feeling accepted by society but it is not donor's real opinion. On the other hand, the second part of the validation test is the same as the first part but in this test, the rater knows the donor's answer given in their speech recording. In this way, the rater may change the previous response.

Finally, the process of labeling is saved in the database, according to the language chosen by rater. The entire process is summarized at the bottom right in Fig. 1. The selected methodology is similar to that used in the manufacturing processes [2]. Using surveys and interviews in order to find customer trends. Some examples of this technique are testing video games, cosmetics and household products. Then, they focus their attention on these interviews and develop or redesign new product strategies and recommendation systems.

Fig. 3. Overview of validation process in the framework.

3.4   Implementation

The developed platform is divided into 4 main sections or web pages: **Home, Speech Data Gathering, Validate Emotions and FAQ**. The first section, *Home*, consists of a scorecard where the user can obtain progress information about the platform as it depicted in Fig. 4. *FAQ*, Frequently Asked Questions, is a help page where the user can find the information related to different procedures. The third and fourth pages are the exercises or procedures which have been explained above.

The application is currently at the test stage. It has not been open yet to the research community. As observed in the introduction section, the main problem at this moment is the Personal Data Protection Act in Spain and the speech recordings custody. Therefore, these recordings and surveys were obtained in offline mode and in a controlled environment. In other words, the validation process has been carried out with a private Intranet server and the assessing process was undertaken by five raters, members of the research group.

From the analysis of the first results, it was made evident that some questions were controversial. Some of them were: "Men at work and women at home?", "Better salary for men, because they are better than women?". The classical questions related to gender issues revealed to be the most productive ones. In other words, these questions have produced more arousal and valence than any others.

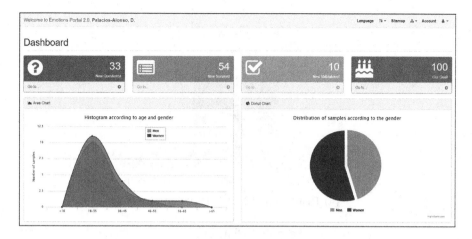

Fig. 4. Overview of online framework for multilingual data acquisition of stress speech

3.5 Corpora

The corpora contain data from sixteen volunteers divided into two groups, female and male, respectively. Therefore, these corpora are gender-balanced. The number of participants was 32 from different ages. The age distributions for males and females are provided in Fig. 5a and b.

In Fig. 6 it is illustrated the distribution of datasets, respectively.

4 Results and Discussion

The results presented in this paper are composed of two parts. In the first part, some of the queries of the database are detailed, where the difference between the replies of volunteers and the raters is explained. On the other hand, in the second part, the summary of the questionnaire about the framework is outlined.

The validation process was performed by four raters, three males (ages: 22, 22 and 43) and a female (35), as shown in Table 1. None of the participants had been evaluated before and they did not know the test methodology in advance.

Table 1. Rater's profiles.

Rater	Gender	Age
A1	Male	22
A2	Male	43
A3	Female	35
A4	Male	22

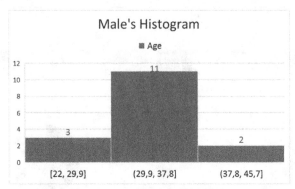

(a) Histogram of Male's Distribution.

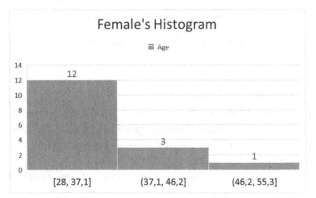

(b) Histogram of Female's Distribution.

Fig. 5. Explanation about corpora.

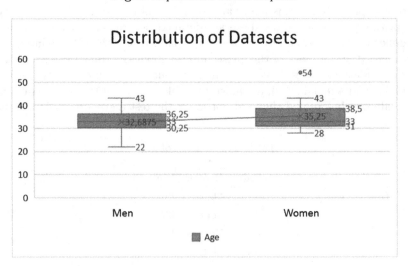

Fig. 6. Distribution datasets divided into male and female corpora.

Raters' scores are given in Table 2. The first rater evaluated 36 speech recordings. Thirty three cases showed a match between users' and raters' answers. However, in three cases, the raters' opinion does not match to the donners' opinion.

The second rater scored eighteen answers, the lowest number respect to the rest of raters. This time, twelve answers showed a user-rater match. In other six the rater considered that the user was defending the opposite idea as far as personal opinions were concerned.

The option *politically correct* was selected in five cases only by the woman rater. In other words, she considered that the user answered with a prefabricated opinion. On the other hand, the users' and the raters' answers matched in 15 of 22 cases, and there were two exceptions.

Finally, the highest number of validation was made by the last rater. The validated 54 speech recordings. The raters' answers coincided in 45 out of 54 cases.

Table 2. Summary of responses between donors and raters.

Rater	Disagreement		Politically correct		Agreement		Total
	Disagree	Agree	Disagree	Agree	Disagree	Agree	
A1	10	3	–	–	–	23	**36**
A2	2	–	–	–	6	10	**18**
A3	7	2	5	–	–	8	**22**
A4	25	4	–	–	5	20	**54**
TOTAL	**44**	**9**	**5**	**-**	**11**	**61**	**130**

The questionnaire used to gather rater's opinion about the methodology and application is the following:

- What do you think about the application?
- What part do you like most, recording or validation?
- What do you think about the registration form, speech recording and record evaluation?
- Have you felt stressed at any moment?
- What do you think about the application's colors and font size?
- What do you think about the speech recordings? Are they done by an actor or a real person?
- What do you think about the methodology to elicit stress?
- Be honest, please. Are you comfortable in sharing your opinions with the research community?

The most interesting graphical responses to the questionnaire are highlighted in Fig. 7. For example, all raters consider the speech recordings original and non-acted. On the other hand, three of four raters liked the methodology to elicit stress and the last one considered the technique difficult to be understood. The response in regard to sharing the voice in a public way is illustrated in the bottom right. Again, three of four raters do not have any doubt in this fact. However, one of them is not sure about this question.

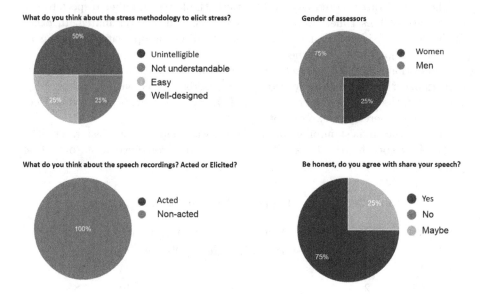

Fig. 7. Screenshot of rater's questionnaire.

5   Conclusions

Acquiring high quality voice data exhibiting emotions is a complex topic to tackle which has not been sufficiently addressed in the research literature. However, it is the key point to progress fast in the research line of emotional and stressed speech recognition. As mentioned before, current databases do not have a standard format and sometimes they are not publicly available, making it very difficult to validate the quality of developed systems for emotion detection because reference samples are different.

This work has presented a collaborative platform where users donate and evaluate their speech. Thanks to this generated open dataset, the research community can better develop their projects. The Internet is a widely accessible resource which we can capitalize on to (a) record a large dataset and (b) label the data accordingly and using some consensus amongst raters in a collaborative process. It is remarkable, the necessity to find a fully efficient and law-compliant approach with the Data Protection Act to ensure this becomes feasible and practical.

The structure of this platform is scalable, flexible and modular. The key point is how to evoke or elicit stress for different languages, cultures, and so on.

A benefit derived from the cooperative characteristic is to be open to ordinary people. Exercises can be carried out without any prior preparation. Therefore, this research can be easily usable by non-expert public. In conclusion, a general methodology has been developed that can be adapted to support multicultural data and addressed to a specific speech emotion target.

Acknowledgments. This work is being funded by grants TEC2016-77791-C4-4-R (MINECO, Spain) and CENIE _ TECA – PARK_55_02 INTERREG V – A Spain – Portugal (POCTEP).

References

1. Ley Orgánica 3/2018, de 5 de diciembre, de Protección de Datos Personales y garantía de los derechos digitales - Agencia Estatal Boletín Oficial del Estado. https://www.boe.es/buscar/act.php?id=BOE-A-2018-16673. Accessed 7 Jan 2019
2. Portal Codec - GFK Group. https://www.portalcodec.com/. Accessed 7 Jan 2019
3. Arciuli, J., Villar, G., Mallard, D.: Lies, lies and more lies. In: Proceedings of the 31st Annual Conference of the Cognitive Science Society (CogSci 2009), pp. 2329–2334 (2009)
4. Burkhardt, F., Paeschke, A., Rolfes, M., Sendlmeier, W.F., Weiss, B.: A database of German emotional speech. In: Interspeech, vol. 5, pp. 1517–1520 (2005)
5. Engberg, I.S., Hansen, A.V.: Documentation of the Danish emotional speech database DES. Internal AAU report, Center for Person Kommunikation, Denmark, p. 22 (1996)
6. Hansen, J.H., Bou-Ghazale, S.E., Sarikaya, R., Pellom, B.: Getting started with SUSAS: a speech under simulated and actual stress database. In: Eurospeech, vol. 97, pp. 1743–1746 (1997)
7. Her - Official Webpage (2013). http://www.herthemovie.com/. Accessed 4 May 2015
8. Hofbauer, K., Petrik, S., Hering, H.: The ATCOSIM corpus of non-prompted clean air traffic control speech. In: LREC (2008)
9. Moore, E., Clements, M.A., Peifer, J.W., Weisser, L.: Critical analysis of the impact of glottal features in the classification of clinical depression in speech. IEEE Trans. Biomed. Eng. **55**(1), 96–107 (2008)
10. Muñoz-Mulas, C., et al.: KPCA vs. PCA study for an age classification of speakers. In: Travieso-González, C.M., Alonso-Hernández, J.B. (eds.) NOLISP 2011. LNCS (LNAI), vol. 7015, pp. 190–198. Springer, Heidelberg (2011). https://doi.org/10.1007/978-3-642-25020-0_25
11. Ramakrishnan, S.: Recognition of emotion from speech: a review. In: Speech Enhancement, Modeling and Recognition-Algorithms and Applications, p. 121 (2012)
12. Robot and Frank - IMDB Webpage (2012). http://www.imdb.com/title/tt1990314/. Accessed 4 May 2015
13. Rodellar, V., Palacios, D., Gomez, P., Bartolome, E.: A methodology for monitoring emotional stress in phonation. In: 2014 5th IEEE Conference on Cognitive Infocommunications (CogInfoCom), pp. 231–236. IEEE (2014)

14. Rodellar-Biarge, V., Palacios-Alonso, D., Nieto-Lluis, V., Gómez-Vilda, P.: Towards the search of detection in speech-relevant features for stress. Expert Syst. **32**, 701–718 (2015)
15. Ververidis, D., Kotropoulos, C.: A review of emotional speech databases. In: Proceedings of the Panhellenic Conference on Informatics (PCI), pp. 560–574 (2003)

Empowering UX of Elderly People with Parkinson's Disease via BCI Touch

Pedro Gómez-López[1(✉)], Francisco Montero[2], and María T. López[2]

[1] Instituto de Investigación en Informática de Albacete,
Universidad de Castilla-La Mancha, 02071 Albacete, Spain
pedro.gomezlopez@uclm.es
[2] Departamento de Sistemas Informáticos, Universidad de Castilla-La Mancha,
02071 Albacete, Spain
{Francisco.MSimarro,Maria.LBonal}@uclm.es

Abstract. The application introduced within this paper, BCI Touch, is based on a prior knowledge base focused on the world of accessibility, within the field of information and communication technologies, EVA Facial Mouse application. Our main objective is to explore new paradigms of interaction, for the specific context of elder people with psycho-motor impairments. Something as routine and humdrum as the use of mobile devices can be an insurmountable barrier depending on the psycho-motor abilities of the user. Therefore, BCI Touch makes use of an innovative data source within the human-computer interaction field, such as brainwaves and brain activity patterns.

Through the processing and adequate treatment of the bio-signals coming from the electroencephalography (EEG), which is recorded by the Emotiv Epoc+ brain-computer interface (BCI), we are able to control events that in turn trigger actions that facilitate interaction with the mobile device. BCI Touch includes a variety of possible interaction mechanisms, ranging from interaction by movement (cursor control with the nose tracker) to interaction using mental commands, passing through interaction through facial expressions. All these capabilities involve a comprehensive solution that considerably improves the technological and personal autonomy of elder people with Parkinson's disease (PD).

Keywords: Elderly people · Ambient assisted living ·
Brain-computer interfaces (BCI) · Wearable systems ·
Applications and case studies

1 Introduction and Motivation

This paper aims to take a step further in the different set of possibilities and functionalities that EVA Facial Mouse [4] offers. EVA allows the user to control an Android device by tracking the facies. It is based on the facial movements captured through the front camera, the app allows the user to control a pointer on the screen (i.e., like a mouse), which provides direct access to most elements

© Springer Nature Switzerland AG 2019
J. M. Ferrández Vicente et al. (Eds.): IWINAC 2019, LNCS 11486, pp. 161–170, 2019.
https://doi.org/10.1007/978-3-030-19591-5_17

of the user interface. EVA is intended to those who cannot use a touchscreen. For instance, people with amputations, cerebral palsy, spinal cord injury, muscular dystrophy, multiple sclerosis, amyotrophic lateral sclerosis (ALS) or other disabilities may benefit from this app. This paper introduces an application that customizes interactive capabilities between people with Parkinson's disease and smartphones. We aim to develop an Android application to improve the way older people interact with mobile devices, making it easier and more accessible their interaction with smartphones. Also, our contribution provides a facial expressions training environment for people with Parkinston's Disease (PD). Stemming from the electric activity registered from a brain computer interface (BCI) device, different and innovative types of interactions will be proposed and evaluated, with the aim of improving the final user autonomy and quality of life. Within this field there exist interesting research in different areas, such as robotic arm control in persons with reduced mobility [10], or more complex systems that integrate multiple devices [2].

The main goal of this paper is to introduce and develop a brain computer interface (BCI) based application to allow disabled people in general and people with Parkinson's Disease in particular, to control mobile devices without using their hands. Parkinson's disease is the second most common neurodegenerative disease of movement disorders, affecting the central nervous system. Parkinson's disease causes masking problems as the progressive loss of motor control extends to the facial muscles as it does to other parts of the body. Masked facies (Hypomimia) can complicate an already difficult situation, alienating acquaintances who may be put off or disturbed by the apparent lack of emotional response. Our application combines a different interaction style and a tool for facial expressions training in older people with PD. In this context, there exist other solutions and proposals that help people with PD in their daily lives, such as the Gyenno spoon [5] or the Emma watch, framed within the Project Emma [9].

The improvement processes and quality contribution activities to be performed on the EVA based application are summarized in the following four major milestones:

1. Training of facial expressions in older people with PD and Slight hypomimia.
2. Detection and implementation of facial expressions as actions that can launch software events (i.e., tap, double tap, etc.).
3. Detection and implementation of mental commands as actions that can launch software events (i.e., click home button, scroll forwards, etc.).
4. Study and evaluation of the wide range of EVA Facial Mouse software events that can be launched by the aforementioned actions.
5. Integration of the previous points with EVA Facial Mouse, to have a high usability and accessibility system in which the most attractive and innovative part consists on tuples of the type action collected by the neuroheadset-software event that improve the interaction mechanisms between the user and the smart phone.

The rest of the paper is organized as follows. First, the brain-computer interaction is presented in Sect. 2. Then, the authoring tool is presented in Sect. 3. BCI Touch evaluation procedures are described and covered in Sect. 4. Finally, Sect. 5 illustrates some conclusions and provides guidelines for future research.

2   Brain-Computer Interface Interaction in BCI Touch

Figure 1 shows a schematic approach to the application operation. On the one hand, the user will use their head to move the mouse pointer displayed on the screen. The way in which this feature is implemented is by using the mobile front camera, which tracks the user nose as a method to control the cursor of the screen, considering aspects such as the head speed movements. But the real innovation component of the application, is the way in which the app uses the Emotiv Epoc+ neuroheadset to control the system. First of all, data collected by the brain computer interface is sent using Bluetooth technology (step 1). That data reaches the smart phone, coming from either the front camera to move the mouse or from the electrical brain activity to trigger specific software events.

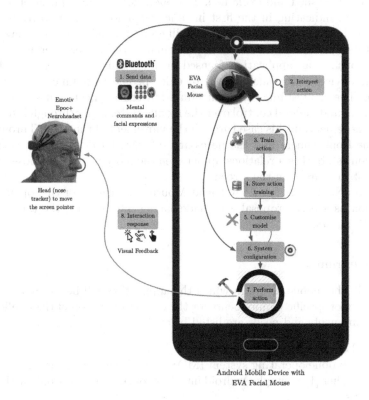

Fig. 1. BCI Touch application behaviour

The application will extend the functionality offered by EVA Facial Mouse application by making use of the Emotiv Epoc+ wearable electroencephalography headset and the whole collection of new interaction mechanisms that it introduces to build a richer and more effective user experience [3]. The set of events sent by the headset via Bluetooth are intended to trigger the execution of different typical gestures that support the touchscreen devices such as tap, double tap, swipe forward, press home button, etc., without actually touching the screen. In other words, the idea is to manage a set of actions sent wirelessly by the EEG that could programmatically trigger software events, which would give rise to different modes of interaction with mobile devices touchscreens. Moreover, our end users, elder people with PD have an environment to train facial expressions and emotions.

3   BCI Touch System Description

In this section, the purpose of the application, its main characteristics, the required resources to execute the application and recommendations to be followed will be detailed and explained. The operation of the application will also be explained, indicating in the first instance what forms of interaction can be used throughout the app. After that we will go into detail about how navigation is done through the different windows that make up the user interface.

BCI Touch is an application focused on improving accessibility in the use of mobile devices with touch screen to elder people with functional diversity problems. The greatest innovation introduced by this application lies in its ability to have a full and integral control over the mobile system only through interaction through movement, in this case through the movement of the head. Through the use of the front camera and the necessary software for detecting our face, the application establishes a relationship between the movement of our nose and the position of the cursor on the screen.

BCI Touch is based on EVA Facial Mouse. The choice of this open source application as a base proposal was made taking into account the target group of potential users.

3.1   Requirements

First of all, the mobile device in which the application will be run must comply with a series of specific requirements for the correct operation of the application, these requirements and needs are listed below:

- Smartphone
- Android mobile operating system (MOS) Jelly Bean 4.1 or higher
- Big Launcher [1], a simple Android interface for seniors and people with vision problems
- Bluetooth as a communication protocol to pair the smartphone with the Emotiv Epoc+

- Front camera with at least 4 megapixels
- Dual-core processor or higher in order to run smoothly

Despite the above requirements, the huge variety of mobile devices with Android as an operating system that include modifications at the software level means that the correct operation of the application cannot be guaranteed in all variety of devices.

3.2 Structure of the Application

The interaction mechanisms that are recognized throughout the application, thanks to the introduction of Emotiv Epoc+ brain-computer interface, have been split into facial expressions and mental commands. But, that said, it should also be pointed that both the application and the mobile system do not respond to tactile interaction as a traditional mobile communication mechanism. It simply loses its meaning due to the target group we are focusing on and the nature of the application we are developing, framed within the accessibility field.

In BCI Touch, all the tactile actions that we would perform through a direct interaction with the touch screen, are replaced by programmed software events that provide us with the same functionality. In fact, these events that are mapped with the Emotiv Epoc+ neuroheadset are not randomly selected. It has been decided to select those that are most used by smartphone users in their basic activities of daily living (BADL), such as, setting of alarms, contact management, make SOS calls, make phone calls, etc.

In the traditional version of EVA Facial Mouse, the interaction mechanism consisted of a controlled pointer with the user's head, which located at a certain point on the screen, performed a specific action once a concrete time had elapsed without moving the cursor. Therefore, the mechanism that controlled the release of the action was a time lapse when the cursor in a fixed position. BCI Touch goes a step further by introducing the novel interaction mechanisms provided by the Emotiv Epoc+ BCI device. The correct control and processing of this new paradigm will provide us with new control mechanisms to launch the actions available in the application. And, without a doubt, the most disruptive attribute is that these control mechanisms are implemented with an exclusive data source, our own brain and its bioelectrical signals.

Therefore, customization and adaptation to the user are assured, due to the unique nature of the biosignals of each person. This flexibility and elasticity fit perfectly with the nature and purpose of the paper. To create particular models of brain activity, it is necessary to previously train the actions, both facial expressions and mental commands. In this sense, there is a specific state called "neutral state", which registers the user's background brain activity to conform an initial pattern. It is a preliminary requirement that must be performed in order to train both facial expressions and mental commands respectively.

Next, we will describe the control mechanisms related to facial expressions. Most BCI devices that use the electroencephalography (EEG) as a technique for reading brain activity remove muscle signals as a step prior to the processing of the purest brain activity. However, Emotiv Epoc+ treats these signals, allowing us to access this data source. It is important to understand that the common denominator between facial expressions and mental commands are biosignals.

In our contributions people with PD and slight hypomimia were specially considered. The three types of facial expressions that has been considered for this paper are smile, smirk right and clench. The procedure for training each of these actions is identical in all three cases. Firstly, and under supervision, the user has to stay a time lapse of eight seconds carrying out the specific action. At the end of this time, the activity pattern will have been generated. The application will ask the user if they accept the training. In the affirmative case, the training is completed, and the Emotiv Epoc+ keeps listening to the arrival of new events. Then users use their mobile phones freely without supervision. In the opposite case, the training is undone and not taken into consideration by BCI Touch.

Once the facial expressions have been described, we will focus our attention on the use of mental commands as a mechanism for interaction and control. The user must remain a time lapse of eight seconds consciously thinking about something concrete, in our case, it is proposed to imagine that a picture is directed to the bottom of the screen (push) or directed in front of the screen (pull). The most important concept to keep in mind is that the Emotiv Epoc+ is continuously sending information through the Bluetooth protocol to the mobile device. This information flow contains data related to the events captured (i.e. facial expressions and/or mental commands) and its intensity. A better description of the idea that we have just mentioned, can be observed in Fig. 2. The figure represents in a graphic way the communication between the different parts of the application, from a relatively high abstraction level.

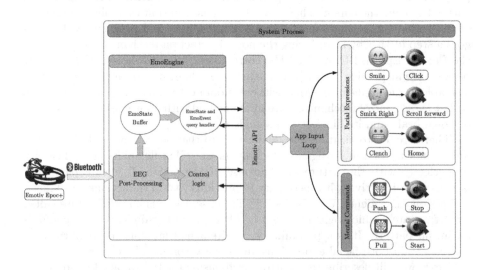

Fig. 2. Conceptual model of the system behaviour

4   BCI Touch System Evaluation with Older People with PD

After the application development an evaluation with final users has been carried out. This proposal would be meaningless if the application performed (at least in an evaluation phase) had not been tested with actual users. Specifically, an evaluation of the quality in use has been performed, with the objective of observing and quantifying the sensations of real users while interacting with the application. The ISO/IEC 25062:2006 international standard [6], according to which this section has been structured, has been taken as a reference for the evaluation.

The evaluation was carried out with one objective in mind: to assess the functional quality of the application in usability terms. The training and conscious control of both facial expressions and mental commands was emphasized, although other elements of the interaction were also evaluated. During the evaluation, the following aspects were verified:

- Facial recognition's and training. The application offers a user-friendly and intuitive interface for facial expressions training and interaction.
- Functionality. Users do not miss any feature during the use of the application, and with each step they take, they are aware that the application is reacting and responding in a correct and adequate way.
- User experience. Users perceive the use of the application as satisfactory or not in order to fully and comprehensively control a mobile device, without the need to request any additional help from an external person.

4.1   Evaluation Method

This section will detail the process followed to conduct the evaluation, including information about the participants, the context in which the evaluation was perform, the tasks that the users had to accomplish, and the metrics that were employed.

Participants

The evaluation was developed with 7 elder people with Parkinson's disease and slight hypomimia from several Day Centers for the elderly (Albacete, Hellín and Almansa). All these participants have previous experience with mobile phones and they must to do facial exercises suggested by their specialists. The strategy behind this approach lies in detecting any type of problem when interacting, whether it originates from a target audience or not. In any case, the wider the sample is, the richer the potential feedback to be obtained will be.

For each user, their age, their level of knowledge in IT and their frequency of use of mobile devices, as well as other parameters such as the hypomimia degree.

Tasks

All participants had to perform three activities (BADLs) after configuration were done: setting up an alarm, find a contact (son, daughter or sister) in your contacts and make a phone call. It is important to take into consideration the fact that before beginning the evaluation, it is necessary to carry out a whole previous process in which the Emotiv Epoc+ is prepared to be used.

The tasks chosen are the same as any user could perform to control a mobile device with a touch screen. The data on the tasks to be performed were provided to the user in an instruction sheet. This sheet shows the objectives that the user should achieve.

Equipment and Devices

The computational equipment used in the evaluation was the following:

- To check the contact quality of the Emotiv Epoc+ electrodes, the Emotiv Control Panel software was used, which was executed on a laptop with macOS Sierra version 10.12.6 operating system, with Intel Core i7 at 2.7 GHz and 16GB of LPDDR3 RAM at 2133 MHz. In addition, we also used the Emotiv SDK Community Edition.
- For the detection of facial expressions, mental commands, and brain activity patterns in general, the brain-computer device Emotiv Epoc+ v1.1 was used, which sent the information to the mobile device through the Bluetooth communication protocol.
- EVA Facial Mouse and BCI Touch were used in the evaluation process. A mobile device with Android v6.0 operating system was used, equipped with an 8-megapixel front camera that integrated the Toshiba T4KA3 FFC sensor, as well as with a 5.5-in. touch screen.

4.2 Results

In this section an analysis of the obtained data is accomplished. First, data obtained during the different evaluation processes are summarized, distinguishing between the three main categories in which data is split (functionality effectiveness, facial recognition's effectiveness and user experience).

Due to the fact that we start from the same set of participants, we have decided to apply a paired samples t-test in order to compare the obtained results from both EVA Facial Mouse and BCI Touch.

Functionality Effectiveness Results. The first parameter analyzed in the evaluation process was the effectiveness of the functionality. In our study, the metric associated with this feature has been the time spent on tasks performance measured in seconds.

The corresponding mean values obtained for EVA Facial Mouse and BCI Touch in this case were $\mu_{EVA} = 486.14$ s for the first and $\mu_{BCI\,Touch} = 365.43$ s for the latter. In this case, the paired samples t-test reflected significant statistical data values (p–value $= 0.0043$). Comparing the analyzed values we can affirm that the time to complete the proposed tasks is lower in the case of BCI Touch, in addition to existing a significant differences with regards to EVA Facial Mouse.

Facial Recognition Effectiveness Results. In order to address the effectiveness of facial expressions as a means of interaction in our application, we have decided to take as a measurement value the number of errors made by participants in the development of the tasks in question.

In this case, the mean values obtained that corresponds to EVA Facial Mouse and BCI Touch were $\mu_{EVA} = 6.86$ for the EVA and $\mu_{BCI\,Touch} = 4.43$ for BCI Touch. In this second scenario, we were retrieved with a meaningful statistical value (p–value $= 0.0074$) which reveals a significant difference between BCI Touch and EVA Facial Mouse.

User Experience Results. Lastly, the participants in the evaluation were asked to complete a spoken-version of a UMUX-Lite questionnaire [8] through which they could score the user experience they had. The Usability Metric for User Experience Lite (UMUX-Lite) is intended to be similar to the SUS questionnaire but is shorter and targeted toward the ISO 9241 definition of usability [7]. It contains two positive items with a 7-point response scale. The two items to be evaluated are "The app capabilities meet my requirements" and "The app is easy to use".

Lewis et al. [8] provided a regression equation to predict SUS scores from the two items (they call the UMUX-Lite) and found that the UMUX-Lite could predict SUS scores with about 99% accuracy. The regression equation is shown below. $SUS_{Score} = 0.65*((Umux_{Item1} + Umux_{Item2} - 2)*(100/12)) + 22.9$ The obtained results in the context of satisfaction are summarized and reported in Fig. 3.

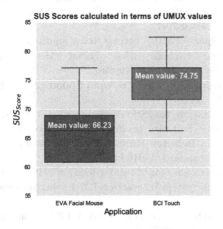

Fig. 3. Distribution of satisfaction values

Discussion and Treats of Validity. It is important to highlight that evaluation has been done with relevant subjects belonging to the main target group and represented by elder people with Parkinson's disease and slight hypomimia.

The results of the UMUX questionnaires are tremendously interesting. These questionnaires reflect that users are more satisfied with the designed solution, which adapts to their personal capabilities, in the sense that they can train actions to interact with the device. These final users value to a much greater extent the positive impact that an application of this characteristics can have on their daily life, despite having aspects that can be improved.

5 Conclusions and Future Work

This paper introduced BCI Touch, a brain computer interface (BCI) based application to allow older people with Parkinson's diseases to control mobile devices. BCI Touch is framed within the field of brain-computer interface devices, as well as in the mobile application category focused on accessibility. It is a relatively new and disruptive field of research, with enormous potential. Using BCI Touch elder people with PD can train their facial expressions in order to avoid "masked facies". There is no doubt about the fact that soon we will begin to see concepts such as thought-based interaction, as a result of applying techniques such as the electroencephalogram (EEG) as the main data asset that nourishes our relationship with technology.

References

1. BIG Launcher: BIG Launcher for Android (2019). http://biglauncher.com/en/
2. de Oliveira Júnior, W.G., de Oliveira, J.M., Munoz, R., de Albuquerque, V.H.C.: A proposal for Internet of Smart Home Things based on BCI system to aid patients with amyotrophic lateral sclerosis. Neural Comput. Appl. 1–11 (2018). https://doi. org/10.1007/s00521-018-3820-7
3. EMOTIV: Emotiv Epoc+ (2019). https://www.emotiv.com/epoc/
4. Fundación Vodafone España: EVA Facial Mouse (2015). http://www. fundacionvodafone.es/app/eva-facial-mouse
5. GYENNO Technologies CO., LTD.: Gyenno Spoon (2018). https://www.gyenno. com/spoon-en.html
6. International Organization for Standardization (ISO): ISO/IEC 25062:2006 - Software engineering – Software product Quality Requirements and Evaluation (SQuaRE) – Common Industry Format (CIF) for usability test reports (2006). https://www.iso.org/standard/43046.html
7. International Organization for Standardization (ISO): ISO 9241-11:2018 - Ergonomics of Human-System Interaction (2018). https://www.iso.org/standard/ 63500.html
8. Lewis, J.R., Utesch, B.S., Maher, D.E.: UMUX-LITE: when there's no time forthe SUS. In: Proceedings of the SIGCHI Conference on Human Factors in Computing Systems - CHI 2013, pp. 2099–2102. ACM Press, New York (2013). https://doi. org/10.1145/2470654.2481287
9. Microsoft Research: Project Emma (2017). https://www.microsoft.com/en-us/ research/project/project-emma/
10. Pelayo, P., Murthy, H., George, K.: Brain-computer interface controlled robotic arm to improve quality of life. In: 2018 IEEE International Conference on Healthcare Informatics (ICHI), pp. 398–399. IEEE, June 2018. https://doi.org/10.1109/ICHI. 2018.00072, https://ieeexplore.ieee.org/document/8419405/

Real-Time Emotional Recognition for Sociable Robotics Based on Deep Neural Networks Ensemble

Nadir Kamel Benamara[1(✉)], Mikel Val-Calvo[2,3],
José Ramón Álvarez-Sánchez[2], Alejandro Díaz-Morcillo[4],
José Manuel Ferrández Vicente[3], Eduardo Fernández-Jover[5],
and Tarik Boudghene Stambouli[1]

[1] Laboratoire Signaux et Images,
Université des Sciences et de la Technologie d'Oran Mohamed Boudiaf,
USTO-MB, BP1505, El M'naouer, 31000 Oran, Algeria
`nadirkamel.benamara@univ-usto.dz`
[2] Dpto. de Inteligencia Artificial,
Universidad Nacional de Educación a Distancia (UNED),
Juan del Rosal, 16, 28040 Madrid, Spain
[3] Dpto. Electrónica, Tecnología de Computadoras y Proyectos,
Univ. Politécnica de Cartagena, Cartagena, Spain
[4] Dpto. Tecnologías de la Información y las Comunicaciones,
Univ. Politécnica de Cartagena, Cartagena, Spain
[5] Instituto de Bioingeniería, Univ. Miguel Hernández, Elche, Spain

Abstract. Recognizing emotions in controlled conditions, based on facial expressions, has achieved high accuracies in the past years. This is still a challenging task for robots working in real-world scenarios due to different factors such as illumination, pose variation or occlusions. One of the next barriers of science is to give sociable robots the ability to fully engage in emotional interactions with users. In this paper a real-time emotion recognition system using a YOLO-based facial detection system and an ensemble CNN for sociable robots, is proposed. Experiments have been carried out on the most challenging database, FER 2013, giving a performance of 72.47% on test sets, achieving current standards.

Keywords: Emotion recognition · Sociable robotics ·
Facial expression · Human-machine interaction

1 Introduction

In the last decades, several applications such as biometrics, biomedical, human-machine interaction, robotics, etc, became dependent on computer vision, and much progress has been made in this field. Recently, considerable attention has been paid to recognizing facial expressions in real environments including illumination and posture variations, and occlusions. The integration of computer vision

© Springer Nature Switzerland AG 2019
J. M. Ferrández Vicente et al. (Eds.): IWINAC 2019, LNCS 11486, pp. 171–180, 2019.
https://doi.org/10.1007/978-3-030-19591-5_18

applications into daily life could improve fields such as behavioral surveillance, education techniques, psychological medicine and sociable robotics.

Emotions play a key role in our lives. The first step in emotion recognition is to set out a reference system; emotional models. Even though a recent study has evidenced that emotional responses are not universal and are dependent on culture [10] and thus many emotional models exist there is a need to narrow down the reference system for a research study. Based on psychological studies, facial expressions are generally divided into six prototypical emotions [5]: anger, disgust, fear, happiness, sadness, surprise, to which neutral emotion has been added.

Many studies have been carried-out in the field of facial expression recognition(FER) under controlled conditions, obtaining high recognition rates [1,15]. However, FER under real conditions is still a challenging task due to the multiple environment variations can affect the information available in the processed image.

Due to recent developments on graphical processing units(GPU), the use of deep learning techniques has been made possible, which has in turn changed the field of computer vision, since deeper convolutional neural networks (CNN) can now be trained. Compared to traditional feature extraction methods, such as local binary patterns (LBP) [17] or histogram of oriented gradients (HOG) [2], deep learning techniques have achieved high and robust recognition rates [13]. Nevertheless, CNN requires a sufficient amount of data to properly generalize the targeted task and avoid overfitting. More recently, a growing interest on ensemble CNN has been noticed since it usually yields an improved recognition rate in comparison to single CNN performance.

In order to compare the obtained results to state of the art, the FER-2013 dataset is used [7]. The performance and accuracy of the proposed model has been compared with the following articles: [22] was the winning submission on Kaggle FER challenge 2013; [3,8,12,16] and [18] achieved the best performances on the FER 2013 database.

This paper proposes an emotion recognition system used in real-world scenarios, based on two stages: facial detection using a YOLO-based model and an ensemble CNN model; for FER in human-robot interaction (HRI).

2   Methods

The proposed emotional recognition system is structured into two main stages: database description, preprocessing, and emotion recognition based on an ensemble deep network approach.

FER 2013 Database. The FER 2013 database was introduced in the ICML 2013 workshop [7] on challenges in representation learning. The database comprises grayscale face images of 48×48 px resolution, with 6+1 different face expressions (angry (AN), disgusted(DI), afraid (AF), happy (HA), sad (SA), surprised (SU) and neutral (NE)) in different real-life scenarios, divided into 3

Table 1. FER 2013 dataset distribution per class

Emotion	AN	DI	AF	HA	SA	SU	NE	Total
Training 1	3995	436	4097	7215	4830	3171	4965	**28709**
Training 2	3983	435	4087	7201	4824	3162	4952	**28644**
Validation	491	55	528	879	594	416	626	**3589**
Test	467	56	496	895	653	415	607	**3589**

subsets: a training set (Training 1) including 28709 face images, a validation set and a test set comprising 3589 face images for the latter two, see Table 1.

2.1 Preprocessing

Preprocessing aims to detect only the region of interest: the face. A face detector based on YOLO architectures trained using a fully annotated face database WIDER DB is used for the following [9,19,25]. Detected faces are cropped and resized to 48 × 48 px, followed by a conversion from RGB to grayscale space with [0, 1] normalization range.

2.2 Ensemble Deep Network

The recognition stage is based on a fully convolutional neural network (FCNN) approach. In CNN, features are extracted from a series of learnable convolution layers and then injected to a fully connected neural network for classification. Early convolution layers extract more general features such as edges and shapes, while the previous layers extract more specific features. In order to find more detailed and discriminative features, the proposed recognition system uses an ensemble of FCNN architectures, where the first convolution layers are fixed and the mapping to the last ones is modified for each model.

After testing many well-known state of the art architectures, a modified version of the proposed architecture ConvPool-CNN-C in [21], with more batch normalization and dropout layers are used for regularization and prevent overfitting, is defined as our baseline (Model A). Each convolution layer uses a number of filters 3 × 3, with same padding and a stride of 1. ReLu activation function is used for all convolution layers except the last one where a softmax activation function is employed to get class probabilities. Furthermore, in this deep model, the fully connected network is replaced by a global average pooling (GAP) that acts as a regularizer [14], and in the same time reduces the number of trainable parameters generated by conventional densely connected networks.

For the training step, categorical cross entropy is employed as loss function with Adam as optimizer, we have trained the models with batch size of 64, for 100 epochs as initial configuration until there is no improvement regarding the validation loss.

Three other FCNN models (Models B, C, and D respectively) are derived from the baseline. The architecture of the model is shown in detail in Table 2. The Nvidia Tesla K80 GPU is used to train the FCNN ensembles.

Table 2. Architecture description of the four FCNN baseline models

Layers	Model A	Model B	Model C	Model D
1	Input $(48, 48, 1)$			
2	Conv 2D $(96, (3 \times 3), relu, same)$			
3	Conv 2D $(96, (3 \times 3), relu, same)$			
4	Conv 2D $(96, (3 \times 3), relu, same)$			
5	BatchNorm			
6	MaxPool 2D $((3 \times 3), 2)$			
7	Dropout (0.5)			
8	Conv 2D $(192, (3 \times 3), relu, same)$			
9	Conv 2D $(192, (3 \times 3), relu, same)$			
10	Conv 2D $(192, (3 \times 3), relu, same)$			
11	BatchNorm			
12	MaxPool 2D $((3 \times 3), 2)$			
13	Dropout (0.5)			
14	Conv 2D $(192, (3 \times 3), relu, same)$			
15	Conv 2D $(192, (1 \times 1), relu, same)$	Conv 2D $(192, (3 \times 3), relu, same)$	Conv 2D $(192, (3 \times 3), relu, same)$	Conv 2D $(192, (3 \times 3), relu, same)$
16		MaxPool 2D $((3 \times 3), 2)$	MaxPool 2D $((3 \times 3), 2)$	MaxPool 2D $((3 \times 3), 2)$
17		Dropout (0.5)	Dropout (0.5)	Dropout (0.5)
18		Conv 2D $(256, (1 \times 1), relu, same)$	Conv 2D $(256, (3 \times 3), relu, same)$	Conv 2D $(256, (3 \times 3), relu, same)$
19			Conv 2D $(256, (1 \times 1), relu, same)$	Conv 2D $(256, (3 \times 3), relu, same)$
20				Dropout (0.5)
21				Conv 2D $(512, (1 \times 1), relu, same)$
Last layers	Conv 2D $(7, (1 \times 1), relu, same)$ BatchNorm GlobalAvgPool 2D Softmax (7)			
Trainable Parameters	$\simeq 1.37m$	$\simeq 1.71m$	$\simeq 2.17m$	$\simeq 2.83m$

3   Experimental Results

To evaluate the proposed approach, experiments have been carried out on the most challenging database FER 2013 [7]. This section presents the results obtained when testing the proposed model with the FER 2013 database.

Using the FER 2013 dataset, experiments have been carried out using multiple trained network configurations on the filtered training set (Training 2). In the first plan, single fully convolutional neural networks (A, B, C, and D respectively) were used giving results on validation and test sets, presented in Table 3, with their confusion matrices in Fig. 1.

In a second plan, all possible ensembles were built based on tested single FCNN networks in the first plan. Average and Maximum score fusion strategies were used for the interpretation of ensemble results. Obtained performances are highlighted in Table 4 and their confusion matrices are illustrated in Fig. 2.

Actually, the ensemble model has achieved comparable results to the best state of the art approaches; quantified in Table 6. The best results are obtained with FCNN ensemble using models A,B and C with the average score fusion strategy, achieving an accuracy of 72.47% on the test set.

4   Discussions

The system is capable of recognizing facial expressions with real time constraints, as shown in Table 5. The average time for the first stage is $238\,ms \pm 191.7$ running on a multicore i7 CPU processor for the YOLO model. That is, $150\,ms$ slower than with Haar Cascade method [24] that runs at $88.3\,ms \pm 12.23$. In contrast, the second stage of the system, the ensemble, needs a total time of $145.7\,ms \pm 111.1$ for the estimation of emotion of a face. This means that the entire system performs the detection of facial emotions at approximately a frequency of $3\,Hz$. This recognition rate is fast enough for the purposes of sociable robotics.

The facial detection stage gives a solution to the impediments encounter when detecting facial emotions in real environments where lighting, occlusions and other factors, make the detection of faces difficult, in Fig. 3. The area of the image that constraints the face, and therefore the facial expression, is detected by the ensemble method using a collaborative scheme.

Although FCNNs are not capable of performing parallel estimation like the YOLO-based model, this can be improved with the use of multi-threading techniques in Python, where the synchronization of the entire set would behave as badly as the slowest model, but at the price of improving the accuracy of the entire system, as measured in Table 6. Based on confusion matrices in Fig. 1, it is noticed that each single model has a better generalization for particular emotions, such as Model A for 'sad'and 'surprised', Model B for 'disgust', 'happy' and 'neutral', Model C for 'afraid', and Model D for 'angry' and 'neutral'. In comparison with the obtained confusion matrices in Fig. 2, the ensembles ABC and ABCD, take the best from every single model and generalize better for each

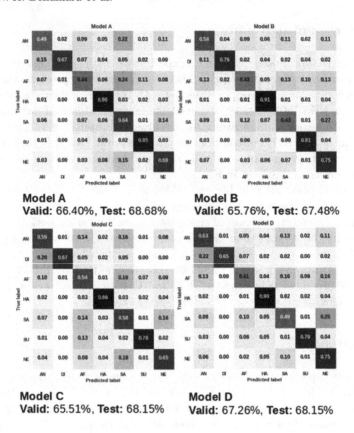

Model A
Valid: 66.40%, Test: 68.68%

Model B
Valid: 65.76%, Test: 67.48%

Model C
Valid: 65.51%, Test: 68.15%

Model D
Valid: 67.26%, Test: 68.15%

Fig. 1. Obtained confusion matrices for FCNN single models

Table 3. Obtained recognition performances for FCNN single models

Model	A	B	C	D
Validation accuracy	66.40%	65.76%	65.51%	67.28%
Test accuracy	68.68%	67.48%	68.15%	68.15%

emotion than using them independently. For a compromise between real-time application and accurate performance, ensemble ABC with average score fusion technique was chosen as the best trained ensemble, since it has the best reported test performance with 72.47%, and requires fewer parameters, 5.25 millions. In comparison, the second best ensemble ABCD requires 8.08 millions.

The subtle differences between facial expressions corresponding to various emotions, offer the main challenge in obtaining a more generalized model. Even though only 435 images are available in the 'Training 2' dataset for the facial expression for 'disgust', most single models perform a better generalization on it than for the 'afraid', 'angry' or 'sad' facial emotions. A possible explanation could

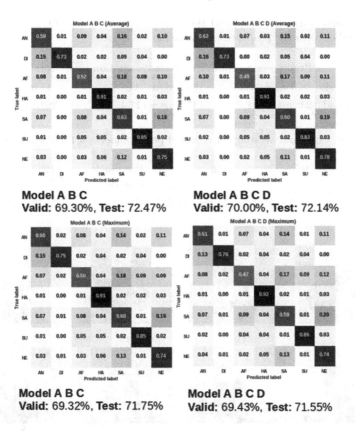

Fig. 2. Obtained confusion matrices for the two best FCNN ensemble models based on test set accuracy (Up : Average fusion strategy, Down : Maximum fusion strategy)

Table 4. Obtained recognition performances for FCNN ensemble models

Ensembles	Validation accuracy		Test accuracy	
	Average	Maximum	Average	Maximum
A B	68.96%	68.65%	70.47%	70.38%
A C	68.93%	68.15%	70.91%	70.97%
A D	69.77%	69.32%	71.11%	70.55%
B C	68.43%	68.04%	70.58%	70.05%
B D	67.46%	67.32%	69.60%	69.43%
C D	68.68%	68.04%	70.08%	69.80%
A B C	69.30%	69.32%	**72.47 %**	71.75%
A B D	69.41%	69.30%	71.08%	70.80%
B C D	68.88%	68.15%	71.50%	70.69%
B D A	69.41%	69.30%	71.08%	70.80%
C A D	69.69%	69.52%	71.66%	71.08%
A B C D	70.00%	69.43%	**72.14 %**	71.55%

Table 5. Comparative study of real time constraints using YOLO model and Haar cascade method with the proposed ensemble model

Method	Preprocessing time	Ensemble recognition time	Total
Haar cascade	88.3 ms ± 12.23	128.6 ms ± 53.6	217 ms ± 54.8
YOLO faced	238 ms ± 191.7	145.7 ms ± 111.1	384.2 ms ± 302.1

Table 6. Comparative study of reported performances on FER 2013 test set

Method	[16]	[3]	[22]	[8]	Proposed method	[12]	[18]
Reported performance	66.4%	67.21%	71.2%	71.33%	72.47%	73.73%	75.2%

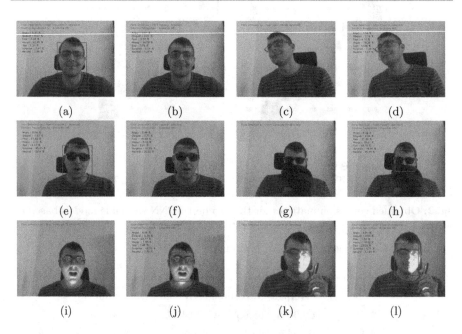

(a)   (b)   (c)   (d)

(e)   (f)   (g)   (h)

(i)   (j)   (k)   (l)

Fig. 3. Experimental emotion detections under real conditions - (a, c, e, g, i, k) using Haar Cascade and (b, d, f, h, j, l) using YOLO based model.

be, that the training, validation and test sets, have different multidimensional distributions in terms of the learned features. This phenomenon could be a bias over the whole database when selecting different sets of data, emphasized by the constraint of having a small dataset relative to the task at hand.

5   Conclusions

An accurate face emotion recognition system could improve human-robot inter-actions(HRI), by rendering the robot accurately aware of the users emotional state, as in therapeutic robotics [11], and by enhancing social interactions in real life scenarios [6,23]. Actually, different kinds of robots are being used as a companion for elder people or in interactions with autists [4,20], alzheimer patients [26], etc.

Dividing and conquering has demonstrated to be a good strategy since the first stage deals only with preprocessing signals in different conditions and allow to focus the second stage only on inferring the emotional state; therefore, sim-plifying the whole process. This system provides both face detection and face emotional recognition and could provide an advanced solution to expand sociable robotics and emotional recognition systems.

The results are comparable to the best state of the art architectures and, furthermore, it faces real-time constraints for accurate emotional recognition in a sociable robotics environments.

Acknowledgements. We want to acknowledge to Programa de Ayudas a Grupos de Excelencia de la Región de Murcia, from Fundación Séneca, Agencia de Ciencia y Tecnología de la Región de Murcia.

References

1. Bartlett, M.S., Littlewort, G., Frank, M., Lainscsek, C., Fasel, I., Movellan, J.: Recognizing facial expression: machine learning and application to spontaneous behavior. In: 2005 IEEE Computer Society Conference on Computer Vision and Pattern Recognition (CVPRV 2005), vol. 2, pp. 568–573, June 2005
2. Dalal, N., Triggs, B.: Histograms of oriented gradients for human detection. In: 2005 IEEE Computer Society Conference on Computer Vision and Pattern Recognition (CVPR 2005), San Diego, CA, USA, vol. 1, pp. 886–893. IEEE (2005)
3. Devries, T., Biswaranjan, K., Taylor, G.W.: Multi-task learning of facial landmarks and expression. In: 2014 Canadian Conference on Computer and Robot Vision, pp. 98–103, May 2014
4. Diehl, J.J., Schmitt, L.M., Villano, M., Crowell, C.R.: The clinical use of robots for individuals with autism spectrum disorders: a critical review. Res. Autism Spectr. Disord. **6**(1), 249–262 (2012)
5. Ekman, P.: Pictures of Facial Affect. Consulting Psychologists Press, Palo Alto (1976)
6. Fong, T., Nourbakhsh, I., Dautenhahn, K.: A survey of socially interactive robots. Robot. Auton. Syst. **42**(3–4), 143–166 (2003)
7. Goodfellow, I.J., et al.: Challenges in representation learning: a report on three machine learning contests. arXiv:1307.0414 [cs, stat], July 2013
8. Guo, Y., Tao, D., Yu, J., Xiong, H., Li, Y., Tao, D.: Deep neural networks with relativity learning for facial expression recognition. In: 2016 IEEE International Conference on Multimedia Expo Workshops (ICMEW), pp. 1–6, July 2016
9. Itzcovich, I.: Yolo-face-detection (2018). https://github.com/iitzco/faced

10. Jack, R.E., Garrod, O.G., Yu, H., Caldara, R., Schyns, P.G.: Facial expressions of emotion are not culturally universal. Proc. Natl. Acad. Sci. **109**(19), 7241–7244 (2012)
11. Jeong, S., et al.: A social robot to mitigate stress, anxiety, and pain in hospital pediatric care. In: Proceedings of the Tenth Annual ACM/IEEE International Conference on Human-Robot Interaction Extended Abstracts - HRI 2015, Extended Abstracts, Portland, Oregon, USA, pp. 103–104. ACM Press (2015)
12. Kim, B.K., Dong, S.Y., Roh, J., Kim, G., Lee, S.Y.: Fusing aligned and non-aligned face information for automatic affect recognition in the wild: a deep learning approach. In: 2016 IEEE Conference on Computer Vision and Pattern Recognition Workshops (CVPRW), Las Vegas, NV, USA, pp. 1499–1508. IEEE, June 2016
13. Li, S., Deng, W.: Deep facial expression recognition: a survey. arXiv:1804.08348 [cs], April 2018
14. Lin, M., Chen, Q., Yan, S.: Network in network. arXiv:1312.4400 [cs], December 2013
15. Lucey, P., Cohn, J.F., Kanade, T., Saragih, J., Ambadar, Z., Matthews, I.: The extended cohn-kanade dataset (CK+): a complete dataset for action unit and emotion-specified expression. In: 2010 IEEE Computer Society Conference on Computer Vision and Pattern Recognition - Workshops, pp. 94–101, June 2010
16. Mollahosseini, A., Chan, D., Mahoor, M.H.: Going deeper in facial expression recognition using deep neural networks. In: 2016 IEEE Winter Conference on Applications of Computer Vision (WACV), pp. 1–10, March 2016
17. Ojala, T., Pietikäinen, M., Harwood, D.: A comparative study of texture measures with classification based on featured distributions. Pattern Recognit. **29**(1), 51–59 (1996)
18. Pramerdorfer, C., Kampel, M.: Facial expression recognition using convolutional neural networks: state of the art. arXiv:1612.02903 [cs], December 2016
19. Redmon, J., Divvala, S., Girshick, R., Farhadi, A.: You only look once: unified, real-time object detection. In: 2016 IEEE Conference on Computer Vision and Pattern Recognition (CVPR), Las Vegas, NV, USA, pp. 779–788. IEEE, June 2016
20. Scassellati, B., Admoni, H., Mataric, M.: Robots for use in autism research. Ann. Rev. Biomed. Eng. **14**(1), 275–294 (2012)
21. Springenberg, J.T., Dosovitskiy, A., Brox, T., Riedmiller, M.: Striving for simplicity: the all convolutional net. arXiv:1412.6806 [cs], December 2014
22. Tang, Y.: Deep learning using linear support vector machines. arXiv:1306.0239 [cs, stat], June 2013
23. Tapus, A., Mataric, M.J., Scassellati, B.: The grand challenges in socially assistive robotics, p. 7
24. Viola, P., Jones, M.: Rapid object detection using a boosted cascade of simple features. In: Proceedings of the 2001 IEEE Computer Society Conference on Computer Vision and Pattern Recognition, CVPR 2001, vol. 1, p. I. IEEE (2001)
25. Yang, S., Luo, P., Loy, C.C., Tang, X.: WIDER FACE: a face detection benchmark. In: 2016 IEEE Conference on Computer Vision and Pattern Recognition (CVPR), Las Vegas, NV, USA, pp. 5525–5533. IEEE, June 2016
26. Yu, R., et al.: Use of a therapeutic, socially assistive pet robot (PARO) in improving mood and stimulating social interaction and communication for people with dementia: study protocol for a randomized controlled trial. JMIR Res. Protoc. **4**(2), e45 (2015)

Advanced Trajectory Generator for Two Carts with RGB-D Sensor on Circular Rail

Ramón Panduro[1], Eva Segura[2], Lidia M. Belmonte[1,2], Paulo Novais[3],
Jesús Benet[2], Antonio Fernández-Caballero[1,2(✉)], and Rafael Morales[1,2]

[1] Instituto de Investigación en Informática de Albacete,
Universidad de Castilla-La Mancha, 02071 Albacete, Spain
antonio.fdez@uclm.es
[2] Escuela Técnica Superior de Ingenieros Industriales,
Universidad de Castilla-La Mancha, 02071 Albacete, Spain
[3] Intelligent Systems Lab, Campus of Gualtar, Universidade do Minho,
4710-057 Braga, Portugal

Abstract. This paper presents a motorised circular rail that generates the motion of two carts with an RGB-D sensor each. The objective of both carts' trajectory generation is to track a person's physical rehabilitation exercises from two points of view and his/her emotional state from one of these viewpoints. The person is moving freely his/her position and posture within the circle drawn by the motorised rail. More specifically, this paper describes the calculation of trajectories for safe motion of the two carts on the motorised circular rail in detail. Lastly, a study case is offered to show the performance of the described control algorithms for trajectory generation.

Keywords: Physical rehabilitation · Facial emotion detection · Moving cart · Motorised circular rail · RGB-D sensor

1 Introduction

Popularity of computer-based physical rehabilitation systems is constantly increasing. Such systems typically use depth cameras to detect and track humans [1–4]. Moreover, some previous works that provide solutions based on RGB-D for monitoring rehabilitation exercises have been presented in the last years [5,6]. In addition, facial emotion detection [7,8] of the human doing exercises is a good way to understand how he/she feels during the rehabilitation program. Our vision-based solutions are based on human detection [9,10] and tracking [11–13]. This paper is also inspired in previous research in multi-robotics [14–16] tracking robotics [17–19] and rehabilitation robotics [20–22].

It is mandatory to continuously provide excellent viewpoints by modifying the camera's angles [23] to monitor people who are undergoing physical rehabilitation programs. RGB-D sensors must be placed in the best positions in an

© Springer Nature Switzerland AG 2019
J. M. Ferrández Vicente et al. (Eds.): IWINAC 2019, LNCS 11486, pp. 181–190, 2019.
https://doi.org/10.1007/978-3-030-19591-5_19

intelligent manner to acquire images of the most relevant parts of the patients' bodies. This is why, mechanical solutions and control strategies are being developed for optimally placing RGB-D sensors during human rehabilitation exercises [24]. Moreover, facial emotion detection determines that one of the viewpoints must be frontal to the patient.

This article describes an advanced trajectory generator for a motorised circular rail capable of smartly relocating two carts equipped with an RGB-D sensor each. The layout of such cart is shown in Fig. 1. The aim is to monitor a patient's face and body from two complementary views [25], one of them being frontal to the patient. In this particular design, a patient can move freely within the rail's circle, so that the carts are placed around him/her to monitor all body gestures from two sights.

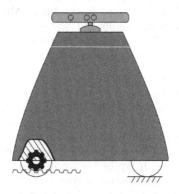

Fig. 1. Layout of a cart equipped with an RGB-D sensor.

2   Trajectory Generator

The proposed trajectory generator must calculate the displacements of both carts to locate them in the optimal position to track the patient's face and physical rehabilitation exercises. For this sake, dynamically one of the carts is assigned the role of master, in front of his/her face, and the other one the role of slave. The patient is described as input vector within the trajectory generation system. It is assumed that both the patient's tracking position and the position of the two carts are known in each instant. Several parameters are considered to correctly carry out the trajectory. These are the tilt and pan movements of the cameras (one per cart), the final angular positions of the carts with respect to the rail, the direction that each cart must follow, and the possible collisions between both carts.

2.1   Angles of the Cameras

First, the location of the patient is defined with respect to the circle's centre (x_p, y_p) and the camera's pan angle γ_c. On the other hand, the camera's tilt

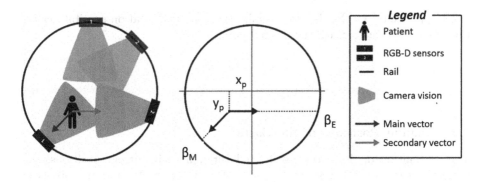

Fig. 2. Vector schemes.

angle α_c is defined by considering the height of the tracked zone. Figure 2 shows an outline of this arrangement.

The formulas that govern the behaviour of the carts are different depending on the master and slave roles assigned. These roles are established according to the current locations of both carts. On the other hand, the angular position of the slave cart must vary when a collision is foreseen with the master cart after the trajectories have been calculated. In this case, the slave cart must follow the opposite path.

In this arrangement, also the camera's pan movement γ_c is calculated as follows. The direction opposite to the RGB-D sensor vector, which angle is $\gamma_c + \pi$, moves until occupying the position of RGB-D sensor vector with angle γ_p. However, as the RGB-D sensor is mounted on a cart rotating around the rail, the turn β_c done by the cart is subtracted, obtaining

$$\Delta\gamma_1 = \gamma_c - (\gamma_p + \pi) - \min(|\Delta\beta_1|, |\Delta\beta_2|); \tag{1}$$

$$\Delta\gamma_2 = \pi - \gamma_c + \gamma_p - \min(|\Delta\beta_1|, |\Delta\beta_2|) \tag{2}$$

where $\Delta\beta_1$ and $\Delta\beta_2$ are magnitudes that will be defined in Sect. 2.2. When calculating the tilt movement of the RGB-D sensor, the height of the tracked zone z_p is considered. The angles of the patient's vector covered by the master and slave carts, named α_{pm} and α_{pe} respectively, are calculated with respect to the RGB-D sensor height z_c. That is,

$$\alpha_{pm} = \arctan \frac{(x_m - x_p)^2 + (y_m - y_p)^2}{z_p - z_c}; \tag{3}$$

$$\alpha_{pe} = \arctan \frac{(x_e - x_p)^2 + (y_e - y_p)^2}{z_p - z_c} \tag{4}$$

Moreover, the movement of the RGB-D sensor is obtained considering that the cart is also moving. Thus, the objective is that α_c occupies the place of the angle opposite to α_p, that is, $-\alpha_p$. Again, there are two rotation possibilities for the RGB-D sensor to reach the desired point:

$$\Delta\alpha_1 = -\alpha_p - \alpha_c \tag{5}$$

$$\Delta\alpha_2 = 2\pi + \alpha_p + \alpha_c \tag{6}$$

2.2   Angular Positions of the Carts

The destination of the carts are defined through their current positions, the patient's position with respect to the centre of the circle, and the observed patient's direction. The new RGB-D sensor position to observe the patient's direction is the angular position of the circle that intersects with the imaginary line that passes through the direction of the patient with origin in his/her current position.

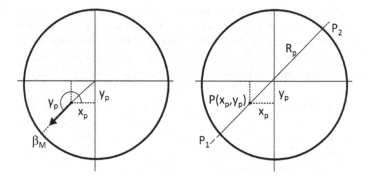

Fig. 3. Angular positions of the carts.

By means of this approach, the two cut points of the line passing through the position of the patient are obtained geometrically, taking the patient as the direction (see Fig. 3). To obtain line R_p, the position of the patient $P = (x_p, y_p)$ and the patient's direction $v_p = (x_v, y_v) = (\cos\gamma_p, \sin\gamma_p)$ are used, obtaining

$$\frac{x - x_p}{x_v} = \frac{y - y_p}{y_v} \tag{7}$$

being x and y the coordinates of the different points that belong to line R_p. On the other hand, the parametrisation of the circular path of radius R is defined as

$$x^2 + y^2 = R^2 \tag{8}$$

Operating with expressions (7) and (8), we get

$$(m^2 + 1)y^2 + 2mny + (n^2 - R^2) = 0 \tag{9}$$

where $m = \frac{x_v}{y_v}$ and $n = x_p - \frac{y_p}{y_v} \cdot x_v$, resulting in cut points $P_1 = (x_1, y_1)$ and $P_2 = (x_2, y_2)$

$$y_1 = \frac{-2mn + \sqrt{4m^2n^2 - 4(m^2 + 1)(n^2 - R^2)}}{2(m^2 + 1)}; \quad x_1 = (y_1 - y_p) \cdot m + x_p \quad (10)$$

$$y_2 = \frac{-2mn - \sqrt{4m^2n^2 - 4(m^2 + 1)(n^2 - R^2)}}{2(m^2 + 1)}; \quad x_2 = (y_2 - y_p) \cdot m + x_p \quad (11)$$

In order to obtain which point is correct, the parametric equation of line R_p with the value of parameter $t = \frac{x_1 - x_p}{x_v} = \frac{y_1 - y_p}{y_v}$ is calculated by substituting in said equation the value of the first calculated point. If the value of parameter t is positive, then point P_1 is the cart's destination point. If it is negative, then the cart must move to P_2.

The next step is using parameter $\beta_m = \arctan \frac{y}{x}$ to convert that point of the circumference into an angular position around the circle. Once we have obtained the point to be addressed, the cart movement has two possible solutions. The first one is $\Delta\beta_1 = \beta_m - \beta_c$. The second one depends on the sign of the first, since it corresponds to the opposite direction. If $\Delta\beta_1$ corresponds to a clockwise turn, we have $\Delta\beta_2 = 2\pi + \beta_m - \beta_c$. If the turn is counter-clockwise, we have $\Delta\beta_2 = -2\pi + \beta_m - \beta_c$. Next, the displacements $\Delta\beta$ of both carts are summed up and the role of each cart is selected as a function of said displacements. The movement function of the master cart is

$$M_{CM} = (\min(|\Delta\beta_1|, |\Delta\beta_2|), \min(|\Delta\alpha_1|, |\Delta\alpha_2|), \min(|\Delta\gamma_1|, |\Delta\gamma_2|)) \quad (12)$$

A similar mathematical development is carried out for the slave cart.

2.3   Selection of the Carts' Roles

The selection of each cart's role is determined according to the following criteria:

i. When the carts' destination points to cover the patient's position have been calculated, firstly the cart closest to the main vector becomes the master. The other cart is assigned the role of slave. However, this may change, as the total route made by both carts is priority when choosing the roles.

ii. Any collision between the carts must be avoided. For this purpose, it is checked that the route used by one cart is not interspersed with the other, avoiding such possible route.

iii. If both carts are at the same distance from point β_M, the cart closest to point β_E becomes the slave.

iv. If both points are at the same distance from the two carts, the one whose speed in the direction of the point is larger is the one that takes the role of master.

v. And, if both carts have the same speed or are quiet, cart 1 will be the master and cart 2 will be the slave.

To explain these situations, two examples are analysed (see Fig. 4), where it is determined which of the two carts should go to each position according to the destination. In example (a) of the figure, the distribution of roles is very simple according to the first rule described. Cart 1 takes the role of master and moves to position β_M since it is the closest one. On the other hand, cart 2 takes the slave role and moves to position β_E. In example (b), the same assignment of roles is done: cart 1 would be the master and go to point β_M, while cart B would take the role of slave and go to point β_E. However, the algorithm foresees a collision of both carts, and immediately changes the trajectory of cart 2 to move to point β_E, which is at least slightly optimal. To avoid such situation, a change of roles is convenient, taking cart 1 the role of slave and cart 2 the role of master. In this way, the total journey made by both carts is much smaller and optimal.

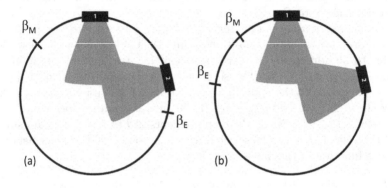

Fig. 4. Examples of role distribution.

3   Study Case

A study case presented to validate the functioning of the advanced trajectory generator. The complete tracking of a patient whose position has moved with respect to the centre of the circular rail is performed. Figure 5a shows the position of the carts and the patient at the initial simulation instant. Figure 5b illustrates the final positions reached, where it can be seen how the carts have reached the desired positions, just as the RGB-D sensor has successfully rotated to point directly to the patient.

The trajectory generator selects the shortest route and gives the role of master to cart Q and that of slave to S. In addition, we compare the values calculated by the algorithm and the final route to check if the system has selected the shortest route. Table 1 collects the aforementioned data. As can be verified, the system selects the shortest path between the possible routes (clockwise or counter-clockwise). This is, the route in counter-clockwise direction for cart Q and the clockwise for cart S, respectively.

Besides, it is checked that the system has correctly selected the roles so that the total distance travelled by both carts is the minimum (see Table 2). Since

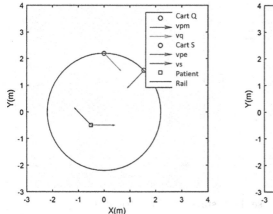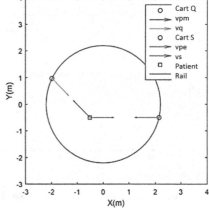

Fig. 5. Positioning graphs of the study case. Left: start positions. Right: final positions.

Table 1. Distance according to path.

Data (rad)	Cart Q	Cart S
Path clockwise	−5.1706	−1.0147
Path counter-clockwise	1.1126	5.2685
Path selected	1.1126	−1.0147

Table 2. Distance according to role.

Data (rad)	Q master, S slave	Q slave, S master
Distance Q	1.1126	−1.8980
Distance S	−1.0147	1.8980
Total distance	2.1273	3.796

cart Q was selected as master and cart S as slave, it is verified that the trajectory generator has correctly selected the shortest distance travelled by both carts.

The next check is related to the tilt of the RGB-D sensor. The data shown in Table 2 throw the graphs shown in Fig. 6. Since the cart's turn is now considered, the tilt angle of the RGB-D sensor must be the opposite of that direction. As can be seen in the graph, the direction of cart Q is tilted until it takes the angle opposite to the patient's master direction. In the same way, cart direction S is tilted to observe the slave vector of the patient.

As with positioning, it is checked that the system is able to select the shortest route. The data obtained for the study are included in Table 3. Finally, the pan angle that the RGB-D sensor takes to focus on the patient must be checked in the same direction but in the opposite sense. As can be seen from the graph, the vector of cart Q tilts until it points directly to the patient's master vector. In the same way, cart S vector is tilted to observe the slave vector of the patient.

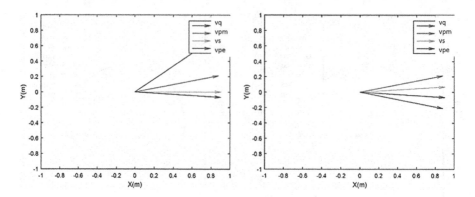

Fig. 6. Tilt graphs of the study case. Left: start positions. Right: final positions.

Table 3. Tilt according to path.

Data (rad)	Cart Q	Cart S
Path clockwise	−0.9337	−6.2076
Path counter-clockwise	5.3495	0.0755
Path selected	−0.933	0.0755

Table 4. Pan according to path.

Data (rad)	Cart Q	Cart S
Path clockwise	−1.1126	6.0539
Path counter-clockwise	5.1706	0.2293
Path selected	−1.1126	0.2293

It is also observed that the system is able to select the shortest route. Table 4 shows that the system has correctly selected the route to travel the smallest possible path. In this case, routes are counter-clockwise and clockwise for carts Q and S, respectively.

The final displacement functions of carts Q and S are called M_{CQ} and M_{CS}, respectively:

$$M_{CQ}(\beta, \alpha, \gamma) = (2.1271, -0.9337, -1.1126) \text{ rad} \tag{13}$$

$$M_{CS}(\beta, \alpha, \gamma) = (3.7960, -0.0755, 0.2293) \text{ rad} \tag{14}$$

4   Conclusions

This paper has presented an advanced trajectory generator for the motion of two carts with an RGB-D sensor aboard on a motorised circular rail. A continuous monitoring of the facial emotion expressed by the patient and the performed physical rehabilitation exercises is the final objective of the described system. This will be a future tool for evaluation of the proper physical exercises by calculating possible deviations of the optimal gestures, and, at the same, the degree of comfort of the patient during rehabilitation through the emotions felt. This is why, the paper has introduced the description of the displacements of both carts and the positioning of the tilt and pan angles of each RGB-D sensor to track the face and the body of the patient from the best viewpoints.

The paper has also described a study case that demonstrates that the proposed advanced trajectory generator offers enough security to ensure that both carts never collide during their tracking of the human undergoing a rehabilitation program.

Acknowledgements. This work was partially supported by Ministerio de Ciencia, Innovación y Universidades, Agencia Estatal de Investigación (AEI) / European Regional Development Fund (FEDER, UE) under DPI2016-80894-R grant.

References

1. Tian, G., Liu, L., Ri, J.H., Liu, Y.: ObjectFusion: an object detection and segmentation framework with RGB-D SLAM and convolutional neural networks. Author links open overlay panel bYiranSuna
2. Freitas, D., et al.: Development and evaluation of a Kinect based motor rehabilitation game. Simposio Brasileiro de Jogos e Entretenimento Digital, pp. 144–153 (2012)
3. Chang, Y., Chen, S., Huang, J.: A Kinect-based system for physical rehabilitation: a pilot study for young adults with motor disabilities. Res. Dev. Disabil. **326**, 2566–2570 (2011)
4. López-Valles, J.M., Fernández, M.A., Fernández-Caballero, A.: Stereovision depth analysis by two-dimensional motion charge memories. Pattern Recognit. Lett. **28**(1), 20–30 (2007)
5. Oliver, M., Montero, F., Molina, J.P., González, P., Fernández-Caballero, A.: Multi-camera systems for rehabilitation therapies: a study of the precision of Microsoft Kinect sensors. Front. Inf. Technol. Electron. Eng. **17**(4), 348–364 (2016)
6. Oliver, M., Montero, F., Fernández-Caballero, A., González, P., Molina, J.P.: RGB-D assistive technologies for acquired brain injury: description and assessment of user experience. Expert Syst. **32**(3), 370–380 (2015)
7. Castillo, J.C., Fernández-Caballero, A., Castro-González, Á., Salichs, M.A., López, M.T.: A framework for recognizing and regulating emotions in the elderly. In: Pecchia, L., Chen, L.L., Nugent, C., Bravo, J. (eds.) IWAAL 2014. LNCS, vol. 8868, pp. 320–327. Springer, Cham (2014). https://doi.org/10.1007/978-3-319-13105-4_46
8. Lozano-Monasor, E., López, M.T., Fernández-Caballero, A., Vigo-Bustos, F.: Facial expression recognition from webcam based on active shape models and support vector machines. In: Pecchia, L., Chen, L.L., Nugent, C., Bravo, J. (eds.) IWAAL 2014. LNCS, vol. 8868, pp. 147–154. Springer, Cham (2014). https://doi.org/10.1007/978-3-319-13105-4_23
9. Wang, P., Li, W., Ogunbona, P., Wan, J., Escalera, S.: RGB-D-based human motion recognition with deep learning: a survey. Comput. Vision Image Underst. **171**, 118–139 (2018)

10. Fernández-Caballero, A., López, M.T., Saiz-Valverde, S.: Dynamic stereoscopic selective visual attention (DSSVA): integrating motion and shape with depth in video segmentation. Expert Syst. Appl. **34**(2), 1394–1402 (2008)

11. Castillo, J.C., Fernández-Caballero, A., Serrano-Cuerda, J., López, M.T., Martínez-Rodrigo, A.: Smart environment architecture for robust people detection by infrared and visible video fusion. J. Ambient Intel. Humanized Comput. **8**(2), 223–237 (2017)

12. Fernández-Caballero, A., López, M.T., Serrano-Cuerda, J.: Thermal-infrared pedestrian ROI extraction through thermal and motion information fusion. Sensors **14**(4), 6666–6676 (2014)

13. Moreno-Garcia, J., Rodriguez-Benitez, L., Fernández-Caballero, A., López, M.T.: Video sequence motion tracking by fuzzification techniques. Appl. Soft Comput. **10**(1), 318–331 (2010)

14. Florea, A.G., Buiu, C.: A distributed approach to the control of multi-robot systems using XP colonies. Integr. Comput.-Aided Eng. **25**(1), 15–29 (2018)

15. Morales, R., Chocoteco, J., Feliu, V., Sira-Ramírez, H.: Obstacle surpassing and posture control of a stair-climbing robotic mechanism. Control Eng. Pract. **21**, 604–621 (2013)

16. Morales, R., González, A., Feliu, V., Pintado, P.: Environment adaptation of a new staircase climbing wheelchair. Auton. Robots **23**, 275–292 (2007)

17. Panwar, R., Sukavanam, N.: Trajectory tracking using artificial neural network for stable human-like gait with upper body motion. Neural Comput. Appl. (2018). https://doi.org/10.1007/s00521-018-3842-1

18. Almansa-Valverde, S., Castillo, J.C., Fernández-Caballero, A.: Mobile robot map building from time-of-flight camera. Expert Syst. Appl. **39**(10), 8835–8843 (2012)

19. Gascueña, J.M., Fernández-Caballero, A.: Agent-oriented modeling and development of a person-following mobile robot. Expert Syst. Appl. **38**(4), 4280–4290 (2011)

20. Morales, R., Somolinos, J.A., Fernández-Caballero, A., Ferraresi, C.: Rehabilitation robotics and systems. J. Healthc. Eng. **2018**, 5370127 (2018)

21. Chocoteco, J., Morales, R., Feliu, V.: Enhancing the trajectory generation of a stair-climbing mobility system. Sensors **17**(1), 1–31 (2017)

22. Chocoteco, J., Morales, R., Feliu, V., Sánchez, L.: Trajectory planning for a stair-climbing mobility system using laser distance sensors. IEEE Syst. J. **10**(3), 944–956 (2016)

23. Benito-Picazo, J., Domínguez, E., Palomo, E.J., López-Rubio, E., Ortiz-de-Lazcano-Lobato, J.M.: Motion detection with low cost hardware for PTZ cameras. Integr. Comput.-Aided Eng. **26**(1), 21–36 (2019)

24. Panduro, R., Oliver, M., Morales, R., González, P., Fernández-Caballero, A.: Motorized multi-camera slider for precise monitoring of physical rehabilitation. In: García, C.R., Caballero-Gil, P., Burmester, M., Quesada-Arencibia, A. (eds.) UCAmI/IWAAL/AmIHEALTH -2016. LNCS, vol. 10070, pp. 21–27. Springer, Cham (2016). https://doi.org/10.1007/978-3-319-48799-1_3

25. Mkhitaryan, A., Burschka, D.: RGB-D sensor data correction and enhancement by introduction of an additional RGB view. In: Proceedings of the IEEE/RSJ International Conference on Intelligent Robots and Systems, pp.1077–1083 (2013)

On the Use of Lateralization for Lightweight and Accurate Methodology for EEG Real Time Emotion Estimation Using Gaussian-Process Classifier

Mikel Val-Calvo[1,2]([⊠]), José Ramón Álvarez-Sánchez[1],
Alejandro Díaz-Morcillo[3], José Manuel Ferrández Vicente[2],
and Eduardo Fernández-Jover[4]

[1] Dpto. de Inteligencia Artificial, Universidad Nacional de Educacióna Distancia
(UNED), Juan del Rosal, 16, 28040 Madrid, Spain
mikel1982mail@gmail.com
[2] Dpto. Electrónica, Tecnología de Computadoras y Proyectos,
Univ. Politécnica de Cartagena, Cartagena, Spain
[3] Dpto. Tecnologías de la Información y las Comunicaciones,
Univ. Politécnica de Cartagena, Cartagena, Spain
[4] Instituto de Bioingeniería, Univ. Miguel Hernández, Elche, Spain

Abstract. Emotional estimation systems based on electroencephalography (EEG) signals are gaining special attention in recent years due to the possibilities they offer. The field of human-robot interactions (HRI) will benefit from a broadened understanding of brain emotional encoding and thus, improve the capabilities of robots to fully engage with the user's emotional reactions. In this paper, a methodology for real-time emotion estimation aimed for its use in the field of HRI is proposed. The proposed methodology takes advantage of the lateralization produced in brain oscillations during emotional stimuli and the use of meaningful features related to intrinsic EEG patterns. In the validation procedure, both DEAP and SEED databases have been used. A mean performance of 88.34% was obtained using four categories of the valence-arousal space, and 97.1% using three discrete categories; both of them obtained with a Gaussian-Process classifier. This lightweight method could run on inexpensive, portable devices such as the openBCI system.

Keywords: Emotion estimation · EEG · Robotics ·
Human-robot interaction

1 Introduction

The increasing use of robots that can interact with human beings is attracting more interest in the application of machine learning techniques for the recognition of human emotions. A recent branch of studies based on the recognition

© Springer Nature Switzerland AG 2019
J. M. Ferrández Vicente et al. (Eds.): IWINAC 2019, LNCS 11486, pp. 191–201, 2019.
https://doi.org/10.1007/978-3-030-19591-5_20

of emotions is being developed to measure and understand how they are produced. These latest developments will advance research into the direction of the emotional human-robot interactions (HRI).

The recognition of emotions in the field of robotics is being studied from different perspectives. For instance, several studies focus on facial emotion recognition, where emotions are related to external cues, such as facial features. In contrast, other approaches study the relationship between emotions and internal cues, i.e. physiological keys related to brain patterns or balances between the parasympathetic and sympathetic autonomous systems.

Different factors make recognition of emotions a challenging task. On one hand, there is no basic truth for self-evaluation, so the assessment of experienced emotions is guided by emotional models developed in the field of psychology. These can be grouped generally as discrete and dimensional models. The former assumes that emotions are qualitatively differentiated neuro-physiological responses which produce independent emotional experiences, while the dimensional approach captures continuous quantified relationships among emotions. However, qualitative differences arise when moving across fuzzy boundaries, between valence and arousal.

Whether brain patterns evoked by emotions can be mapped onto specific brain regions still remains unresolved. In fact, current studies suggest that information encoded during emotional experiences spread over cortical and subcortical areas [12]. There is still no clear evidence on which of the local and global distributions of brain patterns are consistent among subjects, both in dimensional and discrete emotion models. Therefore, there is not yet a consensus on the relevant brain pattern features and brain regions suitable for emotion detection, invariant across subjects.

There are significant variations for each individual in terms of the properties of the measured signals and their related emotional encoding properties, therefore, the studies differ in methodology. To find the invariant relationships across individuals, subject-independent analysis is performed while for user-adapted HRI applications, subject-dependent analysis is done.

The main objective of this research is to focus on developing an accurate methodology for real-time emotion recognition that will be used in the domain of HRI with the openBCI system, taking that into account the preprocessing and feature extraction techniques must be performed with real time feasible techniques. For validation of the methodology, DEAP and SEED databases have been chosen.

2   State of the Art

In order to compare the obtained results, a set of the latest best state of the art articles have been used. First, Zheng et al. [17] used Deep Belief Neural Networks (DBNs) for the classification of three discrete categories on their own produced from SEED database. Critical frequency bands and channels were selected through the weight distributions of the trained DBNs. The best obtained accuracy result was 86.65% with a selection of 12 channels.

Later, Zheng et al. [19] systematically evaluated the performance with a set of popular features used in the domain of electroencephalography (EEG) emotion recognition. Analysis was performed for DEAP and SEED databases. In conclusion, the combination of the differential entropy feature and the Graph regularized Extreme Learning Machine (GELM) classifier outperformed state of the art results. A mean accuracy of 69.67% was obtained using DEAP database for the four quadrants of the valence-arousal dimensional space and 91.07% for SEED database.

Third, Tripathi et al. [15] focused on Deep and Convolutional neural networks (DNN, CNN) to compare the obtained performances and robustness using DEAP database. With the CNN model, 81.46% valence was obtained and 73.12% arousal classifications. With the CNN model 81.46% valence and 73.36% arousal were best obtained results. The DNN model provided more consistent results as the performance was between 65–80% per subject, while the CNN model performance rating was less robust despite having a higher performance average. The valence and arousal dimensions were split into three categories. Self assessments higher than 6 become category 1, ratings between 6 and 4 as category 2, and ratings below 4 as category 3. The DNN model achieved 58.44% and 55.70%, while the CNN model achieved 66.79% and 57.58%, respectively.

Fourth, Khosrowabadi et al. [10] proposed a novel approach called ERNN. EEG data from 57 subjects were produced with emotionally tagged audio-visual stimuli having an average performance of 70.83% for arousal and 71.43% for valence dimensional spaces.

Finally, Song et al. [14] developed a novel Dynamical Graph Convolutional Neural Network (DGCNN). Performances were tested over SEED database. Differential entropy features of five frequency bands were combined resulting in an average recognition accuracy of 90.40% for the case of subject-dependent experiments.

3   Methods

The proposed methodology has been applied to two databases and it comprises four main steps: preprocessing data, feature extraction, feature selection and classification.

3.1   DEAP and SEED Databases

The DEAP database contains 32 different subjects which were stimulated with a set of 40 emotionally-tagged videos, each of them 60 s long. During the experiments, each individual quantified the experienced emotion based on the dimensional valence-arousal model. For the sake of this paper, the database has been classified into four labels by the discretization of the dimensional space: low valence-low arousal (LVLA), low valence-high arousal (LVHA), high valence-low arousal (HVLA) and high valence-high arousal (HVHA).

On the other hand, the SEED database has 15 subjects but the experiment was performed three times each, with a time interval of one week. Emotions were quantified in terms of three discrete categories: POSITIVE, NEGATIVE and NEUTRAL. A set of 15 emotional-tagged videos were employed, each approximately 180 s long. Both studies used the international 10–20 system for EEG acquisition, however 32 channels were used for the DEAP database and 62 channels for the SEED database.

3.2   Preprocessing

EEG signals are arranged in a three dimensional matrix containing n trials, c channels and s samples at a sample frequency f_s. First, given that each signal has it's own scaling factor values, signals are standardized using z-score method. Second, a filter bank, based on sixth-order Butterworth filters, is applied for all n, c and s, within a set of 4 non-overlapping bandwidths of $B = \{4-8, 8-16, 16-32, 32-45\}$Hz.

3.3   Feature Extraction

Once the data-set has been preprocessed, a set of features are computed based on the oscillatory properties of brain signals: differential entropy, estimations (using Hilbert Transform) of instantaneous amplitude and frequency, and lagged-coherence for measuring rhythmicity in neural oscillations.

The differential entropy for a signal X, whose values have a probability density function similar to a Gaussian distribution, $N(\mu, \sigma^2)$, as is the case for EEG signals, can be defined as $h(X) = log(2 * \pi * e * \sigma^2)/2$.

The estimated values for the instantaneous amplitude and frequency of a signal can be obtained through the analytic representation of the signal (or Gabor's complex signal) that uses the Hilbert transform of the signal [3]. Instantaneous amplitude or envelope can be computed from the modulus of the analytic signal, and instantaneous frequency can be computed from the discrete approximation for the derivative of the instantaneous angular phase (argument of analytic signal). The mean values along each time interval of the instantaneous amplitude, $a(X)$, and instantaneous frequency, $f(X)$, for a signal X are used for the features.

Lagged-coherence, $\lambda(X)$, is a metric related to the rhythmicity of neural oscillations as defined by Fransen et al. [7]. It is a frequency-indexed measure that estimates the phase of a signal with a particular window length, where the rhythmicity is evaluated as the consistency of the measured phases across adjacent non-overlapping time windows of fixed length.

Following the proposed strategy by Zheng et al. [19], lateralization in brain oscillations during emotional stimuli is used for feature computation. The set of features is defined as follows:

$$h_A = h(X_{\text{left}}) - h(X_{\text{right}}) \qquad\qquad f_A = a(X_{\text{left}}) - f(X_{\text{right}})$$

$$h_R = h(X_{\text{left}})/h(X_{\text{right}}) \qquad\qquad f_R = h(X_{\text{left}})/f(X_{\text{right}})$$

$$a_A = a(X_{\text{left}}) - a(X_{\text{right}}) \qquad\qquad \lambda_A = a(X_{\text{left}}) - \lambda(X_{\text{right}})$$

$$a_R = a(X_{\text{left}})/a(X_{\text{right}}) \qquad\qquad \lambda_R = h(X_{\text{left}})/\lambda(X_{\text{right}})$$

Where h_A is the differential entropy asymmetry, h_R is the differential entropy asymmetry ratio, a_A is the mean instantaneous amplitude asymmetry, a_R is the mean instantaneous amplitude asymmetry ratio, f_A is mean instantaneous frequency asymmetry, f_R is the mean instantaneous frequency asymmetry ratio, λ_A is the lagged coherence asymmetry, and λ_R is the lagged coherence asymmetry. Where X_{left} uses ('Fp1', 'AF3', 'F7', 'F3', 'FC1', 'FC5', 'T7', 'C3', 'CP1', 'CP5', 'P7', 'P3', 'PO3', 'O1') and X_{right} uses ('Fp2', 'AF4', 'F8', 'F4', 'FC2', 'FC6', 'T8', 'C4', 'CP2', 'CP6', 'P8', 'P4', 'PO4', 'O2') channels.

All features have been computed using a sliding window of 6 s as suggested by Candra et al. [4], with a step size of 1 s.

Each training sample represents the computed features for each time window. Features are computed for each band/channel and later concatenated for each training sample. Thus, resulting in feature sets of 2200 samples with 416 features, and 2250 samples with 864 features, for DEAP and SEED databases respectively. Finally, normalization is performed using the Quantile-Transform method (histogram equalization to uniform distribution) over feature sets.

Features related to instantaneous amplitude, instantaneous frequency and lagged-coherence have been computed with the Neuro Digital Signal Processing Toolbox (neurodsp) python library [16] developed at Voytek's Lab. Classification process has been done using the scikit-learn python library [13].

3.4   Feature Selection

A key step in machine learning is the dimensional reduction process. Care must be taken while choosing the number of features relative to the number of samples in the training data set. This problem is directly related with the course of dimensionality [11], where feature distributions in hyper-space can become non meaningful in terms of the geometrical distances. At some degree, all classification techniques have to deal with this problem, but some are more sensitive than others, if they are based on geometrical distances over the euclidean space, i.e. the K-nearest neighbour as is demonstrated by Beyer et al. in [2]. Moreover, as Babyak et al. [1] suggests, there are two main factor to achieve a model that generates accurate estimates of the unknown, that is, over new samples. The first one is the number of samples of the population relative to the objective task, and the second one, the ratio between the samples and variables where some statisticians uses the rule "One in ten", meaning that at least, 10 samples are needed for each dimension. Based on this drawback, the ratio between samples and features is chosen to be at least higher than 100 samples/dimension, to prevent that the model will not over-fit. Therefore, a set of best 15 selected features have been used in this study, making a ratio of 146.6 and 150 samples/dimension on DEAP and SEED cases, respectively.

3.5 Classification

Classification processes have been performed using a set of 10 classifiers: Multi Layer Perceptron, K-nearest neighbors, Support Vector Machine with linear and radial basis function kernels, Gaussian-Process, Decision Trees, Random Forests, Ada-Boost, Gaussian Naive-Bayes and Quadratic Discriminant Analysis.

The performance has been evaluated as the average accuracy over all participants for each experiment, taking into account POSITIVE, NEGATIVE and NEUTRAL labels for the SEED database and LVLA, LVHA, HVLA and HVHA for the DEAP database. Results have been obtained with default hyperparameter values.

4   Experimental Results

In Fig. 1 the results obtained on the DEAP and SEED databases are shown as an average score on each label over all subjects. For both databases the best results were obtained with the Gaussian-Process classifier. In order to illustrate the robustness in terms of the generalization of the different labels, the confusion matrices are shown in Fig. 2, both for the subjects with best and worst performance on the DEAP and SEED databases. The final average accuracy is shown in Table 1, where state of the art performances are compared with our proposed methodology, in the context of subject dependent EEG emotion recognition.

Table 1. Obtained recognition performances on EEG databases.

Study	Model	Databases	Categories	Performance
Zheng et al. [17]	DBN	SEED	3	86.65%
Zheng et al. [19]	GELM	SEED, DEAP	3	91.07%, 69.67%
Tripathi et al. [15]	CNN	DEAP	2	73.36–81.46%
Khosrowabadi et al. [10]	ERNN	Own produced database	2	70.83–71.43%
Song et al. [14]	DGCNN	SEED	3	90.40%
Proposed method	GPC	SEED, DEAP	3, 4	**97.1%, 91.2%**

As our purpose was to create a computationally light method and meaningful features for future use on the openBCI system, the classification process was repeated taking into account the constraints of this particular system in terms of the number of electrodes available, 8 in total. Selected channels positions were ('FP2', 'F4', 'C4', 'F8') for X_{right} and ('FP1', 'F2', 'C3', 'F7') for X_{left}. The corresponding confusion matrices for these cases are shown in Fig. 3.

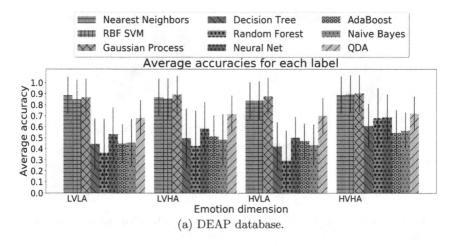

(a) DEAP database.

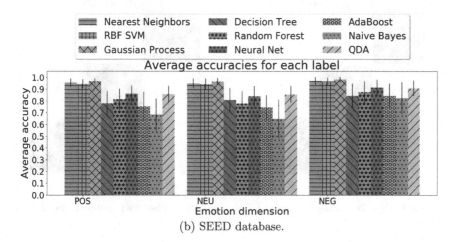

(b) SEED database.

Fig. 1. Average accuracies over all subjects on each label with the set of classifiers selected.

5   Discussion

Our proposed method is optimal in terms of accuracy results in the context of subject dependent analysis. Moreover, it still remains robust when only a subset of electrodes are selected. The average classification accuracy is 95.07% and 78.86% for the SEED and DEAP databases, respectively, when only a subset of 8 electrodes are employed.

The set of selected features are easy to compute in any type of computer and can be easily implemented in any programming language, allowing the quick development of portable systems with high accuracy results, as is the case for the openBCI system. In addition, these features allow for the interpretation of

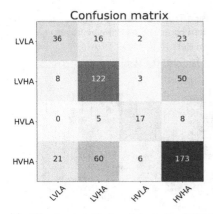

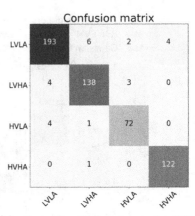

(a) Worst classified subject in DEAP database.

(b) Best classified subject in DEAP database.

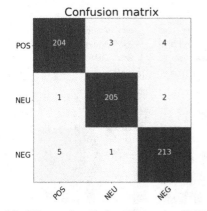

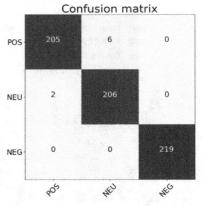

(c) Worst classified subject in SEED database.

(d) Best classified subject in SEED database.

Fig. 2. Confusion matrices for DEAP and SEED databases, using all channels, over worst and best subjects. Rows correspond to True labels while columns to predicted labels.

the phenomenon under study, as they are direct measurements of the properties of brain patterns, being far from black-box techniques using deep-learning approaches such as auto-encoders [5], or very complex features with difficult interpretation in biological terms [18].

A limitation in the domain of EEG signal analysis is often related with the high dimensional space that must be covered due to the great number of electrodes employed. Such signals are complicated in their structure as their intrinsic properties are non-linear and non-stationary. Thus, one of the main limitations is the obligation to construct high dimensional space of features that then must be treated carefully with feature reduction techniques; often biased by the statis-

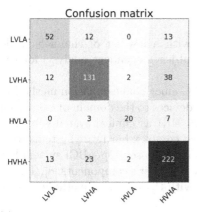

(a) Worst classified subject in DEAP database.

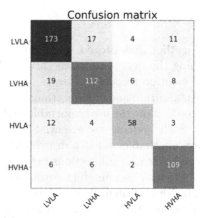

(b) Best classified subject in DEAP database.

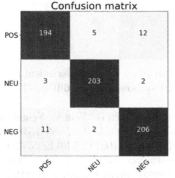

(c) Worst classified subject in SEED database.

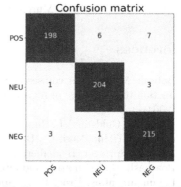

(d) Best classified subject in SEED database.

Fig. 3. Confusion matrices for DEAP and SEED databases, restricted to OpenBCI channels, over worst and best subjects. Rows correspond to True labels while columns to predicted labels.

tics in hand [6]. The proposed methodology shows that it is not necessary to have a large number of electrodes but rather a set of carefully chosen ones and a set of well inter-related meaningful features, to emphasize the differences of brain pattern properties in the task at hand. In this way, after proving that the robustness of the methodology remains almost unchanged when only a subset of 8 electrodes is used, a feature space with less dimensions provides the possibility to further the analysis of where and how each feature is related to an emotional state. Thus, mathematical analysis such as factor analysis, to find invariant relationships among variables, can be performed in a less complex statistical domain.

6   Conclusions

Our method has proved to be robust even with a low set of channels while reaching the best state of the art results in subject dependent analysis for the EEG emotion recognition task.

An accurate and computationally light EEG emotional estimation methodology could allow the use of portable and cheap devices to the domain of emotional HRI. Such systems are essential in emotional HRI as clinical systems are not always affordable and as a drawback they need complex hardware systems with also complex wire connections between them and the user. OpenBCI system has proved to have meaningful information carried out by it's components [8]. Therefore, it is an optimal device for HRI [9], and, with the proposed methodology, it could further the research in this field.

Acknowledgments. We want to acknowledge to Programa de Ayudas a Grupos de Excelencia de la Región de Murcia, from Fundación Séneca, Agencia de Ciencia y Tecnología de la Región de Murcia.

References

1. Babyak, M.A.: What you see may not be what you get: a brief, nontechnical introduction to overfitting in regression-type models. Psychosom. Med. **66**(3), 411–421 (2004)
2. Beyer, K., Goldstein, J., Ramakrishnan, R., Shaft, U.: When is "Nearest Neighbor" meaningful? In: Beeri, C., Buneman, P. (eds.) ICDT 1999. LNCS, vol. 1540, pp. 217–235. Springer, Heidelberg (1999). https://doi.org/10.1007/3-540-49257-7_15
3. Boashash, B.: Estimating and interpreting the instantaneous frequency of a signal. I. Fundamentals. Proc. IEEE **80**(4), 520–538 (1992). https://doi.org/10.1109/5. 135376
4. Candra, H., et al.: Investigation of window size in classification of EEG-emotion signal with wavelet entropy and support vector machine. In: 2015 37th Annual International Conference of the IEEE Engineering in Medicine and Biology Society (EMBC), pp. 7250–7253. IEEE (2015)
5. Chai, X., Wang, Q., Zhao, Y., Liu, X., Bai, O., Li, Y.: Unsupervised domain adaptation techniques based on auto-encoder for non-stationary EEG-based emotion recognition. Comput. Biol. Med. **79**, 205–214 (2016)
6. Fan, J., Li, R.: Statistical challenges with high dimensionality: feature selection in knowledge discovery. arXiv preprint math/0602133 (2006)
7. Fransen, A.M., van Ede, F., Maris, E.: Identifying neuronal oscillations using rhythmicity. Neuroimage **118**, 256–267 (2015)
8. Frey, J.: Comparison of an open-hardware electroencephalography amplifier with medical grade device in brain-computer interface applications. arXiv preprint arXiv:1606.02438 (2016)
9. Jukiewicz, M., Cysewska-Sobusiak, A.: Stimuli design for SSVEP-based brain computer-interface. Int. J. Electron. Telecommun. **62**(2), 109–113 (2016)
10. Khosrowabadi, R., Quek, C., Ang, K.K., Wahab, A.: ERNN: a biologically inspired feedforward neural network to discriminate emotion from EEG signal. IEEE Trans. Neural Netw. Learn. Syst. **25**(3), 609–620 (2014)

11. Köppen, M.: The curse of dimensionality. In: 5th Online World Conference on Soft Computing in Industrial Applications (WSC5), vol. 1, pp. 4–8 (2000)
12. Kragel, P.A., LaBar, K.S.: Decoding the nature of emotion in the brain. Trends Cogn. Sci. **20**(6), 444–455 (2016)
13. Pedregosa, F., et al.: Scikit-learn: machine learning in Python. J. Mach. Learn. Res. **12**, 2825–2830 (2011)
14. Song, T., Zheng, W., Song, P., Cui, Z.: EEG emotion recognition using dynamical graph convolutional neural networks. IEEE Trans. Affect. Comput. (2018)
15. Tripathi, S., Acharya, S., Sharma, R.D., Mittal, S., Bhattacharya, S.: Using deep and convolutional neural networks for accurate emotion classification on DEAP dataset. In: AAAI, pp. 4746–4752 (2017)
16. VoytekLab: Neuro digital signal processing toolbox (2018). https://github.com/ neurodsp-tools/neurodsp
17. Zheng, W.L., Lu, B.L.: Investigating critical frequency bands and channels for eeg-based emotion recognition with deep neural networks. IEEE Trans. Autonom. Mental Dev. **7**(3), 162–175 (2015)
18. Zheng, W.L., Zhang, Y.Q., Zhu, J.Y., Lu, B.L.: Transfer components between subjects for EEG-based emotion recognition. In: 2015 International Conference on Affective Computing and Intelligent Interaction (ACII), pp. 917–922. IEEE (2015)
19. Zheng, W.L., Zhu, J.Y., Lu, B.L.: Identifying stable patterns over time for emotion recognition from EEG. IEEE Trans. Affect. Comput. (2017)

Stress Identification from Electrodermal Activity by Support Vector Machines

Roberto Sánchez-Reolid[1,2], Arturo Martínez-Rodrigo[1,3],
and Antonio Fernández-Caballero[1,2,4(✉)]

[1] Departamento de Sistemas Informáticos, Universidad de Castilla-La Mancha,
02071 Albacete, Spain
antonio.fdez@uclm.es
[2] Instituto de Investigación en Informática de Albacete,
Universidad de Castilla-La Mancha, 02071 Albacete, Spain
[3] Instituto de Tecnologías Audiovisuales, Universidad de Castilla-La Mancha,
16002 Cuenca, Spain
[4] CIBERSAM (Biomedical Research Networking Centre in Mental Health),
Madrid, Spain

Abstract. Continuous atmosphere of competitiveness, job pressure, economic status and social judgment in modern societies leads many people to a frenetic life rhythm, thus favoring the appearance of stress. Consequently, early detection of calm and negative stress is useful to prevent long-term mental illness as depression or anxiety. This paper describes the acquisition of electrodermal activity (EDA) signals from a commercial wearable, and their storage and processing. Several time-domain, frequency-domain and morphological features are extracted over the skin conductance response component of the EDA signals. Afterwards, classification is undergone by using several support vector machines (SVMs). The International Affective Pictures System has been used to evoke calmness and distress to validate the classification results. The best results obtained during training and validation for each of the SVMs report around 87.7% accuracy for Gaussian and cubic kernels.

Keywords: Electrodermal activity · Support vector machines ·
Calmness · Distress

1 Introduction

Early stress detection prevents health problems related to negative stress. There is a great need to create and adapt technologies to monitor and detect conditions of negative stress in everyday life [3,22]. Such early detection helps in the process of emotional self-regulation of the individual under stressful conditions [4,9]. Fortunately, advances have been made in stress detection without disturbing people [16,17]. The use of non-invasive wearable devices allows a constant monitoring of people arousal state. These wearable are well valued as

© Springer Nature Switzerland AG 2019
J. M. Ferrández Vicente et al. (Eds.): IWINAC 2019, LNCS 11486, pp. 202–211, 2019.
https://doi.org/10.1007/978-3-030-19591-5_21

they are comfortable, lightweight, provide long battery life and allow wireless communication.

Lately, many methods and methodologies have been used to determine levels of arousal through detecting alterations of the central nervous system. One of the most commonly used physiological variables to determine arousal is electrodermal activity (EDA). Moreover, this marker is able to quantify changes in the sympathetic nervous system by measuring the conductivity of the skin. In this paper, it has been decided to use a commercial wearable device to record these EDA variations. Empatica E4 [7] is a wristband dedicated to the measurement of several physiological signals (e.g. electrodermal activity, heart rate, skin temperature).

Concretely, this paper describes how to detect calmness and negative stress conditions using a wearable, signal processing techniques and advanced classifiers. The use of advanced classifiers, based on supervised learning, brings an innovative approach against a more classic statistical treatment of the signal features [15,16]. We consider that these classifiers can be implemented in new tools to allow a rapid detection of negative stress conditions.

This paper is structured as follows. Section 2 introduces a description of all materials and software used to identify stress through electrodermal activity acquired from the wearable. In Sect. 3, there is a detailed explanation of the signal processing, feature extraction and classification methods used to validate the developed emotional model. Then, Sect. 4 offers several approaches to segment EDA signals. In addition, the results obtained with the different classifier configurations are shown. Finally, Sect. 5 includes the most relevant conclusions related to this work.

2   Materials for EDA Signals Acquisition and Processing

A fundamental part of this work is EDA signal acquisition and processing. For data acquisition (see Sect. 1) a commercial device [7] has been selected. The Empatica E4 wristband (see Fig. 1) is a wearable designed to measure and collect physiological signals. The wearable is widely used in clinical and domestic research. It incorporates a variety of sensors that provide great versatility like a photoplethysmograph to measure blood volume pulse, as well as electrodermal activity (EDA), three-axis accelerometer and metallic temperature sensors. Each of the sensors has a different sampling frequency. The blood volume pulse works at 64 Hz, the accelerometer at 32 Hz, the skin temperature at 4 Hz and the EDA sensor at 4 Hz. Empatica E4 must be securely attached to the wrist so that the electrodes touch the skin. Otherwise, if the device is not properly connected, the device does not sample well and data are not valid.

On the other hand, we have used the EmoSys software suite as data processing tool. EmoSys software has been developed by some authors of this paper for the integration of a series of devices to acquire both physiological and neurophysiological signals. As shown in Fig. 2, the functionality of EmoSys application is quite simple. EmoSys obtains the physiological signals and stores them into.

CSV (comma-separated values) files. These files will be segmented and analyzed using signal processing techniques and artificial intelligence (AI) [20].

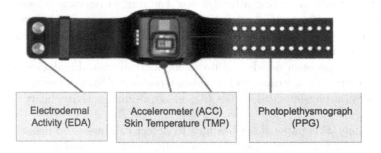

Fig. 1. Empatica E4 wearable (see [7]).

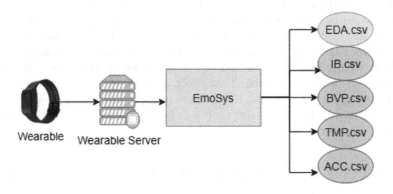

Fig. 2. Acquisition system using Empatica E4 and EmoSys software.

3   Methods and Experiment Design

3.1   Participants

A total number of sixteen participants were recruited to carry out this study, concretely 43.75% women(mean $= 31.4$ SD $= 8.03$) and 56.25% men (mean $= 27.3$ SD $= 4.99$). All participants enrolled voluntarily and no one received financial compensation. All of them were in good physical and mental condition. The participants signed a participation agreement to take part in the study. The agreement form provided information about the risks associated with participating. It described the type of images shown and the possibility to stop the experiment at any time. This experiment was designed following the protocols of Helsinki Declaration and it was approved by the Ethical Committee in Clinical Research according to European and Spanish legislation [20].

The experiment was carried out in a controlled environment. Each participant was seated in a comfortable space avoiding external stimuli that could interfere in the correct development of the study. Once the wearable was placed on a volunteer, he/she was left alone to perform the experiment.

3.2   E-Prime and IAPS

In order to validate the results in this article, we decided to use two tools widely used in the field of Psychology and Affective Computing. Firstly, E-Prime is a software used in psychological experimentation [21]. This software allows to control experiments and their experimental conditions. It covers the design phase of the experiment and the execution phase too. It allows to create slide to show, show videos and make customized questionnaires to be offered during the experiment.

The International Affective Picture System (IAPS) image library is used to evoke a feeling of calmness or distress in the participant [14]. Indeed, the IAPS image database is commonly used to perform and induce emotions. It consists in a huge set of color images grouped into categories that evoke specific emotional states [2]. The database was originally validated using a graphic scale named Self-Assessment Manikin (SAM) [13]. This questionnaire consist of a to rate how pleasant/unpleasant (valence), calm/excited (arousal) and controlled (dominance) they felt when looking at each of them.

In our experiment, different batches of images that have similar values of valence, arousal and dominance were selected. To evaluate if images induce the state of calmness/distress, two conditions were established: LH for low arousal and high valence (stress condition), HL for high arousal and low valence (calm condition) [18]. Dominance in all conditions took usually medium values. Table 1 shows the average and standard deviation values for each group consisting of 25 images.

Table 1. Mean value and standard deviation of valence, arousal and dominance for each IAPS images group.

Experimental condition	Valence	Arousal	Dominance
HL	7.23 (1.54)	3.26 (2.22)	6.44 (2.10)
LH	1.67 (1.21)	6.93 (2.22)	2.79 (2.11)

3.3   Experiment Design

The objective of this experiment is to determine calmness and stress conditions by exposing each participant to a set of images from the IAPS library. The experiment uses the tools described before. As explained before, our idea is to expose every subject to different levels of valence and arousal. Two conditions are established to appear randomly in the experiment. The first condition is to induce stress, the second one to induce calmness in the participant.

The experiment starts when the participant is seated and the wearable have been placed on his/her wrist. When the wearable gets connected to the server (see Fig. 3), E-Prime takes over the execution of the experiment. The experiment begins by showing the participant a brief description and how to respond to the SAM questionnaires. After this, the batch of neutral images is shown. These types of images are used to establish a baseline and induce a neutral emotional state in the participant. Once this has been reached, the first SAM questionnaire is answered. Next, E-Prime offers a distracting task with the purpose of eliminating the induced emotional state. This task forces the subject to concentrate and stop thinking about the images shown previously. Then, the system starts to randomly repeat each of the image blocks (HL, LH). When each blocks is finished, the SAM questionnaire is answered.

At the same time the experiment is being performed, physiological data are collected using the EmoSys software. The signals are synchronized with the events related to the occurrence of each batch of images. This synchronization will help to detect calmness and stress conditions.

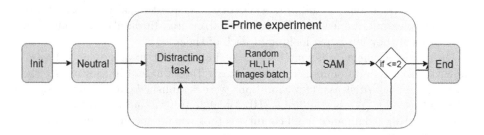

Fig. 3. Flowchart of experiment design as used in E-Prime.

3.4 Electrodermal Activity Processing and Feature Extraction

EDA is one of the most used measurement to identify the affective state of a person, specially when the arousal level is needed. Previous studies have used EDA to characterize changes in emotional experiences [4,5,8]. EDA signals are obtained by measuring the potential drop that occurs when a small current is applied between two electrodes located on the wearable across two metallic electrodes (see Fig. 1).

Prior to analyzing this physiological response, the data typically undergo several processing steps. Rapid gesture and body movements may introduce signal artifacts in the form of high frequency changes that need to be considered. Therefore, the EDA signals must be filtered. To do this a low-pass filter with a cut-off frequency of 4 Hz and a Gaussian filter to smooth the signal have been applied to attenuate these artifacts.

Electrodermal signals are composed of two components, one is the skin conductance level, commonly referred to tonic signal, and the other component is called skin conductance response (SCR), also known as phasic signal. SCR is considered the effective signal for establishing an individual's response to a stimulus [1]. We will have to perform a continuous deconvolution operation to obtain the two components of an EDA signal (see Fig. 4). This operation prepares the signal for the next stage, the extraction of features.

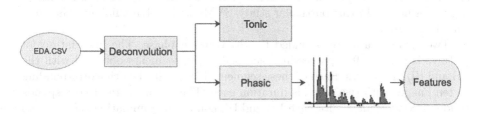

Fig. 4. Flowchart of feature extraction from EDA signals.

In this paper, the signal is processed to obtain all the parameters shown in Table 2 to gain better emotion pattern classification performance. This characterizes each of the signal segments and makes it possible to differentiate the difference between calmness and stress when classifying [23].

Table 2. Features obtained from phasic signals (SCR).

Analysis	Features
Temporal	M, SD, MA, MI, DR, D1, D2, FM, FD, SM, SSD
Morphological	AL, IN, AP, RM, IL, EL, SK, KU, MO
Frequency	F1, F2, F3

As shown in Table 2, several time-domain, frequency-domain and morphological metrics are computed over the SCR component. Firstly the name of temporal parameters over SCR are mean value (M), standard deviation (SD), maximum peak value (MA), minimum peak value (MI), and dynamic range (DR), which is the difference between maximum and minimum value. To see the tendencies in skin conductivity we computed the first and second derivative (D1 and D2), their means (FM and FD), and their standard deviations (SM and SSD). In addition, several morphological features were chosen: arc length (AL), integral area (IN), normalized mean power (AP), perimeter and area ratio (IL), energy and perimeter ratio (EL) and ,finally, two statistic parameters, skewness (SK) and kurtosis (KU). Lastly, in relation to the frequency, we calculated the fast Fourier transform (FFT) through bandwidths F1(0.1,0.2), F2(0.2,0.3) and F3(0.3,0.4) [23].

3.5   Stress Identification by Support Vector Machines

Support vector machines (SVMS) are one of the most well-known machine learning methods. Indeed, this method is used in a large number of fields [10,11]. One remarkable property of SVMs is their ability to learn independently of the dimensionality of the feature space [12]. It has been decided to use SVMs due to the high number of input parameters (23 signal features, as depicted in Table 2) and two classes (calm and distressed). To prevent overfitting, several configuration settings for cross-validation are selected. These settings allow to optimize learning performance. In this particular study, SVMs with polynomial and Gaussian kernels are used.

Two sets of data are provided for the training phase. The first dataset of features is gotten after processing each one of the segments obtained with the LH and HL image sets. Each of these segments have a 20-s length, corresponding to ten images with two seconds duration each. The second dataset corresponds to four second segments for each LH and HL condition, eliminating the first two and last seconds in each section.

4   Results

Once the signals have been processed, the training accuracy of the different SVM topologies is analyzed. Moreover, thirty repetitions are performed for each different SVM and every cross-validation set to ensure that the data obtained are robust.

Table 3 shows the training results with segments 20 s long. It can be observed that the SVM with higher performance is the Gaussian type with 70.8% accuracy for a set of cross-validation (C.V) of 5. For a C.V set of 7, the best result is provided by the a linear kernel SVM with an average accuracy of 75.0%. Finally, the accuracy remains at 75.0% for the cubic kernel using a C.V. of 10.

Table 3. Results using segment lengths of 20 s.

SVM type	C.V.	Accuracy	C.V.	Accuracy	C.V.	Accuracy
Linear	5	54.2%	7	**75.0%**	10	70.0%
Quadratic	5	66.7%	7	70.8%	10	58.3%
Cubic	5	50.0%	7	70.8%	10	**75.0%**
Fine Gaussian	5	**70.8%**	7	62.5%	10	70.8%
Medium Gaussian	5	62.5%	7	62.5%	10	62.5%
Coarse Gaussian	5	62.5%	7	62.5%	10	62.5%

On the other hand, Table 4 shows the training results with segments longing 4 s. The SVM that works best is the quadratic one with an accuracy of 87.7% for a set of C.V. of 5. Also for a C.V. of 7, two other SVMs work quite well, the linear and the fine Gaussian, both offering 87.7% accuracy. At last, for a cross-validation set of 10 folds, the best result comes from a from a cubic kernel (again 87.7% accuracy). None of the three cases do we see any improvement in the precision of the training.

Table 4. Results of interval segments of 4 s.

SVM type	C.V.	Accuracy	C.V.	Accuracy	C.V.	Accuracy
Linear	5	84.6%	7	**87.7%**	10	86.2%
Quadratic	5	**87.7%**	7	81.5%	10	86.2%
Cubic	5	78.5%	7	80.8%	10	**87.7%**
Fine Gaussian	5	70.8%	7	**87.7%**	10	86.2%
Medium Gaussian	5	82.6%	7	70.8%	10	72.3%
Coarse Gaussian	5	58.5%	7	61.5%	10	61.5%

5   Conclusions

There is numerous literature for stress detection. Most works agree that stress is a very complex subject and measuring it is not an easy task. There are many markers that can be used, many algorithms that can be applied, and many forms of stress that can be observed [6,15,16,19]. Due to the existence of many ways to produce distress, the results provided in all these works should be taken with caution. In this sense, we can say that the results obtained in this paper has given an accuracy of 87.5%. If we compare this work with the results obtained in other related studies, it is possible to conclude that outcomes obtained using the approach proposed in this works are comparable and slightly better than others works. In other similar approaches, stress detection rates range between 70% and 95%. Our approach uses solely skin conductance response features to achieve a high performance comparable to other works.

The most prominent aspect of our contribution is the development of a complete acquisition system [20], a signal processing and a classification model based on SVMs with a high capacity to discriminate between the two calmness and distress conditions. The simplicity of the classification model allows this system to work in the long term. Another relevant aspect found is that the use of such non-invasive device enables to constantly monitor electrodermal activity and have a larger database to work with.

On the other hand, we must consider a number of limitations. Firstly, the experiment has taken place in a controlled environment on middle-aged subjects. For this reason, the results cannot be generalized beyond the age range of the participants (18 to 44 years old). The second limitation is the quality of the data obtained. In acquisition systems based on physiological signals, it is common that artifacts that damage or worsen the signal occur. To be able to detect these problems in time will help to improve the rest of the process.

As a final conclusion, let us highlight that this study has helped to design an experiment that allows us to detect states of calm and stress. Throughout the study we have verified that there are many factors that can influence this classification, although the results are very acceptable. In our opinion, during the previous treatment of the EDA signal, a correct filtering and smoothing of the signal must be carried out to avoid problems. Also, it is necessary to avoid artifacts and events of disconnection of the electrodes with the skin. We must understand that good practices have to be adopted from the beginning. If any of the previous processes fails, it will induce errors in the following stages, increasing the global error and decreasing the accuracy.

Acknowledgments. This work has been partially supported by Spanish Ministerio de Ciencia, Innovación y Universidades, Agencia Estatal de Investigación (AEI)/European Regional Development Fund (FEDER, UE) under DPI2016-80894-R grant, and by CIBERSAM of the Instituto de Salud Carlos III. Roberto Sánchez-Reolid holds BES-2017-081958 scholarship from Spanish Ministerio de Educación y Formación Profesional. Arturo Martínez-Rodrigo holds 2018/11744 grant from European Regional Development Fund (FEDER, UE).

References

1. Boucsein, W., et al.: Publication recommendations for electrodermal measurements. Psychophysiology **49**(8), 1017–1034 (2012)
2. Bradley, M., Lang, P.: The international affective picture system (IAPS) in the study of emotion and attention. In: Handbook of Emotion Elicitation and Assessment, pp. 29–46. Oxford University Press (2007)
3. Carneiro, D., Castillo, J.C., Novais, P., Fernández-Caballero, A., Neves, J., López, M.T.: Stress monitoring in conflict resolution situations. In: Novais, P., Hallenborg, K., Tapia, D., Rodríguez, J. (eds.) Ambient Intelligence - Software and Applications, pp. 137–144. Springer, Heidelberg (2012). https://doi.org/10.1007/978-3-642-28783-1_17
4. Castillo, J.C., et al.: Software architecture for smart emotion recognition and regulation of the ageing adult. Cogn. Comput. **8**(2), 357–367 (2016)
5. Castillo, J.C., Fernández-Caballero, A., Castro-González, Á., Salichs, M.A., López, M.T.: A framework for recognizing and regulating emotions in the elderly. In: Pecchia, L., Chen, L.L., Nugent, C., Bravo, J. (eds.) IWAAL 2014. LNCS, vol. 8868, pp. 320–327. Springer, Cham (2014). https://doi.org/10.1007/978-3-319-13105-4_46
6. Eisenbarth, H., Chang, L.J., Wager, T.D.: Multivariate brain prediction of heart rate and skin conductance responses to social threat. J. Neurosci. **36**(47), 11987–11998 (2016)
7. empatica: E4 wristband from empatica (2019). https://www.empatica.com/en-eu/research/e4/
8. Fernández-Caballero, A., et al.: Smart environment architecture for emotion recognition and regulation. J. Biomed. Inform. **64**, 55–73 (2016)
9. Fernández-Sotos, A., Fernández-Caballero, A., Latorre, J.M.: Elicitation of emotions through music: the influence of note value. In: Ferrández Vicente, J.M., Álvarez-Sánchez, J.R., de la Paz López, F., Toledo-Moreo, F.J., Adeli, H. (eds.) IWINAC 2015. LNCS, vol. 9107, pp. 488–497. Springer, Cham (2015). https://doi.org/10.1007/978-3-319-18914-7_51

10. Gola, J., et al.: Objective microstructure classification by support vector machine (SVM) using a combination of morphological parameters and textural features for low carbon steels. Comput. Mater. Sci. **160**, 186–196 (2019)
11. Hernandez, J., Riobo, I., Rozga, A., Abowd, G.D., Picard, R.W.: Using electrodermal activity to recognize ease of engagement in children during social interactions. In: 2014 ACM International Joint Conference on Pervasive and Ubiquitous Computing, pp. 307–317. ACM (2014)
12. Joachims, T.: Text categorization with support vector machines: learning with many relevant features. In: Nédellec, C., Rouveirol, C. (eds.) ECML 1998. LNCS, vol. 1398, pp. 137–142. Springer, Heidelberg (1998). https://doi.org/10.1007/BFb0026683
13. Lang, P.J.: Behavioral treatment and bio-behavioral assessment: Computer applications. In: Technology in Mental Health Care Delivery Systems, pp. 119–137. Ablex (1980)
14. Lang, P., Bradley, M., Cuthbert, B.: International affective picture system (IAPS): affective ratings of pictures and instruction manual. Center for the Study of Emotion & Attention, NIMH (2005)
15. Martínez-Rodrigo, A., Fernández-Caballero, A., Silva, F., Novais, P.: Monitoring electrodermal activity for stress recognition using a wearable. In: Intelligent Environments, pp. 416–425. IOS Press (2016). https://doi.org/10.3233/978-1-61499-690-3-416
16. Martínez-Rodrigo, A., Zangróniz, R., Pastor, J.M., Fernández-Caballero, A.: Arousal level classification in the ageing adult by measuring electrodermal skin conductivity. In: Bravo, J., Hervás, R., Villarreal, V. (eds.) AmIHEALTH 2015. LNCS, vol. 9456, pp. 213–223. Springer, Cham (2015). https://doi.org/10.1007/978-3-319-26508-7_21
17. Martínez-Rodrigo, A., Zangróniz, R., Pastor, J.M., Latorre, J.M., Fernández-Caballero, A.: Emotion detection in ageing adults from physiological sensors. In: Mohamed, A., Novais, P., Pereira, A., Villarrubia González, G., Fernández-Caballero, A. (eds.) Ambient Intelligence - Software and Applications. AISC, vol. 376, pp. 253–261. Springer, Cham (2015). https://doi.org/10.1007/978-3-319-19695-4_26
18. Russell, J.A.: A circumplex model of affect. J. Pers. Soc. Psychol. **39**(6), 1161 (1980)
19. Salai, M., Vassányi, I., Kósa, I.: Stress detection using low cost heart rate sensors. J. Healthc. Eng. (2016). https://doi.org/10.1155/2016/5136705. Article no. 5136705
20. Sánchez-Reolid, R., et al.: Artificial neural networks to assess emotional states from brain-computer interface. Electronics **7**(12), 384 (2018)
21. Schneider, W., Eschman, A., Zuccolotto, A.: E-Prime: User's Guide. Psychology Software Incorporated (2002)
22. Sokolova, M.V., Fernández-Caballero, A.: A review on the role of color and light in affective computing. Appl. Sci. **5**(3), 275–293 (2015)
23. Zangróniz, R., Martínez-Rodrigo, A., Pastor, J., López, M., Fernández-Caballero, A.: Electrodermal activity sensor for classification of calm/distress condition. Sensors **17**(10), 2324 (2017)

Trajectory Planning of a Quadrotor to Monitor Dependent People

Lidia M. Belmonte[1,2], Rafael Morales[1,2], Arturo S. García[1,2], Eva Segura[1,2], Paulo Novais[3], and Antonio Fernández-Caballero[1,2(✉)]

[1] Instituto de Investigación en Informática de Albacete,
Universidad de Castilla-La Mancha, 02071 Albacete, Spain
antonio.fdez@uclm.es
[2] Escuela Técnica Superior de Ingenieros Industriales,
Universidad de Castilla-La Mancha, 02071 Albacete, Spain
[3] Escola de Engenharia, Universidade do Minho,
Campus de Gualtar, 4710-057 Braga, Portugal

Abstract. This article introduces a framework for assisting dependent people at home through a vision-based autonomous unmanned aerial vehicle (UAV). Such an aircraft equipped with onboard cameras can be useful for monitoring and recognizing a dependent's activity. This work is focused on the problem of planning the flight path of a quadrotor to perform monitoring tasks. The objective is to design a trajectory planning algorithm that allows the UAV to position itself for the sake of capturing images of the dependent person's face. These images will be later treated by a base station to evaluate the persons emotional state, together with his/her behavior, this way determining the assistance needed in each situation. Numerical simulations have been carried out to validate the proposed algorithms. The results show the effectiveness of the trajectory planner to generate smooth references to our previously designed GPI (generalized proportional integral) controller. This demonstrates that a quadrotor is able to perform monitoring flights with a high motion precision.

Keywords: Home assistance · Dependent people ·
Unmanned aerial vehicles · Quadrotor · Trajectory planning ·
Generalized proportional integrated controller

1 Introduction

Inability to perform daily tasks reduces the autonomy and quality of life of dependent people. These people require daily help that has traditionally been provided by health personnel in specialized care centers. However, this kind of care forces dependents to leave their homes, which is an additional problem, since this is not usually the habitual preference. To counteract this situation, family members are usually those who dedicate their time to assist the dependent person. But, in many cases, this is not the ideal solution either. Family

J. M. Ferrández Vicente et al. (Eds.): IWINAC 2019, LNCS 11486, pp. 212–221, 2019.
https://doi.org/10.1007/978-3-030-19591-5_22

caregivers, who cope with a lack of resources and preparation, are sometimes overwhelmed by the situation. Consequently, their quality of life is also affected. In addition, every day the number of cases of dependent people living alone is more frequent. Therefore, they must obligatory move to specialized centers to receive the necessary care.

Hence, it is necessary to focus research on the development of home care strategies that allow assistance to dependents. In this way, their personal autonomy is increased. They can stay at home as long as possible and improve their quality of life. In this sense, new technologies provide novel solutions for the care and support of dependents [11,16,23,25]. Assistance robotics is fundamental at this point. However, it is essential to work with methods that allow the correct monitoring and identification of the dependent's condition for designing systems that respond to their needs [21,28]. One of them is automatic recognition of emotions, a non-invasive method in which our research group has extensive experience [6,7,13,18]. This approach requires taking photographs of the person's face for further analyzing the information collected. Thus, the person's mood is detected and the necessary assistance is determined under each situation.

In this context, unmanned aerial vehicles (UAVs) may suppose a new model of home care [17,20,30]. Indeed, an UAV equipped with an on-board camera [1,2], can be very useful in home monitoring. This type of vision-based aircraft allows, unlike other static vision systems, access to remote points, avoid dead angles, and position itself in front of the person [14,15]. The taking of snapshots allows a subsequent recognition of emotions [22]. For this purpose, this article describes a trajectory planner for the flight of a quadrocopter equipped with a camera to capture snapshots of the person's face. The aim is to generate smoothed reference trajectories for a generalized proportional integral (GPI) control algorithm [12], so that the UAV performs the simulation of a flight aimed at monitoring the person. The proposed approach is validated by numerical simulations in MALTAB/Simulink environment [3–5]. This work is part of an ongoing research to design autonomous UAVs for their future use as home assistance for dependent people.

2   Quadrotor Dynamics

A quadrotor [12,31] is a rotatory-wing UAV formed by four rotors arranged in the shape of a cross and equidistant from the center of mass of the aircraft, as shown in Fig. 1. Such a vehicle allows vertical take-off and landing, and is characterized by high maneuverability, agility, and versatility. In addition, it can move at low speed, reducing the risk of collision in flight, and improving the quality of the image recorded by a camera aboard. For all these reasons, it has been considered suitable for the proposed approach.

The quadrotor's thrust is generated by the four fixed-angle propellers of the rotors. The lift forces are modified by changing the propellers rotation speed, thus achieving the three possible movements, namely, pitch, roll, and yaw. As shown in Fig. 1, by increasing (reducing) the speed of the propeller [1] while reducing (increasing) the speed of the propeller [3] the pitch movement is obtained. In

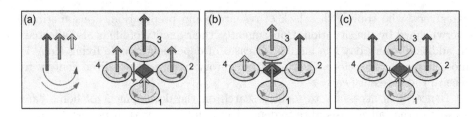

Fig. 1. Quadrotor's motion principles.

the case of increasing (reducing) the speed of the propeller [2] while reducing (increasing) the speed of the propeller [4], the roll movement is produced. And finally, by increasing (decreasing) the speed between each pair of propellers, it is possible to modify the yaw angle. The system of equations that model this dynamic behavior has been obtained through the Euler-Lagrange approach [8, 19], resulting in:

$$m\ddot{x} = -u\sin\theta \qquad\qquad \ddot{\psi} = \tau_\psi$$
$$m\ddot{y} = u\cos\theta\sin\phi \qquad\qquad \ddot{\theta} = \tau_\theta$$
$$m\ddot{z} = u\cos\theta\cos\phi \qquad\qquad \ddot{\phi} = \tau_\phi$$

where m is the mass, g is the gravity acceleration, x and y are coordinates in the horizontal plane, z is the vertical position, the angles ϕ, θ and ψ express the independent orientation angles, u is defined as the total thrust and τ_ψ, τ_θ and τ_ϕ denote the angular moments (yawing moment, pitching moment and rolling moment, respectively). Moreover, the following assumption has been considered: orientation angles θ and ϕ are upper and lower bounded in intervals $-\frac{\pi}{2} < \phi < \frac{\pi}{2}$ and $-\frac{\pi}{2} < \theta < \frac{\pi}{2}$.

3   Control Algorithm

A control scheme is necessary for regulating and tracking the trajectory that will be generated by the planner (which will be detailed in the next section) to perform a precise flight that allows monitoring a dependent in the proposed assistance system. For this purpose, we have selected a generalized proportional integral (GPI) controller, which is based on the theory of differential flatness, and which has demonstrated good performance in the control of nonlinear systems, which is the case od a quadrotor. GPI control sidesteps the need for traditional asymptotic state observers and proceeds directly to use structural state estimates in place of the actual state variables [26, 27]. The effect of such structural estimates in the controller is neglected in the feedback control law by means of suitable integral output tracking error feedback control actions.

The complete design of the GPI controller can be consulted in detail in our previous work [12]. The results of this research demonstrated the effectiveness of the proposed approach in comparison with the classical PID control in the

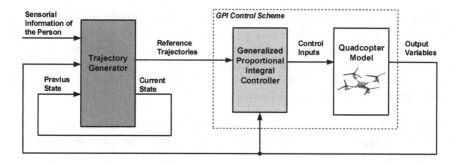

Fig. 2. General control scheme.

following terms: (a) stabilization and trajectory tracking tasks; (b) performance when the measured signals are corrupted by noise; and (c) dynamic response when atmospheric disturbances such as gusty wind affect the quadrotor.

4   Trajectory Planning

Planning trajectories is one of the problems to necessarily resolve when designing autonomous mechatronic systems and mobile robots. For this reason, it is a field that has attracted the interest of the research community in recent years [9,10, 24,29]. Thus, this section describes the trajectory planning algorithm designed for the quadrotor. The overall goal is to make a flight for monitoring a dependent person. To do this, the UAV, which will initially be in a base position on the ground, must take off, approach the person and surround him/her until finding the face. Then, the UAV will take a photograph of the face that will be sent to a base station for analysis. Finally, the UAV must conclude the circular motion around the person and return to its base.

During the planner's development, the following considerations have been considered. (i) The sensors provide the information of the person's position defined by the face's center coordinates (x_p, y_p, z_p); (ii) the person remains static during the monitoring process; (iii) there are not obstacles at the monitoring height at which the UAV works; (iv) a safety radius, R, is defined during the whole monitoring process to avoid collisions between the UAV and the person; and, (v) when the UAV does not perform any monitoring task, it remains in the base position whose coordinates are (x_b, y_b, z_b).

The trajectory planner is based on a state machine. The states define the maneuvers to be performed by the UAV during the monitoring process. For each state, the planner generates smoothed reference trajectories for the position (coordinates x, y, z) and the yaw angle (ψ) of the UAV. These references are the inputs to the GPI algorithm, which determines the required inputs to control the UAV's flight. The general control scheme of the quadrotor is illustrated in Fig. 2.

As shown in the figure, the trajectory generator depends on the person's information provided by the sensors (x_p, y_p, z_p), the UAV's output variables (x, y, z, ψ), and the previous machine state. The planner defines the references trajectories during the monitoring process so that the UAV's camera focus points towards the UAV's forward direction or the person. The considered states for the trajectory planner are the following.

- **State 0: Home.** It defines the initial state of the UAV located on its base. When it receives the instruction to start the monitoring process, it transits to state 1.
- **State 1: Takeoff.** Generation of the trajectory for the take-off of the UAV. When the quadrotor reaches the face's height defined by z_p coordinate, it transits to state 2.
- **State 2: Person Search.** The UAV is requested to rotate its position, that is, to vary its yaw angle to find the person. When the cameras center is aligned with the person, it transits to state 3.
- **State 3: Approximation.** The UAV performs an approach maneuver advancing in a straight line towards the person. The objective is to reach the Safety Position located in the circumference of radius R defined around the person. When this position is reached, it transits to state 4.
- **State 4: Waiting in Safety Position.** Intermediate state in which the UAV stops before starting the circular movement around the person in order to search his/her face. Once the programmed timeout has elapsed, it transits to state 5.
- **State 5: Face Search.** The UAV is requested to perform a circular movement around the person while varying the yaw angle so that the camera on board points towards the person. When the UAV is in front of the face, it transits to state 6.
- **State 6: Data Capture.** The UAV stops for a while to take a picture of the person's face. This image is transmitted to a base station for analysis. After the time required for data capture elapses, it transits to state 7.
- **State 7: Motion to Safety Position.** Continuation of the circular movement until the turn is completed and the previously defined safety position has been reached. In that position, it transits to state 8.
- **State 8: Base Search.** Keeping the position, the UAV is requested to modify its yaw angle until the camera is focused towards the base; then, it transits to state 9.
- **State 9: Return to Base.** The UAV must advance in a straight line until it is positioned on the base. When the UAV is on position (x_b, y_b, z_p), it transits to state 9.
- **State 10: Yaw Angle Adjustment.** The UAV is requested to modify its yaw angle so that it can subsequently land on the base correctly and be ready for the next monitoring process.
- **State 11: Landing.** The UAV lands at the base position and transits to the initial state (0) for the next monitoring process.

5   Numerical Simulations

The numerical simulations carried out to evaluate the trajectory planning for the quadrotor are detailed in this section. These simulations were performed within the MATLAB/Simulink environment. The parameters used are defined in Table 1.

Table 1. Parameters defined in the MATLAB/Simulink trials.

Planner's parameters
Safety radius, $R = 2$ [m]
Base position, $(x_b, y_b, z_b) = (0, 0, 0)$ [m]
Velocity in Z axis, $v_z = 6.8 \cdot 10^{-2}$ [m/s]
Velocity in diagonal motion (x, y), $v_d = 7 \cdot 10^{-2}$ [m/s]
Angular velocity for yaw adjustment, $\omega_\psi = 3 \cdot \pi/100$ [rad/s]
Angular velocity for circular motion, $\omega_{circle} = 3 \cdot \pi/100$ [rad/s]
Period of time for State 4 (waiting in safety position), $t_{s4} = 15$ [s]
Period of time for State 6 (data capture), $t_{s6} = 30$ [s]
Person's parameters
Face's position, $(x_p, y_p, z_p) = (4, -4, 1.7)$ [m]
Face's orientation, $\alpha_p = \pi/4$ [rad]
UAV's parameters
Initial position, $(x(0), y(0), z(0)) = (x_b, y_b, z_b)$ [m]
Initial yaw angle, $\psi(0) = 0$ [rad]
Camera's angle, $\alpha_{camera} = \pi/4$ [rad]
Controller's parameters
The same design parameters used in our previous work [12]
Simulation parameters
Sample time, $Ts = 0.01$ [s]
Simulation time, $t = 300$ [s]

Figure 3 illustrates the reference trajectory generated by the planner and the trajectory performed by the UAV, both in a 3D representation. In this picture, the planner's highlight points are detailed. Firstly, there is the base position in which the UAV remains between each monitoring process. Second, we have the person's face position and the direction (where he/she is looking at), which is represented by an arrow. In third place, there is the safety position reached by the UAV in the approximation maneuver and the same position where the UAV returns after taking the photo. Finally, we have the position where the UAV stops to capture that data.

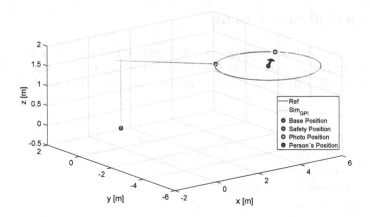

Fig. 3. 3D center of mass of the quadrotor trajectory.

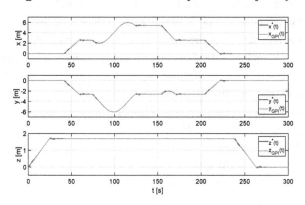

Fig. 4. Position and reference variables of the center of mass of the quadrotor.

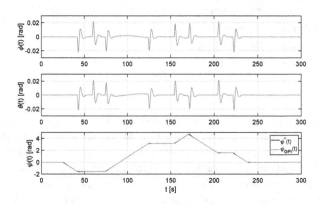

Fig. 5. Attitude variables of the quadrotor.

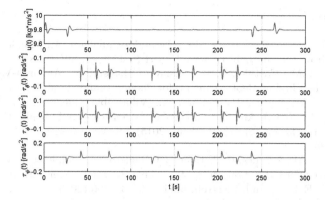

Fig. 6. Applied control inputs.

In Figs. 4 and 5 it is possible to appreciate the precision of the GPI controller for trajectory tracking of the quadrotor's position and orientation. And, finally, the control inputs applied to the UAV model are detailed in Fig. 6.

6 Conclusions

The need of novel home care strategies for dependent people has motivated this work. We have designed a trajectory planner for a quadrotor aimed to monitor dependents. The final aim is to perform an autonomous flight to observe the person and take a photo of his/her face that will be later analyzed to determine the person's mood. That information will allow providing the assistance required at each moment.

Despite being the first development of the trajectory planner, the results of the simulations are positive. The planner is able to generate smoothed reference trajectories that allow performing precise flights of the UAV governed by a GPI controller. In future works, it will be necessary to improve the planner in the following aspects: (a) to increase the planner's detail to consider the transitions between states as a consequence of the movement of the person during the monitoring process; (b) to develop a strategy for detecting obstacles and avoiding collisions in the flight environment; (c) to perform an experimentation of the proposed approach in virtual reality environments before moving to real scenarios.

Acknowledgments. This work has been partially supported by Spanish Ministerio de Ciencia, Innovación y Universidades, Agencia Estatal de Investigación (AEI)/European Regional Development Fund (FEDER, UE) under DPI2016-80894-R grant. Lidia M. Belmonte holds FPU014/05283 scholarship from Spanish Ministerio de Educación y Formación Profesional.

References

1. Almansa-Valverde, S., Castillo, J.C., Fernndez-Caballero, A.: Mobile robot map building from time-of-flight camera. Expert Syst. Appl. **39**(10), 8835–8843 (2012)
2. Belmonte, L.M., Castillo, J.C., Fernández-Caballero, A., Almansa-Valverde, S., Morales, R.: Flying depth camera for indoor mapping and localization. In: Mohamed, A., Novais, P., Pereira, A., Villarrubia González, G., Fernández-Caballero, A. (eds.) Ambient Intelligence - Software and Applications. AISC, vol. 376, pp. 243–251. Springer, Cham (2015). https://doi.org/10.1007/978-3-319-19695-4_25
3. Belmonte, L.M., Morales, R., Fernández-Caballero, A., Somolinos, J.A.: A tandem active disturbance rejection control for a laboratory helicopter with variable speed rotors. IEEE Trans. Ind. Electron. **63**(10), 6395–6406 (2016)
4. Belmonte, L.M., Morales, R., Fernández-Caballero, A., Somolinos, J.A.: Robust decentralized nonlinear control for a twin rotor MIMO system. Sensors **16**(8) (2016). Article 1160
5. Belmonte, L.M., Morales, R., Fernández-Caballero, A., Somolinos, J.A.: Nonlinear cascade-based control for a twin rotor MIMO system. In: Nonlinear Systems - Design, Analysis, Estimation and Control, pp. 265–292. In-Tech (2016)
6. Castillo, J.C., Castro-González, Á., Alonso-Martín, F., Fernández-Caballero, A., Salichs, M.Á.: Emotion detection and regulation from personal assistant robot in smart environment. In: Costa, A., Julian, V., Novais, P. (eds.) Personal Assistants: Emerging Computational Technologies. ISRL, vol. 132, pp. 179–195. Springer, Cham (2018). https://doi.org/10.1007/978-3-319-62530-0_10
7. Castillo, J.C., et al.: Software architecture for smart emotion recognition and regulation of the ageing adult. Cogn. Comput. **8**(2), 357–367 (2016)
8. Castillo, P., Dzul, A., Lozano, R.: Real-time stabilization and tracking of a four rotor mini rotorcraft. IEEE Trans. Control Syst. **12**(4), 510–516 (2004)
9. Chocoteco, J., Morales, R., Feliu, V.: Enhancing the trajectory generation of a stair-climbing mobility system. Sensors **17**(1), 1–31 (2017)
10. Chocoteco, J., Morales, R., Feliu, V., Sánchez, L.: Trajectory planning for a stair-climbing mobility system using laser distance sensors. IEEE Sens. J. **10**(3), 944–956 (2016)
11. Chocoteco, J., Morales, R., Feliu, V.: Improving the climbing/descent performance of stair-climbing systems confronting architectural barriers with geometric disturbances. Mechatronics **30**, 11–26 (2015)
12. Fernández-Caballero, A., Belmonte, L.M., Morales, R., Somolinos, J.A.: Generalized proportional integral control for an unmanned quadrotor system. Int. J. Adv. Robot. Syst. **12** (2015). Article 85
13. Fernández-Caballero, A., et al.: Smart environment architecture for emotion recognition and regulation. J. Biomed. Inform. **64**, 55–73 (2016)
14. Gascueña, J.M., Fernández-Caballero, A.: Agent-oriented modeling and development of a person-following mobile robot. Expert Syst. Appl. **38**(4), 4280–4290 (2011)
15. Gascueña, J.M., Fernández-Caballero, A.: Agent-based modeling of a mobile robot to detect and follow humans. In: Håkansson, A., Nguyen, N.T., Hartung, R.L., Howlett, R.J., Jain, L.C. (eds.) KES-AMSTA 2009. LNCS (LNAI), vol. 5559, pp. 80–89. Springer, Heidelberg (2009). https://doi.org/10.1007/978-3-642-01665-3_9
16. Igual, R., Plaza, I., Medrano, C., Rubio, M.A.: Personalizable smartphone-based system adapted to assist dependent people. J. Ambient. Intell. Smart Environ. **6**(6), 569–593 (2014)

17. Kim, S.J., Lim, G.J., Cho, J., Côté, M.J.: Drone-aided healthcare services for patients with chronic diseases in rural areas. J. Intell. Robot. Syst. **88**(1), 163–180 (2017)
18. Lozano-Monasor, E., López, M.T., Vigo-Bustos, F., Fernández-Caballero, A.: Facial expression recognition in ageing adults: from lab to ambient assisted living. J. Ambient. Intell. Humaniz. Comput. **8**(4), 567–578 (2017)
19. Lozano, R.: Unmanned Aerial Vehicles-Embedded Control. Wiley, Hoboken (2010)
20. Todd, C., et al.: Towards an autonomous UAV for indoor flight in healthcare: a review of research challenges and approaches. Int. J. Emerging Technol. Adv. Eng. **5**(8), 21–28 (2015)
21. Maglogiannis, I., Ioannou, C., Tsanakas, P.: Fall detection and activity identification using wearable and hand-held devices. Integr. Comput. Aided Eng. **23**(2), 161–172 (2016)
22. Martínez-Gómez, J., Fernández-Caballero, A., García-Varea, I., Rodríguez, L., Romero-González, C.: A taxonomy of vision systems for ground mobile robots. Int. J. Adv. Robot. Syst. **11**, 111 (2014)
23. Morales, R., Chocoteco, J., Feliu, V., Sira-Ramrez, H.: Obstacle surpassing and posture control of a stair-climbing robotic mechanism. Control Eng. Pract. **21**, 604–621 (2013)
24. Morales, R., Feliu, V., González, A.: Optimized obstacle avoidance trajectory generation for a reconfigurable staircase climbing wheelchair. Robot. Auton. Syst. **58**, 97–114 (2010)
25. Morales, R., González, A., Feliu, V., Pintado, P.: Environment adaptation of a new staircase climbing wheelchair. Auton. Robot. **23**, 275–292 (2007)
26. Morales, R., Sira-Ramírez, H.: Trajectory tracking for the magnetic ball levitation system via exact feedforward linearization and GPI control. Int. J. Control **83**, 1155–1166 (2010)
27. Morales, R., Sira-Ramírez, H., Feliu, V., González, A.: Adaptive control based on fast online algebraic identification and GPI control for magnetic levitation systems with time-varying input gain. Int. J. Control **87**, 1604–1621 (2014)
28. Rodriguez, F.J., Rico, F.M., Olivera, V.M.: Neural networks for recognizing human activities in home-like environments. Integr. Comput. Aided Eng. **26**(1), 37–47 (2019)
29. Solea, R., Nunes, U.: Trajectory planning and sliding-mode control based trajectory-tracking for cybercars. Integr. Comput. Aided Eng. **14**(1), 33–47 (2007)
30. Todd, C., et al.: A proposed UAV for indoor patient care. Technol. Health Care (2015). https://doi.org/10.3233/THC1046
31. Zemalache, K.M., Beji, L., Maaref, H.: Two inertial models of X4-flyers dynamics, motion planning and control. Integr. Comput. Aided Eng. **14**(2), 107–119 (2007)

Development and Validation of Basic Virtual Human Facial Emotion Expressions

Miguel Á. Vicente-Querol[1], Arturo S. García[1,2], Patricia Fernández-Sotos[3,4],
Roberto Rodriguez-Jimenez[3,4,5], and Antonio Fernández-Caballero[1,2,4(✉)]

[1] Instituto de Investigación en Informática de Albacete,
Universidad de Castilla-La Mancha, 02071 Albacete, Spain
[2] Departamento de Sistemas Informáticos,
Universidad de Castilla-La Mancha, 02071 Albacete, Spain
[3] Department of Psychiatry,
Instituto de Investigación Sanitaria Hospital 12 de Octubre (imas12), Madrid, Spain
[4] CIBERSAM (Biomedical Research Networking Centre in Mental Health),
Madrid, Spain
antonio.fdez@uclm.es
[5] CogPsy-Group, Universidad Complutense de Madrid, Madrid, Spain

Abstract. This paper introduces the design process of facial expressions on virtual humans to play basic emotions. The design of the emotions is grounded on the Facial Action Coding System that enables describing facial expressions based on Action Units. All the tools employed to attain the final human avatar expressions are detailed. Then, an experiment with healthy volunteers is carried out to validate the designed virtual human facial emotions. As result, we obtained that the faces are correctly interpreted by healthy people with an accuracy of 83.56%. Thus, as recognition works quite well with this small sample of healthy people, this paper is a first step towards validating and enhancing the avatar characters generated, experimenting with a sufficient number of healthy persons, and, then, designing therapies based on human avatars to enhance facial affect recognition in patients with deficits in facial affect recognition.

Keywords: Virtual human · Avatar · Facial expression ·
Facial affect recognition · Virtual reality

1 Introduction

Facial emotion recognition is the ability to identify and recognize basic forms of affective expression in faces [26]. This capacity, used daily by individuals, is crucial for effective social interaction, determining a large part of social functioning [27]. Thus, the way an individual recognizes emotional states in others affects his/her social success, which is relevant for adaptation to the community [33].

© Springer Nature Switzerland AG 2019
J. M. Ferrández Vicente et al. (Eds.): IWINAC 2019, LNCS 11486, pp. 222–231, 2019.
https://doi.org/10.1007/978-3-030-19591-5_23

There is consistent evidence that patients with different neuropsychiatric disorders have significant difficulty in accurately recognizing emotions expressed by others. This generates a misinterpretation of social situations that favors the appearance of psychotic symptoms and reduction of social functioning [6].

This deficit in facial recognition of emotions has been extensively studied in psychotic disorders, especially in schizophrenia and related disorders [23]. The impairment seems to be stable in the course of the disorder, not related to psychopathology or pharmacological treatment, and independent of general cognitive deficits [5].

This is why multiple psychological interventions have been designed to improve facial affect recognition in patients with schizophrenia. Indeed, recent meta-analyzes have shown promising results of these psychotherapeutic approaches improving facial affect recognition and functionality [6]. Considering these results, the design and evaluation of facial emotion recognition have an important relevance in order to improve social functioning and quality of life of several neuropsychiatric disorders. For this sake, computer-based therapies seem to be appropriate to date. In fact, access to digital technology and the Internet to people suffering from mental disorders [16] enables new computer-based approaches to tackle with their illness.

Frameworks for emotion [7,14,29] and facial emotion detection [22] have been at the center of our research. The creation of systems based on virtual humans for facial affect recognition [3,21] is also one of current main interests. In the last years, some works on the creation of multimodal avatars for social cognition therapies [18,19] as well as proposals for using avatars to describe hallucinations in schizophrenia patients [13,15] have been introduced.

The first attempt to recreate human faces in 3D using computer graphics imagery was probably more than 45 years ago [25]. Since then, 3D human faces have been extensively used in video games and movies. Current advances in graphic technology are climbing out of the uncanny valley, as virtual characters rendered in real time become more and more realistic. However, a lack of human-like facial expressions depicted by virtual characters increases the level of strangeness perceived despite physical realism [31]. Moreover, physical realism should be accompanied by behavioural realism [20], as people expectations about realistic movements or behaviours are raised by the degree of physical realism [28]. Several physical models describing facial expressions from the point of view of muscle activation have been proposed and can be used to achieve a higher degree of realism. One of the most popular model in the literature is the one by Ekman et al. [10]. However, conveying emotions using virtual characters is not an easy task, and this may be related to the lack of knowledge about the time course of facial movements and the affective content perceived from those movements [30].

This paper presents the design process of facial expressions on virtual humans for demonstrating basic emotions. Then, an experiment is carried out with healthy people to validate that the designed facial emotions are correctly interpreted by persons who have no social cognitive deficits. Should the results be concluding, our virtual human emotional faces could be used as comparison to patients with schizophrenia. This would be a first step towards designing a complete therapy to enhance facial affect recognition in these patients.

2   Virtual Human Facial Expressions

2.1   Facial Action Coding System

Humans are social creatures, and to socialize they need to convey emotions. People express emotions in different ways and the face plays an important role in how emotions are transmitted both in verbal and non-verbal communications. Emotions have been studied in the field of Psychology and Psychiatry. For instance, Ekman et al. arrived to the conclusion that there exist six universal basic emotions (anger, disgust, fear, happiness, sadness, and surprise) [11]. Facial muscles are used to show these emotions, changing that way the appearance in the face. Several studies tried to find a system to quantify the different changes in the face using several approximations (linguistically based, anatomically based, etc.) [9].

To recreate the changes in the face, our study is not based in an accurate representation and study of the muscles, but in the so-called Facial Action Coding System (FACS). We chose this system because it is the most widely used and has proven its efficacy. Hence, it provides more information than other systems about the changes in the face such as intensity [9]. Indeed, the Facial Action Units System (FACS), designed in 1978 [17], and revised and improved in 2002 [10], is a well known and used system that categorizes facial movements based on different Action Units (AUs), teaching how to recognize and score them.

Each AU defines a group of muscles that work together to make a change on the facial appearance. The different AUs are grouped according to the location of the facial muscles which are divided in upper and lower face muscles. Upper face muscles include eyebrows, forehead, eye cover fold, and upper and lower lids. The lower face includes the muscles around mouth and lips, and it is divided in other categories according to the movement directions of these muscles. There are other AUs based on muscles that move the neck and the gaze direction.

2.2   Facial Expressions from FACS

Among other uses, FACS is used to describe facial expressions based on AUs. Only fifteen AUs from the twenty-eight main AUs are required to describe the six emotions and neutral expression used in this research. These emotions are the six basic emotions (anger, disgust, fear, happiness, sadness, and surprise) and the neutral one. The AUs used and their relation with each emotion is shown in Table 1. The table shows that:

- Fourteen animations were modelled.
- For each emotion two animations were designed, levels (1, 2), expect for happiness, where three animations were modelled, levels (1, 2, 3).
- For modelling the neutral emotion no AU was needed.

- Each level indicates the emotion intensity; a higher number shows greater emotional intensity $((3) > (2) > (1))$.
- For some emotions new AUs are added, indicating that more muscles are moved and more facial changes appear.

Table 1. Action Units used to describe the six basic emotions (based on [9,10,12]).

AU	Name	Surprise	Fear	Happiness	Sadness	Disgust	Anger
1	Inner Brow Raiser	(1,2)	(1,2)		(1,2)		
2	Outer Brow Raiser	(1,2)	(1,2)				
4	Brow Lowerer		(1,2)		(1,2)		(1,2)
5	Upper Lid Raiser	(1,2)	(1,2)				(1,2)
6	Cheek Raiser			(1,2,3)			
7	Lid Tightener						(1,2)
9	Nose Wrinkler					(1,2)	
12	Lip Corner Puller			(1,2,3)			
15	Lip Corner Depressor				(1,2)	(1,2)	
16	Lower Lip Depressor					(1,2)	
17	Chin Raiser				(2)		(1)
20	Lip Stretcher		(1,2)				
23	Lip Tightener						(1,2)
25	Lips Part						(2)
26	Jaw Drop	(1,2)	(1,2)				

2.3 Creation of Affective Virtual Humans

The work flow for the creation of the affective virtual humans used in this proposal is described next. We started by selecting two predefined characters available in Adobe Fuse [1]. This is a software tool mainly aimed at video game developers that enables users to create 3D characters using an advanced character creation editor. The characters obtained by using this tool take advantage of many visual characteristics that are standard in recent high-end video games, namely high-resolution textures, normal maps, ambient occlusion maps, and so on. Moreover, they are fully configurable, from the face to the length of the arms, torso or the clothes they wear.

For this work, predefined avatars were selected and not modified apart from choosing clothes and selecting a haircut that did not occlude important parts of the face (i.e. the forehead and the eyes). The characters were then taken to Mixamo [2], a web platform that provides an auto-rigging of humanoid 3D models. Then, an idle animation was selected from the available ones. This platform also provides some basic facial animation to the models. However, it is not based on FACS so that there is no direct correspondence between them.

After that, the resulting 3D character is brought into 3D Studio Max [4] authoring tool to create the AUs, starting from the neutral facial expression. For this aim, we used blendshapes, also known as morph animation targets, that consist in modifying the mesh accordingly and storing the vertex positions for each AU. Then, these AUs are smoothly morphed and combined to form the desired facial animation. Other options to implement AUs are the use of a muscle-based animation system or a hierarchy of bones to modify the geometry.

A blendshape animation system was used due to its simplicity and the possibility to combine AUs to create complex facial expressions.

Once all the AUs were included in the virtual human models, they were exported and imported into Unity 3D [32], the 3D real-time engine used to play the animations. This software tool allows using the initial idle animation included in Mixamo as well as the blendshapes included in 3D Studio Max. Then, the facial expressions were enhanced by adding wrinkles to the models. For this, a shader that made use of several Normal Map textures was created in Unity. Each one included a different wrinkle pattern associated to every emotion. Normal maps are used to simulate details in the objects surface by changing the vertices' normal and, therefore, affecting light calculation on the surface.

The Nvidia Normal Map Filter for Adobe Photoshop [24] was used to create the normal maps based on photographs of people depicting the facial emotion and based on the wrinkle descriptions given by Ekman et al. [12]. Finally, the shader smoothly interpolated between the neutral normal map and each facial expression normal map, simulating a dynamic generation of wrinkles. As an example, Fig. 1 shows how the surprise and disgust facial expressions are improved by using wrinkles.

Fig. 1. Male virtual human depicting the surprise emotion (first and second images) and female avatar depicting disgust (third and fourth). Both pairs of pictures show how they look without (first and third) and with (second and fourth) normal maps. Notice the wrinkles on the forehead and on both sides of the mouth in the male avatar, and the wrinkles around the nose and mouth in the female avatar.

3   Preliminary Validation of Facial Expressions

A preliminary validation of the system was performed to assess its suitability to propose a clinical therapy for enhancing facial affect recognition in people with schizophrenia. This is why, in first term it is mandatory to evaluate the recognizability of the human facial expressions with healthy people.

3.1   Participants

Twenty three people took part in this preliminary validation of the system ($N = 23$), 14 males (60.9%) and 9 females (39.1%). The mean age of the participants was $M = 26.3$ ($SD = 8.2$). As we already stated, this validation was intended for healthy people. They were all volunteers and did not receive any compensation for their participation. Exclusion criteria consisted in reporting a neuropsychiatric disorder or any somatic disorders that could interfere in emotion recognition. This study was conducted in accordance with the Declaration of Helsinki, and, as no patients was involved, the approval of an Ethics Committee in Clinical Research was not required according to Spanish and European legislation.

3.2 Experiment Design

Two virtual humans, a male and a female, were used in this validation process. As previously described in Sect. 2.2, the virtual characters were used to express six basic emotions and neutral. In reality, several intensities of the six emotions plus neutral expression were implemented, showing fourteen different facial emotional expressions. These were neutral, surprise1, surprise2, fear1, fear2, anger1, anger2, disgust1, disgust2, happiness1, happiness2, happiness3, sadness1, and sadness2.

Each of these facial expressions was presented to the participants four times as described next. Two frontal views of each facial emotion and two lateral, one from each side. The lateral views show the face turned in one direction so that the nose is almost touching the outline of the cheek on the far side. This summed a total amount of fifty-six facial expressions that were randomly presented to the participants. For each of these facial expressions, both virtual humans were used exactly half of the times in a randomized way (see, for instance, the female faces created in Fig. 2).

Fig. 2. Female's facial expressions. First row: neutral, surprise1, surprise2, fear1, fear2, anger1, anger2. Second row: disgust1, disgust2, happiness1, happiness2, happiness3, sadness1, sadness2.

The validation process starts with a black screen in which a simple menu is used by the participant to start the experiment. Each time a new facial expression is shown, the character's face is faded in from a black background. A transition is made from the neutral expression to the new expression (lasting 0.4 s), which is held for 1.5 s and, then, there is a new transition to neutral expression (again, 0.4 s). This is in accordance with transition studied in the past [8], as expression time longs between 0.5 and 4 s.

Once this process had finished, a panel was shown to the participant asking for the expression just offered by the virtual human. This panel also included a button for each of the six basic emotions, the neutral one and an "I don't know" button. After a participant clicks on an option, the character face is faded out. This process is repeated for each of the fifty-six facial expressions. Once the system had presented all the facial expressions to the participant, the experiment finished and a sociodemographic questionnaire was filled out.

We used the same idle animation for both virtual humans. This animation is subtle enough to not distract the participants, while it adds a slight swing that provides more realism to the character. Similarly, a blinking animation was also added, but only for the time while the system was waiting for a participant's response, not during the actual expression of the emotion.

4   Results and Discussion

Table 2 shows the successful recognition for each of the six basic emotions plus neutral expression, with an average rate of 83.56% accuracy. The results show that most of the facial emotion expressions were perceived with high recognition accuracy by the participants (over 80%), except for disgust (69.6%) and sadness (62%). This was expected for disgust, since it is also confused with anger in previous works by other authors [3,21], but was surprising for sadness, which is mainly confused with disgust and fear.

Table 2. Emotion recognition confusion matrix for each emotion.

	Neutral	Surprise	Fear	Anger	Disgust	Happiness	Sadness	I dont know
Neutral	98.9	0.0	0.0	0.0	0.0	0.0	1.1	0.0
Surprise	0.0	95.1	4.3	0.0	0.0	0.5	0.0	0.0
Fear	0.0	15.8	81.0	0.0	3.3	0.0	0.0	0.0
Anger	0.0	0.0	0.0	91.3	4.9	0.0	1.6	2.2
Disgust	0.0	0.0	0.5	28.3	69.6	0.0	0.0	1.6
Happiness	10.5	0.4	0.7	0.0	0.4	87.0	0.0	1.1
Sadness	1.6	0.5	15.2	0.5	17.9	0.0	62.0	2.2

Moreover, Table 3 is created to find out whether a single animation of the two that compose sadness is responsible for the bad classification. As can be noted, sadness2 is the one that is confused with disgust and fear, obtaining a recognition percentage of 31.5% as opposed to 92.4% for sadness1. Possibly, the way the AUs were combined to create sadness2 was not correct enough and, thus, it needs to be redone. This situation was, again, expected to happen, as creating blendshapes is a skillful and laborious task that usually takes weeks or even months to an experienced 3D artist.

A closer look to Table 3 shows that happiness1 obtains low recognition accuracy as well (67.7%) compared to happiness2 (98.9%) and happiness3 (94.6%). Happiness1 depicts a subtle smile in which AU6 (cheek riser) and AU12 (lip corner puller) are applied at their lowest intensity. In fact, they did not affect the eyes and no wrinkles (crow's feet) were noticeable. It was confused mainly with the neutral expression (31.5%), which may reflect that, even if the participants were able to notice the smile, it was not strong enough to be considered a sign of joy. Therefore, even though this subtle smile is described by Ekman and Friesen [12], we will consider removing it in future works. It is interesting to note that after removing the results of happiness1 and sadness2, the global accuracy increases up to 89.3%.

The results of our experiment are consistent with those obtained by other authors in previous works with regards to emotion recognition accuracy using virtual humans. We obtained an accuracy of 83.56%, while other authors reached 73.22% [21] and 83.8% [3].

Table 3. Emotion recognition confusion matrix for the 14 animations created.

	Neutral	Surprise	Fear	Anger	Disgust	Happiness	Sadness	I dont know
Neutral	98,9	0.0	0.0	0.0	0.0	0.0	1,1	0.0
Surprise1	0.0	97,8	1,1	0.0	0.0	1,1	0.0	0.0
Surprise2	0.0	92,4	7,6	0.0	0.0	0.0	0.0	0.0
Fear1	0.0	9,8	83,7	0.0	6,5	0.0	0.0	0.0
Fear2	0.0	21,7	78,3	0.0	0.0	0.0	0.0	0.0
Anger1	0.0	0.0	0.0	85,9	6,5	0.0	3,3	4,3
Anger2	0.0	0.0	0.0	96,7	3,3	0.0	0.0	0.0
Disgust1	0.0	0.0	0.0	27.2	70,7	0.0	0.0	2,2
Disgust2	0.0	0.0	1.1	29.3	68,5	0.0	0.0	1,1
Happiness1	31,5	0.0	0.0	0.0	0.0	67,7	0.0	1,1
Happiness2	0.0	0.0	0.0	0.0	0.0	98,9	0.0	1,1
Happiness3	0.0	1,1	2,2	0.0	1,1	94,6	0.0	1,1
Sadness1	2,2	1,1	3,3	0.0	0.0	0.0	92,4	1,1
Sadness2	1,1	0.0	27,2	1,1	35,9	0.0	31,5	3,3

5 Conclusions

This paper has detailed the complete design process of a couple of human avatars expressing facial emotions. The human avatars play the basic emotions (anger, disgust, fear, happiness, sadness, and surprise) plus the neutral state. The design of the proper emotions was based on the well-known Facial Action Coding System, where facial expressions are described as Action Units. In addition, the paper has described in detail all the tools employed to obtain the human avatar expressions.

Afterwards, an experiment to validate the designed virtual human facial emotions has been described. For this sake, healthy volunteers have visualized fourteen different facial emotional expressions (different intensities of the expressions) four times: two frontal and two lateral views each. Each volunteer had to push one of the six basic emotions, the neutral one or an "I don't know" button as response to every stimulus. The results showed that the human avatar facial emotions are correctly interpreted by persons who have no social cognitive deficits with an accuracy of 83.56%.

Based on these results, a validation study is proposed in healthy volunteers with a larger sample, representative of the general population. Once this validation was done, the use of this tool would be considered to be used in cognitive rehabilitation programs in patients with a deficit in facial affect recognition.

Acknowledgments. This work was partially supported by Spanish Ministerio de Ciencia, Innovación y Universidades, Agencia Estatal de Investigación (AEI)/European Regional Development Fund (FEDER, UE) under DPI2016-80894-R and TIN2015-72931-EXP grants, and by Biomedical Research Networking Centre in Mental Health (CIBERSAM) of the Instituto de Salud Carlos III.

References

1. Adobe: Fuse (2019). https://www.adobe.com/es/products/fuse.html
2. Adobe: Mixamo (2019). https://www.mixamo.com
3. Amini, R., Lisetti, C., Ruiz, G.: HapFACS 3.0: FACS-based facial expression generator for 3D speaking virtual characters. IEEE Trans. Affect. Comput. **6**(4), 348–360 (2015)
4. Autodesk: 3D Studio Max (2019). https://www.autodesk.es/products/3ds-max/overview
5. Barkhof, E., de Sonneville, L.M., Meijer, C.J., de Haan, L.: Specificity of facial emotion recognition impairments in patients with multi-episode schizophrenia. Schizophr. Res.: Cogn. **2**(1), 12–19 (2015)
6. Bordon, N., O'Rourke, S., Hutton, P.: The feasibility and clinical benefits of improving facial affect recognition impairments in schizophrenia: systematic review and meta-analysis. Schizophr. Res. **188**, 3–12 (2017)
7. Castillo, J.C., Fernández-Caballero, A., Castro-González, Á., Salichs, M.A., López, M.T.: A framework for recognizing and regulating emotions in the elderly. In: Ambient Assisted Living and Daily Activities, pp. 320–327 (2014)
8. Ekman, P.: Emotions Revealed: Recognizing Faces and Feelings to Improve Communication and Emotional Life. Times Books, New York (2003)
9. Ekman, P., Friesen, W., Hager, J.: Facial action coding system investigator's guide. Technical report, Research Nexus (2002)
10. Ekman, P., Friesen, W., Hager, J.: Facial action coding system: the manual on CD rom. Technical report, A Human Face (2002)
11. Ekman, P., Friesen, W.V.: Constants across cultures in the face and emotion. J. Pers. Soc. Psychol. **17**(2), 124 (1971)
12. Ekman, P., Friesen, W.V.: Unmasking the Face: A Guide to Recognizing Emotions from Facial Clues. ISHK (2003)
13. Fernández-Caballero, A., et al.: Human-avatar symbiosis in cognitive cybertherapies: proof of concept for auditory verbal hallucinations. In: Ubiquitous Computing and Ambient Intelligence, pp. 742–753 (2017)
14. Fernández-Caballero, A., Latorre, J.M., Pastor, J.M., Fernández-Sotos, A.: Improvement of the elderly quality of life and care through smart emotion regulation. In: Ambient Assisted Living and Daily Activities, pp. 348–355 (2014)
15. Fernández-Caballero, A., et al.: Human-avatar symbiosis for the treatment of auditory verbal hallucinations in schizophrenia through virtual/augmented reality and brain-computer interfaces. Front. Neuroinformatics **11**, 64 (2017)

16. Fernández-Sotos, P., et al.: Digital technology for Internet access by patients with early stage schizophrenia in Spain: a multicenter research study. J. Med. Internet Res. **21**, e11824 (2019)

17. Friesen, E., Ekman, P.: Facial Action Coding System: a Technique for the Measurement of Facial Movement. Consulting Psychologists Press, Palo Alto (1978)

18. García, A.S., Navarro, E., Fernández-Caballero, A., González, P.: Towards the design of avatar-based therapies for enhancing facial affect recognition. In: Ambient Intelligence - Software and Applications - 9th International Symposium on Ambient Intelligence, pp. 306–313 (2019)

19. García-Sánchez, M., Teruel, M.A., Navarro, E., González, P., Fernández-Caballero, A.: A distributed tool to perform dynamic therapies for social cognitive deficit through avatars. In: Ubiquitous Computing and Ambient Intelligence, pp. 731–741 (2017)

20. Guadagno, R.E., Swinth, K.R., Blascovich, J.: Social evaluations of embodied agents and avatars. Comput. Hum. Behav. **27**(6), 2380–2385 (2011)

21. Gutiérrez-Maldonado, J., Rus-Calafell, M., González-Conde, J.: Creation of a new set of dynamic virtual reality faces for the assessment and training of facial emotion recognition ability. Virtual Reality **18**(1), 61–71 (2014)

22. Lozano-Monasor, E., López, M.T., Fernández-Caballero, A., Vigo-Bustos, F.: Facial expression recognition from webcam based on active shape models and support vector machines. In: Ambient Assisted Living and Daily Activities, pp. 147–154 (2014)

23. Marwick, K., Hall, J.: Social cognition in schizophrenia: a review of face processing. Br. Med. Bull. **88**(1), 43–58 (2008)

24. NVIDIA: Texture Tools for Adobe Photoshop (2019). https://developer.nvidia.com/nvidia-texture-tools-adobe-photoshop

25. Parke, F.I.: Computer generated animation of faces. In: Proceedings of the ACM Annual Conference. vol. 1, pp. 451–457. ACM (1972)

26. Russell, J.A.: Is there universal recognition of emotion from facial expression? A review of the cross-cultural studies. Psychol. Bull. **115**(1), 102 (1994)

27. Sachs, G., et al.: Training of affect recognition (TAR) in schizophrenia-impact on functional outcome. Schizophr. Res. **138**(2–3), 262–267 (2012)

28. Slater, M., Steed, A.: Meeting people virtually: experiments in shared virtual environments. In: Schroeder R. (eds.) The Social Life of Avatars, pp. 146–171 (2002)

29. Sokolova, M.V., Fernández-Caballero, A.: A review on the role of color and light in affective computing. Appl. Sci. **5**(3), 275–293 (2015)

30. Tessier, M.H., Gingras, C., Robitaille, N., Jackson, P.L.: Toward dynamic pain expressions in avatars: perceived realism and pain level of different action unit orders. Comput. Hum. Behav. **96**, 95–109 (2019)

31. Tinwell, A., Grimshaw, M., Williams, A.: Uncanny behaviour in survival horror games. J. Gaming Virtual Worlds **2**(1), 3–25 (2010)

32. Unity3d: Unity 3D (2019). https://unity3d.com

33. Wölwer, W., et al.: Neurophysiological correlates of impaired facial affect recognition in individuals at risk for schizophrenia. Schizophr. Bull. **38**(5), 1021–1029 (2011)

Brushstrokes of the Emotional Brain: Cortical Asymmetries for Valence Dimension

Jennifer Sorinas[1,2]([envelope]) [ORCID], José Manuel Ferrández Vicente[2] [ORCID],
and Eduardo Fernández-Jover[1] [ORCID]

[1] Institute of Bioengineering,
University Miguel Hernández and CIBER BBN Avenida de la Universidad,
03202 Elche, Spain
jennifersorinas@gmail.com, e.fernandez@umh.es
[2] Department of Electronics and Computer Technology, University of Cartagena,
Cartagena, Spain
jm.ferrandez@upct.es

Abstract. Understanding the neurophysiology of emotions, the neuronal structures involved in the processing of emotional information and the circuits by which they act, is key to design applications in the field of affective neuroscience, both to advance in new treatments and in applications of brain-computer interactions. With this objective, we have carried out a study of cortical asymmetries based on the spectral power and differential entropy (DE) of the electroencephalographic signal of 24 subjects stimulated with videos of positive and negative emotional content. The results have shown different interhemispheric asymmetries throughout the cortex, presenting opposite patterns for both emotional categories. In addition, increased activity has also been observed in the right hemisphere and in anterior cortical regions during emotion processing. These preliminary results are encouraging for elucidating the neuronal circuits of the emotional brain.

Keywords: Asymmetries · Differential entropy · EEG · Emotions · Valence dimension

1 Introduction

Emotions are a key part of people's daily lives, they regulate our behavior, through modulating and influencing our attention [1,2], mood and decision making [3]; and our social behavior through communication, tone of voice, gestures and facial expressions [4]. It is for this reason that more and more importance has been given to the detection, recognition and classification of emotions. Less than 30 years ago a new branch known as affective neuroscience emerged [5], which tries to understand the psychobiology of emotions, together with the development of affective brain computer interface (aBCI) applications [6,7]. However,

© Springer Nature Switzerland AG 2019
J. M. Ferrández Vicente et al. (Eds.): IWINAC 2019, LNCS 11486, pp. 232–243, 2019.
https://doi.org/10.1007/978-3-030-19591-5_24

despite many advances in aBCI, little is known about the brain mechanisms, structures, and neural networks that underlie the processing of emotions. In order to achieve its mission, affective neuroscience has relied mainly on neuroimaging techniques such as functional magnetic resonance and electroencephalography (EEG), the latter being especially noteworthy for its applicability in BCI systems. The EEG is the most widely used technique given its advantages over other neuroimaging systems [8]; it has a temporal resolution of the order of milliseconds which allows applications in realtime; there are wireless versions, so that its use is not restricted to clinical or laboratory environments; it is non-invasive and has a relatively low cost; thus the results obtained are susceptible to be implemented for real applications.

Different brain structures, both cortical and subcortical, have been identified as relevant, or at least, have shown involvement, in the processing of emotions [9,10]. However, due to the lack of consensus in the very definition of the term [11] and taxonomy of emotions [12,13], finding the key to the neurophysiology of emotion is a complicated task. The authors devoted to the study of the neurophysiology of emotions have based themselves mainly on two models, the discrete theory and the dimensional theory of emotions. Discrete theory holds that there are a number of basic, innate and universal emotions, which possess a unique physiological signature [14], and are encoded by a specific brain circuit [15]. Although for some of these discrete emotions, such as disgust and fear, specific circuits have been found, there has not been as much luck or consensus for the rest [16,17]; this is why this emotional model is not the most widespread in the applications of affective neuroscience. On the other hand, the dimensional theory of emotions holds that emotions are defined on the basis of two main dimensions, valence (pleasure/positive vs displeasure/negative) and arousal (calm vs excited) [18,19]. As for the arousal dimension, it is believed that as such it has no representation in a specific neuronal circuit or structure, but is more related to the general state or level of activity of the emotional system [20]. Valence has been related to specific brain regions, especially with asymmetries between both brain hemispheres; as for example in frontal and temporal regions in the alpha band of the EEG, in which positive-approach emotions lateralize towards the left hemisphere and negative-withdrawal towards the right [21].

Previous studies have allowed us to develop a model for recognition of biphasic emotions based on EEG, focused on applications in real-time [22] (unpublished). The obtained results showed a set of cortical regions involved in the processing of these emotions, spread throughout the cerebral cortex and encoded in almost the entire frequency spectrum of the EEG signal. These results, together with those of other authors such as Mauss and Robinson [8], indicate that emotions probably involve neuronal circuits rather than individual brain regions. The present work consists of a preliminary study with the aim of defining the substrates and cortical circuits of the dimension of emotional valence. To this end, we have undertaken the study of interhemispheric and rostro-caudal asymmetries related to the processing of positive and negative emotions, using two methodologies: (1) the traditional way of studying asymmetries based on the spectral power of the different EEG frequency bands [23]; and (2) a new methodology that is beginning to gain popularity in EEG, based on the DE of certain fragments of the signal in specific frequency ranges [24].

2   Materials and Methods

2.1   Experimental Setup

We used the database used in previous work [22,25], consisting of a sample of 24 subjects, who were stimulated audio-visually with a total of 14 videos of positive and negative emotional content. During stimulation, the brain activity of the participants was recorded by means of a 64-channel electroencephalography system (NeuroScan SynAmps EEG amplifier (Compumedics, Charlotte, NC, USA)), with a sampling frequency of 1000 Hz and following the 10/10 positioning system [26]. EEG signals were filtered between 0.5 Hz and 45 Hz; and artifacts derived from nearby muscle activity and flickering were eliminated by selecting independent components. However, 10 channels were eliminated due to the presence of noise.

After pre-processing, the signal corresponding to each video was extracted in the 52 electrodes and standardized by means of a z-score with respect to the baseline. The electrodes were grouped into 13 functional sets (left prefrontal, right prefrontal, left frontal, right frontal, frontal midline, central linear midline, parieto-occipital midline, left central, right central, left parietal, right parietal, left occipital and right occipital), calculating the regional means. The resulting signal was segmented into two data matrices depending on the size of the segment; on the one hand, 1-s trials were obtained, and on the other, 12-s fragments were created using a 1-s sliding window. In both sets, the characteristics corresponding to the spectral power of the signal in 6 frequency bands (delta, theta, alpha, beta1, beta2, gamma) were extracted using the Level 8 wavelet packets decomposition method, using the mother wavelet known as db4 (Daubechies order 4). See previous work for details (unpublished). For the following analyses, the data set of all subjects was used, adopting an independent subject model for the calculation of asymmetries. All analyses were carried out using the Matlab software (The MathWorks Inc.).

2.2   Asymmetry Index (AI)

Asymmetries have usually been studied by comparing spectral power in different frequency bands on contralateral inter-hemispheric sides. However, in order to see the direction and magnitude of the asymmetry, the AI is used, so that the result of the difference between the power of left and right hemisphere homologous regions is divided for the sum of the total power [23].

$$AI = \frac{right - left}{right + left} \tag{1}$$

Spectral power values in the 6 studied frequency bands with the window size of 12 s were used as inputs to calculate AI in the hemispheric prefrontal, frontal, central, parietal and occipital pairs. The outliers were replaced by the median value for each variable. After the AI calculation, the Mann-Whitney statistical test [27] was performed to analyze the differences between the positive and negative emotional videos. On the other hand, the same test was applied to the spectral power data proving the existence of significant differences in the different frequency bands in homologous regions within the same emotional category.

2.3   Differential Entropy

Lately, there are authors who are beginning to apply the DE parameter, used to measure the complexity of a variable, to the EEG signals, obtaining results that are not negligible and even improving those obtained with the classic parameters of spectral power when classifying emotions [24,28]. We calculated the DE according to the formula (2) described by [24], where hi(X) is the differential entropy of the corresponding EEG signal, e is a constant and i is the variance of that signal, all for a given frequency band and in a specific segment of time [29]. We have used sets of 12 s of signal spectral power extracted for each bandwidth, in the trials of 1 s, that is to say, every 12 s of signal we obtain a value of entropy. The outliers were replaced by the median value for each variable. With the DE values we studied the asymmetry features DASM (differential asymmetry) (3), RASM (rational asymmetry) (4) and fronto-posterior asymmetry, DCAU (differential caudality) (5).

$$h_i(X) = \frac{1}{2}log(2\pi e\sigma_i^2) \tag{2}$$

$$DASM = DE(X_{left}) - DE(X_{right}) \tag{3}$$

$$RASM = \frac{DE(X_{left})}{DE(X_{right})} \tag{4}$$

$$DCAU = DE(X_{frontal}) - DE(X_{posterior}) \tag{5}$$

For DASM and RASM variables, we analyzed the DE in 5 homologous functional sets (prefrontal (PF), frontal (F), central (C), parietal (P) and occipital (O)), for the 6 frequency bands of study, obtaining a total of 30 features for each asymmetry parameter. We use absolute values to work with the RASM results. On the other hand, we studied the differences between rostral and caudal regions in 9 pairs (PF-O left, PF-O right, F-O left, F-O right, F-O midline, PF-P left, PF-P right, F-P left, F-P right), for all frequency bands, obtaining a total of 54 DCAU features. In order to study the differences in positive and negative emotional conditions in the different asymmetry parameters and the intra-emotional differences in DE, we performed the Mann-Whitney statistical test.

3 Results

3.1 Classical Asymmetry Index

The interpretation of the results of the asymmetry index is complex, due to the different possibilities regarding the punctuation sign of the spectral power, which when positive indicates an increase of the spectral power with respect to the baseline and a decrease when negative. We will say that there is a lateralization towards a concrete hemisphere when this one possesses greater amount of spectral power with respect to the other one, in a certain band of frequency. Figure 1 shows the results obtained for the IA of the 30 pairs of frequency-region for both emotional categories. Table 1 indicates the lateralization direction of those pairs that have shown significant differences. In most pairs, the activity is opposite in the studied emotional conditions, i.e. the different frequency bands in the same cortical regions lateralize towards opposite hemispheres when dealing with positive and negative emotions; excepting three pairs, PF-theta, C-theta and P-gamma.

In prefrontal regions we found increased activity in the left hemisphere during stimulation with positive valence emotions and increased activity in the right hemisphere when dealing with negative emotions; specifically, in the alpha and beta2 frequency bands. At the frontal level, we also found asymmetries in the spectral power of the delta and beta1 bands. However, although the PF pattern was maintained for the low frequencies, it was shown to be opposite in the high frequencies. In central areas, opposite contralateral activations were also observed when comparing positive and negative emotions, however, each frequency seems to act independently to any pattern. In the parietal lobe, we again observed a pattern of lateralization towards the right hemisphere of the low frequencies (delta and theta) in positive emotions and towards the left in negative emotions. And on the contrary, the lateralization was reversed for the high frequency beta2, increasing its activity in the left hemisphere in positive emotions and in the right in negative emotions. The same pattern found for high and low frequencies in parietal zones was maintained in the occipital region. In positive emotions the activity of lower frequencies such as delta, alpha and beta1 lateralized towards the right hemisphere and that of the highest, gamma, towards the left hemisphere. Conversely, in the negative emotions, the increase in activity of the delta, alpha and beta1 frequencies occurred in the left hemisphere, while the increase in gamma occurred in the right hemisphere. Finally, interhemispheric differences that presented significant differences within the same emotional category are shown in Table 2. Here it is worth noting the lateralization towards the left hemisphere in more rostral regions and towards the right in caudal zones in the positive emotions. And, on the contrary, lateralization towards the left hemisphere in caudal regions and towards the right in rostral regions in the negative emotional category.

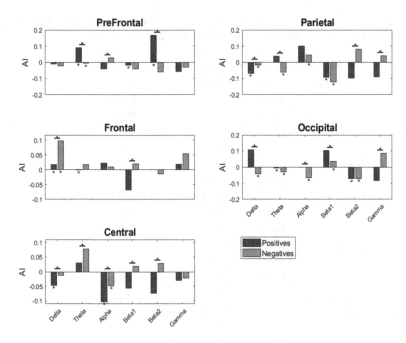

Fig. 1. AI in the five study regions for the 6 frequency bands into which we divide the EEG signal corresponding to positive and negative emotions. The bracket with the asterisk above, which joins two bars of the histogram, indicates those pairs that have shown significant differences (p-value < 0.05) between the positive-negative conditions. Asterisks on the bars indicate significant differences (p-value < 0.05) between interhemispheric, intra-condition (positive-positive or negative-negative).

3.2 DASM and RASM

With respect to asymmetry metrics derived from DE, positive DASM values indicate greater DE in the left hemisphere; conversely, negative values would indicate greater DE values in the right hemisphere. When comparing the emotional categories of study (Fig. 2), we found significant differences in all the cortical regions, although, unlike the results obtained with the IA, there are no opposite directions in the lateralization, but there were differences in the magnitude of ED, that is to say, one category presented greater activity than the other. The same occurs within the same emotional category, no opposing differences were observed in positive and negative emotions, but there was lateralization in terms of the activity of the oscillations of the cerebral hemispheres.

Table 1. Interhemispheric asymmetries between emotional categories. Left or right refers to the hemisphere with the greatest spectral power.

Cortical region	Bandwidth	Positive emotion	Negative emotion
Pre-frontal	Theta	Right	Right
	Alpha	Left	Right
	Beta2	Left	Right
Frontal	Delta	Left	Right
	Beta1	Right	left
Central	Delta	Left	Right
	Theta	Left	left
	Alpha	Right	Left
	Beta1	Left	Right
	Beta2	Right	Left
Parietal	Delta	Right	Left
	Theta	Right	Left
	Beta2	Left	Right
	Gamma	Left	Left
Occipital	Delta	Right	Left
	Alpha	Right	Left
	Beta1	Right	Left
	Gamma	Left	Right

Table 2. Lateralization within the same emotional category.

Cortical region	Bandwidth	Positive emotion	Negative emotion
Pre-frontal	Theta	Right	Right
	Beta1	Left	
	Beta2	Left	
Frontal	Delta	Left	Right
	Theta	Left	
Central	Delta	Left	
	Alpha	Right	Left
Parietal	Delta	Right	Left
	Theta		Left
	Alpha		Left
	Beta1	Right	Left
Occipital	Delta		Left
	Theta	Right	Left
	Alpha		Left
	Beta1		Left
	Beta2	Right	Left

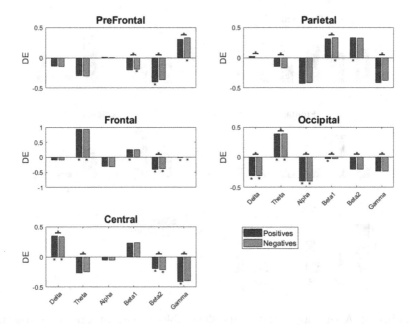

Fig. 2. DASM. Results for the DASM asymmetry feature for the 24 subjects in the 30 variables in the positive and negative emotional conditions. The bracket with the asterisk above, which joins two bars of the histogram, indicates those pairs that have shown significant differences (p-value < 0.05) between the positive-negative conditions. Asterisks on the bars indicate significant differences (p-value < 0.05) between interhemispheric, intracondition (positive-positive or negative-negative).

There were also significant differences in interhemispheric frequency ratios when comparing both emotional categories (Fig. 3). In this case, values greater than the unit would indicate greater activity in the left hemisphere and lower values in the right hemisphere. In general, we could observe how in most regions and frequencies, except for the alpha-prefrontal, theta-frontal, delta-central, beta1 and gamma parietal and theta-occipital pairs; the right hemisphere presented greater activity than the left while processing both positive and negative emotions.

3.3   DCAU

Finally, significant differences were also found comparing caudality between positive and negative emotional conditions (Fig. 4). Positive DCAU values would reflect greater frontal or anterior activity, and negative values, greater posterior activity. In general, we can observe that there is greater activity at all frequencies in the prefrontal and frontal areas compared to the parietal and occipital areas in both hemispheres and in both types of emotion.

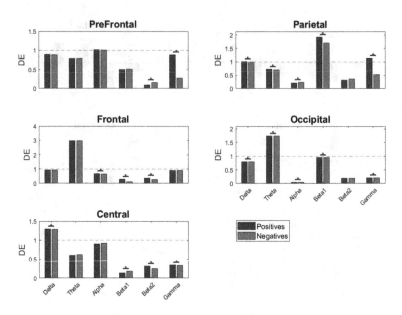

Fig. 3. RASM. Asymmetry ratios for the 30 variables (5 cortical regions × 6 frequency bands) of study in both emotional conditions. The bracket with the asterisk above, which joins two bars of the histogram, indicates those pairs that have shown significant differences (p-value < 0.05) between the positive-negative conditions. The red dotted line indicates the unit value. (Color figure online)

4 Discussion

The study of neural substrates underlying the processing of emotions is key to understanding the neurophysiology and structure of emotions, in order to implement aBCI systems that would be more faithful to neuroscience and therefore provide better performance; as well as to design more specific treatments for the broad spectrum of emotional disorders, as autism or depression.

Studies related to emotional asymmetries based on the EEG signal have focused mainly on the frontal lobe, supporting the evidence that the frontal asymmetry present in the EEG can serve as a moderator and mediator in emotions and motivations [21,30]. Using other neuroimaging techniques such as PET and fMRI, it has also found an increase in activity throughout the left hemisphere to emotions that provoke approach responses; however, no differential results have been found between the activation of the left and right hemispheres, to emotions that trigger a withdrawal response [17]. Our results showed a lateralization pattern towards the left hemisphere of positive emotions and towards the right of negative emotions in prefrontal zones that coincides with the theory of Davidson. In addition, we saw how this pattern changed as we moved toward more posterior regions. Already at frontal level, the low frequencies changed the laterality in the positive and negative emotions conferring a pattern opposite to the one presented at prefrontal regions and, nevertheless, the higher frequencies

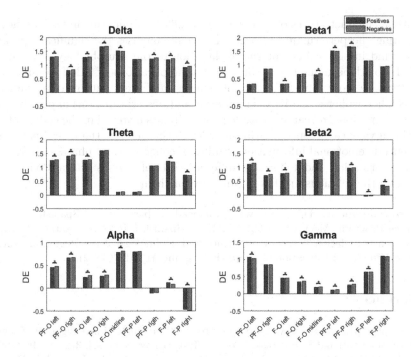

Fig. 4. Differences in fronto-posterior rate for the 54 location-frequency pairs of positive and negative emotions. The bracket with the asterisk above, which joins two bars of the histogram, indicates those pairs that have shown significant differences (p-value < 0.05) between the positive-negative conditions.

did maintain the prefrontal pattern. The exception to this pattern was found in central motor regions, in which, although there was interhemispheric lateralization of the entire frequency spectrum, except for the gamma band, there was no clear pattern between positive and negative emotions.

With respect to the results obtained by the different parameters calculated from the DE feature, no differences have been found in the direction of lateralization of the EEG activity in positive and negative emotions, but the same lateralization pattern has been found in all frequencies and the difference between emotional categories would lie in the magnitude of the complexity of the signal. The results of the DASM and RASM parameters suggest increased activity of the right hemisphere compared to the left hemisphere during emotion processing. On the other hand, the DCAU results suggest a greater involvement of the rostral, prefrontal and frontal cortical regions, in emotion processing compared to the more caudal, parietal and occipital cortical regions.

The interpretation of the IA is clearer and seems to provide more information than the DE, however, it has been seen that, when using this information to classify positive, negative and neutral emotions, the characteristics of DE provide higher percentages of success and with less standard deviation than the traditional characteristics of spectral power [28]. Preliminarily, in the absence of comparing the performance of a classification that uses the significant parameters found in this paper, for the explanation of the neurobiology of emotion, the AI would be more useful, but for real applications of aBCI possibly the DE would be more robust. Our results suggest a distinct pattern of asymmetry between hemispheres and between anterior and posterior regions in positive and negative emotions, revealing possible neural circuits involved in the coding of the emotional valence dimension. Still, in order to characterize the neural pathways that encode emotional information, studies of coherence and phases can provide useful information about how the different cortical regions interact with each other and the relationship that exists between them.

Acknowledgement. This work was supported in part by the Spanish National Research Program (MAT2015-69967-C3-1), the Spanish Blind Organization (ONCE), the Seneca Foundation - Agency of Science and Technology of the Region of Murcia and the Ministry of Education of Spain (FPU grant AP2013/01842).

References

1. Compton, R.J., et al.: Paying attention to emotion: an fMRI investigation of cognitive and emotional Stroop tasks. Cogn. Affect. Behav. Neurosci. **3**(2), 81–96 (2003)
2. Schupp, H.T., Stockburger, J., Codispoti, M., Junghofer, M., Weike, A.I., Hamm, A.O.: Selective visual attention to emotion. J. Neurosci. **27**(5), 1082–1089 (2007)
3. Schwarz, N.: Emotion, cognition, and decision making. Cogn. Emot. **14**, 433–440 (2000)
4. Ekman, P.: Expression and the nature of emotion. Approaches Emot. **3**, 19–344 (1984)
5. Panksepp, J.A.: A critical role for affective neuroscience in resolving what is basic about emotions. Psychol. Rev. **99**, 554–560 (1992)
6. Picard, R.W., Vyzas, E., Healey, J.: Toward machine emotional intelligence: analysis of affective and physiological state. IEEE Trans. Pattern Anal. Mach. Intell. **23**(10), 1175–1191 (2001)
7. Nijboer, F., Morin, F.O., Carmien, S.P., Koene, R.A., Leon, E., Hoffmann, U.: Affective braincomputer interfaces: psychophysiological markers of emotion in healthy persons and in persons with amyotrophic lateral sclerosis. In: Proceedings of 2009 3rd International Conference on Affective Computing and Intelligent Interaction and Workshops, ACII 2009 (2009)
8. Mauss, I.B., Robinson, M.D.: Measures of emotion: a review. Cogn. Emot. **23**(2), 209–237 (2009)
9. Kober, H., Barrett, L.F., Joseph, J., Bliss-Moreau, E., Lindquist, K., Wager, T.D.: Functional grouping and cortical-subcortical interactions in emotion: a meta-analysis of neuroimaging studies. Neuroimage **42**(2), 998–1031 (2008)
10. Kleinginna, P.R., Kleinginna, A.M.: A categorized list of motivation definitions, with a suggestion for a consensual definition. Trends Cogn. Sci. **16**(11), 533–540 (2012)
11. Lindquist, K.A., Barrett, L.F.: A functional architecture of the human brain: emerging insights from the science of emotion. Motiv. Emot. **5**(3), 263–291 (1981)
12. Dalgleish, T.: The emotional brain. Nat. Rev. Neurosci. **5**, 283–289 (2004)

13. Scherer, K.R.: What are emotions? And how can they be measured? Soc. Sci. Inf. **44**(4), 695–729 (2005)
14. Ekman, P., Levenson, R.W., Friesen, W.V.: Autonomic nervous system activity distinguishes among emotions. Science **221**(4616), 1208–1210 (1983)
15. Panksepp, J.: Emotions as natural kinds within the mammalian brain. In: Handbook of Emotions, 2nd ed, pp. 137–156. Lewis & J. M. Haviland-Jones/Guilford Press, New York (2000)
16. Phan, K.L., Wager, T., Taylor, S.F., Liberzon, I.: Functional neuroanatomy of emotion: a metaanalysis of emotion activation studies in PET and fMRI. Neuroimage **16**, 331–348 (2002)
17. Murphy, F.C., Nimmo-Smith, I., Lawrence, A.D.: Functional neuroanatomy of emotions: a meta-analysis. Cogn. Affect. Behav. Neurosci. **3**(3), 207–233 (2003)
18. Russell, J.: A circumplex model of affect. J. Pers. Soc. Psychol. **39**(6), 1161 (1980)
19. Rolls, E.T.: A theory of emotion, and its application to understanding the neural basis of emotion. Cogn. Emot. **4**, 161–190 (1990)
20. Lang, P.J., Bradley, M.M., Cuthbert, B.N.: Emotion, motivation, and anxiety: brain mechanisms and psychophysiology. Biol. Psychiatry **44**(12), 1248–1263 (1998)
21. Davidson, R.J., Ekman, P., Saron, C.D., Senulis, J.A., Friesen, W.V.: Approach-withdrawal and cerebral asymmetry: emotional expression and brain physiology. I. J. Pers. Soc. Psychol. **58**, 330–341 (1990)
22. Sorinas, J., Grima, M.D., Ferrandez, J.M., Fernandez, E.: Identifying suitable brain regions and trial size segmentation for positive/negative emotion recognition. Int. J. Neural Syst. **29**(2), 1–14 (2019)
23. Davidson, R.J.: EEG measures of cerebral asymmetry. Int. J. Neurosci. **39**(1986), 71–89 (1988)
24. Shi, L.-C., Jiao, Y.-Y., Lu, B.-L.: Differential entropy feature for EEG-based emotion classification. In: International IEEE/EMBS Conference on Neural Engineering NER, pp. 81–84 (2013)
25. Sorinas, J., et al.: Setting the parameters for an accurate EEG (electroencephalography)-based emotion recognition system. In: Ferrández Vicente, J.M., Álvarez-Sánchez, J.R., de la Paz López, F., Toledo Moreo, J., Adeli, H. (eds.) IWINAC 2017. LNCS, vol. 10337, pp. 265–273. Springer, Cham (2017). https://doi.org/10.1007/978-3-319-59740-9_26
26. Chatrian, G.E., Lettich, E., Nelson, P.L.: Ten percent electrode system for topographic studies of spontaneous and evoked EEG activities. Am. J. EEG Technol. **25**, 83–92 (1985)
27. Hollander, M., Wolfe, D.A.: Nonparametric Statistical Methods. Wiley, Hoboken (1999)
28. Zheng, W., Zhu, J., Lu, B., Member, S.: Identifying stable patterns over time for emotion recognition from EEG. IEEE Trans. Affect Comput. (2017)
29. Duan, R.-N., Zhu, J.-Y., Lu, B.-L.: Differential entropy feature for EEG-based emotion classification. In: Proceedings of 6th International IEEE/EMBS Conference on Neural Engineering, pp. 81–84 (2013)
30. Coan, J.A., Allen, J.J.B.: Frontal EEG asymmetry as a moderator and mediator of emotion. Biol. Psychol. **67**(1–2), 7–49 (2004)

Multiple-Instance Lasso Regularization
via Embedded Instance Selection
for Emotion Recognition

J. Caicedo-Acosta[1(✉)], D. Cárdenas-Peña[1], D. Collazos-Huertas[1],
J. I. Padilla-Buritica[1], G. Castaño-Duque[2], and G. Castellanos-Dominguez[1]

[1] Signal Processing and Recognition Group, Universidad Nacional de Colombia,
Km 9 Vía al Aeropuerto la Nubia, Manizales, Colombia
{juccaicedoac,dcardenasp,dfcollazosh,jipadilla,gacastanod,
cgcastellanosd}@unal.edu.co
[2] Universidad Nacional de Colombia, Manizales, Colombia

Abstract. Since emotions affect physical and psychologically the health of people, their identification is crucial for understanding human behavior. Despite the several systems developed in this regard, most of them underperform on people with disabilities, their setup is sensitive to noise or non-emotional stimuli. Recent studies consider electroencephalographic (EEG) signals for understanding emotional responses due to reflecting the activity of the central nervous system. However, the non-stationary nature of EEG signals demand elaborated signal processing approaches because not all time instants hold information related to the stimulus-response. This work proposes a temporal analysis approach, termed MILRES, based on the Multi-Instance Learning framework that includes a multiple instance Regularization with LASSO penalty and an Embedded instance Selection. We test MILRES in discriminating two states (high and low) of the valence and arousal emotional dimensions from the DEAP dataset. The proposed approach reaches 84.4% accuracy and 79.5% F1-score for valence, and 81.9% accuracy 67.9% for arousal. Such results evidence that MILRES outperforms other EEG-based emotion recognition approaches from the state-of-the-art, with the additional benefit of identifying the brain areas involved in processing emotions.

Keywords: Electroencephalography · Emotion recognition ·
Multi-Instance learning · Feature selection

1 Introduction

Emotions are a fundamental part of people's mental health affecting physically and psychologically social behavior and making decisions. Thus, identifying emotions is crucial to understand and interpret human behavior in different scenarios. As an example of clinical applications, the measurement of emotional perception may improve the treatment of social cognition impairments in patients with traumatic brain injury [1]. In the education scenario, the Media and Information Literacy methodology proposed

J. M. Ferrández Vicente et al. (Eds.): IWINAC 2019, LNCS 11486, pp. 244–251, 2019.
https://doi.org/10.1007/978-3-030-19591-5_25

by the UNESCO covers the competencies that are vital for people to be effectively engaged in all aspects of human development [2]. In this sense, affective learning models the affective dimension of learning to enhance the knowledge transfer and student's development [3]. Also, applications such as data-driven animation, neuromarketing, interactive games, and sociable robotics rely on emotion recognition from human facial expression [4].

Above applications demand the analysis of human biosignals to suitably identify emotions, as video and audio signals for recording facial expressions [5] and voice changes [6]. Despite the high recognition rates, audio and video-based systems wrongly perform on mute people or with facial paralysis [7]. Researches based on the autonomic nervous system (ANS) variables (heart rate, skin temperature, respiration patterns, blood volume pressure, and galvanic skin response) attempt to overcome such an issue [8]. However, the nervous system response to non-emotional stimuli (e.g., physical activity) highly hampers the performance of ANS-based approaches [9]. More recently, electroencephalography (EEG) recordings draw attention for the analysis of emotions as they reflect the activity of the central nervous system and allows understanding the internal brain activity before emotional stimuli [10].

Among the reported EGG-based approaches, some of them analyze the EEG in time domain using, for instance, fractal dimension [11], sample entropy [12], nonstationary index [13], and Hjort features [14]. Also, frequency features as the power spectral density suitably perform on emotion recognition [15]. Further, some researchers have gathered both time and frequency analysis based on Short-time Fourier transform [16], Hilbert-Huang transform [17], Discrete Wavelet Transform [18], and Wigner-Ville distribution [19]. However, these approaches assume stationarity of time series, which hardly applies to brain activity from external stimuli [20]. A straightforward solution is carrying out a piece-wise analysis [21], at the cost of reduced performance because not all time segments hold information about the stimulus response, that is noisy segments [22].

Aiming to identify relevant samples that cope with the previous issue, multiple instance learning (MIL) analyzes independent instances to predict the label of bags without information about instance labels. MIL has been widely used in fields such as video-based visual tracking [23], image-based object recognition [24], and text-based language recognition [25]. Particularly for EEG-based emotion recognition, MIL considers as bags the whole EEG recording and as instances its time windows [22]. Despite its evident premise, MIL strongly depends on the instance representation and demands a subject-wise feature extraction to deal with the inter-subject variability [19].

In this paper, we propose a time-window analysis based on a multi-instance framework with LASSO penalty approach and embedded instance selection (MILRES). Our method allows selecting relevant information of each EEG channel through the least absolute shrinkage and selection operator (LASSO) from the quadratic time-frequency distribution of each time window.

2   Materials and Methods

2.1   DEAP Dataset and Preprocessing

In this work, we consider EEG from the Database for Emotion Analysis using Physiological Signals (DEAP) [26]. DEAP records physiological signal from 32 subjects (16 males and 16 females) while watching 40 videos, selected to evoke specific emotional states. For each subject, the EEG recording related to a video represents a trial lasting 63 s (summing up to 1280 trials). At each trial, the BioSemi ActiveTwo system records 32 channels (using the 10–20 system) for a three-seconds baseline period followed by a 60-s stimulus response. After the stimulus, each subject quantified the emotional response for valence, arousal, dominance, and linking in a continuous interval from 1 to 9. Since the two-dimensional valence-arousal model represents several emotional states [27], we carry out our experiment as two binary classification task, namely, high valence ($[6 - 9]$) vs. low valence ($[1 - 5]$), and high arousal vs. low arousal.

For the signal preprocessing, we apply a three-stage pipeline. Firstly, we downsampled the raw EEG signals to 128 Hz and excluded the first three seconds of baseline. Secondly, we attenuated the electrooculographic artifacts and band-passed the signals from 4 to 45 Hz so reducing the high-frequency electromyographic noise [26]. Lastly, we referenced all channels to the common average and selected 22 symmetric ones (6 parietal, 12 frontal, 2 temporal, and 2 occipital) [19]. Therefore, the i-th trial becomes a matrix of $T = 7680$ time instants and $C = 22$ channels, $\mathbf{Z}_i \in \mathbb{R}^{T \times C}$, where $i \in [1, 40]$.

2.2   Feature Extraction

For each trial matrix, we compute the quadratic time-frequency features that are known to suitably perform in the emotion recognition task [19]. Particularly, the Choi-Williams transform (CWD) extracts the quadratic time-frequency distribution at 512 time instants for 1024 frequency bins as:

$$CWD_z(t,f) = \int_{-\infty}^{\infty} \int_{-\infty}^{\infty} WVD_z(\phi, \tau) \xi(\phi, \tau) e^{j2\pi(t\phi - f\tau)} \partial_\tau \partial_\phi, \tag{1}$$

$$\xi(t,f) = \exp\left(-\frac{t^2 f^2}{\alpha^2}\right),$$

where $WVD_z(t,f)$ is the Wigner-Ville distribution of the signal z, $\xi(t,f)$ is a exponential kernel and α is a parameter that controls the suppression of the cross-terms fixed to 0.5 [19]. Then, we estimate the following set of 13 CWD-based frequency features at four-second sliding windows with 50% overlap within the channel-wise CWD [19]: mean, variance, skewness, kurtosis, the sum of logarithmic amplitudes, median absolute deviation, inter-quartile range of the CWD, root mean square value, flatness, flux, spectral roll-off, normalized Renyi entropy, and energy concentration. As a result, each trial becomes a set of vectors $\mathbf{B}_i = \{\mathbf{x}_{ij} \in \mathbb{R}^D : j = 1 \ldots M\}$, being $D = 13 \times C$ and $M = 29$ the number of sliding windows in a trial.

2.3 Multiple Instance Learning-Based Representation

The MIL framework defines the i-th EEG trial $\boldsymbol{B}_i$ as a bag composed of M instances extracted $\boldsymbol{x}_{ij}$, and the provided bag label as $y_i \in \{0,1\}$. To estimate the bag label, the Multiple-Instance Logistic Regression with LASSO Penalty (MILR-LASSO) aggregates the approximated instance labels as $\tilde{y}_i = I\left(\sum_{j=1}^{M} y_{ij} > 0\right)$, where $I(x)=1$ if $x > 0$ and $I(x)=0$ in otherwise, and y_{ij} results from the logistic regression [28]: $y_{ij} \sim Bernoulli(p_{ij})$, being $p_{ij}=p\left(\beta_0 + \boldsymbol{x}_{ij}^\top \boldsymbol{\beta}\right)$, $p(x)=1/(1+e^{-x})$, β_0 the bias term, and $\boldsymbol{\beta} \in \mathbb{R}^D$ the coefficient vector. Therefore, finding the regression paramters becomes a quadratic optimization problem [29]:

$$\min_{\beta_0, \boldsymbol{\beta}} \left(-Q_q\left(\beta_0, \boldsymbol{\beta} | \beta_0^t, \boldsymbol{\beta}^t\right) + \lambda \sum_{d=1}^{D} |\beta_d| \right), \tag{2}$$

$$Q\left(\beta_0, \boldsymbol{\beta} | \beta_0^t, \boldsymbol{\beta}^t\right) = \sum_{i=1}^{N} \sum_{j=1}^{M_i} y_i \gamma_{ij}^t \left(\beta_0 + \boldsymbol{x}_{ij}^\top \boldsymbol{\beta}\right) - \log\left(1 + e^{(\beta_0 + \boldsymbol{x}_{ij}^\top \boldsymbol{\beta})}\right), \tag{3}$$

where Q_q is the quadratic approximation of Q, γ_{ij} is the conditional expectation given $y_i = 1$, $\gamma_{ij} = p_{ij}/(1 - \prod_{j=1}^{M_i} q_{ij})$, and $\beta_0^t, \boldsymbol{\beta}^t$ are the parameters at iteration t. We solved the optimization problem using the iterative coordinate decent algorithm [30]. Given that the larger the magnitud of β_d - the more relevant the feature to regress the instance labels, we select the features with a coefficient exceeding a predefined threshold, yielding instances with selected features, $\widetilde{\boldsymbol{x}}_{ij}$.

From the resulting feature selection stage, we embed trials in a vector space aiming to apply conventional classification machines [31]. To this end, the MIL via embedded instance selection represents bags in terms their similarity against training instances $\widetilde{\boldsymbol{x}}_k$ $\boldsymbol{s}_i = \{\max_j \exp\left(-\|\widetilde{\boldsymbol{x}}_{ij} - \widetilde{\boldsymbol{x}}_k\|^2/\sigma^2\right) : k=1 \ldots M\}$, where vector $\boldsymbol{s}_i \in \mathbb{R}^M$ corresponds to the representation of the i-th trial and $\sigma \in \mathbb{R}^+$ a bandwidth parameter.

2.4 Classification and Performance Assessment

After the MIL representation, vectors $\boldsymbol{s}_i$ feed a support vector machine classifier with a Gaussian kernel to discriminate the emotional states. To tune the regularization parameter λ, the threshold ε, and kernel bandwidth, we carried out a 5-fold cross-validation grid search. Due to class imbalance impacts classification results, we reported the F1-score as the performance measure along with the conventional accuracy rate. Besides, we compare our approach against performance results reported for Citation-kNN (C-kNN) [32], mi-SVM [22], and MILR-LASSO [29] in the same classification tasks.

3 Results and Discussion

Figure 1 compares C-kNN, mi-SVM, MILR-LASSO, and the proposed MILRES in terms of their performed accuracy and F1-score for discriminating High vs Low valence and High vs Low arousal. For the valence dimension in Fig. 1(a), MILRES outperforms the compared approaches from 3% to 12% in both, accuracy and F1-score. Regarding the arousal dimension in Fig. 1(b), MILRES reaches a larger accuracy (81.9%) than MILR-LASSO (78.2%), mi-SVM (77.5%), and C-kNN (76.3%). However, mi-SVM (73.65%) and C-kNN (70.25%) better perform in F1-score than MILR-LASSO (64.89%) and MILRES (67.94%). Such a fact is due to the class imbalance in the arousal discrimination problem that implies a smaller number of training instances for the minority class. Therefore, the similarity representation biases towards the larger class, so increasing the average accuracy but reducing the F1-score.

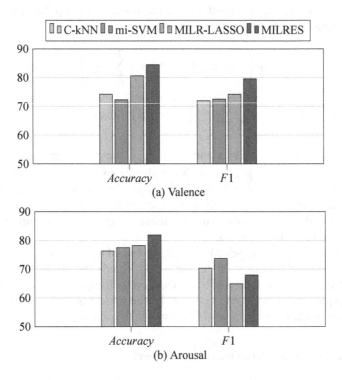

Fig. 1. Comparison of classification accuracies and F1-scores obtained by C-kNN, mi-SVM, MILR-LASSO, and MILRES.

Since we compute the feature set in Sect. 2.2 at the channel level, MILRES allows interpreting the relevance of each EEG channel for discriminating emotional states according to its corresponding regression coefficients β_d. In this regard, the topographic plots in Fig. 2 illustrate the channel-wise sum of absolute regression coefficients for four subjects. Our results indicate that the frontal, prefrontal, temporal, parietal and occipital regions contribute the most in identifying the emotional response, which agrees with previous studies [33,34]. Particularly, the subjects 13 and 12 (Fig. 2(a) and (c) respectively) highly concentrate the relevant information in the frontal, prefrontal, and parietal areas, processing the emotional stimuli, self-reflection, and activation from pleasant and unpleasant emotions [35]. Also, the proposed MILRES identifies discriminant information all over the 22 channels for subjects 11 and 7 (Fig. 2(b) and (d) respectively) that include parietal, temporal, and occipital. Those areas involve the emotional working memory [36], decision making based on emotions [37], experiencing emotional states [38], visual processing of emotional images [39], and emotional attachment [40]. Therefore, our proposed approach not only suitably discriminates states within an emotional dimension but also identifies the brain areas involved in the process.

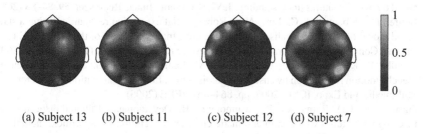

(a) Subject 13   (b) Subject 11   (c) Subject 12   (d) Subject 7

Fig. 2. Channel-based spatial activation relevance for two subjects in valence (a, b) and arousal (c, d) using the proposed MILRES.

4   Conclusions and Future Work

This work proposes a temporal analysis of EEG signals based on a multi-instance framework including LASSO regularization for feature selection at the instance level and the embedded instance selection for the similarity representation of trials. Joining the MIL representation and the feature selection possess two main advantages: First, the instance representation as an overlapping temporal segmentation allows each time-segment to be analyzed individually to account for the appearance of stimulus response. Second, the feature selection allows identifying information improving the discrimination of emotional states with interpretability from the brain physiology.

As a future work, we plan to extend the MIL framework to multi-class and regression problems for modeling emotional dimensions at a finer level. Also, we will work on a temporal relevance analysis that provides information about the stimulus-response for education and neuromarketing applications.

Acknowledgment. This work is developed within the framework of the research project "programa reconstrucción del tejido social en zonas de pos-conflicto en Colombia del proyecto Fortalecimiento docente desde la alfabetización mediática Informacional y la CTel, como estrategia didáctico-pedagógica y soporte para la recuperación de la confianza del tejido social afectado por el conflicto, Código SIGP 58950" funded by "Fondo Nacional de Financiamiento para la Ciencia, la Tecnología y la Innovación, Fondo Francisco José de Caldas con contrato No 213-2018 con Código 58960".

References

1. Vallat-Azouvi, C., Azouvi, P., Le-Bornec, G., Brunet-Gouet, E.: Treatment of social cognition impairments in patients with traumatic brain injury: a critical review. Brain injury **33**(1), 87–93 (2019)
2. Frau-Meigs, D.: Media education. A kit for teachers, students parents and professionals. UNESCO (2007)
3. Picard, R.W., et al.: Affective learning-a manifesto. BT Technol. J. **22**(4), 253–269 (2004)
4. Wang, F., Lv, J., Ying, G., Chen, S., Zhang, C.: Facial expression recognition from image based on hybrid features understanding. J. Vis. Commun. Image Represent. **59**, 84–88 (2019)
5. Bourel, F., Chibelushi, C.C., Low, A.A.: Robust facial expression recognition using a state-based model of spatially-localised facial dynamics. In: Proceedings of the Fifth IEEE International Conference on Automatic Face and Gesture Recognition, pp. 113–118. IEEE (2002)
6. Schuller, B., Reiter, S., Muller, R., Al-Hames, M., Lang, M., Rigoll, G.: Speaker independent speech emotion recognition by ensemble classification. In: IEEE International Conference on Multimedia and Expo, ICME 2005, pp. 864–867. IEEE (2005)
7. Purnamasari, P.D., Ratna, A.A.P., Kusumoputro, B.: Development of filtered bispectrum for EEG signal feature extraction in automatic emotion recognition using artificial neural networks. Algorithms **10**(2), 63 (2017)
8. Nasoz, F., Lisetti, C., Alvarez, K., Finkelstein, N.: Emotion recognition from physiological signals for user modeling of affect. In: proceedings of the 9th International Conference on User Model, Pittsburg, USA, pp. 22–26 (2003)
9. Petrantonakis, P.C., Hadjileontiadis, L.J.: Emotion recognition from EEG using higher order crossings. IEEE Trans. Inf. Technol. Biomed. **14**(2), 186–197 (2010)
10. Paus, T., Sipila, P., Strafella, A.: Synchronization of neuronal activity in the human primary motor cortex by transcranial magnetic stimulation: an eeg study. J. Neurophysiol. **86**(4), 1983–1990 (2001)
11. Sourina, O., Liu, Y.: A fractal-based algorithm of emotion recognition from EEG using arousal-valence model. In: Biosignals, pp. 209–214 (2011)
12. Jie, X., Cao, R., Li, L.: Emotion recognition based on the sample entropy of EEG. Bio-med. Mater. Eng. **24**(1), 1185–1192 (2014)
13. Kroupi, E., Yazdani, A., Ebrahimi, T.: EEG correlates of different emotional states elicited during watching music videos. In: D'Mello, S., Graesser, A., Schuller, B., Martin, J.-C. (eds.) ACII 2011. LNCS, vol. 6975, pp. 457–466. Springer, Heidelberg (2011). https://doi.org/10. 1007/978-3-642-24571-8_58
14. Hjorth, B.: EEG analysis based on time domain properties. Electroencephalogr. Clin. Neurophysiol. **29**(3), 306–310 (1970)
15. Wang, X.-W., Nie, D., Lu, B.-L.: EEG-based emotion recognition using frequency domain features and support vector machines. In: Lu, B.-L., Zhang, L., Kwok, J. (eds.) ICONIP 2011. LNCS, vol. 7062, pp. 734–743. Springer, Heidelberg (2011). https://doi.org/10.1007/978-3-642-24955-6_87
16. Chanel, G., Ansari-Asl, K., Pun, T.: Valence-arousal evaluation using physiological signals in an emotion recall paradigm. In: IEEE International Conference on Systems, Man and Cybernetics, ISIC, pp. 2662–2667. IEEE (2007)
17. Hadjidimitriou, S.K., Hadjileontiadis, L.J.: Toward an EEG-based recognition of music liking using time-frequency analysis. IEEE Trans. Biomed. Eng. **59**(12), 3498–3510 (2012)
18. Mohammadi, Z., Frounchi, J., Amiri, M.: Wavelet-based emotion recognition system using eeg signal. Neural Comput. Appl. **28**(8), 1985–1990 (2017)
19. Alazrai, R., Homoud, R., Alwanni, H., Daoud, M.: EEG-based emotion recognition using quadratic time-frequency distribution. Sensors **18**(8), 2739 (2018)

20. Kaplan, A.Y., Fingelkurts, A.A., Fingelkurts, A.A., Borisov, S.V., Darkhovsky, B.S.: Non-stationary nature of the brain activity as revealed by EEG/MEG: methodological, practical and conceptual challenges. Signal Process. **85**(11), 2190–2212 (2005)

21. Sanei, S., Chambers, J.: Fundamentals of EEG Signal Processing, pp. 35–125. Wiley, Hoboken (2013). Chapter 2

22. Zhang, X., et al.: Emotion recognition based on electroencephalogram using a multiple instance learning framework. In: Huang, De-Shuang, Jo, Kang-Hyun, Zhang, Xiao-Long (eds.) ICIC 2018. LNCS, vol. 10955, pp. 570–578. Springer, Cham (2018). https://doi.org/10.1007/978-3-319-95933-7_66

23. Babenko, B., Yang, M.-H., Belongie, S.: Robust object tracking with online multiple instance learning. IEEE Trans. Pattern Anal. Mach. Intell. **33**(8), 1619–1632 (2011)

24. Zhang, C., Platt, J.C., Viola, P.A.: Multiple instance boosting for object detection. In: Advances in Neural Information Processing Systems, pp. 1417–1424 (2006)

25. Pappas, N., Popescu-Belis, A.: Explicit document modeling through weighted multiple-instance learning. J. Artif. Intell. Res. **58**, 591–626 (2017)

26. Koelstra, S., et al.: DEAP: a database for emotion analysis; using physiological signals. IEEE Trans. Affect. Comput. **3**(1), 18–31 (2012)

27. Lang, P.J.: The emotion probe: studies of motivation and attention. Am. Psychol. **50**(5), 372 (1995)

28. Chen, R.-B., et al.:Multiple-instance logistic regression with lasso penalty. arXiv preprint arXiv:1607.03615 (2016)

29. Chen, P.-Y., Chen, C.-C., Yang, C.-H., Chang, S.-M., Lee, K.-J.: milr: Multiple-instance logistic regression with lasso penalty. R J. **9**(1), 446–457 (2017)

30. Friedman, J., Hastie, T., Tibshirani, R.: Regularization paths for generalized linear models via coordinate descent. J. Stat. Softw. **33**(1), 1 (2010)

31. Chen, Y., Bi, J., Wang, J.Z.: MILES: multiple-instance learning via embedded instance selection. IEEE Trans. Pattern Anal. Mach. Intell. **28**(12), 1931–1947 (2006)

32. Wang, J., Zucker, J.-D.: Solving multiple-instance problem: a lazy learning approach (2000)

33. Zheng, W.-L., Zhu, J.-Y., Lu, B.-L.: Identifying stable patterns over time for emotion recognition from EEG. IEEE Trans. Affect. Comput. (2017)

34. Zhuang, N., Zeng, Y., Tong, L., Zhang, C., Zhang, H., Yan, B.: Emotion recognition from EEG signals using multidimensional information in EMD domain. BioMed Res. Int. (2017)

35. Bermpohl, F., et al.: Attentional modulation of emotional stimulus processing: an fmri study using emotional expectancy. Hum. Brain Mapp. **27**(8), 662–677 (2006)

36. Rämä, P., Martinkauppi, S., Linnankoski, I., Koivisto, J., Aronen, H.J., Carlson, S.: Working memory of identification of emotional vocal expressions: an fMRI study. Neuroimage **13**(6), 1090–1101 (2001)

37. Deppe, M., Schwindt, W., Kugel, H., Plassmann, H., Kenning, P.: Nonlinear responses within the medial prefrontal cortex reveal when specific implicit information influences economic decision making. J. Neuroimag. **15**(2), 171–182 (2005)

38. Pelletier, M., et al.: Separate neural circuits for primary emotions? Brain activity during self-induced sadness and happiness in professional actors. Neuroreport **14**(8), 1111–1116 (2003)

39. Lane, R.D., Chua, P.M., Dolan, R.J.: Common effects of emotional valence, arousal and attention on neural activation during visual processing of pictures. Neuropsychologia **37**(9), 989–997 (1999)

40. Gillath, O., Bunge, S.A., Shaver, P.R., Wendelken, C., Mikulincer, M.: Attachment-style differences in the ability to suppress negative thoughts: exploring the neural correlates. Neuroimage **28**(4), 835–847 (2005)

Emotion Detection in Aging Adults Through Continuous Monitoring of Electro-Dermal Activity and Heart-Rate Variability

Luz Fernández-Aguilar[1], Arturo Martínez-Rodrigo[2,3], José Moncho-Bogani[1], Antonio Fernández-Caballero[2,4(✉)], and José Miguel Latorre[1]

[1] Departamento de Psicología, Universidad de Castilla-La Mancha,
02071 Albacete, Spain
[2] Departamento de Sistemas Informáticos, Universidad de Castilla-La Mancha,
02071 Albacete, Spain
[3] Instituto de Tecnologías Audiovisuales, Universidad de Castilla-La Mancha,
16002 Cuenca, Spain
[4] Instituto de Investigación en Informática de Albacete,
Universidad de Castilla-La Mancha, 02071 Albacete, Spain
antonio.fdez@uclm.es

Abstract. This paper introduces a system composed of hardware, control software, signal processing and classification for the deployment of a wearable with a high ability to discriminate among seven emotional states (neutral, affection, amusement, anger, disgust, fear and sadness). The study described in this proposal focuses on comparing the emotional states of young and older people by means of two physiological parameters, namely electro-dermal activity and heart-rate variability, both captured from the wearable. The wearable emotion detection system is trained by eliciting the desired emotions on eighty young (16 to 26 years old) and fifty older adults (aged 60 to 84) through a film mood induction procedure. Seventeen features are calculated on skin conductance response and heart-rate variability data. Then, these features are classified by a support vector machines. State amusement reached a high number of hits (87.4%), whilst affection received the lowest rate of hits (82.5%). The negative emotion with lowest value is anger (82.4%) and the highest is disgust (85.9%).

Keywords: Electro-dermal activity · Heart-rate variability ·
Emotion detection · Aging adults

1 Introduction

Population aging is a recent concern in developed countries due to decreasing birth rate and higher life expectancy. The growth of older population is attributable to the joint action of various factors, including advances in health

J. M. Ferrández Vicente et al. (Eds.): IWINAC 2019, LNCS 11486, pp. 252–261, 2019.
https://doi.org/10.1007/978-3-030-19591-5_26

systems, public hygiene, and sanitation, regularization of income, and improved nutrition [1]. This phenomenon relates to a shift in the structure of the population ages, where basically those groups with greater ages grow, while younger population is reduced. Although improvements in nutrition and health care enable aging with high quality of life, there are cases in which some health-related issues require close and personalized supervision. Indeed, Ambient Assisted Living (AAL) approaches are gaining importance in recent years as they provide a personalized support to older people, mainly at home [2]. We believe that perceiving and enhancing the quality of life of the elderly who lives at home is possible through automatic emotion recognition and regulation using different means [3,4].

From an individual perspective, quality of life can be considered in terms of well-being. It includes emotional (self-esteem, emotional intelligence, mindset), social (friends, family, community) and physical (health, physical safety) aspects in a person's life. Indeed, it has been largely studied that positive emotional states promote healthy perceptions, beliefs and physical well-being [5,6]. In the context of research on well-being in old age, the need of a specific software architecture for emotion recognition and regulation tasks is justified. Besides, we have introduced a new gerontechnological approach for monitoring the elderly at home. In first place, the goal is to detect the elder's emotions by analyzing their physiological signals, facial expression, behavior and voice [2].

Nowadays, human emotions are present in countless daily situations, like communications, learning processes or rational decision-making [5]. Researching on smart environments, home automation, ambient intelligence, and entertainment systems or e-health care assistance are trying to relief social isolation and/or exclusion suffered by elderly who decide to stay at their homes [6]. Aging adults living alone are prone to develop mental illness as they experiment negative emotions like disgust, sadness, anger and/or fear. Technological paradigms aforementioned often lack from emotional intelligence, being unable to recognize the human emotional states [5]. Therefore, they fail to properly decide which actions to execute depending on the emotion, and adequate their behavior to the mood of elderly.

This is where the paradigm of affective computing raises, trying to provide emotional intelligence to machines for improving human-machine interaction. However, the first step towards a machine emotional intelligence is the development of mathematical models able to classify human feelings. This is not an easy task, because feeling emotions involves a number of complex physiological processes that may variate depending on age, memory or past experiences. Indeed, the same stimulus may affect disparately to different people [7].

It is important to understand the differences between young and older adults in emotional states and reactions. Many theoretical models studying emotional experience across adulthood predict changes throughout this life stage. A growing number of studies find that the way we understand, manage, and react to positive and negative events changes as we age. Previous findings clearly show that film clips evoke differential emotional responses in younger and older adults, and corroborate the importance of measuring the baseline state of each participant using neutral stimuli. Only by considering the baseline state can the strength of the emotion induction be identified, since this takes into account the distance between affect at baseline and after induction [7, 8].

Emotion detection requires continuous monitoring of relevant physiological data. Besides other bio-potentials, electro-dermal activity (EDA) and heart-rate variability (HRV) are some of the most used, because they are linked with the central nervous system through sympathetic and parasympathetic components [9]. More concretely, it has been reported that EDA is exclusively linked to the sympathetic component whilst HRV seems to be related to the parasympathetic, such that both variables cover the autonomous nervous system. Thanks to the recent advances on microelectronics, communications and low-power devices, EDA and HRV sensors use to be embedded into wearables, providing an easy and non-intrusive way to continuously acquire physiological data [10–15].

In this work, we present a classification system of EDA and HRV physiological responses in young and older caused by exposure to seven types of emotions by using films as inductors. Based on previous research, we expect to find high levels of accuracy of the metrics [11, 14, 15]. For this, a novel mathematical model in which the responses of the two physiological parameters are combined is used. In summary, this study introduces a wearable technology and an emotional model, specifically tailored to detect a series of emotions in elders. The proposed system is trained through eliciting emotions using films that have demonstrated to induce mood in aging adults and young people [7, 8].

2 Method

2.1 Participants

The final sample comprises 130 volunteers aged between 18 and 84 years (M = 39.02, SD = 25.32, 68.83% women). From the initial sample, 4 older adults and 7 young adults were excluded due to depressive symptoms. The participants were recruited from a research volunteer pool at the Department of Psychology, University of Castilla- La Mancha (UCLM) Medical School, from an association at the "Universidad de Mayores" (a university program for older adults) and two socio-cultural centers in the city of Albacete. Participants were divided into age groups to form a younger group of 80 participants aged 18–26 (M = 18.87, SD = 1.63, 69.9% women) and an older group of 50 participants aged 60–84 years (M = 69.74, SD = 6.56, 68.4% women).

Participants were receiving no psychotropic treatment or drug use and had no previous history of psychological, psychiatric or neurological disorder, according to the criteria of the Diagnostic and Statistical Manual of Mental Disorders Fifth Edition (DSM-V). They presented no auditory or visual impairments other than requiring corrective lenses. All were of Caucasian ethnicity and native Spanish speakers. They gave voluntary consent to take part in the study without obtaining any type of remuneration and according to the requirements of the approved ethics procedure of the Clinical Research Ethics Committee of the Albacete University Hospital.

2.2 Procedure

The experiment is performed in a small room equipped with a comfortable armchair and a 27-inches screen monitor. Upon arrival of the participants, they are welcomed by offering an overview of the experiment and they sign a written consent. Before starting the experimental session, Beck Depression Inventory (BDI) and Positive and Negative Affect Schedule (PANAS) are administered to know the participant's current emotional state. Moreover, if the participant is older than 60, Mini-Mental State Examination (MMSE) is administered to rule out any cognitive impairment. The experimental task has an average duration of 50 min depending on the participant who may answer the complete questionnaire quicker or slower. The experiment has been designed with software E-Prime 2.0 professional, which includes the instructions on the experiment for each event.

We selected 54 scenes from HD films dubbed in Spanish with an average length of 2'38". These fragments were a battery of audio-visual stimuli, previously validated in a population of young Spanish adults [16]. The selected excerpts maintained the same features used in previous studies [17,18]. Furthermore, we added a scene from film '127 h' to the disgust category, which presented the characteristics of this stimulus used in previous studies. In accordance with the previously published film clip batteries, each segment was expected to induce an emotion from a specific category: amusement, affection, anger, sadness, disgust, fear and neutral state.

2.3 Physiological Measures

EDA. Electro-dermal activity (EDA) measures the changes in conductivity produced in the skin derived from the increase in the activity of the sweat glands. The sudomotor nerve activity (SMNA) is responsible for triggering the sudomotor fibers which activate the sweat glands. Nevertheless, it has been reported that SMNA is linked to emotional states, particularly influencing the arousal dimension [19]. EDA signals are composed by the superposition of two different components. On the one hand, the skin conductance response (SCR) can be observed when the sudomotor nerve is activated [12–15]. From a morphological point of view, SCR is represented by a peak or a burst of peaks with different amplitudes, slopes and decays depending of the stimulus intensity.

On the other hand, the tonic component, or skin conductance level (SCL), represents the base line of the skin conductance. SCL varies among people, depending on their physiological states and autonomic regulation [11]. Finally, EDA morphology is represented by a fast-changing SCR signal modulated by a slowly varying SCL component. Given the slow response of the SCL component, the useful information ranges from 0 to 0.05 Hz. Similarly, the energy of the SCR component ranges from 0.05 to 1.5 Hz.

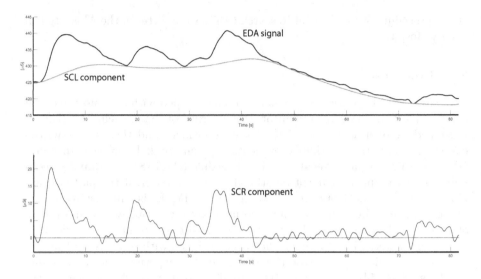

Fig. 1. Extraction of SCR component.

In this study, EDA signal are acquired by using a direct-current exosomatic technique, using a couple of Ag/AgCl disc electrodes with contact diameter of 10 mm attached to medial phalanges in palm of non-dominant hand, as it is described in [11,12]. Signals are acquired to a sampling frequency of 10 Hz to accomplish with Nyquist criteria. Then, signals are filtered by using a 1.5 cut-off low-pass finite impulse response filter with order N = 32. Considering that SCL could behavior as a confounding factor, it is separated from SCR component using a deconvolution approach [20] (Fig. 1).

HRV. The heart rate (HR) represents the successive heart polarization and depolarization caused by the electrical impulses generated on the sinoatrial node and transmitted to the ventricles [21]. During ventricular polarization, blood is pumped into the cells throughout the circulatory system. This process is reflected in the electrocardiogram as the QRS complex, where R-peaks are the most significant points within this wave. However, in recent years and thanks to the emerging of wearable technologies, one of the most extended approaches to measure the HR consists in measuring the blood volume changes caused by the circulatory system functioning in veins or capillaries [9,12,21].

In this work, raw blood pumping signals are obtained by using a photoplethysmography (PPG) technique, able to measure small variations in the reflected/transmitted light intensity, associated with changes in the blood pumping function. The signals are recording using a sampling frequency of 60 Hz, since useful information is located between 0 Hz and 30 Hz. Then, signals are filtered in order to remove possible interferences, such as power line interference or ambient electromagnetic signals. Maximums of signals corresponds with pulse pumping, and they are highly correlate with the R-R series in the electrocardiogram [22].

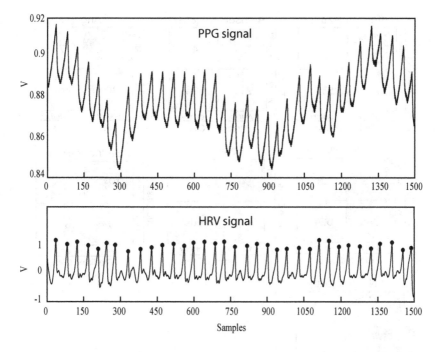

Fig. 2. Obtaining of HRV series.

Therefore, maximums of PPG signal are located by using a robust and reliable peak detection, able to deal with different signal morphologies [12]. Finally, the heart rate variability (HRV) is estimated by measuring the variation in consecutive PPG peaks (Fig. 2).

2.4   Feature Extraction and Statistical Analysis

With the aim of characterizing the processed information, seventeen features were calculated on skin conductance response (SCR) and heart-rate variability (HRV) data, grouped into five statistical, four temporal and eight morphological features.

Statistical features measure the level sample distribution and may provide relevant information about how the samples are distributed, and their deviations. In this category, mean (MEN), standard deviation (STD), maximum (MAX), minimum (MIN) and dynamic range (DRG) are computed. Furthermore, temporal features emphasize the sudden changes on the data series and provide important information regarding evolution of data along time. This group contains the computation of mean and standard deviation of the first derivative (FRD and FRS, respectively) and mean and standard deviation of the second derivative (SDM and SDS, respectively). Finally, morphological characteristics focus on highlighting the shape and form of the data. In this group, arc-length (ARC), integral (INT), potency (POT), root mean square (RMS), area-perimeter ratio

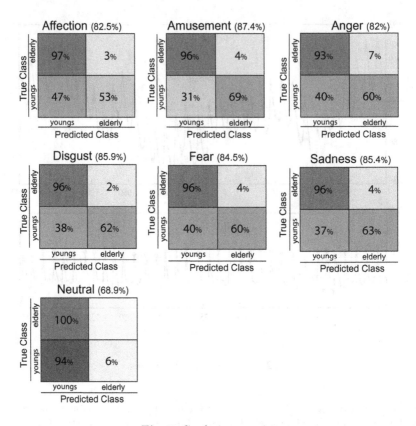

Fig. 3. Confusion matrix.

(APR), energy-perimeter ratio (EPR) are computed. It is worth noting that these features were always normalised by the length of the sample, since the duration of the data may variate depending on the duration of the stimulus. Finally, the asymmetry (ASY) and kurtosis (KUR) of the data distribution was computed.

A multi-parametric model was considered to build an algorithm able to discriminate among different emotions. Thus, aforementioned features, calculated for both physiological variables EDA and HRV, were used to feed a support vector machine (SVM). This classifier was latter run using a cubic kernel function and kernel scale one.

3   Results

Using an advanced quadratic SVM classifier with normalized data, seven matrices are obtained, one for each of the emotions studied.: affection, amusement, anger, disgust, fear and neutral. Moreover, by means of a confusion matrix, Fig. 3 shows the performance of the SVM classifier.

As shown in the figure, the overall accuracy varies from 68.9% for 'neutral' to a maximum of 87.4% for 'amusement'. In 'affection' the overall accuracy is 82.5% (graph 1). For 'amusement' the overall accuracy is 87.4%. The overall accuracy is 82.0% for 'anger'. For 'disgust', we obtain an overall accuracy of 85.9%. 'Fear' offers an overall accuracy of 84.5%. For 'sadness' the overall accuracy is 85.4%. Finally, the overall accuracy is 68.9% for 'neutral'.

4 Conclusions

In this work, a complete system composed of hardware, control software, signal processing and classification model has been considered to deploy a wearable with a remarkable ability to discriminate among seven considered emotional states (neutral, affection, amusement, anger, disgust, fear and sadness). Moreover, contrary to most algorithms usually trained with a non-targeted sample, in this study the experimentation and results are completely focused on comparing young and older people in two joint physiological parameters, namely, EDA and HRV. Indeed, it has been already reported that a reaction against a specific stimulus of a young individual is different from the reaction shown by an older person [8]. Therefore, most models by other authors cannot be extrapolated.

The classification results for each detected emotion have been explained through previous psychological evidences. The results have shown that the present system achieves 82.4% global accuracy for all emotions, including the neutral one. This value is in line with some theoretical models predicting emotional responses in aging adults. Nevertheless, the results have shown a different trend for positive emotions. As in some previous research, amusement reached a high number of hits (87.4%) whilst affection received the lowest rate of hits (82.5%). For negative emotions, the one with the lowest value is anger (82.4%) and the highest is disgust (85.9%).

In conclusion, this work is in line with previous results [14,23], and demonstrates that the proposed wearable emotion detection system can be used by aging adults, especially for detecting negative emotions that usually deteriorate health and wellness and lead to social isolation.

Acknowledgments. This work has been partially supported by Spanish Ministerio de Ciencia, Innovación y Universidades, Agencia Estatal de Investigación (AEI)/European Regional Development Fund (FEDER, UE) under DPI2016-80894-R grant. Arturo Martínez-Rodrigo holds 2018/11744 grant from European Regional Development Fund (FEDER, UE).

References

1. Serrano, J.P., Latorre, J.M., Gatz, M.: Spain: promoting the welfare of older adults in the context of population aging. Gerontologist **54**(5), 733–740 (2014). https://doi.org/10.1093/geront/gnu010

2. Castillo, J.C., Castro-Gonzalez, A., Fernandez-Caballero, A., Latorre, J.M., Pastor, J.M., Fernandez-Santos, A., Salichs, M.A.: Software architecture for smart emotion recognition and regulation of the ageing adult. Cogn. Comput. **8**(2), 357–367 (2016). https://doi.org/10.1007/s12559-016-9383-y
3. Sokolova, M.V., Fernández-Caballero, A.: A review on the role of color and light in affective computing. Appl. Sci. **5**(3), 275–293 (2015). https://doi.org/10.3390/app5030275
4. Fernández-Sotos, A., Fernández-Caballero, A., Latorre, J.M.: Influence of tempo and rhythmic unit in musical emotion regulation. Front. Comput. Neurosci. **10**, 80 (2016). https://doi.org/10.3389/fncom.2016.00080
5. Fernández-Caballero, A., et al.: Smart environment architecture for emotion detection and regulation. J. Biomed. Inform. **64**, 55–73 (2016). https://doi.org/10.1016/j.jbi.2016.09.015
6. Fernández-Caballero, A., Latorre, J.M., Pastor, J.M., Fernández-Sotos, A.: Improvement of the elderly quality of life and care through smart emotion regulation. In: Pecchia, L., Chen, L.L., Nugent, C., Bravo, J. (eds.) IWAAL 2014. LNCS, vol. 8868, pp. 348–355. Springer, Cham (2014). https://doi.org/10.1007/978-3-319-13105-4_50
7. Fernández-Aguilar, L., et al.: Emotional induction through films: a model for the regulation of emotions. In: Chen, Y.-W., Tanaka, S., Howlett, R.J., Jain, L.C. (eds.) Innovation in Medicine and Healthcare 2016. SIST, vol. 60, pp. 15–23. Springer, Cham (2016). https://doi.org/10.1007/978-3-319-39687-3_2
8. Fernández-Aguilar, L., Ricarte, J.J., Ros, L., Latorre, J.M.: Emotional differences in young and older adults: films as mood induction procedure. Front. Psychol. **9**, 1110 (2018). https://doi.org/10.3389/fpsyg.2018.01110
9. Malik, M., et al.: Heart rate variability standards of measurement, physiological interpretation, and clinical use. Eur. Heart J. **17**, 354–381 (1996)
10. Zangróniz, R., Martínez-Rodrigo, A., López, M.T., Pastor, J.M., Fernández-Caballero, A.: Estimation of mental distress from photoplethysmography. Appl. Sci. **8**, 69 (2018). https://doi.org/10.3390/app8010069
11. Zangróniz, R., Martínez-Rodrigo, A., Pastor, J.M., López, M.T., Fernández-Caballero, A.: Electrodermal activity sensor for classification of calm/distress condition. Sensors **17**, 2324 (2017). https://doi.org/10.3390/s17102324
12. Martínez-Rodrigo, A., Alcaraz, R., Rieta, J.J.: Application of the phasor transform for automatic delineation of single lead ECG fiducial points. Physiol. Meas. **31**, 1467 (2010). https://doi.org/10.1088/0967-3334/31/11/005
13. Martínez-Rodrigo, A., Fernández-Caballero, A., Silva, F., Novais, P.: Monitoring electrodermal activity for stress recognition using a wearable. In: Ambient Intelligence and Smart Environments, pp. 416–425 (2016). https://doi.org/10.3233/978-1-61499-690-3-416
14. Martínez-Rodrigo, A., Zangróniz, R., Pastor, J.M., Fernández-Caballero, A.: Arousal level classification in the ageing adult by measuring electrodermal skin conductivity. In: Bravo, J., Hervás, R., Villarreal, V. (eds.) AmIHEALTH 2015. LNCS, vol. 9456, pp. 213–223. Springer, Cham (2015). https://doi.org/10.1007/978-3-319-26508-7_21
15. Martínez-Rodrigo, A., Zangróniz, R., Pastor, J.M., Sokolova, M.V.: Arousal level classification of the aging adult from electro-dermal activity: from hardware development to software architecture. Pervasive Mob. Comput. **34**, 46–59 (2017). https://doi.org/10.1016/j.pmcj.2016.04.006
16. Fernández, C.F., Mateos, J.C.P., Ribaudi, J.S., Fernández-Abascal, E.G.: Spanish validation of an emotion-eliciting set of films. Psicothema **23**, 778–785 (2011)

17. Gross, J.J., Levenson, R.W.: Emotion elicitation using films. Cogn. Emot. **9**, 87–108 (1995). https://doi.org/10.1080/02699939508408966

18. Schaefer, A., Nils, F., Sanchez, X., Philippot, P.: Assessing the effectiveness of a large database of emotion-eliciting films: a new tool for emotion researchers. Cogn. Emot. **24**, 1153–1172 (2010). https://doi.org/10.1080/02699930903274322

19. Boucsein, W.: Electrodermal Activity. Springer, Heidelberg (2012). https://doi.org/10.1007/978-1-4614-1126-0

20. Benedek, M., Kaernbach, C.: A continuous measure of phasic electrodermal activity. J. Neurosci. Methods **190**, 80–91 (2010). https://doi.org/10.1016/j.jneumeth.2010.04.028

21. Malik, M.: Heart rate variability. Ann. Noninvasive Electrocardiol. **1**, 151–181 (1996). https://doi.org/10.1111/j.1542-474X.1996.tb00275.x

22. Allen, J.: Photoplethysmography and its application in clinical physiological measurement. Physiol. Meas. **28**, R1 (2007). https://doi.org/10.1088/0967-3334/28/3/R01

23. Martínez-Rodrigo, A., Zangróniz, R., Pastor, J.M., Latorre, J.M., Fernández-Caballero, A.: Emotion detection in ageing adults from physiological sensors. In: Mohamed, A., Novais, P., Pereira, A., Villarrubia González, G., Fernández-Caballero, A. (eds.) Ambient Intelligence - Software and Applications. AISC, vol. 376, pp. 253–261. Springer, Cham (2015). https://doi.org/10.1007/978-3-319-19695-4_26

Game-Based Human-Robot Interaction Promotes Self-disclosure in People with Visual Impairments and Intellectual Disabilities

Jelle-Jan De Groot[1], Emilia Barakova[1(✉)], Tino Lourens[2],
Evelien van Wingerden[3], and Paula Sterkenburg[3]

[1] Eindhoven University of Technology, P.O. Box 513, Eindhoven, The Netherlands
j.j.a.d.groot@student.tue.nl, e.i.barakova@tue.nl
[2] TiViPE, Kanaaldijk ZW 11, Helmond, The Netherlands
tino@tivipe.com
[3] Faculty of Behavioural and Movement Sciences, Clinical Child and Family Studies,
Vrije Universiteit Amsterdam, Amsterdam, The Netherlands
{e.van.wingerden,p.s.sterkenburg}@vu.nl

Abstract. The willingness to share personal information about negative social experiences is of great importance for the effectiveness of robot-mediated social therapies. This paper reports the results of a pilot test on the effectiveness of using a game or a conversation on achieving a higher self-disclosure in people with visual and intellectual disabilities. The participants interacted with a humanoid robot NAO. Comparable game-based and conversation-based interaction were implemented. We measured the length of the self-disclosing sentences during the two interactions. The majority of the participants said that they preferred the conversation-based over the game-based interaction. The results indicate that during the game-based interaction the participants used much longer self-disclosing sentences in comparison with the to be conversation-based interaction. The outcomes of this pilot will help to improve the human-robot interactions for promoting self-disclosure as the first step in a research project that aims to alleviate worrying behavior in this user group.

1 Introduction

Self-disclosure is defined as the process by which people reveal personal information to others and is important in all types and stages of social relationships. Reciprocity via effective self-disclosure can lead to positive outcomes in interactions and promote further disclosure and relationship building [1,2]. Willingness to share personal information about negative social experiences with the robot is especially important for the effectiveness of social therapies. Robots might play a positive role in this process – a person might more easily engage in self-disclosure with a robot than with a human even if s/he realizes that the robot might be

© Springer Nature Switzerland AG 2019
J. M. Ferrández Vicente et al. (Eds.): IWINAC 2019, LNCS 11486, pp. 262–272, 2019.
https://doi.org/10.1007/978-3-030-19591-5_27

teleoperated by a human [3]. In this project we target to achieve self-disclosure as the first step towards alleviating worrying behavior – the persons first need to disclose what is troubling them, before the robot or the therapist can offer a set of solutions. The question that arises at this stage of the research is how can we design robot behaviors and human-robot interaction that contributes to better self-disclosure and engagement in this activity in such a way that the robot can be used effectively in robot-mediated therapies. As stated in [4]: 'The challenge in building effective social and behavioral therapies with robots is mainly in the difficulties of bridging social interaction studies, and clinical expertise to computational models that the robots can utilize' [4]. Methods from user-centered design can contribute to solving this challenge. By using participatory research through design method as proposed in [5], we aim to develop effective human-robot interaction scenarios that can improve the quality of self-disclosure, and thus the therapy.

Two user research methods, shadowing and empathy map, described in the Materials and Methods section, and previous research about the usability of robots in care for persons with a visual and intellectual disability led to the initial idea to see if game-based interactions that incorporate these techniques could also be beneficial for this user group. Previous research has shown that also conversation-based interactions are well-suited for people with visual impairments and intellectual disability since many contemporary therapies are conversation-based. For instance, Kumazaki et al. [6] found that robots might be useful in eliciting and promoting self-disclosure for adolescents with autism spectrum disorder (ASD). In this study, adolescents with ASD and a typically developing group of participants communicated with two types of humanoid robots or with a human interviewer. Inspired by the study of Kumazaki et al. [6] we measure the differences of an impression of emotional state and the measured length of self-disclosing statements to gain insight in the amount of self-disclosure the participants would show. We propose an additional measure of the content of the self-disclosing sentences through analysis of the transcripts of the answers, to evaluate the quality of the disclosed information. With this pilot experiment, we want to get an indication whether the game-based or conversation-based approach will bring to better self-disclosure.

2 Materials and Methods

2.1 Participants

Six participants with visual impairments and intellectual disabilities from the Bartiméus expertise center were recruited for the experiment. Bartiméus is an organization providing care for persons with a visual impairment, but often the clients have more complex conditions. For this experiment, three participants took part in the conversation-based interaction (P1, P3, P6), and the other three in the game-based interaction (P2, P4, P5). This order was randomly chosen. Of the six participants, there were five men and one woman (P1). The participants were young adults and adults. Their specific ages are not recorded. Four of the participants had mild intellectual disability (P1, P2, P3, P4); two had moderate intellectual disability (P5, P6). All participants had visual impairment below a certain cut-off point of 6/18 according to the World Health Organization criteria [7]. The exact specifications of the visual and intellectual disability are not of much importance yet, as the goal of this study is to get a general overview of the self-disclosure towards the robot. The research ethics committee at Bartiméus approved this pilot study. All the participants signed an informed consent where they agreed to participate and to be filmed while interacting with the robot. The parents of the participants also signed consent forms.

2.2   Aim of the Study

The main goal of the pilot study is to find ways for increasing the amount and the level of detail of self-disclosed information and engagement the participant would show during the interactions. The outcomes of the pilot are expected to help us understand how we might improve the robot interactions on the effectiveness of self-disclosure and engagement in robot-mediated therapies for people with visual impairments and intellectual disability and how to improve the interaction design in follow-up research.

The topics of both interactions are about dealing with positive and negative social experiences in everyday life. We measured the amount of self-disclosure the participants would show during a self-disclosing question towards the robot by counting the number of words the participant spoke while answering a self-disclosing question in both conditions. For the word counting, transcribed audio from the interactions with the robot was used. In addition, after each interaction with a participant, a 5-point smiley preference scale was used for measuring the levels of enjoyment, embarrassment, stress, and boredom of the conversation-based and game-based interaction. Also, a preference for one of the two different interactions was asked for. The sessions were recorded, and qualitative analysis of the answers was made as well.

2.3   Human-Robot Interactions Design Methods

The participatory research through design approach was done in close collaboration with clinical/psychological experts from the Bartiméus expertise center and the Vrije Universiteit in Amsterdam. Technical expertise in the design of a task-appropriate human-robot interaction came from the Technical University of Eindhoven and the TiViPE company.

In the early stages of interaction development, several results were gathered. An Empathy map with professional caregivers from the Bartiméus expertise center was used to find out what characteristics the robot should have and what kind of skills it should possess while interacting with people with a visual and intellectual disability [8]. The outcomes from the empathy mapping gave some practical guidelines - the robot should speak slowly, in simple, short sentences to the participants. The robot should appear to be friendly and funny. The Shadowing technique was used to elicit information about the everyday life of the participants [9]. Based on this input, the participants showed a preference for playing games, and enjoyment of music. The circle of security was taken into account while developing the interactions [10,11], which implies that the robot should respond supportive and reassuring to the answers a participant will give.

2.4 Materials

For this research project, an NAO robot from Softbank robotics was used. This robot has a humanoid appearance and movements. The robot can express through the head and bodily gestures, speech and LED light. Two sets of interaction scenarios were developed. The robot was teleoperated to ensure more natural speech-based interaction. At the end of each interaction, the robot would dance with a large onset of the limbs so the visually impaired participants could see the dance. The interactions were created with TiViPE environment [12] since it will make possible high level of autonomy and interaction fluency of the behaviors at the final test.

For the game-based interaction, four cards, each containing one question were used (Fig. 1). These cards were inspired by card games like Unstuck and Cards of Calm. They were designed to be large so even persons with impaired vision can read them, although during the game the robot read the text. In collaboration with the clinical experts, these questions were fine-tuned to be clear for this user group.

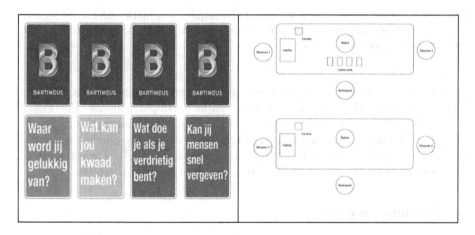

Fig. 1. (a) The design of the question cards used in the game-based interaction. From left to right: What makes you happy? What makes you angry? What do you do when you are sad? Can you forgive people quickly? (b) Experimental setup in the two conditions Game condition – above.

2.5   Procedure and Data Collection

Each participant was welcomed by two researchers and a small introduction about the interaction with the robot was provided. The participant was seated in front of the robot during both interactions. On a separate table, one of the researchers operated the robot from a computer, and a video camera recorded the interaction between the participant and the robot (Fig. 1b). By switching the order of the interactions for each participant, we excluded bias from the novelty effect of the robot. Also, the robot would wear a blue t-shirt during the game-based interactions and white one during the conversation based interaction to appear as a different robot.

After the first interaction, the participant was offered a drink, and meanwhile, the researchers set up the robot for the second interaction. After each interaction, each participant was asked to rate the interaction with a five-point smiley scale (Fig. 2) on the level of joy, embarrassment, stress, and boredom they felt during the interactions with the robot. At the end of the second interaction, each participant was asked whether they prefer the game or the conversation-based interaction with the robot.

Fig. 2. Five-point smiley face scale was set to acquire information about the experienced level of joy, embarrassment, stress and boredom. Retrieved from https://www.shutterstock.com/search/smiley+face.

Both types of interaction scenarios were recorded using a GoPro camera. This resulted in 142.85 min of video material form six participants. The videos recorded during the interactions were first transcribed to analyze the measured length of self-disclosure statements and to check whether the participant would respond to a question or maybe interprets the question wrongly. The interactions were viewed twice by one researcher to transcribe the audio correctly.

3   Implementation

Previously we developed a robot controller that can facilitate the robot therapy co-creation process [13]. This means that persons with a different level of technical skills can develop human-robot interaction scenarios using either the main program or one of the interfaces [14], which will result in simpler program, for instance without interpretation of sensory information and low cyclomatic complexity [14]. To allow the creation of realistic interactions with a robot we adopted the event-based finite state machine approach. In this approach, a state diagram, which is a graphical representation of a finite state machine, is used as a basic concept for the creation of all training scenarios for both technical professionals and end-users. All the sensory and motor information from the robot is continuously available and updated 5–10 times per second, and can provide triggers for state change.

Both visual programming and end-user interfaces to TiViPE are designed so that the state diagram is incorporated in a loop that constantly updates of all sensory and motor information of the robot. The robot actuators information is available to the robot as proprioceptive sensory information defining the current 3D positioning (state) of the robot [15]. This implies that sensory information from the outside environment or the robot proprioceptive sensing can be an event that causes a transition to a new state. Once a task is accomplished, the scenario proceeds to the next state or set of states if no event occurs. The state concept makes it possible to handle every event more flexible than for instance if-than-else loops, since these only support applications with only one trigger and one action and lacks real-time feedback from the outside world.

Clinical psychologists who design the therapies usually define the progression of therapy with a flowchart. The difference between a state machine and a flowchart is that the state machine performs actions in response to explicit events (such as sensory readings) and the current state. In contrast, the flowchart does not need explicit events; it makes transitions from node to node in its graph automatically upon completion of activities. Therefore, the difference in defining a state machine or a flowchart by therapists or other end-users is that they always need to specify with which another state the flow continues. Another difference is that in a state machine the scenario can be repeated from the step it was not functioning – for instance, if the person did not hear the last sentence, the robot would repeat it until the person understands it. Another example, the robot can point to the cards, if it is sitting or standing, so if the user has pushed the robot and it has fallen, the robot will first need to go from state laying on the ground to sitting state before it can proceed with pointing to a card. In a flow-chart based behavior definition, such a failure should result either in the human intervention or in restarting the whole scenario from the beginning.

In robotics (social robotics in particular), the behavior can consist of more than one parallel action (like movement and speech) and can be triggered by different events. With such a system design we aim to reach a better match with the user's mental models when they want to specify how the interactive robot should behave according to the objects and situations available in the context of use.

In summary, the created robot behaviors are constantly updated for changes in the environment or the robot state. This means that the changes in the environment are determining the robot actions in real-time. For the end-user programmers as the clinical psychologists and occupational therapists, who are accustomed to thinking in the flow-chart framework, the transition to the new concept of event-based state diagram is accomplished by them explicitly giving the next state if it is not only the one that follows in the flow-chart representation.

The state diagram of the actual interaction was as follows. To start of the game-based interaction, the robot introduces itself to the participant first. The robot asks if the participant has talked to a robot before. Based on the participant's reaction, the robot will respond in a friendly manner. After that, the robot invites the participant to play a game to get to know each other better. The robot will explain the rules of the game, and asks if it needs to repeat the rules again if it is unclear for the participant. The participant asks one of the questions on the cards to the robot. For the game-based interaction, the four cards, each containing one questions are used. The robot gives an example of self-disclosure by answering one of the questions (on the cards) in the game. In the next round, the participant has to answer a question from the cards in the game, in predefined order. The participant does this by showing the question card to the robot, so the robot can ask the question to the participant. When the participant answered the question, the robot will give a reward by colorful blinking LED's and playing a happy tune. The player lays the card down, and the next self-disclosing question will be asked in the indicated order. Several rounds will be played where all the self-disclosing questions will be answered by the participant.

4   Results

4.1   Interview Questions and Five-Point Smiley Face Scale

The results of the smiley-scale rating and the preferences are shown in Fig. 3. The five smileys are transcribed to numbers weighting from factors 1 (very low) to 5 (very high).

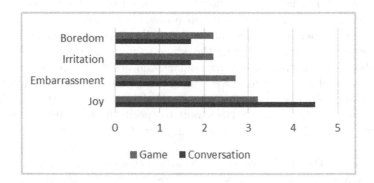

Fig. 3. Emotions reported after both interactions using a 5 point smiley scale. Each participant rated their level of Joy, Embarrassment, Irritation, and Boredom (1- Low, 5 High).

By asking about what could be improved in the interaction Participant 1 proposed that the robot was sweet and kind, but she did find annoying that she had to wait for a while before the robot responded. Participant 2 said the speech of the robot could be clearer. He wanted to get to know the robot even better. Participant 3 liked both interactions just as much. Participant 4 preferred if the robot would ask a bit more about a particular conversation topic. He said it would be nice if the robot can ask how your day was, and what your hobbies are. Participant 4 could hear the robot clearly, but he did prefer a human voice over a robot voice. He also stated that he prefers to talk with a human when something is bothering him compared to the robot. Participant 5 also mentioned that he prefers a human voice over a robot voice. He said he had to get used to interacting with the robot, but in the end, he said he enjoyed it very much. Participant 6 also said to prefer a human voice over a robot voice. Participant 6 mentioned several times that he would like to ask the robot what time it is.

4.2 Audio Transcription Self-disclosing Statements

Each interaction with the robot was recorded with a GoPro camera, which resulted in video material for the game-based and conversation-based interaction for each participant. During the conversation-based and game-based interaction, several self-disclosing questions were asked. The questions were asked in Dutch but transcribed in this paper in English. Figure 4 visualizes the total number of words in the answers of the participants to the questions on the same topic that were asked in both interactions.

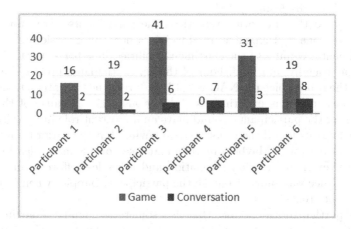

Fig. 4. Graphical representation on the number of self-disclosing words used in both interactions to answer the same 2 questions. The Game-based interaction triggers much longer self-disclosing statements.

5 Discussion

This is to the best of our knowledge the first study that attempts to provoke self-disclosure in persons with visual impairments and intellectual disability through interaction with a robot. There are several studies showing that children with a medical condition and high IQ initiated dialogue with a robot or increased the level of self-disclosure [12], but experiments with adults with such a complex condition have not been performed before.

The results show that the self-disclosing statements by the participants with visual impairments and intellectual disability are not very long or detailed. Since in the game interaction the participants and the robot took turns, the participants answered half of the questions that were asked. To see the differences, we calculated the descriptive statistics (Mean and Standard Deviation) which are independent from the number of the answers, and we can see that by the Game interaction the mean length of the answers is much higher 12.6 vs. 2.48 words, which indicates that Game-based interaction might be a better choice for promoting self-disclosure. This paper also offers a methodological improvement in comparison with the related work reported in [6]. While in the referred study the number of words in the answers were counted, we also analyzed the content of the transcripts of the answers. The number of words in the responses of self-disclosing questions were counted after we evaluated whether the sentence contains self-disclosing information.

In both interactions, there were correspondingly two and three occasions when the participant did not answer. This might be because the participants found it difficult to interpret the questions that aim self-disclosure properly. The personality of the participants could also be taken into account for explaining the length of self-disclosing questions.

We observed that in both interactions the participants were impressed by the robot, and one participant wanted to join a new robot session when he saw the experimenter coming to the Bartiméus facilities. The participants described the robot as friendly and kind. Four of the six participants preferred a human voice over the robot-voice the NAO-robot had during the two interactions, which is in line with previous experiments [16], see also [17]. Because of the visual impairment of the participants, sound plays an important role in their lives. Not all the participants found the robot voice annoying, but the majority preferred a more human-like voice. Maybe a more human-like voice is more pleasing to the ear, can convey more emotion/intonation and takes less effort to understand. The human voice was shown to make the participants happier when interacting with the robot [16].

Several participants mentioned that they sometimes found it annoying to wait for a reaction from the robot, which we will improve for the main experiment. There could be a link between the rating of irritation and boredom with the smiley-scale and the time a participant had to wait before the robot responded. This aspect could also have had an impact on the affective state and user experience of the participant. The level of irritation and boredom scored higher in the game-based interaction compared to the conversation-based interaction.

The level of joy was also rated higher during the conversation-based interaction compared to the game-based interaction. This was not expected, as we had assumed that the gaming elements of surprise and structure would influence the interaction more positively compared to a conversational robot interaction. The type of self-disclosing questions the robot would ask during the interactions could also have influenced the kind of experience the participant had.

There were some limitations to the design process. Due to the exploratory nature of this preliminary study, the robot interaction was not programmed to have quick reaction times and autonomy. Another limitation of the study is that although similar in meaning, the self-disclosing questions by game-based and conversation-based interaction slightly differ, although they address the same problem. A more extensive behavioral analysis of engagement could be done to look at the level of engagement while the robot asks a self-disclosing question. Because of the limitations in the reflective capabilities of the participants, it was hard to ask specific and reflection-promoting questions about the interaction. Also, the participants needed guidance when using the 5-point smiley scale.

Acknowledgments. We thank the six participants in this study for participating and contributing to this research. We also thank Bartiméus expertise center for facilitating the research and Bartiméus Sonneheerdt Foundation for the Grant nr 2017075B.

References

1. Sprecher, S., Hendrick, S.S.: Self-disclosure in intimate relationships: associations with individual and relationship characteristics over time. J. Soc. Clin. Psychol. **23**(6), 857–877 (2004)
2. Sprecher, S., Treger, S., Wondra, J.D., Hilaire, N., Wallpe, K.: Taking turns: reciprocal self-disclosure promotes liking in initial interactions. J. Soc. Clin. Psychol. **49**(5), 860–866 (2013)
3. Aroyo, A.M., Rea, F., Sandini, G., Sciutti, A.: Trust and social engineering in human robot interaction: will a robot make you disclose sensitive information, conform to its recommendations or gamble? IEEE Robot. Autom. Lett. **3**(4), 3701–3708 (2018)
4. Barakova, E.I., Bajracharya, P., Willemsen, M., Lourens, T., Huskens, B.: Long-term LEGO therapy with humanoid robot for children with ASD. Expert Syst. **32**(6), 698–709 (2015)
5. Zimmerman, J., Forlizzi, J., Evenson, S.: Research through design as a method for interaction design research in HCI. In: Proceedings of the SIGCHI Conference on Human Factors in Computing Systems, pp. 493–502. ACM (2007)
6. Kumazaki, H., et al.: Can robotic systems promote self-disclosure in adolescents with autism spectrum disorder? A pilot study. Front. Psychiatry **9**(2018), 36 (2018)
7. World Health Organization, et al.: International classification of impairments, disabilities, and handicaps: a manual of classification relating to the consequences of disease, published in accordance with resolution wha29. 35 of the twenty-ninth world health assembly, May 1976 (1980)
8. Ferreira, B., Silva, W., Oliveira Jr, E.A., Conte, T.: Designing personas with empathy map. In: SEKE, vol. 152 (2015)
9. McDonald, S.: Studying actions in context: a qualitative shadowing method for organizational research. Qual. Res. **5**(4), 455–473 (2005)
10. Kearsley, G., Shneiderman, B.: Engagement theory: a framework for technology-based teaching and learning. Educ. Technol. **38**(5), 20–23 (1998)

11. Cooper, G., Hoffman, K., Powell, B., Marvin, R.: The Circle of Security Intervention. Disorganized Attachment and Caregiving, p. 318 (2011)
12. Lourens, T., Barakova, E.: User-friendly robot environment for creation of social scenarios. In: Ferrández, J.M., Álvarez Sánchez, J.R., de la Paz, F., Toledo, F.J. (eds.) IWINAC 2011. LNCS, vol. 6686, pp. 212–221. Springer, Heidelberg (2011). https://doi.org/10.1007/978-3-642-21344-1_23
13. Kim, M.-G., et al.: Designing robot-assisted pivotal response training in game activity for children with autism. In: 2014 IEEE International Conference on Systems, Man, and Cybernetics (SMC), pp. 1101–1106. IEEE (2014)
14. Buchina, N., Kamel, S., Barakova, E.: Design and evaluation of an end-user friendly tool for robot programming. In: 2016 25th IEEE International Symposium on Robot and Human Interactive Communication (RO-MAN), pp. 185–191. IEEE (2016)
15. Barakova, E.I., Lourens, T.: Event based self-supervised temporal integration for multimodal sensor data. J. Integr. Neurosci. 4(02), 265–282 (2005)
16. Straten, C.L., Smeekens, I., Barakova, E., Glennon, J., Buitelaar, J., Chen, A.: Effects of robots' intonation and bodily appearance on robot-mediated communicative treatment outcomes for children with autism spectrum disorder. Pers. Ubiquitous Comput. 22(2), 379–390 (2018)
17. Marchi, E., Ringeval, F., Schuller, B., Neustein, A.: Voice-enabled assistive robots for handling autism spectrum conditions: an examination of the role of prosody. In: Neustein, A. (ed.) Speech and Automata in the Health Care, pp. 207–236. Walter de Gruyter GmbH & Co KG, Berlin (2014)

Neuroethology

A Short Review of Some Aspects of Computational Neuroethology

Manuel Graña[1,2]([✉]) and Javier de Lope Asiain[1,2]

[1] Computational Intelligence Group, University of the Basque Country,
(UPV/EHU), San Sebastián, Spain
`manuel.grana@ehu.es`
[2] Polytechnical University Madrid (UPM), Madrid, Spain

Abstract. Computational Neuroethology comprises a wide variety of devices, computational tools and techniques used in studies aiming to understand the neural substrate of the observable behavior. In this short review we focus on the description of available computational tools in a landscape of resources that is steadily growing as the scientific community recognizes this Computational Neuroethology as one of the frontiers of scientific endeavor. We comment on the biological basis and some examples of studies reported in the literature before providing a description and taxonomy of resources and tools.

1 Introduction

Ethology is the study of behavior that allows animals to survive and reproduce in natural environments (i.e., adaptive behavior). Neuroethology is the study of the neural basis of adaptive behavior. Computational neuroethology is the use of modeling and simulation to study the neural control of adaptive behavior [48]. Traditionally, neuroethology tries to find the neural basis for behavior by direct intervention or by accidental observation. For instance, the ablation of the pretectum in zebra fish [38] abolishes the prey capture behavior even with intact hyothalamus (that regulates food intake), hence showing that prey related information flow is interrupted.

Under the label of computational neuroethology there are some very abstract attempts to stablish a brain-behavior model, that try to relate mathematical dyanmical models of behaviors (such as the dynamics of finger tapping) with neural dynamics [31], however such abstract approach is limited in the scope of the modeling target. These models follow from a tradition of attempts to reproduce neural mechanisms underlying biological behaviors by artificial mechanical/computational systems, such as Arbib's *rana computatrix* [6] attempt to produce a computational explanation of language evolution, the attempt to model autism via surrogate robot models [27], or modeling the spatiotemporal map building process of honeybees [34]. A more general approach is to try to find correlations between behavioral observations and neural activity measurements

© Springer Nature Switzerland AG 2019
J. M. Ferrández Vicente et al. (Eds.): IWINAC 2019, LNCS 11486, pp. 275–283, 2019.
https://doi.org/10.1007/978-3-030-19591-5_28

obtained from a variety of synchronized sensors. Hence the predominant approach is a data science based approach, using statistics and machine learning
tools.

Behaviors develop because they have some evolutionary advantage that
allows the animal/human to survive and reproduce. For instance, there are quite
diverse behavioral reactions triggered by fear in predator-prey encounters which
are mediated by the specifically optimal environment survival strategy [36]. It
is only natural that an entire field called behavioral ecology has emerged from
the need to explain the interaction between individual and social behavior in
an evolutionary framework, strongly interwined with innovative computational
methods biologically inspired [33].

Neuroethology is increasingly used as a tool to evaluate the effect of treatments to a diversity of brain diseases or injuries, such as the hipoxia-isquemia
in newborns [52]. Objective behavior impairment measures, such as the Longa
score, can be correlated to brain damage observed via postmortem histology, or
via EEG measurement through electrode implants.

2   Animal and Human Models

The behaviors arising in the predator-prey interaction is one of the computational ethology topics studied more intensely [36]. It is a key evolutive scenario,
where complex decision making process are emerging from the survival pulsion.
In this setting, early behavioral neuroscience models found that fear inhibits pain
and injury related behaviors [9], and a ranking of steretyped behaviors according
to the threat imminence continuum [21]. Current studies have identified several
brain circuits involving the amygdala and hypothalamus and other cortex areas
as survival circuits responsible for the flight-fight-freeze behaviors of the prey
as a function of predator distance through experiments carried out on rodents
and humans. Animal models consists in the presentation of the predator or some
surrogate sensorial correlate, such as odour or a shape. For instance, a human
model described in [36] was the presentation of a tarantula at the foot of a human
subject under fMRI scanning. An animal model of fear, also reported in [36], was
a rat presented with a robot simulating a predator performing aggressive moves
when the rat approaches the food pellets.

Ecological laboratory models covering the relation of the social and individual
behaviors benefited from the advances in image and video processing to a large
scale that actually allows to track individual larvae or fly, but the real challenge
is the tracking in the wild [18] under uncontrolled conditions and with great
sparsity of the actual animal observations. Social relations and their neural correlate are of outmost importance. The ability to intervene on the brain pathways
is illustrated in [26] where optical fiber implants allow to activate or shutdown
groups of neurons in the amigdala of genetically modified mice, showing that
antagonistic groups of neurons control the social role of grooming.

Emotion is topic that is gathering a lot of attention from the neuroethological point of view [4]. Emotion is characterized by an internal brain state and

external behavioral manifestations. There is the question of whether animals suffer emotional states analogous to human emotions, which can be attacked with neuroethology tools to find the "emotion primitives" that are the building blocks of emotion, so that emotion in animal models could be investigated without referring to anthopocentric labels. The investigation aims to identify the "central emotion states" in species as far of humans as *Drosophila*, which, paradoxically, allow for more precise identification of neural correlates of specific emotional behaviors.

A growing concern worldwide is the aging population, which poses many problems such as brain degenerative diseases and the need to monitor the elder people in a non intrusive way. The kinect sensor has been shown accurate enough for the latter task [39,51]. Table 1 summarizes the variety of animal and human models that have been studied in the literature.

Table 1. Human and animal models in the literature

Models	Study target
Wild animals	Locomotion [15]; Deep-sea [1]
Fish	Motion [15]; Larvae, predation and feeding [38]; Swim evolution [22]; Abnormal school behavior [58]; Drug induced behavior [50,56]
Human	Fear [36]; Foraging [35]; Team behavior [5]; Locomotion and age [30]; Impact of robot interaction [23,55]
Mice	Social behavior [26,40]; Pain [3]; Home cage behavior [7]; Object recognition [8]; Olfactory research [14]; Grooming [29]; Spinal cord injury [24]; Stroke [19]; Parkinson [25]
Rat	Fear [36]
C elegans	Seasonality an the brain [53]; Locomotion [10,16]
Spider	Foraging [49]
Drosophila	Social behavior [20], Courtship [54] and Aggression [17]
Honeybees	Communication [57]

3   Data Resources

There have been early attempts to setup data repositories that could be used for training of students and professionals, such as the video database of behaviors[1] presented in [37] dedicated to farm animals. The database was also intended to develop multitarget tracking of animals in natural farm environments. More recently, Caltech Resident-Intruder Mouse dataset (CRIM13)[2], a big annotated

---

[1] http://www.ansc.purdue.edu/USDA-LBRU/vdb/video3.htm.
[2] http://www.vision.caltech.edu/Video_Datasets/CRIM13/CRIM13/Main.html.

video recording dataset of experiments regarding aggression and courtship in mice has been produced by Caltech researchers [11]. It consists of 237×2 videos recoded synchronously from top and side views. Another extensive dataset[3] of hom-cage behavior of mice is reported in [28] provides extensive samples of videos as well as a software prototype for the automated analysis of the videos which can be used for additional developments.

4   Computational and Data Capture Systems

The general structure of a computational neuroethological observation system has two main concurrent modules, one is devoted to the capture and analysis of the neural activation, often via Electorencephalogram (EEG) sensors, which can be external or internally implanted. In some animal models it is possible to produce mutant individuals whose neural activity can be observed optically in specific apparatus, such as fluorescent micrscopy [38].

The second module is devoted to the observation of the behavior, for instance by some imaging method. Image processing is a key technology for the development of the ecological behavior observation, allowing identification of individuals, tracking and classification of their behaviors using supervised and unsupervised approaches [18]. There is a wide variety of sensors providing the imaging sources besides the optical cameras, such as infrared camera/illumination, X-ray imaging for animals embedded in the soil, thermal imaging for video shooting in darkness [11], sonar signals for underwater monitoring, sensitive pressure sensors for micromotion detection [12], catwalk systems for animal gait analysis [25]. Sometimes, ingenuity allows to improve data capture, such as adding lateral mirrors that help to obtain 3D information in aquariums [59]. For instance, radar pulses are used customarily to track honeybees [44], and functional Magnetic Resonance Imaging (fMRI) has been used for neuroethological experiments in humans [35].

Thirdly, specific computational modules are devoted to extract the correlation between observed behavior and neural activity. Specific behaviors have to be codified and calibrated in the observation hardware/software. An example, fear produces immobility, but calibration of the system in order to distinguish between fear induced immobility and other conditions needs a careful calibration [43].

Some systems provide some machine learning enhancement to the video annotation by human observers [29], which a time consuming and error prone process, but the current research interest is in the fully automated behavior analysis. For instance, the continuous recognition of social behavior on video recordings without human intervention [11]. This fully automated systems are specially desirable if you plan to do experiments over long periods of time, such when studying the social interactions in a mildy restricted environment [40] approaching as much as possible to the wild conditions. Machine learning techniques are of paramount value for the automated interpretation of observation data. Characterization of

---

[3] http://cbcl.mit.edu/software-datasets/mouse/.

the observation data, aka feature extraction, has been approached from a diversity of points of view. For instance, fractal dimension has been used in [30] to characterize walking path tortuosity of aging person walks. Rather classical approaches, such as Fourier descriptors and a k-NN classifier provided good results in the detection of bottom-of-the-sea wandering animals [1]. Conditional random field models have been exploited for human motion recognition [47], because they can jump over the restrictive and artificious independence assumptions of other models. The application of innovative machine learning includes deep learning techniques, such as the convolutional neural networks (CNN) [2], or the spatio-temporal bags of words used by [11] for the automated construction of ethograms from continuous video, recognizing the behavior building blocks by an Adaboost trained classifier. Another deep learning application to behavior understanding is the application of short time long memory (STLM) recurrent neural networks to the modeling of abnormal behaviors in schools of fish [58]. However, also traditional techniques like hierarchical clustering and K-means have produced good results discriminating behaviors of zebra fish under some antidepresant drugs [56]. Unsupervised techniques are quite useful as discovery tools when no labeled information is accesible, which often is the case in behavioral sciences. Some systems, however, use a plethora of approaches, such the catwalk gait analysis system in [25] which uses gradient boosting engine, random forests, and elastic nets for the catwalk data analysis in order to discriminate gait types from control and Parkinson model animals.

Some early human centered techniques, such as facial image processing, have been translated into animal behavior characterization, such as the analysis of mice facial expressions to assess pain intensity [2,3], or the use of the Kinect, originally a game oriented device, for the monitoring of fishes in an aquarium [45].

All these improved computational techniques lead to the goal of fully automation of the experimental observation, such as the long term observation of behaviors in hone cages [7] which will allow detailed phenotypic characterizations. Many of the current experiments use quite conventional image processing techniques, such as binarization and detection of the tip point for mouse nose detection in exploratory environments [8], using the image processing toolbox of MATLAB to develop custom solutions [32], or the direct use of open source resources (i.e. OpenCV [15]). There are also commercial solutions[4][5] that provide the behavior observation summary that are customary in laboratory research, but no one that carries out the synchronized neural activation and behavior measurement.

Tracking of many individuals in the field of view requires to use accurate and robust motion prediction process, while the body pose needs specific models, such as the misture of gaussians proposed in [54], or accurate geometrical modeling of zebra fish for the study of swimming evolution [22]. Human pose decomposition into body parts (head, hands, etc.) can be made on depth data

---

[4] https://www.harvardapparatus.com/smart-video-tracking-system.html.

[5] https://www.noldus.com/animal-behavior-research/products/ethovision-xt.

obtained from instruments such as Kinect [46]. Occlusions and crossings of the images corresponding to the individuals is a big problem in tracking multiple animals, such as fishes, flies, and ants. A patented software claims to have solved this issue by identification of each animal through a fingerprinting process that is carried online [42]. A more down to the earth solution to the individual tracking problem is to mark each individual with a specific bleach pattern that is learnt by the system by simple pattern recognition [40]. Similar approach was followed in [57] where the objective is to carry out a study of honeybee communication dances inside the hive. They tag the bees to be identified with a binary image code. This allows quite accurate social behavior analysis in a long time frame.

A tracking and velocity analysis method carries out the composition of time subsampled video frames into a single image containing the time variation of fish positions [13]. Trying to remove the effect of the human presence in the recorded experiments may be a concern when dealing with fish populations whose motion may be conditioned by human presence. To achieve this, remote visualization and control of the cameras via web services is proposed [41].

5   Concluding Remarks

Computational neurothology has deep roots in computational models of brain and behavior relations, but it is also deeply related to neuroscience search for neural mechanisms and biological behavior analysis. In fact, it is a convergence point of many computational models and data capture devices and techniques which produces an extraordinary fertile ground for new research ideas, which eventually become products that are changing our lives, such as new ways to validate drug effect in the fight against degenerative brain diseases, which are becoming highly prevalent as the aging population grows worldwide.

References

1. Aguzzi, J., Costa, C., Fujiwara, Y., Iwase, R., Ramirez-Llorda, E., Menesatti, P.: A novel morphometry-based protocol of automated video-image analysis for species recognition and activity rhythms monitoring in deep-sea fauna. Sensors **9**(11), 8438–8455 (2009)
2. Akkaya, B., Tabar, Y.R., Gharbalchi, F., Ulusoy, I., Halici, U.: Tracking mice face in video. In: 20th National Biomedical Engineering Meeting (BIYOMUT), pp. 1–4, November 2016
3. Akkaya, İ.B., Halici, U.: Mouse face tracking using convolutional neural networks. IET Comput. Vis. **12**(2), 153–161 (2018)
4. Anderson, D.J., Adolphs, R.: A framework for studying emotions across species. Cell **157**(1), 187–200 (2014)
5. Andrienko, G., et al.: Visual analysis of pressure in football. Data Min. Knowl. Discov. **31**(6), 1793–1839 (2017)
6. Arbib, M.A.: Rana computatrix to human language: towards a computational neuroethology of language evolution. Philos. Trans. R. Soc. Lond. A: Math. Phys. Eng. Sci. **361**(1811), 2345–2379 (2003)

7. Bains, R.S., et al.: Assessing mouse behaviour throughout the light/dark cycle using automated in-cage analysis tools. J. Neurosci. Methods **300**, 37–47 (2018). Measuring Behaviour 2016

8. Benice, T.S., Raber, J.: Object recognition analysis in mice using nose-point digital video tracking. J. Neurosci. Methods **168**(2), 422–430 (2008)

9. Bolles, R.C., Fanselow, M.S.: A perceptual-defensive-recuperative model of fear and pain. Behav. Brain Sci. **3**(2), 291–301 (1980)

10. Brown, A.E.X., Yemini, E.I., Grundy, L.J., Jucikas, T., Schafer, W.R.: A dictionary of behavioral motifs reveals clusters of genes affecting caenorhabditis elegans locomotion. Proc. Natl. Acad. Sci. **110**(2), 791–796 (2013)

11. Burgos-Artizzu, X.P., Dollár, P., Lin, D., Anderson, D.J., Perona, P.: Social behavior recognition in continuous video. In: 2012 IEEE Conference on Computer Vision and Pattern Recognition, pp. 1322–1329, June 2012

12. Carreno, M.I., et al.: First approach to the analysis of spontaneous activity of mice based on permutation entropy. In: 2015 4th International Work Conference on Bioinspired Intelligence (IWOBI), pp. 197–204, June 2015

13. Cha, B.J., Bae, B.S., Cho, S.K., Oh, J.K.: A simple method to quantify fish behavior by forming time-lapse images. Aquac. Eng. **51**, 15–20 (2012)

14. Cho, H.-J., et al.: Newly developed method for mouse olfactory behavior tests using an automatic video tracking system. Auris Nasus Larynx **45**(1), 103–110 (2018)

15. Conklin, E.E., Lee, K.L., Schlabach, S.A., Woods, I.G.: Videohacking: automated tracking and quantification of locomotor behavior with open source software and off-the-shelf video equipment. J. Undergrad. Neurosci. Educ. **13**(3), A120–A125 (2015). PMID: 26240518

16. Cronin, C.J., Feng, Z., Schafer, W.R.: Automated Imaging of C. elegans Behavior, pp. 241–251. Humana Press, Totowa (2006)

17. Dankert, H., Wang, L., Hoopfer, E.D., Anderson, D.J., Perona, P.: Automated monitoring and analysis of social behavior in drosophila. Nat. Methods **6**, 297 (2009)

18. Dell, A.I., et al.: Automated image-based tracking and its application in ecology. Trends Ecol. Evol. **29**(7), 417–428 (2014)

19. Desland, F.A., Afzal, A., Warraich, Z., Mocco, J.: Manual versus automated rodent behavioral assessment: comparing efficacy and ease of Bederson and Garcia neurological deficit scores to an open field video-tracking system. J. Cent. Nerv. Syst. Dis. **6**, 7–14 (2014). PMID: 24526841

20. Eyjolfsdottir, Eyrun, et al.: Detecting social actions of fruit flies. In: Fleet, D., Pajdla, T., Schiele, B., Tuytelaars, T. (eds.) ECCV 2014. LNCS, vol. 8690, pp. 772–787. Springer, Cham (2014). https://doi.org/10.1007/978-3-319-10605-2_50

21. Fanselow, M.S., Lester, L.S.: A functional behavioristic approach to aversively motivated behavior: predatory imminence as a determinant of the topography of defensive behavior. In: Bolles, R.C., Beecher, M.D. (eds.) Evol. Learn., pp. 185–212. Lawrence Erlbaum Associates Inc., Hillsdale (1988)

22. Fontaine, E., et al.: Automated visual tracking for studying the ontogeny of zebrafish swimming. J. Exp. Biol. **211**(8), 1305–1316 (2008)

23. Manuel Graña for CybSPEED: On The Proposed Cybspeed Project Experimental Research Protocols. Zenodo (2018). https://doi.org/10.5281/zenodo.1405505. Accessed Aug 2018

24. Fournely, M., Petit, Y., Wagnac, É., Laurin, J., Callot, V., Arnoux, P.-J.: High-speed video analysis improves the accuracy of spinal cord compression measurement in a mouse contusion model. J. Neurosci. Methods **293**, 1–5 (2018)

25. Fröhlich, H., Claes, K., De Wolf, C., Van Damme, X., Michel, A.: A machine learning approach to automated gait analysis for the Noldus catwalk system. IEEE Trans. Biomed. Eng. **65**(5), 1133–1139 (2018)
26. Hong, W., Kim, D.-W., Anderson, D.J.: Antagonistic control of social versus repetitive self-grooming behaviors by separable amygdala neuronal subsets. Cell **158**(6), 1348–1361 (2014)
27. Idei, H., Murata, S., Chen, Y., Yamashita, Y., Tani, J., Ogata, T.: Reduced behavioral flexibility by aberrant sensory precision in autism spectrum disorder: a neurorobotics experiment. In: 2017 Joint IEEE International Conference on Development and Learning and Epigenetic Robotics (ICDL-EpiRob), pp. 271–276, September 2017
28. Jhuang, H., et al.: Automated home-cage behavioural phenotyping of mice. Nat. Commun. **1**, 68 (2010)
29. Kabra, M., Robie, A.A., Rivera-Alba, M., Branson, S., Branson, K.: JAABA: interactive machine learning for automatic annotation of animal behavior. Nat. Methods **10**, 64 (2012)
30. Kearns, W.D., Fozard, J.L., Nams, V.O.: Movement path tortuosity in free ambulation: relationships to age and brain disease. IEEE J. Biomed. Health Inform. **21**(2), 539–548 (2017)
31. Kelso, J.A.S., Dumas, G., Tognoli, E.: Outline of a general theory of behavior and brain coordination. Neural Netw. **37**, 120–131 (2013). Twenty-fifth Anniversay Commemorative Issue
32. Cario, C.L., Farrell, T.C., Milanese, C., Burton, E.A.: Automated measurement of zebrash larval movement. J. Physiol. **589**(15), 3703–3708 (2011)
33. (Sam) Ma, Z.: Towards computational models of animal cognition, an introduction for computer scientists. Cognit. Syst. Res. **33**, 42–69 (2015)
34. Menzel, R., Greggers, U.: The memory structure of navigation in honeybees. J. Comp. Physiol. A **201**(6), 547–561 (2015)
35. Mobbs, D.: Foraging under competition: the neural basis of input-matching in humans. J. Neurosci. **33**(23), 9866–9872 (2013)
36. Mobbs, D., Kim, J.J.: Neuroethological studies of fear, anxiety, and risky decision-making in rodents and humans. Curr. Opin. Behav. Sci. **5**, 8–15 (2015). Neuroeconomics
37. Morrow-Tesch, J., Dailey, J.W., Jiang, H.: A video data base system for studying animal behavior. J. Anim. Sci. **76**(10), 2605–2608 (1998)
38. Muto, A., Lal, P., Ailani, D., Abe, G., Itoh, M., Kawakami, K.: Activation of the hypothalamic feeding centre upon visual prey detection. Nat. Commun. **8**, 15029 (2017)
39. Obdržálek, S.: Accuracy and robustness of kinect pose estimation in the context of coaching of elderly population. In: Conference Proceedings: ... Annual International Conference of the IEEE Engineering in Medicine and Biology Society. IEEE Engineering in Medicine and Biology Society. Conference, pp. 1188–1193 (2012)
40. Ohayon, S., Avni, O., Taylor, A.L., Perona, P., Roian, S.E.: Automated multi-day tracking of marked mice for the analysis of social behaviour. J. Neurosci. Methods **219**(1), 10–19 (2013)
41. Papadakis, V.M., Papadakis, I.E., Lamprianidou, F., Glaropoulos, A., Kentouri, M.: A computer-vision system and methodology for the analysis of fish behavior. Aquac. Eng. **46**, 53–59 (2012)
42. Pérez-Escudero, A., Vicente-Page, J., Hinz, R.C., Arganda, S., de Polavieja, G.G.: idtracker: tracking individuals in a group by automatic identification of unmarked animals. Nat. Methods **11**, 743 (2014)

43. Pham, J., Cabrera, S.M., Sanchis-Segura, C., Wood, M.A.: Automated scoring of fear-related behavior using ethovision software. J. Neurosci. Methods **178**(2), 323–326 (2009)
44. Riley, J.R.: Tracking bees with harmonic radar. Nature **379**, 29 (1996)
45. Saberioon, M.M., Cisar, P.: Automated multiple fish tracking in three-dimension using a structured light sensor. Comput. Electron. Agric. **121**, 215–221 (2016)
46. Shotton, J., et al.: Real-time human pose recognition in parts from single depth images. In: Cipolla, R., Battiato, S., Farinella, G. (eds.) Machine Learning for Computer Vision. Studies in Computational Intelligence, vol. 411, pp. 119–135. Springer, Heidelberg (2013). https://doi.org/10.1007/978-3-642-28661-2_5
47. Sminchisescu, C., Kanaujia, A., Li, Z., Metaxas, D.: Conditional models for contextual human motion recognition. In: Tenth IEEE International Conference on Computer Vision (ICCV 2005), vol. 1, vol. 2, pp. 1808–1815, October 2005
48. Squire, L.R.: Encyclopedia of Neuroscience. In: Encyclopedia of Neuroscience, vol. 3. Elsevier/Academic Press (2009)
49. Stafstrom, J.A., Michalik, P., Hebets, E.A.: Sensory system plasticity in a visually specialized, nocturnal spider. Sci. Rep. **7**, 46627 (2017)
50. Stewart, A.M.: A novel 3D method of locomotor analysis in adult zebrafish. J. Neurosci. Methods **255**, 66–74 (2015)
51. Stone, E.E., Skubic, M.: Unobtrusive, continuous, in-home gait measurement using the microsoft kinect. IEEE Trans. Biomed. Eng. **60**(10), 2925–2932 (2013)
52. Tang, B.: An in vivo study of hypoxia-inducible factor-1α signaling in ginsenoside Rg1-mediated brain repair after hypoxia/ischemia brain injury. Pediatr. Res. **81**, 120 (2016)
53. Todd, P.A.C., McCue, H.V., Haynes, L.P., Barclay, J.W., Burgoyne, R.D.: Interaction of ARF-1.1 and neuronal calcium sensor-1 in the control of the temperature-dependency of locomotion in caenorhabditis elegans. Sci. Rep. **6**, 30023 (2016)
54. Tsai, H.-Y., Huang, Y.-W.: Image tracking study on courtship behavior of drosophila. PLoS One **7**(4), 1–8 (2012)
55. Urgen, B., Plank, M., Ishiguro, H., Poizner, H., Saygin, A.: EEG theta and Mu oscillations during perception of human and robot actions. Front. Neurorobotics **7**, 19 (2013)
56. Wang, Y.-N.: Behavioural screening of zebrafish using neuroactive traditional Chinese medicine prescriptions and biological targets. Sci. Rep. **4**, 5311 (2014)
57. Wario, F., Wild, B., Couvillon, M., Rojas, R., Landgraf, T.: Automatic methods for long-term tracking and the detection and decoding of communication dances in honeybees. Front. Ecol. Evol. **3**, 103 (2015)
58. Zhao, J., et al.: Modified motion influence map and recurrent neural network-based monitoring of the local unusual behaviors for fish school in intensive aquaculture. Aquaculture **493**, 165–175 (2018)
59. Zhu, L., Weng, W.: Catadioptric stereo-vision system for the real-time monitoring of 3D behavior in aquatic animals. Physiol. Behav. **91**(1), 106–119 (2007)

Deep Learning Prediction of Gait Based on Inertial Measurements

Pedro Romero-Hernandez[1], Javier de Lope Asiain[1], and Manuel Graña[2]([⊠])

[1] Artificial Intelligence Department, Madrid Polytechnic University, Madrid, Spain
[2] Computer Science Department, University of the Basque Country,
San Sebastian, Spain
manuel.grana@ehu.es

Abstract. We report the application of recurrent deep learning networks, namely long term short memories (LSTM) for the modeling of gait synchronization of legs using a basic configuration of off-the-shelf inertial measurement units (IMU) providing six acceleration and rotation parameters. The proposed system copes with noisy and missing data due to high sampling rate, before applying the training of LSTM. We report accurate testing results on one experimental subject. This model can be transferred to robotised prostheses and assistive robotics devices in order to achieve quick stabilization and robust transfer of control algorithms to new users.

1 Introduction

Aging population is pushing research towards improving quality of life of dependent and fragile people, such as the elderly. One such research avenues is assistive robotics, where the aim is to develop autonomous or semi-autonomous devices that may help the patients or users to achive normal activity performance. For instance, walking may be assisted by exoeskeletons in persons suffering of reduced mobility of the legs [8]. Fine tuning of the control of such devices may be guided by the actual measurements from healthy persons. The approach taken in this paper is to produce a generative model of walking patterns that may be used for the fine control of the assistive devices. This generative model takes the form of a predictive non-linear model implemented as a deep neural network and trained from the actual walking gait measurements of a healthy person. It has been shown that inertial measurement units (IMUs) allow to characterize human motion fort activity recognition [7]. In this paper we propose a minimal configuration of IMUs that allow the characterization of gait and the construction of the predictive model.

2 Gait Characterization

Gait is a complex activity involving several parts of the body, including upper and lower limbs. Upper limps have an effect on the body dynamics during the

© Springer Nature Switzerland AG 2019
J. M. Ferrández Vicente et al. (Eds.): IWINAC 2019, LNCS 11486, pp. 284–290, 2019.
https://doi.org/10.1007/978-3-030-19591-5_29

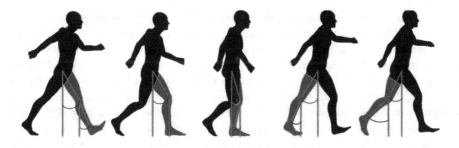

Fig. 1. Gait parametrization

displacement, helping to maintain the equilibrium in some of the critical positions or to give additional impulse. However, they are usually not considered in the characterization of gait, which often refers to the lower limbs dynamics. Figure 1 illustrates the typical states of the lower limbs at some of the critical instants of gait steps, i.e. when there is a change in the limb's parts relative motion and the articulation angle variation. We have chosen to parameterize the gait motion instantaneous state by the angles of the knee and ankle joints relative to the hips. These angles provide enough information to induce the remaining leg component positions and dynamics. Our goal is to estimate the correlation of the dynamics of both legs in a balanced gait, so that we can predict the desired position of one leg knowing the position of the other. This prediction will provide us with the desired control commands for an exoskeleton to produce a balanced gait motion. Measurement of the gait parameters is carried out by a minimal set of IMUs placed in specific positions of the leg.

3   Human Activity Recognition Using IMUs

Inertial sensors (i.e. accelerometers and gyroscopes) provide acceleration and oritetation of the motion. This information has been used by researcher for the recognition of specific human activities. Up to now, Markovian modeling tools have been the most used, but next generation approaches, based on deep learning architectures are under extensive testing. Some authors [7] use fuzzy logic classifiers to recognize daily human activities from using instantaneous information of the IMU sensors constellation. Other authors have used artificial neural networks [9] achieving discrimination between dynamic and static activities with an specific feature selection process, while other use classical decision trees [10] for instantaneous activity modeling. Comparative evaluation of static classifiers is provided in [13], including support vector machines (SVM), k Nearest neighbors (KNN), and random forests, which are found best performing. However, dynamic activity modelling is better achieved with Hidden Markov Models [11,12]. On the other hand, histogram modeling and classification using kNN [14,15] allows for long term activity modeling using inertial sensors. Smartphone emergence in our daily life has also been profitted by some researchers in order to obtain motion information without requiring the need to put the sensors on the subject body. Careful noise filtering and the use of an heterogeneous ensemble of classifiers allows great precision in human activity recognition [16]. Additionally, combining with GPS information improves recognition (using Random Forest) of outdoor activities [17]. A critical issue is the online adaptation to drifts in behavior, in other words to non stationary feature distribution. It has been shown that Adaboost can cope with this time changes successfully [18] using up to 300 weak classifiers. More recent trends apply deep learning approaches, specifically convolutional neural networks [4]. In this paper we are not strictly concerned with activity classification, but with modeling gait dynamics in order to use this model for the steering of the exoskeletons.

4   System Description

The system hardware is composed of four IMUs connected to a multiplexor for simulating parallel inputs to an Arduino board. The computations have carried out in an Intel Core i5-3330 with a GTX750i graphics board. The software platform for deep neural network training is Keras. Figure 2 shows the position of the IMUs and their connectivity. Firstly, we apply.

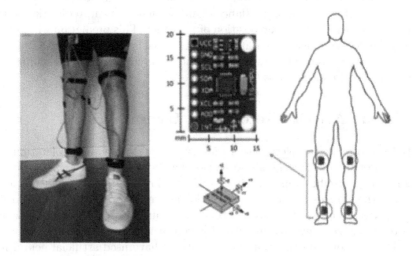

Fig. 2. Positioning of the inertial units

Figure 3 shows the overall process of training and validation pipeline. Data capture has been done at the maximum allowable velocity of the IMU sensors, resulting in some instances of missing data. When there is some IMU sensor data missing in a time instant, the entire reading for the four IMUs is dropped,

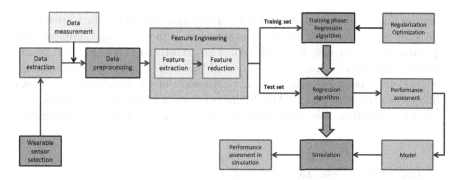

Fig. 3. Pipeline of the system training and validation

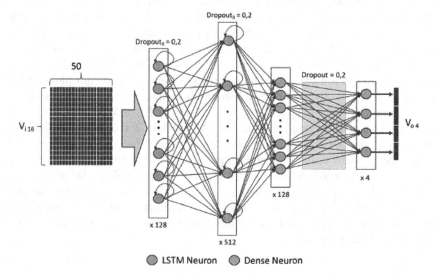

Fig. 4. Architecture of the deep neural network trained and tested in the experiments.

ensuring complete data stream. The next step, is noise removal from the data. We use a combination of low pass and high pass filtering of the accelerometer and gyroscopes in order to remove noise and drift of the data. Moreover, for the preprocessing of the data, in order to reduce measurement error, we use the complementary filter [5].

The recurrent neural network that we use is the long term short memories (LSTM) [1] which has been widely used in time series analysis as well as in natural language processing. Recent works have reported also the use of convolutional neural networks to human activity recognition [4]. However, the cyclic nature of gait lends itself to the modeling by a recurrent neural network.

Figure 4 presents the actual architecture of the deep neural network. Input is a given by a sliding window of size 50, for each time instant the feature vectors are the acceleration and orientation of the left leg IMUs. The output are the inclination angles (saggittal and coronal) of the right leg. These data are enough to check for the correct coordination between legs while walking. Complete right leg parameters could also be predicted. The architecture is composed of two hidden layers of LSTM units fully connected that inject to a non-recurrent fully connected outer layer carrying the final regression of the right leg parameters. Training was carried out using ADAM optimization and we used a validation set to test for overfitting. We have used dropout as the regularization mechanism [2,3].

5   Empirical Results

The data for training and testing corresponds to several walking gaits performed by the same subject. The training uses a validation dataset to stop the training before overfitting effects occcur. Besides the root mean square error (RMSE) whose evolution is shown in Fig. 5, we also computed the coefficient of determination of the output to ensure significant convergence of the training process. Figure 6 shows the prediction of the right leg parameters (bottom plot) and the original data of left and right leg during a short interval of the test (unknown gait). Therefore it can be appreciated that the model is able to approximate the real gait parameters of one leg from the observation of the other leg for a gait that was not part of the training data. This means that the system would be able to adapt to new situations, and even new users. Predicting one leg motion is very useful for situations where one leg is being substituted by the robotic prosthesis. In this situation, the predicted motion parameters maybe used to guide the motion of the robotic prostheses to be in harmony with the biological one. This model may be retrained on the actual subject motions in order to obtain fine tuning of the predictions.

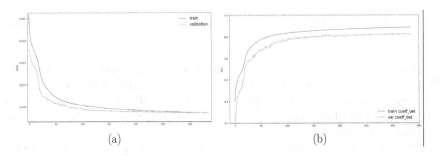

(a)   (b)

Fig. 5. Evolution of (a) training and validation error; (b) training and validation coefficient of determination.

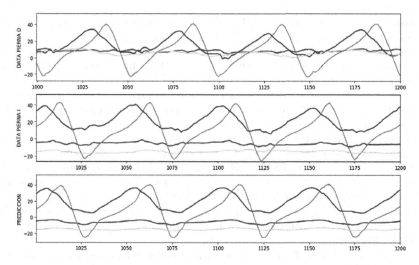

Fig. 6. Example prediction interval, from top to bottom, data from the first and second legs, and the predictions for the second leg. The curves are the angles in the saggital plane of knee (blue) and ankle (green) joints, and the angles in the coronal plane of the knee (cyan) and ankle (yellow) joints (Color figure online).

6   Conclusions

We show that it is possible to model accurately the time evolution of motion parameters of the legs, i.e. acceleration and angles of the knee and ankle joints, using off-the-shelf IMUs whose data is fed to a recurrent neural network architecture. Prediction appears to be very robust, achieving high accuracy in unseen gait movements. Further testing is necessary, adding general population recruited subjects. However, the approach may be useful to provide initial models for fine tuning of the prostheses control [6].

Acknowledgements. This work has been partially supported by FEDER funds through MINECO project TIN2017-85827-P.

References

1. Hochreiter, S., Schmidhuber, J.: Long short-term memory. Neural Comput. **9**(8), 1735–1780 (1997)
2. Cheng, G., Peddinti, V., Povey, D., Manohar, V., Khudanpur, S., Yan, Y.: An exploration of dropout with LSTMs. In: Proceedings of Interspeech 2017 (2017)
3. Gal, Y., Ghahramani, Z.: A theoretically grounded application of dropout in recurrent neural networks. In: Advances in Neural Information Processing Systems, pp. 1019–1027 (2016)
4. Ignatov, A.: Real-time human activity recognition from accelerometer data using convolutional neural networks. Appl. Soft Comput. **62**, 915–922 (2018)

5. Kok, M., Hol, J. D., Sch öon, T.B.: Using inertial sensors for position and orientation estimation. arXiv preprint arXiv:1704.06053 (2017)
6. Ikehara, T., et al.: Development of closed-fitting-type walking assistance device for legs and evaluation of muscle activity. In: 2011 IEEE International Conference on Rehabilitation Robotics (ICORR), pp. 1–7. IEEE, June 2011
7. Chen, Y.P., Yang, J.Y., Liou, S.N., Lee, G.Y., Wang, J.S.: Online classifier construction algorithm for human activity detection using a tri-axial accelerometer. Appl. Math. Comput. **205**(2), 849–860 (2008)
8. Dollar, A.M., Herr, H.: Lower extremity exoskeletons and active orthoses: challenges and state-of-the-art. IEEE Trans. Rob. **24**(1), 144–158 (2008)
9. Yang, J.Y., Wang, J.S., Chen, Y.P.: Using acceleration measurements for activity recognition: an effective learning algorithm for constructing neural classifiers. Pattern Recogn. Lett. **29**(16), 2213–2220 (2008)
10. Godfrey, A., Del Din, S., Barry, G., Mathers, J.C., Rochester, L.: Instrumenting gait with an accelerometer: a system and algorithm examination. Med. Eng. Phys. **37**(4), 400–407 (2015)
11. Mannini, A., Sabatini, A.M.: Machine learning methods for classifying human physical activity from on-body accelerometers. Sensors **10**(2), 1154–1175 (2010)
12. Wang, J., Chen, R., Sun, X., She, M.F., Wu, Y.: Recognizing human daily activities from accelerometer signal. Proc. Eng. **15**, 1780–1786 (2011)
13. Erdas, C.B., Atasoy, I., Acici, K., Ogul, H.: Integrating features for accelerometer-based activity recognition. Proc. Comput. Sci. **98**, 522–527 (2016)
14. Garcia-Ceja, E., Brena, R.: Long-term activity recognition from accelerometer data. Proc. Technol. **7**, 248–256 (2013)
15. Zhang, M., Sawchuk, A.A.: A feature selection-based framework for human activity recognition using wearable multimodal sensors. In: Proceedings of the 6th International Conference on Body Area Networks, pp. 92–98. ICST (Institute for Computer Sciences, Social-Informatics and Telecommunications Engineering) (2011)
16. Bayat, A., Pomplun, M., Tran, D.A.: A study on human activity recognition using accelerometer data from smartphones. Proc. Comput. Sci. **34**, 450–457 (2014)
17. Lee, K., Kwan, M.P.: Physical activity classification in free-living conditions using smartphone accelerometer data and exploration of predicted results. Comput. Environ. Urban Syst. **6**, 124–131 (2018)
18. Wen, J., Wang, Z.: Sensor-based adaptive activity recognition with dynamically available sensors. Neurocomputing **218**, 307–317 (2016)

Recognizing Cognitive Activities Through Eye Tracking

Sara Moraleda[1], Javier de Lope Asiain[1(✉)], and Manuel Graña[2]

[1] Computational Cognitive Robotics Group, Department of Artificial Intelligence,
Universidad Politécnica de Madrid (UPM), Madrid, Spain
`javier.delope@upm.es`
[2] Computational Intelligence Group, University of the Basque Country (UPV/EHU),
San Sebastián, Spain

Abstract. Eye detection and tracking is usually performed by using specific devices that allow to determine the pupil position in many different situations. We propose to use these techniques for recognizing cognitive activities that a potential user is carrying out in front of a computer. We use the images captured by a conventional web camera located over the computer display. Those image are processed and, after the face and facial landmarks are found, the user gaze is analyzed and the ethogram and several statistics associated to the eyes and gaze destination are computed. They are used for determining what is doing the user from a set of predefined activities.

Keywords: Neuroethology · Activities recognition · Eye tracking · Screen-based eye tracker · Non-invasive techniques

1 Introduction

Nowadays faces and facial landmarks detection is becoming a usual task. It is performed by most of smartphones and handheld cameras. Once the facial landmarks are localized, it is possible to analyze if the subject is smiling or where he or she is looking at. Thus, we can determine what kind of behaviors and activities are been carried out. For instance, it is common to analyze the visual behavior of users while visiting a web page, i.e. where they are looking at and which areas are demanding his or her attention. We may get data on what is looking at the visitor, what was previously demanding his or her interest, which are his or her real motivations, or even where must be located the most valuable content, surely the advertising. Also it can be used to know if the visual contents in the web page drive efficiently in the visit or if the visitor is able to localize the data that he or she is looking for.

Real world examples of these analyzers are applied to different areas, for example, to find where the people's visual attention in web search results is focused to be applied to digital neuromarketing [1], to determine students' visual attention and how it may influence the school failure [2], to evaluate the decision

© Springer Nature Switzerland AG 2019
J. M. Ferrández Vicente et al. (Eds.): IWINAC 2019, LNCS 11486, pp. 291–300, 2019.
https://doi.org/10.1007/978-3-030-19591-5_30

making process during sports playing [3], or to contribute to the analysis of general cognitive processes [4]. The latter is probably the area that receives a greater number of applications, which are focused on the discovering mechanisms in which visual memory, visual attention and learning are based on.

Eye tracking defines the changes in the gaze direction, i.e., it does not determine the exact gaze direction. Both conventional techniques [5–8] and artificial neural networks [9–12] have been used to develop systems for eye tracking.

The most used techniques for finding the iris are generally based on electro-oculography (EOG) and video-oculography (VOG) [13]. EOG uses a series of electrodes situated in the user's face to measure the eye movement. Usually pairs of electrodes are placed either to the left and right of eye or above and below the eye. It is considered as an invasive method. On the other hand VOG employs a head-mounted mask that is equipped with small cameras. Although it is considered as a non-invasive method for medical purposes, it is not directly applicable for everyday use.

Generally, an initial calibration process is required in order to record the approximate destination point associated to the gaze position. This calibration process could be challenging.

Commercial eye trackers for research are also available. They use special near-infrared lighting and additional hardware for detecting the iris. The light is directed towards the pupil, infrared cameras are used to track the reflections produced in the cornea and estimate the gaze direction. There exist screen-based eye trackers (also called *desktop* or *stationary eye trackers*) that are used when the user interacts with a screen-based content, and eye tracking glasses (generally known as *head-mounted eye trackers*) that are mobile devices usually mounted onto eyeglass frames that are fitted near the user eyes.

We propose an adaptation of conventional screen-based or desktop eye trackers that uses conventional cameras. Thus, the infrared lighting is not longer needed and the users annoyance generated by this special lighting or the use of head-mounted trackers is eliminated. The results may be quite comparable depending on the camera resolution and processing used.

The rest of the paper is organized as follows. Firstly, we define some concepts concerning eye movements and gaze analysis. Then, we determine the methods for finding faces and facial landmarks in images. The method for defining and recognizing cognitive activities in front of a computer is described in the next sections. Finally, we summarize the experiments carried out for validating the proposal and discuss the experimental results and conclusions.

2 Identifying Eye Movements

In order to analyze the eye movements and recognize the activity that is been carried out, it is important to identify the different types of eye movements. There exist three basic types of eye movements that can be easily detected: saccadic eye movements, fixations and blinking.

Saccades are quick, simultaneous movement of both eyes between two or more phases of fixation in the same direction [14]. When someone is reading a book or watching a movie, the eyes perform several saccades per second for inspecting the paper or the screen. The duration of each saccade is about 10–100 ms and the peak angular speed of the eye reaches up 900 °/s. It is not retrieved information from the stimulus with these movements.

After a saccade, a fixation occurs. A *visual fixation* is the maintaining of the gaze on a single location and it is when the information retrieval is carried out. The averaged duration of fixations is about 200 ms.

The third eye movement considered is the blinking. *Blinking* is a semi-autonomic rapid closing of the eyelid. Its function helps spread tears across and remove irritants from the surface of the cornea and conjunctiva. It basically keeps the eye lubricated and avoids that the eyes became irritated and tired, which may produce a loss of sharpness of eyesight and blurred vision. Blinking depends on environmental factors such as the relative humidity, the temperature or the bright but also the physical activity, the fatigue or the intensity of cognitive work. Generally the rate of blinking is about 12–18 blinks per minute, although it may decrease to about 3–4 times per minute when the eyes are focused on an object for an extended period of time, such as when reading, this is the major reason that eyes dry out and become fatigued. The averaged duration of blinking is about 200–300 ms.

3 Getting Features from Images

In order to detect the eyes in an image, the first step is to localize the face. It can be achieved in a number of ways. We use a pre-trained detector based on histograms of oriented gradients and linear support vector machines [15].

Once the face is localized in the image, the next step deals with the problem of face alignment for images. Here, we use the method proposed by Kazemi and Sullivan [16], which uses an ensemble of regression trees to estimate the face's landmarks positions directly from a sparse subset of pixels intensities. The method has been deeply tested and it is well-known by it performance and high quality predictions. The method returns 68 pairs of coordinates referred to the image that describe the facial landmarks. These coordinates can be used to localize the eyes, eyebrows, nose, mouth and jawline. For the purpose of the current work we only employ the pairs corresponding to the eyes.

Then, the eye aspect ratio (EAR) is computed [17]. This ratio between height and width of the eye is used to determine if it is open (the value is mostly constant) or it is closing (the value will be getting close to zero). The ratio is computed as shown in (1).

$$\mathrm{EAR} = \frac{\|p_2 - p_6\| + \|p_3 - p_5\|}{2 \, \|p_1 - p_4\|} \tag{1}$$

where $p_1, \ldots, p_6$ are the points that describe the eye position that have been detected in the previous step. p_1 and p_4 correspond to the left and right edges of the eye, p_2 and p_3 are two points above the eye about the intersection between the eyelid and the pupil, and p_6 and p_5 are the points below the eye relative to the two previous ones. The points are numbered clockwise starting from the leftmost one as shown in Fig. 1.

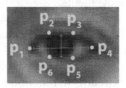

Fig. 1. Points used to compute the eye aspect ratio (EAR) as proposed in [17].

The EAR will be used as one of the descriptors due to it is very helpful in order to determine if the gaze destination is the top or the bottom of the display. The greater EAR, the higher the gaze destination (the EAR is zero when the eye is closed).

We continuously check the EAR values of both eye. When they go to about zero, it can be considered that a blinking movement has been performed. As we stated above the duration of blinking is about 200–300 ms. Thus, we use this estimation to determine if the user is just blinking or if he or she almost closed the eyes. We count the blinking during the experiment when appropriate.

The next step is to localize the center of each pupil in the image. It is performed by applying basic image processing techniques in the area surrounding the eyes. The final result of this process is shown in Fig. 2.

Fig. 2. The coordinates in the image of the center of the pupil are computed after applying basic image processing techniques in the area around the eyes are detected.

Summarizing, firstly, we detect the face and its facial landmarks in the image. Then, we compute the EAR of both eyes and the center of the pupil coordinates in the image. The EAR and the center of the pupil will be used as some of the features to classify the gaze. Also, we compute the times that the user blinks although this value is not currently used for the gaze classification, just as an index of the user fatigue.

4 Defining Activities

The final purpose of our system is to define what activities is carrying out the user in front of the computer. We have empirically determined that it is not needed to get the exact gaze destination as for example if it would used in a HCI context where it could be used to choose an option or to gain access to a specific feature. Thus, we have defined a set of targets to which the gaze is associated. These targets are shown in Fig. 3. The target will be also a feature that will be used for the classifier in order to identify the gaze destination.

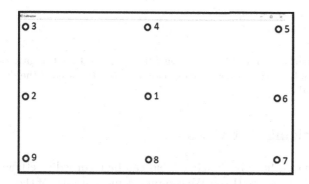

Fig. 3. Template with the targets to identify the gaze destination. Note that the target number has been arbitrarily assigned to each target to reduce the user fatigue during the calibration stage.

A calibration or training stage is needed for getting samples to train the classifier. This procedure is performed as follows. Each target is displayed for about 3 s. The system takes 60 samples for each target. We have considered interesting that the user follows the order shown in Fig. 3 for the fixations to minimize the fatigue and to reduce the length of eye movements between targets.

For each sample the center of the pupil coordinates and the EAR are computed. Note that blinking is also estimated. These values are used as features to determine the target destination of the gaze. We use a k-NN classifier. We have compared the classifier performance with values from $k = 1$ to $k = 5$ and leave-one-out as cross-validation and we get the best results for $k = 1$.

Once that we can determine the approximate display area that the user is looking at, the next step is to try to define which activity is carrying out. To do that we introduce the concept of ethogram. An *ethogram* is a representation of the different actions that occur during an activity or activities, which indicates the frequency or probability with which each action is followed by other action (either the same or a different one) [18]. In our case the actions are determined by the target that is associated to the current gaze destination of the user during an experiment, and the activity is what the user is doing in that experiment. Figure 4 depicts an ethogram that has been recorded while the user is reading a text, which is the activity. The destination target (from 1 to 9) is the action and is shown on the vertical axis, the horizontal one shows the time when the samples are taken.

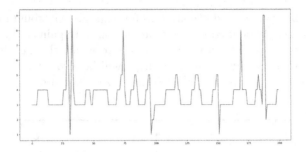

Fig. 4. Ethogram associated to a reading activity. Note that the gaze destination of this user is mainly in the targets corresponding to the top area if the display, namely targets 3, 4, and 5.

5   Recognizing Activities

Once the activities have been defined and can be recorded as ethograms we can focus on how to compare them. We compute some statistics of the data gathered while generating the ethogram: the pupil coordinates and the EAR as well as the targets. Those statistics are used to compose a feature vector, which is used to determine the activity. Again, we use a k-NN classifier.

We define three kind of activities to be performed in front of a computer display: reading a text, watching a movie and typing a text. All of them are very common activities in a office-like environment. Figure 5 show the ethograms recorded during an experiment in which the experimental subject is reading a text. Figures 6 and 7 are the ethograms for the movie watching and text typing activities, respectively.

The experiments are carried out in an office during the workday with conventional light and temperature conditions. The experimental subjects are seated in front of a conventional computer with a 15.6 in. display. They are to a distance between 40–60 cm of the display. The camera is situated to a height equivalent determined for each subject, thus the eye aspect ratio and position can be computed more efficiently. The head movements are restricted during the experiments in order to improve the sensibility of the whole system.

After a calibrating or training procedure defined above, the experimental subject is recorded for about 2 min for each activity. The recording is repeated several times. Then, as the ethograms as the feature vector are computed for creating the dataset for the classifier.

As can be observed these activities generate very different ethograms. While reading a text (Fig. 5) the experimental subjects tend to visit more frequently the target 4. Probably it is due to the fact that the text starts in the top of the display and the subject was scrolling the text.

During the video watching activity (Fig. 6) the experimental subjects tend to visit more frequently the targets 1 and 8. Moreover, there are many gaze changes between both targets. Target 1 corresponds to the center of the display,

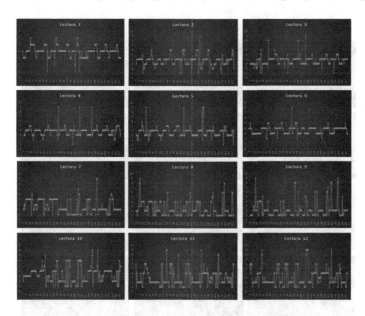

Fig. 5. Ethograms associated to reading activity.

so it is an expectable output. It is where the visual field is wider and higher in comparison to the other targets and where can gather much more information.

The ethograms relative to the typing activity (Fig. 7) show that the user tend to focus to targets 7, 8 and 9. These targets are in the bottom of the display. Probably the output is also expectable. Once the area in which the text must be typed has been filled, we use the bottom most line in the document. Moreover, it is usual that some users also watch to the keyboard while typing. On the other hand, this set of experiments has a number of blinking movements much lower than the experiments concerning reading and movie watching, probably because the gaze destination was in the bottom of the display.

All the above mentioned experiments have been repeated also for a duration about 7 min. No fundamental difference has been found between both sets of ethograms and statistics.

Table 1 shows some examples of featured vectors computed from the data gathered in the experiments with a duration of 2 min. The averaged EAR is practically the same for each type of activity. As the averaged pupil coordinates as the targets are also quite similar for the same activities.

The best classification results with the k-NN classifier are again with $k = 1$ (from $k = 1$ to $k = 5$). We get an averaged performance of 94.526 and a standard deviation equals to 6.594. We get a pretty good performance in many situation, very near to 100%, but several experiments give certainly bad performance. After analyzing those situations it seems it could be related to the image processing step and the eye color of the experimental subjects. The median performance with $k = 1$ is 97.220.

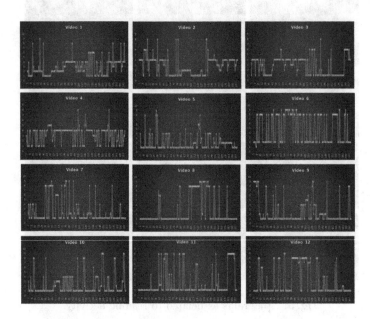

Fig. 6. Ethograms associated to video watching activity.

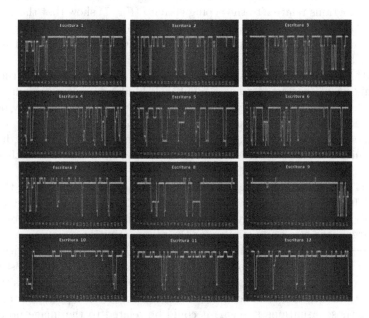

Fig. 7. Ethograms associated to the typing activity.

Table 1. Some examples of feature vectors computed from three experiments of the analyzed activities (averaged values).

Activity	X	Y	Ear	Target
Reading	23	11	32	2
Reading	25	14	32	3
Reading	23	11	32	2
Video watching	22	11	37	2
Video watching	24	11	31	1
Video watching	21	10	27	1
Typing	27	8	21	9
Typing	25	10	24.5	8
Typing	27	6	14	8

6   Conclusions and Further Work

A system for recognizing cognitive activities in front of a computer by means of eye tracking has been presented. The system uses images captured by a conventional web camera. Once a face is detected in the image, several facial landmarks are localized. Then, the gaze is analyzed in order to create an ethogram and several statistics associated to the eyes and gaze destination. The data is used for classifying the activity that a potential user in front of the computer is carrying out.

Based on the experimental results it is concluded that the system is able to classify a reduced number of activities in normal office-like conditions and several experimental subjects with different physical characteristics as color of the skin and eyes, form of the face, and so on.

Future work is planned towards improving the image processing techniques that are used in order to detect the face and facial landmarks in the image. Currently the head movements are restricted in order to improve the results. If the user turns the head several degrees, the face is not detected and no data is gathered. It can be easily accomplished by updating the dataset with more samples. Now it only includes samples with frontal face images.

Also, we are currently working with other templates that with more targets and different target structure. We have to trade off the low resolution of the employed equipment and the detection of gaze destination. We are also considering to use directly an estimation of the display area of the gaze destination and to overcome the use of landmarks.

Finally we want to increase the number and diversity of activities. Although the selected ones for this work are quite representatives, they are just some activities that an user performs in front of a computer.

Acknowledgments. This work has been partially supported by FEDER funds through MINECO project TIN2017-85827-P.

References

1. Hof, R.: How do you Google? New eye tracking study reveals huge changes. https://www.forbes.com/sites/roberthof/2015/03/03/how-do-you-google-new-eye-tracking-study-reveals-huge-changes/. Accessed 11 Feb 2019
2. Tsai, M.-J., Hou, H.-T., Lai, M.-L., Liu, W.-Y., Yang, F.-Y.: Visual attention for solving multiple-choice science problem: an eye-tracking analysis. Comput. Educ. **58**, 375–385 (2012)
3. Weigel, P., Raab, M., Wollny, R.: Tactical decision making in team sports: a model of cognitive processes. Int. J. Sports Sci. **5**(49), 128–138 (2015)
4. Gidlöf, K., Wallin, A., Dewhurst, R., Holmqvist, K.: Using eye tracking to trace a cognitive process: Gaze behaviour during decision making in a natural environment. J. Eye Mov. Res. **6**(1), 1–14 (2013)
5. Al-Rahayfeh, A., Faezipour, M.: Eye tracking and head movement detection: a state-of-art survey. IEEE J. Transl. Eng. Health Med. **1**, 1–12 (2013)
6. Krafka, K., et al.: Eye tracking for everyone. In: IEEE Conference on Computer Vision and Pattern Recognition (CVPR), pp. 2176–2184 (2016)
7. Ferhat, O., Vilariño, F.: Low cost eye tracking: the current panorama. Comput. Intell. Neurosci. **2016**, 1–14 (2016)
8. Obaidellah, U., Al Haek, M., Cheng, P.C.-H.: A survey on the usage of eye-tracking in computer programming. ACM Comput. Surv. **51**(1), 1–58 (2018)
9. Baluja, S., Pomerleau, D.: Non-intrusive gaze tracking using artificial neural networks. Technical report CMU-CS-94-102. Carnegie Mellon University. Pittsburgh, Pennsylvania (1994)
10. Sewell, W., Komogortsev, O.: Real-time eye gaze tracking with anunmodified commodity webcam employing a neural network. In: ACM CHI Conference Human Factors in Computing Systems, pp. 3739–3744. Atlanta, Georgia (2010)
11. Vora, S., Rangesh, A., Trivedi, M.M.: On generalizing driver gaze zone estimation using convolutional neural networks. In: IEEE Intelligent Vehicles Symposium, pp. 849–854. Redondo Beach, California (2017)
12. Naqvi, R.A., Arsalan, M., Batchuluun, G., Yoon, H.S., Park, K.R.: Deep learning-based gaze detection systems for automobile drivers using a NIR camera sensor. Sensors **18**, 1–34 (2018)
13. Blakley, B.W., Chan, L.: Methods considerations for nystagmography. J. Otolaryngol. Head Neck Surg. **44**, 25 (2015)
14. Cassin, B., Solomon, S.: Dictionary of Eye Terminology. Triad Publishing Company, Gainesville (1990)
15. Dalal, N., Triggs, B.: Histogram of Oriented Gradients for Human Detection. In: IEEE Conference on Computer Vision and Pattern Recognition (CVPR), pp. 886–893 (2005)
16. Kazemi, V., Sullivan, J.: One millisecond face alignment with anensemble of regression trees. In: IEEE Conference on Computer Vision and Pattern Recognition (CVPR), pp. 1867–1874. Ohio, USA (2014)
17. Soukupová, T., Čech, J.: Real-time eye blink detection using facial landmarks. In: 21st Computer Vision Winter Workshop (2016)
18. Anderson, D.J., Perona, P.: Toward a science of computational ethology. Neuron **84**, 18–31 (2014)

An Approach to Teach Nao Dialogue Skills

Manuel Graña[✉] and Alexander Triguero

Computational Intelligence Group, Department of CCIA,
University of the Basque Country, San Sebastián, Spain
manuel.grana@ehu.es

Abstract. Endowing social robots with natural interaction abilities, such as following a dialogue that gives the human user a sense of natural interaction, is a current interest in many areas. We are interested in developing the dialogue skills of the Nao robot for its potential use in treatment of children with special educational needs and elder people at risk of isolation. Corpora based dialog system development approaches are not adequate for personalization. In our approach we propose a teacher and introspection approach that may be able to produce highly personalized and entertaining dialog systems. The introspection module would run in the background using generative randomized systems creating new dialog pathways from the patterns learnt by direct teaching interaction.

1 Introduction

In order to set the stage for our work, we would like to remind the reader about the two basic categories of dialogue systems that appear in the literature [17]:

- Task oriented systems, where the conversation has some specific goal that has to be achieved through the dialogue interaction. Commercial assistant systems propsoed by companies such as Google, Apple or Amazon, are intended to help the user to search for specific information items or to patronize them in routine tasks, such as looking for the nearest restaurant, or to coordinate events, such as planning an appointment or a date [11]. Other examples of automated dialog services are technical support services, and goal-free systems, such as language learning tools or computer game characters [22]. The iteration always reaches a termination state when the user achieves its goals. The dialogue system is an interface to other digital services, such as entertainment, travel, and house maintenance. They are typically designed according to a structured ontology (or a database schema), which defines the domain that the system can talk about [25]. Getting the info is usually achieved using slot-filling, where a dialogue state is a set of slots to be filled during dialogue [3].
- Conversational systems, on the other hand, have no specific goal for the conversation. Hence, the user-machine iteration can evolve indefinitely, though it

© Springer Nature Switzerland AG 2019
J. M. Ferrández Vicente et al. (Eds.): IWINAC 2019, LNCS 11486, pp. 301–308, 2019.
https://doi.org/10.1007/978-3-030-19591-5_31

is expected that the iterations would produce some evolution of both the user and the automated agent internal states. For instance, if the dialog agent is used for some kind of therapeutic purpose, we expect that the user has some benefit from the dialog. As an example, consider the treatment of children with autism spectrum disorders (ASD) by interaction with anthropomorphic robots in order to achieve better social skills. After some interactions, we expect some permanent changes in the child social abilities. The main feature that we want from conversational systems is that they engage the user and are entertaining [27].

From the technological point of view, dialog systems have been boosted in performance and capabilities by the current explosion of data driven machine learning approaches, foremost the resurgence of deep learning [3] techniques, architectures, and tools for training and development following their success in natural language procesing, machine translation [8,20,22], language interpretation [18], and response generation [13,14,23]. Though there have been some attempts to use convolutional neural networks (CNN) [20], most successful applications are based on the well known long-short term memory recurrent neural networks (LSTM) [10]. LSTMs are well suited to learn sequential information and provide great flexibility. They have been used for humor prediction in dialogues [2], sentence embedding [18] The other computational advance has been deep reinforcement learning approaches [5,12,13], and the use of adversarial networks [14].

One of the keystones to build data driven systems is the availability of data for system training. Specifically, data repositories (corpora) for dialog systems are scarce [21] and they are often topic specific [15], hence training based on them are prone to introduce bias and artifacts in the dialog. For this reason we interested in approaches that build the systems from scratch personalizing it to the user as much as possible. Besides, dialog corpora in Spanish are non-existent.

Intended Contribution. The aim of the work in this article is to present our current work towards the implementation of an open dialog system in the Nao robot that will be tailored to the user from scratch. We are using of-the-shelf tools provided by the Nao development environment, as well as some widely used machine learning tools, such as the keras python package for deep learning, and tools for speech recognition and speech synthesis that are well integrated in the Nao development environment. The current language is Spanish, and the aim of the system is to assist in some experimental treatments of children with special educational needs or elder people at risk of isolation.

The contents of the paper are as follows: Sect. 2 discusses system architectures, and evaluation issues. Finally, Sect. 3 discusses some future challenges.

2   Architectures of Dialogue Systems

The traditional architecture for dialogue systems is composed of a series of modules, each with specific functionality:

- Speech Recognizer, in charge of providing the lexical units for the system extracting them from the voice signal,
- Language Interpreter, in charge of extracting meaning from the stream of lexical units by Natural Language Processing techniques,
- State Tracker, in charge of modelling the dialogue state and dynamics, it keeps track of the goal in task oriented systems and of the contextual information in task-free systems. It is the semantic backbone of the dialog system, setting the stage for understanding the messages [9].
- Response Generator, produces a semantically grounded response to a current input,
- Language Generator, formulates the response in correct language constructs by Natural Language Generation techniques, and
- Speech Synthesizer generates a recognizable voice signal for the communication with the human side.

We intend that our Nao based system has an interface as natural as possible, so Speech Recognizer and Speech Synthesizer modules are required in voice-based dialogue systems. Text based dialogue systems do not need them. Each of these modules can be tackled with as an independent problem, hence they have been approached using different techniques. Lately, the mainstream approach was statistical modeling of diverse flavors, until the eclosion of deep learning approaches.

One critical issue is that of the time and resources required for training the systems, and the need to overcome the inherent semantic limitations of given corpora. A bold approach is to tackle it in an incremental process [1], where the system is in a continuous learning process. If we recognize that dialog processes may change the actors, then the dialog is per se an open-end learning process, where actors (humans or automata) must be able to understand and answer new inputs, generating also innovative responses.

It seems that end-to-end architectures [3,7,22,24,29] provide the required flexibility due to its data driven approach. Drifting of the conversation patterns is possible by direct application of the same training process, and does not need additional engineering, such as identifying the new semantic domain. Such flexibility is a requirement for social robot dialog applications [4]. The greatest flexibility is achieved by end-to-end systems that decompose the response into utterances that are selected probilistically, i.e. by maximization of the posterior probability among all possible utterances. Most either rule-based or corpus-based chatbots tend to do very little modelling of the conversational context. Instead they tend to focus on generating a single response turn that is appropriate given the user's immediately previous utterance. For this reason they are often called response generation systems [11]. Given the lack of precise goals, the conversational systems can be formulated as sequence-to-sequence transductors (SEQ2SEQ). However the SEQ2SEQ models tend to generate generic responses, which closes the conversation, or become stuck in an infinite loop of repetitive responses [13].

Some approaches to dialog system evaluation use quality measures developed for machine translation systems, such as the bilingual evaluation understudy

(BLEU), assuming that the dialogue process is akin to a translation between the system generated responses and the natural ones from humans. Other use the word perplexity measure [22] from probabilistic word modelling. This approach requires big corpora often unavailable for conversational dialogue systems, and scarce for task oriented systems. Most of the corpora available for dialogue system training and tuning come from very specific domains (e.g chats about technical problems such as the Ubuntu IRC chats, or restaurant/movie picking) or were designed for other purposes such as automatic speech recognition system training [21].

Reinforcement Learning (RL) approaches [14,24,26] only require rewards at some point in time, such as the successful task achievement or some negative rewards when the task-free dialogue becomes senseless, and the estimation of the policy gradient, often done by a likelihood trick. RL allow to treat dialogue system training as an optimisation problem. Moreover, RL-based systems can improve their performance over time with experience [6] following a life-long learning approach. However, training dialogue policies in an efficient, scalable and effective way across domains remains an unsolved problem as often requires significant time to explore the state-action space, which is a critical issue when the system is trained on-line with real users where learning costs are expensive [26].

Reinforcement learning approaches need some mechanism to generate the reward function values. The natural approach is to use human operators that provide rewards according to some quality criteria (i.e. easy of answering, coherence, informativeness, keyword retrieval) but in general it is difficult to extend the approach to wide open dialogue systems. A way to automate the process is to apply adversarial approaches [11,14] mimicking the Turing test of indistinguishability of the machine responses from the human responses. For example in [14] the authors use a generator (a neural SEQ2SEQ model) that defines the probability of generating a dialogue sequence, and a discriminator analogous to the human evaluator in the Turing test that labels dialogues as human-generated or machine-generated. The generator is driven by the discriminator to generate utterances indistinguishable from human generated dialogues. In the end the human evaluation is the gold standard for all approaches, despite the high cost and inconvenience of having to deal with humans in the loop.

3   Social Robots and Children with ASD

Recent reviews [19] have found that there are positive effects of the interaction between social robots and children with ASD:

- they often performed better with a robot partner rather than a human partner;
- sometimes, they show toward robots, behaviors that TD patients had toward human caretakers;
- they had a lot of social behaviors toward robots;

- during robotic sessions, ASDs showed reduced repetitive and stereotyped behaviors and;
- interaction with social robots improved spontaneous language during therapy sessions.

Therefore, robots provide a way to connect with ASD subjects. But it seems that studies in this area are still insufficient. Besides small sample sizes [16], it is necessary to assess the influence of other covariants such as age, sex, and IQ. Also, it is required to assess if the outcome of the therapy are still observable outside the clinical/experimental context.

Moreover, robots were operated mostly in a wizard-of-Oz setting or in an open loop automata behavior, with no real autonomy or feedback interaction, so it is mostly the esthetic aspects that were evaluated. A long term interaction will become stuck if only a few robot behavior patterns are available. Next step for this kind of studies is the contact with a truly evolving and autonomously interacting robot. In this setting, we are working on endowing the Nao with an adaptive and evolving dialog interface whose elements will be described below.

4   On Going Development of Spoken Dialog Interface for the Nao

We are working on the Python interface to the Naoqui API for Nao and other Aldebaran social robotics products. Nao has been a highly exploited robot in experiments with ASD children. The company has marketed a product for dealing with experiments and treatment of ASD children. However, the review of

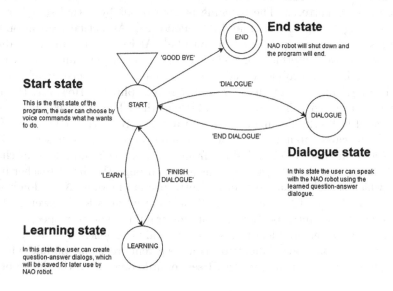

Fig. 1. Early Nao dialog structure

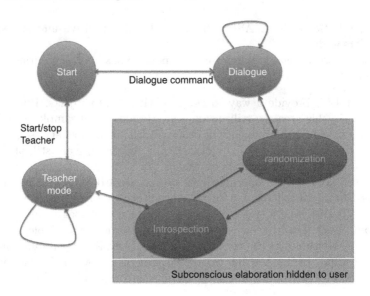

Fig. 2. Proposed architecture of the dialog system.

the literature shows that in fact the robot has been used in open loop behaviors, with no autonomy or little feedback of what is happening in the experimental room. In fact, it is little different from a nineteen century automaton regarding autonomous behavior. Figure 1 shows the actual structure of the dialog system, which consists in two separate modules that can be reached by voice commands. The LEARNING module asks for new pairs of phrases that are to be used as question-answer patterns. The teaching is carried out by actual speech recognition. Coding details can be found at zenodo [28]. An actual realization of a simple session has been published in youtube[1]. At its current state, the dialog system is a spoken interface for collection of input/output pairs, that can be make a little bit more robust by adding some sequence distance search to cope with errors in the recognition such as incomplete phrases. However, the next step that we are envisaging tries to go a little further. The proposed architecture is illustrated in Fig. 2. The main issue we want to solve is the generation of the system from scarce input information. The solution we seek to implement is an introspective module which is hidden from the user. This module is in charge of elaborating over the response pairs acquired through the direct teacher interaction, which sets the standards for the introspection module. A randomization module is in charge of the generation of randomized question/answer patterns that are fed to the introspection module for training. The introspection module will run an adversarial learning scheme to train the generative network [14]. The hidden subconscious elaboration is a deep reinforcement module which is running in between user interactions. User reward comes from the dialog or the

---

[1] https://www.youtube.com/watch?v=RbfM-9gaxzY.

teaching mode. Updates to the current system will be published in the same zenodo reference.

5 Conclusions

We are working towards the implementation of a dialog system that learns from scratch to carry out spoken dialogues. We have reviewed in this paper the current trends in dialogue system design. The deep reinforcement learning with adversarial learning is the approach that offers greater flexibility and potential for our purposes. The aim is the development of truly autonomous dialog systems embedded in the Nao robot for the treatment of children with special educational needs that may be benefitting from humanoid robot interaction. A target population are the children with ASD, whose positive reaction to social robot interaction has been noted by many researchers.

Acknowledgments. This work has been partially supported by the EC through project CybSPEED funded by the MSCA-RISE grant agreement No 777720.

References

1. Baumann, T., Kennington, C., Hough, J., Schlangen, D.: Recognising conversational speech: what an incremental ASR should do for a dialogue system and how to get there. In: Jokinen, K., Wilcock, G. (eds.) Dialogues with Social Robots. LNEE, vol. 999, pp. 421–432. Springer, Singapore (2017). https://doi.org/10.1007/978-981-10-2585-3_35
2. Bertero, D., Fung, P.: A long short-term memory framework for predicting humor in dialogues. In: Proceedings of the 2016 Conference of the North American Chapter of the Association for Computational Linguistics: Human Language Technologies, pp. 130–135 (2016)
3. Bordes, A., Boureau, Y.L., Weston, J.: Learning end-to-end goal-oriented dialog. arXiv preprint arXiv:1605.07683 (2016)
4. Bowden, K.K., Oraby, S., Misra, A., Wu, J., Lukin, S.: Data-driven dialogue systems for social agents. arXiv preprint arXiv:1709.03190 (2017)
5. Cuayáhuitl, H.: Deep reinforcement learning for conversational robots playing games. In: 2017 IEEE-RAS 17th International Conference on Humanoid Robotics (Humanoids), pp. 771–776, November 2017
6. Cuayáhuitl, H.: *SimpleDS*: a simple deep reinforcement learning dialogue system. In: Jokinen, K., Wilcock, G. (eds.) Dialogues with Social Robots. LNEE, vol. 999, pp. 109–118. Springer, Singapore (2017). https://doi.org/10.1007/978-981-10-2585-3_8
7. Dodge, J., et al. Evaluating prerequisite qualities for learning end-to-end dialog systems. arXiv preprint arXiv:1511.06931 (2015)
8. Graves, A., Mohamed, A.R., Hinton, G.: Speech recognition with deep recurrent neural networks. In: 2013 IEEE International Conference on Acoustics, speech and signal processing (ICASSP), pp. 6645–6649. IEEE (2013)
9. Henderson, M.: Machine learning for dialog state tracking: a review. In: Proceedings of The First International Workshop on Machine Learning in Spoken Language Processing (2015)

10. Hochreiter, S., Schmidhuber, J.: Long short-term memory. Neural Comput. **9**(8), 1735–1780 (1997)
11. Jurafsky, D., Martin, J.H.: Dialog systems and chatbots. In: Speech and Language Processing, vol. 3. Pearson, London (2014)
12. Khouzaimi, H., Laroche, R., Lefèvre, F.: A methodology for turn-taking capabilities enhancement in spoken dialogue systems using reinforcement learning. Comput. Speech Lang. **47**, 93–111 (2018)
13. Li, J., Monroe, W., Ritter, A., Galley, M., Gao, J., Jurafsky, D.: Deep reinforcement learning for dialogue generation. arXiv preprint arXiv:1606.01541 (2016)
14. Li, J., Monroe, W., Shi, T., Ritter, A.,Jurafsky, D.: Adversarial learning for neural dialogue generation. arXiv preprint arXiv:1701.06547 (2017)
15. Lowe, R., Pow, N., Serban, I., Pineau, J.: The Ubuntu dialogue corpus: a large dataset for research in unstructured multi-turn dialogue systems. arXiv preprint arXiv:1506.08909 (2015)
16. Cruz, A.M., Rincon, A.M.R., Duenas, W.R.R., Torres, D.A.Q., Bohorquez-Heredia, A.F.: What does the literature say about using robots on children with disabilities? Disabil. Rehabil. Assist. Technol. **12**(5), 429–440 (2017)
17. Ozaeta, L., Graña, M.: A view of the state of the art of dialogue systems. In: de Cos Juez, F.J., et al. (eds.) Hybrid Artificial Intelligent Systems, pp. 706–715. Springer, Cham (2018). https://doi.org/10.1007/978-3-319-92639-1_59
18. Palangi, H., et al.: Deep sentence embedding using long short-term memory networks: analysis and application to information retrieval. IEEE/ACM Transact. Audio Speech Lang. Process. (TASLP) **24**(4), 694–707 (2016)
19. Pennisi, P., et al.: Autism and social robotics: a systematic review. Autism Res. **9**(2), 165–183 (2016)
20. Sainath, T.N., Vinyals, O., Senior, A., Sak, H.: Convolutional, long short-term memory, fully connected deep neural networks. In: 2015 IEEE International Conference on Acoustics, Speech and Signal Processing (ICASSP), pp. 4580–4584. IEEE (2015)
21. Serban, I.V., Lowe, R., Henderson, P., Charlin, L., Pineau, J.: A survey of available corpora for building data-driven dialogue systems. arXiv preprint arXiv:1512.05742 (2015)
22. Serban, I.V., Sordoni, A., Bengio, Y., Courville, A.C., Pineau, J.: Building end-to-end dialogue systems using generative hierarchical neural network models. In: AAAI, vol. 16, pp. 3776–3784 (2016)
23. Serban, I.V., et al.: A hierarchical latent variable encoder-decoder model for generating dialogues. In: AAAI, pp. 3295–3301 (2017)
24. Strub, F., De Vries, H., Mary, J., Piot, B., Courville, A., Pietquin, O.: End-to-end optimization of goal-driven and visually grounded dialogue systems. arXiv preprint arXiv:1703.05423 (2017)
25. Su, P.-H., et al.: On-line active reward learning for policy optimisation in spoken dialogue systems. arXiv preprint arXiv:1605.07669 (2016)
26. Su, P.-H., Vandyke, D., Gasic, M., Mrksic, N., Wen, T.-H., Young, S.: Reward shaping with recurrent neural networks for speeding up on-line policy learning in spoken dialogue systems. arXiv preprint arXiv:1508.03391 (2015)
27. Trieu, H.-L., Iida, H., Bao, N.P.H., Nguyen, L.-M.: Towards developing dialogue systems with entertaining conversations. ICAART **2**, 511–518 (2017)
28. Triguero, A., Graña, M.: Teaching NAO to answer. https://doi.org/10.5281/zenodo.2567595. February 2019
29. Wen, T.-H., et al.: A network-based end-to-end trainable task-oriented dialogue system. arXiv preprint arXiv:1604.04562 (2016)

Boosting Object Detection in Cyberphysical Systems

José M. Buenaposada[1]([✉])[ID] and Luis Baumela[2]

[1] Univ. Rey Juan Carlos,
Móstoles, Spain
josemiguel.buenaposada@urjc.es
[2] Univ. Politécnica de Madrid,
Madrid, Spain
lbaumela@fi.upm.es

Abstract. The construction of Cyberphysical systems requires providing intelligent behavior to physical agents at the smallest scale and, therefore, the need to develop very efficient and resource-aware algorithms. In this paper we present an object detection algorithm that may endow an agent with perceptual object detection capabilities at a small computational cost. To this end we adapt a recent Multi-class Boosting scheme to create an efficient detector with the capability of regressing the object bounding box. In the experiments we prove that the resulting algorithm shows Average Precision (AP) improvements in a multi-view car detection problem.

Keywords: Object detection · Multi-class boosting · Cyberphysical systems

1 Introduction

The last years have witnessed such evolution in internet technology that almost everything can now be connected transparently and seamlessly through the Internet of Things (IoT). In parallel, advances in Artificial Intelligence enable the construction of autonomous agents that perceive and take actions in the real world. In this context Cyberphysical (CBP) systems emerge as an evolution of the IoT in which physical objects not only have computing and communication abilities, but also sensing and operation capacities, enabling them to co-operate in the construction of distributed and autonomous ecosystems [11,15].

Perceptual skills, such as for example detecting and recognizing objects of interest, is a requirement for a CBP agent to interact with the environment. Powered by the use of deep neural nets, modern object detection algorithms have achieved remarkable performance [8]. However, these approaches require advanced computational resources such as Graphical Processing Units (GPUs). Although there is an ever-increasing number of devices shipping GPUs, it is also true that such intelligent behavior is required at the smallest scale, such as in

---

The original version of this chapter was revised: The "Acknowledgment" was inserted. The correction to this chapter is available at https://doi.org/10.1007/978-3-030-19591-5_44

J. M. Ferrández Vicente et al. (Eds.): IWINAC 2019, LNCS 11486, pp. 309–318, 2019.
https://doi.org/10.1007/978-3-030-19591-5_32

micro-scale mobile robots, that are inherently limited in powering and computational capabilities [2]. Hence, the necessity of developing very efficient algorithms, that are aware of the time and energy required for their execution [15].

In this paper we propose a detection algorithm based on Viola and Jones seminal Boosting scheme [12]. Boosting classifiers have been extensively used for building multi-class object detectors [14]. This approach has received much attention because it is very efficient and achieves very good performance in various object detection problems [1,9]. The key for its success is the exploitation of the feature selection capabilities of Boosting together with efficient image descriptions such as the *Integral Channel Features* [3]. The usual framework for Boosting-based object detection uses binary classification (e.g. AdaBoost). In this regard, multi-class detection problems are usually solved with K detectors, one per object view or positive class. Here we propose the use of a single multi-class Boosting algorithm.

A key methodological advance in object detection is the bounding box refinement. When dealing with objects that can present different aspect ratios depending on their pose or configuration, the bounding box refinement step is crucial to get better precision. Recent CNN-based detectors already perform bounding box parameters regression, e.g. [10].

In this paper we improve the Boosting-based object detection paradigm [12] in two ways. First using BAdaCost [4], a recent multi-class cost-sensitive Boosting algorithm. With it we get a precise control over class boundaries (e.g. errors between positive classes). Hence improving the performance compared to approaches based on plain binary classifiers, e.g. [7]. Second, we extend BAdaCost so it is able to regress the detected target bounding box. We present our approach in a car detection problem and evaluate it with the KITTI benchmark. In the experiments we show that our approach results in an improvement in AP from previous baseline results.

2   Multi-class Boosting Algorithm

A Boosting algorithm is a supervised learning scheme that requires N training data instances $\{(\mathbf{x}_i, l_i)\}_{i=1}^{N}$, where $\mathbf{x}_i \in X$ encodes the object to be classified with class label $l_i \in L = \{1, 2, \ldots, K\}$. Each label $l \in L$ has a corresponding margin vector $\mathbf{y}_l \in Y$ where $Y = \{\mathbf{y}_1, \ldots, \mathbf{y}_K\}$ [4]. $\mathbf{y}_l$ has a value 1 in the l-th coordinate and $\frac{-1}{K-1}$ elsewhere. So, if $l = 1$, the margin vector representing class 1 is $\mathbf{y}_1 = \left(1, \frac{-1}{K-1}, \ldots, \frac{-1}{K-1}\right)^{\top}$. Hence, it is immediate to see the equivalence between classifiers G defined over L and classifiers $\mathbf{g}$ defined over Y, $G(\mathbf{x}) = l \in L \Leftrightarrow \mathbf{g}(\mathbf{x}) = \mathbf{y}_l \in Y$.

2.1   BAdaCost: Cost-Sensitive Multi-class Boosting Classification

Cost-sensitive classification endows the traditional Boosting scheme with the capability to to modify pair-wise class boundaries. In this way, we can reduce the number of errors between positive classes (e.g. different target orientations) and improve recall when object classes have different aspect ratios. To this end we use BAdaCost [4] (Boosting Adapted for Cost matrix), a recently introduced multi-class cost-sensitive Boosting classifier. In this section we briefly introduce it.

The costs are encoded in a $K \times K$-matrix $\mathbf{C}$, where each entry $C(i,j)$ represents the cost of miss-classifying an instance with real label i as j. Here it is assumed that $C(i,i) = 0, \forall i \in L$, i.e. the cost of correct classifications is zero.

Let $\mathbf{C}^*$ be a $K \times K$-matrix defined in the following way

$$C^*(i,j) = \begin{cases} C(i,j) & \text{if } i \neq j \\ -\sum_{h=1}^{K} C(j,h) & \text{if } i = j \end{cases}, \ \forall i,j \in L. \tag{1}$$

In a cost-sensitive classification problem each value $C^*(j,j)$ represents a "reward" associated to a correct classification. The j-th row in $\mathbf{C}^*$, denoted as $\mathbf{C}(j,-)$, is a margin vector that encodes the costs associated to the j-th label. The multi-class cost-sensitive margin associated to instance $(\mathbf{x}, l)$ is given by $z_C := \mathbf{C}^*(l,-) \cdot \mathbf{g}(\mathbf{x})$. It is easy to verify that if $\mathbf{g}(\mathbf{x}) = \mathbf{y}_i \in Y$, for a certain $i \in L$, then $\mathbf{C}^*(l,-) \cdot \mathbf{g}(\mathbf{x}) = \frac{K}{K-1} \mathbf{C}^*(l,i)$. Hence, using this generalized margin, BAdaCost defines a *Cost-sensitive Multi-Class Exponential Loss Function* (*CMELF*):

$$\mathcal{L}_C(l, \mathbf{g}(\mathbf{x})) := \exp(z_C) = \exp\left(\mathbf{C}^*(l,-) \cdot \mathbf{g}(\mathbf{x})\right) = \exp\left(\frac{K}{K-1} \mathbf{C}^*(l, G(\mathbf{x}))\right). \tag{2}$$

The margin, z_C, yields negative values when the classification is correct under the cost-sensitive point of view, and positive values for costly (wrong) outcomes. The CMELF is a generalization of the Multi-class Exponential Loss introduced in [17].

BAdaCost resorts to the CMELF (2) for evaluating classifications encoded with margin vectors. The expected loss is minimized using a stage-wise additive gradient descent approach. The strong classier that arises has the following structure:

$$\mathbf{H}(\mathbf{x}) = \arg\min_k \left(\mathbf{C}^*(k,-) \cdot \sum_{m=1}^{M} \beta_m \mathbf{g}_m(\mathbf{x})\right) = \arg\min_k \left(\mathbf{C}^*(k,-) \cdot \mathbf{f}(\mathbf{x})\right), \tag{3}$$

where $\mathbf{f}(\mathbf{x})$ is a linear combination of M cost-sensitive weak learners, $\{\mathbf{g}_m(\mathbf{x})\}_{m=1}^{M}$, that the algorithm learns incrementally. In this case $\mathbf{f}(\mathbf{x})$ is a vector with the estimated per-class costs from the feature vector $\mathbf{x}$.

2.2 Object Detection Score for BAdaCost

When building an object detector it is necessary to have a confidence measure or detection score. In BAdaCost the predicted costs incurred when classifying sample $\mathbf{x}$ in one of the K classes are given by the vector:

$$\mathbf{c} = \mathbf{C}^* \cdot \mathbf{f}(\mathbf{x}) = (c_1, \ldots, c_K)^\top. \tag{4}$$

From now on, in multi-class detection problems, we assume that the background (negative) class has label $l = 1$ and the object classes (e.g. different views of a car) have label $l > 1$. Therefore, we can compute the score of $\mathbf{x}$ as

$$s(\mathbf{x}) = (c_1 - min(c_2, \ldots, c_K)). \tag{5}$$

This score has desirable properties for detection problems: (1) $s(\mathbf{x}) > 0$ when the winner class (i.e. the class with lowest cost) has label $l > 1$; (2) $s(\mathbf{x}) < 0$ when the winner class is $l = 1$. Given that score definition, we can use any cascade calibration algorithm for Boosting, for example [16], and stop execution of weak learners whenever the score falls below a calibrated threshold.

3   Bounding Box Aspect Ratio Estimation

In our experiments we build a multi-view car detector. One of the challenges in the car detection problem is that the bounding box aspect ratio (AR) changes with the view (i.e. frontal cars have lower AR than side view ones). By posing a classification problem where the labels are the 20 car views (plus no-car label), we can also compute information related to the AR in the Boosted tree leaves. The overall approach to simultaneous detection and AR estimation is shown in Fig. 1.

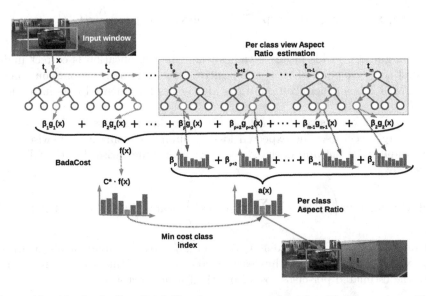

Fig. 1. Algorithmic pipeline. BAdaCost learns an ensemble of multi-class cost-sensitive trees. The estimation of AR distribution is computed using all the trees starting with the t_p one. The final AR is the one of the the minimal cost class.

The classifier learns m weak-learners that are cost-sensitive decision trees. The split measure used in each tree node is the Gini impurity. The modifications of the tree to make it cost-sensitive are two-fold:

1. On each split node S the probability of class l, $p(l)$, is multiplied by the percentage of costs associated to class l (i.e. sum of a row in the cost matrix), $c(l)$:

$$p'(l) = \underbrace{\frac{\sum_{i \in S} w_i \Delta I(y_i = l)}{\sum_{i \in S} w_i}}_{p(l)} \underbrace{\frac{\sum_{k=1}^{K} C(l, k)}{\sum_{i=1}^{K} \sum_{j=1}^{K} C(i, j)}}_{c(l)}, \tag{6}$$

where $I()$ is the indicator function.

2. On each leaf node the minimum cost rule is applied for classification:

$$h = \arg \min_l \mathbf{C}(l, -)(p(1), \ldots, p(K))^\top. \tag{7}$$

During the training phase, for every decision tree and leaf node S, we store: (1) the minimum cost label, h_S and (2) a $K \times 1$ vector, $\mathbf{a}_S$, with the mean AR of each view class. During the detection phase, the trees are traversed with the feature vector $\mathbf{x}$ corresponding to a candidate window (see Fig. 1). As we have seen in Sect. 2, the vector $\mathbf{f}(\mathbf{x})$ is computed as a linear combination of tree labels outputs h, codified as its corresponding margin vector $\mathbf{g}(\mathbf{x}) = \mathbf{y}_h \in Y$. Vector $\mathbf{f}(\mathbf{x})$ is then used in Eq. (3) to obtain the minimum cost view class estimation.

Our procedure to estimate the aspect ratio follows a similar approach. Let $\mathbf{a}_t(\mathbf{x})$ be the per class view aspect ratios stored in the leaf node of t-th tree in which $\mathbf{x}$ ends. After traversing the weak learners trees, the vector of class aspect ratios is computed as a linear combination: $\mathbf{a}(\mathbf{x}) = \sum_{i=t_p}^{M} \beta_i \mathbf{a}_i(\mathbf{x})$. If h is the class estimated by the BAdaCost strong learner, $H(\mathbf{x})$, then the estimated AR is given by $\mathbf{a}(h)$. Note here that we drop all the trees below the t_p-th one. The rationale is that in the first trees the strong classifier are not accurate enough. In the experimental section we will see that this is in fact true and it is better to use only the final trees in the ensemble to estimate the AR.

4   Experiments

In our experiments we have modified Piotr Dollar's Matlab Toolbox[1] with BAda-Cost (e.g adding cost-sensitive decision trees and multi-class detection). Our modified implementation with the BAdaCost detectors is already available[2].

In the experiments we use a detection problem in which the target object changes its Bounding Box AR depending on the view angle. Car detection in the KITTI dataset [6] is a good example of this kind of problem. The database presents three subsets: easy, moderate and hard (easy $\subset$ moderate $\subset$ hard). We carry out the evaluation in each level separately. In total there are 7481 images for training and 7518 for testing. Since the testing images have no ground truth, we split the train set in training and validation subsets: cars in the first 6733 images (90%) to train (KITTI-train90) and the last 748 images (10%) as validation (KITTI-train10).

---

[1] https://github.com/pdollar/toolbox.
[2] https://github.com/jmbuena/toolbox.badacost.public.

Fig. 2. KITTI cars classes we use in our experiments.

We divide the images into $K = 20$ view classes (see Fig. 2). With the BAda-Cost algorithm we use cost-sensitive decision tree weak learners that select features from LDCF channels [13]. In all the experiments we train a car model of size 48×84 pixels, $AR = 1.75$. We start the pyramid one octave above the actual image size, to detect cars 25 pixel high. This approach produces detection bounding boxes with fixed AR of 1.75 (Fixed-Equal approach). On the other hand, since the multi-class detector outputs the view class, we can correct the fixed size window to the training mean (Fixed-Class-Mean approach) AR of the predicted class view as done in [5,9].

We train the classifier storing the mean AR of each class in tree leaves as explained in Sect. 3. During training we perform 4 rounds of hard negatives mining with the KITTI training image subset (KITTI-train90). We set the number of cost-sensitive trees to $T = 1024$ (4 rounds with 32, 128, 256 and T weak learners, respectively), tree depth to $D = 8$, the number of negatives per round to add to $N = 7500$ and the total amount of negatives to $NA = 30000$.

The costs matrix is set to weight up gross errors between view classes. This is important because estimating the wrong class will output a Bounding Box with the wrong AR (e.g. frontal car, $AR = 1.0$, to left side car, $AR \gg 1.0$). We show the cost matrix we use in Fig. 3. The non-car class has label 1. Positive classes have the labels shown in Fig. 2 plus one.

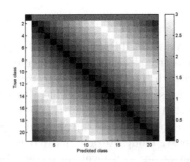

Fig. 3. Costs matrix used in our experiments.

First, we train only one detector with the mean aspect ratio of each view class stored on the tree leaves. The detector uses KITTI-train90 for training and KITTI-train10 for testing. We set the detection threshold to an entersection over union (IoU) value 0.7, es established in the KITTI benchmark. Then, we use different strategies to estimate the ARs using this detector. First we test the AR estimation algorithm introduced Sect. 3 with different values of t_p (first tree to use in the estimation). In Fig. 4 we show that neither using all the trees nor using the last few trees are the best strategies. We can see that, in the Moderate KITTI car detection problem, using all trees starting with $t_p = 950$ we get the best result.

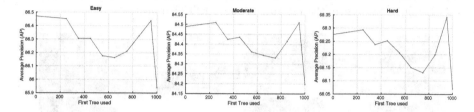

Fig. 4. Using different number of weak learners for estimating the detections AR. Here we train in KITTI-train90 and test in the validation subset, KITTI-train10.

Secondly, once we have found the best t_p value we can compare it with other AR estimation strategies: use the output of the fixed size sliding window detector (Fixed-Equal), modify the fixed aspect ratio window with the estimated class view aspect ratio (Fixed-Class-Mean) and, finally, our proposal (Estimated-AR). In Fig. 5 we confirm that a fixed aspect ratio detector as Fixed-Equal, gets the worst results. We get a much better result in the Moderate KITTI subset (the one used for ranking) with the Fixed-Class-Mean procedure. On the other hand, we can improve even further the AP by using our Estimated-AR strategy. We get an better AP by 1.7%, 1.2% and 1.1%, respectively, in the Easy, Moderate and Hard settings. Given that our procedure is computationally cheap it is a significant improvement. On Fig. 6 we show results of the different methods on images were our method (Estimated-AR) improves over the baseline (Fixed-Class-Mean).

To further analyze the performance of our procedure (Estimated-AR) with respect to the baseline (Fixed-Class-Mean), we have performed an additional experiment varying the IoU threshold (see Table 1). The good behavior of our approach is more evident when we look for higher overlapping in the detection. With a threshold of IoU = 0.8, Estimated-AR, in Moderate subset, is better by 11,53% (from 44.2% to 49.3%) and with IoU = 0.9 it is better by 63.15% (from 1.9% to 3.1%).

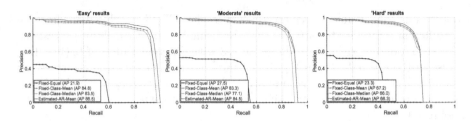

Fig. 5. Comparing different strategies to compute the detection AR. Here we train in KITTI-train90 and test in the validation subset, KITTI-train10.

Fig. 6. Sample car detection improvement with AR estimation on KITTI-train10. In green, red and yellow we show respectively the ground truth, Estimated-AR-Mean and Fixed-Class-Mean true positives for the data base moderate settings. (Color figure online)

Table 1. AP for different IoU values on the KITTI train90/train10 experiment

	Algorithm/IoU	0.5	0.6	0.7	0.8	0.9
Easy	Fixed-Class-Mean	95.6 %	94.9 %	84.8 %	44.2 %	1.5 %
	Estimated-AR	95.6 %	94.8 %	86.4 %	49.3 %	2.8 %
Moderate	Fixed-Class-Mean	90.3 %	89.8 %	83.3 %	44.2 %	1.9 %
	Estimated-AR	90.3 %	89.8 %	84.5 %	47.7 %	3.1 %
Hard	Fixed-Class-Mean	79.5 %	78.2 %	67.2 %	36.9 %	1.7 %
	Estimated-AR	79.5 %	78.1 %	68.3 %	39.1 %	2.9 %

5   Conclusions

Detection algorithms have evolved over time by changing various components of the pipeline. Some of these improvements, however, have been exploited only in the context of modern deep neural nets. In this paper we improve the performance of Boosting-based detectors by refining the target bounding box using a new cost-sensitive multi-class boosting scheme. This is a relevant result in the construction of Cyberphysical Systems, given the computational efficiency of this family of algorithms.

In the experiments we show that our approach improves the detection AP with respect to the baseline Fixed-Class-Mean regressor. Moreover, it beats the results of its closest Boosting competitor [7]. This Boosting-based detector achieves 52.9% AP in the moderate KITTI testing set, where as our result is 67.23%.

If we analyze the results in the moderate set in Table 1 we can see that for an IoU of 0.5, we achieve a result above 90% AP. However, as the IoU threshold increases, the AP goes down to 3.1% in the most demanding case, $IoU = 0.9$. This means that most of the detections are correct, but the accurate location of the object bounding box is an important source of errors that should be further studied in the future.

The use of proper data augmentation and alternative and more accurate bounding box regression algorithms are future research avenues that will further improve AP with no extra computing cost.

Acknowledgments. The authors gratefully acknowledge funding from the Spanish *Ministerio de Economía y Competitividad*, project TIN2016-75982-C2-2-R.

References

1. Benenson, R., Mathias, M., Timofte, R., Van Gool, L.: Pedestrian detection at 100 frames per second. In: Proceedings of the IEEE Conference on Computer Vision and Pattern Recognition (2012)
2. Diller, E., Metin Sitti, M.: Micro-scale mobile robotics. Found. Trends Robot. **2**(3), 143–259 (2013)
3. Dollar, P., Appel, R., Belongie, S., Perona, P.: Fast feature pyramids for object detection. IEEE Trans. Pattern Anal. Mach. Intell. **36**(8), 1532–1545 (2014)
4. Fernández-Baldera, A., Buenaposada, J.M., Baumela, L.: Multi-class boosting for imbalanced data. In: Paredes, R., Cardoso, J.S., Pardo, X.M. (eds.) IbPRIA 2015. LNCS, vol. 9117, pp. 57–64. Springer, Cham (2015). https://doi.org/10.1007/978-3-319-19390-8_7
5. Fernández-Baldera, A., Buenaposada, J.M., Baumela, L.: BAdaCost: multi-class boosting with costs. Pattern Recogn. **79**, 467–479 (2018)
6. Geiger, A., Lenz, P., Urtasun, R.: Are we ready for autonomous driving? the kitti vision benchmark suite. In: Proceedings of the IEEE Conference on Computer Vision and Pattern Recognition (2012)
7. Juranek, R., Herout, A., Dubska, M., Zemcik, P.: Real-time pose estimation piggy-backed on object detection. In: Proceedings of the International Conference Computer Vision, December 2015
8. Liu, L., et al.: Deep learning for generic object detection: a survey. CoRR abs/1809.02165 (2018). http://arxiv.org/abs/1809.02165
9. Ohn-Bar, E., Trivedi, M.: Learning to detect vehicles by clustering appearance patterns. IEEE Trans. Intell. Transp. Syst. **16**(5), 2511–2521 (2015)

10. Ren, S., He, K., Girshick, R., Sun, J.: Faster R-CNN: towards real-time object detection with region proposal networks. In: Conference on Neural Information Processing Systems (2015)
11. Serpanos, D.: The cyber-physical systems revolution. Computer **51**(3), 70–73 (2018)
12. Viola, P.A., Jones, M.J.: Fast and robust classification using asymmetric AdaBoost and a detector cascade. In: Conference on Neural Information Processing Systems, pp. 1311–1318 (2001)
13. Nam, W., Dollar, P., Han, J.H.: Local decorrelation for improved pedestrian detection. In: Conference on Neural Information Processing Systems (2014)
14. Wang, X., Yang, M., Zhu, S., Lin, Y.: Regionlets for generic object detection. IEEE Trans. Pattern Anal. Mach. Intell. **37**(10), 2071–2084 (2015)
15. Wolf, W.: Cyber-physical systems. Computer **42**(3), 88–89 (2009)
16. Zhang, C., Viola, P.A.: Multiple-instance pruning for learning efficient cascade detectors. In: Conference on Neural Information Processing Systems, pp. 1681–1688 (2007)
17. Zhu, J., Zou, H., Rosset, S., Hastie, T.: Multi-class AdaBoost. Stat. Interface **2**, 349–360 (2009)

Fusion of Inertial Motion Sensors and Electroencephalogram for Activity Detection

Ibai Baglietto Araquistain[1], Xabier Garmendia[1], Manuel Graña[1(✉)], and Javier de Lope Asiain[2]

[1] Computational Intelligence Group,
University of the Basque Country, (UPV/EHU), San Sebastián, Spain
`manuel.grana@ehu.es`
[2] Computational Cognitive Robotics Group, Department of Artificial Intelligence,
Universidad Politécnica de Madrid (UPM), Madrid, Spain

Abstract. A central issue in Computational Neuroethology is the fusion of information coming from a wide variety of devices, by computational tools and techniques aiming to correlate the neural substrate and the observable behavior. In this paper we are concerned with the fusion of information from two specific commercial devices, the Emotiv EPOC+ EEG recorder, and the Rokoko motion capture suite based on inertial motion units (IMU). We have built an ad hoc system for synchronized data capture. We test the system on the recognition of simple activities. We are able to confirm that the fusion of the neural activity information and the motion information improves the activity recognition.

1 Introduction

Traditionally, neuroethology tries to find the neural basis for behavior by direct intervention or by accidental observation. Neuroethology is increasingly used as a tool to evaluate the effect of treatments to a diversity of brain diseases or injuries, such as the hipoxia-isquemia in newborns [12]. Objective behavior impairment measures can be correlated to brain damage observed via postmortem histology, or via EEG measurement through electrode implants.

Under the label of computational neuroethology there are some very abstract attempts to establish a brain-behavior model, that try to relate mathematical dynamical models of behaviors (such as the dynamics of finger tapping) with neural dynamics [8], however such abstract approach is quite limited to some modeling targets. A more general approach is to try to find correlations between behavioral observations and neural activity measurements obtained from a variety of synchronized sensors. Hence the predominant approach is a data science based approach, using statistics and machine learning tools. Animal or human models are designed to gather data that can be subjected to statistical analysis or machine learning predictive modeling. For instance, animal models of fear consists in the presentation of the predator or some surrogate sensorial correlate,

J. M. Ferrández Vicente et al. (Eds.): IWINAC 2019, LNCS 11486, pp. 319–326, 2019.
https://doi.org/10.1007/978-3-030-19591-5_33

such as odor or a shape, or a robot simulating the predator performing aggressive moves [10]. A human model of fear was the presentation of a tarantula at the foot of a human subject whose neural activity was recorded by fMRI [10].

We are interested in the development of tools that may allow the study of how some treatments affect subjects with brain degenerative diseases, and children with special needs. Many of these conditions show typical external behavioral traits that can be objectively measured by means of motion capture devices, allowing to measure changes in behavior due to treatment with great accuracy. Simultaneous recording of brain activity allows to measure how the changes in behavior correlate with neural activity changes.

In this paper we report on going work devoted to the identification of activities based on two commercial devices: an inertial motion capture and an electroencephalogram (EEG) recorder. Both have wireless connection via wifi protocol allowing for broad and natural mobility of the subject under study. Code developed for data capture is published in Zenodo [2]. We report exploratory results on the identification of some basic behaviors.

The paper structure is as follows: Sect. 2 presents the data capture and data processing systems employed in our work. Section 3 presents results on preliminary testing data collected in-house with the proposed system. Section 4 gives some conclusions and further work.

2   Data Capture and Data Processing

The general structure of a computational neuroethological observation system has the following main concurrent modules,

- One module is devoted to the capture and analysis of the neural activity, often via Electroencephalogram (EEG) sensors, which can be external or internally

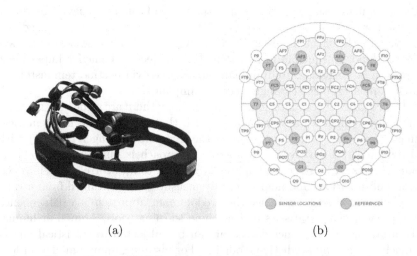

(a)   (b)

Fig. 1. Emotiv EPOC+ (a) the device, (b) the recording channels

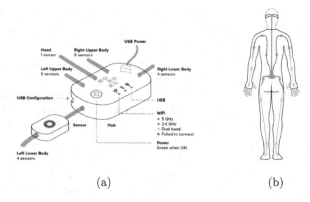

(a)   (b)

Fig. 2. Rokoko elements (a) the hub collecting information from IMU sensors, (b) the placement of the sensors in the suit

implanted. Functional Magnetic Resonance Imaging (fMRI) has been used for neuroethological experiments in humans [9]. We use the Emotiv EPCO+[1] wireless EEG recorder, a minimally invasive device allowing natural mobility of the subjects. Figure 1 shows the actual device and the channels that are recorded. Instead of the raw EEG signals[2], we will be working with the neural activity band activities as computed by the Emotiv API, which are computed at 10 Hz:

- Theta (4–7 Hz): Associated with first stages of sleep.
- Alpha (8–13 Hz): Associated with cortex activity in resting state.
- Low Beta (12.5–16 Hz) y High Beta (20.5–28 Hz): Associated with waken conscious state.
- Gamma (32–100 Hz): Related with the conscious cognition processes.

Taking into account that we have 17 channels, as illustrated in Fig. 1(b), we may end up with 85 features for classification building characterizing the neural activity state each 0.1 s. In the computational results reported below we make several combinations of this channel information with the behavior measurement information.

- The second module is devoted to the quantitative observation of the subject behavior. Image processing is a key technology for the development of the ecological behavior observation, allowing identification of individuals, tracking and classification of their behaviors using supervised and unsupervised approaches [5]. There is a wide variety of imaging sensors providing the motion capture besides the optical cameras, such as infrared camera/illumination, X-ray imaging for animals embedded in the soil, thermal imaging for video shooting in darkness [3], sonar signals for underwater monitoring, sensitive pressure sensors for micromotion detection [4], catwalk systems for animal gait analysis [6]. We use the Rokoko motion capture suit[3]. Figure 2 shows the

---

[1] https://www.emotiv.com/epoc/.

[2] Raw signals need a specific license which we can not pay at this time.

[3] https://www.rokoko.com.

schema of the central hub collecting the information from the 9 degrees of freedom inertial measurement units (IMU) and sending it via wifi connection, and the placement of the IMU on the body. The IMU are embedded in the textile's suite, which can be tightly adjusted to minimize noise from random motions. The system needs no anatomical calibration, and can be setup in a few minutes. Calibration of the initial pose is easy. The sampling frequency is 100 Hz, much higher than that of the EPOC+ computation of EEG bands, so some synchronization problems need to be solved. Besides, Rokoko suite shows some drifting effects, greater in lab conditions with many electromagnetic sources nearby. Information fusion with optical sensing to help to correct the drift is under development. The suite contains 19 IMU providing XYZ spatial information as well as motion quaternions vectors (discarded in this paper) at up to 25 body positions. For synchronization with the neural readings, we carry out subsampling of the position readings to 10 Hz. We keep the differences between positions at each sampling time, i.e. we use differential instead of instantaneous information. Hence we have up to 75 position features each 0.1 s.

- Thirdly, specific computational modules are devoted to extract the correlation between observed behavior and neural activity. Specific behaviors have to be codified and calibrated in the observation hardware/software [7]. Machine learning techniques are of paramount value for the automated interpretation of observation data. Characterization of the observation data, aka feature extraction, has been approached from a diversity of points of view. For instance, fractal dimension has been used in [7] to characterize walking path tortuosity of aging person. Conditional random field models have been exploited for human motion recognition [11], avoiding restrictive and artificious independence assumptions. The application of innovative machine learning includes deep learning techniques, such as the convolutional neural networks (CNN) [1], or the spatio-temporal bags of words used by [3] for the automated construction of ethograms from continuous video, recognizing the behavior building blocks by an Adaboost trained classifier. In our work, we have used a machine learning approach testing several classifiers which are available at the scikit-learn Python package[4]. Namely, we have applied logistic regression, nearest neighbors, linear SVM, gradient boosting (estimators = 1000), decision trees, random forest (estimators = 1000), multilayer perceptron (MLP) (alpha = 1), and naive bayes. We tried to predict the actual activity state of the subject from several combinations of motion and neural activity features.

3   Some Preliminary Results

To test our system we have designed a simple task. We want to discriminate three activity states of the subject: standing, advancing forward, and advancing

---

[4] https://scikit-learn.org/.

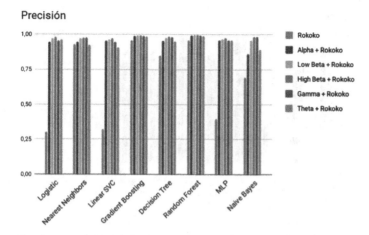

Fig. 3. Precision of all classifiers for different combinations of Rokoko and Emotiv EPOC+ features.

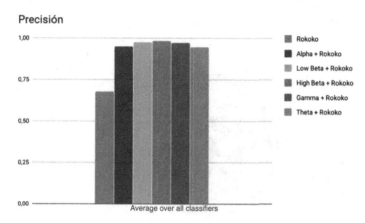

Fig. 4. Average precision over all classifiers for each combination of features

backwards. The dataset is well balanced as the time spent in each activity is the same. We have repeated the process ten times with one subject. For validation we follow a 50% holdout approach, repeated ten times, so we report the average results of the holdout training and validation. The classification task is instantaneous, that is, we classify the activity at each time point independently. Hence, all the data points conform the validation dataset. Figure 3 shows the plot of the average holdout precision for each classifier tested and each one-to-one combination of rokoko data, including the rokoko data alone. It can be appreciated that some classifiers (logistic regression, linear SVM, MLP, and naive bayes) give very bad results when using only rokoko data. Another salient feature of the plot is that all classifiers improve their results when some neural activity band is added to the set of features. This effect is more notorious in Fig. 4 where we plot the

Precisión

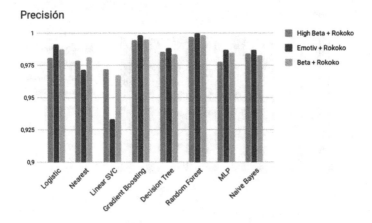

Fig. 5. Precision of classifiers achieved with Rokoko combined with high-beta versus high-beta and low-beta (denoted beta in the figure), versus all neural activity bands (denoted Emotiv in the figure)

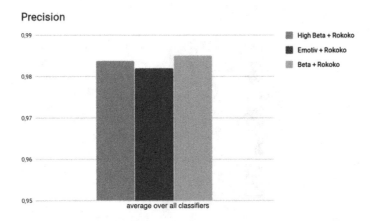

Fig. 6. Average over all classifiers of the precision achieved with high beta versus high-beta and low-beta (denoted beta in the figure), versus all bands (denoted Emotiv in the figure)

average of the results achieved by all classifiers over each combination of features. It appears that high-beta is the neural activity band that produces the best results when added to the rokoko motion features. Regarding classifiers, it is apparent that random forest and gradient boosting are the ones providing best results. However, our interest is on the actual features selected. The question already positively answered is "do neural activity features add some information over motion capture, thus enhancing classifier performance?". The next question is "what is the optimal feature selection?". Figure 5 shows the precision achieved by the classifiers under three conditions: adding only high-beta band data, adding high-beta and low-beta bands (denoted beta in the figure), and adding all bands (denoted emotiv in the figure). The effect is unclear, as adding all the bands improves the precision of the best classifiers, but decreases on others. To summarize, we plot in Fig. 6 the average results over all classifiers. The results are in favor of using the two beta bands as the most robust feature selection. It seems that this selection is also well grounded on the interpretation of the bands. Beta bands correspond to wake and conscious activity, therefore are quite relevant for the activities performed. On the other hand, it must be noted that even the theta band associated with deep sleep, has some information regarding instantaneous classification of activity.

4   Concluding Remarks

Computational neuroethology has deep roots in computational models of brain and behavior relations, but it is also deeply related to neuroscience search for neural mechanisms and biological behavior analysis. It can be of great use in the detailed quantitative analysis of the effect of treatments to patients suffering a wide spectrum of brain related conditions. In this paper we have introduced a system that is based on inertial motion capture and EEG recording. The devices are wirelessly connected, which allows natural motion of the subjects. A preliminary evaluation on a simple task is quite successful, showing that the combination of both motion and neural activity information provides improved activity classification capabilities. Future works will be aiming to adapt the system to various experimental settings, so that it can be used for actual evaluation of treatments. One potential setting is the evaluation of the impact of social robots on children with special needs, specially children with autistic spectrum disorder.

Acknowledgments. This work has been partially supported by FEDER funds through MINECO project TIN2017-85827-P, and project KK-2018/00071 of the Elkartek 2018 funding program of the Basque Government

References

1. Akkaya, B., Tabar, Y.R., Gharbalchi, F., Ulusoy, I., Halici, U.: Tracking mice face in video. In: 20th National Biomedical Engineering Meeting (BIYOMUT), pp. 1–4, November 2016
2. Baglietto, I., Garmendia, X., Graña, M.: A synchronized capture system for Emotiv+, Kinect, and Rokoko motion capture, Jaunary 2019. https://doi.org/10.5281/zenodo.2548964
3. Burgos-Artizzu, X.P., Dollár, P., Lin, D., Anderson, D.J., Perona, P.: Social behavior recognition in continuous video. In: 2012 IEEE Conference on Computer Vision and Pattern Recognition, pp. 1322–1329, June 2012
4. Carreno, M.I., et al.: First approach to the analysis of spontaneous activity of mice based on permutation entropy. In: 2015 4th International Work Conference on Bioinspired Intelligence (IWOBI), pp. 197–204, June 2015
5. Dell, A.I., et al.: Automated image-based tracking and its application in ecology. Trends Ecol. Evol. **29**(7), 417–428 (2014)

6. Fröhlich, H., Claes, K., De Wolf, C., Van Damme, X., Michel, A.: A machine learning approach to automated gait analysis for the Noldus Catwalk system. IEEE Trans. Biomed. Eng. **65**(5), 1133–1139 (2018)
7. Kearns, W.D., Fozard, J.L., Nams, V.O.: Movement path tortuosity in free ambulation: relationships to age and brain disease. IEEE J. Biomed. Health Inform. **21**(2), 539–548 (2017)
8. Kelso, J.A.S., Dumas, G., Tognoli, E.: Outline of a general theory of behavior and brain coordination. Neural Netw. **37**, 120–131 (2013). Twenty-fifth Anniversay Commemorative Issue
9. Mobbs, D., et al.: Foraging under competition: the neural basis of input-matching in humans. J. Neurosci. **33**(23), 9866–9872 (2013)
10. Mobbs, D., Kim, J.J.: Neuroethological studies of fear, anxiety, and risky decision-making in rodents and humans. Curr. Opin. Behav. Sci. **5**, 8–15 (2015). Neuroeconomics
11. Sminchisescu, C.: Conditional models for contextual human motion recognition. In: Tenth IEEE International Conference on Computer Vision (ICCV 2005), Volume 1, vol. 2, pp. 1808–1815, October 2005
12. Tang, B., et al.: An in vivo study of hypoxia-inducible factor-1α signaling in ginsenoside Rg1-mediated brain repair after hypoxia/ischemia brain injury. Pediatric Res. **81**, 120 (2016)

BIOTHINGS: A Pipeline Creation Tool for PAR-CLIP Sequence Analsys

Oier Echaniz[1,2] and Manuel Graña[1,2(✉)]

[1] Grupo de Inteligencia Computacional (GIC),
Universidad del País Vasco (UPV/EHU), San Sebastián, Spain
`manuel.grana@ehu.es`
[2] Asociación de Ciencias de la programación Python San Sebastian (ACPYSS),
San Sebastián, Spain

Abstract. Bioinformatics pipelines dealing with analysis of sequences of aminoacids are tricky. It is not easy to match the input and outputs of stand-alone applications that sometimes were developed for quite different kinds of sequences. In this paper we propose a tool for the guided and safe composition of pipelines to treat a specific kind of sequences. This tool can easily extend to more general bioinformatics setting. Cross-Linking Immuno Precipitation associated to high-throughput sequencing (CLIP-seq) has been recently developed aiming to uncover the RNA-protein interaction genome-wide. Specifically PhotoActivable-Ribonucleoside-enhanced-CLIP (PAR-CLIP) has been proposed to achieve single-nucleotide resolution. A critical step in the analysis of PAR-CLIP sequences is peak calling. Specific methods propose probabilistic models based on its substitution properties, allowing for a more accurate detection of RNA-protein interaction sites. The pipeline construction tool proposed here can be used for systematic comparison of the effect of the choice of peak calling method.

1 Introduction

1.1 What Is PAR-CLIP?

RNA-binding proteins (RBPs) bind RNAs to regulate their fate, function, localization or secondary structure, therefore they influence many biological processes including cell apoptosis, growth, fate and differentiation. Cross-Linking Immune Precipitation associated to high-throughput sequencing (CLIP-seq) has been recently developed aiming to uncover the RNA-protein interaction genome-wide. CLIP-seq protocol has many steps involving sample preparation, sequencing and bioinformatics analysis. The main workflow of a CLIP bio-chemical protocol starts with UV radiation of the cell or tissue culture, which induces covalent crosslinks between RBPs and their bound RNAs. This is followed by immuno-precipitation of the RBP-RNA complexes and partial RNase digestion to narrow down the binding sites to appropriate sequencing and mapping lengths. Further steps aim at stringent purification, including radioactive labeling, recovery by

© Springer Nature Switzerland AG 2019
J. M. Ferrández Vicente et al. (Eds.): IWINAC 2019, LNCS 11486, pp. 327–336, 2019.
https://doi.org/10.1007/978-3-030-19591-5_34

SDS–PAGE, transfer to nitrocellulose membrane to abolish loose RNA fragments, excision and proteinase K treatment to remove the RBP and recover the trimmed RNA fragments. Finally, the fragments are reverse-transcribed and their cDNAs are subjected to deep sequencing. The resulting sequencing data is then analysed to obtain RBP sites which can be identified based on the mapped read profiles.

PhotoActivable-Ribonucleoside-enhanced-CLIP (PAR-CLIP) [13,16] is an experimental procedure based on next-generation sequencing (NGS) targeting the RNA interaction sites of a given protein. To increase crosslinking efficiency, cells are additionally supplemented with 4-thiouridine (4SU), and UV radiation is applied at 365 nm instead of 256 nm. Interestingly, these modifications also lead to a high number of thymidine to cytidine transitions (T => C) in the cDNA at the crosslink sites, which can be exploited in a subsequent mutational analysis for pinpointing the crosslink position, thus basically enabling PAR-CLIP to achieve single-nucleotide resolution. PAR-CLIP has allowed new discoveries, such as the role of Nrd1-Nab3-dependent transcription termination in the regulation of the expression of hundreds of protein coding genes in yeast [21].

1.2   Contributions in this Paper

This paper presents a new tool for the composition of computational pipelines for bioinformatics, specifically for the comparison of PAR-CLIP sequence analysis alternatives. The need of such a tool became apparent while working in a previous paper on the comparison of peak calling algorithms [10]. Besides, this paper icludes a breief review of the most relevant computational proposals for peak calling which have been applied over PAR-CLIP data. Section 2 gives an overview of the PAR-CLIP data processing elements and its natural sequence. Section 3 gives an overview of peak calling algoritms that can be applied to PAR-CLIP sequences. Section 4 describes some aspects of BIOTHINGS. Section 5 gives some conclusions of the paper.

2   Data Processing General Schema

After high-throughput sequencing, the bioinformatics analysis workflow illustrated in Fig. 1 starts by a preprocessing aimed to filter out the low quality and duplicate reads, and to map them onto the genome or the transcriptome of reference. Afterward, to assess real signal over the noise background, the reads are processed by peak-calling programs. Called peaks are further analyzed for functional, structural and biochemical characterizations of the RNA–protein interaction, including motif discovery, expression profile and gene ontology. Short explanation of each step in de workflow follows:

1. Preprocessing: involves adapter removal, filtering raw data according to read quality scores and collapsing reads with the exact sequence. While for the adapter removal, specific programs have been developed such as cutadapt [6] or Trimmomatic [3], for the quality filtering, usually bioinformaticians develop ad hoc scripts.

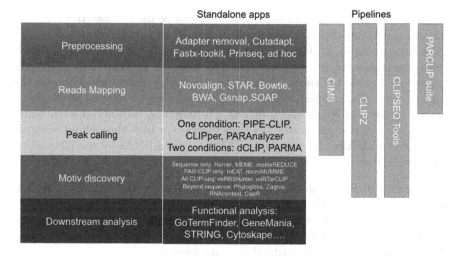

Fig. 1. General dataflow for CLIP data (extracted from [4])

2. Reads Mapping: Reads that survive the preprocessing steps are mapped onto the reference sequences that can be the complete genome, the transcriptome or sequences belonging to specific categories. The most common algorithms used to perform this task are Novoalign (http://www.novocraft.com/products/novoalign/), STAR [9], Bowtie [17], and RMAP [20].

3. Peak calling (Clustering): Assessing peaks is a central step of the analysis to determine specific signal over the noise background for the identification of real binding sites. The number of identified peaks increases with the sequencing depth because weaker sites become statistically significant with a greater number of reads [19]. However, the optimal sequencing depth can only be experimentally evaluated, as it depends on the noise background of the antibody. The most common strategy is to analyze distribution profiles to find clusters of reads that belong to the same peak. This strategy is used by different programs, including PIPE-CLIP [5], Pyicos [1] for all CLIP-seq protocol variants, and WavClusteR [7], PARalyzer [8], PARma [12], and BMix [14] designed for PAR-CLIP data. PIPE-CLIP and Pyicos group the reads based on positional overlap. To discriminate enriched read clusters over the background, the peak-calling programs use different statistical models.

4. Motif discovery: Following the peak calling, the analysis mainly focuses on the characterization of the RBP-RNA interactions, especially looking for possible binding sequence signature(s), using a candidate screening or a de novo motifs identification. For the candidate screening approach, programs like FIMO [15] can be used to screen peak sequences for the identification of known RNA binding motifs. If the user is looking for unknown RNA-binding motifs, a *de novo* motif identification could be performed. For this task, two main parameters should be calibrated before launching the analysis. The first parameter is the nucleotide length of the motif. The second parameter to take into account

is the so-called 'background sequences' that can be used as negative template in which it is not expected to contain the enriched motif sequence(s).

5. Downstream analysis: The last step of CLIP-seq analysis involves functional characterization of the target RNAs identified to provide clues about the molecular function of the RBP(s) or the miRNA(s) of interest. Although not always routinely updated, many resources have been developed for the functional analysis of RBPs and miRNAs. For instance, miRonTop is an online Java Web tool that integrates DNA microarrays or high-throughput sequencing data to identify the potential miRNA target mRNAs by complementary between the seed and the 30 UTR sequences.

As illustrated in Fig. 1, there are some pipelines that deal with some of the general process steps using specific solutions and applications. Our goal is to easy the construction of such pipelines aiming to a fair comparison of different solutions to the same bioinformatics processing tasks. An example are the peak calling algorithms, which are critical in some aspects.

3 Algorithms for Peak Calling

If the CLIP experiment was performed for a specific RBP, the generated reads should agglomerate in regions to which the RBP binds. Many reads appear from unspecific binding and thus have to be discarded, which is done in the process of peak calling. This task can typically be divided into two parts: one first extracts potentially interesting peaks based on peak shape or height and then filters the resulting peaks such that only sites enriched over a certain threshold or background are kept. Once the peaks are identified, they can be quantified and their statistical significance should be evaluated by comparing them to a control experiment. Depending on the biological question and sample conditions, scientists may need to tune the parameters of the different peak-calling programs to find the best set to perform this task such as the P value and the minimal number are significant.

3.1 BMix

BMix [14] is a probabilistic method which explicitly accounts for the sources of noise in PAR-CLIP data and distinguishes cross-link induced T => C substitutions from low and high-frequency erroneous alterations in PAR-CLIP cDNA sequencing reads. After alignment to the reference genome, the observed nucleotide can either match or differ from the reference at each position in an aligned read. In order to detect RNA-protein cross-link-induced T => C substitutions, BMix models for each position i in the genome where the genomic reference r_i is different from C, the probability of the observed T => C, A => C or G => C substitution. Denote x_i as the sequencing coverage at position i, y_i as the number of times the reference nucleotide is substituted with C in all the reads covering position i, and latent random variable $z_i \in \{1, 2, 3\}$ corresponding to the three possible reasons that can explain the observed C nucleotide at locus i on the genome. Specifically, for reference $r_i = T$ positions, $z_i = 1$ refers to background substitutions, $z_i = 2$ corresponds to a sequence variant, and $z_i = 3$ refers to an RNA-RBP cross-link. For reference $r_i = A$ or $r_i = G$ positions, only $z_i = 1$ and $z_i = 2$ are possible. Denote ϵ as the probability of a substitution due to sequencing noise. Thus, the probability of substitution at sequence variant loci becomes $1 - 3\epsilon$. Finally, at cross-link loci ($z_i = 3$), which can, at the same time, be affected by sequencing errors, T => C substitutions occur with probability $\theta = (1 - \gamma)\epsilon + (1 - 3\epsilon)\gamma$ where γ corresponds to the probability of a T nucleotide to be mutated to C following photo-activation and cross-link during PAR-CLIP. The probability of an observation is:

$$P\left((x_i, y_i) | r_i = T\right) = \sum_{i=1}^{3} P\left((x_i, y_i) | z_i, r_i = T\right) P\left(z_i | r_i = T\right) \qquad (1)$$

Model parameters can be estimated by likelihood maximization. The classification of each T locus is done choosing the class with maximum a posteriori probability.

3.2   PARalyzer

The rationale of PARalyzer [8] is to examine the pattern of T => C conversions in order to spot, with high confidence, RNA–protein interaction sites. A kernel-density-based classifier is used to characterize crosslinked regions, identified by T => C conversions (the signal), against not crosslinked ones, characterized by the absence of T => C conversions (the background). Class-specific densities (one for the signal and one for the background) are assessed by employing a Gaussian kernel density estimator with globally fixed precision parameter $\lambda = 3$ that, for each reference T nucleotide, considers the number of T => C conversions and the number of non T => C conversions in the aligned reads. To exploit available read data in an effective way, PARalyzer utilizes relatively lenient alignment parameters allowing reads to be as short as 13 nucleotides after adapter stripping, and a read may contain up to 2 mismatches restricted to T => C conversions. Nucleotides within the read groups that maintain a minimum read depth, and where the likelihood of T => C conversion is higher than non-conversion, are considered interaction sites.

WavClusteR

WavClusteR [7,18] is an R implementation of peak calling procedures for PAR-CLIP data. Let $A = A, C, G, T$ be the nucleotide alphabet and $S = (g, r) | g, r \in A \& g \neq r$ be the set of substitutions of any base g in the reference genome to any other base r contained in the already mapped read. The relative substitution frequency (RSF) can be computed as $\hat{x}_{s,i} = \frac{y_{s,i}}{z_i}, s \in S$, where $y_{s,i}$ indicates the total number of observed substitutions s at position i and z_i represents the total coverage at position i. At any position the number of substitutions can be regarded as a independent binomially distributed random variables $y_{s,i} \sim Bin(z_i, x_{s,i})$ parametrized by sample size z_i and probability

$x_{s,i}$. Consequently, $\hat{x}_{s,i}$ represents the maximum likelihood estimate (MLE) of $x_{s,i}$. Since the variance of the MLE is a function of the coverage it was required that $z_i \geq c$, where $c = 20$ was chosen in this study, as regions of low coverage will give rise to MLE with high variance. Considering all genomic positions exhibiting a particular substitution, the parameter x_s will be distributed according to some probability density function (PDF) p_s, $x_s \sim p_s$. Therefore, p_s can be expressed as mixture of two components $p_s(x) = \lambda_{s,1}p_{s,1}(x) + \lambda_{s,2}p_{s,2}(x)$, subject to $\lambda_{s,k} \geq 0$ and $\sum_k \lambda_{s,k} = 1$. Here, the first component accounts for non-experimentally induced substitutions, whereas the second component models experimentally induced substitutions. The estimation of the PDFs is carried out following a Bayesian approach that uses a beta prior.

Binding sites identified by PAR-CLIP appear as narrow regions exhibiting jump discontinuities and often localize within broader regions of non-zero coverage. Geometric properties of the coverage function at binding sites can be used for two purposes: (i) proximal binding sites can be resolved and regions exhibiting low signal-to-noise ratio can be excluded, referred to as peak calling and (ii) the coverage function at high confidence interaction sites can be utilized to determine cluster boundaries. Peak calling is performed within the time-scale domain using the continuous wavelet transform (CWT) of the coverage function. Time corresponds to the reference genome position. Prior to peak calling, ridges are identified as local maxima of CWT coefficients connected across scale dimension. The set of all ridges constitutes the branches of a tree, employed for peak detection, i.e. branches are pruned starting from small scales until a specified signal-to-noise ratio is exceeded. The time coordinate corresponding to the scale coordinate closest to zero is returned as peak location.

PIPE-CLIP

The aim of PIPE-CLIP [5] is to provide a public web-based resource to process and analyze CLIP-seq data. It provides a unified pipeline for PAR-CLIP, HITS-CLIP and iCLIP, with the following features: (1) user-specified parameters for customized analysis; (2) statistical methods to reduce the number of false positive cross-linking sites; (3) statistical significance levels for each binding site to facilitate planning of future experimental follow-ups; and (4) a user-friendly interface and reproducibility features.

To identify enriched peaks, the adjacent mapped reads are clustered together if they overlap each other by at least one nucleotide. The clusters are used for further analysis. Let r_i denote the total number of reads within the ith cluster of length s_i. Longer clusters tend to have greater read counts, so the variable s_i needs to be used to adjust the length effect on modeling r_i. Given that all clusters receive at least one read, PIPE-CLIP proposes a model based on the zero-truncated negative binomial (ZTNB) likelihood. We assume the ZTNB regression of r on s with mean μ_s and dispersion θ_s^{-1}. The length effect is incorporated into the model by link functions for μ_s and θ_s as follows: $\log \mu_s = \alpha + \log f(s)$ and $\log \theta_s = \beta + \log f(s)$ where $f(s)$ is used as an explanatory variable that represents the functional dependence of the read count on the cluster length. This model allows us to test whether a cluster is significantly enriched by reads, while adjusting the span of the cluster. For clusters of length s_i and read count r_i, the P-value is defined as the probability of observing read counts $\geq r_i$. That is, the P-value $= P(r \geq r_i | s = s_i)$. For the model inference, first we estimate $f(s)$ using the local liner regression of r on s. Then, the estimate $\hat{f}(s)$ is plugged into the ZTNB regression as a predictor. To obtain maximum likelihood estimates (MLEs) of α and β, the conditional maximization method is implemented along with the Fisher's scoring method for α and the Newton-Raphson method for β. False discovery rates are calculated using the Benjamin- Hochberg procedure [2].

4   BIOTHINGS

We propose a Python tool that enables the seamlessly construction of PAR-CLIP sequence treatment pipelines. The first version of this tool has been published in zenodo [11] and development continues in github. Figure 2 shows the general procedure for the creation of the pipeline, which starts creating an empty process graph, to which new elements are added. If the compilation of the entire pipeline is correct the user may proceed to pipeline execution. If it is not correct, the user needs to come back to pipeline definition. The process of adding new modules to the pipeline is illustrated in Fig. 3, where some natural order of insertion is recommended (yellow line) preserving the order explained in Fig. 1, i.e. preprocessing followed by mapping followed by peak calling. Some comparison modules can be also included that allow the quantitative comparison between approaches. Finally, Fig. 4 shows an example pipeline produced with BIOTHINGS. There a preprocessing step uses cutadapt, the mapping process uses bowtie, and there are three alternative peack calling algorithms (Bmix, WavclusteR, and Paralyzer) to be tested and compared by the final two modules that measure the differences in hits.

MAIN FUNCTIONALITY

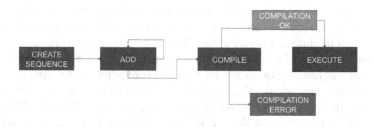

Fig. 2. General processing steps for the construction of a pipeline

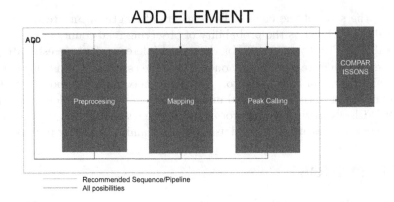

Fig. 3. Adding new modules to the pipeline

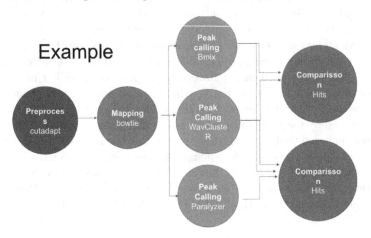

Fig. 4. Example pipeline

5   Conclusions

Bioinformatics pipeline creation is a tricky process. We propose a tool that helps to put together the diverse pieces ensuring the seamlessly integration into a working pipeline. The code has been published in its early stage [11]. Besides, we have revised the definition of four approaches to peak calling in PAR-CLIP data. Each of these approaches propose a model for the probability of the matching reads to the reference genomic data taking into account the number of substitutions, and specifically the $T => C$ substitutions, which are induced by the PAR-CLIP protocol. The comparison of these peak callling processes is a good example of the usefulness of the proposed tool.

Acknowledgments. This work has been partially supported by FEDER funds through MINECO project TIN2017-85827-P.

References

1. Althammer, S., González-Vallinas, J., Ballaré, C., Beato, M., Eyras, E.: Pyicos: a versatile toolkit for the analysis of high-throughput sequencing data. Bioinformatics **27**(24), 3333–3340 (2011)
2. Benjamini, Y., Hochberg, Y.: Controlling the false discovery rate: a practical and powerful approach to multiple testing. J. Roy. Stat. Soc. Ser. B (Methodol.) **57**(1), 289–300 (1995)
3. Bolger, A.M., Lohse, M., Usadel, B.: Trimmomatic: a flexible trimmer for illumina sequence data. Bioinformatics **30**(15), 2114–2120 (2014)
4. Bottini, S., Pratella, D., Grandjean, V., Repetto, E., Trabucchi, M.: Recent computational developments on CLIP-seq data analysis and microRNA targeting implications. Briefings Bioinf. **19**(6), 1290–1301 (2017)
5. Chen, B., Yun, J., Kim, M.S., Mendell, J.T., Xie, Y.: PIPE-CLIP: a comprehensive online tool for CLIP-seq data analysis. Genome Biol. **15**, R18 (2014)
6. Chen, C., Khaleel, S.S., Huang, H., Cathy, H.W.: Software for pre-processing illumina next-generation sequencing short read sequences. Source Code Biol. Med. **9**(1), 8 (2014)
7. Comoglio, F., Sievers, C., Paro, R.: Sensitive and highly resolved identification of RNA-protein interaction sites in PAR-CLIP data. BMC Bioinf. **16**, 32 (2015)
8. Corcoran, D.L., et al.: PARalyzer: definition of RNA binding sites from PAR-CLIP short-read sequence data. Genome Biol. **12**, R79 (2011)
9. Dobin, A., et al.: STAR: ultrafast universal RNA-seq aligner. Bioinformatics **29**(1), 15–21 (2013)
10. Echaniz, O., Graña, M.: A comparison of par-clip peak calling approaches on noisy data. In: 2018 IEEE International Conference on Bioinformatics and Biomedicine (BIBM), pp. 2017–2023, December 2018
11. Echaniz, O., Graña, M.: BIOTHINGS: a tool to create safe and sound bioinformatics pipelines, February 2019. https://doi.org/10.5281/zenodo.2580383
12. Erhard, F., Dölken, L., Jaskiewicz, L., Zimmer, R.: PARma: identification of microRNA target sites in AGO-PAR-CLIP data. Genome Biol. **14**, R79 (2013)
13. Garzia, A., Morozov, P., Sajek, M., Meyer, C., Tuschl, T.: PAR-CLIP for discovering target sites of RNA-binding proteins. In: Lamandé, S.R. (ed.) mRNA Decay. MMB, vol. 1720, pp. 55–75. Springer, New York (2018). https://doi.org/10.1007/978-1-4939-7540-2_5
14. Golumbeanu, M., Mohammadi, P., Beerenwinkel, N.: BMix: probabilistic modeling of occurring substitutions in PAR-CLIP data. Bioinformatics **32**(7), 976–983 (2016)
15. Charles, G.E., Bailey, T.L., Noble, W.S.: FIMO: scanning for occurrences of a given motif. Bioinformatics **27**(7), 1017–1018 (2011)
16. Hafner, M., et al.: Transcriptome-wide identification of RNA-binding protein and microRNA target sites by PAR-CLIP. Cell **141**(1), 129–141 (2010)
17. Langmead, B., Trapnell, C., Pop, M., Salzberg, S.L.: Ultrafast and memory-efficient alignment of short DNA sequences to the human genome. Genome Biol. **10**(3), R25 (2009)
18. Sievers, C., Schlumpf, T., Sawarkar, R., Comoglio, F., Paro, R.: Mixture models and wavelet transforms reveal high confidence RNA-protein interaction sites in MOV10 PAR-CLIP data. Nucleic Acids Res. **40**(20), e160 (2012)
19. Sims, D., Sudbery, I., Ilott, N.E., Heger, A., Ponting, C.P.: Sequencing depth and coverage: key considerations in genomic analyses. Nat. Rev. Genet. **15**, 121 (2014)

20. Smith, A.D., et al.: Updates to the RMAP short-read mapping software. Bioinformatics **25**(21), 2841–2842 (2009)
21. Webb, S., Hector, R.D., Kudla, G., Granneman, S.: PAR-CLIP data indicate that Nrd1-Nab3-dependent transcription termination regulates expression of hundreds of protein coding genes in yeast. Genome Biol. **15**, R8 (2014)

Machine Learning in Neuroscience

Automating Autoencoder Architecture Configuration: An Evolutionary Approach

Francisco Charte[(✉)] [iD], Antonio J. Rivera [iD], Francisco Martínez [iD], and María J. del Jesus [iD]

Andalusian Research Institute in Data Science and Computational Intelligence, Computer Science Department, Universidad de Jaén, Campus Las Lagunillas, s/n, 23071 Jaén, Spain
{fcharte,arivera,fmartin,mjjesus}@ujaen.es

Abstract. Learning from existing data allows building models able to classify patterns, infer association rules, predict future values in time series and much more. Choosing the right features is a vital step of the learning process, specially while dealing with high-dimensional spaces. Autoencoders (AEs) have shown ability to conduct manifold learning, compressing the original feature space without losing useful information. However, there is no optimal AE architecture for all datasets. In this paper we show how to use evolutionary approaches to automate AE architecture configuration. First, a coding to embed the AE configuration in a chromosome is proposed. Then, two evolutionary alternatives are compared against exhaustive search. The results show the great superiority of the evolutionary way.

Keywords: Deep learning · Autoencoder · Optimization · Evolutionary

1 Introduction

The performance of many machine learning methods mostly depends on the quality of the data patterns. Hence the prevalence of feature engineering (FE) [7] techniques in late years. Feeding the training model with good features greatly improves its predictive ability. This is specially important with high-dimensional and other nonstandard problems [4]. The subset of features can be picked up from the original set of attributes through feature selection [10] procedures. A new reduced set of features holding more information can also be obtained [11], e.g. relying on algorithms such as *Principal Component Analysis* (PCA) [13].

Representation learning [2] is an inherent capability of numerous artificial neural networks (ANNs). Many of them generate this representation as an intermediate step in the full learning process, such is the case of two Deep Learning (DL) models, *Convolutional Neural Networks* and *Deep Belief Networks*. There

This work is supported by the Spanish National Research Project TIN2015-68454-R.

J. M. Ferrández Vicente et al. (Eds.): IWINAC 2019, LNCS 11486, pp. 339–349, 2019.
https://doi.org/10.1007/978-3-030-19591-5_35

are a plethora of DL applications in the neuroscience field, and the high dimensionality problem is usually present in them [17].

In this context *Autoencoders* (AEs) [5] are an interesting tool, since they are mostly devoted to learn new data representations. AEs work in unsupervised fashion, trying to reconstruct the input into the output the best they can while preserving certain restrictions in the coding (hidden) layer. The benefits of AEs compared to classic alternatives such as PCA, specifically in brain disease diagnosis, have been also demonstrated [15].

As usually happens with most ANNs, adjusting the architecture of an AE is not an easy work. There are too many options to perform an exhaustive search of parameters. Therefore, the design frequently is entrusted to the experience of the practitioner or researcher. However, there is no a best AE architecture to all cases as the traits of the data to be processed vary.

Our proposal is to lean on evolutionary approaches (EAs) [1], that usually provide good results in many optimization problems, to design the best AE for every specific data. The main contributions of this paper are the introduction of an scheme to represent the AE architecture as a chromosome and the conducted experiments. These demonstrate that evolutionary methods are able to find good AE configurations in acceptable time.

The rest of this paper is structured as follows. Basic concepts related to FE, AEs and EAs are provided in Sect. 2. Section 3 describes the proposal, detailing the chromosome codification, the EAs to be used and their configuration. The conducted experimentation and its results are covered in Sect. 4. Some final thoughts in Sect. 5 close this work.

2   Preliminaries

This section provides a concise introduction to a few essential concepts, including how FE has been faced until now, what AEs are and the foundations of EAs. Some basic references useful for further study in these fields are supplied.

2.1   Feature Engineering

Feature engineering is a manual or automated task aimed to obtain a set of features better than the original one. Feature selection [10] consists in choosing a subset of attributes while maintaining most useful information in the data. It can be manually performed by an expert in the field, but mostly is faced with automated methods based on feature correlation [12] and mutual information [16]. By contrast, feature extraction methods transform the original data features to produce a new, usually reduced, set of attributes. Popular algorithms to do this are PCA and LDA, whose mathematical foundations are relatively easy to understand.

More advanced studies work with the hypothesis that the distribution of variables in the original data lies along a lower-dimensional space, usually known as *manifold*. A manifold space works with the parameters that produce the data points in the original high-dimensional space. Finding this embedded space is the task of manifold learning [3] algorithms. Unlike PCA or LDA, manifold methods apply non-linear transformations, so they fall into the non-linear dimensionality reduction [14] category.

2.2 Autoencoders

Autoencoders, as detailed in [5], are ANNs having a symmetric architecture, as shown in Fig. 1. The input and output layers have as many units as features there are in the data. Inner layers usually have fewer units, so that a more compact representation of the information hold in the data is produced. The goal is to reconstruct the input patterns into the output as faithfully as possible.

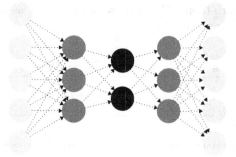

Fig. 1. Classic architecture for an AE. Black nodes denote a 2-variable encoding layer.

Although AEs have many practical applications, the most common one is to perform feature fusion [5], searching the manifold in which the parameters to rebuild the data are found. AEs can be configured with a variable amount of inner layers, each of them having different lengths. The proper architecture will mostly depend on the complexity of the patterns to be reconstructed and the restrictions imposed by the codification layer.

2.3 Evolutionary Optimization

Finding the best parameters to tune a machine learning model is an uphill battle. Performing a grid search through an internal validation process is an usual approach. However, it is useful only for limited sets of parameters taking known ranges of values. Evolutionary algorithms [8] have been used to optimize hyperparameters for many years, for instance for support vector machines [9] and more recently for deep learning networks [18].

Even though EAs have been also used to optimize ANNs, and even AEs, most of the proposals have been focused on learning the weights linked to each connection. By contrast, the proposal described in the following section is based on EAs to evolve the AE architecture, while weights are learned through the usual back-propagation algorithm.

3 Learning AE Configuration Through Evolution

Next, the approach used to code an AE configuration in a chromosome and the evolutionary methods used to search good configurations are described.

3.1 Coding AE Structure in a Chromosome

Evolutionary algorithms usually work with binary or real-valued genes. A set of genes builds a chromosome or individual of the population. In our case each chromosome will code the configuration of an AE. However, an integer gene representation is used rather than binary or real-valued genes.

The chromosome will be made up of 14 genes, as shown in Fig. 2. The number of each gene is shown above, their names inside and just below the range of values that can be assigned to them. The purpose of each gene, as well as the meaning of its values, are portrayed in Table 1.

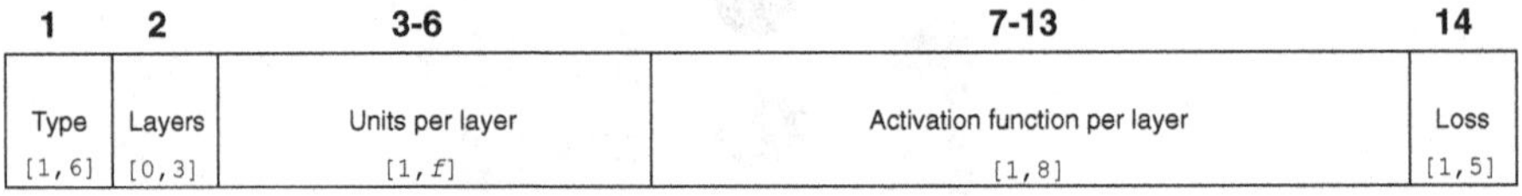

1	2	3-6	7-13	14
Type	Layers	Units per layer	Activation function per layer	Loss
[1,6]	[0,3]	[1,f]	[1,8]	[1,5]

Fig. 2. Chromosome genes, name and interval of values they can get.

Table 1. Purpose of each gene and description of their values.

Name	Purpose	Values
Type	Sets the type of AE to be used	(1) Basic, (2) Denoising, (3) Contractive, (4) Robust, (5) Sparse, (6) Variational
Layers	Number of additional layers in coder/decoder	(0) Only a coding layer, (1–3) Additional layers in both coder and decoder
Units	Set the number of units per layer, with f being the amount of features in the dataset	The first integer (gen 3) configures the number of units in the outer layer, while the last one (gen 6) sets the coding length
Activ.	Activation function to use in each layer, both for the coder and decoder	(1) linear, (2) sigmoid, (3) tanh, (4) relu, (5) selu, (6) elu, (7) softplus, (8) softsign
Loss	Loss function to evaluate during fitting	(1) Mean squared error, (2) Mean absolute error, (3) Mean absolute percentage error, (4) Binary crossentropy, (5) Cosine proximity

As can be easily seen, the search space is huge. Excluding genes 3–6, whose values would vary depending on the number of features in the dataset, there are more than 250 million combinations: $Type \times Layers \times Activation^7 \times Loss$. For small datasets having only a few dozens of attributes, this number will grow to several billions, reaching the trillions of solutions or even more for high-dimensional datasets. Evaluating all those solutions to find the best one is currently unfeasible. Therefore, searching the optimal AE configuration will be not always possible by brute force. However, we could find good enough solutions through optimization mechanisms based on evolution strategies.

3.2 Evolutionary Approaches

We propose two different evolutionary ways of attacking the outlined problem. Both of them will use the former chromosome representation. These two approaches are:

- **Genetic algorithm (GA).** A classical genetic algorithm, in which a population of individuals evolves through a crossover operator, to give rise to new ones, and to which a mutation operator is applied with a certain probability.
- **Evolution strategy (ES).** An aggressive solution-seeking procedure, working with a few individuals who give rise to new ones exclusively through mutation.

Table 2 summarizes the main parameters used to run these methods. Each gene in the chromosome is mutated with a probability of 1/15, value based on the chromosome length itself. Elitism is used in the GA to preserve the tenth percent of individuals having better fitness.

For the GA, crossover points have been established according to the diagram in Fig. 2. This allows the two individuals acting as parents to interchange several of their genes to produce childhood.

Table 2. Main parameters of the evolutionary algorithms.

Parameter	GA	ES
Population size	50	4
Iterations	100	500
Prob. mutation	1/15	1/15
Elitism (individuals)	5	NA
Termination cost	0	0

Regarding the fitness function that will decide the quality of the solutions, it will be computed as shown in (1), where *trainloss* is the reconstruction loss produced by the AE with training data, *Layers* is the number of additional hidden layers (gen 2), *Unitscode* is the size of the codification layer (gen 6), and α is a coefficient setting the level of penalization applied according to the complexity of the AE.

$$fitness = trainloss + \alpha(Layers \times Unitscode) \qquad (1)$$

4   Experiments

In order to test the ability of evolutionary algorithms to find good solutions in a reasonable time, two experiments have been carried out. The first one is a small-scale experiment with the `sonar` dataset, while the second is a large-scale one using the well-known `MNIST` dataset. Exactly the same hardware[1] and software[2] configuration has been used in both cases. The high-level interface provided by the `ruta` [6] package has been used to configure the AEs. The penalization factor has been set as $\alpha = 1 \times 10^{-4}$, so that simpler architectures are preferred over complex ones for AEs with similar performance.

Three runs are made for each experiment. One will use the GA to look up for a solution, other will rely on the ES approach, and the last one will try an exhaustive search. In the latter case the experiment is run for 24 hours, since it is impossible to evaluate all existing configurations. Publicly available training/test partitions were used.

4.1   Small-Scale Case Study

As it happens with all neural networks having several layers, adjusting AE parameters through training is a time consuming process. The more units there are in these layers the longer it will take. Because of this our first experiment is small-scale with the `sonar` dataset, having only 60 input features. This will be the number of units in the input and output layers, as well as it would be the maximum amount of units in the hidden layers. The goal is to obtain a lower-dimensional codification preserving enough information to reconstruct the original data.

Having at most 60 units per layer implies that there will be 3.26×10^{15} possible AE configurations. Assuming we were able to evaluate one AE per millisecond in a machine running 24/7, we would need $> 100\,000$ years to find the optimal solution.

The plots in Fig. 3 give a clear glimpse of each algorithm behavior. The top row shows the quality[3] (Y axis) of evaluated solutions by each approach through the running time (X axis). The GA tests some bad solutions at the beginning (left), but it quickly focuses on the better ones. ES only uses mutation and it produces some bad solutions from time to time, but most of them are quite good. By contrast, the exhaustive search is not guided by any strategy, so quite heterogeneous results are obtained.

---

[1] 1 PC, CPU Core i5, 16 GB RAM, GPU Nvidia RTX-2080.

[2] GNU/Linux, Tensorflow and Keras.

[3] Measured by the reconstruction mean squared error expressed as percentage.

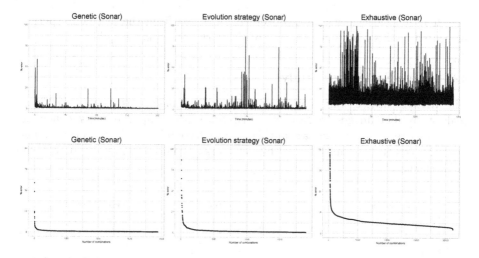

Fig. 3. Analysis of results from the Sonar dataset.

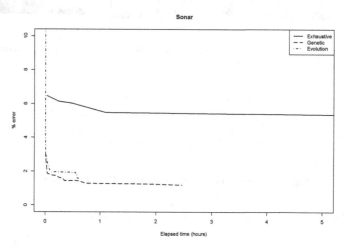

Fig. 4. Comparative convergence of three approaches on the Sonar dataset.

The bottom row in Fig. 3 shows the same data but with all tested configurations sorted by committed error. As can be seen, both the GA and the ES have most of the configurations close to the baseline of the Y axis (% error), while the exhaustive search is not able to reach this point.

In addition to the quality of the solutions, it is also interesting to know how quickly each method converges to the best solution they are able to find. This is represented in Fig. 4. It can be noted that ES is the first method to complete its work. It is quite fast at the beginning, mutating the initial bad solutions into others much better. The GA takes a little more time and it is able to find solutions a little more precise than the ES. The convergence of the exhaustive search is too slow, and the improvement achieved from the 5th hour (period presented in this plot) until the end of the 24th hour was negligible.

4.2 Large-Scale Case Study

The MNIST dataset, containing handwritten digit images, was used for the large-scale study. The images are 28×28 pixels, so it has 784 input features. Following the former reasoning for `sonar`, in this case we have 9.51×10^{19} potential configurations. It will take more than 3 billion years of computation time to evaluate all of them.

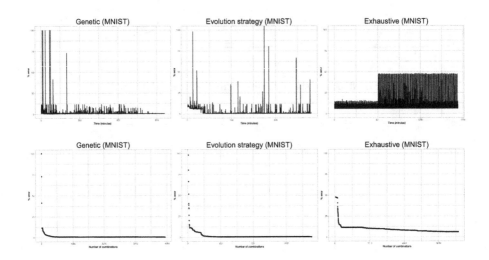

Fig. 5. Analysis of results from the MNIST dataset.

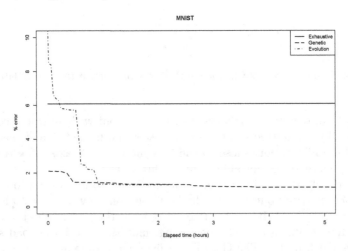

Fig. 6. Comparative convergence of three approaches on the MNIST dataset.

Solutions tested through time and all solutions sorted by quality have been represented in Fig. 5. Once again, the GA forgets bad solutions faster than the ES does. Moreover, it seems that the ES takes longer to reach the same baseline than the GA. The exhaustive approach, with its non-guided search, explores lots of bad solutions through time.

The convergence plot for this dataset (see Fig. 6) is quite similar to that of sonar. Once again, the ES quickly reduces the error and it achieves better solutions than the GA in less time. The GA spends more time, and eventually it seems to reach the same performance as the ES but several hours later. As it would be expected after analyzing its behavior in Fig. 5, the exhaustive search almost stalled in the same error level for all the running time.

4.3   Summary of Results

The exact running time, number of evaluated configurations and error percentage for the best one are provided in Table 3. From the analysis of these results the following consequences can be drawn:

- The non-guided exhaustive search evaluates a larger amount of AE configurations, but it is not able to reach the reconstruction performance level of GA and ES.
- GA and ES almost achieve the same error levels. The GA returned a slightly better configuration for sonar, while the ES found the best one for MNIST.
- Although it starts with worse solutions than the GA, the ES takes less time to hit at the same level.

Table 3. Summary of results.

	Approach	Running time	Configurations	Error (%)
Sonar	Exhaustive	24 h	21 262	7.093
	Genetic algorithm	3 h 21 m	4 505	1.180
	Evolution strategy	1 h 16 m	4 001	1.553
MNIST	Exhaustive	24 h	7 153	6.084
	Genetic algorithm	10 h 39 m	4 505	0.607
	Evolution strategy	4 h 40 m	4 001	0.560

Overall, if we are willing to sacrifice a minimal performance advantage in some cases, the ES seems the best approach to find a good AE configuration for any dataset, even in cases as MNIST with hundreds of features and several dozens of thousands of instances.

5 Final Thoughts

AEs are a useful tool to perform manifold learning, but setting the most appropriate AE architecture for every case is a difficult task. Internal cross-validation is an usual approach for tuning hyper-parameters. However, when the structure of the AE has to be adjusted the search space is huge. Therefore, more powerful ways of facing this problem are needed.

In this paper we propose the use of EAs to find the best AE architecture for each dataset. This may not be the optimal, but it is the best that can be found in a reasonable time. The conducted experiments demonstrate that ES and GA are competitive methods to accomplish the job.

References

1. Bäck, T., Schwefel, H.P.: An overview of evolutionary algorithms for parameter optimization. Evol. Comput. **1**, 1–23 (1993)
2. Bengio, Y., Courville, A., Vincent, P.: Representation learning: a review and new perspectives. IEEE Trans. Pattern Anal. Mach. Intell. **35**(8), 1798–1828 (2013)
3. Cayton, L.: Algorithms for manifold learning. Technical report, University of California at San Diego (2005)
4. Charte, D., Charte, F., García, S., Herrera, F.: A snapshot on nonstandard supervised learning problems: taxonomy, relationships, problem transformations and algorithm adaptations. Prog. Artif. Intell. **8**(1), 1–14 (2018). https://doi.org/10.1007/s13748-018-00167-7
5. Charte, D., Charte, F., García, S., del Jesus, M.J., Herrera, F.: A practical tutorial on autoencoders for nonlinear feature fusion: taxonomy, models, software and guidelines. Inf. Fusion **44**, 78–96 (2018)
6. Charte, D., Herrera, F., Charte, F.: Ruta: implementations of neural autoencoders in R. Knowl.-Based Syst. **174**, 4–8 (2019, in press). https://doi.org/10.1016/j.knosys.2019.01.014
7. Domingos, P.: A few useful things to know about machine learning. Commun. ACM **55**(10), 78–87 (2012)
8. Freitas, A.A.: A review of evolutionary algorithms for data mining. In: Maimon, O., Rokach, L. (eds.) Data Mining and Knowledge Discovery Handbook, pp. 371–400. Springer, Boston (2009). https://doi.org/10.1007/978-0-387-09823-4_19
9. Friedrichs, F., Igel, C.: Evolutionary tuning of multiple svm parameters. Neurocomputing **64**, 107–117 (2005)
10. García, S., Luengo, J., Herrera, F.: Data Preprocessing in Data Mining. Springer, Cham (2015). https://doi.org/10.1007/978-3-319-10247-4
11. Guyon, I., Elisseeff, A.: An introduction to feature extraction. In: Guyon, I., Nikravesh, M., Gunn, S., Zadeh, L.A. (eds.) Feature Extraction, pp. 1–25. Springer, Heidelberg (2006). https://doi.org/10.1007/978-3-540-35488-8_1
12. Hall, M.A.: Correlation-based feature selection for machine learning. Ph.D. thesis, University of Waikato Hamilton (1999)
13. Hotelling, H.: Analysis of a complex of statistical variables into principal components. J. Educ. Psychol. **24**(6), 417 (1933)
14. Lee, J.A., Verleysen, M.: Nonlinear Dimensionality Reduction. Springer, New York (2007). https://doi.org/10.1007/978-0-387-39351-3

15. Martinez-Murcia, F.J., et al.: Deep convolutional autoencoders vs PCA in a highly-unbalanced Parkinson's disease dataset: a DaTSCAN study. In: Graña, M., et al. (eds.) SOCO'18-CISIS'18-ICEUTE'18 2018. AISC, vol. 771, pp. 47–56. Springer, Cham (2019). https://doi.org/10.1007/978-3-319-94120-2_5

16. Peng, H., Long, F., Ding, C.H.Q.: Feature selection based on mutual information criteria of max-dependency, max-relevance, and min-redundancy. IEEE Trans. Pattern Anal. Mach. Intell. **27**, 1226–1238 (2005)

17. Segovia, F., Górriz, J., Ramírez, J., Martinez-Murcia, F., García-Pérez, M.: Using deep neural networks along with dimensionality reduction techniques to assist the diagnosis of neurodegenerative disorders. Logic J. IGPL **26**(6), 618–628 (2018)

18. Young, S.R., Rose, D.C., Karnowski, T.P., Lim, S.H., Patton, R.M.: Optimizing deep learning hyper-parameters through an evolutionary algorithm. In: Proceedings of the Workshop on Machine Learning in High-Performance Computing Environments, p. 4. ACM (2015)

Periodogram Connectivity of EEG Signals for the Detection of Dyslexia

F. J. Martinez-Murcia[1]([✉])([iD]), A. Ortiz[1], R. Morales-Ortega[4,5], P. J. López[2],
J. L. Luque[2], D. Castillo-Barnes[3], F. Segovia[3], I. A. Illan[3], J. Ortega[4],
J. Ramirez[3], and J. M. Gorriz[3]

[1] Department of Communications Engineering, University of Malaga, Málaga, Spain
fjmm@ic.uma.es
[2] Department of Developmental Psychology, University of Malaga, Málaga, Spain
[3] Department of Signal Theory, Networking and Communications,
University of Granada, Granada, Spain
[4] Department of Computer Architecture, University of Granada, Granada, Spain
[5] Department of Computer Science and Electronics, Universidad de la Costa CUC,
Barranquilla, Colombia

Abstract. Electroencephalography (EEG) signals provide an important source of information of brain activity at different areas. This information can be used to diagnose brain disorders according to different activation patterns found in controls and patients. This acquisition technology can be also used to explore the neural basis of less evident learning disabilities such as Developmental Dyslexia (DD). DD is a specific difficulty in the acquisition of reading skills not related to mental age or inadequate schooling, whose prevalent is estimated between 5% and 12% of the population. In this paper we propose a method to extract discriminative features from EEG signals based on the relationship among the spectral density at each channel. This relationship is computed by means of different correlation measures, inferring connectivity-like markers that are eventually selected and classified by a linear support vector machine. The experiments performed shown AUC values up to 0.7, demonstrating the applicability of the proposed approach for objective DD diagnosis.

Keywords: Periodogram · EEG · Connectivity ·
Principal Component Analysis · Dyslexia

1 Introduction

Developmental dyslexia (DD) is a learning disability, specifically related to the acquisition of reading skills. Its prevalence is estimated between 5% and 12% of the population [11], with an important social impact. Furthermore, it may determine school failure. Usually, DD is diagnosed using specifically designed tests to measure different behavioural variables involved in the reading process. Nevertheless, the results of the tests depend on the motivation and the mood of the

© Springer Nature Switzerland AG 2019
J. M. Ferrández Vicente et al. (Eds.): IWINAC 2019, LNCS 11486, pp. 350–359, 2019.
https://doi.org/10.1007/978-3-030-19591-5_36

child when performing the benchmark tasks, which implies an important source of error in the final diagnosis. On the other hand, early diagnosis allows starting specific learning tasks to leverage the intellectual and personal development of the affected children [15]. This way, objective diagnosis methods, based on biological markers play a decisive role not only to improve the diagnosis accuracy but also in the best knowledge of the biological basis of DD.

Recent models of neuronal speech coding suggest that dyslexia originates from the atypical dominant neuronal entrainment in the right hemisphere to the slow-rhythmic prosodic (delta band, 0.5–1 Hz), syllabic (theta band, 4–8 Hz) or the phoneme (gamma band, 12–40 Hz), speech modulations, which are defined by the time of increase in amplitude (i.e., the envelope) generated by the speech rhythm [2,3]. Thus, we compared the cortical entrainment to a modulated white-noise at a fixed rate in the delta (2 Hz). In a sample composed of 7 years old children, listened to stimuli obtained by rhythmically modulating the amplitude (AM) of white-noise sound either in the delta, theta and gamma band.

Machine learning, e.g. classification models, has been extensively for signal processing [4]. In EEG, the classification of spectral power features is widely documented [1,17]. In this regard, functional connectivity could reveal new patterns in the EEG spectrum. Functional connectivity analysis was originally applied in neuroimaging [10] and progressive extended to other fields such as EEG [6,12,13]. It revealed that the co-variances between the signals acquired at each region of the brain (e.g., EEG or the BOLD activation in fMRI) were indicative of the underlying neural circuitry, supporting the modelling of the brain as a network.

In this proposal we assume that the connectivity of the spectral density estimation acquired at each electrode under a 2 Hz auditory stimulation could be indicative of differences in the brain function of children affected with dyslexia and those not affected at all. To do so, we built a system composed of a spectral estimator (via a modified Welch's method), the computation of several connectivity measures (that is, correlation, covariance and precision -also known as inverse covariance-) and a further reduction of the features by using Principal Component Analysis (PCA). These last features are then analysed and classified using a Support Vector Classifier (SVC).

2   Materials and Methods

2.1   EEG Dataset

The present experiment was carried out with the understanding and written consent of each child's legal guardian and in the presence thereof. Forty-eight participants took part in the present study, including 32 skilled readers (17 males) and 16 dyslexic readers (7 males) matched in age ($t = -1.4, p > 0.05$). The mean age of the control group was $94, 1 \pm 3.3$ months, and $95, 6 \pm 2.9$ months for the dyslexic group. All participants were right-handed Spanish native speakers with no hearing impairments and normal or corrected-to-normal vision. Dyslexic children in this study had all received a formal diagnosis of dyslexia in the school. None of the skilled readers reported reading or spelling difficulties or had received a previous formal diagnosis of dyslexia.

In this work, we only used data from children listening to AM white-noise at a fixed rate in the delta/prosodic (2 Hz) band. We proceeded with the elimination of ocular and non-ocular artifacts, and a number of 5-sec segments were obtained for each subject. Neither averaging nor grand averaging was used.

2.2   Spectral Estimation

In order to estimate the spectral density of each subject's signals, we applied a modification of the Welch's method [16], a robust estimator which improves the standard periodogram by reducing the noise, but at the cost of reducing the spectral resolution.

In the original method, the signal is divided into different overlapping segments. Then, a modified periodogram is computed for each windowed segment, and the resulting periodograms are averaged. Here, we computed the modified periodogram over each subject's 5-sec segment. Here, the 'Hanning' window is used, and then the average periodogram per subject is used as feature for computing the spectral connectivity in the following steps.

2.3   Connectivity Features

When assessing connectivity in neuroimaging or EEG [12,13], three measures appear consistently: correlation, covariance and precision. In this work, we use the Ledoit-Wolf shrunk covariance estimator [7] in order to compute all these three measures. The shrinkage overcomes some of the pitfalls of empirical covariance estimators, which frequently fail at estimating the eigenvalues of the covariance matrix, resulting in problems to obtain the inverse covariance. The shrinkage can be defined mathematically as a simple convex transformation:

$$\Sigma_S = (1 - \delta)\mathbf{S} + \delta\mathbf{F} \tag{1}$$

in which the Σ_S is the shrunk covariance, δ is the amount of shrinkage (controlling a bias-variance trade-off), $\mathbf{S}$ is the sample covariance. $\mathbf{F}$ is a highly structured estimator whose diagonal elements f_{ii} are the same as those of $\mathbf{S}$, $f_{ii} = s_{ii}$ and the rest are defined as $fij = \bar{r}\sqrt{s_{ii}s_{jj}}$, where $\bar{r}$ is:

$$\bar{r} = \frac{2}{(N-1)N} \sum_{i=1}^{N-1} \sum_{j=i+1}^{N} \left(\frac{s_{ij}}{\sqrt{s_{ii}s_{jj}}} \right) \tag{2}$$

Then, the shrinkage parameter δ is automatically selected using the Ledoit-Wolf formula [7].

The covariance Σ_S is directly estimated and the precision is defined as its inverse. Finally, the correlation $\mathbf{R}$ is obtained from the covariance matrix as:

$$\mathbf{R} = \Sigma_S \mathbf{d}\mathbf{d}' \quad where \quad \mathbf{d} = \frac{1}{\sqrt{diag(\Sigma_S)}} \tag{3}$$

2.4   Principal Component Analysis

Principal Component Analysis (PCA) is a well known technique for feature reduction in many studies [5,8]. It intuitively defines a new space in which each dimension (better known as component) explains the maximum variance in the data; the second will account for most of the remaining variance and so on. These components are meant to be uncorrelated, and the coordinates of a dataset in the new space can be computed as:

$$\mathbf{S} = \mathbf{X}\mathbf{W} \tag{4}$$

where $\mathbf{S}$ are the $K \times M$ set of new coordinates, $\mathbf{X}$ is the original data matrix (containing K samples of length N) and $\mathbf{W}$ is the basis of the new space, a $N \times M$ matrix whose columns contains the so-called 'principal components'. An efficient and popular way of computing the PCA is via the Singular Value Decomposition (SVD) of the data matrix $\mathbf{X}$.

The feature reduction is then achieved via a truncated reconstruction, in which the C first components (ranked by their eigenvalues) are retained, which generates a new set $\mathbf{S}_C$ of size $K \times C$ where C is small:

$$\mathbf{S}_C = \mathbf{X}\mathbf{W}_C \tag{5}$$

where $\mathbf{S}_C$ is a truncated estimate of the dataset in the PCA space, containing K samples of C features, and $\mathbf{W}_C$ contains only the C first columns of $\mathbf{W}$.

2.5   Experimental Setup and Evaluation

Two models will be tested in this work:

- A **baseline** model, in which we estimate the periodogram, and then the connectivity features, but they are directly fed to a linear Support Vector Classifier (SVC) [14].
- The **PCA+SVC** model, similar to the baseline, but in which PCA is applied to reduce the spectral feature vector and then, the reduced vector is used as input in the SVC.

In order to evaluate the ability of system in detecting dyslexia, we have used a leave-one-out cross-validation procedure. It estimates the generalization ability of the classifier by training the system with all but one of the feature vectors, and then estimates the class of the one remaining. It is important to note that in the PCA+SVC model, the whole PCA is estimated over the training set, not the whole dataset. By repeating this procedure for all subjects, we obtain the performance of the system.

We have used the following classification performance metrics: accuracy, sensitivity, specificity, balanced accuracy, precision and F1, all derived from the confusion matrix, and additionally, the area under the Receiver-Operating Characteristic (ROC) curve (AUC). To compare between different features, we have also plot the ROC curve at the operation point.

3   Results and Discussion

3.1   Classification Results

To evaluate the performance of our EEG-based dyslexia detection system, we have obtained several performance measures as stated in Sect. 2.5. The system combines spectral connectivity analysis in order to extract features from the EEG signals, and then performs PCA to reduce the feature space. Since the number of PCA components is key in this task, we have tested the performance of the model (via AUC) when varying the number of components C for each of the connectivity features.

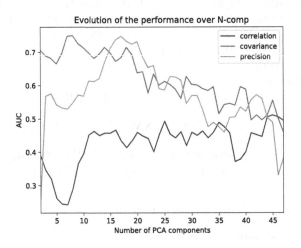

Fig. 1. Evolution of the performance when varying the number of components in the PCA decomposition.

In Fig. 1, we depict the evolution of the AUC when increasing the number of components C in the model. The three features vary in their behaviour. Covariance has a relatively large range of components in which the performance is relatively high (between 2 and 20 components), standing out clearly for 7 and 8. For its part, correlation only starts to increase performance after 13 components and then remaining stable, but small. Finally, precision achieves its best performance after 16, and substantially degrades after 20 or so.

Since the number of components is related to the variability of the dataset, the behaviour is coherent with what was expected. Correlation seems not to have significant information for dyslexia diagnosis, regardless of the number of components used. However, covariance and precision, both of which have been extensively used in connectome analyses, achieve large performance. Covariance needs much less components (8) to achieve a maximum, whereas precision needs some more, indicating that there is more variability in the precision than in the covariance matrices. In order to continue with the analysis we will use 45, 8 and 17 PCA components for correlation, covariance and precision respectively.

For this values we obtain the performance displayed at Table 1, where it is compared with the baseline system (as commented before, the same system with no PCA reduction).

Table 1. Performance of the baseline model compared to the PCA+SVC system.

Feature	C	AUC	CR	Sens.	Spec.	Prec.	F1	Bal-Acc
Correlation	-	0.494	0.520	0.318	0.679	0.497	0.388	0.498
Covariance	-	0.575	0.600	0.400	0.733	0.600	0.480	0.567
Precision	-	0.522	0.560	0.375	0.731	0.582	0.456	0.553
Correlation	45	0.511	0.580	0.333	0.686	0.515	0.405	0.510
Covariance	8	0.750	0.680	0.500	0.800	0.714	0.588	0.650
Precision	17	0.748	0.760	0.667	0.789	0.760	0.710	0.728

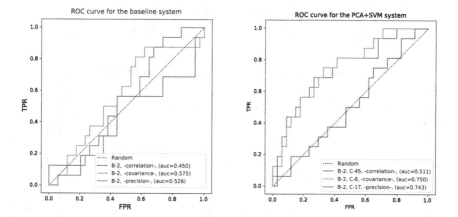

Fig. 2. Comparison of the performance of the three spectral connectivity features at the operation point (where B is the excitation band -2Hz- and C is the number of PCA components).

From the table we can infer that the introduction of the PCA model generally improves the performance of the system, but more substantially with the covariance and precision features. It particularly improves the sensitivity of all systems, which one of the main problems in an imbalanced dataset. The balanced accuracy (average of sensitivity and specificity) is therefore also higher. So we can conclude that summarizing the variability within the connectivity features has significant effects on the performance, especially in the case of correlation,

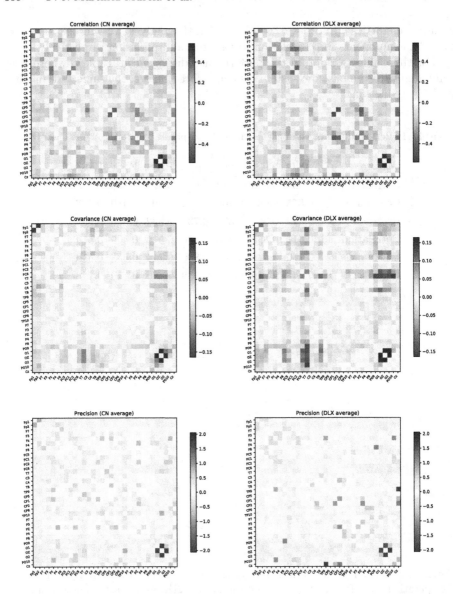

Fig. 3. Comparison of the average of the connectivity matrices per group and feature under the same scale.

when the feature reduction is large and the information is key. To obtain a more detailed view of this comparison, the ROC curves of these combinations (for the baseline and PCA+SVC model) are provided in Fig. 2.

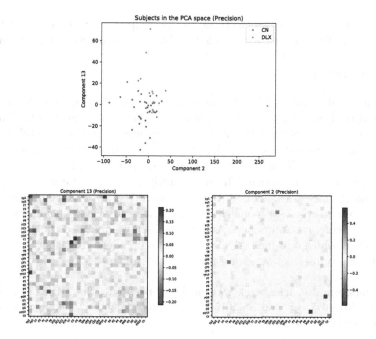

Fig. 4. Comparison of the average of the connectivity matrices per group and feature under the same scale.

3.2 Visual Analysis of the Differences

In order to provide a further understanding of the differences between classes, we have computed the average connectivity matrix per group for each of the spectral connectivity features. These are displayed at Fig. 3.

In that figure we observe what we already saw in the classification results. There are few differences between the average correlation matrices, which is consistent with the small classification performance of this feature. However, there are significant differences between the covariance matrices that can explain why these features lead to larger performance. In the case of the precision matrices, the differences are large but in very few places, mainly due to their sparsity.

Finally, to model the separability of the classes in the PCA space, we focus on the 'precision' matrices. Since they stand for the sparse inverse covariance in many cases, the variability in these matrices could account for relevant inter-relations between the spectral density of the different electrodes. Therefore, in Fig. 4 we display all subjects in the database in the PCA space. Note that only two components are visualized (of all 17 which were used), and they were selected by means of the separability, modelled via a Mann-Whitney-Wilcoxon U-Test [9].

In Fig. 4 we observe that subjects are well separated via components 2 and 13. Component 13 weights many links, and its analysis might be long. But component 2 provides the better separability, and highlights mainly two connections:

CP1 to Fz, that connects an electrode in the occipital lobe to the frontal lobe, and PO9 to PO10, which corresponds to a bilateral symmetric connection.

4   Conclusions

Electroencephalography (EEG) has been key to study many kinds of brain disorders and neurological diseases. In this work, we analyse a series of EEG signals in order to prove their ability in the differential diagnosis of Developmental Dyslexia (DD). To do so, we propose a method to extract a series of discriminative features from the raw EEG signals, based mainly on the spectral density computed at each channel of the device. The relationship between these measures, using correlation-like measures, allowed to extract a series of spectral connectivity features that could serve as a biomarker for DD. After further reducing the feature space using Principal Component Analysis (PCA), we analysed the performance of a classifier, which obtained AUC values up to 0.7, demonstrating the applicability of the proposed approach for objective DD diagnosis.

Acknowledgements. This work was partly supported by the MINECO/ FEDER under TEC2015-64718-R and PSI2015-65848-R projects and the Juan de la Cierva - Formación postdoctoral programme.

References

1. Acharya, U.R., Oh, S.L., Hagiwara, Y., Tan, J.H., Adeli, H.: Deep convolutional neural network for the automated detection and diagnosis of seizure using EEG signals. Comput. Biol. Med. (2017). https://doi.org/10.1016/j.compbiomed.2017.09.017
2. Di Liberto, G., Peter, V., Kalashnikova, M., Goswami, U., Burnham, D., Lalor, E.: Atypical cortical entrainment to speech in the right hemisphere underpins phonemic deficits in dyslexia. NeuroImage **175**, 70–79 (2018)
3. Flanagan, S., Goswami, U.: The role of phase synchronisation between low frequency amplitude modulations in child phonology and morphology speech tasks. J. Acoust. Soc. Am. **143**, 1366–1375 (2018). https://doi.org/10.1121/1.5026239
4. De la Hoz, E., de la Hoz, E., Ortiz, A., Ortega, J., Martínez-Álvarez, A.: Feature selection by multi-objective optimisation: application to network anomaly detection by hierarchical self-organising maps. Knowl.-Based Syst. **71**, 322–338 (2014)
5. Illán, I., et al.: 18F-FDG PET imaging analysis for computer aided Alzheimer's diagnosis. Inf. Sci. **181**(4), 903–916 (2011)
6. Lafuente, V., Gorriz, J.M., Ramirez, J., Gonzalez, E.: P300 brainwave extraction from EEG signals: an unsupervised approach. Expert Syst. Appl. **74**, 1–10 (2017). https://doi.org/10.1016/j.eswa.2016.12.038
7. Ledoit, O., Wolf, M.: A well-conditioned estimator for large-dimensional covariance matrices. J. Multivar. Anal. **88**(2), 365–411 (2004). https://doi.org/10.1016/s0047-259x(03)00096-4
8. Markiewicz, P., Matthews, J., Declerck, J., Herholz, K.: Robustness of multivariate image analysis assessed by resampling techniques and applied to FDG-PET scans of patients with Alzheimer's disease. Neuroimage **46**, 472–485 (2009). http://www.sciencedirect.com/science/article/B6WNP-4VFK7X3-3/2/e7833cb1d62f98e28326352e45981d00

9. Martínez-Murcia, F., Górriz, J., Ramírez, J., Puntonet, C., Salas-González, D.: Computer aided diagnosis tool for Alzheimer's disease based on Mann-Whitney-Wilcoxon U-test. Expert Syst. Appl. **39**(10), 9676–9685 (2012). https://doi.org/10.1016/j.eswa.2012.02.153

10. Ortiz, A., Munilla, J., Martínez-Murcia, F.J., Górriz, J.M., Ramírez, J.: Learning longitudinal MRI patterns by SICE and deep learning: assessing the Alzheimer's disease progression. In: Valdés Hernández, M., González-Castro, V. (eds.) MIUA 2017. CCIS, vol. 723, pp. 413–424. Springer, Cham (2017). https://doi.org/10.1007/978-3-319-60964-5_36

11. Peterson, R., Pennington, B.: Developmental dyslexia. Lancet **379**, 1997–2007 (2012)

12. Sakkalis, V.: Review of advanced techniques for the estimation of brain connectivity measured with EEG/MEG. Comput. Biol. Med. **41**(12), 1110–1117 (2011). https://doi.org/10.1016/j.compbiomed.2011.06.020

13. Schoffelen, J.M., Gross, J.: Source connectivity analysis with MEG and EEG. Hum. Brain Mapp. **30**(6), 1857–1865 (2009). https://doi.org/10.1002/hbm.20745

14. Stoeckel, J., Ayache, N., Malandain, G., Koulibaly, P.M., Ebmeier, K.P., Darcourt, J.: Automatic classification of SPECT images of Alzheimer's disease patients and control subjects. In: Barillot, C., Haynor, D.R., Hellier, P. (eds.) MICCAI 2004. LNCS, vol. 3217, pp. 654–662. Springer, Heidelberg (2004). https://doi.org/10.1007/978-3-540-30136-3_80

15. Thompson, P.A., Hulme, C., Nash, H.M., Gooch, D., Hayiou-Thomas, E., Snowling, M.J.: Developmental dyslexia: predicting individual risk. J. Child Psychol. Psychiatry **56**(9), 976–987 (2015)

16. Welch, P.: The use of fast fourier transform for the estimation of power spectra: a method based on time averaging over short, modified periodograms. IEEE Trans. Audio Electroacoust. **15**(2), 70–73 (1967). https://doi.org/10.1109/tau.1967.1161901

17. Zhou, S.M., Gan, J.Q., Sepulveda, F.: Classifying mental tasks based on features of higher-order statistics from EEG signals in brain-computer interface. Inf. Sci. **178**(6), 1629–1640 (2008). https://doi.org/10.1016/j.ins.2007.11.012

Isosurface Modelling of DatSCAN Images for Parkinson Disease Diagnosis

M. Martínez-Ibañez[1], A. Ortiz[1(✉)], J. Munilla[1], Diego Salas-Gonzalez[2], J. M. Górriz[2], and J. Ramírez[2]

[1] Communications Engineering Department,
University of Málaga, 29004 Málaga, Spain
`aortiz@ic.uma.es`
[2] Department of Signal Theory, Communications and Networking,
University of Granada, 18060 Granada, Spain

Abstract. This paper proposes the computing of isosurfaces as a way to extract relevant features from 3D brain images. These isosurfaces are then used to implement a Computer aided diagnosis system to assist in the diagnosis of Parkinson's Disease (PD) which uses a most well-known Convolutional Neural Networks (CNN) architecture, LeNet, to classify DaTScan images with an average accuracy of 95.1% and AUC = 97%, obtaining comparable (slightly better) values to those obtained for most of the recently proposed systems. It can be concluded therefore that the computation of isosurfaces reduces the complexity of the inputs significantly, resulting in high classification accuracies with reduced computational burden.

Keywords: Deep learning · Convolutional networks · Isosurfaces · Parkinson's Disease

1 Introduction

In recent years, different works have analyzed DaTSCAN (3D) images for early diagnosis of PD. Thus, a range of semi-quantification methods can be found in the literature [22]. These methods compute SBRs (Striatal Binding Ratios) from both, with and without consideration of the caudates, and use different methods and establish certain limits and likelihood of disease being present. The clinician must eventually interpret the results to come to an overall decision. At this point, machine learning algorithms can be used to help with such decision. Machine learning algorithms can combine multiple input variables describing different features to produce a single value that helps the clinician.

The development of novel architectures and effective training algorithms, has enabled to use multi-layer neural networks or deep neural networks (aka deep learning) for a wide range of applications, such as speech recognition, drug discovery and genomics, but it is in the field of computer vision and image classification where deep learning, and particularly convolutional neural networks (CNN),

© Springer Nature Switzerland AG 2019
J. M. Ferrández Vicente et al. (Eds.): IWINAC 2019, LNCS 11486, pp. 360–368, 2019.
https://doi.org/10.1007/978-3-030-19591-5_37

has undergone a real revolution of the state of the art. CNNs are biologically-inspired models that resemble the human vision system, computing image features at different abstraction levels by means of the convolution operator, which is subsequently applied to the response of the previous layer. Nowadays, these architectures have practically reached, or even surpassed, human-level performance in object recognition. Two of the most famous CNN architectures are LeNet-5 [7] and AlexNet [6]. They have been well-studied and provide good results compared to other machine learning algorithms and even more complex CNNs.

This work analyzes DaTSCAN (3D) images and identifies features which are suitable for use in a computer-aided classification system intended to classify between positive and negative cases of PD. In particular, this is realized through the identification of isosurfaces and the extraction of descriptive features from these by using CNN architectures based on LeNet-5 and AlexNet. Isosurfaces connect voxels that have the specified intensity or value much the way contour lines connect points of equal elevation. This work culminates in the implementation of a classification system which uses supervised learning through CNN architectures to classify DaTSCAN images with an average accuracy of 95.1%. Sensitivity and specificity of the system have been also calculated resulting at an average of 95.5% and 94.8% respectively.

The rest of the paper is structured as follows. Section 2 reviews related works. Section 3 shows details on the database used and the applied preprocessing. Then, Sect. 4 describes the computing of isosurfaces, the analyzed architectures and their training process. Section 5 presents and discusses the classification results, and finally, Sect. 6 draws the main conclusions.

2 Related Work

Two of the first works to analyze the possibilities of machine learning algorithms with DaTSCAN were Palumbo et al. in 2010 [17] and Towey et al. in 2011 [23]. The former compared a probabilistic neural network (PNN) with a classification tree (CIT) to differentiate between PD and essential tremor. Striatal binding ratios for caudate and putamina on 3 slices were used as image features. The latter used Naïve-Bayes with PCA decomposition of the voxels in the striatal region. These were followed for a series of works where SVMs were used as the main classifier tool, with linear or RBF kernel and different image features: [4,13] used voxel-as-features, [5,21] used Partial Least Square (PLS), [19] proposed the use of 2D empical mode decomposition and [9] decomposed the DaTSCAN images into statistically independent components which revealed patterns associated to PD. A more recent approach also based on multivariate decomposition techniques is proposed in [15], where the use of functional principal component analysis and fractal curves on 3D images is proposed. Striatal binding ratios for both caudates and putamina were used in [2,16,18]. [8] proposed the extraction of 3D textural-based features (Haralick texture features) for the characterization of the dopamine transporters concentration in the image.

And finishing with those based on SVM, [1] used univariate (voxel-wise) statistical parametric mapping and multivariate pattern recognition using linear discriminant classifiers to differentiate among different Parkinsonian syndromes.

More recently, and in line with general trends, methods based on neural networks, especially deep learning-based methods, have paved the way to discover complex patterns and, consequently, to outperform the diagnosis accuracy obtained by classical statistical methodologies. [24] proposes a classifier based on a single layer neural network and voxel-as-features from different slices. [10,11] propose the use of CNNs to discover patterns associated to PD. Increasing the accuracy requires the use of deeper networks, but this increment also makes the network prone to overfitting and the limitations of the training algorithms arise.

3 Materials

Data used in the preparation of this article was obtained from the Parkinson's Progression Markers Initiative (PPMI) (www.ppmi-info.org/data). A total of $N = 269$ DaTSCAN images from this database were used in the preparation of the article. Specifically, the baseline acquisition from 158 subjects suffering from PD and 111 normal controls (NC) was used.

Spatial normalization is frequently used in neuroimaging studies to eliminate differences in shape and size of brain, as well as local inhomogeneities due to individual anatomic particularities. The DaTSCAN images from the PPMI dataset are roughly realigned. We further preprocessed the images using the SPM12 [12] New Normalize procedure with default parameters, which applied affine and local deformations to achieve the best warping of the images and a custom DaTSCAN template defined in [20]. After this, the regions of interests, those which reveal dopaminergic activity (intensity values which are not close to zero), were selected. As a result, the original size of (95,69,79) were converted into images of size (29,25,41).

Intensity normalization is also important to ensure that the same intensity levels corresponds to similar drug uptakes, so that intensities can be compared as an indirect measure of the neurophysical activity. This paper uses Integral Normalization [4], where the intensity normalization values is computed independently for each subject as the mean of the whole image (in an approximation of the integral). Sometimes, for Parkinson, I_n is set to the average of the brain without the striatum; although the influence of this is small and it can be approximated by the mean of the whole image. Finally, in this work, the resulting values are further normalized within [0 1].

4 Methods

4.1 Feature Extraction Using Isosurfaces

DaTSCAN SPECT images contains an enormous amount of information. The extraction and selection of features is an important and determinant part in any classification method, which allows reducing this complexity. This results in lower computational burden, more efficient training algorithms and less proneness to overfitting.

For feature extraction, this paper proposes the use of isosurfaces. Isosurfaces connect voxels that have the specified intensity or value much the way contour lines connect points of equal elevation. Roughly, this implies to set a threshold at a certain level and take the surface that envelops the remaining voxels above that threshold (see Fig. 1 for an example). In this work, however, a refined version for computing isosurfaces is used where interpolation is employed instead of just thresholding. When different thresholds are used, isolines are preferred for representation. Isolines are simply 2D slices of the corresponding isosurfaces (see Fig. 1).

The following characteristics can be observed in isosurfaces/isolines: (i) they define closed volumes/areas, (ii) they do not cross each other (iii) the same threshold can result in several isosurfaces/isolines, and (iv) the proximity between isosurfaces/isolines provides information about intensity gradients; the closer they are, the faster the changes. Regarding the diagnosis of PD, it can be observed in previous figures, that isosurfaces and isolines from PD patients, in contrast with those from NC subjects, are characterized by a loss of symmetry between hemispheres.

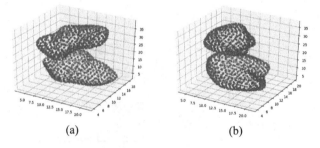

Fig. 1. Examples of isosurfaces (threshold = 0.5) for NC subject (a) and PD patient (b)

For feature selection classification results using isosurfaces computed with different thresholds have been compared, choosing those that provide the best classification results, with forward (starting with one and then adding one each time) and backward (starting with all of them and then removing one each time) selection.

4.2 CNNs for Classification

Method based on CNNs are becoming more and more popular for the development of new early diagnosis tools [14]. The election and configuration of the CNN architecture are, however, not trivial tasks. The best performances are obtained with balanced architectures; that is, architectures complex enough to reveal the relevant patterns but not so complex that it cannot be conveniently trained with certain guarantees of non-overfitting. In this paper, two 3D versions based on the well-known LeNet architecture has been tested.

The LeNeT architecture comprises 7 layers, not counting the input (see Fig. 2): 2 convolutional layers (1st and 3rd), 2 subsampling layers (2nd and 4th), 1 flatten layer (5th) and 2 full connected layers (6th and 7t). The 2 convolutional layer use five 3D-kernels of [3 × 3 × 3] to sweep over the input topologies and transform them into feature maps. Stride of (1,1,1) and padding are employed with the convolution so that the output feature maps keep the size of the input. For the second convolutional layer (3DCONV_2), each unit is connected to the entire set of input feature maps (not just a subset). The number of trainable parameters of these two layers are 140 (for a single input volume) and 680, respectively. The two subsampling layers apply max-pooling with a [2 × 2 × 2] window. After the learning phase, feature maps are flattened into a feature vector with 3050 neurons, which is followed by two fully-connected layers of 4096 and 2 neurons, respectively. These two layers have 12,6190,776 and 8194 trainable parameters, respectively. Between these two layers there is a dropout interphase with 0.5 dropout probability. The last layer yields the prediction probability using softmax activation. The total number of trainable parameters of this CNN is 12,628,790.

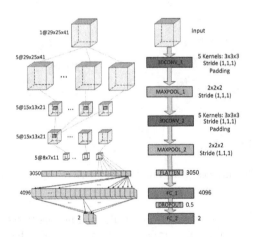

Fig. 2. CNN architecture based on LeNet.

Classification performance is evaluated by means of the accuracy, sensitivity and specificity. Resulting from these values, Receiver Operating Curves (ROC) and the Areas Under the ROC Curves are also computed. Classification experiments conducted in this work have been assessed by k-fold cross-validation (k = 10) to avoid double-dipping and determine the generalization ability of the proposed method. More specifically, resampling by stratified cross-validation has been used to ensure that the proportion of both classes is preserved in each fold.

5   Results and Discussion

Classification results were firstly compared with single input volumes to determine which of the computed isosurfaces (see Sect. 4.1) provided more significant information and performance (see Fig. 3). Intermediate values of isosurfaces, i.e. 0.5, 0.6 and 0.7, seem to contain the most relevant information providing slightly better classification results.

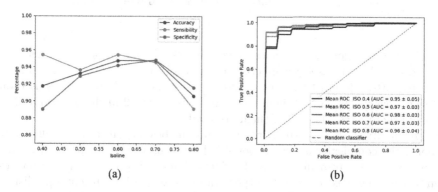

Fig. 3. Results of the LeNet-based architecture using as input a single isosurface: sensibilities, sensitivities and accuracies (a) and ROC curves (b)

Then, classification performances obtained when different isosurfaces were combined at the input were compared. Note that, although the introduction of more isosurfaces adds more information, it also increases the complexity of the CNN (number of trainable parameters of the first layer) so that the best results are only obtained when the input has an optimum trade-off between the information it provides and the complexity that it introduces. Thus, many

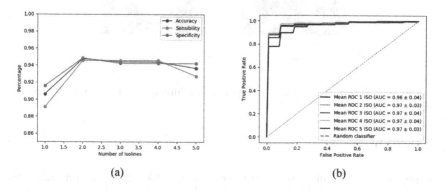

Fig. 4. Results of the LeNet-based architecture using as input several isosurfaces: sensibilities, sensitivities and accuracies (a) and ROC curves (b)

Table 1. Classification results using different methods

Method	Accuracy	Sensitivity	Specificity	AUC
EMD [19]	0.95	0.95	0.94	0.94
Significance M. [9]	0.92	0.95	0.89	0.90
Brahim et al. [3]	0.92	0.94	0.91	-
EfPCA [15]	0.93	0.97	0.88	0.94
LeNet-based	**0.948**	**0.945**	**0.948**	**0.97**

possible combinations of isosurfaces have been tested. One of these tests is shown in Fig. 4 for LeNet-based architecture using a forward selection from top level (0.8) to bottom level (0.4); that is, first the isosurface with level 0.8 is used on its own (marked as 1 in the figures), then 0.7 is added (2 in the figures) and so on (5 in the figures when all of them are used).

The inputs chosen eventually as providing the best classification results while keeping the complexity as low as possible have been the combination of isosurfaces 0.8 and 0.7, providing an AUC of 0.95. These classification performances can be considered as very good, outperforming most methods recently published in the bibliography for the detection of Parkinsonism [3,9,19]. Table 1 collects the different performance classifications.

Finally, and for the sake of completeness, the saliency maps for the last layer of the Lenet-based architecture are computed (see Fig. 5 for the Lenet-based). Saliency maps use the gradient of output category with respect to input image to determine the regions of the input image that have a greater impact on the output class.

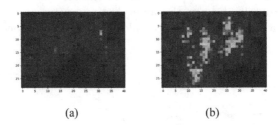

(a)   (b)

Fig. 5. Saliency maps of the LeNet-based architecture: NC (a) and PD (b)

6 Conclusions

This paper proposes the use of isosurfaces as a way to extract the relevant information from 3D DatSCAN images so that they can be used as inputs of CNN architectures. As a result, a classification system that uses LeNet-based CNN architectures has been implemented. This system achieves accuracy of 95.1%, providing comparable (slightly better) vales to those obtained for recently proposed systems. It can be concluded, therefore, that the computation of isosurfaces reduces the complexity of the inputs significantly while keeping the relevant information, resulting in high classification accuracies with reduced computational burden. Finally, in order to determine which areas of the input brain images has a greater impact on the predicted output class, saliency maps of the last two-neuron layer are also computed.

Acknowledgments. This work was partly supported by the MINECO/FEDER under TEC2015-64718-R and PSI2015-65848-R projects. We gratefully acknowledge the support of NVIDIA Corporation with the donation of one of the GPUs used for this research. PPMI - a public - private partnership - is funded by The Michael J. Fox Foundation for Parkinson's Research and funding partners, including Abbott, Biogen Idec, F. Hoffman-La Roche Ltd., GE Healthcare, Genentech and Pfizer Inc.

References

1. Badoud, S., Ville, D.V.D., Nicastro, N., Garibotto, V., Burkhard, P.R., Haller, S.: Discriminating among degenerative parkinsonisms using advanced 123i-ioflupane SPECT analyses. NeuroImage: Clin. **12**, 234–240 (2016)
2. Bhalchandra, N.A., Prashanth, R., Roy, S.D., Noronha, S.: Early detection of Parkinson's disease through shape based features from 123I-Ioflupane SPECT imaging. In: 2015 IEEE 12th International Symposium on Biomedical Imaging (ISBI), pp. 963–966, April 2015. https://doi.org/10.1109/ISBI.2015.7164031
3. Brahim, A., Ramírez, J., Górriz, J., Khedher, L., Salas-Gonzalez, D.: Comparison between different intensity normalization methods in 123I-Ioflupane imaging for the automatic detection of Parkinsonism. PLoS One **10**(6: e0130274), 1–20 (2015)
4. Illán, I.A., Górriz, J.M., Ramírez, J., Segovia, F., Hoyuela, J.M.J., Lozano, S.J.O.: Automatic assistance to Parkinsons disease diagnosis in DaTSCAN SPECT imaging. Med. Phys. **39**(10), 5971–5980 (2012). https://doi.org/10.1118/1.4742055
5. Khedher, L., Ramírez, J., Górriz, J., Brahim, A., Segovia, F.: Early diagnosis of disease based on partial least squares, principal component analysis and support vector machine using segmented MRI images. Neurocomputing **151**, 139–150 (2015). https://doi.org/10.1016/j.neucom.2014.09.072
6. Krizhevsky, A., Sutskever, I., Hinton, G.E.: ImageNet classification with deep convolutional neural networks. In: Proceedings of the 25th International Conference on Neural Information Processing Systems, NIPS 2012, vol. 1, pp. 1097–1105. Curran Associates Inc., USA (2012)
7. LeCun, Y., Bottou, L., Bengio, Y., Haffner, P.: Gradient-based learning applied to document recognition. Proc. IEEE **86**(11), 2278–2324 (1998)
8. Martinez-Murcia, F.J., Górriz, J.M., Ramírez, J., Moreno-Caballero, M., Gómez-Río, M.: Parametrization of textural patterns in 123I-Ioflupane imaging for the automatic detection of Parkinsonism. Med. Phys. **41**(1) (2014)
9. Martínez-Murcia, F., Górriz, J., Ramírez, J., Illán, I., Ortiz, A.: Automatic detection of Parkinsonism using significance measures and component analysis in DaTSCAN imaging. Neurocomputing **126**, 58–70 (2014). https://doi.org/10.1016/j.neucom.2013.01.054. Recent trends in Intelligent Data Analysis Online Data Processing

10. Martinez-Murcia, F.J., Górriz, J.M., Ramírez, J., Ortiz, A.: Convolutional neural networks for neuroimaging in Parkinson's disease: is preprocessing needed? Int. J. Neural Syst. (2018). https://doi.org/10.1142/s0129065718500351
11. Martinez-Murcia, F.J., et al.: A 3D convolutional neural network approach for the diagnosis of Parkinson's disease. In: Ferrández Vicente, J.M., Álvarez-Sánchez, J.R., de la Paz López, F., Toledo Moreo, J., Adeli, H. (eds.) IWINAC 2017. LNCS, vol. 10337, pp. 324–333. Springer, Cham (2017). https://doi.org/10.1007/978-3-319-59740-9_32
12. London Institute of Neurology, UCL: Statistical parametrix mapping (2012). http://fil.ion.ucl.ac.uk/spm/
13. Oliveira, F.P.M., Castelo-Branco, M.: Computer-aided diagnosis of Parkinson's disease based on [(123)I]FP-CIT SPECT binding potential images, using the voxels-as-features approach and support vector machines. J. Neural Eng. 12(2) (2015). https://doi.org/10.1088/1741-2560/12/2/026008
14. Ortiz, A., Martínez-Murcia, F.J., García-Tarifa, M.J., Lozano, F., Górriz, J.M., Ramírez, J.: Automated diagnosis of Parkinsonian syndromes by deep sparse filtering-based features. In: Chen, Y.-W., Tanaka, S., Howlett, R.J., Jain, L.C. (eds.) Innovation in Medicine and Healthcare 2016. SIST, vol. 60, pp. 249–258. Springer, Cham (2016). https://doi.org/10.1007/978-3-319-39687-3_24
15. Ortiz, A., Munilla, J., Martinez-Murcia, F.J., Górriz, J.M., Ramírez, J.: Empirical functional PCA for 3D image feature extraction through fractal sampling. Int. J. Neural Syst. 1–22 (2019). https://doi.org/10.1142/S0129065718500405
16. Palumbo, B., et al.: Diagnostic accuracy of Parkinson disease by support vector machine (SVM) analysis of 123I-FP-CIT brain SPECT data: implications of putaminal findings and age. Medicine 93(27), e228 (2014). https://doi.org/10.1097/MD.0000000000000228
17. Palumbo, B., et al.: Comparison of two neural network classifiers in the differential diagnosis of essential tremor and Parkinson's disease by (123)I-FP-CIT brain SPECT. Eur. J. Nuclear Med. Mol. Imaging 37(11), 2146–2153 (2010). https://doi.org/10.1007/s00259-010-1481-6
18. Prashanth, R., Dutta Roy, S., Mandal, P.K., Ghosh, S.: Automatic classification and prediction models for early Parkinson's disease diagnosis from SPECT imaging. Expert Syst. Appl. 41(7), 3333–3342 (2014). https://doi.org/10.1016/j.eswa.2013.11.031
19. Rojas, A., et al.: Application of empirical mode decomposition (EMD) on DaTSCAN SPECT images to explore Parkinson disease. Expert Syst. Appl. 40(7), 2756–2766 (2013)
20. Salas-Gonzalez, D., et al.: Building a FP-CIT SPECT brain template using a posterization approach. Neuroinformatics 13(4), 391–402 (2015)
21. Segovia, F., Górriz, J.M., Ramírez, J., Chaves, R., Illán, I.Á.: Automatic differentiation between controls and Parkinson's disease DaTSCAN images using a partial least squares scheme and the fisher discriminant ratio. In: KES, pp. 2241–2250 (2012)
22. Taylor, J.C., Fenner, J.W.: Comparison of machine learning and semi-quantification algorithms for (I123)FP-CIT classification: the beginning of the end for semi-quantification? EJNMMI Phys. 4, 29 (2017). https://doi.org/10.1212/01.CON.0000436152.24038.e0
23. Towey, D.J., Bain, P.G., Nijran, K.S.: Automatic classification of 123I-FP-CIT (DaTSCAN) SPECT images. Nuclear Med. Commun. 32(8), 699–707 (2011)
24. Zhang, Y.C., Kagen, A.C.: Machine learning interface for medical image analysis. J. Digit. Imaging 30(5), 615–621 (2017). https://doi.org/10.1007/s10278-016-9910-0

An Anomaly Detection Approach
for Dyslexia Diagnosis Using EEG Signals

A. Ortiz[1]([✉]), P. J. López[2], J. L. Luque[2], F. J. Martínez-Murcia[1],
D. A. Aquino-Britez[3], and J. Ortega[3]

[1] Communications Engineering Department, University of Málaga, Málaga, Spain
aortiz@ic.uma.es
[2] Department of Developmental Psychology, University of Málaga, Málaga, Spain
[3] Department of Computer Architecture, University of Granada, Granada, Spain

Abstract. Developmental dyslexia (DD) is a specific difficulty in the acquisition of reading skills not related to mental age or inadequate schooling. Its prevalence is estimated between 5% and 12% of the population. Currently, biological causes and processes of DD are not well known and it is usually diagnosed by means of specifically designed tests to measure different behavioural variables involved in the reading process. Thus, the diagnosis results depend on the analysis of the test results which is a time-consuming task and prone to error. In this paper we use EEG signals to search for brain activation patterns related to DD that could result useful for differential diagnosis by an objective test. Specifically, we extract spectral features from each electrode. Moreover, the exploration of the activation levels at different brain areas constitutes an step towards the best knowledge of the brain proccesses involved in DD.

Keywords: EEG · Dyslexia · One-Class-SVM · Automatic diagnosis

1 Introduction

Developmental dyslexia (DD) is a specific difficulty in the acquisition of reading skills not related to mental age or inadequate schooling. Its prevalence is estimated between 5% and 12% of the population [7], depending on the reading performance benchmark. It has an important social impact and may determine school failure. In addition, it has harmful effects in the self-esteem of affected children. Early diagnosis and prognosis to start an adequate, early and individualized, intervention is decisive in the in the personal and intellectual development of these children. Currently, biological causes and processes of DD are not well known. It is usually diagnosed by means of specifically designed tests to measure different behavioural variables involved in the reading process. Examples of these variables are reading efficiency, or the ability to split words in their constituent syllables. These tests are individually applied by specialists who need further time to analyze the results and usually, diagnosis is established by means of cut-off points computed over a non very large population. On the other hand,

J. M. Ferrández Vicente et al. (Eds.): IWINAC 2019, LNCS 11486, pp. 369–378, 2019.
https://doi.org/10.1007/978-3-030-19591-5_38

the results of the tests depend on the motivation and the mood of the child when performing the benchmark tasks. As a result, classical diagnosis methods are time-consuming and prone to error, and it is usual that children with specific difficulties in the acquisition of reading skills are neither correctly diagnosed nor treated, what affects their cognitive and emotional development. In addition, most benchmarks are designed for readers, limiting the minimum age for the early diagnosis. Hence, research work oriented towards obtaining results which allow an early diagnosis and an individualized intervention would have a theoretical and a practical impact [10]. There is an active research activity in search of objective, quantifiable measures with diagnostic capability, to improve the diagnosis accuracy and eventually, to reveal unknown aspects of the DD related to its neural basis. Additionally, the research in the biological causes of dyslexia can offer valuable information for a better understanding of the differences between dyslexic and non-dyslexic subjects, with special application in the design of individualized intervention tasks. These quantifiable measures are known as biomarkers, and different studies carried out in the last years used different techniques to extract them. Recent studies searching for DD-related patterns in EEG signals [1,8] have shown differences in readers due to cognitive impairment of the phonological representation of word forms. Speech encoding which is related to speech prosody and sensorimotor synchronization problems can be revealed by finding patterns in EEG channels at different sub-bands as it provides enough time resolution. In this work, we used EEG signals recorded by a 32 active electrodes BrainVision equipment during 5 min sessions, while presenting an auditive stimulus to the subject. These signals are then pre-processed and analyzed in the frequency domain. Spectral features extracted from the EEG signals are then used to classify the subjects between Controls (CN) and Dyslexic (DD).

The rest of the paper is structured as follows. Section 2 shows details on the database used and the applied preprocessing. Then, this section describes the auditive stimulus, EEG preprocessing and post-processing (feature extraction) as well as the classification method. Section 4 presents and discusses the classification results, and finally, Sect. 5 draws the main conclusions.

2   Materials and Methods

2.1   Database

The present experiment was carried out with the understanding and written consent of each child's legal guardian and in the presence thereof. Forty-eight participants took part in the present study, including 32 skilled readers (17 males) and 16 dyslexic readers (7 males) matched in age ($t(1) = -1.4, p > 0.05$, age range: 88–100 months). The mean age of the control group was $94, 1 \pm 3.3$ months, and $95, 6 \pm 2.9$ months for the dyslexic group. All participants were right-handed Spanish native speakers with no hearing impairments and normal or corrected-to-normal vision. Dyslexic children in this study had all received a formal diagnosis of dyslexia in the school. None of the skilled readers reported reading or spelling difficulties or had received a previous formal diagnosis of dyslexia.

3 Methods

DD is a reading disorder often characterized by reduced awareness of speech units [6]. Recent models of neuronal speech coding suggest that dyslexia originates from the atypical dominant neuronal entrainment in the right hemisphere to the slow-rhythmic prosodic (delta band, 0.5–1 Hz), syllabic (theta band, 4–8 Hz) or the phoneme (gamma band, 12–40 Hz), speech modulations, which are defined by the time of increase in amplitude (i.e., the envelope) generated by the speech rhythm [2,4]. Thus, we compared the cortical entrainment to AM white-noise at a fixed rate in delta (2 Hz), theta (8 Hz) and gamma (20 Hz) bands. In a sample composed of 7 years old children, listened to stimuli obtained by rhythmically modulating the amplitude (AM) of white-noise sound either in the delta, theta and gamma band. Our hypothesis was that the quality of the oscillatory neural processes measured through AM modulations contribute to the optimal construction of predictions of incoming auditory information (such as linguistic sequences or their simplification through AM modulations), these neurophysiological responses should explain the manifestations of the temporal processing deficits described in dyslexia. Then, we recorded EEG signals using a 32 active electrodes (BrainVision actiCAP, https://www.brainproducts.com) while presenting the auditory stimulus. Figure 1 shows the construction of a 8 Hz auditive stimulus, which is based on the AM modulation of bandwidth-limited white noise.

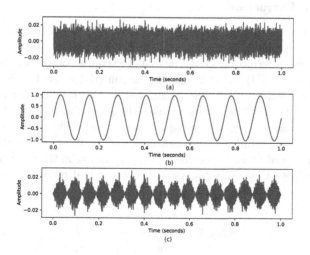

Fig. 1. Stimulus example (a) bandwidth-limited noise, (b) 8 Hz modulating signal, (c) 8 Hz AM Modulated noise

EEG signals were pre-processed in order to remove artefacts related to eye blinking and impedance variations due to movements. Since eye blinking signal is recorded along with EEG signals, these artefact are removed by blind source separation using Independent Component Analysis (ICA) [5]. Other artefacts required the removal of EEG segments. Afterwards, the remaining, cleaned signals were segmented into 5 s excerpts. As a result, a different number of segments are available for different subjects.

Figure 2 shows the average activation levels by frequency bands for the 2 Hz stimulus.

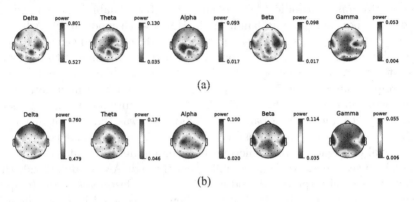

(a)

(b)

Fig. 2. Average activation patterns computed for 2 Hz stimulus by different bands for (a) Controls and (b) Dyslexic subjects. Multitaper [11] method is used to estimate the PSD.

3.1   Feature Extraction

In this section, we show features extracted from each segment. Since we expect differences in the power spectrum at different frequency bands, we extracted different spectral descriptors. Thus, the first step consist on estimating the Power Spectral Density (PSD). This is usually computed by the Fourier transform. However, the reliability of the PSD computed by this method is reduced by (1) high variance of the estimate, which makes the spectrum noisy and (2) the bias created by the leakage of energy across frequencies [11]. The solution proposed in [11] consist on using windows (also called *tapers*) in the time domain, reducing the leakage produced by multiple side lobes of a window in the frequency domain. This is also achieved by using tapers with low spectral power in the side lobes. Thus, the PSD can be computed as:

$$PSD(\omega) = \left| \sum_{t=0}^{N-1} x(t)a(t)e^{-j\omega t} \right|^2 \qquad (1)$$

where $x(t)$ is the N-samples time series corresponding to the signal and $a(t)$ is the window (taper) in the time domain. The total energy of these tappers is normalized to keep the total power invariant. This approach can be extended to reduce the variance of the estimate at each frequency by using multiple tapers. Specifically, Thomson proposed the use of K orthogonal tapers, providing K orthogonal samples of the data $x(t)$. As a result, we have K spectral estimations $PSD_k(\omega)$ that can be averaged to reduce the variance. Furthermore, the method devised by Thomson includes an optimization step to find the tapers that minimize the leakage by maximizing the energy within a specific bandwidth.

Once PSD is computed, two features are extracted to characterize the spectrum of each band for each electrode. The first feature is the *spectral centroid*, (SC) that indicates where the location of the *center of mass* of the spectrum (i.e. the frequency where the PSD is concentrated). This can be calculated as the weighted average of the amplitude spectrum:

$$SC = \frac{\sum_{k=1}^{N} k \cdot w \cdot PSD(k)}{\sum_{k=1}^{N} PSD(K)} \tag{2}$$

where $PSD(k)$ and w are the PSD estimated for the k-bin and the width of each spectral bin, respectively.

Moreover, the mean PSD for each band is also computed and used as a feature.

This way, a feature vector can be composed for the electrode l as

$$f_l = (SC_l^\Delta, PSD_l^\Delta, SC_l^\theta, PSD_l^\theta, SC_l^\alpha, PSD_l^\alpha, SC_l^\beta, PSD_l^\beta, SC_l^\gamma, PSD_l^\gamma) \tag{3}$$

for the Delta, Theta, Alpha, Beta and Gamma bands.

3.2 Feature Selection

Feature selection is addressed by keeping those electrodes presenting a small spectral coherence when comparing Controls and DD. Spectral coherence is a statistic with many applications in neuroscience [3] that measures the relation between the signals acquired from two electrodes $x(t)$ and $y(t)$:

$$C_{xy} = \frac{|C_{xy}|^2}{C_{xx}C_{yy}} \tag{4}$$

where C_{xx} and C_{yy} are the power spectral densities of signals x and y, respectively, and C_{xy} is the cross-spectral density, which can be calculated as the power spectrum of the cross-correlation function between x and y.

As shown in this figure, different electrodes present different coherence values depending on the frequency band. This indicates that signals acquired by different electrodes contain information regarding different bands. Thus, electrode selection can be addressed by keeping the electrodes that present the lower coherence when comparing CN to DD subjects. Hence, Fig. 3 shows the coherence only for the bands presenting the lowest values.

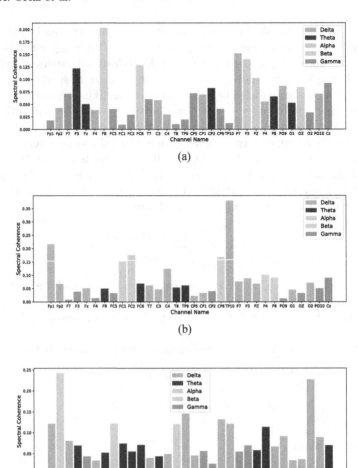

Fig. 3. Minimum coherence bands for each electrode for (a) 2 Hz stimulus, (b) 8 Hz stimulus and (c) 20 Hz stimulus

3.3   Classification

Class imbalance is an usual problem in biomedical engineering, where databases normally contains more controls than experimental subjects. On the other hand, it is not straightforward to balance the database by obtaining more experimental subjects, due to the distribution of controls and experimental subjects in the general population. As a result, models generated from unbalanced databases are biased, showing special affinity to the most probable class. There are different methods to mitigate the biasing effect such as using cost sensitive objective functions by assigning different weights to miss-classification of samples from different classes. An alternative method to overcome the biasing effect while taking advantage of it consists on modelling the most probable class and then, identify whether a new sample belongs to that distribution or not. This is also known as anomaly detection.

In this work, we used the One-Class SVM [9], a variant of the Support Vector Classifier (SVC) [12] devised to identify outliers with respect to the training dataset. This method separates all datapoints of the training dataset from the origin in the feature space, maximizing the distance from the computed hyperplane to the origin. This is addressed by solving the quadratic programming, minimization problem:

$$\min_{\omega, \xi_i, b} \left\{ \frac{1}{2} \|\omega\| + \frac{a}{\nu N} \sum_{i=1}^{N} \xi_i - b \right\} \tag{5}$$

subject to:

$$(\omega \cdot \phi(x_i)) \geq b - \xi_i \quad i \in \{1, ..., N\}$$
$$\xi_i > 0, \nu \in (0, 1] \quad i \in \{1, ..., N\}$$

where ξ_i are non-zero variables to control the margin, and ν controls the number of support vectors and the fraction of training samples considered as outliers. Additionally, ϕ is the kernel function.

Hence, a decision function can be constructed to produce a different value for samples belonging to the same distribution of the training samples that for out-of-class samples, using the hyperplane defined by ω and b parameters

$$f(z) = sign\{(\omega \cdot \phi(z)) - b\} \tag{6}$$

In our experiments, a Radial Basis Function was used for the kernel.

4   Results and Discussion

In this section, we present the experimental results obtained when classifying the subjects by means of the features extracted from the EEG signals. These classification experiments used EEG features from signals acquired during the 2 Hz, 8 Hz and 20 Hz stimuli as explained in Sect. 3. Moreover, experiments using all the features and the selection provided by the method described in Sect. 3.2 are shown here. The classification method exposed here has been assessed by stratified k-fold cross-validation (k = 5) to ensure the database independence and to avoid double dipping in the training-testing process.

Thus, Figs. 4a, b and c, shows the ROC curves obtained when classifying the subjects using th 2 Hz, 8 Hz and 20 Hz stimuli, respectively.

The feature selection method based on using only the band that shows the lowest coherence between CN and DD subjects, improves the performance of the classifier with respect to the use of all the features for 2 Hz and 8 Hz. The improvement of the performance comes from the reduction of the dimensionality and the use of more discriminative features. Nevertheless, the use of all

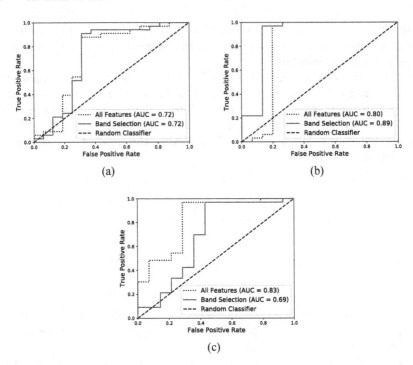

Fig. 4. ROC curves obtained with the (a) 2 Hz, (b) 8 Hz and (c) 20 Hz stimuli. All features vs. per electrode band selection method is shown.

the features (i.e. all bands for all the electrodes) provides higher AUC values for the 20 Hz stimulus. Moreover, Table 1 shows the classification performance in terms of accuracy, sensitivity and specificity. As shown in this table, the feature selection method improves the sensitivity and specificity for 2 Hz and 8 Hz, while decreases the performance in the 20 Hz case. This suggest that discriminative information regarding electrode inter-dependence is present when the 20 Hz stimulus is used.

Table 1. Classification results

Stimulus	Accuracy	Sensitivity	Specificity	AUC
2 Hz (All features)	0.62	0.66	0.60	0.72
2 Hz (Band Selection)	0.70	0.66	0.69	0.72
8 Hz (All Features)	0.63	0.80	0.55	0.80
8 Hz (Band Selection)	0.66	0.86	0.56	0.89
20 Hz (All Features)	0.78	0.66	0.81	0.83
20 Hz (Band Selection)	0.71	0.53	0.78	0.69

5 Conclusions and Future Work

In this paper, EEG signals have been recorded during the presentation of different stimulus related to the frequency of neural oscillations generated at different brain areas during language processing. Then, a feature extraction process directed to characterize the signals from each electrode in terms of the predominant brainwave. Moreover, these features are selected by computing the spectral coherence for all electrodes between controls and experimental subjects. The feature extraction and selection method used in this work improves the classification performance for 2 Hz and 8 Hz stimulus, which suggest that discriminative information regarding DD diagnosis is in the distribution of power along different bands. In fact, the proposed method always provides AUC values up to 0.89, showing its diagnostic utility. In addition, the 20 Hz seems to produce effects beyond the spectral distribution and thus, a different feature selection method has to be used. In a future work, we will explore the use of different, time-frequency features and different descriptors to characterize the power distribution along different bands, as well as to compute electrode synchronicity among different brain areas.

Acknowledgments. This work was partly supported by the MINECO/FEDER under PSI2015-65848-R and TEC2015-64718-R projects.

References

1. Cutini, S., Szűcs, D., Mead, N., Huss, M., Goswami, U.: Atypical right hemisphere response to slow temporal modulations in children with developmental dyslexia. NeuroImage **143**, 40–49 (2016)
2. Di Liberto, G., Peter, V., Kalashnikova, M., Goswami, U., Burnham, D., Lalor, E.: Atypical cortical entrainment to speech in the right hemisphere underpins phonemic deficits in dyslexia. NeuroImage **175**, 70–79 (2018)
3. Engel, A.K., Fries, P., Singer, W.: Dynamic predictions: oscillations and synchrony in top-down processing. Nat. Rev. Neurosci. **2**, 704–716 (2001)
4. Flanagan, S., Goswami, U.: The role of phase synchronisation between low frequency amplitude modulations in child phonology and morphology speech tasks. J. Acoust. Soc. Am. **143**, 1366–1375 (2018). https://doi.org/10.1121/1.5026239
5. Li, R., Principe, J.C.: Blinking artifact removal in cognitive EEG data using ICA. In: 2006 International Conference of the IEEE Engineering in Medicine and Biology Society, pp. 5273–5276 (2006)
6. Molinaro, N., Lizarazu, M., Lallier, M., Bourguignon, M., Carreiras, M.: Out-of-synchrony speech entrainment in developmental dyslexia. Hum. Brain Mapp. **37**, 2767–2783 (2016)
7. Peterson, R., Pennington, B.: Developmental dyslexia. Lancet **379**, 1997–2007 (2012)
8. Power, A.J., Colling, L., Mead, N., Barnes, L., Goswami, U.: Neural encoding of the speech envelope by children with developmental dyslexia. Brain Lang. **160**, 1–10 (2016)

9. Schölkopf, B., Williamson, R., Smola, A., Shawe-Taylor, J., Platt, J.: Support vector method for novelty detection. In: Proceedings of the 12th International Conference on Neural Information Processing Systems, NIPS 1999, pp. 582–588. MIT Press, Cambridge (1999)
10. Thompson, P.A., Hulme, C., Nash, H.M., Gooch, D., Hayiou-Thomas, E., Snowling, M.J.: Developmental dyslexia: predicting individual risk. J. Child Psychol. Psychiatry **56**(9), 976–987 (2015)
11. Thomson, D.: Spectrum estimation and harmonic analysis. Proc. IEEE **70**, 1055–1096 (1982)
12. Vapnik, V.N.: Statistical Learning Theory. Wiley, New York (1998)

Comparison Between Affine and Non-affine Transformations Applied to I[123]-FP-CIT SPECT Images Used for Parkinson's Disease Diagnosis

Diego Castillo-Barnes[✉], Francisco J. Martinez-Murcia, Fermin Segovia, Ignacio A. Illán, Diego Salas-Gonzalez, Juan M. Górriz, and Javier Ramírez

Department of Signal Theory, Networking and Communications, University of Granada, Periodista Daniel Saucedo Aranda, S/N, 18071 Granada, Spain
diegoc@ugr.es

Abstract. In recent years, the use of I[123]-FP-CIT or I[123]-Ioflupane SPECT images has emerged as an effective support tool for Parkinson's Disease diagnosis. Many works in this field have consisted on comparing different images obtained from subjects both Healthy Control (HC) subjects and patients with Parkinsonism (PD) and using them to obtain measures (features) able to discern among them. In this scenario, spatial normalization of I[123]-FP-CIT images is fundamental to match equivalent areas of the brain from different subjects.

This work tries to compare the two most common ways to make the spatial normalization of SPECT images from PD and HC subjects in the study of Parkinsonism: affine and non-affine transformations. For that, these two approaches have been applied to a set of 20 images obtained from 20 different subjects (11 HC and 9 with PD) and measured how volume of new voxels, when applying normalization to a reference template, has changed.

Despite the accurate match obtained when using a non-affine spatial normalization procedure, using this method involves that some parts of the brain are compressed or stretched in excess to fit the template. This effect is even more pronounced when using PD images than HC. Using the affine procedure, *striatum* area preserves better its morphology and can be used to obtain more reliable morphological features.

Keywords: Neuroimaging · Normalization · Single Photon Emission Computed Tomography (SPECT) · Statistical analysis · Parkinson's Disease · Striatum

1 Introduction

In recent years, the use of medical procedures based on medical imaging have strengthened due to their practical considerations in diagnosis of a great amount

© Springer Nature Switzerland AG 2019
J. M. Ferrández Vicente et al. (Eds.): IWINAC 2019, LNCS 11486, pp. 379–388, 2019.
https://doi.org/10.1007/978-3-030-19591-5_39

of illnesses. This is the case of Parkinson's Disease which can be defined as a chronic neurodegenerative disorder that affects an estimated 6.3 million people worldwide, according to the European Parkinson's Disease Association [1].

An extended tool for Parkinson's Disease diagnosis is based on the use of $I^{[123]}$-FP-CIT or $I^{[123]}$-Ioflupane SPECT images [2,3]. These images make use of the radio-ligand Iodine-123-fluoropropyl-carbomethoxy-3-β-(4-iodophenyltropane) that presents a high binding affinity for presynaptic dopamine transporters (DAT) in the brain. Because of this affinity, the radio-oligand is able to give us a quantitative measure of the spatial distribution of the dopaminergic neurons whose loss is related to Parkinson's Disease onset. This information will be used to discern between subjects with probable PD and HC [4].

The emergence of Computer-Aided Diagnosis (CAD) systems based on image analysis techniques have also had a positive impact on the study of Parkinsonism [5–9]. Generally, structure of these works is organized starting with the spatial normalization of $I^{[123]}$-Ioflupane SPECT images. This let to compare all subjects between them or just to obtain comparative measures (features) about *striatum* area in the brain. As this region has a high relevance in PD pathogenesis [10], many of the works are focused almost exclusively on this region [11,12].

Focusing on *striatum* area, or not, the more common scenario is that a set of images from several subjects are fitted to a reference template to compare them lately. In these cases, some parts of *striatum* area might be deformed in excess. This process is even more apparent in the case of PD subject images with a highlighted reduction of dopamine transporters, as an small area like the *striatum* has to be adjusted to a bigger one in the template.

With this aim, this paper compares the two main approaches about spatial normalization: affine and non-affine transformation and check which of them preserves better the shape of *striatum* area. In order that, both approaches (affine and non-affine) have been applied to a set of 20 $I^{[123]}$-FP-CIT SPECT images and compared between them. All the images used in this work have been previously diagnosed and labelled by experts from Hospital Virgen de la Victoria (Málaga, Spain).

2 Methods

2.1 Dataset

This work includes imaging acquisition of 20 subjects from Hospital Virgen de la Victoria (Málaga, Spain). All images has been labeled by three experienced clinicians from the Nuclear Medicine department of the hospital as: Control Subjects (labelled as HC or CS) and Parkinsonian patients (labelled as PKS or PD). Demographics have been included in Table 1.

Neuroimaging data were acquired 3–4 h after the radiopharmaceutical injection of 185 MBq (5 mCi) of $I^{[123]}$-Ioflupane using a gamma camera[1] equiped with

---

[1] Millennium model from General Electric.

Table 1. Demographics.

	Number			Age (years)	
	Total	Male	Female	Mean	Std
HC	11	5	6	70.73	5.83
PD	9	5	4	71.89	5.01

a dual head and general purpose collimator. All the images have been reconstructed by means of filtered back-projection algorithms without attenuation
correction and a Hanning filter (with frequency of 0.7) has also been applied.

Informed consents to clinical testing and neuroimaging prior to participation
of the study were obtained and approved by the institutional review boards
(IRB) from Hospital Virgen de la Victoria[2]. During the acquisition of $I^{[123]}$-
Ioflupane images, no subject was on treatment with drugs that could interfere
with any imaging test result.

2.2 Spatial Normalization

For each $I^{[123]}$-FP-CIT input image, it has been studied two different spatial
normalization procedures: affine and non-affine transformations.

Affine Transformation. Consists of the combination of different procedures
including: (a) traslation $\mathbf{M_t}$; (b) rotation $\mathbf{M_r}$; (c) enlargement (or zoom) $\mathbf{M_z}$;
and (d) shears $\mathbf{M_s}$. As any of these procedures come from rigid transformations
with general expression as shown in (1), it can be used a matrix notation $\mathbf{y} = \mathbf{Mx}$
with $\mathbf{M}$ equal to the product of matrices that correspond to each transformation
as follows in (2):

$$\begin{bmatrix} y_1 \\ y_2 \\ y_3 \\ 1 \end{bmatrix} = \begin{bmatrix} M_{1,1} & M_{1,2} & M_{1,3} & M_{1,4} \\ M_{2,1} & M_{2,2} & M_{2,3} & M_{2,4} \\ M_{3,1} & M_{3,2} & M_{3,3} & M_{3,4} \\ 0 & 0 & 0 & 1 \end{bmatrix} \begin{bmatrix} x_1 \\ x_2 \\ x_3 \\ 1 \end{bmatrix} \quad (1)$$

$$\mathbf{M_r} = \begin{bmatrix} 1 & 0 & 0 & 0 \\ 0 & cos(r_1) & sin(r_1) & 0 \\ 0 & -sin(r_1) & cos(r_1) & 0 \\ 0 & 0 & 0 & 1 \end{bmatrix} \begin{bmatrix} cos(r_2) & 0 & sin(r_2) & 0 \\ 0 & 1 & 0 & 0 \\ -sin(r_2) & 0 & cos(r_2) & 0 \\ 0 & 0 & 0 & 1 \end{bmatrix} \begin{bmatrix} cos(r_3) & sin(r_3) & 0 & 0 \\ -sin(r_3) & cos(r_3) & 0 & 0 \\ 0 & 0 & 1 & 0 \\ 0 & 0 & 0 & 1 \end{bmatrix}$$

$$\mathbf{M_t} = \begin{bmatrix} 1 & 0 & 0 & t_1 \\ 0 & 1 & 0 & t_2 \\ 0 & 0 & 1 & t_3 \\ 0 & 0 & 0 & 1 \end{bmatrix} \quad \mathbf{M_z} = \begin{bmatrix} z_1 & 0 & 0 & 0 \\ 0 & z_2 & 0 & 0 \\ 0 & 0 & z_3 & 0 \\ 0 & 0 & 0 & 1 \end{bmatrix} \quad \mathbf{M_s} = \begin{bmatrix} 0 & c_1 & c_2 & 0 \\ 0 & 1 & c_3 & 0 \\ 0 & 0 & 1 & 0 \\ 0 & 0 & 0 & 1 \end{bmatrix}$$

$$\quad (2)$$

---

[2] For more info, visit: http://www.huvv.es/

Since the registration of a 3D-image using an affine transformation can be explained as a geometric transformation of an Euclidean space [13,14], next step will be determining how to calculate the parameters that optimize the fitting between a $I^{[123]}$-FP-CIT image and a reference template.

Using Gauss-Newton approach, suppose a function $b_i(q)$ that describes differences between an objective image and a reference one for voxel i when using a transformation parameters vector q. For each voxel, it can be used the first approximation of Taylor theorem to estimate the value of this difference when q is lessen by a factor of t as shown in expression (3):

$$b_i(q-t) \cong b_i(q) - t_1 \frac{\partial b_i(q)}{\partial q_1} - t_2 \frac{\partial b_i(q)}{\partial q_2} - \dots \tag{3}$$

This expression allows to determine a set of simultaneous equations ($\mathbf{A}t \cong \mathbf{B}$) to estimate t that minimizes $\sum_i b_i(q-t)^2$. This is described in expressions (4) and (5). Note that the process is repeated until convergence although it is not sure that convergence conditions will be reached in all cases [15].

$$\mathbf{A} = \begin{bmatrix} \frac{\partial b_1(q)}{\partial q_1} & \frac{\partial b_1(q)}{\partial q_2} & \dots \\ \frac{\partial b_2(q)}{\partial q_1} & \frac{\partial b_2(q)}{\partial q_2} & \dots \\ \vdots & \vdots & \ddots \end{bmatrix} \quad \mathbf{B} = \begin{bmatrix} b_1(q) \\ b_2(q) \\ \vdots \end{bmatrix} \tag{4}$$

$$q^{n+1} = q^n - (\mathbf{A}^T \mathbf{A})^{-1} \mathbf{A}^T \mathbf{B} \tag{5}$$

Non-affine Transformation. Once the image has been registered using the 12 parameters affine registration, it can be performed a non-affine spatial registration using a small-deformation approach [17]. In this case, the inverse transformation is usually approximated by subtracting the displacement. In addition, the regularization is by the bending energy of the displacement field [16,18]. In this case. The deformations are parameterized using a three-dimensinoal cosine transform bases. The non-linear spatial transformation from voxels in the original image $\mathbf{x}$ to transformed positions of the voxels $\mathbf{y}$ is given by expression (6) where $\alpha_{m,k}$ is the coefficient m for dimension $k = [1,2,3]$ and $\phi_m(\mathbf{x})$ is the cosine transform bases as shown in expression (7).

$$\begin{aligned} y_1(\mathbf{x}, \alpha) &= x_1 + u_1 = x_1 + \sum_{m=1}^{M} \alpha_{m,1}\, \phi_m(\mathbf{x}) \\ y_2(\mathbf{x}, \alpha) &= x_2 + u_2 = x_2 + \sum_{m=1}^{M} \alpha_{m,2}\, \phi_m(\mathbf{x}) \\ y_3(\mathbf{x}, \alpha) &= x_3 + u_3 = x_3 + \sum_{m=1}^{M} \alpha_{m,3}\, \phi_m(\mathbf{x}) \end{aligned} \tag{6}$$

$$\phi_m(x) = \phi_{m,3}(x_3)\, \phi_{m,2}(x_2)\, \phi_{m,1}(x_1)$$

$$\phi_1(i) = \frac{1}{\sqrt{I}} \qquad i = 1, \dots, I \tag{7}$$

$$\phi_m(i) = \sqrt{\tfrac{2}{I}} \cos\left(\tfrac{\pi(2i-1)(m-1)}{2I}\right) \qquad i = 1, \dots, I \quad m = 2, \dots, M$$

2.3   Evaluation

In order to compare the two approaches, the spatial normalization of 20 SPECT images has been carried out considering the two approaches. Deformation fields have also been applied to prebuilt 3D cubes. Figure 1 shows how an original image is deformed when applying an affine or a non-affine transformation. These cubes have been designed to measure the compression of each voxel in the original image.

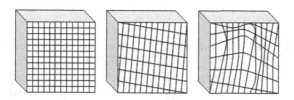

Fig. 1. Original (left), affine transformation (center), non-affine transformation (right).

Next steps describes this process:

– First, a 3D matrix filled with zeros is created. This matrix has a size equal to its subject SPECT image. Then, each voxel (s_v) is filled with an unique value, u_i with $u_i = 1, 2, 3, \ldots, N$ where N is equivalent to the total size of its input subject image.
– Second, the 3D matrix is expanded by a factor of 3. This process defines for each voxel a neighbourhood of voxels which will be defined here as "supervoxels". These supervoxels that present the same value, have a size of $3 \times 3 \times 3$ voxels as shown in Fig. 2.

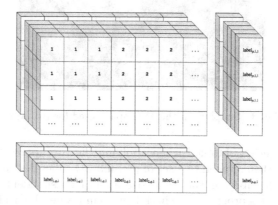

Fig. 2. 3D cube labelled using a $3 \times 3 \times 3$ grid.

- Once cubes are created for all subjects, next step consists on apply the same deformation fields that SPM computes when normalizing original subjects images to a reference template. This process is performed for both affine and non-affine approaches.
- A loop is used to measure how many voxels present the intensity given by label u_i. High values correspond with more expanded voxels.
- Finally, histograms are used to compare the volumes given by these two approaches.

3   Results

For this work it has been compared the affine and the non-affine transformations applied to a set of 20 $I^{[123]}$-Ioflupane SPECT images from subjects using the Statistical Parametric Mapping (SPM) software tool available from its website[1]. With this aim, each image has been spatially normalized to a reference template twice: one for the affine transformation and other for the non-affine. This template has been built following the approach proposed in [19]. An axial slice of this template is shown in Fig. 3.

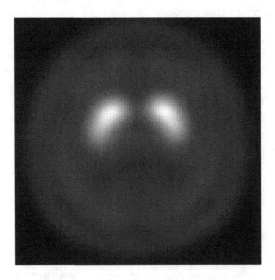

Fig. 3. Template in the MNI space used for this work.

Deformation fields obtained when applying the two approaches (affine and non-affine) were then applied to a set of prebuilt 3D cubes designed as explained in Sect. 2.3. Each cube has the same size as its correspondent subject image. The objective of this process is to check how volume of each voxel in the original image increases or decreases when the spatial normalization is applied.

[1] Website: https://www.fil.ion.ucl.ac.uk/spm/. Documentation about SPM, manuals and references are also available from this URL.

Figure 4 shows distribution of supervoxels volume in prebuilt 3D cubes for affine and non-affine normalization.

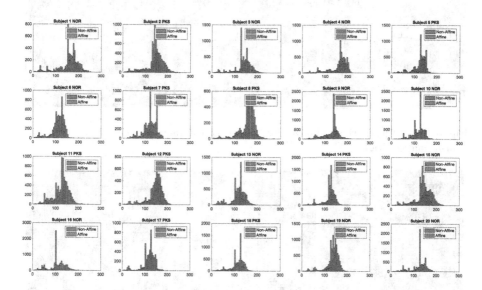

Fig. 4. Volume histograms for all subjects using affine and non-affine transformations.

A direct comparison of deformation fields applied to two subjects (a HC subject and a patient with PD) is depicted in Figs. 5 and 6.

4   Discusion

As stated in introduction section, sometimes shape differences between subjects are interesting in the diagnosis of many neurological disorders [10]. This is the case of Parkinsonism where measuring not only the size of *striatum* area but also its shape could be indicative of suffering this disorder or not [11]. Thus, in order to compare subjects as precise as possible, it is important to select an spatial normalization method that preserves as well as possible structures and, more precisely, voxels from original images.

If focusing on histogram results in Fig. 4, it can be observed that affine approach preserves better voxel volumes: affine histograms are more tight while non-affine results present a distribution more similar to a soft gaussian distribution. This can be explained as parts of the brain have been comprised in excess while others have been stretched. In Fig. 6 it can be observed this effect. In fact, centering on *striatum* area, it can be checked that some voxels have grown trying to cover the most part of the *striatum* area of our reference template at the cost of comprising the region situated around prefrontal cortex. This effect is even more highlighted as less DAT levels are detected in subjects with advanced PD.

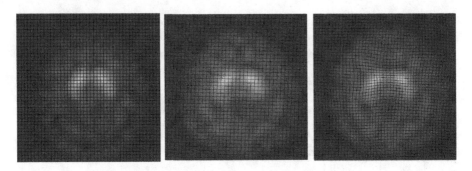

Fig. 5. HC subject: original image (left), affine transformation (center) and non-affine transformation (right).

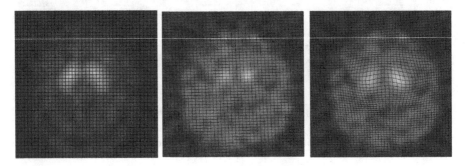

Fig. 6. Subject with PD: original image (left), affine transformation (center) and non-affine transformation (right).

5 Conclusions

Spatial normalization is one of the most important steps in the current analysis of neurological images for the development of novel and accurate automated diagnosis systems. This technique allows us to compare different subjects images between them and describing in an standarized way, for example, how intensities of functional images are distributed. However, as this work proposes, not all techniques are able to preserve, in the same way, the morphology of structures like *striatum* area that could be useful for their analysis using ML algorithms [20].

When morphology of *striatum* region is an important feature of the study, it is better to use an spatial normalization procedure based on an affine-registration. This method preserves better the contour of the region and do not compress or stretch other brain parts in excess to fit the objective image to a reference template. This idea is reinforced when considering works in which new imaging biomarkers for Parkinsonism are proposed [21,22].

Acknowledgment. This work has been supported by the MINECO/FEDER under the TEC2015-64718-R project.

References

1. Feigin, V.L., et al.: Global, regional, and national burden of neurological disorders during 1990–2015: a systematic analysis for the global burden of disease study 2015. Lancet Neurol. **16**(11), 877–897 (2017)
2. Sixel-Döring, F., et al.: The role of ^{123}I-FP-CIT-SPECT in the differential diagnosis of Parkinson and tremor syndromes: a critical assessment of 125 cases. J. Neurol. **258**(12), 2147–2154 (2011)
3. Booth, T.C., et al.: The role of functional dopamine-transporter SPECT imaging in Parkinsonian syndromes, part 2. Am. J. Neuroradiol. **36**(2), 236–244 (2015)
4. Marek, K.L., et al.: [^{123}I]β-CIT SPECT imaging assessment of the rate of Parkinson's disease progression. Neurology **57**(11), 2089–2094 (2001)
5. Badoud, S., et al.: Discriminating among degenerative Parkinsonisms using advanced ^{123}I-ioflupane SPECT analyses. NeuroImage Clin. **12**(Suppl. C), 234–240 (2016)
6. Augimeri, A., et al.: CADA-computer-aided DaTSCAN analysis. EJNMMI Phys. **3**(1), 2197–7364 (2016)
7. Martinez-Murcia, F., et al.: A 3D convolutional neural network approach for the diagnosis of Parkinson's disease. In: Ferrández Vicente, J.M., Álvarez-Sánchez, J.R., de la Paz López, F., Toledo Moreo, J., Adeli, H. (eds.) IWINAC 2017. LNCS, vol. 10337, pp. 324–333. Springer, Cham (2017). https://doi.org/10.1007/978-3-319-59740-9_32
8. Segovia, F., et al.: Multivariate analysis of ^{18}F-DMFP PET data to assist the diagnosis of Parkinsonism. Front. Neuroinform. **11**, 23 (2017)
9. Castillo-Barnes, D., et al.: Robust ensemble classification methodology for I^{123}-ioflupane SPECT images and multiple heterogeneous biomarkers in the diagnosis of Parkinson's disease. Front. Neuroinform. **12**, 53 (2018)
10. Owens-Walton, C., et al.: Striatal changes in Parkinson disease: an investigation of morphology, functional connectivity and their relationship to clinical symptoms. Psychiatry Res.: Neuroimaging **275**, 5–13 (2018)
11. Segovia, F., et al.: Automatic separation of Parkinsonian patients and control subjects based on the striatal morphology. In: Ferrández Vicente, J.M., Álvarez-Sánchez, J.R., de la Paz López, F., Toledo Moreo, J., Adeli, H. (eds.) IWINAC 2017. LNCS, vol. 10337, pp. 345–352. Springer, Cham (2017). https://doi.org/10.1007/978-3-319-59740-9_34
12. Castillo-Barnes, D., Segovia, F., Martinez-Murcia, F.J., Salas-Gonzalez, D., Ramírez, J., Górriz, J.M.: Classification improvement for Parkinson's disease diagnosis using the gradient magnitude in DaTSCAN SPECT images. In: Graña, M., et al. (eds.) SOCO'18-CISIS'18-ICEUTE'18. AISC, vol. 771, pp. 100–109. Springer, Cham (2019). https://doi.org/10.1007/978-3-319-94120-2_10
13. Friston, K.J., et al.: Spatial registration and normalization of images. Hum. Brain Mapp. **3**(3), 165–189 (1995)
14. Woods, R.P., et al.: Automated image registration: I. General methods and intra-subject, intramodality validation. J. Comput. Assist. Tomogr. **22**(1), 139–152 (1998)
15. Friston, K.J., et al.: Statistical Parametric Mapping. Elsevier Ltd., Oxford (2006)
16. Ashburner, J., Friston, K.J.: Non-linear registration. In: Statistical Parmetric Mapping, Chap. 5. Elsevier (2007)
17. Ashburner, J., et al.: Incorporating prior knowledge into image registration. Neuroimage **6**(4), 344–352 (1997)

18. Ashburner, J., et al.: Nonlinear spatial normalization using basis functions. Hum. Brain Mapp. **7**, 254–266 (1999)
19. Salas-Gonzalez, D., et al.: Building a FP-CIT SPECT brain template using a posterization approach. Neuroinformatics **13**(4), 391–402 (2015)
20. Sakai, K., et al.: Machine learning studies on major brain diseases: 5-year trends of 2014–2018. Jpn. J. Radiol. **37**(1), 34–72 (2018)
21. Saeed, U., et al.: Imaging biomarkers in Parkinson's disease and Parkinsonian syndromes: current and emerging concepts. Transl. Neurodegener. **6**(1), 8 (2017)
22. Burciu, R.G., et al.: Progression marker of Parkinson's disease: a 4-year multi-site imaging study. Brain **140**(8), 2183–2192 (2017)

Deep Learning on Brain Images in Autism: What Do Large Samples Reveal of Its Complexity?

Matthew Leming$^{(\boxtimes)}$ ⓘ and John Suckling ⓘ

Department of Psychiatry, Cambridge University, Cambridge CB20SZ, UK
ml784@cam.ac.uk

Abstract. Deep learning models for image classification face two recurring problems: they are typically limited by low sample size and are abstracted by their own complexity (the "black box problem"). We address these problems with the largest functional MRI connectome dataset ever compiled, classifying it across gender and Task vs rest (no task) to ascertain its performance, and then apply the model to a cross-sectional comparison of autism vs typically developing (TD) controls that has proved difficult to characterise with inferential statistics. Employing class-balancing to build a training set, a convolutional neural network was classified fMRI connectivity with overall accuracies of 76.35% (AUROC 0.8401), 90.71% (AUROC 0.9573), and 67.65% (AUROC 0.7162) for gender, task vs rest, and autism vs TD, respectively. Salience maps demonstrated that the deep learning model is capable of distinguishing complex patterns across either wide networks or localized areas of the brain, and, by analyzing maximal activations of the hidden layers, that the deep learning model partitions data at an early stage in its classification.

Keywords: Autism · Big data · Functional connectivity ·
Deep learning

1 Introduction

Motivated by reports of increased head circumference in children diagnosed with autism, the first measurements with MRI reported increased total brain, total tissue, and total lateral ventricle volumes in autistic adults [31]. Many similar studies followed, leading to a general consensus that brain volume was increased in autism. Moreover, in a highly cited article [8], increases in brain volume were suggested to occur in the first few years of life when diagnostic symptoms - social communication challenges, restricted and repetitive behaviours - also emerge. Since then, as further evidence has accumulated, the period of early brain overgrowth has been restricted to the first year of life [35], although large-scale longitudinal studies have failed to reproduce these meta-analytic findings [2,13]. Localising putative changes to brain structure has proved to be an even greater

© Springer Nature Switzerland AG 2019
J. M. Ferrández Vicente et al. (Eds.): IWINAC 2019, LNCS 11486, pp. 389–402, 2019.
https://doi.org/10.1007/978-3-030-19591-5_40

difficultly, with discrepancies between meta-analyses even though there is a significant overlap in the primary literature [6,10,41].

To address variations in data acquisition and processing that make between study comparisons less powerful, publicly available large-sample datasets are now a key aspect of imaging research. The ABIDE (http://fcon_1000. projects.nitrc.org/indi/abide/) multi-centre initiative has made available over 2000 images in two releases, but cross-sectional analyses of structural MRI have failed to observe significant differences [17,42]. The majority of these studies have used the established voxel brain morphometry technique (VBM), to estimate voxelwise tissue occupancies, and mass-univariate statistical testing. Other morphological properties of the cortex may yield greater sensitivity [25].

The measurement of correlation, or 'functional connectivity', between time-series of blood oxygenation level dependent (BOLD) endogenous contrast estimated from brain regions whilst in resting wakefulness has been demonstrated as a reproducible measurement on an individual basis [16]. Functional connectivity estimates represented as undirected graphs (connectomes) of nodes (brain regions) and edges (connectivity strengths) show promise in localising differences in resting activity to specific large-scale brain networks [40], and although there is cautionary evidence using the ABIDE dataset and others [32], it would appear that statistically significant differences in connectivity are generally observable, although variable in their presentation.

Computing power and access to large datasets have led to a resurgence in the popularity of neural networks (NNs) as a tool for data classification. In parallel, because of their wide applicability in representing complex data such as proteins and social networks, connectors have undergone significant development in terms of global and local characteristics. Some recent work has used NNs for processing connectomes, including whole-graph classification, clustering into sub-graphs, and node-wise classification [4,9,19,21,26,29].

In this article, we leverage publicly available datasets to amass and automatically pre-process a total of 39,461 functional MRIs from nine different multi-centre collections. We first classify them based on gender and task vs rest (no task) as a test of the validity of the application NNs to imaging data due to the known connectivity differences identified using inferential statistics [1,37]. We then classify autistic individuals from typically developing (TD) controls. All classifications were undertaken using a convolutional neural network (CNN) that uniquely encodes multi-layered connectivity matrices, an extension of the deep learning architecture previously described in [23]. To incentivise the model to classify based on phenotypic differences rather than site differences, class balancing techniques were used when building the training and test sets and compared against the fully-inclusive samples. Key outputs of the CNN were salience maps [23,38] that highlighted areas of the connectome the model preferentially focused on when performing its classification, and activation maximization [15] of a hidden layer inspected to visualize how the model partitioned the dataset following classification.

Table 1. Populations present in each dataset. Note that this represents the data that was successfully preprocessed and does not include data that failed this stage.

Collection	Subjs	Conns	Rest	Task	Age Min	Max	Mean	Stddev	Sex F	M	Disorders Depr	ASD	Alzh
1000 FC	833	833	833	0	7.88	85	26.47	11.22	475	358	0	0	0
ABCD	1424	11789	5142	6647	0.42	11.08	10.05	0.64	5553	6236	1557	124	0
ABIDE	658	658	658	0	6	64	17.18	7.94	84	574	0	307	0
ABIDE II	646	674	674	0	5.32	55	14.48	7.63	155	464	0	293	0
ADNI	158	309	309	0	56	95	73.38	7.22	171	138	0	0	157
BioBank	11275	11275	11275	0	40	70	54.93	7.50	6172	5103	1486	0	0
ICBM	83	353	0	353	19	74	43.53	14.58	169	184	0	0	0
OPEN FMRI	1409	6548	997	5551	5.89	78	27.11	10.47	2774	3037	182	81	0
NDAR	1284	7022	5080	1942	0.25	53.42	20.51	8.05	3434	3588	0	404	0
All	**17770**	**39461**	**24968**	**14493**	**0.25**	**95**	**28.97**	**19.88**	**18987**	**19682**	**3225**	**1209**	**157**

In attempting to classify components of this accumulated dataset, we sought to address the following questions: (1) How effective is a machine learning paradigm at classifying fMRI connectomes? (2) Which areas or networks of the brain do models focus on when undertaking classifications? (3) How does the model partition large datasets during classification? (4) Can the model effectively classify functional connectivities taken from multiple sources without relying explicitly on site differences to do so? (5) What is the best current evidence for cross-sectional differences in functional connectivity that characterise autism?

2   Methods

2.1   Datasets and Preprocessing

Datasets were acquired from OpenFMRI [33,34]; the Alzheimer's Disease Neuroimaging Initiative (ADNI); ABIDE [12]; ABIDE II [11]; the Adolescent Brain Cognitive Development (ABCD) Study [5]; the NIMH Data Archive, including the Research Domain Criteria Database (RDoCdb), the National Database for Clinical Trials (NDCT), and, most predominantly, the National Database for Autism Research (NDAR) [18]; the 1000 Functional Connectomes Project [14]; the International Consortium for Brain Mapping database (ICBM); and the UK Biobank; we refer to each of these sets as *collections*. OpenFMRI, NDAR, ICBM, and the 1000 Functional Connectomes Project are collections that comprise different datasets submitted from unrelated research groups; ADNI, ABIDE, ABIDE II, ABCD, and the UK Biobank are collections that were acquired as part of a larger research initiative.

Data were preprocessed using the fMRI Signal Processing Toolbox and the Brain Wavelet Toolbox [30] and parcellated with the 116-area Automated Anatomical Labelling (AAL) atlas that defined the nodes of the connectome, with the edges weighted by the correlation of the wavelet coefficients from the decomposition of the pre-processed BOLD time-series in each of four temporal scales: 0.1–0.2 Hz, 0.05–0.1 Hz, 0.03–0.05 Hz, and 0.01–0.03 Hz.

Datasets with regional dropout or which otherwise failed the parcellation stage were omitted from the analysis. Redundant datasets across collections were discarded. Multiple instances of connectivity matrices from the same individuals were used, though contributions from the same individuals were not shared between the training, validation, and test sets. The numbers of participants, total numbers of datasets used as well as phenotypic distributions, are shown in Table 1.

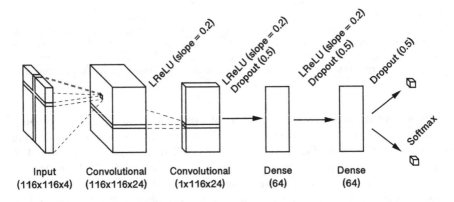

Fig. 1. The structure of the neural network, based on BrainNetCNN.

2.2   Neural Network Model and Training

The data used for training and testing the CNN were $4 \times 116 \times 116$ (4 wavelet scales and 116 nodes) symmetric connectivity (wavelet coefficient correlation) matrices with values scaled on $[0, 1]$.

To classify data, we employed a CNN with cross-shaped filters described in [23]; to allow the network to train on connectivity matrices (Fig. 1. We re-implemented the architecture of [23] using Keras [7], a popular machine learning library, leveraging the advantages of other software libraries that support Keras. Additionally, this re-implementation extended the model to include multiple channels in the inputs, as opposed to single connectivity matrices.

The CNN was constructed with: 24 edge-to-edge filters; 24 edge-to-node filters; 2 fully-connected layers, each with 64 nodes; and a final softmax layer. Three leaky rectified linear unit (ReLU) layers, with a slope of 0.2, and three dropout layers, with a dropout rate of 0.5, were also used in the network. Specifications are shown in Fig. 1. The model was trained using an Adam optimizer with batch sizes of 64, otherwise Keras defaults were used. Models were trained for 250 epochs, and the epoch with the highest validation accuracy was selected.

2.3   Set Division

Datasets were partitioned into three sets: the training set, comprised of two-thirds of the data and used to train the model; the validation set, comprised of one-sixth of the data and used to select the epoch at which training stopped; and the test set, used to assess the trained classifier performance.

For all classifications, balancing was used such that each class comprised approximately half of the datasets. To account for gender, age, and possible scanning site differences between datasets, we report the inter-dataset classification accuracy as well as the global accuracy. Two different class-balancing approaches were used when building the sets: one selected two age-matched cases for gender and task vs rest classification, and the other selected a case and corresponding control from the same collection for the autism vs TD classification.

2.4   Test Set Evaluation

Inter-data Classification. Following the training of the models, the accuracy and the area under the receiver operating characteristic curve (AUROC) were calculated as measures of machine learning performance on the test set. This was to determine if one group in the classification outperformed the other in training leading to a biasing of the overall accuracy.

Activation Maximization. Activation maximization [15] is a technique to determine the maximally activated hidden units in response to the test set of the CNN layers following training. Activation maximization was applied to the 116×24 second layer of our network (Fig. 1) as this two-dimensional convolutional layer acts as a bottleneck, and is thus easier to interpret and visualize. This layer is naturally stratified by 24 *filters*, each with 116 nodes that correspond to parcellated brain areas. To offset the influence of spurious maximizations, we opted to record the 10 datasets that maximally activated each hidden unit, displaying their mode, collection, gender, age group, and task/rest; for example, if 6 connectomes that maximally activated a unit were from Biobank and four from Open fMRI, Biobank would be displayed as maximally activating that unit.

Salience Maps. We deployed salience maps [23,28,38] using a previous Keras implementation [27] to display the parts of the connectivity matrix the CNN emphasised in its classification of the test set. Class saliency extractions operate by taking the derivative of the CNN classification function (approximated as a first-order Taylor expansion, estimated via back-propagation) with respect to an input matrix, with the output being the same dimensions as the input [38]. Saliency extractions are particularly advantageous when applied to connectivity matrices, because unlike typical 2D images these matrices are spatially static (i.e. each part of the matrix represents the same connection in the brain, across all datasets), and thus global tendencies of the model can be visualized. Saliency maps for each adjacency matrix were averaged and displayed to demonstrate on which aspects of the connectome the CNN was most focused when performing the classification.

Table 2. Populations present in the training set for each round of classification, with and without class balancing

	With class balancing						Without class balancing					
	Autism		Rest v Task		Gender		Autism		Rest v Task		Gender	
	non-ASD	ASD	Rest	non-Rest	Female	Male	non-ASD	ASD	Rest	non-Rest	Female	Male
1000 FC	0	0	507	0	320	271	0	0	625	0	358	272
ABCD	61	82	3088	3634	3370	3275	7301	82	3091	4292	3416	3991
ABIDE	232	229	461	0	62	375	263	230	493	0	60	434
ABIDE II	221	218	408	0	113	303	284	221	505	0	117	346
ADNI	0	0	4	0	106	88	0	0	230	0	135	95
BIOBANK	3	3	597	0	3967	3704	0	0	8458	0	4633	3825
ICBM	0	0	0	185	99	105	0	0	0	217	121	94
NDAR	122	130	2164	909	2194	2020	4307	138	3215	1230	2180	2240
OPEN FMRI	61	62	372	2792	1977	2059	0	0	883	4030	2059	2299
TOTAL	**700**	**724**	**7601**	**7520**	**12208**	**12200**	**12155**	**671**	**17500**	**9769**	**13079**	**13596**

2.5   Experiments

We performed the classification on class-balanced datasets that then classified based on gender, task vs rest, and autism vs TD controls. For gender and task vs rest classifications, we also balanced classes by age; that is, the distribution of ages for each group was the same. For autism vs TD controls, we balanced across collections to minimise site differences, and also as a proxy for age whilst maximising the sample size.

Additionally, we trained models without the use of class balancing, only excluding collections that entirely lacked a particular class. The number of connectomes used in each experiment's training set, with and without class balancing, are given in Table 2. Where training was successful, we report the overall classification accuracy and AUROC for the balanced and unbalanced test sets.

3   Results

The results displayed a tendency of the model to use particular filters to sequester data by different variables, especially if it were attempting to classify by that variable, although the model divided data across certain filters independent of the classification variable. While gender, task vs rest, and autism vs TD controls each have a small proportion of their filters wholly activated by the datapoints of a single collection (which may be easy to distinguish based on differences between MRI scanners), the majority of filters were activated by a variety of different collections, indicating the effective synthesis of data from different sources. Those comparisons that saw the highest classification accuracy tended to activate individual filters in most nodes, indicating the network's tendency to group data early in the architecture, prior to the fully-connected layers.

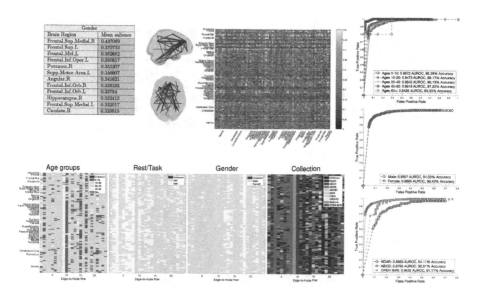

Fig. 2. Activation maximization, salience map, and ROC-curve results on gender classification

3.1 Gender Comparison

With class balancing, classification accuracy on the test group was 76.35% (AUROC 0.8401). Classification was most successful on the UK Biobank collection (87.31% accuracy). When stratifying by age, the CNN was able to obtain higher performance distinguishing gender in older age groups than younger age groups, and better able to achieve classification of gender in resting than task-based fMRI (78.96% versus 71.44%).

In activation maximization Fig. 2, filters 3/8, 9, and 10 were almost entirely dedicated to the classification of OPEN fMRI, Biobank, and ABCD collections, respectively. Filter 18 was activated by females, whilst most other filters are activated by males. Filter 3 was activated by task-based fMRI from OPEN fMRI, while filter 15 as activated by resting-state fMRI from no particular collection. Salience maps indicated that gender classification utilized a wider spread of areas, focusing on networks in the frontal lobe.

Without class balancing, the results on gender were a comparable 0.8406 AUROC and 76.88% accuracy.

3.2 Task vs Rest (No Task)

With balanced classes, task vs rest fMRI classification was successful with 90.71% (AUROC 0.9573) of the test set correctly assigned. The training set, whilst balanced by age, had a high imbalance between collections. The AUROC of those collections that contributed substantial amounts both resting-state and task participants - i.e., NDAR, ABCD, and Open fMRI - had comparable AUROCs to

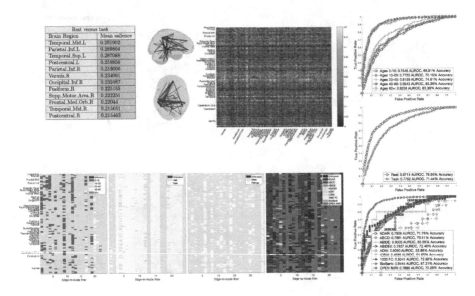

Fig. 3. Activation maximization, salience map, and ROC-curve results on resting-state-versus-task classification

that obtained overall. Furthermore, the salience map focused on the default mode network in the left hemisphere and its connection to the right frontal medial orbital area. Together, this suggests that the main influence in classification was not site differences.

In activation maximization six filters were dedicated to the resting-state class, fourteen to task-based fMRI, and four were mixed Fig. 3. This is likely indicative of the deep learning model using a simpler characterization of resting-state fMRI than task-based, which used more of its internal memory to capture the distinguishing patterns.

Without class balancing, the model achieved a higher 0.9792 AUROC, presumably displaying the effects of using more data on these models, as the age-balancing technique applied effectively discarded nearly half the training set data. However, a classification based partially on age groups is also possible.

3.3 Autism vs TD Controls

With class balancing, the overall performance on the test set was 67.65% (AUROC 0.7162). Autism classifications were highly dependent on the collection used, though the final accuracies were above chance for all collections. Class balancing was necessary, as data from autistic individuals comprised a relatively low percentage; collections with data from autistic individuals - Open fMRI, ABIDE I and II, NDAR, and ABCD - had <10%. Without class balancing the model failed to converge, simply classifying every datapoint as a TD control.

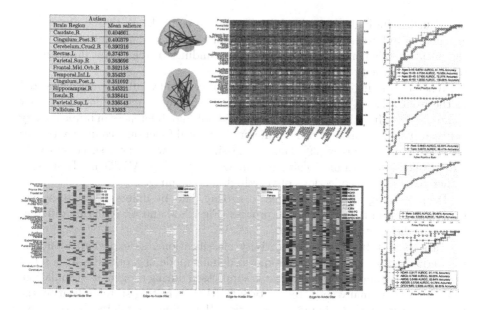

Fig. 4. Activation maximization, salience map, and ROC-curve results on autism classification

In activation maximization of the second layer, autism classification used filters 1, 5, 9, and 23 for the ABIDE collection, and filters 7, 18, and 24 were mostly used for females from the Open fMRI coillection Fig. 4. The majority of nodes were maximally activated by data from the ABIDE I and II collections, although a disproportionately high number were used to classify Open fMRI autism data, which comprised < 10% of the total. A surprisingly low proportion of data from the NDAR and ABCD collections maximally activated the nodes, even though its classification was relatively successful and comprised a more substantial portion of the dataset. Most other nodes were maximally activated by the male resting-state data, which reflects the autism dataset as a whole. The salience maps indicate autism was classified using specific, localised regions of the brain; notably, bilateral posterior cingulum and the right caudate nucleus.

4 Discussion

This work describes how large and diverse imaging data might be analyzed by deep learning models, encouraging the aggregation of publicly available collections. Data were partitioned based on clear and logical features of the images, and that, even with imperfect classification accuracies, deep learning models are capable of recognizing highly complex patterns in large datasets representing large-scale brain networks and localized structures.

The neuroscientific objective of this study was to use the available imaging data with deep learning to describe the pattern of functional brain changes that distinguishes individuals with autism from TD controls. With the absence of any gold standard in the cross-sectional comparison, we first undertook other classifications that have more secure, robust findings in the extant literature to confirm the veracity of the developed methods.

When classifying gender, the model was influenced by diffuse areas connected to the frontal lobe (Fig. 2). This is consistent with previous findings in gender comparisons of functional imaging, which did not find differences in brain activity between specific areas, but rather differences in local functional connectivity over large areas of the cortex [39]. Gender classifications were most successful with larger collections with more consistent image quality (e.g. ABCD and BioBank), rather than smaller collections of very high-quality images.

Deep learning models are prone to sorting data by different variables relatively early on in the classification process (Figs. 2, 3, and 4), reserving different filters for different classes of data.

Task vs rest functional connectivity classifications, as expected, identified the major components of the well-known default mode network (Fig. 3), a set of bilateral and symmetric regions that is suppressed during exogenous stimulation. More filters maximally activated by task fMRI than resting-state, indicating the greater variation that characterizes task fMRI, which is related to cognitive performance [20]. The high classification accuracies and detected patterns gives credibility to the use CNN with neuroimages.

Bilateral areas with some correspondence to the default mode network, particularly parietal, temporal and frontal medial regions, were identified as salient to the comparison of the autism vs TD controls: Figs. 3 and 4. Notably, autistic individuals were additionally classified by connections to the cerebellum and deep structures (caudate and hippocampus). Prior cross-sectional studies of functional connectivity in autistic individuals have primarily thresholded connectivity estimates (i.e. correlations), whereas here all existing connections were included, both positive and negative. A comparison of connectors using a highly matched sub-set of the ABIDE II collection [24] found global differences, and reduced network segregation within the default mode network and primary auditory and somatosensory cortical regions, and between these regions and other large networks.

Model accuracy was lower compared to the highest rates reported in literature [3,22,28], although this result should be viewed with several caveats. The dataset used in this analysis was larger and more complex than any other previously analyzed, consisting of data from many collections. Direct comparisons of machine learning classification methods is difficult as there are no universally accepted methods to divide collections into training and test sets (unlike standardized competitions in other fields, such as the ImageNet Large Scale Visual Recognition Challenge (ILSVRC) [36]). Furthermore, our exclusion criteria differed, and, because we opted to use multiple scanning sessions from single subjects during training, we also used data in ABIDE not employed in previous studies. Class balancing may also have significantly affected the classification accuracy. Nevertheless, this was necessary to avoid spuriously large accuracies due to the highly skewed ratio of autism:TD, where high rates of classification the larger groups lead to biases to the overall rate. Lastly, preprocessing methods and exclusion criteria are not typically shared across studies, and thus differences due to the input data cannot be discounted.

More generally, our deep learning model employed multichannel input. Although this has long been the standard in 2D image classification (for instance, RGB images), it has not been utilized before in the classification of connectomes. Theoretically, this provides an advantage, since it encodes more information about the underlying timeseries. In practice, multichannel inputs generally increased the accuracy of our model by 2–3% over the single-channel models tested.

We used salience maps [38] to identify connections and areas that the model incorporated in its classification; this method has previously been used in deep learning on functional connectivity [23, 28] as is an effective method of dissecting neural networks. However, a caveat to this is that salience maps are imperfect indicators of areas of importance in the data that may not give a complete depiction of the distinguishing features.

One of the key methods we used to interrogate the results from our deep learning model was activation maximization. Previously, activation maximization has been used for intuiting the internal configuration of neural networks rather than for interpretation purposes [15]. In this study, while some filters were solely activated by data from single collections, the majority by mixed data from different collections suggesting an ability to account for site differences during classification. Deployment of activation maximisation here led to specific observations: variation of task-based fMRI is far greater than during rest (six filters maximally activated by rsfMRI and 14 by tasks); dataset sequestering happens even without successful classification; the number of filters activated maximally by a particular dataset is not necessarily proportional to the classification accuracy of that dataset.

5 Conclusion

With careful class-balancing, deep learning models are capable of good quality classifications across mixed collections detecting differences in brain networks, and functions of localized structures, or functional connections over large areas. Salience maps highlighted key spatial elements of the classification and activation maximisation gave insights into the types of features on which the CNN based its classification. This deep learning model is an example of the apparatus to leverage publicly accessible large volumes of data for discovery science.

Acknowledgements. This study used publicly available datasets, each with their own acknowledgements. For brevity, we have not included the full text, but recognise the contributions of the Alzheimer's Disease Neuroimaging Initiative, International Consortium for Brain Mapping, National Database for Autism Research, NIH Pediatric MRI Data Repository, National Database for Clinical Trials, Research Domain Criteria Database, Adolescent Brain Cognitive Development Study, UK Biobank Resource, 1000

Functional Connectomes Project, ABIDE I and II, and Open fMRI. This research was co-funded by the NIHR Cambridge Biomedical Research Centre and Marmaduke Sheild. ML is supported by a Gates Cambridge Scholarship from the University of Cambridge.

References

1. Arbabshirani, M., Havlicek, M., Kiehl, K., Pearlson, G., Calhoun, V.: Functional network connectivity during rest and task conditions: a comparative study. Hum. Brain Mapp. **34**, 2959–2971 (2012). https://doi.org/10.1002/hbm.22118
2. Blanken, L., et al.: A prospective study of fetal head growth, autistic traits and autism spectrum disorder. Autism Res. **11**, 602–612 (2018). https://doi.org/10.1002/aur.1921
3. Brown, C., Kawahara, J., Hamarneh, G.: Connectome priors in deep neural networks to predict autism. In: 2018 IEEE 15th International Symposium on Biomedical Imaging (ISBI 2018) (2018). https://doi.org/10.1109/ISBI.2018.8363534
4. Bruna, J., Zaremba, W., Szlam, A., LeCun, Y.: Spectral networks and locally connected networks on graphs. In: ICLR (2014)
5. Casey, B., Dale, A.: The adolescent brain cognitive development (ABCD) study: imaging acquisition across 21 sites. Dev. Cogn. Neurosci. **32**, 43–54 (2018). https://doi.org/10.1016/j.dcn.2018.03.001
6. Cauda, F., et al.: Grey matter abnormality in autism spectrum disorder: an activation likelihood estimation meta-analysis study. J. Neurol. Neurosurg. Psychiatry **82**, 1304–1313 (2011). https://doi.org/10.1136/jnnp.2010.239111
7. Chollet, F.: Keras (2015). https://github.com/fchollet/keras
8. Courchesne, E., Carper, R., Akshoomoff, N.: Evidence of brain overgrowth in the first year of life in autism. JAMA **290**, 337–344 (2003). https://doi.org/10.1001/jama.290.3.337
9. Defferrard, M., Bresson, P., Vandergheynst, X.: Convolutional neural networks on graphs with fast localized spectral filtering. In: NIPS, pp. 3844–3852 (2016)
10. DeRamus, T., Kana, R.: Anatomical likelihood estimation meta-analysis of grey and white matter anomalies in autism spectrum disorders author links open overlay panel. NeuroImage: Clin. **7**, 525–536 (2015). https://doi.org/10.1016/j.nicl.2014.11.004
11. Di Martino, A., et al.: Enhancing studies of the connectome in autism using the autism brain imaging data exchange II. Sci. Data **4**, 170010 (2017). https://doi.org/10.1038/sdata.2017.10
12. Di Martino, A., et al.: The autism brain imaging data exchange: towards a large-scale evaluation of the intrinsic brain architecture in autism. Mol. Psychiatry **19**, 659–67 (2014). https://doi.org/10.1038/mp.2013.78
13. Dinstein, I., Haar, S., Atsmon, S., Schtaerman, H.: No evidence of early head circumference enlargements in children later diagnosed with autism in Israel. Mol. Autism **8** (2018). https://doi.org/10.1186/s13229-017-0129-9
14. Dolgin, E.: This is your brain online: the functional connectomes project. Nat. Med. **16**, 351 (2010). https://doi.org/10.1038/nm0410-351b
15. Erhan, D., Bengio, Y., Courville, A., Vincent, P.: Visualizing higher-layer features of a deep network. Technical report 1341, University of Montreal (2009)
16. Finn, E., et al.: Functional connectome fingerprinting: identifying individuals using patterns of brain connectivity. Nat Neurosci. **18**, 1664–1671 (2015). https://doi.org/10.1038/nn.4135

17. Haar, S., Berman, S., Behrmann, M., Dinstein, I.: Anatomical abnormalities in autism? Cereb. Cortex **26**, 1440–1452 (2016). https://doi.org/10.1093/cercor/bhu242
18. Hall, D., Huerta, M., McAuliffe, M., Farber, G.: Sharing heterogeneous data: the national database for autism research. Neuroinformatics **10**, 331–339 (2012). https://doi.org/10.1007/s12021-012-9151-4
19. Hamilton, W., Ying, R., Leskovec, J.: Representation learning on graphs: methods and applications. Bulletin of the IEEE Computer Society Technical Committee on Data Engineering (2017)
20. Hasson, U., Nusbaum, H., Small, S.: Task-dependent organization of brain regions active during rest. PNAS **106**, 10841–10846 (2009). https://doi.org/10.1073/pnas.0903253106
21. Hechtlinger, Y., Chakravarti, P., Qin, J.: A generalization of convolutional neural networks to graph-structured data. arXiv (2017)
22. Heinsfeld, A., Franco, A., Craddock, R., Buchweitz, A., Meneguzzia, F.: Identification of autism spectrum disorder using deep learning and the abide dataset. NeuroImage: Clin. **17**, 16–23 (2018). https://doi.org/10.1016/j.nicl.2017.08.017
23. Kawahara, J., et al.: BrainNetCNN: convolutional neural networks for brain networks; towards predicting neurodevelopment. NeuroImage **146**, 1038–1049 (2017). https://doi.org/10.1016/j.neuroimage.2016.09.046
24. Keown, C., Datko, M., Chen, C., Maximo, J., Jahedi, A., Müller, R.: Network organization is globally atypical in autism: a graph theory study of intrinsic functional connectivity. Biol. Psychiatry: Cogn. Neurosci. Neuroimaging **2**, 66–75 (2017). https://doi.org/10.1016/j.bpsc.2016.07.008
25. Khundrakpam, B., Lewis, J., Kostopoulos, P., Carbonell, F., Evans, A.: Cortical thickness abnormalities in autism spectrum disorders through late childhood, adolescence, and adulthood: a large-scale MRI study. Cereb. Cortex **27**, 1721–1731 (2017). https://doi.org/10.1093/cercor/bhx038
26. Kipf, T., Welling, M.: Semi-supervised classification with graph convolutional neural networks. In: ICLR 2017 (2017)
27. Kotikalapudi, R., Contributors: keras-vis (2017). https://github.com/raghakot/keras-vis
28. Khosla, M., Jamison, K., Kuceyeski, A., Sabuncu, M.R.: 3D convolutional neural networks for classification of functional connectomes. In: Stoyanov, D., et al. (eds.) DLMIA/ML-CDS-2018. LNCS, vol. 11045, pp. 137–145. Springer, Cham (2018). https://doi.org/10.1007/978-3-030-00889-5_16
29. Nikolentzos, G., Meladianos, P., Tixier, A.J.-P., Skianis, K., Vazirgiannis, M.: Kernel graph convolutional neural networks. In: Kůrková, V., Manolopoulos, Y., Hammer, B., Iliadis, L., Maglogiannis, I. (eds.) ICANN 2018. LNCS, vol. 11139, pp. 22–32. Springer, Cham (2018). https://doi.org/10.1007/978-3-030-01418-6_3
30. Patel, A., Bullmore, E.: A wavelet-based estimator of the degrees of freedom in denoised fmri time series for probabilistic testing of functional connectivity and brain graphs. NeuroImage **142**, 14–26 (2016). https://doi.org/10.1016/j.neuroimage.2015.04.052
31. Piven, J., Arndt, S., Bailey, J., Havercamp, S., Andreasen, N., Palmer, P.: An MRI study of brain size in autism. Am. J. Psychiatry **152**, 1145–1149 (1995). https://doi.org/10.1176/ajp.152.8.1145
32. Plitt, M., Barnes, K., Martin, A.: Functional connectivity classification of autism identifies highly predictive brain features but falls short of biomarker standards. NeuroImage Clin. **7**, 359–66 (2015). https://doi.org/10.1016/j.nicl.2014.12.013

33. Poldrack, R., et al.: Toward open sharing of task-based fMRI data: the OpenfMRI project. Front. Neuroinform. **7** (2013). https://doi.org/10.3389/fninf.2013.00012
34. Poldrack, R., Gorgolewski, K.: OpenfMRI: open sharing of task fMRI data. NeuroImage **144**, 259–261 (2017). https://doi.org/10.1016/j.neuroimage.2015.05.073
35. Redcay, E., Courchesne, E.: Biol. Psychiatry **58**, 1–9 (2005). https://doi.org/10.1016/j.biopsych.2005.03.026
36. Russakovsky, O., et al.: ImageNet large scale visual recognition challenge. Int. J. Comput. Vis. **115**, 211–252 (2015). https://doi.org/10.1007/s11263-015-0816-y
37. Satterthwaite, T., et al.: Linked sex differences in cognition and functional connectivity in youth. Cereb. Cortex **25**, 2383–2394 (2015). https://doi.org/10.1093/cercor/bhu036
38. Simonyan, K., Vedaldi, A., Zisserman, A.: Deep inside convolutional networks: visualising image classification models and saliency maps. In: Workshop at International Conference on Learning Representations (2014)
39. Tomasi, D., Volkow, N.: Gender differences in brain functional connectivity density. Hum. Brain Mapp. **33**, 849–860 (2013). https://doi.org/10.1002/hbm.21252
40. Wang, W., et al.: Altered resting-state functional activity in patients with autism spectrum disorder: a quantitative meta-analysis. Front. Neurol. **9**, 556 (2018). https://doi.org/10.3389/fneur.2018.00556
41. Yang, J., Hofmann, J.: Action observation and imitation in autism spectrum disorders: an ALE meta-analysis of fMRI studies. Brain Imaging Behav. **10**, 960–969 (2016). https://doi.org/10.1007/s11682-015-9456-7
42. Zhang, W., Groen, W., Mennes, M., Greven, C., Buitelaar, J., Rommelse, N.: Revisiting subcortical brain volume correlates of autism in the abide dataset: effects of age and sex. Psychol. Med. **48**, 654–668 (2018). https://doi.org/10.1017/S003329171700201X

Multivariate Pattern Analysis of Electroencephalography Data in a Demand-Selection Task

David López-García[1], Alberto Sobrado[1], J. M. González-Peñalver[1],
Juan Manuel Górriz[2], and María Ruz[1(✉)]

[1] Mind, Brain and Behavior Research Center (CIMCYC),
University of Granada, Granada, Spain
{dlopez,mruz}@ugr.es
[2] Signal Theory, Telematics and Communications Department (TSTC),
University of Granada, Granada, Spain
gorriz@ugr.es

Abstract. Cognitive effort is costly and partly aversive, and thus humans usually avoid it if given the chance. In Demand-Selection Tasks (DST), participants tend to choose the easy option over the hard one. The neural underpinnings of this effect, however, are not well understood. The current study is an initial approximation to adapt a DST to a format that allows measuring concurrent high-density electroencephalography. We used multivariate pattern analysis (MVPA) to decode conflict-related neural processes associated with congruent or incongruent events in a time-frequency resolved way and determined how different frequency bands contribute to the overall decoding accuracy. The decoding analysis involved the use of Support Vector Machines, a supervised learning algorithm that provides a theoretically elegant, computationally efficient, and very effective solution for many practical pattern recognition problems. Preliminary results show significant differences in activation patterns for congruent and incongruent trials, yielding 80% of decoding accuracy 400 ms after the stimulus onset. The results of frequency bands contribution analysis suggest that context-dependent proportion of congruency effect may rely on neural processes operating in Delta and Theta-band frequencies.

Keywords: Multivariate pattern analysis · Electroencephalography ·
Classification · Support Vector Machine · Demand-Selection Task

1 Introduction

Cognitive effort is costly and partly aversive, and thus humans usually avoid it if given the chance. In Demand-Selection Tasks (DST)[1], participants tend to choose the easy option over the hard one. The neural underpinnings of this effect, however, are not well understood. The current study is an initial approximation to adapt a DST to a format that allows measuring concurrent high-density

© Springer Nature Switzerland AG 2019
J. M. Ferrández Vicente et al. (Eds.): IWINAC 2019, LNCS 11486, pp. 403–411, 2019.
https://doi.org/10.1007/978-3-030-19591-5_41

electroencephalography. Supervised machine learning algorithms, more specifically Support Vector Machines (Vapnik, 1979), in conjunction with several neuroimaging techniques, such as functional Magnetic Resonance Imaging (fMRI), Electroencephalography (EEG) or Magnetoencephalography (MEG), have been widely and successfully applied in clinical applications, such as computer-aided diagnosis of Alzheimer's disease [2–5], automatic sleep stages classification [6,7] or automatic detection of sleep disorders [8]. Recently, these techniques are gaining popularity in Cognitive Neuroscience, especially in fMRI studies. However, the poor temporal resolution of the fMRI signal prevents an accurate time-resolved study of the cognitive precesses. For this reason, the use of these techniques is spreading and they are being applied to M/EEG signals, studying the neural dynamics of face detection [9], the process of memory retrieval [10], the representational dynamics of task and object processing in humans [11] or decoding spoken words in bilingual listeners [12].

This study uses multivariate pattern analysis (MVPA) to decode conflict-related neural processes associated to congruent or incongruent events in a time-frequency resolved way. Due to the noisy nature of the EEG signal, a trial averaging approach has been carried out during the feature extraction stage, increasing the signal-to-noise ratio (SNR). In addition, we determined how different frequency bands contribute to the overall decoding accuracy, showing that context-dependent proportion of congruency effect may rely on neural processes operating in Delta and Theta frequency bands [13].

2   Materials and Methods

Participants. Thirty-two healthy individuals (21 females, 29 right-handed, mean age = 24.65, SD = 4.57) were recruited for the experiment. Subjects had normal or corrected-to-normal vision and none reported any neurological or psychiatric disorder. All of them provided informed, written consent before the beginning of the experiment and received a 10-euro payment or course credits in exchange for their participation. The experiment was approved by the Ethics Committee of the University of Granada.

Experimental Setup. Stimuli presentation and behavioral data collection were carried out using MATLAB (MathWorks) in conjunction with Phychtoolbox-3 Toolbox [14], in a magnetically shielded room. The visual stimuli were presented in an LCD screen (Benq, 1920 × 1080 resolution, 60 Hz refresh rate) and placed 68.31±5.37 cm away of subject's Glabella. Using a photodetector, the stimuli onset lag was measured at 8 ms, which corresponds to half of the refresh rate of the monitor. Triggers were sent from the presentation computer to the EEG recording system through an 8-bit parallel port and using a custom MATLAB function in conjunction with inpoutx64 driver [15].

Stimuli. The predictive cue acted as a difficulty selector, and consisted of two squares of different colors stacked and presented in the center of the screen (visual angle ∼ 5°). In forced blocks, a small white indicator (circle 50% or

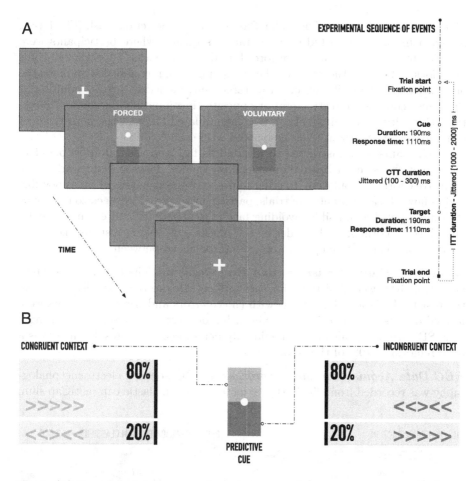

Fig. 1. (A) Experimental sequence of events in case of a correct response on both cue and stimulus flanker. A trial starts width a fixation point, followed by a cue, witch act as a color picker. Subjects have to choose (freely or forced, depending on the block type) the possible color of the upcoming target stimulus. Finally, after a variable time interval (100–300 ms) the target stimulus appears and subjects have to respond accordingly to the orientation of the central arrow. Another variable time interval started before the beginning of the next trial. The cue and the target stimulus remained in the screen for 190 ms. (B) Cognitive effort manipulation through the percentage of congruent and incongruent trials. Each cue color is associated to a high and low conflict context. (Color figure online)

square 50%) appeared on top of the color that had to be chosen. In voluntary blocks, this indicator appeared between the two colored squares (see Fig. 1). Each target stimulus consisted of five arrows pointing left or rightwards, which were displayed at the center of the screen (visual angle ∼6°). The color of the target stimulus depended on the previously selected color.

Experimental Design. The Color-Based Demand-Selection Task [Fig. 1 (a)], modified from [1], consisted of a cue-target sequence where participants were required to choose (voluntarily or forced, in different blocks: 4 blocks, 240 trials per block, ~90 min) the color of the upcoming stimulus and discriminate the orientation (right or left) of an arrow target surrounded by arrows pointing at the same (compatible distracters) or opposite (incompatible distracters) direction. Difficulty, or cognitive effort, was manipulated through the percentage of congruent or incongruent trials associated with each color.

Participants were instructed to respond as fast and accurately as possible, and to not choose color based on personal preference. They were unaware of the cognitive effort manipulation. In order to preserve the signals as clean as possible and remove the least number of trials, participants were encouraged to remain as still and relaxed as possible, avoiding face muscle activity and eye movements, but blinking normally. The order of the blocks, cue colors, response keys and color-conflict context mappings were counterbalanced between subjects.

Behavioral Data Acquisition and Preprocessing. The reaction time (RT) and error rates were registered for each subject. Before the statistical analysis, the first trial of each block, trials with choice errors and trials after errors were filtered out, as suggested in [16]. Finally, RT outliers were also rejected using a ±2.5 SD threshold, calculated individually per subject. As a result, there was a total removal of 19% of the trials.

EEG Data Acquisition and Preprocessing. High-density electroencephalography was recorded from 65 electrodes mounted on an elastic cap (actiCap slim,

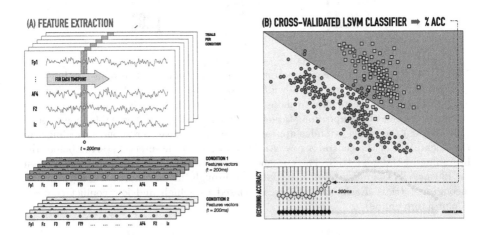

Fig. 2. (A) Feature extraction process in simulated data. The feature vectors of each condition and time point consisted of an z-scored voltage array for all the scalp electrodes. For an improved SNR, five trials were averaged before the feature extraction. (B) Cross-validated LSVM classifier. For each time point, a LSVM was trained and tested (stratified k-fold cross-validation, k = 10). Chance level was calculated permuting the labels.

Brain Products). The TP9 and TP10 electrodes were used to record the electrooculogram (EOG) and were placed below and next to the left eye of the subject. Impedances were kept below 5 k. EEG activity was referenced to the FCz electrode and signals were digitalized at a sampling rate of 1 KHz.

Electroencephalography recordings were average referenced, downsampled to 256 Hz, and digitally filtered using a bandpass FIR filter [0.5–40 Hz], preserving the phase information. No channel was interpolated for any subject. EEG recordings were epoched [−1000, 2000 ms centered at the target arrows] and baseline corrected [−200, 0 ms], extracting data only from correct trials. A total of 90 518 epochs (target, cue and cue response) were extracted. To remove blinks from the remaining data, Independent Component Analysis (ICA) was computed using the *runica* algorithm from EEGLAB [17], excluding TP9 and TP10 channels. Artifactual components were rejected by visual inspection of raw activity of each component, scalp maps and power spectrum. Then, an automatic trial rejection process was performed, pruning the data from no stereotypical artifacts. The trial rejection procedure was based on (1) extreme values: all trials with amplitudes in any electrode out of $\pm75\mu V$ range were automatically rejected ($\sim7\%$ of the total sample); (2) abnormal spectra: the spectrum should not deviate from baseline by ±50 dB in the 0–2 Hz frequency window (which is optimal for localizing any remaining eye movements) and should not deviate by -100 dB or $+25$ dB in 20–40 Hz (useful for detecting muscle activity) ($<1\%$ of the total sample).

Multivariate Pattern Analysis (MVPA). The MVPA for the decoding analysis was performed in MATLAB by a custom-developed set of linear Support Vector Machines (LSVM), trained to discriminate between congruent and incongruent target stimuli. To avoid skewed classification results due to a possible unbalanced dataset, the prior probabilities of each class were set to uniform. The rest of the classification parameters remained by default. The generalization performance of the classifiers was calculated through cross-validation technique (stratified k-fold, $k = 10$).

To obtain the classification performance in a time-resolved way, the feature vectors were extracted as shown in Fig. 2. Thus, the classification procedure, for each subject, ran as follows: (1) For each timepoint and trial, we generated two feature vectors (one for each condition or class) consisting of the raw potential measured in all electrodes (excluding EOG electrodes: TP9 and TP10). (2) Features vector containing raw potential values were normalized (z-score). (3) LSVMs were trained and cross-validated, resulting in a single value of accuracy for each timepoint and subject. (4) Finally, a single measure of accuracy for each timepoint was calculated by averaging the classification performance over all the subjects. The chance level was calculated following the former analysis but using randomly permuted labels for each trial.

In a second analysis, to increase the signal-to-noise ratio [18] (SNR), improving the overall decoding performance and reducing the computational load, each subjects dataset was reduced by randomly averaging a number of trials belonging to the same condition. The number of trials to average is a trade-off between

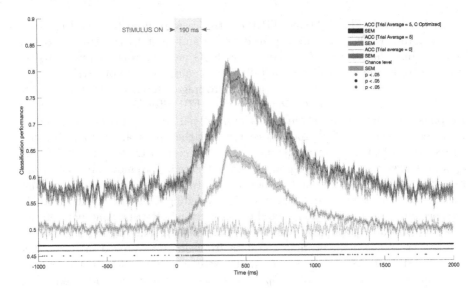

Fig. 3. Classification performance. The green line represents the classification results when no trial average was carried out. An improved classification performance is shown in orange, averaging 5 trials before the feature extraction. Finally, the former analysis was repeated optimizing the cost parameter C (fivefold cross-validated), shown in blue. The gray line represents the classifier chance level, calculated through permuted labels. The shaded areas show the standard error. The statistically significant regions are indicated on the bottom of the figure by colored dots. (Color figure online)

an increased classification performance (due to an increased SNR) and the variance in the classifier performance, since reducing the trial per condition typically increases the variance in (within-subject) classifier performance [19]. The optimal number of trials to average depends on the data. In our dataset (~500 trials per condition and subject) considering that averaging more trials does not increment the decoding performance linearly, we found that averaging 5 trials is a good trade-off between SNR and trials per conditions (~100 trials per condition and subject). Finally, a search-grid based cost parameter (C) optimization was carried out using fivefold cross-validation on the training set and increasing the final decoding accuracy.

Frequency Contribution Analysis. The contribution of each frequency band to the overall decoding accuracy was assessed through a sliding filter approach. We designed a band-stop FIR filter (4 Hz bandwidth, 0.5 Hz transition band, 2816 filter order, Blackman window) and pre-filtered the EEG data (37 overlapped frequency bands, between 2–40 Hz and logarithmically spaced steps) producing 37 filtered versions of the original EEG dataset. The former decoding analysis was repeated for each filtered version and the importance of each filtered-out band was quantified computing the difference in decoding accuracy between the filtered and the original datasets.

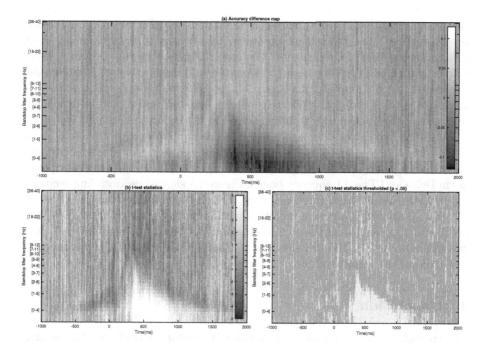

Fig. 4. Frequency contribution analysis. (A) Classification differences when a specific frequency band is filtered-out. (B) T-test statistics showing significant differences in classification at each time point and frequency band. (C) $p < .05$ thresholded significance map.

3   Results and Discussion

The behavioral results replicate well-known conflict effects linked to context-dependence congruency. Effort avoidance was observed in voluntary decision blocks (percentage of choice of easy 57.11% SEM = 2.93 vs difficult 42.88% SEM = 2.93 contexts; $t = 2.42$, $p = .021$). Planned comparisons show significant differences in reaction time between contexts for both congruent ($F(1,31) = 12.76$, $p = .001$, $\eta_p^2 = .292$) and incongruent trials ($F(1,31) = 10.72$, $p = .003$, $\eta_p^2 = .257$) and interaction of context and congruency, showing the context-dependent congruency effect.

The electrophysiological analyses (Fig. 3) show significant differences ($p < 0.05$) in activation patterns for congruent and incongruent trials, peaking 400 ms after the stimulus onset. A paired t-test was computed comparing the classification performance mean at each time point with the classifier chance level, which was calculated through permuted labels. The significant region extends from stimulus onset ($t = 0$ ms) to 1500 ms later, when no trial average was carried out. When the signal to noise ratio was increased by trial averaging, this significant region extends throughout the entire analyzed temporal window, which suggests that neural patterns associated to congruent or incongruent trials are significantly different even before the stimulus presentation. These results are reasonable, since the stimulus onset is preceded by a predictive cue, which indicates with 80% of validity, once the context is chosen (easy or hard), if the following trial will be congruent or incongruent. These activation patterns differences between conditions may relay on the differences in preparatory neural mechanisms triggered by the selected context, reasserting the context-dependent congruency effects in reaction times showed in the behavioral results.

A sliding bandstop filter approach was followed to study the contribution of each frequency band to the overall decoding accuracy, showing that context-dependent proportion of congruency effect may rely on neural processes operating in Delta and Theta frequency bands. Figure 4A shows how decoding accuracy significantly drops when frequencies up to 8 Hz were filtered-out. A paired t-test was computed comparing the classification performance mean at each time point and frequency band with the classifier performance when no frequency was filtered-out (Fig. 4B). Finally, Fig. 4C shows a thresholded significance map ($p < 0.05$) of the former analysis.

4   Conclusion

The current study is an initial approximation to adapt a DST to a format that allows measuring concurrent high-density electroencephalography. We used multivariate pattern analysis (MVPA) to decode conflict-related neural processes associated with congruent or incongruent events in a time-frequency resolved way, yielding 80% of decoding accuracy 400 ms after the stimulus onset. Our preliminarily results of frequency bands contribution analysis suggest that context-dependent proportion of congruency effect may rely on neural processes operating in Delta and Theta-band frequencies. For a better understanding of preparation processes and conflict effects, it would be of interest to continue analyzing our data, focusing not only on the target stimulus, but also on the cue. Further detailed analyses should be carried out to study the activation differences between forced and voluntary blocks or high and low congruency contexts.

Acknowledgments. This research was supported by the Spanish Ministry of Economy and Business under the TEC2015-64718-R and PSI2016-78236-P projects. The first author of this work is supported by a grant from the Spanish Ministry of Economy and Business (BES-2017-079769).

References

1. Kool, W., McGuire, J.T., Rosen, Z.B., Botvinick, M.M.: Decision making and the avoidance of cognitive demand. J. Exp. Psychol.: Gen. **139**(4), 665 (2010)
2. Ramírez, J., et al.: Computer-aided diagnosis of Alzheimer's type dementia combining support vector machines and discriminant set of features. Inf. Sci. **237**, 59–72 (2013)

3. Chaves, R., et al.: SVM-based computer-aided diagnosis of the Alzheimer's disease using t-test nmse feature selection with feature correlation weighting. Neurosci. Lett. **461**(3), 293–297 (2009)

4. Salas-Gonzalez, D., et al.: Computer-aided diagnosis of Alzheimer's disease using support vector machines and classification trees. Phys. Med. Biol. **55**(10), 2807 (2010)

5. Álvarez, I., et al.: Alzheimer's diagnosis using eigenbrains and support vector machines. Electron. Lett. **45**(7), 342–343 (2009)

6. Koley, B., Dey, D.: An ensemble system for automatic sleep stage classification using single channel EEG signal. Comput. Biol. Med. **42**(12), 1186–1195 (2012)

7. Aboalayon, K.A.I., Ocbagabir, H.T., Faezipour, M.: Efficient sleep stage classification based on EEG signals. In: IEEE Long Island Systems, Applications and Technology (LISAT) Conference 2014, pp. 1–6. IEEE (2014)

8. López-García, D., Ruz, M., de Inestrosa, J.R.P., Sáez, J.M.G.: Automatic detection of sleep disorders: multi-class automatic classification algorithms based on support vector machines. In: International Conference on Time Series and Forecasting (ITISE 2018), vol. 3, pp. 1270–1280 (2018)

9. Cauchoix, M., Barragan-Jason, G., Serre, T., Barbeau, E.J.: The neural dynamics of face detection in the wild revealed by MVPA. J. Neurosci. **34**(3), 846–854 (2014)

10. Kerrén, C., Linde-Domingo, J., Hanslmayr, S., Wimber, M.: An optimal oscillatory phase for pattern reactivation during memory retrieval. Curr. Biol. **28**(21), 3383–3392 (2018)

11. Hebart, M.N., Bankson, B.B., Harel, A., Baker, C.I., Cichy, R.M.: The representational dynamics of task and object processing in humans. Elife **7**, e32816 (2018)

12. Correia, J.M., Jansma, B., Hausfeld, L., Kikkert, S., Bonte, M.: EEG decoding of spoken words in bilingual listeners: from words to language invariant semantic-conceptual representations. Front. Psychol. **6**, 71 (2015)

13. Cohen, M.X., Donner, T.H.: Midfrontal conflict-related theta-band power reflects neural oscillations that predict behavior. Am. J. Physiol.-Heart Circ. Physiol. **110**, 2752–2763 (2013)

14. Kleiner, M., Brainard, D., Pelli, D., Ingling, A., Murray, R., Broussard, C., et al.: What's new in psychtoolbox-3. Perception **36**(14), 1 (2007)

15. Logix4U, Gibbons, P.: Inpout32 is an open source windows DLL and driver to give direct access to hardware ports

16. Schouppe, N., Demanet, J., Boehler, C.N., Ridderinkhof, K.R., Notebaert, W.: The role of the striatum in effort-based decision-making in the absence of reward. J. Neurosci. **34**(6), 2148–2154 (2014)

17. Delorme, A., Makeig, S.: EEGLAB: an open source toolbox for analysis of single-trial EEG dynamics including independent component analysis. J. Neurosci. Methods **134**(1), 9–21 (2004)

18. Isik, L., Meyers, E.M., Leibo, J.Z., Poggio, T.A.: The dynamics of invariant object recognition in the human visual system. Am. J. Physiol.-Heart Circ. Physiol. **111**, 91–102 (2013)

19. Grootswagers, T., Wardle, S.G., Carlson, T.A.: Decoding dynamic brain patterns from evoked responses: a tutorial on multivariate pattern analysis applied to time series neuroimaging data. J. Cogn. Neurosci. **29**(4), 677–697 (2017)

Support Vector Machine Failure
in Imbalanced Datasets

I. A. Illan[✉], J. M. Gorriz, J. Ramirez, F. J. Martinez-Murcia,
D. Castillo-Barnes, F. Segovia, and D. Salas-Gonzalez

Departamento de Teoria de la señal y Comunicaciones,
Universidad de Granada, Granada, Spain
`illan@ugr.es`

Abstract. Imbalanced datasets often pose challenges in classification problems. In this work we study and quantify the problem of imbalanced classification using support vector machines (SVM). We identify the conditions under which a SVM failure occur, both theoretically and experimentally, and show that it can be relevant even in cases of very weakly imbalanced data. The guidelines for exploratory data analysis are presented to avoid the SVM failure.

Keywords: Support vector machines · Imbalanced data · SVM ·
Data analysis · SVM failure

1 Introduction

Often in statistical learning, the available training data set has few samples in a high dimensional space, allowing very poor estimations on probability distribution functions. Non-parametric approaches based on statistical learning theory, such as neural networks or SVMs, have been proven to be very succesful solving classification problems. However, in the case of unbalanced training datasets, some difficulties arise if the learning algorithms are straightforwardly applied. For example, the soft margin solution in SVM [4,9] for non-separable classes, includes a term in the lagrangian that accounts for the classification error rate together with the structural risk minimization. If the learning algorithm is optimized to minimize the risk of misclassifying samples, some additional constraints must be imposed to avoid the trivial solution in imbalanced datasets. The trivial solution is achieved when all samples are classified as the dominant class. In that undesirable case, the misclassification error can be very small if the dominant class outnumbers the scarce class in several orders of magnitude, thus masking the problem. It is however possible that the trivial solution is achieved in cases of weakly imbalanced data.

A common practice in SVM imbalanced classification is to apply penalties to the classification errors on the scarce class, so that the risk of classification errors is weighted. Usually, no other method or theoretical ground for class weight estimation but trial-and-error is proposed. Moreover, it has been shown that

© Springer Nature Switzerland AG 2019
J. M. Ferrández Vicente et al. (Eds.): IWINAC 2019, LNCS 11486, pp. 412–419, 2019.
https://doi.org/10.1007/978-3-030-19591-5_42

applying class weights is equivalent to use fuzzy-SVMs [6]. The importance of the data properties has been studied in imbalanced data [7], although the use of weights in SVM is usually reserved to heavily imbalanced data.

In this work we study the relevant properties of the data for SVM imbalanced classification and its theoretical relation to the trivial solution.

2   Methods

The methodology followed in this study is as following: first a review on SVM is given, fixing the notation. Secondly, a definition of SVM failure is given, together with a theoretical derivation of the conditions that cause it. Lastly, a experimental set is proposed to illustrate the effects of the SVM failure and the circumstances around it.

2.1   Support Vector Machines

SVM is a machine learning algorithm that separates a given set of binary labeled training data with a hyper-plane that is maximally distant from the two classes (known as the maximal margin hyper-plane). In the C-SVM formulation, the problem of finding the maximal margin hyperplane is solved by quadratic programming algorithms that try to minimize the dual of the cost function J:

$$J(\boldsymbol{w}, w_0, \xi) = \frac{1}{2}||\boldsymbol{w}||^2 + C \sum_{i=1}^{l} \xi_i, \tag{1}$$

subject to the inequality constraints:

$$y_i[\boldsymbol{w} \cdot \mathbf{x}_i + w_0] \geq 1 - \xi_i, \quad \xi_i \geq 0 \quad i = 1, 2, ..., l. \tag{2}$$

where the slack variables ξ_i make the margin "soft", by incorporating to the optimization those feature vectors that are not separable, leading to the soft margin solution (details can be found in [10] and [9]).

By applying Lagrange duality and introducing kernel methods, the following dual optimization problem is obtained:

$$\min_{\alpha} \frac{1}{2} \sum_{j=1}^{l} \sum_{i=1}^{l} y_i y_j \alpha_i \alpha_j K(\mathbf{x}_i, \mathbf{x}_j) - \sum_{i=1}^{l} \alpha_i \tag{3}$$

subject to the KKT dual conditions:

$$\sum_{i=1}^{l} y_i \alpha_i = 0, \quad \text{and} \quad 0 \leq \alpha_i \leq C, \quad i = 1, ..., l \tag{4}$$

where $K(.,.)$ is the kernel function and α_i are the Lagrange multipliers that need to be solved. The dual conditions will be related to the primal problem as:

$$\alpha_i = 0 \quad \rightarrow \quad y_i[\mathbf{w} \cdot \mathbf{x}_i + w_0] \geq 1 \tag{5}$$
$$\alpha_i = C \quad \rightarrow \quad y_i[\mathbf{w} \cdot \mathbf{x}_i + w_0] \leq 1 \tag{6}$$
$$0 < \alpha_i < C \quad \rightarrow \quad y_i[\mathbf{w} \cdot \mathbf{x}_i + w_0] = 1 \tag{7}$$

Common kernels that are used by SVM practitioners for the nonlinear feature mapping are:

– Polynomial
$$K(\boldsymbol{x}, \boldsymbol{y}) = [\gamma(\boldsymbol{x} \cdot \boldsymbol{y}) + c]^d. \tag{8}$$

– Radial basis function (RBF)
$$K(\boldsymbol{x}, \boldsymbol{y}) = \exp(-\gamma||\boldsymbol{x} - \boldsymbol{y}||^2). \tag{9}$$

as well as the linear kernel.

The solution to that problem can be expressed by a linear combination of a subset of vectors, called support vectors:

$$d(\mathbf{x}) = \sum_{i=1}^{N_S} \alpha_i y_i K(\mathbf{s}_i, \mathbf{x}) + w_0 \tag{10}$$

where $\mathbf{s}_i$ are the N_S support vectors; those vectors with $\alpha_i > 0$. Taking the sign of the function $d(\mathbf{x})$ leads to the binary classification solution [10]. The solution may also be expressed as:

$$y(\mathbf{x}) = \text{sign}(\varphi(\mathbf{x}) \cdot \mathbf{w} + w_0) \tag{11}$$

where:

$$\mathbf{w} = \sum_{i=1}^{l} \alpha_i y_i \varphi(\mathbf{x}_i) \tag{12}$$

with $K(\mathbf{x}_i, \mathbf{x}_j) = \varphi(\mathbf{x}_i) \cdot \varphi(\mathbf{x}_j)$ being the kernel mapping that will be the identity in the linear case.

3   SVM Failure

The solution given in 13 can be split into its positive and negative class fractions as:

$$\mathbf{w} = \sum_{i=1}^{l} \alpha_i^+ \varphi(\mathbf{x}_i^+) - \sum_{i=1}^{l} \alpha_i^- \varphi(\mathbf{x}_i^-) \tag{13}$$

where $\mathbf{x}_i^-$ and $\mathbf{x}_i^+$ are the negative and positive training examples. The sign of the vector $\mathbf{w}$ will determine how the positive and negative labels are assigned in reference to the hyperplane. Ideally, the vector $\mathbf{w}$ will point *from* the negative class *to* the positive class. However, there will be some special cases where the vector **w** will point in the wrong direction, that is, from the positive class towards the negative class. In those cases, the training of the SVM will fail, and the only possible adjustment is to set w_0 so that all the training examples are classified as positive (or negative). We will call that situation *SVM failure*. There are several properties of the training data involved in a SVM failure, namely: the proportion between training samples and the overlap between them. We will show here how this undesirable situation occurs when the difference in support vector density between classes reaches a threshold inside the margin.

Let us first consider the simpler case of linear SVM. In accordance with the dual KKT conditions, $\alpha_i = C$ for all the training examples inside the margin, including those in the wrong side of the margin. The constraints imposed in Eq. 4 to the solution of Eq. 10 make it possible to express the vector **w** as:

$$\mathbf{w} = C(\bar{\mathbf{x}}_s^+ - \bar{\mathbf{x}}_s^-) \tag{14}$$

where $\bar{\mathbf{x}}_s^+$ and $\bar{\mathbf{x}}_s^+$ are the average positive and negative support vectors respectively, and where we have neglected those support vectors with $0 < \alpha_i < C$ for reasons that will become clear later. Intuitively, **w** can be thought as the difference vector between the average positive support vector and the average negative support vector, up to a factor. However, to guarantee the optimal performance of the SVM, the sign of the vector **w** must be the same as the sign of the vector **v** defined as:

$$\mathbf{v} = \sum_{i=1}^{n^+} \mathbf{x}_i^+ - \sum_{i=1}^{n^-} \mathbf{x}_i^- \tag{15}$$

where n^+ is the total number of samples in the positive class and n^- is the total number of samples in the negative class. In oder words, we expect the classifier to be somewhere between the average positive class and the average negative class, thus dividing both point clouds. To understand when this condition is not met, it is useful to analyze the different scenarios in which the Eq. 14 vanishes. For Eq. 14 to vanish, the classes are required to be non-separable. It is easier to analyze first the simpler case of imbalanced data in which all the samples of the scarce class are support vectors, and then discuss the more general case in which Eq. 14 can vanish but there are a non-negligible number of samples that are not support vectors.

3.1   All Support Vectors

In the case of a complete overlap between classes, it is a consequence of the constraints 2 that all the samples of at least one class must be support vectors. Take the negative class to be the scarce one. In that case, one of the terms of Eq. 14 can be calculated explicitly from the data only, the $\bar{\mathbf{x}}_s^-$ term. Therefore, if it was possible to calculate the $\bar{\mathbf{x}}_s^+$ term, it would be possible to predict if the classifier will fall into a SVM failure. The smallest value of the second term can be achieved only for no support vectors outside the margin, or all $\alpha_i = C$, neglecting smaller values of α_i as mentioned earlier. If we define the subset of one class samples that are in the region of the feature space delimited by the hyperplane located at a distance C of the furthest negative sample in the $\mathbf{v}$ direction as $\mathcal{L}$, then the SVM failure condition is:

$$\sum_{i \in \mathcal{L}} \mathbf{x}_i^+ = \sum_{i=1}^{n^-} \mathbf{x}_i^- \tag{16}$$

4   Experiments

We performed simulations of real case scenarios in which the different properties of the data are varied, as the imbalance proportion between classes or their overlap. To model the data we used multidimensional Gaussian distributions, that allowed us to control the aforementioned characteristics. Two classes w_1 and w_2 were modeled with Gaussian distributions with different mean and covariance, and described by:

$$p(w_1 \mid \mathbf{x}) = \frac{1}{2\pi |\Sigma_1|^{\frac{1}{2}}} \exp\left(-\frac{1}{2}(\mathbf{x} - \mu_1)^T \Sigma_1^{-1} (\mathbf{x} - \mu_1)\right) \tag{17}$$

$$p(w_2 \mid \mathbf{x}) = \frac{1}{2\pi |\Sigma_2|^{\frac{1}{2}}} \exp\left(-\frac{1}{2}(\mathbf{x} - \mu_2)^T \Sigma_2^{-1} (\mathbf{x} - \mu_2)\right) \tag{18}$$

Experiment 1: $\mu_1 = \begin{pmatrix} 0 & 0 \\ 0 & 0 \end{pmatrix}$, $\mu_2 = \begin{pmatrix} 1 & 0 \\ 0 & 1 \end{pmatrix}$ and $\Sigma_1 = \begin{pmatrix} 2 & 0 \\ 0 & 1 \end{pmatrix}$ $\Sigma_2 = \begin{pmatrix} 0.25 & 0 \\ 0 & 0.5 \end{pmatrix}$.
The training set is built by joining a varying number b of w_1 samples and a fixed number $m = 100$ of w_2 samples. 400 different trained SVM are built by modifying the proportion $\rho = b/m$ ranging form $\rho = 1$ to $\rho = 5$ in 0.01 increments. (see Fig. 1)

Experiment 2: $\Sigma_1 = \begin{pmatrix} 2 & 0 \\ 0 & 1 \end{pmatrix}$ $\Sigma_2 = \begin{pmatrix} 0.25 & 0 \\ 0 & 0.5 \end{pmatrix}$, and $m = 100$ $b = 125$. The training set is built by varying the value of μ_2 while keeping $\mu_1 = \begin{pmatrix} 0 & 0 \\ 0 & 0 \end{pmatrix}$. 300 different trained SVM are built by modifying the value of μ_2 according to $\mu_2 = \begin{pmatrix} a & 0 \\ 0 & a \end{pmatrix}$, with a ranging from 0 to 3 in 0.01 increments. (see Fig. 1)

For each variation of the parameters a and ρ, a SVM was trained, and the accuracy, sensitivity and specificity of each classifier on the trained data was acquired. The results are shown in Fig. 2. To perform the experiments we used the SVC implementation of scikit-learn [8] based on libsvm [3].

Although the data is synthetic, these kind of datasets can represent real data. Such an example can be realized in dynamic-contrast-enchancing magnetic-resonance-imaging (DCE-MRI) for breast cancer diagnosis [5]. Consider a DCE-MRI patient image with N voxels. In such case, the classification problem reduces

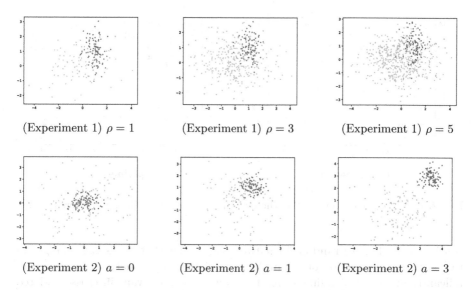

Fig. 1. Illustration of simulated data for different parameter settings and different experiments.

to separate healthy tissues from malignant ones. A set of voxels m belonging to a malignant region constitutes a tumor. It is expected that the number of voxels b belonging to benign regions outnumber the voxels in malignant regions, so that $n/b << 1$ in either the training set or the unseen case. However, the size of the tumor is unknown in unseen cases, and do not have to match necessarily the size of tumors in the training set. Therefore, the proportion n/b is variable as well as its overlapping.

5   Discussion

Results showed in Fig. 2 illustrate the effect of a SVM failure when the conditions are met. For this particular datasets, SVM failure occurs for $\rho \approx 4.5$ in Experiment 1 and when $a \approx 0.4$ in Experiment 2.

For $\rho \approx 4.5$ in Experiment 1 Eq. 16 is fulfilled. By varying the imbalance proportion while keeping the overlap between classes fixed, there is a limit in which there are not enough support vectors in the scarce class to balance the density of support vectors of the dominant class inside the margin, and the sign of $\mathbf{w}$ gets reversed producing the failure. This situation is easier to predict and quantify, since the number of samples in the scarce class establishes a fixed limit.

In the circumstances of Experiment 2, it is harder to predict the SVM failure since it depends on the particular realization of the data, adding to it the limitation to Gaussian distributions of this study. It is however showed that Eq. 14 can vanish in some particular configurations of the data, independently from its imbalanced proportion between classes. It also shows that SVM failure is less

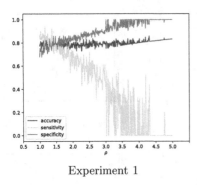
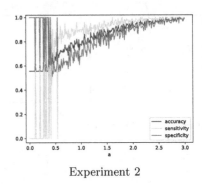

Experiment 1   Experiment 2

Fig. 2. Performance of the SVM on the training set by varying the parameters ρ and a.

consistent, and more random in nature, suggesting that the small changes in the particular realization of the probability distribution function can affect significantly in the SVM failure. This fact can be very relevant in cross-validated studies, where subsampling the data into cross validation folds can produce SVM failure.

A common practice in SVM imbalanced classification is the use of class-weights. This solution is equivalent to the FSVM problem [6] or more precisely, the latter problem is more general and includes the former as an special case. In the light of this interpretation, applying different weights to class-slack variables is the same as decreasing the membership level of one class, say the w_1 class, misclassified samples, while keeping the w_0 membership not fuzzy.

The FSVM-CIL method proposed in [2] explicitly makes use of this correspondence, and propose three different functions to estimate the membership function s_i; distance to class center, distance to estimated hyperplane and distance to actual hyperplane. To tackle the imbalanced problem, they propose to use different upper bound values in the membership function for each class so that the ratio corresponds with the ratio on the priors, in concordance with [1].

However, the solutions to the imbalanced SVM classification problem do not usually study the conditions under which the solutions should be applied. Here we show that even weakly imbalanced data can require of a imbalanced solution as FSVM or weighted-SVM if certain conditions are met, suggesting that balanced classes in SVM are important in guaranteeing its performance.

Here, we have limited the analysis to the simpler linear case, but all the arguments are extrapolable to the non-linear case by including the use of kernels, without modifying any fundamental idea.

6   Conclusion

We have established the theoretical conditions for SVM failure and showed experimentally the circumstances under which it may occur. We have shown that not only the imbalanced proportion between classes is relevant for predicting the

SVM failure, but also their overlap. We have shown that SVM failure can be produced even for weakly imbalanced data, suggesting that balancing or weighting the data is always recommendable as a default option in SVM classification.

References

1. Akbani, R., Kwek, S., Japkowicz, N.: Applying support vector machines to imbalanced datasets. In: Boulicaut, J.-F., Esposito, F., Giannotti, F., Pedreschi, D. (eds.) ECML 2004. LNCS (LNAI), vol. 3201, pp. 39–50. Springer, Heidelberg (2004). https://doi.org/10.1007/978-3-540-30115-8_7
2. Batuwita, R., Palade, V.: FSVM-CIL: fuzzy support vector machines for class imbalance learning. IEEE Trans. Fuzzy Syst. 18(3), 558–571 (2010)
3. Chang, C.C., Lin, C.J.: LIBSVM: a library for support vector machines. ACM Trans. Intell. Syst. Technol. 2(3), 27:1–27:27 (2011). https://doi.org/10.1145/1961189.1961199
4. Cortes, C., Vapnik, V.: Support-vector networks. Mach. Learn. 20(3), 273–297 (1995). https://doi.org/10.1023/A:1022627411411
5. Illan, I.A., et al.: Automated detection and segmentation of nonmass-enhancing breast tumors with dynamic contrast-enhanced magnetic resonance imaging (2018). https://www.hindawi.com/journals/cmmi/2018/5308517/
6. Lin, C.F., Wang, S.D.: Fuzzy support vector machines. IEEE Trans. Neural Netw. 13(2), 464–471 (2002)
7. López, V., Fernández, A., García, S., Palade, V., Herrera, F.: An insight into classification with imbalanced data: empirical results and current trends on using data intrinsic characteristics. Inf. Sci. 250, 113–141 (2013). http://www.sciencedirect.com/science/article/pii/S0020025513005124
8. Pedregosa, F., et al.: Scikit-learn: machine learning in Python. J. Mach. Learn. Res. 12, 2825–2830 (2011)
9. Schölkopf, B., Smola, A.J., Williamson, R.C., Bartlett, P.L.: New support vector algorithms. Neural Comput. 12(5), 1207–1245 (2000). https://doi.org/10.1162/089976600300015565
10. Vapnik, V.N.: Statistical Learning Theory. Wiley, New York (1998)

Machine Learning Methods for Environmental-Enrichment-Related Variations in Behavioral Responses of Laboratory Rats

Karmele López-de-Ipiña[1(✉)], Hodei Cepeda[2], Catalina Requejo[2],
Elsa Fernandez[1], Pilar Maria Calvo[1], and Jose Vicente Lafuente[2]

[1] EleKin Research Group, Department of Systems Engineering and Automatics,
University of the Basque Country (UPV/EHU), 20018 Donostia, Spain
karmele.ipina@ehu.eus
[2] Neuroscience Department, University of the Basque Country (UPV/EHU),
Campus de Leioa, B Sarriena, 48940 Leioa, Spain

Abstract. Environmental enrichment (EE) paradigms are designed to enhance laboratory animals surroundings to encourage natural behaviors. Some enrichment paradigms also include a social component, based on the social interactions typical of the genus and species. Novel automatic methodologies based on image are becoming useful tools to improve laboratory works. This paper present a first approach to the automatic image analysis of laboratory rats in EE: behaviour, drug effects and pathology. The new methodology is based on image and Machine Learning paradigms and will become a useful tool for Neuroscience issues.

Keywords: Entropy · Nonlinear analysis · Image analysis ·
Clustering · Optical flow · Pattern recognition · Intelligent methods ·
Environmental monitoring

1 Introduction

New and rapid developments in neuroscience, psychology, genetics, and pharmacology have led to growing demands for automated analysis of animal behavioral in scientific and preclinical research experiments, while maintain to surpassing the accuracy of expert human observer [6]. Key applications of such algorithms include research on addiction and drug abuse and a variety of medical interventions, such as development of new medications [7]. Being small, low cost, and easy to breed mammals, rodent species, such as rats and mice, have been widely used in experiments, further supported by the fact that their genome sequences are widely available [1,3]. At present, most physical behavioral assessment is conducted by expert human annotations, making the process labor-intensive,

J. M. Ferrández Vicente et al. (Eds.): IWINAC 2019, LNCS 11486, pp. 420–427, 2019.
https://doi.org/10.1007/978-3-030-19591-5_43

tedious, and yet subjective. As a result, manual assessment of rodent behavior suffers from being time consuming, costly, low throughput (one animal at a time), and poorly reproducible.

Environmental enrichment (EE) paradigms are designed to enhance laboratory animals surroundings to encourage natural behaviors. Some enrichment paradigms also include a social component, based on the social interactions typical of the genus and species. For example, wild mice and rats generally live in colonies, whereas hamsters are known to be social with unfamiliar animals only during mating.

Adverse environmental conditions have been shown to affect the susceptibility of animals exposed to diverse stress regimes, reflected in their behavioral, physiologic, and biochemical responses in a strain-dependent manner. Therefore, a diverse environment might be expected to alter their response to such stressors. A review of the literature reveals few behavioral investigations of the effects of EE on response to a stressor, and the results of biochemical studies in this context have generally been inconsistent. For example, some laboratories have reported no difference in corticosterone levels between EE- and standard-housed animals after exposure to a stressor, whereas others have observed a reduction in the corticosterone levels of SpragueDawley rats or even elevated levels of plasma corticosterone in enriched Wistar rats.32 These differences may be due to length of EE exposure or in-strain responsivity to stress. Therefore, the first aim of the present set of experiments was to investigate whether rat strain influences the behavioral and physiologic measures typically used to assess stress responses. Novel automatic methodologies based on image are becoming useful tools to improve laboratory works [2]. This paper present a first approach to the automatic image analysis of laboratory rats in EE.

Section 2 describes the materials and methods. Section 3 analyze the results and finally Sect. 4 presents the conclusions and future works.

2 Materials and Methods

2.1 Experimental Design and Housing Conditions

A total of 20 adult male Sprague-Dawley rats at 3-month-old (280–300g) were randomly and equally assigned to the following groups: Saline group (n = 10) as a control and 6-OHDA group (n = 10) including animals injected with 6-OHDA to describe the proposed model. After saline solution or 6-OHDA administration, all the animals were housed for two weeks in monitored enriched environment (EE) cages under 12 h light/12 h dark cycle with access to food and water ad libitum. EE cages (790 mm × 460 mm × 640 mm) consisted of two floors, which were connected by a plastic ramp that enabled rats to move from one level to the next and an external running wheel as previously described (requejo C). There were 10 animals placed in every EE cage, one per group. In addition, EE cages were supplied with an additional infrared camera system (developed by our group) to collect pictures accurately every 10 s to be later analyzed by a novel specific software in order to measure changes in the activity.

Fig. 1. Model of a enriched environment cage

2.2   Image Processing

The schematic diagram of the working procedure is described in Fig. 2. The video sequences and images were acquired using.

The methodology used from image acquisition to the rats centroids. trajectories estimation was based on that described in [2].

From the point of view of image segmentation and object detection, and due to the nature of the set up, (a biological experiment in a real, small-scale industrial environment) there were three main problems: noise, artifacts and occlusions. The main source of noise was generated by the sand moved with the movements of the rats. This creates a uniform noise after binarization that can be eliminated very easily. There were three main types of artifacts (anomalies introduced in the signal or in the data by the equipment or the technique): The first was caused by the sand that the rats move when they move. The second (very similar to the first but larger) was caused by the objects that are inside the cage and which moves the rat when moving, and the third by the difference in lighting between night and day. During the night a spotlight illuminates the cages.

2.3   Clustering and Trajectory Generation

We decided to use a clustering method to identify the fish group and calculate the groups centroid. The centroids positions were estimated by k-means because this algorithm is robust, with a good relationship between speed and stability and it works well with large amounts of data. Thus, once the centers of the objects were calculated, and knowing their coordinates in the two axes within each frame, k-means was applied to find the center of the entire group. In our particular case, the dataset were the objects centers in each frame, from the first frame to the last one. K-means clustering operates on actual observations (rather than on a larger set of dissimilarity measures), and creates a single level of clusters.

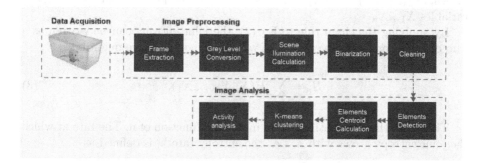

Fig. 2. Data acquisition, preprocessing and analysis workflow.

2.4   Non-linear Trajectory Analysis–Calculation of the Shannon Entropy

SE was selected as the best parameter to analyze the trajectories due to its low computational load and robustness [2]. As proposed by Shannon on his studies on languages [4], the SE allows the estimation of the average minimum number of bits needed to encode a string of symbols based, in his case, on the alphabet size and the frequency of the symbols. This indicated the minimal number of bits per symbol needed to encode the information in binary form in case the logarithm base were 2. Shannon used this entropy measurement to estimate redundancy in the English language [5]. Formally, the entropy $H(X)$ of a single discrete random variable X is a measure of its average uncertainty. Shannon entropy [4] was calculated as described by Eguiraun et al. [2]. It follows a detailed description of the equations used to perform the calculations.

$$H(X) = - \sum_{x_i \in \Theta} p(x_i) \, log_p(x_i) = -E[log_p(x_i)], \tag{1}$$

where X represents a random variable with a set of values Θ and probability mass function $p(x_i) = P_r\{X = x_i\}, x_i \in \Theta$, and E represents the expectation operator. Note that $p \, log_p = 0$ if p=0.

For a time series representing the output of a stochastic process, that is, an indexed sequence of n random variables, $X_i = X_1...X_n$, with a set of values $\theta 1,...,\theta n$, respectively, and $X_i \in \theta i$, the joint entropy is defined by

$$H_n = H(X_1...X_n) = - \sum_{x_i \in \Theta} ... \sum_{x_n \in \Theta n} p(x_1...x_n) \, log_p(x_1...x_n), \tag{2}$$

where $p(x_1...x_n) = P\{X_1 = x_1...X_n = x_n\}$ is the joint probability for the n variables $X_1...X_n$.

By applying the chain rule to Eq. (2), the joint entropy can be written as a sum of conditional entropies, each of which is a non-negative quantity:

$$H_n = \sum_{i=1}^{n} H(X_i|X_{i-1}...X_1), \tag{3}$$

Therefore, the joint entropy is an increasing function of n. The rate at which the joint entropy grows with n, *i.e.*, the entropy rate h, is defined as

$$h = \lim_{n \to \infty} \frac{H_n}{n} \tag{4}$$

It must be said that for stationary ergodic processes as random processes, the evaluation of the rate of entropy has proven to be a very useful parameter.

The trajectories of the response to the stochastic event were measured both in the control case C_1 and in the treated C_2.

2.5   Machine Learning Paradigms

Two classifiers will be used to analyses pathological and control behaviour: Support Vector Machines (SVM) and Multilayer Perceptron (MLP). The results were evaluated using Classification Error Rate (CER, %). For training and validation steps we used k-fold cross-validation with k = 10.

3   Results and Discussion

In the experimentation the materials described in sub-Section 2.1 are used. In the first stage the image processing is carried out and trajectories are created. Then the following linear and non-linear features are extracted: centroid-x - centroid-y speed acceleration activity area entropy. Figures 3 and 4 show the obtained results for the groups: Activity and Entropy. In the second stage Machine Learning algorithms are applied to detect pathological behavior with a CER (%) of around 87% for MLP for 2 layers of 100 neurons that outperforms SVM with around 85% and less computational cost. The results are hopeful, stable, good and balanced for all of them.

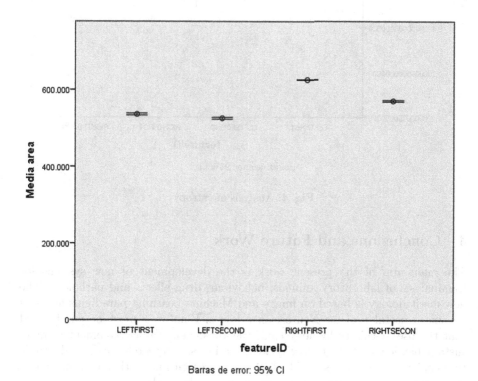

Fig. 3. Analysis of area activation

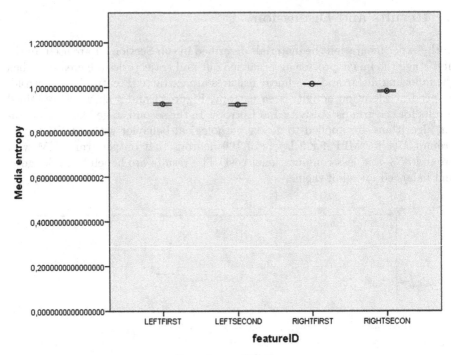

Barras de error: 95% CI

Fig. 4. Analysis of entropy

4   Conclusions and Future Work

The main aim of the present work is the development of new systems for the analysis of laboratory animals: behaviour, drug effects and pathology. The new methodology is based on image and Machine Learning paradigms and will become a useful tool for Neuroscience issues. Finally, it must be emphasized that the use of this technology could clearly benefit the development of more sustainable, low cost, high quality, and non-invasive researcher easily adaptable to complex environments as EE. In future research lines, other non-linear features and automatic selection of algorithms will be explored.

References

1. Baker, M.: Animal models: inside the minds of mice and men. Nature **475**, 123–128 (2011). https://doi.org/10.1038/475123a. https://www.nature.com/articles/475123a
2. Eguiraun, H., López-de-Ipiña, K., Martinez, I.: Application of entropy and fractal dimension analyses to the pattern recognition of contaminated fish responses in aquaculture. Entropy **16**(11), 6133–6151 (2014). https://doi.org/10.3390/e16116133. https://www.mdpi.com/1099-4300/16/11/6133

3. Rat genome sequencing project consortium: genome sequence of the Brown Norway rat yields insights into mammalian evolution. Nature **428**(6982), 493–521 (2004). https://doi.org/10.1038/nature02426. https://www.nature.com/articles/nature02426
4. Shannon, C.E.: A mathematical theory of communication. Bell Syst. Tech. J. **27**(3), 379–423 (1948). https://doi.org/10.1002/j.1538-7305.1948.tb01338.x
5. Shannon, C.E.: Prediction and entropy of printed English. Bell Syst. Tech. J. **30**(1), 50–64 (1951). https://doi.org/10.1002/j.1538-7305.1951.tb01366.x
6. Tecott, L.H., Nestler, E.J.: Neurobehavioral assessment in the information age. Nature Neuroscience **7**(5), 462–466 (2004). https://doi.org/10.1038/nn1225. https://www.nature.com/articles/nn1225
7. Van Meer, P.J.K., Graham, M.L., Schuurman, H.J.: The safety, efficacy and regulatory triangle in drug development: impact for animal models and the use of animals. Eur. J. Pharmacol. **759**, 3–13 (2015). https://doi.org/10.1016/j.ejphar.2015.02.055. http://www.sciencedirect.com/science/article/pii/S0014299915002551

Correction to: Boosting Object Detection in Cyberphysical Systems

José M. Buenaposada⬤ and Luis Baumela

Correction to:
Chapter "Boosting Object Detection in Cyberphysical Systems" in: J. M. Ferrández Vicente et al. (Eds.):
Understanding the Brain Function and Emotions, **LNCS 11486,**
https://doi.org/10.1007/978-3-030-19591-5_32

In the original version of this paper that originally has been published, the funding information was missing. This has now been corrected.

The updated version of this chapter can be found at
https://doi.org/10.1007/978-3-030-19591-5_32

© Springer Nature Switzerland AG 2020
J. M. Ferrández Vicente et al. (Eds.): IWINAC 2019, LNCS 11486, p. C1, 2020.
https://doi.org/10.1007/978-3-030-19591-5_44

Author Index

Printed in the United States
By Bookmasters